The *CLSC Exam Certification Guide* uses detailed explanations of exam objectives, challenging questions, and a test simulation on the accompanying CD-ROM to help you master the CLSC exam objectives. All exam objectives are up-to-date and covered, and are pointed out like this:

Objective 27: Describe configuration rules for demand nodes and resource nodes.

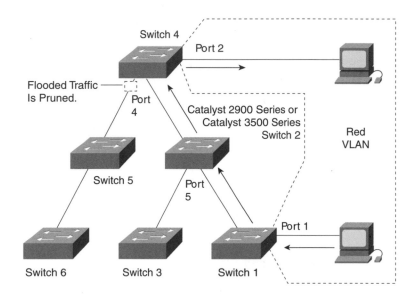

In addition, the CD-ROM provides a simulation of the CLSC exam with multiple-choice questions to help ensure your mastery of the exam objectives. For example:

Q. Full-duplex Ethernet connection supports a transmit circuit connection wired directly to the _____ circuit at the other end of the connection.

    a. receiver

    b. transmitter

    c. loop-back

    d. cross-over

The book's chapters are organized by topic area: Switching Concepts, VLANs, Placing Catalyst 5000 Series Switches in Your Network, Catalyst 5000 Series Switch Architecture, Catalyst 5000 Series Switch Hardware, Configuring The Catalyst 5000 Series Switches, Catalyst 5000 Series Switch Software, Managing the Catalyst 5000 Series Switch Family, Troubleshooting, Catalyst 5000 Series Switch FDDI Module, ATM Networking, Catalyst 1900 and 2820 Switches, and Catalyst 3000 Series Switches. By working through the information, exercises, and questions, you should feel confident as you prepare to take the exam and acquire your CLSC certification.

CLSC Exam Certification Guide

Kevin Downes, CCIE #1987, and Tim Boyles, CCNP

Cisco Press
201 West 103rd Street
Indianapolis, IN 46290 USA

CLSC Exam Certification Guide

Kevin Downes and Tim Boyles

Copyright© 1999 Cisco Press

Cisco Press logo is a trademark of Cisco Systems, Inc.

Published by:
Cisco Press
201 West 103rd Street
Indianapolis, IN 46290 USA

Printed in the United States of America 2 3 4 5 6 7 8 9 0

Library of Congress Cataloging-in-Publication Number: 99-61725

ISBN: 0-7357-0875-4

Warning and Disclaimer

This book is designed to provide information about CLSC certification. Every effort has been made to make this book as complete and as accurate as possible, but no warranty or fitness is implied.

The information is provided on an "as is" basis. The author, Cisco Press, and Cisco Systems, Inc., shall have neither liability nor responsibility to any person or entity with respect to any loss or damages arising from the information contained in this book or from the use of the discs or programs that may accompany it.

The opinions expressed in this book belong to the author and are not necessarily those of Cisco Systems, Inc.

Trademark Acknowledgments

All terms mentioned in this book that are known to be trademarks or service marks have been appropriately capitalized. Cisco Press or Cisco Systems, Inc., cannot attest to the accuracy of this information. Use of a term in this book should not be regarded as affecting the validity of any trademark or service mark.

Feedback Information

At Cisco Press, our goal is to create in-depth technical books of the highest quality and value. Each book is crafted with care and precision, undergoing rigorous development that involves the unique expertise of members from the professional technical community.

Readers' feedback is a natural continuation of this process. If you have any comments regarding how we could improve the quality of this book, or otherwise alter it to better suit your needs, you can contact us through e-mail at ciscopress@mcp.com. Please make sure to include the book title and ISBN in your message.

We greatly appreciate your assistance.

Publisher	John Wait
Executive Editor	John Kane
Cisco Systems Program Manager	Jim LeValley
Managing Editor	Patrick Kanouse
Acquisitions Editor	Brett Bartow
Development Editor	Howard Jones
Project Editor	Jen Nuckles
Copy Editor	Krista Hansing
Technical Editors	Stephen Daleo
	Carole Warner Reece
	Casimir Sammanasu
	David Hucaby
	Ron McCarty
Team Coordinator	Amy Lewis
Book Designer	Scott Cook
Cover Designer	Aren Howell
Compositor	Steve Gifford
Indexer	Cheryl Jackson
Proofreader	Bob LaRoche

CISCO SYSTEMS

CISCO PRESS

Corporate Headquarters
Cisco Systems, Inc.
170 West Tasman Drive
San Jose, CA 95134-1706
USA
http://www.cisco.com
Tel: 408 526-4000
      800 553-NETS (6387)
Fax: 408 526-4100

European Headquarters
Cisco Systems Europe s.a.r.l.
Parc Evolic, Batiment L1/L2
16 Avenue du Quebec
Villebon, BP 706
91961 Courtaboeuf Cedex
France
http://www-europe.cisco.com
Tel: 33 1 69 18 61 00
Fax: 33 1 69 28 83 26

**Americas
Headquarters**
Cisco Systems, Inc.
170 West Tasman Drive
San Jose, CA 95134-1706
USA
http://www.cisco.com
Tel: 408 526-7660
Fax: 408 527-0883

Asia Headquarters
Nihon Cisco Systems K.K.
Fuji Building, 9th Floor
3-2-3 Marunouchi
Chiyoda-ku, Tokyo 100
Japan
http://www.cisco.com
Tel: 81 3 5219 6250
Fax: 81 3 5219 6001

Cisco Systems has more than 200 offices in the following countries. Addresses, phone numbers, and fax numbers are listed on the Cisco Connection Online Web site at http://www.cisco.com/offices.

Argentina • Australia • Austria • Belgium • Brazil • Canada • Chile • China • Colombia • Costa Rica • Croatia • Czech Republic • Denmark • Dubai, UAE Finland • France • Germany • Greece • Hong Kong • Hungary • India • Indonesia • Ireland • Israel • Italy • Japan • Korea • Luxembourg • Malaysia Mexico • The Netherlands • New Zealand • Norway • Peru • Philippines • Poland • Portugal • Puerto Rico • Romania • Russia • Saudi Arabia • Singapore Slovakia • Slovenia • South Africa • Spain • Sweden • Switzerland • Taiwan • Thailand • Turkey • Ukraine • United Kingdom • United States • Venezuela

About the Author

Kevin Downes, CCIE #1987, is a senior network systems consultant with International Network Services (INS), where he provides network design, traffic analysis, and troubleshooting of large-scale enterprise networks. His network certifications include CCIE, Bay Network CRS, Certified Network Expert (CNX), Ethernet, Novell CNE, and Banyan Systems CBE. He has published several articles on network infrastructure design, network operating systems, and Internet Protocol (IP). Kevin has also contributed to several Cisco Press titles, including *Internetworking Troubleshooting Handbook* and *Internetworking Troubleshooting Handbook, Second Edition*.

Tim Boyles is a Senior Network Systems Consultant with International Network Services (INS). He has been working in the industry for more than 15 years with experience at the U.S. Navy, Rockwell Automation, Aquila Technologies, and now INS. He has been involved in many network projects over the years and recently was a project manager for a Cisco Catalyst rollout of 20,000 switched ports for a major computer services firm. He is the author of several articles on the subjects of technologies and design. He holds a B.S. in Engineering Management from the University of Missouri-Rolla and an MBA from California State University. He is the holder of several industry certifications including the Cisco Certified Network Professional (CCNP).

About the Technical Reviewers

Stephen Daleo is a Cisco Certified Systems Instructor (CCSI) and consultant with Chesapeake Computer Consultants, Inc. Stephen has been teaching most of the recommended training courses for Cisco Career Certifications since 1996, including ICRC, ACRC, CLSC, and CIT. Previous to joining Chesapeake, Stephen worked as a Network Systems Analyst for North Broward Hospital District, where he designed and implemented their Metropolitan WAN consisting of four major sites and ten smaller remote sites. Stephen has a B.S. in Computer Science from Florida International University and a M.S. in Computer Technology from Barry University.

Carole Warner Reece is a consultant for Chesapeake Computer Consultants and has been involved in the networking and telecommunications industry for over 10 years. She has most recently been responsible for the development of MentorLabs' vLabs, which provide practice scenarios to help students hone their networking skills. Carole has written about 40 labs to date ranging from basic to advanced level, including one on switching. Carole has a B.S. in Electrical Engineering from Case Western Reserve University, and a M.S. in Telecommunications from the University of Pittsburgh. She is currently pursuing her CCIE certification.

Casimir Sammanasu is a Product Marketing Engineer for Cisco Systems, Inc., and manages the Video Solutions Lab showcasing video conferencing and video streaming (IP/TV) over IP networks. Prior to his current responsibilities, Casimir was a Program

Manager in the Customer Advocacy group and developed a CD/web-based multimedia training for LAN Switching with simulated lab exercises and voice instructions. As a Technical Course Developer for Cisco's Worldwide Training Division, he developed the "Technical Essentials: Switching" course and co-developed the "Cisco LAN Switch Configuration (CLSC)" course. Casimir has a B.A. in Education from the University of Madras, India, an M.S. in Computer Science from DePaul University in Chicago, and an M.B.A. from the University of Dallas. He has accrued over 16 years of training and course development experience.

David Hucaby, CCIE #4594, is a Senior Network Consultant for The Information Connection, where he provides consulting and troubleshooting services for a variety of clientele. He has extensive design, implementation, and management experience with switched and routed enterprise networks using Cisco Catalyst switches, routers, and firewalls. He has implemented network operations center services for multiple clients. Prior to his current position, David designed, implemented, and maintained networks for the University of Kentucky Hospital using Cisco routers and switches and IBM devices. David has a B.S. and M.S. in Electrical Engineering from the University of Kentucky.

Ronald W. McCarty, Jr., is a network engineer and project manager at Software Spectrum Incorporated. His responsibilities include designing and implementing network solutions to support Software Spectrum's growing global network. Prior to Software Spectrum, Ronald worked at FreiNet GmbH, an ISP in Freiburg, Germany, where he planned and implemented edge networks and Internet services. He received his bachelor's degree in Computer Information Systems from the University of Maryland's international campus at Schwaebisch Gmuend, Germany. Ronald is also a CCNA. In addition, he has published articles on the RADIUS protocol, packet filtering with Cisco routers, IP Security, and intrusion detection.

Contents at a Glance

Table of Contents

Introduction: Overview of Cisco Certifications

Professional certifications have been an important part of the computing industry for many years and will continue to become increasingly more important. Many reasons exist for these certifications, but the most popularly cited reason is credibility. All other considerations equal, the certified employee, consultant, or job candidate is considered more valuable than one who is not.

Cisco Certifications: Training Paths and Exams

The *Cisco Certified Internetwork Expert (CCIE)* certification program has been available since the early 1990s. This long-standing certification has maintained a high degree of credibility and is recognized as a certification that lives up to the name "expert." The CCIE certification process requires passing a computer-based test and a two-day hands-on lab. Recertification is required every two years to ensure that the individual has kept pertinent skills updated.

Many problems were created by having one highly credible but difficult to pass certification. One problem was that there was no way to distinguish between a novice and someone who was almost ready to pass CCIE. The CCIE lab test is meant to prove that the individual has not only mastery of many topics, but also the ability to learn and unravel situations quickly and under pressure. Many highly respected engineers have failed the CCIE lab on the first attempt. Employers wanting to reward employees based on certification, employers looking at prospective new employees, and network managers trying to choose between competing consulting companies have had too few Cisco-related certifications on which they could base their decisions.

Certification Exams

In an effort to solve these problems, Cisco Systems has created several new Cisco Career Certifications. Included in these new certifications is a series of certifications related to routing and switching. The *Cisco Certified Network Professional (CCNP)* and *Cisco Certified Design Professional (CCDP)* certifications, accomplished by passing computer-based exams, are two of these certifications oriented toward routing and switching

Figure I-1 lists the various Cisco certifications relating to routing and switching. This figure also lists with the exams required, including the exams that must be passed to become a CCNP or CCDP.

Figure I-1 *Cisco Certifications and Exams on the Routing and Switching Career Track*

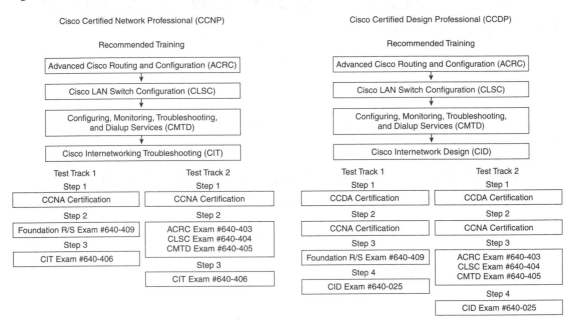

In addition to these certifications and exams, a CCNP can choose to go onto one of five available career specializations: Security, LAN ATM, Voice Access, SNA Solutions, and Network Management. These require CCNP certification and passing a specific exam. See Cisco's web site (www.cisco.com) for exam details. Some reasons for passing the Cisco LAN Switch Configuration (CLSC) exam and achieving CCNP or CCDP certification are listed here:

1 To prove your mastery of advanced networking concepts.

2 To create a more impressive entry in your résumé.

3 To prove that, beyond simply taking a Cisco-certified course, you understood the topics in the class.

4 To demonstrate that you have equivalent experience and expertise to those who have taken the Cisco-certified courses.

5 To obtain a Cisco certification while you gain the experience needed to pass the CCIE Routing and Switching or CCIE ISP Dial certifications. (Unless you want to shoot for the stars and take a CCIE test now.)

6 To encourage self-discipline in your study as you try to become CCIE-certified.

7 For consultants, to provide a marketing edge compared to competitors by asserting that a Cisco-certified individual will be working with a particular prospective client.

Certification Training Paths

Cisco suggests training paths that include courses and exams for each certification. See Cisco's web site at www.cisco.com/training for information and updates.

The *Cisco Certified Network Associate (CCNA)* certification is used to prove mastery over network implementation issues for basic networks. The courses suggested in the training path defined by Cisco for CCNA are Internetworking Technology Multimedia (ITM), Cisco Routing and LAN Switching (CRLS), Introduction to Cisco Router Configuration (ICRC), and High-Performance Solutions for Desktop Connectivity (HPSDC).

Because the CCNA is the entry-level Cisco certification, candidates may also find an ample amount of training to become a CCNA though on-the-job experience. Finally, Cisco's Networking Academies are designed for high school and university students, with the goal of providing a learning path that grants students valuable Cisco skills, ready to use in the marketplace at CCNA level.

The *Cisco Certified Networking Professional (CCNP)* certification is used to prove mastery of more complex networks. In this case, "complex" means topics covered in the prerequisite courses. As with the CCNA, the CCNP certification is oriented toward proving the skills needed to implement internetworks. CCNA certification is a prerequisite to becoming a CCNP.

The following courses are suggested by Cisco for CCNP to prepare for the CNNP certification:

1 A training path leading to CCNA certification

2 The Advanced Cisco Router Configuration (ACRC) course

3 The Cisco LAN Switching Course (CLSC) course

4 The Configuring, Monitoring, and Troubleshooting Dial-up Services (CMTD) course

5 The Cisco Internetwork Troubleshooting (CIT) course

The *Cisco Certified Design Associate (CCDA)* exam is used to prove mastery over network design issues for basic networks. It is similar to CCNA, but is focused on design issues. This certification is particularly important for those with pre-sales–oriented jobs.

The following courses are suggested by Cisco to prepare for the CCDA certification:

1 The Internetworking Technology Multimedia (ITM) CD-based course

2 The Designing Cisco Networks (DCN) course

The *Cisco Certified Design Professional (CCDP)* exam is used to prove mastery over design issues for more advanced networks. This certification proves mastery of design issues in complex networks. In this case, "complex" means topics covered in the prerequisite courses. This certification is particularly important for those with pre-sales–oriented jobs. CCDA and CCNA certification are prerequisites to becoming a CCDP.

The following courses are suggested by Cisco to prepare for CCDP certification:

1 A training path leading to CCDA and CCNA certification

2 The Advanced Cisco Router Configuration (ACRC) course

3 The Cisco LAN Switching Course (CLSC) course

4 The Configuring, Monitoring, and Troubleshooting Dial-up Services (CMTD) course

5 The Cisco Internetwork Design (CID) course

A Few Words on the Various Cisco Certifications

You should note the following when considering CCNA, CCNP, CCDA, and CCDP Cisco routing and switching certifications:

Most people will not pursue all four of these certifications—Most people will first get CCNA certification and then will focus on either the design certifications or the implementation certifications.

None of these certifications require you to take any Cisco classes—However, the new certification exams happen to cover the content taught in Cisco Systems Certified Courses, so there is a definite benefit to taking the courses suggested by Cisco before taking the exam.

The old CCIE is now CCIE-Routing and Switching (R/S)—Cisco added the designation R/S for routing and switching, which includes both LAN and ATM switching. This is the CCIE of old. A separate CCIE-ISP Dial certification covers dial issues in more depth, as well as exterior routing protocols. CCIE-WAN, which entails a separate career path of recommended courses and exams altogether, covers WAN switching and voice.

Only the CCIE certifications require a hands-on lab exam—CCIE-R/S, CCIE-ISP Dial, and CCIE-WAN all require passing a hands-on lab exam after passing a written (computer-based) exam. Recertification for CCIE of any kind currently does not require a hands-on lab, but rather demands a more detailed written test in an area of specialization.

In the future, CCNA might be required before taking CCIE—Today, you can take the CCIE written exam at any time. The reason these new certifications are currently not required before taking the CCIE exam is that people who have prepared for CCIE would then have to back up and take other tests. It is possible, however, that one day Cisco will require CCDP or CCNP certification before taking the CCIE written and lab exams. Of course, the CCNP certification requires CCNA certification first, and the CCDP requires the CCDA and CCNA certifications first.

There is also a WAN Switching Career Certifications path—There is a whole other set of certifications with the acronym WAN in the title, which refers to the WAN switching topics and the functions of what was once the Stratacom product line (which was bought by Cisco). CCNA-WAN, CCNP-WAN, CCDP-WAN, and CCIE-WAN are the certifications; only a CCDA-WAN is missing as compared to the routing/switching certifications outlined previously. These certifications are similar in concept to the others outlined previously, but because the technology concerned is WAN switching, there are different exams and courses for the Career Certification levels. Please see Cisco's web site (www.cisco.com) for more details.

Objectives

The objective of this book is to help you fully understand, remember, and recall all the details of the exam objectives covered on the CLSC exam.

When that objective is reached, passing the CLSC exam should follow. The CLSC exam will be a stepping stone for most people as they progress through the other Cisco certifications; passing the exam because of a thorough understanding and recall of the topics will be incredibly valuable at the next steps.

This book will help you pass the CLSC exam, by doing the following:

- Helping you discover which test topics you have not mastered

- Providing explanations and information to fill in your knowledge gaps

- Supplying exercises that enhance your ability to recall and deduce the answers to test questions

- Providing practice exercises on the topics and the testing process via online test questions (delivered on the CD-ROM)

Who Should Read This Book?

This book is not designed to be a general networking topics book, although it can be used for that purpose. This book is intended to tremendously increase your chances of passing the CLSC exam. This book is intended for an audience who has taken the CLSC course or who has an equivalent level of on-the-job experience. Although others may benefit from using this book, the book is written with the assumption that you want to pass the exam.

So, why should you want to pass CLSC? Numerous reasons exist:

- To get a raise
- To show your manager you are working hard to increase your skills
- To fulfill a requirement from your manager before the company will spend money on another course
- To enhance your résumé
- Because you work in a pre-sales job at a reseller and want to become CCDA- and CCDP-certified
- To prove you know the topic, if you learned via on-the-job experience rather than from taking the prerequisite classes
- Or one of many other reasons

Have You Mastered All the Exam Objectives?

The exam will test you on a wide variety of topics; most people will not remember all the topics on the exam. Because some study will be required, this book focuses on helping you obtain the maximum benefit from the time you spend preparing for the exam. Of course, there are many sources for the information covered in the exam; for example, you could read the Cisco Documentation CD. However, this book is the most effective way to prepare for the exam.

You should begin your exam preparation by reading Chapter 1, "The Cisco LAN Switch Configuration (CLSC) Exam Overview," and by spending ample time reviewing the exam objectives listed there. Check out Cisco's web site (www.cisco.com) for any future changes to the list of objectives.

How This Book Is Organized

The book begins with a chapter that has a general definition of the topics that will be covered by the CLSC exam, including all the objectives. Before studying for any exam, knowing the topics that could be covered is vitally important. With the CLSC exam, knowing what is on the exam is seemingly straightforward because Cisco publishes a list of CLSC objectives. However, the objectives are certainly open to interpretation.

The chapters directly follow Cisco's CLSC exam objectives and provide detailed information on each. Each chapter begins with a quiz so that you can quickly determine your current level of readiness.

Appendix A, "Answers to 'Do I Know This Already?' Quizzes and Q & A Sections," provides the answers to the various chapter quizzes. Example test questions and the testing engine on the CD-ROM also allow simulated exams for final practice.

Approach

Retention and recall are the two features of human memory most closely related to performance on tests. This exam preparation guide focuses on increasing both retention and recall of the topics on the exam.

Adult retention is typically less than that of children. As an example, it is common for 4-year-olds to pick up basic language skills in a new country faster than their parents. Children retain facts as an end unto itself; adults typically either need a stronger reason to remember a fact or must have a reason to think about that fact several times to retain it in memory. For these reasons, a student who attends a typical Cisco course and retains 50 percent of the material is actually quite an amazing student!

Memory recall is based on connectors to the information that must be recalled. For example, if the exam asks what ARP stands for, we automatically add information to the question. We know the topic is networking because of the test. We may recall the term "ARP broadcast," which implies that it is the name of something that flows in a network. Maybe we do not recall all three words in the acronym, but we recall that it has something to do with addressing. Of course, because the test is multiple choice, if only one answer begins with "address," we have a pretty good guess. Having read the answer, "Address Resolution Protocol," then we may even have the infamous "Aha!" experience, in which we are then sure that our answer is correct (and possibly a brightly lit light bulb is hovering over our head!). All these added facts and assumptions are the connectors that eventually lead our brains to the fact needed to be recalled.

Of course, recall and retention work together. If you do not retain the knowledge, it will be difficult to recall it!

This book is designed with features to help you increase retention and recall. It does that in the following ways:

- Providing succinct and complete methods of helping you decide what you already know and what you do not know.

- Giving references to the exact passages in this book that review those concepts you did not recall, so that you can quickly be reminded about a fact or concept.

- Including exercise questions that supply fewer connectors than multiple choice questions. This helps you exercise recall and avoids giving you a false sense of confidence, as a multiple-choice exercise might do. For example, fill-in-the-blank questions require you to have better recall than a multiple choice question.

- Finally, accompanying this book is a CD-ROM that contains online exam-like multiple choice questions that you can use to practice taking the exam and to work on getting accustomed to the time restrictions imposed while you take the exam.

Features and Conventions of This Book

The various features of this book are listed as follows:

Cross-reference to CLSC objectives—Cisco lists the objectives of the CLSC exam on its web site (www.cisco.com). That list is also included in Chapter 1. A section of each core chapter will include a reference to the CLSC objectives discussed in that chapter. Each major section also begins with a list of the objectives covered there.

Do I Know This Already? Quiz—This beginning section of each chapter is designed to thoroughly quiz you on all topics in that chapter. Use your score on these questions to determine your relative need to study this topic further.

Foundation Topics—This section in each chapter explains and reviews topics that will be covered in the exam. If you feel the need for some review of the topics listed in that chapter, read through the explanations in the section. If you do not feel as much need to review these topics, review the Foundation Summaries section in each chapter, and then proceed directly to the exercises at the end of the chapter.

Q&A—Thinking about the same fact in many different ways increases recall; as we've already discussed, recall is a very important factor during a timed test. During study time, increasing retention is most important so that there is something in memory you can recall in the future. These end-of-the-chapter questions focus on recall, covering topics in the Foundation Topics section by using several types of questions.

Test questions—Using the test preparation test engine on the CD, you can take simulated exams or choose to be presented with several questions on a topic you need to work on more. The testing tool will provide you with practice that will make you more comfortable when you actually take the CLSC exam.

Guidance through using each chapter—Use the chapters to discover gaps in your knowledge, fill those gaps, and practice recalling the new information. Figure I-2 describes how to use each of these chapters best.

Figure I-2 *How to Use Each Chapter*

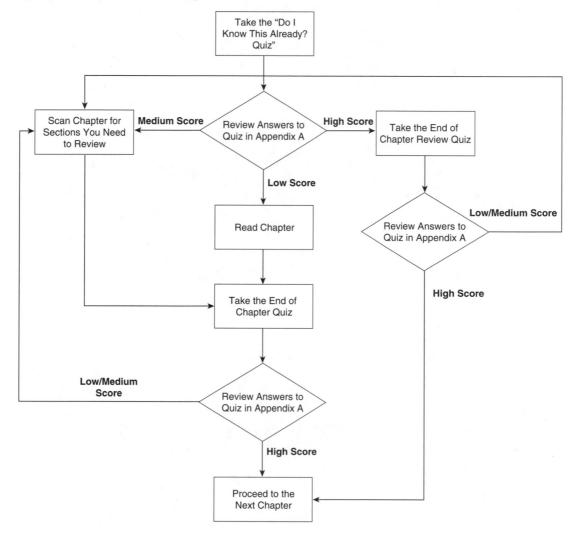

By following this process, you can gain confidence, fill the holes in your knowledge, and know when you are ready to take the exam.

Knowing Cisco is not enough; knowing Cisco, and being able to prove that you know it—both at your job and with credentials—is vitally important in the job markets of the 21st Century. The days of working an entire career at one firm are most likely gone, and your skills—both professional and technical—will be invaluable as your career evolves. Being certified is a key to getting the right opportunities inside your company, with your clients, and with your next job move!

CHAPTER 1

The Cisco LAN Switch Configuration (CLSC) Exam Overview

The CLSC exam evaluates the internetworking knowledge of network administrators, network specialists, and technicians who configure and support multiprotocol internetworks. The candidates attempting the CLSC exam must possess the skills to perform the following tasks:

- Describe the major features of the Catalyst switches

- Describe the architecture and functions of the major components of the Catalyst switches

- Place Catalyst series switches in a network for optimal performance benefit

- Use the command-line or menu-driven interface to configure the Catalyst series switches and their switching modules

- Use the command-line or menu-driven interface to configure trunks, virtual LANs, and ATM LAN Emulation

- Maintain Catalyst series switches and perform basic troubleshooting

Suggested Cisco Training Paths for Prior Preparation

This book assumes that you have a familiar level of understanding of the CLSC objectives, through either the CLSC course or an equivalent level of on-the-job training, and that you are now ready to master the CLSC exam objectives and become a CCNP or CCDP. Table 1-1 outlines the three training paths you can take to become a CCNP, including the various courses available.

Table 1-1   *Training Paths for Becoming a CCNP*

Training Path	What Is Involved
1 CCNP Path	As defined by Cisco Systems, this involves taking these courses: Advanced Cisco Router Configuration (ACRC) Cisco LAN Switch Configuration (CLSC) Configuring, Monitoring, and Troubleshooting Dialup Services (CMTD) Cisco Internetworking Troubleshooting (CIT) The candidate then would take a test for each class attended. (Note that the ACRC, CLSC, and CMTD exams can be taken all together as the Foundation Routing and Switching [FRS] exam.)
2 On-the-job training	The courses are not required to take the exams, but the exams require a large amount of specific knowledge. Candidates who have not taken the courses should use this book to make sure they are familiar with all the objectives. When the candidate is familiar with the exam objectives, he or she would take the same exams listed at the bottom of Step 1.

The CCDP training path is the same as the CCNP path, but it substitutes a Cisco Internetwork Design (CID) course and exam for the Cisco Internetworking Troubleshooting (CIT) course and exam.

CLSC Exam Philosophy

The exam objectives create a great tool for preparation. If you are going to prepare only slightly, making sure that you can address all objectives is an obvious thing to do. However, what each objective means, and the breadth of questions that could be asked based on an individual objective, is open to interpretation. This book generally follows the CLSC course to determine the depth of coverage for various objectives.

A full definition of exactly what topics are on the exam will probably never be stated by Cisco. Cisco does want candidates to succeed at passing the CLSC exam, but not at the expense of making the Cisco career certification an easily attained paper diploma. Cisco's goal is that passing the CLSC exam should reflect the fact that you have internalized and mastered the concepts, not that you can read a book and memorize well. To protect against the CCDP and CCNP losing credibility due to people just reading a book and passing the test, Cisco will probably always avoid an exact definition of the topics on the exam. Giving a general definition only will reward those who understand networks; those who prefer to memorize will be less likely to pass the test.

Naturally, the objectives will change as time goes on. As this happens, a higher percentage of the test questions will not be in the list of objectives found in this book. Of course, Cisco will change or add to the objective list at its discretion, so pulling the latest CLSC objectives list from Cisco's web site (http://www.cisco.com) is worth the effort.

The CLSC exam topics will closely match what is covered in the recommended prerequisite training course. Cisco Worldwide Training (WWT) is the Cisco organization with responsibility for the certifications. Many of the certification exams evolved from exams covering a particular course. It is reasonable to expect, with good benefits to us, that CLSC and the other certifications will cover the topics in the prerequisite classes.

The following list encapsulates the basic philosophy behind preparing for the CLSC exam, based on what Cisco is willing to disclose:

- While open to interpretation, the CLSC objectives define the main topics covered on the exam. At a minimum, you should know about each subject covered in these objectives.

- The depth of knowledge on each topic is comparable to what is covered in the prerequisite courses. The book attempts to cover the topics to a slightly deeper level, to make sure you know more than enough.

- Getting the latest copy of Cisco's CLSC objectives from the company's web site (http://www.cisco.com) is very useful. Comparing that list to the one used for this book will let you know the topics you will need to spend additional time studying.

- Do not expect to pass the exam if your only preparation has been to read this book. Use one of the suggested training paths, and work with routers and switches for the best chance at success.

CLSC Exam Preparation

This book contains many solid tools to help you prepare for the CLSC exam. Some of the key features to help you are outlined in the next few sections.

Chapters Follow the Objectives

Each chapter clearly follows the CLSC exam objectives so that you can stay on track with the material that will be covered in the exam. You'll know clearly what objective each section is covering.

Determining Your Strengths and Weaknesses

You may feel confident about one topic and less confident about another. However, that may be a confidence problem, not a knowledge problem! One key to using your time well is to determine whether you truly need more study or not—and if so, how much?

The chapters are designed to guide you through the process of determining what you need to study. Suggestions are made as to how to study a topic based on your personal strengths. Each chapter begins with a quiz that helps you decide how well you recall the topics in that chapter. From there, you can choose to fully read the entire chapter, to ignore that chapter because you know it already, or something in between. Much of the factual information is summarized into lists and charts in the Foundations Summaries sections, so a review of the chapter is easy. Also, exercises at the end of the chapter provide an excellent tool for practice and for quick review.

Questions and Exercises That Are Harder Than the Actual Exam

The exercises in this book are intended to make you stretch beyond what the exam requires. Do not be discouraged as you take the quizzes and exercises in the book; they are *intended* to be harder than the exam. If, by the end of your study time, you are getting 70 or 80 percent of these harder non-multiple choice questions correct, you should find the CLSC exam easier to handle. You will probably want to validate your readiness by using the testing engine included on the CD-ROM with this book.

The main purpose for making this book's exams harder than the CLSC exam is not by asking for facts or concepts you will never see on the CLSC exam; it is by asking for information in ways that will not imply the correct answer. You will get some questions correct on the CLSC exam just because the multiple answers will trigger your memory to the correct information. By answering questions that are not multiple choice, however, and by providing the same information in different ways, you will exercise your memory so that the multiple choice exam is easy!

Simulated Testing on the CD-ROM

Of course, if you never practice using actual exams, you will not be fully prepared. The test engine on the CD-ROM can be used in two ways to help you prepare for the actual test. First, it will give you a timed test of the same length as the actual CLSC exam and will score the exam for you. Secondly, you can tell the tool to feed you questions on a particular subject so that you can do some intensive review.

The CLSC Exam Objectives

Cisco System's published CLSC exam objectives are currently listed on Cisco's web site (http://www.cisco.com).

The objectives intend to test your ability to install, configure, operate, and troubleshoot switched LANs.

The CLSC exam includes 85 objectives, and you will be tested on the following areas:

- Basic switching concepts
- Virtual LANs
- Placing Catalyst switches in your network
- The Catalyst 5000 series switch overview
- The Catalyst 5000 series switch architecture
- The Catalyst 5000 series switch hardware
- Configuring the Supervisor module and Fast Ethernet
- The Catalyst 5000 switch series software
- Managing the Catalyst 5000 series switch
- Troubleshooting the Catalyst 5000 series switch
- The Catalyst 5000 FDDI module
- ATM LAN Emulation concepts
- The Catalyst 5000 series ATM LANE module
- Configuring the Catalyst 5000 series ATM LANE modules
- Catalyst 2820 and Catalyst 1900 features
- Configuring Catalyst 2820 and Catalyst 1900 switches
- Catalyst 3000 series switches
- Configuring the Catalyst 3000 series switch

List of the CLSC Exam Objectives

Table 1-2 lists all the CLSC exam objectives. These are the objectives this book will help you master to pass the CLSC exam. Each chapter also begins with a list of which objectives are covered in that chapter.

Table 1-2   *List of CLSC Exam Objectives*

1	Describe the major features of the Catalyst switches.
2	Describe the architecture and functions of the major components of the Catalyst switches.
3	Place Catalyst series switches in a network for optimal performance benefit.
4	Use the command-line or menu-driven interface to configure the Catalyst series switches and their switching modules.
5	Use the command-line or menu-driven interface to configure trunks, virtual LANs, and ATM LAN Emulation.
6	Maintain Catalyst series switches and perform basic troubleshooting.
7	Describe the advantages of LAN segmentation.
8	Describe LAN segmentation using bridges.
9	Describe LAN segmentation routers.
10	Describe LAN segmentation using switches.
11	Name and describe two switching methods.
12	Describe full- and half-duplex Ethernet operation.
13	Describe Token Ring switching concepts.
14	Define VLANs.
15	Name seven reasons to create VLANs.
16	Describe the role switches play in the creation of VLANs.
17	Describe VLAN frame filtering and VLAN frame tagging.
18	Describe how switches can be used with hubs.
19	Name the five components of VLAN implementations.
20	Describe static and dynamic VLANs.
21	Describe the VLAN technologies.
22	Describe Token Ring VLANs.
23	Describe Cisco's VLAN architecture.
24	Describe demand nodes and resource nodes.
25	Describe configuration rules for demand nodes and resource nodes.

Table 1-2   *List of CLSC Exam Objectives (Continued)*

26	Describe local resources and remote resources.
27	Describe configuration rules for local resources and remote resources.
28	Name five applications for Catalyst 5000 series switches.
29	Describe Catalyst 5000 series switch product evolution.
30	Describe Catalyst 5000 product features.
31	Describe Catalyst 5002 product features.
32	Describe Catalyst 5500 product features.
33	Describe the architecture and function of major components of the Catalyst 5000 series switch: • Processors: NMP, MCP, and LCP • Logic Units: LTL, CBL, Arbiter, and EARL • ASICs: SAINT, SAGE, SAMBA, and Phoenix
34	Trace a frame's progress through a Catalyst 5000 series switch.
35	Describe the hardware features, functions, and benefits of Catalyst 5000 series switches.
36	Describe the hardware features and functions of the Supervisor engine.
37	Describe the hardware features and functions of the modules in the Catalyst 5000 series switches.
38	Prepare network connections.
39	Establish a serial connection.
40	Use the Catalyst 5000 switch CLI to: • Enter privileged mode. • Set system information. • Configure interface types.
41	Upon completion of this module, you will be able to describe the different ways of managing the Catalyst 5000 series switch, including: • Out-of-band management (console port) • In-band management (network connection using SNMP) • RMON • SPAN • CWSI

continues

Table 1-2   *List of CLSC Exam Objectives (Continued)*

42	Upon completion of this module, you will be able to: • Describe the approach for troubleshooting Catalyst. • Describe the physical-layer problem areas. • Use the **show** commands to troubleshoot problems. • Describe the switch hardware status. • Describe network test equipment.
43	Describe the major features and functions of the Catalyst 5000 FDDI/CDDI Module.
44	Describe IEEE 802.10 VLANs.
45	Configure the Catalyst 5000 FDDI/CDDI Module.
46	Define LAN Emulation.
47	Describe the LAN Emulation components.
48	Describe the start-up procedure of a LAN Emulation Client.
49	Describe how one LEC establishes communication with another LEC.
50	Discuss how internetworking is achieved in a LANE environment.
51	List the features of the Catalyst 5000 LANE module.
52	Outline the performance ratings for the ATM bus and the switching bus.
53	Describe how to access the CLI for the LANE.
54	Describe the Simple Server Redundancy Protocol (SSRP).
55	Explain ATM address structure.
56	Describe how ATM addresses are automatically assigned.
57	Describe the rules for assigning ATM components to interfaces.
58	Configure LANE components on a Catalyst 5000 switch.
59	Describe the major features and benefits of the Catalyst 1900 and Catalyst 2820 switches.
60	Describe the hardware components and their functions of the Catalyst 1900 and Catalyst 2820 switches.
61	Describe the architecture.

Table 1-2   *List of CLSC Exam Objectives (Continued)*

62	Describe the following key features and applications of the Catalyst 1900 and 2820 switches:

- Switching modes
- Virtual LANs
- Multicast packet filtering and registration
- Broadcast storm control
- Management support, CDP, and CGMP

63	Trace a frame's progress through a Catalyst 1900 or Catalyst 2820 switch.
64	Use the Catalyst 1900 and Catalyst 2820 switch menus for configuration.
65	Configure IP addresses and ports on the Catalyst 1900 and Catalyst 2820 switches.
66	Configure VLANs on the Catalyst 1900 and Catalyst 2820 switches.
67	View the Catalyst 1900 and Catalyst 2820 switch reports and summaries.
68	Configure the ATM LANE module on the Catalyst 2820 switch.
69	Describe Catalyst 3000 series LAN switch products.
70	Describe Catalyst 3000 series LAN switch product differences.
71	Describe the Catalyst Stack System.
72	Perform initial setup of a Catalyst 3000 series switch.
73	Configure the switch for management.
74	Configure port parameters.
75	Configure VLANs and trunk links.
76	Configure the ATM LANE module.
77	Perform basic router module configuration.
78	Describe the POST and diagnostic messages on the Catalyst 1900 and Catalyst 2820 switches.
79	Describe the cabling guidelines for the Catalyst 1900 and Catalyst 2820 switches.
80	Use the statistics and reports to maintain the Catalyst 1900 and Catalyst 2820 switches.
81	Describe the firmware upgrade procedures for the Catalyst 1900 and Catalyst 2820 switches.
82	Troubleshooting the Catalyst 3000 series switch subsystems.
83	Troubleshooting network interfaces and connections.
84	Use the switch LEDs to isolate problems.
85	Isolate network segment problems.

The CLSC Exam

The CLSC exam is an exam that tests for knowledge on the Catalyst 5000 series switch, with a minor accent on smaller and older switches such as the 3000 series switches and the 1900/2820 series switches. Because the switches are largely based on Ethernet, you can expect most questions to be based on Ethernet functions. However, FDDI and ATM modules are included, and you are expected to know both modules and how to configure both services.

Not surprisingly, the CLSC exam is based almost exclusively on the course material taught in the Cisco CLSC course taught by Cisco Training Partners.

The exam itself is 70 questions long. The test is broken down into 19 sections, as detailed in Table 1-3, which shows an estimated number of questions in each section:

Table 1-3   *CLSC Exam Sections*

Section Number	Section Title	Number of Questions
1	Introduction to Switching Concepts	5
2	Virtual LANs	2
3	Placing Catalyst 5000 Series Switches in Your Network	4
4	Catalyst 5000 Series Switch Overview	2
5	Catalyst 5000 Series Switch Architecture	6
6	Catalyst 5000 Series Switch Hardware	2
7	Configuring the Catalyst 5000 Series Switch	5
8	Catalyst 5000 Series Switch Software	4
9	Managing the Catalyst 5000 Series Switches	4
10	Troubleshooting the Catalyst 5000 Series Switches	2
11	Catalyst 5000 Series Switch FDDI Module	4
12	ATM LANE Concepts	3
13	Catalyst 5000 Series Switch ATM LANE Module	4

Table 1-3   *CLSC Exam Sections (Continued)*

Section Number	Section Title	Number of Questions
14	Configuring the Catalyst 5000 Series Switch ATM LANE Module	6
15	Catalyst 2820 and Catalyst 1900 Hardware	3
16	Catalyst 2820 and Catalyst 1900 Features	4
17	Configuring Catalyst 2820 and Catalyst 1900 Switches	3
18	Catalyst 3000 Series Switches	3
19	Configuring the Catalyst 3000 Series Switches	4

Cross-Reference to Objectives Covered in Each Chapter of the Book

Table 1-4 provides a breakdown of where the test objectives fall in each chapter. (For convenience, the objectives also are listed at the beginning of each chapter.)

Table 1-4   *CLSC Exam Objectives Cross-Reference List*

Chapter	Objectives Covered
2	7–13
3	14–23
4	3, 24–28
5	2, 33, 34
6	1, 29–32, 35–37
7	4, 5, 38–40
8	4
9	41
10	6, 42
11	43–45
12	46–58
13	59–68, 78–81
14	69–77, 82–85

Where Do I Go From Here?

After passing the CLSC exam, you should choose to proceed directly to passing all the exams that allow you to be a CCNP or CCDP (see the exams listed in Table 1-1). Then, with the proper amount of experience and training, the CCIE exam should be your next step.

The objectives of the Cisco LAN Switch Configuration (CLSC) exam are taken from the Cisco web site, at the Cisco career certification and training area. The following table shows the exam objectives covered in this chapter:

Objective	Description
7	Describe the advantages of LAN segmentation.
8	Describe LAN segmentation using bridges.
9	Describe LAN segmentation routers.
10	Describe LAN segmentation using switches.
11	Name and describe two switching methods.
12	Describe full- and half-duplex Ethernet operation.
13	Describe Token Ring switching concepts.

CHAPTER 2

Introduction to Switching Concepts

In the past, network designers had only a limited number of hardware options when purchasing a technology for their campus networks. Hubs were for wiring closets, and routers were for the data center or main telecommunications operations. The increasing power of desktop processors and the requirements of client-server and multimedia applications, however, have driven the need for greater bandwidth in traditional shared-media environments. These requirements are prompting network designers to replace hubs in their wiring closets with switches.

Switching is a technology that alleviates congestion in Ethernet, Token Ring, and Fiber Distributed Data Interface (FDDI) LANs by reducing traffic and increasing bandwidth. Such switches, known as LAN switches, are designed to work with existing cable infrastructures so that they can be installed with minimal disruption of existing networks.

How to Best Use This Chapter

By taking the following steps, you can make better use of your study time:

- Keep your notes and the answers for all your work with this book in one place, for easy reference.

- Take the quiz, and write down your answers. Studies show that retention is significantly increased through writing down facts and concepts, even if you never look at the information again.

- Use the diagram in Figure 2-1 to guide you to the next step.

Figure 2-1 *How to Best Use This Chapter in Preparation for the CLSC Exam*

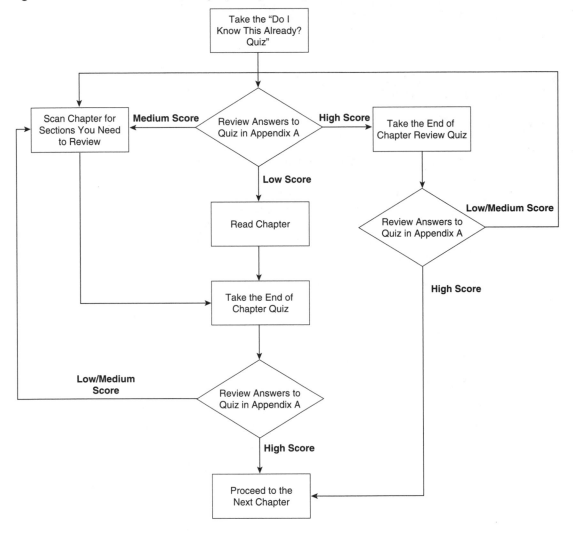

Do I Know This Already? Quiz

You can find the answers to this quiz in Appendix A, "Answers to 'Do I Know This Already?' Quizzes and Q & A Sections." Review the answers, grade your quiz, and choose an appropriate next step in this chapter based on the suggestions diagrammed in Figure 2-1.

  1 An advantage to LAN segmentation is:

   a. It places more internetworking devices between clients and servers.

   b. It provides more bandwidth per user.

   c. It reduces WAN costs.

   d. It increases the number of dumb terminals on the network.

2 Segmenting LANs with bridges:

   a. Occurs at OSI Layer 3.

   b. Reduces the propagation of multicast and broadcast frames.

   c. Provides fewer users per segment.

   d. Uses address tables that associate segment end stations with protocol types.

3 Segmenting LANs with routers (configured as routers):

   a. Occurs at OSI Layer 2.

   b. Has no effect on the propagation of multicast and broadcast frames.

   c. Typically costs less per port than using bridges or switches.

   d. Allows multiple active paths.

4 Segmenting LANs with switches:

   a. Enables multiple high-speed data exchanges.

   b. Increases the number of users per segment.

   c. Occurs at OSI Layer 3.

   d. Requires replacing 802.3-compliant NICs and cabling.

5 A switch that receives a frame completely before forwarding it uses what switching technology?

   a. Cut-through

   b. In and out

   c. Receive-and-send

   d. Store-and-forward

6 Using full-duplex Ethernet:

   a. Requires the attached node to be directly attached to a repeater hub.

   b. Requires the attached node to have an installed network interface card that supports full-duplex Ethernet.

   c. Provides the same performance as half-duplex Ethernet.

   d. Increases contention on Ethernet point-to-point links.

7 Full-duplex port connections can use which of the following media types to provide point-to-point links between switches or end nodes:

   a. 10BaseT

   b. 10BaseFL

   c. 100BaseTX

   d. 100BaseFX

   e. ATM

   f. Token Ring

8 To implement full-duplex Ethernet, which of the following are required?

   a. Two 10 Mbps or 100 Mbps data paths

   b. Full-duplex Ethernet controllers, or an Ethernet controller for each path

   c. Loopback and collision detection disabled

   d. Software network interface drivers supporting two simultaneous data paths

   e. All of the above

9 Cut-through switching is supported on which of the following Catalyst platforms:

   a. 1900

   b. 2820

   c. 3000

   d. 5000

   e. 5500

10 Store-and-forward switching is supported on which of the following Catalyst platforms:

   a. 1900

   b. 2820

   c. 3000

   d. 5000

   e. 5500

Using the answer key in Appendix A, grade your answers.

- **5 or less correct**—Read this chapter.

- **6, 7, or 8 correct**—Review this chapter, looking at the charts and diagrams that summarize most of the concepts and facts in this chapter.

- **9 or more correct**—If you want more review on these topics, skip to the Q&A section at the end of this chapter. If you do not want more review on these topics, skip this chapter.

Foundation Topics

Bridging and Switching Basics

The material presented here is intended to help the reader understand switch features; however, it is not directly related to one of the objectives.

Bridges and switches are data communications devices that operate principally at Layer 2 of the OSI reference model. As such, they are widely referred to as data link layer devices.

Bridges became commercially available in the early 1980s. At the time of their introduction, bridges connected and enabled packet forwarding between homogeneous networks. More recently, bridging between different networks also has been defined and standardized.

Bridges and switches are not complicated devices. They analyze incoming frames, make forwarding decisions based on information contained in the frames, and forward the frames toward the destination. In some cases, such as source-route bridging, the entire path to the destination is contained in each frame. In other cases, such as transparent bridging, frames are forwarded one hop at a time toward the destination, if known. If the destination is unknown, the frames are flooded to all ports except the receiving port.

Upper-layer protocol transparency is a primary advantage of both bridging and switching. Because both device types operate at the link layer, they are not required to examine upper-layer information. This means that they can rapidly forward traffic representing any network-layer protocol. It is not uncommon for a bridge to move AppleTalk, DECnet, TCP/IP, XNS, and other traffic between two or more networks.

Bridges are capable of filtering frames based on any Layer 2 fields. A bridge, for example, can be programmed to reject (not forward) all frames sourced from a particular network. Because link-layer information often includes a reference to an upper-layer protocol, bridges usually can filter on this parameter. Furthermore, filters can be helpful in dealing with unnecessary broadcast and multicast packets.

By dividing large networks into self-contained units, bridges and switches provide several advantages. Because only a certain percentage of traffic is forwarded, a bridge or switch diminishes the traffic experienced by devices on all connected segments. The bridge or switch acts as a firewall for some potentially damaging network errors, and both accommodate communication among a larger number of devices than would be supported on any single LAN connected to the bridge. Bridges and switches extend the effective length of a LAN, permitting the attachment of distant stations that were not previously permitted.

Several kinds of bridging have proven important as internetworking devices. *Transparent bridging* is found primarily in Ethernet environments, while *source-route bridging* occurs primarily in Token Ring environments. *Translational bridging* provides translation between the formats and transit principles of different media types (usually Ethernet and

Token Ring). Finally, *source-route transparent bridging* combines the algorithms of transparent bridging and source-route bridging to enable communication in mixed Ethernet/Token Ring environments.

Today, switching technology has emerged as the evolutionary heir to bridging-based internetworking solutions. Switching implementations now dominate applications in which bridging technologies were implemented in prior network designs. Superior throughput performance, higher port density, lower per-port cost, and greater flexibility have contributed to the emergence of switches as replacement technology for bridges and as complements to routing technology.

Internetworking Device Comparison

Internetworking devices offer communication between local-area network (LAN) segments. Four primary types of internetworking devices exist: *repeaters*, *bridges*, *routers*, and *gateways*. These devices can be differentiated very generally by the *Open System Interconnection* (OSI) layer at which they establish the LAN-to-LAN connection. Repeaters connect LANs at OSI Layer 1; bridges connect LANs at Layer 2; routers connect LANs at Layer 3; and gateways connect LANs at Layers 4–7. Each device offers the functionality found at its layer(s) of connection and uses the functionality of all lower layers.

OSI Layers

Now that the network equipment that services each layer of the OSI model has been described, each individual OSI layer and its functions can be discussed. Each layer has a predetermined set of functions it must perform for communication to occur.

Application Layer

The application layer is the OSI layer closest to the user. It differs from the other layers in that it does not provide services to any other OSI layer, but rather to application processes lying outside the scope of the OSI model. Examples of such application processes include spreadsheet programs, word-processing programs, banking terminal programs, and so on.

The application layer identifies and establishes the availability of intended communication partners, synchronizes cooperating applications, and establishes agreement on procedures for error recovery and control of data integrity. Also, the application layer determines whether sufficient resources for the intended communication exist.

Presentation Layer

The presentation layer ensures that information sent by the application layer of one system will be readable by the application layer of another system. If necessary, the presentation layer translates among multiple data representation formats by using a common data representation format. The presentation layer concerns itself not only with the format and representation of actual user data, but also with data structures used by programs. Therefore, in addition to actual data format transformation (if necessary), the presentation layer negotiates data transfer syntax for the application layer.

Session Layer

As its name implies, the session layer establishes, manages, and terminates sessions between applications. Sessions consist of dialogue between two or more presentation entities (recall that the session layer provides its services to the presentation layer). The session layer synchronizes dialogue between presentation layer entities and manages their data exchange. In addition to basic regulation of conversations (sessions), the session layer offers provisions for data expedition, class of service, and exception reporting of session-layer, presentation-layer, and application-layer problems.

Transport Layer

The boundary between the session layer and the transport layer can be thought of as the boundary between application-layer protocols and lower-layer protocols. Whereas the application, presentation, and session layers are concerned with application issues, the lower four layers are concerned with data transport issues.

The transport layer attempts to provide a data transport service that shields the upper layers from transport implementation details. Specifically, issues such as how reliable transport over an internetwork is accomplished are the concern of the transport layer. In providing reliable service, the transport layer provides mechanisms for the establishment, maintenance, and orderly termination of virtual circuits, transport fault detection and recovery, and information flow control (to prevent one system from overrunning another with data).

Network Layer

The network layer is a complex layer that provides connectivity and path selection between two end systems that may be located on geographically diverse *subnetworks*. A subnetwork, in this instance, is essentially a single network cable (sometimes called a *segment*).

Because a substantial geographic distance and many subnetworks can separate two end systems desiring communication, the network layer is the domain of routing. Routing protocols select optimal paths through the series of interconnected subnetworks. Traditional network-layer protocols then move information along these paths.

Link Layer

The link layer (formally referred to as the *data link layer*) provides reliable transit of data across a physical link. In so doing, the link layer is concerned with *physical* (as opposed to *network*, or *logical*) addressing, network topology, line discipline (how end systems will use the network link), error notification, ordered delivery of frames, and flow control.

Physical Layer

The physical layer defines the electrical, mechanical, procedural, and functional specifications for activating, maintaining, and deactivating the physical link between end systems. Such characteristics as voltage levels, timing of voltage changes, physical data rates, maximum transmission distances, physical connectors, and other similar attributes are defined by physical layer specifications.

Broadcasts in Switched LAN Internetworks

CLSC Objectives Covered in This Section

7	Describe the advantages of LAN segmentation.

To communicate with all or part of the network, protocols use broadcast and multicast datagrams at Layer 2 of the OSI model. When a node needs to communicate with the entire network, it sends a datagram to MAC address 0xFFFFFFFF (a broadcast), an address to which the network interface card (NIC) of every host must respond. When a host needs to communicate with part of the network, it sends a datagram to address 0xFFFFFFFF, with the leading bit of the vendor ID set to 1 (a multicast). Most NICs with that vendor ID respond to a multicast by processing the multicast to its group address.

Because switches work like bridges, they must flood all broadcast and multicast traffic. The accumulation of broadcast and multicast traffic from each device in the network is referred to as *broadcast radiation*.

Because the NIC must interrupt the CPU to process each broadcast or multicast, broadcast radiation affects the performance of hosts in the network. Most often, the host does not benefit from processing the broadcast or multicast—that is, because the host is not the destination being sought, it doesn't care about the service that is being advertised, or it already knows about the service. High levels of broadcast radiation can noticeably degrade host performance.

The following sections describe how the desktop protocols—IP, Novell, and AppleTalk—use broadcast and multicast packets to locate hosts and advertise services. The sections also discuss how broadcast and multicast traffic affects the CPU performance of hosts on the network.

Using Broadcasts with IP Networks

Three sources of broadcasts and multicasts exist in IP networks:

- *Workstations*—An IP workstation broadcasts an Address Resolution Protocol (ARP) request every time it needs to locate a new IP address on the network. For example, the command telnet mumble.com translates into an IP address through a Domain Name System (DNS) search, and then an ARP request is broadcast to find the actual station. Generally, IP workstations cache 10 to 100 addresses for about two hours. The ARP rate for a typical workstation might be about 50 addresses every two hours, or 0.007 ARPs per second. Thus, 2000 IP end stations produce about 14 ARPs per second.

- *Routers*—An IP router is any router or workstation that runs an IP routing protocol, such as RIP. Some administrators configure all workstations to run RIP as a redundancy and reachability policy. Every 30 seconds, RIP uses broadcasts to retransmit the entire RIP routing table to other RIP routers. If 2000 workstations were configured to run RIP, and if 50 packets were required to retransmit the routing table, the workstations would generate 3333 broadcasts per second. Most network administrators configure a small number of routers—usually 5 to 10—to run RIP. For a routing table that requires 50 packets to hold it, 10 RIP routers would generate about 16 broadcasts per second.

- *Multicast applications*—IP multicast applications can adversely affect the performance of large, scaled, switched networks. Although multicasting is an efficient way to send a stream of multimedia (video data) to many users on a shared-media hub, it affects every user on a flat-switched network. A particular packet video application can generate a 7 MB stream of multicast data that, in a switched network, would be sent to every segment, resulting in severe congestion.

Figure 2-2 shows the results of tests that Cisco conducted on the effect of broadcast radiation on a Sun SPARCstation 2 with a standard built-in Ethernet card. The SPARCstation was running SunOS version 4.1.3 without IP multicast enabled. If IP multicast had been enabled, for example, by running Solaris 2.x, multicast packets would have affected CPU performance.

As indicated by the results shown in Figure 2-2, an IP workstation can be effectively shut down by broadcasts flooding the network. Although extreme, broadcast peaks of thousands of broadcasts per second have been observed during *broadcast storms*. Testing in a controlled environment with a range of broadcasts and multicasts on the network shows measurable system degradation with as few as 100 broadcasts or multicasts per second.

Figure 2-2   *Effect of Broadcast Radiation on Hosts in IP Networks*

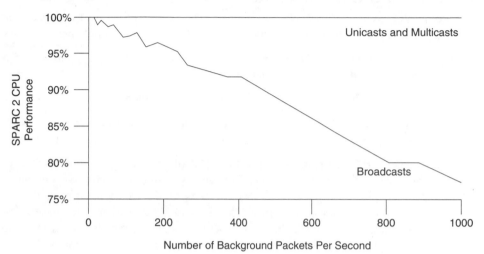

Table 2-1 shows the effect of broadcasts and multicasts for IP networks. As the number of hosts increases, the percentage of CPU loss becomes more significant, due to dealing with with broadcasts and multicasts.

Table 2-1   *Average Number of Broadcasts and Multicasts for IP Networks*

Number of Hosts	Average Percentage of CPU Loss Per Host
100	.14%
1000	.96%
10,000	9.15%

Although the numbers in Table 2-1 might appear low, they represent an average, well-designed IP network that is not running RIP. When broadcast and multicast traffic peak due to "storm" behavior, peak CPU loss can be orders of magnitude greater than average. Broadcast storms can be caused by a device requesting information from a network that has grown too large. So many responses are sent to the original request that the device cannot process them, or the first request triggers similar requests from other devices that effectively block normal traffic flow on the network.

Using Broadcasts with Novell Networks

Many PC-based LANs use Novell's Network Operating System (NOS) and NetWare servers. Novell technology poses the following unique scaling problems:

- NetWare servers use broadcast packets to identify themselves and to advertise their services and routes to other networks.

- NetWare clients use broadcasts to find NetWare servers.

- Version 4.0 of Novell's SNMP-based network management applications, such as NetExplorer, periodically broadcast packets to discover changes in the network.

An idle network with a single server with one shared volume and no print services generates one broadcast packet every 4 seconds. A large LAN with high-end servers might have up to 150 users per PC server. If the LAN has 900 users with a reasonably even distribution, it would have six or seven servers. In an idle state with multiple shared volumes and printers, this might average out to four broadcasts per second, uniformly distributed. In a busy network with route and service requests made frequently, the rate would peak at 15 to 20 broadcasts per second.

Figure 2-3 shows the results of tests that Cisco conducted on the effect of broadcast radiation on the performance of an 80386 CPU running at 25 MHz. Performance was measured with the Norton Utilities System Information utility. Background traffic was generated with a Network General Sniffer and consisted of a broadcast destination packet and a multicast destination packet, with data of all zeros. CPU performance was measurably affected by as few as 30 broadcast or multicast packets per second. Multicast packets had a slightly worse effect than broadcast packets.

Figure 2-3   *Effect of Broadcast Radiation on Hosts in Novell Networks*

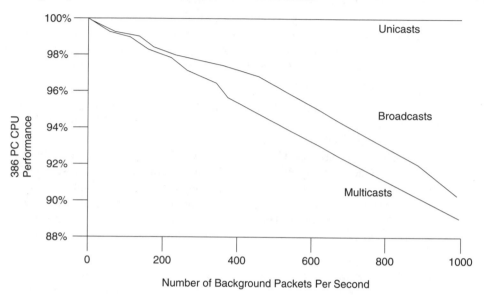

Table 2-2 shows the effect of broadcasts and multicasts for Novell networks. As the number of hosts increases, the percentage of CPU loss becomes more significant, due to dealing with broadcasts and multicasts.

Table 2-2   *Average Number of Broadcasts and Multicasts for Novell Networks*

Number of Hosts	Average Percentage of CPU Loss Per Host
100	.12%
1000	.22%
10,000	3.15%

The results listed in Table 2-2 represent multi-hour, average operation. Peak traffic load and CPU loss per workstation can be orders of magnitude greater than with average traffic loads. A common scenario is that at 9 a.m. on Monday, everyone starts their computers. Normally, in circumstances with an average level of utilization or demand, the network can handle a reasonable number of stations. However, in circumstances in which everyone requires service at once (a demand peak), the available network capacity can support a much lower number of stations. In determining network capacity requirements, peak demand levels and duration can be more important than average serviceability requirements.

Using Broadcasts with AppleTalk Networks

AppleTalk uses multicasting extensively to advertise services, request services, and resolve addresses. On startup, an AppleTalk host transmits a series of at least 20 packets aimed at resolving its network address (a Layer 3 AppleTalk node number) and obtaining local zone information. Except for the first packet, which is addressed to itself, these functions are resolved through AppleTalk multicasts.

In terms of overall network traffic, the AppleTalk Chooser is particularly broadcast-intensive. The Chooser is the software interface that allows the user to select shared network services. It uses AppleTalk multicasts to find file servers, printers, and other services. When the user opens the Chooser and selects a type of service (for example, a printer), the Chooser transmits 45 multicasts at a rate of one packet per second. If left open, the Chooser sends a five-packet burst with a progressively longer delay. If left open for several minutes, the Chooser reaches its maximum delay and transmits a five-packet burst every 270 seconds. By itself, this does not pose a problem, but in a large network, these packets add to the total amount of broadcast radiation that each host must interpret and then discard.

Other AppleTalk protocols—such as the Name Binding Protocol, which is used to bind a client to a server; and the Router Discovery Protocol, a RIP implementation that is transmitted by all routers and listened to by each station—are broadcast-intensive. The system in it, called AutoRemounter (part of the Macintosh operating system), is also broadcast-intensive.

NOTE   The AppleTalk stack is more efficient than the Novell stack because the AppleTalk stack discards non-AppleTalk broadcasts earlier than the Novell stack discards non-Novell broadcasts.

Figure 2-4 shows the results of tests that Cisco conducted on the effect of broadcast radiation on the performance of a Power Macintosh 8100 and a Macintosh IIci. Both CPUs were measurably affected by as few as 15 broadcast or multicast frames per second.

Figure 2-4   *Effect of Broadcast Radiation on Hosts in AppleTalk Networks*

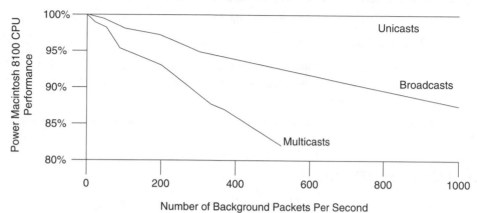

Table 2-3 shows the effect of broadcasts and multicasts for AppleTalk networks. As the number of hosts increases, the percentage of CPU loss become more significant, due to dealing with broadcasts and multicasts. Note that peaks can be as high as 100 percent for 10,000 hosts.

Table 2-3   *Average Number of Broadcasts and Multicasts for AppleTalk Networks*

Number of Hosts	Average Percentage of CPU Loss per Host	Peak Percentage of CPU Loss Per Host
100	.28%	6.00%
1000	2.10%	58.00%
10,000	16.94%	100.00%

Slow LocalTalk-to-Ethernet connection devices are a major problem in large-scale AppleTalk networks. These devices fail in large AppleTalk networks because they have limited ARP caches and can process only a few broadcasts per second. Major broadcast storms arise when these devices lose their capability to receive Routing Table Maintenance Protocol (RTMP) updates. After this occurs, these devices send ARP requests for all known devices, thereby accelerating the network degradation because they cause their neighbor devices to fail and send their own ARP requests.

Using Broadcasts with Multiprotocol Networks

The following can be said about the interaction of AppleTalk, IPX, and IP:

- AppleTalk stacks ignore any other Layer 3 protocol.

- AppleTalk and IP broadcast and multicast packets affect the operation of IP and IPX stacks. AppleTalk and IP packets enter the stack and then are discarded, which consumes CPU resources.

These findings show that AppleTalk has a cumulative effect on IPX and IP networks.

LAN Segmentation

CLSC Objectives Covered in This Section

8	Describe LAN segmentation using bridges.
9	Describe LAN segmentation routers.
10	Describe LAN segmentation using switches.

Because Ethernet is a shared-medium technology, only one station can transmit at a time. Ethernet provides a best-effort delivery service. In the early years of Ethernet implementation, attaching multiple workstations to a LAN to share the 10 Mbps bandwidth was quite sufficient for sending electronic mail, making file transfers, sharing printers, and performing tasks expected to take place on a network.

Recent years have seen a rise in the use of client/server architecture. Technology advancements are producing faster, more intelligent desktop computers and workstations. Audio and video now accompany data on the network. The changes in how networks are used increase network utilization. The increased utilization causes an increase in network congestion, as more users access the same network resources. Response times become slow or variable, file transfers take longer, and network users become less productive. Congestion generates the demand for more LAN bandwidth. By distributing hosts and clients carefully, you can use this simple method of dividing up a network to reduce overall network congestion.

Three main methods exist for segmenting an Ethernet LAN to increase available bandwidth:

- Segmentation with bridges

- Segmentation with routers

- Segmentation with switches

Segmentation with Bridges

Bridges were once widely used to segment Ethernet LANs to provide more bandwidth per user. They have now been replaced in the marketplace by switches.

Bridges perform segmentation by building address tables that associate segment end stations with the segment's port connection. Bridges—unlike routers—operate at OSI Layer 2. Therefore, they are protocol-independent and transport to end stations in the network. Network installation of a bridge is a simple task because the bridge learns its connected topology. A typical bridged network is shown in Figure 2-5.

Figure 2-5   *A Network Segmented with a Bridge*

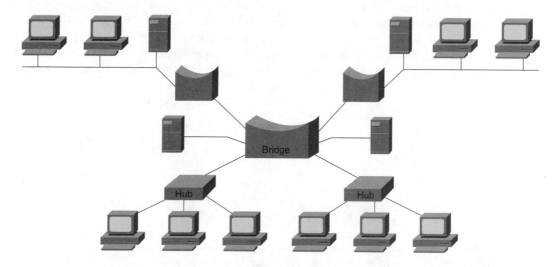

A frame transmitted on the attached segment is received by the bridge in its entirety before processing starts. Bridges use the source address to build a table of device addresses attached to a port. The destination address is used to make a forwarding decision. If the destination address is on the same segment as the source station, the frame is discarded. If the destination address is associated with another port on the bridge, the frame is forwarded to that port. If the frame is a broadcast or multicast frame, or if its destination address is unknown, it is forwarded on all ports except the receiving port.

Bridges introduce a latency penalty due to processing overhead. The latency is about 20 to 30 percent in loss of throughput for acknowledgement-oriented protocols, and 10 to 20 percent for sliding window protocols. This delay can increase significantly if the frame cannot be immediately forwarded due to current activity on the destination segment.

Bridges forward multicast and broadcast frames. This characteristic may actually diminish the bandwidth gains realized as a result of segmentation. Multicast and broadcast addresses are never used as source addresses; hence, they never appear in the address tables associated with the bridge ports. Broadcast storms can result as these frames propagate throughout the network. Filters to restrict propagation of multicast frames can effectively isolate them to the originating segment, but filter processing by the bridge can reduce throughput. This phenomenon can also affect switches.

Segmentation with Routers

Routers operate at OSI Layer 3, the network layer. They are used to extend across multiple links, finding routes between the source and destination stations on an internetwork. Routers typically perform functions associated with bridging, such as making forwarding decisions based on table lookup. Unlike a bridge, the router is known to the stations using its services, and a well-defined protocol must be used among the stations and the router. A typical routed network is shown in Figure 2-6.

Figure 2-6   *A Network Segmented with a Router*

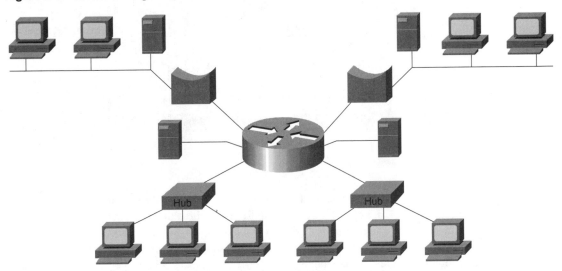

Routers offer the following advantages in a network:

- *Manageability*—Explicit protocols operate among routers, giving the network administrator greater control over path selection and making network routing behavior more visible.

- *Functionality*—Routers can implement mechanisms to provide flow control, error and congestion control, fragmentation and reassembly services, and explicit packet lifetime control.

- *Multiple active paths*—Network topologies can offer more than one path between stations. Operating at the network layer, routers can examine protocol, destination service access point (DSAP), source service access point (SSAP), and path metric information before forwarding or filtering decisions.

To provide these advantages, routers must be more complex and more software-intensive than bridges. Routers provide a lower level of performance in terms of the numbers of frames or packets that can be processed per unit. Compared with a bridge, a router must examine the syntax and interpret the semantics of more fields in a packet. The penalty for this added functionality is a 30 to 40 percent loss of throughput for acknowledgement-oriented protocols, and 20 to 30 percent for sliding window protocols.

To reduce this latency, NetFlow Switching (a Cisco IOS software mechanism) identifies traffic flows between hosts. Then, on a connection-oriented basis, it switches packets in this flow. Packets are switched and services are applied to them in tandem by a single task. This streamlined way of handling packets enables Cisco routers to greatly increase performance for network services.

Segmentation with Switches

The most recently introduced technology for LAN segmentation is the LAN switch, which enables high-speed data exchanges. Servers in a properly configured switched environment achieve full access to the bandwidth of the medium being used. Cut-through switches forward frames by reading the destination MAC address and forwarding the frame to the correct outgoing port. Frames with the source and destination addresses on the same segment are filtered. The Catalyst 5000 series switch uses a bus-based store-and-forward architecture. A typical switched network is shown in Figure 2-7.

Figure 2-7   *Network Segmented with a Switch*

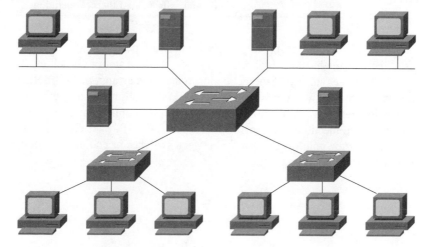

The term "switching" has been applied to several network concepts:

- *Port configuration switching*—Enables a port to be assigned to a physical network segment under software control. This is a very simplistic form of switching.

- *Frame switching*—Primarily used to increase available bandwidth on the network. Frame switching enables multiple transmissions to occur in parallel. This is the type of switching performed by Catalyst switches.

- *Cell switching (ATM)*—Similar to frame switching. In ATM, small cells of a fixed length are switched on the network. This type of switching is performed by all Cisco LightStream switches.

Ethernet switching increases the available bandwidth of a network by creating dedicated network segments and interconnecting the segments. Some devices, such as the Catalyst 3000 series switch (but not the Catalyst 5000 series switch), use high-speed virtual circuits to connect the segments. Each segment can compromise one or more nodes. As long as the total bandwidth of the switch is not exceeded, each dedicated segment added to the network through the switch increases the aggregate speed of the network.

An Ethernet switch works with existing 802.3-compliant network interface cards and cabling. The capability to use existing resources provides increased network performance at a lower cost than most alternatives. More effective utilization of the available medium bandwidth and greater flexibility in the network infrastructure are additional benefits of switching.

Full-Duplex and Half-Duplex Ethernet Overview

CLSC Objectives Covered in This Section

12	Describe full- and half-duplex Ethernet operation.

Full-duplex Ethernet significantly improves network performance without the expense of installing new media. Full-duplex transmission between stations is achieved by using point-to-point Ethernet and Fast Ethernet connections. This arrangement is collision-free—frames sent by the two connected end nodes do not collide because there is not a physical connection between the two nodes. Each full-duplex connection uses only one port. Full-duplex port connections can use 10BaseT, 10BaseFL, 100BaseTX, 100BaseFX, and ATM media to provide point-to-point links between switches or end nodes, but not between shared hubs.

Before examining full-duplex circuitry, it is important to have a clear understanding of how half-duplex Ethernet works. The Ethernet physical connector provides several circuits, as shown in Figure 2-8. Each circuit is used for a specific purpose. The most important circuits are receive (RX), transmit (TX), and collision detection. When the station is not transmitting, its RX circuit is active (performing the carrier-sense aspect of CSMA/CD). Logically, these circuits feed into a single cable, creating a situation similar to a narrow one-way bridge.

Figure 2-8   *Half-Duplex Ethernet*

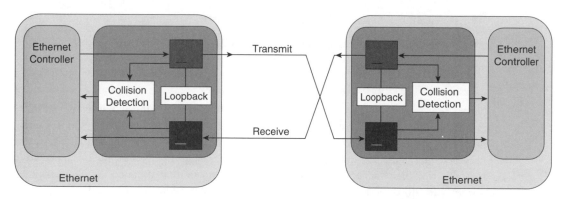

Full-duplex Ethernet technology provides a transmit circuit connection wired directly to the receiver circuit at the other end of the connection (illustrated in Figure 2-9). Because just two stations are connected in this arrangement, a collision-free environment is created. Unlike half-duplex Ethernet, the conditions for multiple transmissions on the same physical medium do not occur.

Figure 2-9   *Full-Duplex Ethernet*

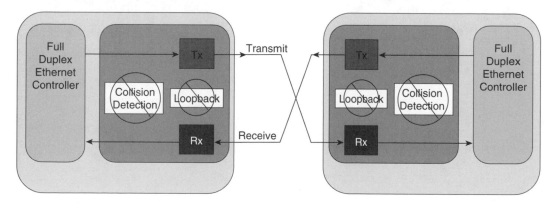

Standard Ethernet configuration efficiency is typically rated at 50 to 60 percent of the 10 Mbps bandwidth. Full-duplex Ethernet offers 100 percent efficiency in both directions (10 Mbps transmit, and 10 Mbps receive).

To implement full-duplex Ethernet, the following are required:

- Two 10 Mbps or 100 Mbps data paths

- Full-duplex Ethernet controllers, or an Ethernet controller for each path

- Loop-back and collision detection disabled

- Software network interface drivers supporting two simultaneous data paths

- Adherence to Ethernet distance constraints:

    — 10BaseT/100BaseT: 100 meters

    — 10BaseFL/100BaseFX: 2 kilometers

Nodes that are directly attached to a dedicated switch port, and those that have network interface cards installed that support full-duplex Ethernet, should be connected to switch ports that are configured to operate in full-duplex mode. Most Ethernet and Fast Ethernet network interface cards sold today offer full-duplex capability. Nodes that are attached to hubs, sharing their connection to a switch port with one or more other nodes, cannot operate properly in full-duplex mode because the end stations must be capable of detecting collisions.

Switching Modes

CLSC Objectives Covered in This Section

11	Name and describe two switching methods.

Two primary operational modes are used to handle frame switching, as illustrated in Figure 2-10:

- Store-and-forward

- Cut-through

Figure 2-10   *Overview of Store-and-Forward and Cut-Through Switching*

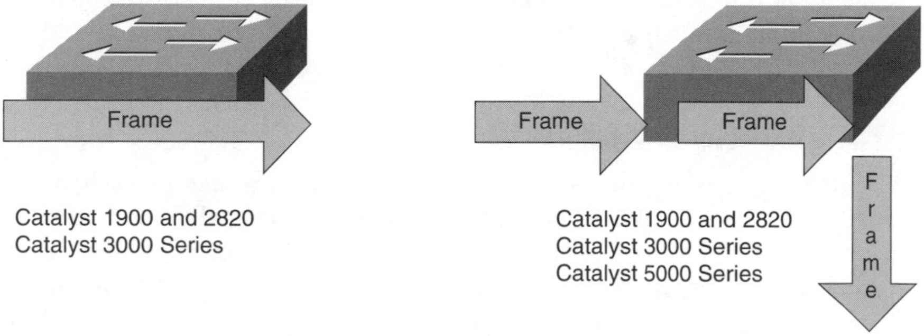

Catalyst 1900 and 2820
Catalyst 3000 Series

Catalyst 1900 and 2820
Catalyst 3000 Series
Catalyst 5000 Series

Store-and-Forward

In the store-and-forward mode, the switch receives the complete frame before forwarding takes place. The destination and source addresses are read, the cyclic redundancy check (CRC) is performed, relevant filters are applied, and the frame is forwarded. If the CRC is bad, the frame is discarded. Latency through the switch varies with frame length. The Catalyst 1900, 2820, 3000 series, and 5000 series support store-and-forward.

Cut-Through

In the cut-through mode, the switch checks the destination address (DA) as soon as the header is received and immediately begins forwarding the frame. Depending on the network transport protocol being used (connectionless or connection-oriented), a significant decrease in latency occurs from input port to output port. The delay in cut-through switching remains constant, regardless of frame size, because this switching mode starts to forward the frame as soon as the switch reads the destination address. (In some switches, just the destination address is read.) Some switches continue to read the CRC and keep a count of errors. If the error rate is too high, the switch can be set to use store-and-forward, either manually or automatically. Other Catalyst switches support combined cut-through and store-and-forward modes. The Catalyst 1900, 2820, and 3000 series switches support the cut-through mode of switching.

Overview of Token Ring Switching

CLSC Objectives Covered in This Section

13	Describe Token Ring switching concepts.

This chapter provides a brief overview of Token Ring switching, and describes the industry standard functions supported by the Catalyst Token Ring switches as well as several functions that are unique to the Catalyst line of Token Ring switches.

Why Use Token Ring Switches?

The traditional method of connecting multiple Token Ring segments is to use a source-routing bridge (SRB). For example, bridges are often used to link workgroup rings to the backbone ring. However, the introduction of the bridge can significantly reduce performance at the user's workstation. Further problems may be introduced by aggregate traffic loading on the backbone ring.

To maintain performance and avoid overloading the backbone ring, you can locate servers on the same ring as the workgroup that needs to access the server. However, dispersing the servers throughout the network makes them more difficult to back up, administer, and secure than if they are located on the backbone ring. Dispersing the servers also limits the number of servers that particular stations can access.

Collapsed backbone routers may offer greater throughput than bridges and can interconnect a larger number of rings without becoming overloaded. Routers provide both bridging and routing functions between rings and have sophisticated broadcast control mechanisms. These mechanisms become increasingly important as the number of devices on the network increases.

The main drawback of using routers as the campus backbone is the relatively high price per port and the fact that the throughput typically does not increase as ports are added. A Token Ring switch is designed to provide wire speed throughput regardless of the number of ports in the switch. In addition, the Catalyst 3900 Token Ring switch can be configured to provide very low latency between Token Ring ports by using cut-through switching.

As a local collapsed backbone device, a Token Ring switch offers a lower per-port cost and can incur lower interstation latency than a router. In addition, the switch can be used to directly attach large numbers of clients or servers, thereby replacing concentrators. Typically, a Token Ring switch is used in conjunction with a router, providing a high-capacity interconnection between Token Ring segments while retaining the broadcast control and wide-area connectivity provided by the router.

History of Token Ring Switching

The term "switching" was originally used to describe packet-switch technologies such as Link Access Procedure, Balanced (LAPB); Frame Relay; Switched Multimegabit Data Service (SMDS); and X.25. Today, LAN switching refers to a technology that is similar to a bridge in many ways.

Like bridges, switches connect LAN segments and use information contained in the frame to determine the segment to which a datagram needs to be transmitted. Switches, however, operate at much higher speeds than bridges and can support new functionality, such as virtual LANs (VLANs).

Token Ring switches first appeared in 1994. The first-generation Token Ring switches can be divided into two basic categories:

- *Processor-based switches*—These switches use reduced instruction set computer (RISC) processors to switch Token Ring frames. Although they typically have a lot of function, they are slow and relatively expensive. These switches have been deployed mainly as backbone switches because of their high cost.

- *Application-specific integrated circuit (ASIC)-based switches with limited functionality*—Fast and relatively inexpensive, these switches have very limited function. Typically, they offer little to no filtering, limited management information, limited support for bridging modes, and limited VLANs. Today, although these switches are less expensive than processor-based switches, they are still too expensive and limited for widespread use of dedicated Token Ring to the desktop.

In 1997, a second generation of Token Ring switches was introduced. Cisco's second-generation Token Ring switches use ASIC-based switching, but they provide increased functionality, resulting in a higher speed and lower cost. They also provide a wider variety of function than their predecessors, including support for multiple bridging modes, Dedicated Token Ring (DTR) on all ports, high port density, high-speed links, filtering, Remote Monitoring (RMON) management, broadcast control, and flexible VLANs.

The family of second-generation Token Ring switches can be used for backbone switching, workgroup microsegmentation, and dedicated Token Ring to the desktop. Token Ring switches currently being offered include these:

- The Catalyst 3900, a stackable workgroup switch that provides support for all switching modes, filtering, RMON, DTR, and SNMP management, as well as support for Asynchronous Transmission Mode (ATM) and Inter-Switch Link (ISL).

- The Catalyst 5000, a modular switch that supports Ethernet, Fast Ethernet, Fiber Distributed Data Interface (FDDI), ATM, and now Token Ring.

Bridging Modes

The Catalyst Token Ring switches support the following bridging modes:

- Source-route bridging (SRB)
- Source-route transparent bridging (SRT)
- Source-route switching

Source-Route Bridging (SRB)

SRB is the original method of bridging used to connect Token Ring segments. A source-route bridge makes all forwarding decisions based upon data in the routing information field (RIF). It does not learn or look up Media Access Control (MAC) addresses. Therefore, SRB frames without a RIF are not forwarded.

With SRB, each port on the switch is assigned a ring number, and the switch itself is assigned one or more bridge numbers. This information is used to build RIFs and to search them to determine when to forward a frame.

Clients or servers that support source routing typically send an explorer frame to determine the path to a given destination. Two types of explorer frames exist: all-routes explorer (ARE) and spanning-tree explorer (STE). SRB bridges copy ARE frames and add their own routing information. For frames that are received from or sent to ports in the spanning-tree forwarding state, bridges copy STE frames and add their own routing information. Because ARE frames traverse all paths between two devices, they are used in path determination. STE frames are used to send datagrams because the spanning tree ensures that only one copy of an STE frame is sent to each ring.

Source-Route Transparent Bridging (SRT)

SRT bridging is an IEEE standard that combines source-route bridging and transparent bridging. An SRT bridge forwards frames that do not contain a RIF based on the destination MAC address. Frames that contain a RIF are forwarded based on source routing.

Two possible problems arise when using SRT:

- Some protocols, such as SNA, attempt to establish a connection using a frame without a RIF. In the SNA case, this test frame is sent to see whether the destination is on the same ring as the source. If no response is received from this test frame, then an ARE test frame with a RIF is sent. If SRT bridging is used, the first test frame without a RIF is forwarded through the bridge to the destination. The destination responds, and the spanning-tree path through the bridges is used. Although this path will work, it may be undesirable. The network may be configured with parallel backbones with the intent that traffic is to be distributed across the backbones. This works well if source-routing is used; however, if the spanning-tree path is used, then only one of the backbones will carry traffic. The other backbone will not be used unless a failure occurs.

- The use of duplicate SNA gateway MAC addresses can cause a problem. SNA requires the user to enter the destination MAC address of the gateway (for example, IBM 3745 Token Ring interface coupler [TIC]). To prevent the user from having to enter a backup address in the case of a gateway failure, many SNA network designers put another gateway on a different ring with the same MAC address. This works with source routing and provides for automatic recovery of a failed gateway. However, SRT does not allow the same MAC address to be on two different rings.

Source-Route Switching

Because standard transparent bridging does not support source-routing information, a new bridging mode—called source-route switching—was created. Source-route switching forwards frames that do not contain routing information based on MAC addresses, the same way that transparent bridging does. All rings that are source-route switched have the same ring number, and the switch learns the MAC addresses of adapters on these rings.

In addition to learning MAC addresses, in source-route switching the switch also learns route descriptors. A route descriptor is a portion of a RIF that indicates a single hop; it is defined as a ring number and a bridge number. When a source-routed frame enters the switch, the switch learns the route descriptor for the hop closest to the switch. Frames received from other ports with the same next-hop route descriptor as their destination are forwarded to that port.

The key difference between SRB and source-route switching is that, while a source-route switch looks at the RIF, it never updates the RIF. Therefore, all ports in a source-route switch group have the same ring number.

Source-route switching provides the following benefits:

- The switch does not need to learn the MAC addresses of the devices on the other side of a source-route bridge. Therefore, the number of MAC addresses that the switch must learn and maintain is significantly reduced.

- The switch can support parallel source-routing paths.

- An existing ring can be partitioned into several segments without requiring a change in the existing ring numbers or the source-route bridges.

- The switch can support duplicate MAC addresses if the stations reside on LAN segments with different LAN IDs (ring numbers).

Forwarding Modes

The Catalyst Token Ring switches support one or more of the following forwarding modes:

- Store-and-forward

- Cut-through

- Adaptive cut-through

Store-and-Forward

Store-and-forward is the traditional mode of operation for a bridge and is one of the modes supported by the Catalyst 3900 and the Catalyst 5000 Token Ring switching cards. In store-and-forward mode, the port adapter reads the entire frame into memory and then determines whether the frame should be forwarded. At this point, the frame is examined for any errors (frames with errors are not forwarded). If the frame contains no errors, it is sent to the destination port for forwarding. While store-and-forward mode reduces the amount of error traffic on the LAN, it also causes a delay in frame forwarding that is dependent upon the length of the frame.

Cut-Through

Cut-through mode is a faster mode of forwarding frames and is supported by the Catalyst 3900. In cut-through mode, the switch transfers non-broadcast packets between ports without buffering the entire frame into memory. When a port on the switch operating in cut-through mode receives the first few bytes of a frame, it analyzes the packet header to determine the destination of the frame, establishes a connection between the input and output ports, and, when the token becomes available, transmits the frame onto the destination ring.

In accordance with specification ISO/IEC 10038, the Catalyst 3900 uses Access Priority 4 to gain priority access to the token on the output ring if the outgoing port is operating in half-duplex (HDX) mode. This increases the proportion of packets that can be forwarded and makes it possible for the switch to reduce the average interstation latency.

In certain circumstances, however, the cut-through mode cannot be applied and the switch must buffer frames into memory. For example, buffering must be performed in the following circumstances:

- When the switch has more than one packet to transmit to the same ring
- When a packet is switched between 4 Mbps and 16 Mbps rings
- When the destination ring is beaconing

Adaptive Cut-Through

Adaptive cut-through mode uses a combination of store-and-forward and cut-through modes and is supported by the Catalyst 3900. With adaptive cut-through mode, the user can configure the switch to automatically use the best forwarding mode based on user-defined thresholds. In adaptive cut-through mode, the ports operate in cut-through mode unless the number of forwarded frames that contain errors exceeds a specified percentage. When this percentage is exceeded, the switch automatically changes the mode of the port to store-and-forward. Then, when the number of frames containing errors falls below a specified percentage, the operation mode of the ports is once again set to cut-through.

Port Operation Modes

A port can operate in one of the following modes:

- *Half-duplex concentrator port*—The port is connected to a single station in HDX. In this case, the port behaves like an active media access unit (MAU) port for classic Token Ring.

- *Half-duplex station emulation*—The port is connected to a port on a MAU. In this case, the port behaves like a station connected to a classic Token Ring segment that contains multiple stations.

- *Full-duplex concentrator port*—The port is connected to a single station in full-duplex (FDX) mode.

- *Full-duplex station emulation*—The port is connected to another Token Ring switch in FDX mode.

Ring In/Ring Out

In addition to the port operation modes listed here, certain ports can operate in Ring In/Ring Out (RI/RO) mode. In RI/RO mode, the port is connected to a traditional main ring path coming from either a MAU or a controlled access unit (CAU).

For the Catalyst 3900, ports 19 and 20 and any of the ports on a fiber expansion module can operate in RI/RO mode. For the Catalyst 5000, any of the ports on the fiber Token Ring module can operate in RI/RO mode.

You can use the RI/RO ports to provide redundancy in a segment. For example, let's assume that you have three MAUs that are daisy-chained together (RO of one MAU is connected to RI of the next), with the RO of the third MAU connected back to RI of the first one. To add a Catalyst 3900 to this configuration, you would remove the cable from the RI port on the first MAU and insert it into port 19 of the Catalyst 3900. Then, you would insert one end of a new cable into the RI port on the first MAU and insert the other end of the same cable into port 20 of the Catalyst 3900.

The result is that port 19 is driving one path through the MAUs that eventually terminates at the receiver of port 20. Port 20 is driving the other path through the MAUs in the opposite direction and terminates at the receiver of port 19. Because both ports must be in the same TrCRF, the duplicate paths are detected by the TrCRF's spanning tree, and one port is placed in blocking mode.

If you then removed a different cable from one of the MAUs, the TrCRF spanning tree would detect that the paths are no longer duplicates, the blocked port would be unblocked, and two rings would form. Because the two rings are still in the same TrCRF, the network would continue to operate normally.

Dedicated Token Ring (DTR)

Classic 4 Mbps and 16 Mbps Token Ring adapters must be connected to a port on a concentrator. These adapters are also limited to operating in HDX mode. In HDX mode, the adapter can only send or receive a frame; it cannot do both simultaneously.

DTR, developed by the IEEE, defines a method in which the switch port can emulate a concentrator port, thereby eliminating the need for an intermediate concentrator. In addition, DTR defines a new FDX data-passing mode called transmit immediate (TXI), which eliminates the need for a token and enables the adapter to transmit and receive simultaneously.

DTR is particularly useful for providing improved access to servers. A server can be attached directly to a switch, enabling the server to take advantage of the full 16 Mbps available for sending and receiving, and resulting in an aggregate bandwidth of 32 Mbps.

Speed Adaptation

In addition to supporting 4 Mbps and 16 Mbps, the Catalyst Token Ring switches can automatically configure the speed of a port by sensing the speed of the ring to which a port is connected.

With Token Ring, however, the speed cannot be changed without closing and reopening the port. Therefore, the following rules apply:

- If a port is closed, the speed can be changed without impact to the port or the network.

- If the port is open and running at a speed equal to the new speed specified, no action is taken.

- If the port is open and running at a speed different from the new speed specified, the port closes and reopens at the new speed. Closing and opening a port on an existing ring at a different speed from which the ring is operating will cause the port to issue a beacon on that ring.

Transmission Priority Queues

To address the needs of delay-sensitive data, such as multimedia, the Token Ring ports of the Catalyst switches have two transmission queues: high-priority and low-priority. The queue for a frame is determined by the value of the priority field in the frame control (FC) byte of the frame. If the FC priority is above a configurable level (the default is 3), the frame is put in the high-priority queue. If an output port becomes congested, you can configure the port to transmit all frames at high priority, regardless of the FC byte contents.

The switch's CPU software monitors the size of the output queue at each Token Ring port to minimize the effects of congestion at output ports. When port congestion is detected, the switch does the following:

- Raises the transmit priority to a higher level for low-priority frames

- Discards the oldest frames when the output queue is almost full

Frame Filtering

Many bridged networks use filtering to reduce broadcast traffic, to block protocols, and to provide simple security. In Token Ring environments, dedicated gateways and servers are often put on their own rings, and filters are used to protect them from unnecessary broadcast traffic from other protocols. The Catalyst Token Ring switches enable users to configure filters based on both MAC address (destination and source address) and protocol (destination service access point [DSAP]/Subnetwork Access Protocol [SNAP] type). Because the filters are implemented in the hardware ASICs, filtering can be done at media speed on a per-port basis to control traffic to certain rings. MAC address filters and broadcast filters can be applied only at input ports. DSAP and SNAP filters can be applied at input ports and output ports.

Broadcast Control

A common design in source-routing networks is parallel backbones. With source routing, the traffic tends to be distributed across both backbones, thereby providing both backup and load distribution. In some cases, these configurations suffer from excessive explorer traffic as the explorer frames are duplicated on the many possible paths through the network. As a result, network managers have had to use hop counts and filters to manage this problem. Second-generation Token Ring switches support the automatic reduction of explorer traffic via the mechanism called Automatic Reduction of Explorer (ARE) reduction.

ARE reduction ensures that the number of ARE frames generated by the switch does not overwhelm the network. The IEEE 802.1d SRT standard specifies the following optional ways of reducing the ARE explosion, which both involve examining the entire RIF to determine where the frame has been:

- The first method is based on whether the frame has been through the bridge before. This is determined by examining the RIF of the received frame for a ring-bridge-ring combination that contains this bridge's number.

- The second method is based on whether the frame has been on any ring attached to the bridge before. This method is more restrictive than the first. Whether the frame has been on an attached ring is determined by examining the RIF of the received frame for a LAN ID that matches any of the LAN IDs associated with the rings attached to the bridge.

The Catalyst Token Ring switches use the simpler of the two, which is to discard any ARE frame that has already been on a ring that is attached to the switch. For example, an ARE frame from ring 1 is sent to switches A and B. The ARE frames are then forwarded to ring 2. When switch B receives the frame from switch A on ring 2, it examines the RIF and determines that this ARE has already been on ring 1. Because switch B is also attached to ring 1, the ARE is discarded. ARE reduction requires no configuration and ensures that only two ARE frames (in this example) are received on each ring. The number of ARE frames is equal to the number of parallel switches between the rings.

If a port on the switch fails or is disabled, the switch will no longer check for this ring number in the RIF. This enables alternate paths to the ring. Therefore, if there are two failures (for example, switch A to ring 1 and switch B to ring 4), there will still be a path between rings 1 and 4 (ring 1 to switch B to ring 2 to switch A to ring 4).

Q&A

As mentioned in Chapter 1, "The Cisco LAN Switch Configuration (CLSC) Exam Overview," the questions and scenarios are more difficult than what you should experience on the actual exam. The questions do not attempt to cover more breadth or depth than the exam; however, the questions are designed to make sure you know the answers. Rather than allowing you to derive the answer from clues hidden inside the question itself, the questions will challenge your understanding and recall of the subject. Questions from the "Do I Know This Already?" quiz from the beginning of the chapter are repeated here to ensure that you have mastered the chapter's topic areas. Hopefully, these questions will help limit the number of exam questions on which you narrow your choices to two options and then guess!

1 Name the three main methods for segmenting an Ethernet LAN to increase available bandwidth.

2 What are the two primary operational modes used to handle frame switching?

3 What Catalyst switch platforms support cut-through switching?

4 What Catalyst switch platforms support store-and-forward switching?

5 Name at least two benefits of implementing Ethernet switching.

6 At which layer of the OSI model do routers operate?

7 At which layer of the OSI model do bridges operate?

8 At which layer of the OSI model do switches operate?

9 What are the four types of bridging?

10 Using full-duplex Ethernet requires the attached node to be directly attached to a repeater hub. (True/False)

11 Define the link layer of the OSI model.

12 Define the network layer of the OSI model.

13 What LAN segmentation device can be utilized to control broadcast?

14 What LAN segmentation device makes forwarding decisions based on Layer 3 information?

15 What LAN segmentation device(s) makes forwarding decisions based on layer 2 information?

Source Material

Some content in this chapter is based on the following sources:

- Broadcasts in Switched LAN Internetworks

  http://www.cisco.com/univercd/cc/td/doc/cisintwk/idg4/nd20e.htm#xtocid93460

- Overview of Token Ring Switching

  http://www.cisco.com/univercd/cc/td/doc/product/lan/trsrb/overview.htm

- Broadcasts in Switched LAN Internetworks

  http://www.cisco.com/univercd/cc/td/doc/ccisintwk/idg4/n20e.htm

- Internetworking Design Basics

  http://www.cisco.com/univercd/cc/td/doc/cisintwk/idg4/nd2002.htm

The objectives of the Cisco LAN Switch Configuration (CLSC) exam are taken from the Cisco web site, at the Cisco career certification and training area. The following table shows the exam objectives covered in this chapter:

Objective	Description
14	Define VLANs.
15	Name seven reasons to create VLANs.
16	Describe the role switches play in the creation of VLANs.
17	Describe VLAN frame filtering and VLAN frame tagging.
18	Describe how switches can be used with hubs.
19	Name the five components of VLAN implementations.
20	Describe static and dynamic VLANs.
21	Describe the VLAN technologies.
22	Describe Token Ring VLANs.
23	Describe Cisco's VLAN architecture.

CHAPTER 3

VLANs

Virtual local-area networks (VLANs) offer significant cost and performance benefits for a majority of the LANs installed today. Network managers realize these benefits as they migrate to switched LAN architectures across the enterprise. And with VLANs working as an integral part of ATM architectures, the concept and much of the technology have been designed into LAN-based switches that offer similar benefits across shared-LAN backbones. In addition, end users' applications need not change to realize these benefits: As part of switching architecture, VLANs are invisible to end users. Finally, VLANs are more than simply a shared hub, routing, switching, or network management solution: The combination of all these components provides powerful segmentation and efficient administration across the network.

This chapter provides an introduction to VLANs and switched internetworking, compares traditional shared LAN configurations with switched LAN configurations, and discusses the benefits of using a switched virtual LAN architecture.

How to Best Use This Chapter

By taking the following steps, you can make better use of your study time:

- Keep your notes and the answers for all your work with this book in one place, for easy reference.

- Take the quiz, and write down your answers. Studies show that retention is significantly increased through writing down facts and concepts, even if you never look at the information again.

- Use the diagram in Figure 3-1 to guide you to the next step.

Figure 3-1 *How to Best Use This Chapter in Preparation for the CLSC Exam*

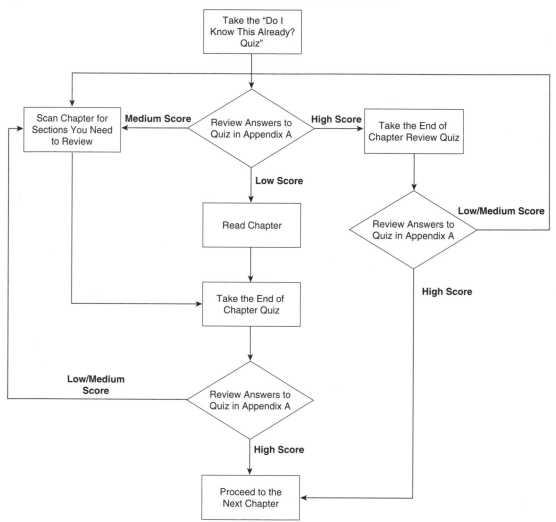

Do I Know This Already? Quiz

You can find the answers to this quiz in Appendix A, "Answers to 'Do I Know This Already?' Quizzes and Q & A Sections." Review the answers, grade your quiz, and choose an appropriate next step in this chapter based on the suggestions diagramed in Figure 3-1.

1 A virtual LAN:

   a. Is a group of ports or users in the same collision domain.

   b. Is a group of ports or users in the same broadcast domain.

   c. Is defined at the application layer (OSI Layer 7).

   d. None of the above.

2 Virtual LANs:

   a. Complicate moves, adds, and changes.

   b. Increase administrative costs.

   c. Loosen network security.

   d. Reduce the propagation of broadcast frames.

3 Frame filtering:

   a. Is used by the Catalyst 5000 series.

   b. Was developed specifically for multi-VLAN, interswitch communications.

   c. Involves comparing frames with table entries.

   d. Places a unique identifier in the header of each frame.

4 Frame tagging:

   a. Is used by the Catalyst 5000 series.

   b. Uses a filtering table developed by each switch.

   c. Involves comparing frames with table entries.

   d. Is a technique that is very similar to that used by bridges and routers.

5 Multisegment hubs:

   a. Are basically useless in a switched network.

   b. Must have all segments attached to the same VLAN.

   c. May have each segment attached to a separate VLAN.

   d. Are useful for establishing inter-VLAN communication.

6 Static VLANs:

   a. Use a VLAN configuration server.

   b. Require less configuration in the wiring closet than do dynamic VLANs.

   c. Provide for automatic notification of a new network user.

   d. Are typically assigned by port.

7 Dynamic VLANs:

   a. Remain configured on a port until the port's configuration is changed.

   b. Typically use a VLAN configuration server.

   c. Are typically assigned by port.

   d. Require more configuration in the wiring closet than static VLANs.

8 ISL is the VLAN transport protocol used across which type of trunk link?

   a. Fast Ethernet

   b. Token Ring

   c. FDDI

   d. ATM

9 IEEE 802.10 is the VLAN transport protocol used across which type of trunk link?

   a. Fast Ethernet

   b. Token Ring

   c. FDDI

   d. ATM

10 LAN Emulation is the VLAN transport protocol used across which type of trunk link?

   a. Fast Ethernet

   b. Token Ring

   c. FDDI

   d. ATM

11 How many instances of spanning tree are supported per VLAN in Cisco's VLAN implementation?

    a. 1 per switch

    b. 1 per VLAN

    c. 64

    d. 255

Using the answer key in Appendix A, grade your answers.

- **5 or less correct**—Read this chapter.

- **6, 7, or 8 correct**—Review this chapter, looking at the charts and diagrams that summarize most of the concepts and facts in this chapter.

- **9 or more correct**—If you want more review on these topics, skip to the Q&A section at the end of this chapter. If you do not want more review on these topics, skip this chapter.

Foundation Topics

VLAN Solutions

CLSC Objectives Covered in This Section	
14	Define VLANs.
15	Name seven reasons to create VLANs.
16	Describe the role switches play in the creation of VLANs.
19	Name the five components of VLAN implementations.

Today's cost-effective, high-performance local-area network (LAN) switches offer users superior microsegmentation, low-latency packet forwarding, and increased bandwidth across the corporate backbone. LAN switches also can segment networks into logically defined virtual workgroups. This logical segmentation, commonly referred to as virtual LAN (VLAN) communication, offers a fundamental change in how LANs are designed, administered, and managed. Although logical segmentation provides substantial benefits in LAN administration, security, and management of network broadcast activity across the enterprise, many components of VLAN solutions must be considered prior to large-scale VLAN deployment.

These additional VLAN components include high-performance switches that logically segment connected end stations; transport protocols that carry VLAN traffic across shared LAN and Asynchronous Transfer Mode (ATM) backbones; Layer 3 routing solutions that extend VLAN communications between workgroups; system compatibility and interoperability with previously installed LAN systems; and network management solutions that offer centralized control, configuration, and traffic management functions. Figure 3-2 summarizes these concepts. All these components are critical for enterprise-wide VLAN solutions because they provide the scalability necessary for migrating from an installed base of shared LAN technologies to the new, emerging architecture of per-user switched communications.

The first section of this chapter briefly discusses the importance of each of these components within VLAN architectures. The second section reviews the benefits of VLANs and their applicability within workgroups and across the enterprise backbone.

Figure 3-2   *VLAN System Components*

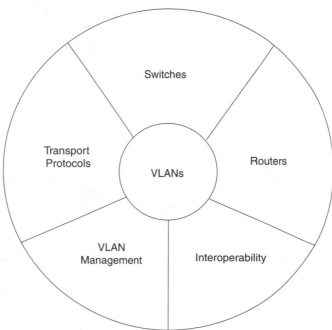

Building VLAN Solutions

Conceptually, VLANs provide greater segmentation and organizational flexibility. VLAN technology enables network managers to group switch ports and users connected to them into logically defined communities of interest. These groupings can be coworkers within the same department, a cross-functional product team, or diverse users sharing the same network application or software (such as Lotus Notes users).

Grouping these ports and users into communities of interest, referred to as VLAN organizations, can be accomplished within a single switch—or more powerfully, between connected switches within the enterprise. By grouping ports and users across multiple switches, VLANs can span single building infrastructures, interconnected buildings, or even wide-area networks (WANs). VLANs completely remove the physical constraints of workgroup communications across the enterprise, as shown in Figure 3-3.

VLANs provide the capability for any organization to be physically dispersed throughout the company while maintaining its group identity. For example, accounting personnel can be located on the shop floor, in the research and development center, in the cash disbursement office, and in the corporate offices, while at the same time all members reside on the same virtual network, sharing traffic only with each other. Figure 3-4 illustrates a typical VLAN architecture that places these employees closer to their assigned areas of management and the people with whom they interact, while yet maintaining communication integrity within their respective organizations. Today's VLANs better match the way that companies are organized and enable network managers to more closely align the network to the way that employees work and communicate.

Figure 3-3 *Logically Defined Networks (VLANs)*

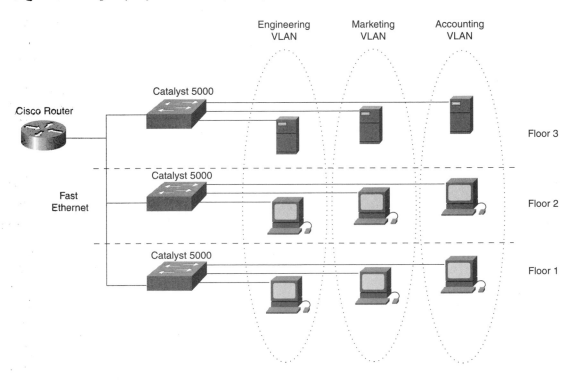

Figure 3-4   *Logical Communication Among Users*

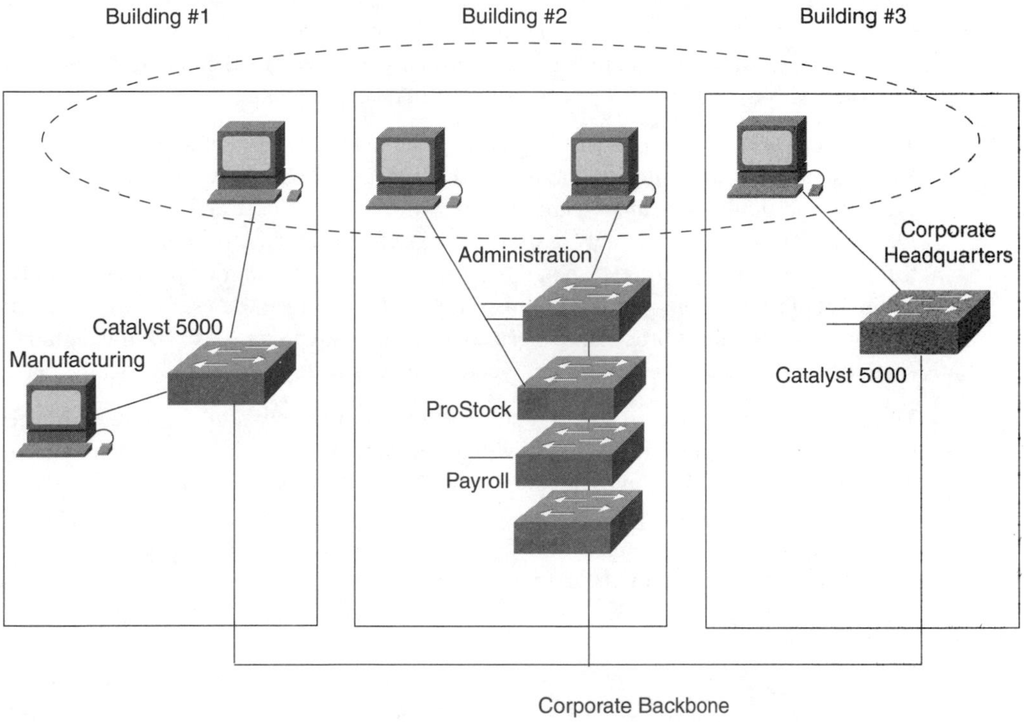

Building #1   Building #2   Building #3

Administration

Corporate
Headquarters

Catalyst 5000

Manufacturing

Catalyst 5000

ProStock

Payroll

Corporate Backbone

Switches: The Core of VLANs

CLSC Objectives Covered in This Section

17	Describe VLAN frame filtering and VLAN frame tagging.

Switches are one of the core components of VLAN communications. They are the entry point for end station devices into the switched fabric and for communication across the enterprise. Switches provide the intelligence to group users, ports, or logical addresses into common communities of interest. Each switch has the intelligence to make filtering and forwarding decisions by frame, based on VLAN metrics defined by network managers, and to communicate this information to other switches and routers within the network.

Although today LAN switches are installed between shared segment hubs and routers located within the backbone, they will take on a larger, more significant role for VLAN segmentation and low-latency forwarding as they are deployed in the wiring closet. LAN switches offer significant increases in performance and dedicated bandwidth across the network, with the intelligence necessary for VLAN segmentation.

The most common approaches for logically grouping users into administratively defined VLANs include frame filtering and frame identification. Frame filtering is a technique that examines particular information about each frame based on user-defined offsets. Frame identification (tagging) uniquely assigns a user-defined ID to each frame. Both of these techniques examine the frame when it is either received or forwarded by the switch. Based on the set of rules defined by the administrator, these techniques determine where the frame is to be sent, filtered, or broadcast. These control mechanisms can be centrally administered (with network management software), yet they are easily deployed throughout the network.

The concept of frame filtering is very similar to that commonly used for routers. A filtering table is developed for each switch, providing a high level of administrative control because it can examine many attributes of each frame. Network managers can group users based upon MAC station addresses, network-layer protocol types, or application types. Managers then can compare table entries with the frames filtered by the switch. The switch takes the appropriate action based on the entries (see Figure 3-5).

Figure 3-5   *Frame Filtering*

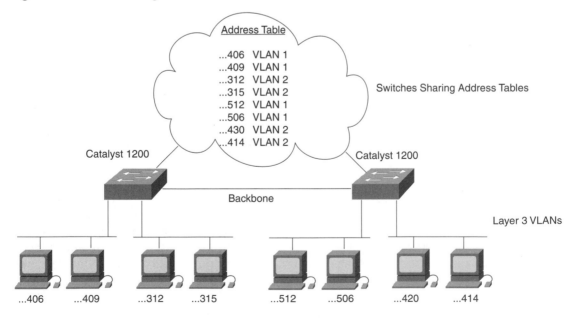

Frame filtering (not supported on the Catalyst 5000 series switches) typically provides an additional layer of switch processing prior to forwarding each frame to another port or switch within the network. This process, which can affect switch latency and overall network performance, becomes more apparent as you filter deeper into each frame. In addition, maintaining address tables adds an extra layer of administration per switch and requires synchronizing tables between switches.

VLAN frame identification (frame tagging), used by the Catalyst 3000 and 5000 series switches, is a relatively new approach that has been specifically developed for switched communications. This approach places a unique identifier in the header of each frame as it is forwarded throughout the switch fabric. Each switch examines and understands the identifier prior to any broadcasts or transmissions to other switches, routers, or end station devices. When the frame exits the switch fabric, the switch removes the identifier before the frame is transmitted to the target end station. Over the past two years, frame identification has gained acceptance as switches have increased in popularity; frame identification functions at Layer 2 and requires little processing or administrative overhead (see Figure 3-6).

The overall benefits of both frame filtering and frame identification provide for VLAN architectures that are nonintrusive to end node applications and communication protocols. Switches provide all the filtering, identification, and forwarding without any modification to the attached end station devices. This delivers a VLAN architecture that easily integrates with existing LAN applications while offering scalability and migration to ATM networks.

Figure 3-6   *Frame Identification*

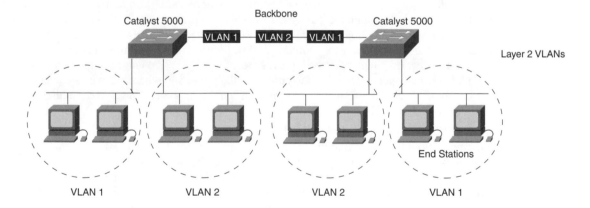

Configuring VLANs

<table>
<tr><td colspan="2" align="center">**CLSC Objectives Covered in This Section**</td></tr>
<tr><td>18</td><td>Describe how switches can be used with hubs.</td></tr>
<tr><td>20</td><td>Describe static and dynamic VLANs.</td></tr>
</table>

Users can be assigned to VLANs using several different configuration options that include static port assignments, dynamic port assignments, and multi-VLAN port assignments. These options are a function of the switch's capabilities (as mentioned in the previous section), the manner in which the stations are attached to each port on the switch, and the capabilities of the VLAN management software.

Stations directly attached to the ports on the switch provide the greatest flexibility for VLAN configuration and management. All stations can be uniquely assigned to VLANs. When they move to other physical locations using other directly attached switch port connections, the stations maintain their VLAN identities irrespective of their new locations. Stations connected to a switch through a shared hub are commonly grouped within the same VLAN because they all share the same switch port. Although this approach is less flexible for each user on the network, it still provides highly desirable VLAN solutions for network managers. Additionally, hubs that provide multibackplane connection options increase the flexibility for unique VLAN assignments. Each backplane connection from the hub to a switch port can be individually assigned to a VLAN.

Static VLANs are ports on a switch that a network manager has statically assigned to a VLAN, either using a VLAN management application or by configuring directly within the switch. These ports maintain their assigned VLAN configurations until the network manager takes another action. Although static VLANs require changes by the network operator, they are secure, easy to configure, and straightforward to monitor. These VLANs work well in networks where network moves are controlled and managed, where there is robust VLAN management software to configure the ports, and where network managers do not want to take on the additional overhead of maintaining end station MAC addresses and custom filtering tables.

Dynamic VLANs are ports on a switch that can automatically determine their VLAN assignments with the aid of intelligent management software. Dynamic VLANs function based on their assignments to end user station MAC addresses, logical addresses, or protocol type. These assignments are entered and maintained in a centralized VLAN management application. When a station is initially connected to an unassigned switch port, the appropriate switch checks the MAC address entry in the VLAN management database and dynamically configures the port with the corresponding VLAN configuration. The major benefits of this approach include less administration within the wiring closet when a user is added or moved, and centralized notification when an unrecognized user is added to the network. Typically, more administration is required up front to set up the database within the VLAN management software and to maintain an accurate database of all network users, as shown in Figure 3-7.

Figure 3-7   *Configuring Ports to VLANs*

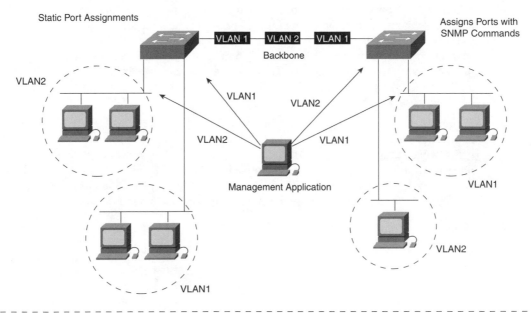

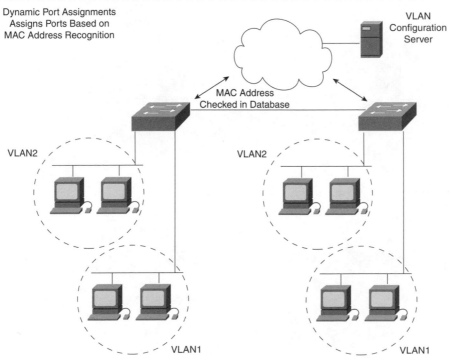

Multi-VLAN port configurations provide communications among multiple VLANs concurrently, from either a single port or a single user (server). This includes shared servers and users who need to belong to multiple workgroups. Several solutions on the market today provide this functionality, but there is an associated trade-off: Concurrent port sharing across multiple groups dramatically reduces the firewalls between workgroups and the security these firewalls provide. These ports act as gateways into other VLAN groups and, in effect, create one larger VLAN. This approach does not scale well as the intersection between these VLAN groups becomes larger and larger.

For resources that need to participate in several VLANs concurrently, a better approach is to attach the end station directly to the backbone and to configure unique communication paths to each individual VLAN, thus providing resource sharing while maintaining the integrity of the VLAN firewalls. This approach has been defined in the ATM LAN Emulation draft standards and is also being evaluated for implementation across shared-LAN backbones and switching architectures, illustrated in Figure 3-8.

Figure 3-8   *Servers as Part of Multiple VLANs*

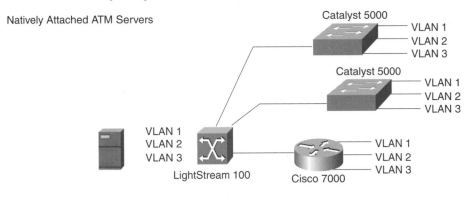

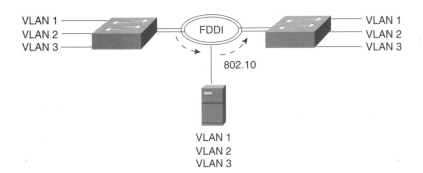

Segmenting with Switching Architectures

Restructuring users according to logical associations across the enterprise rather than physical location is a fundamental shift away from the topologies deployed today. A large majority of networks currently installed provide very limited logical segmentation. Users are commonly grouped based on their connections into the shared hub and the router ports between these hubs. In addition, users on two different hubs segmented with a router cannot be connected to the same LAN segment.

This topology provides segmentation only between the hubs, which are typically located on separate floors and not between users connected to the same hub. This setup imposes physical constraints on the network and greatly limits the manner in which users can be grouped. And although some shared hub architectures provide a small degree of grouping capabilities, network managers are restricted in the way they can configure logically defined workgroups.

Switches remove the physical constraints imposed by a shared-hub architecture because they logically group users and ports across the enterprise. As a replacement for shared hubs, switches remove the physical barriers imposed within each wiring closet. Additionally, the role of the router evolves beyond the more traditional role of firewalls and broadcast suppression to policy-based control, broadcast management, and route processing and distribution. Equally important, routers remain vital for switched architectures configured as VLANs because they provide the communication between logically defined workgroups (VLANs). Routers also provide VLAN access to shared resources such as servers and hosts, and they connect to other parts of the network that are logically segmented with the more traditional subnet approach or that require access to remote sites across wide-area links. Layer 3 communication, either embedded in the switch or provided externally, is an integral part of any high-performance switching architecture.

External routers can be cost-effectively integrated into the switching architecture using one or multiple high-speed backbone connections; these are typically FDDI, Fast Ethernet, or ATM-type connections. These connections increase the throughput between switches and routers, provide a one-to-one logical association between the configured VLANs and Layer 3 subnets, and consolidate the overall number of physical router ports required for communication between VLANs. As illustrated in Figure 3-9, this architecture not only provides logical segmentation, but it also greatly enhances the efficiency of the network.

Figure 3-9 *Topology Changes of LANs*

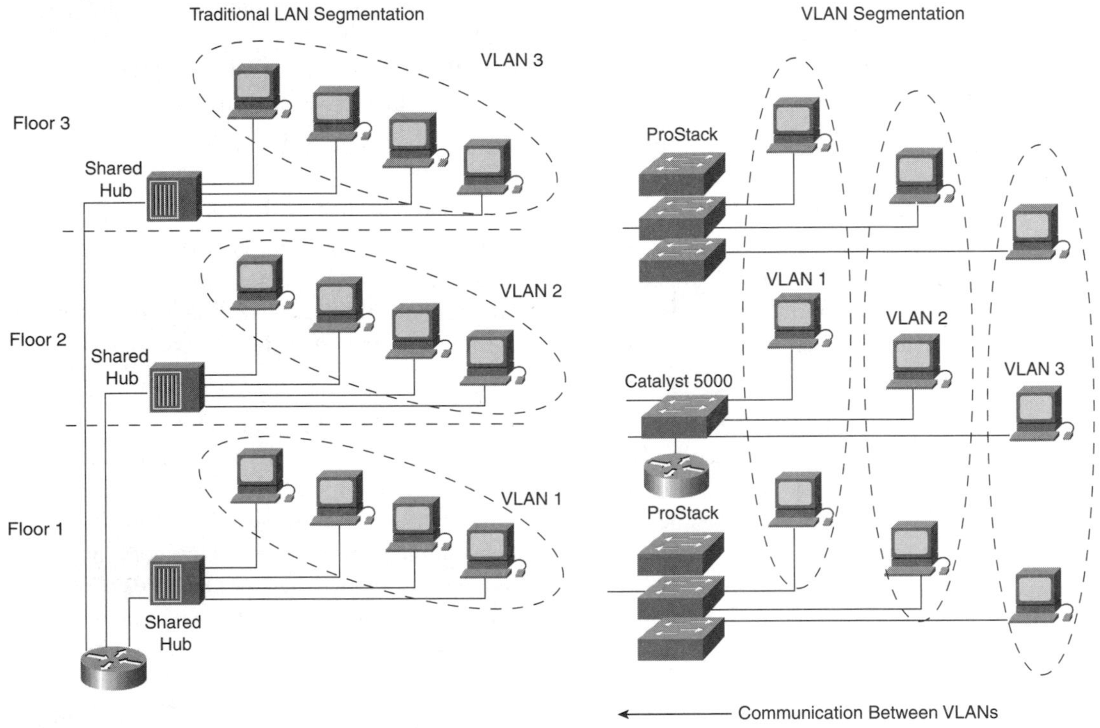

VLANs Across the Backbone

Important to any VLAN architecture is the capability to transport VLAN information between interconnected switches and routers that reside on the corporate backbone. (The VLAN transport enables enterprise-wide VLAN communications.) These transport capabilities remove the physical boundaries between users, increase the configuration flexibility of a VLAN solution when users move, and provide mechanisms for interoperability between backbone system components. The backbone commonly acts as the aggregation point for large volumes of traffic, and it also carries end-user VLAN information and identification between switches, routers, and directly attached servers.

Within the backbone, high-bandwidth, high-capacity links are typically chosen to carry the traffic throughout the enterprise. The three most popular high-bandwidth options include Fast Ethernet, Fiber Distributed Data Interface (FDDI), Copper Distributed Data Interface (CDDI), and ATM. Because switches and routers directly attach to the backbone, they must be capable of transporting VLAN information and interoperating with other network components.

In response to these requirements, several different transport mechanisms are being considered for communicating VLAN information across high-performance backbones. Among them is the LAN Emulation draft standard that has recently been approved by the ATM Forum, and the IEEE 802.10 protocol, which provides VLAN communication across shared backbones. Both of these define an interoperable mechanism for configuring and transporting VLANs across different backbone technologies.

The 802.10 proposal has been recommended by switching, routing, and hub vendors. Figure 3-10 shows typical applications for 802.10. This proposal defines a 32-bit addressing scheme within an 802.10 frame for VLAN identification, an addressing scheme non-intrusive to existing backbone architectures; however, it requires that switches include built-in software intelligence for enterprise VLAN communications. With the standardization of these two transport protocols, network managers can implement VLANs within individual workgroups across the enterprise backbone and can gain access to WANs. In addition, Cisco has developed the inter-switch link (ISL) VLAN transport protocol to deliver efficient communication across Fast Ethernet backbones. Cisco will implement this as a de facto standard and has made the specification available to vendors who want to interoperate.

Figure 3-10 *VLANs Across FDDI Backbones*

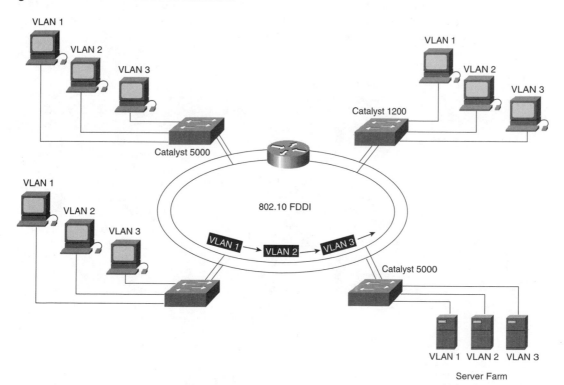

Using ISL

21	Describe the VLAN technologies.

ISL, originally developed for Ethernet switches, uses a Fast Ethernet interface to provide connectivity between switches. ISL extends the VLAN capabilities of the switch by tagging the standard Fast Ethernet frame with the necessary VLAN information. Like ATM, this technology can provide a high-speed link between switches. Unlike ATM, ISL forwards the data across the high-speed link without breaking the frames into cells. The entire frame is sent intact across the ISL connection.

An ISL port is considered a trunk port. A *trunk* is a physical link that carries the traffic of multiple VLANs between two switches, between a switch and a server, or between a switch and a router, thereby allowing the VLANs to be extended across switches. Trunks use high-speed interfaces such as Fast Ethernet, FDDI, or ATM.

The ISL protocol is a frame-tagging protocol that contains a standard Ethernet or Token Ring frame and the VLAN information associated with that frame.

The ISL backbone design looks much like an ATM design; however, ISL is less expensive than ATM and avoids the need for LAN Emulation (LANE) services. It is primarily intended for network managers who do not want an ATM backbone for the campus. In the future, routing between Token Ring VLANs will be provided via an ISL-attached router or the route-switch module in the Catalyst 5500.

Figure 3-11   *ISL Backbone Design*

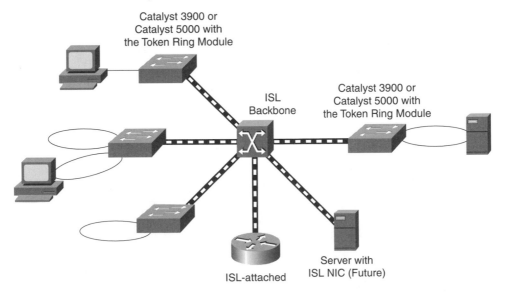

The Catalyst 5000 family of switches should be used to provide the ISL backbone. The Catalyst 3900 switch can then be connected to this backbone via the dual 100 Mbps ISL expansion module. In addition, vendors are developing ISL network interface cards (NICs) that support both Token Ring and Ethernet VLANs and that can be used for high-speed attachment to servers. For the Catalyst 5000, any of the ports on its Fast Ethernet modules can be configured as trunk ports that use ISL.

The Catalyst 3900 two-port 100 Mbps Token Ring ISL module supports the encapsulation of Token Ring frames on a standard Fast Ethernet link to enable VLANs to be distributed across multiple platforms and devices. The module is available with a fiber or UTP copper media interface. The ports of the ISL module can be connected to the ports of another ISL module in another router or switch.

Although your Catalyst 3900 can contain both an ATM expansion module and an ISL expansion module, you cannot use both in a parallel configuration. If the ATM module and the ISL module are configured for parallel connections, the Spanning-Tree Protocol will allow only one of the trunk ports to be active at a time.

Because ISL is used to propagate VLAN trunking information, it is important for the ISL module to be the active path in an ISL-ATM parallel connection. Therefore, the path cost is calculated based on a 200 Mbps connection, which results in a path cost of 5 and causes the Spanning-Tree Protocol to place the ISL port in forwarding mode and the ATM port in blocked mode (a separate instance of STP runs within each configured VLAN). Appendix D, "Configuring Spanning Tree," provides an overview of the Spanning Tree Protocol and explains how to customize the configuration on a Catalyst 5000 series switch.

VLAN Integration

Traditional network architectures are experiencing significant changes as they evolve toward greater microsegmentation, more capacity across the backbone, and dedicated circuit switching with the adoption of ATM. At the core of these changes are LAN-based switches with wiring closet applications, backbone switches for greater throughput performance, and ATM switches for dedicated circuit switching. As network managers migrate to these products, VLANs become a reality. Typically, the integration of VLANs begins with the first switch installation in a department or building. As the number of switches grows throughout the enterprise, VLANs become an enterprise-wide solution. These enterprise-wide VLANs require the transport mechanism, management tools, and Layer 3 communication for logical segmentation and access across the network.

VLANs become a natural inclusion for LAN architectures as network designers and managers seek dedicated bandwidth to the desktop and segmentation based upon logical workgroups across the enterprise. Switching architectures that are VLAN-capable, along with routing solutions that interconnect VLANs, are evolutionary design changes compared with the physical segmentation that a majority of networks have in place today. VLANs are one of the essential technologies for breaking today's restrictive paradigm.

The Benefits of VLANs

CLSC Objectives Covered in This Section	
15	Name seven reasons to create VLANs.
16	Describe the role switches play in the creation of VLANs.
23	Describe Cisco's VLAN architecture.

VLANs are often positioned as solving the problems associated with moves, adds, and changes. They certainly do reduce a large part of the administration costs when users change locations within a building or campus, but VLAN technology provides many internetworking benefits that are equally as compelling. In addition to the reduced costs of administration, VLAN benefits include tighter network security with establishment of secure user groups, better management and control of broadcast activity, micro-segmentation of the network without sacrificing scalability, load distribution of traffic across traffic-intensive switches ("hot spots" within the network), and the relocation of workgroup servers into secured, centralized locations.

Improved Administration Efficiencies

Companies continuously reorganize as they seek productivity improvements. On average, between 20 and 40 percent of the workforce is physically moved every year. These moves, adds, and changes are one of a network manager's biggest headaches and one of the largest expenses relative to managing the network. Many moves require recabling, and almost all moves require new station addressing and hub and router reconfigurations. Invariably, about the time managers stabilize their networks, more changes are requested.

VLANs provide an effective mechanism for controlling these changes and reducing much of the cost associated with hub and router reconfigurations. Users in a VLAN can share the same network "address space" regardless of their location. When users in a VLAN move from one location to another, their network addresses do not change, as long as they remain within the same VLAN and are connected to a switch port. Location changes can be as simple as plugging a user into a port on a VLAN-capable switch or simply configuring the port on the switch to that VLAN, as shown in Figure 3-12. This greatly simplifies the rewiring, configuration, and debugging necessary to get the user back online. It also marks a significant improvement over the techniques used within the wiring closet today. Moreover, router configuration remains intact; a simple move of a user from one location to another does not create any configuration modifications in the router as long as the user resides within the same VLAN.

Figure 3-12   *Port Configuration for Greater Administration Efficiency*

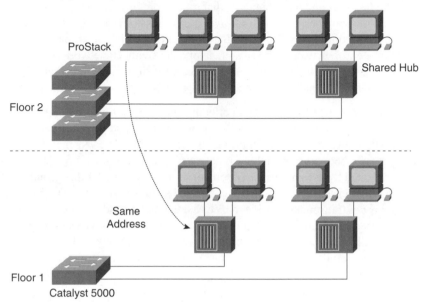

Controlling Broadcast Activity

Whether broadcast traffic is controlled through effective segmentation or by pruning an application's behavior, it occurs in every network. Broadcast frequency depends on the types of applications, the types of servers, the amount of logical segmentation, and how these network resources are used. While applications have been fine-tuned over the last few years to reduce the number of broadcasts they send out, new multimedia applications are being developed that are broadcast- and multicast-intensive. Operationally, broadcasts can occur as a result of faulty network interface cards and communication devices. If not properly managed, they can seriously degrade network performance and can potentially bring down an entire network. This type of failure is primarily due to inadequate firewalls, internetworking loops, faulty network devices, or broadcast-intensive applications.

Network managers must take preventive measures to ensure against broadcast-related problems. One of the most effective measures is to properly segment the network with protective firewalls that minimize problems on one segment from damaging other parts of the network. Thus, although one segment may exhibit excessive broadcast conditions as a result of a faulty network device or a mismanaged application, the rest of the network is protected with a firewall, commonly provided by a router. Firewall segmentation provides reliability, safeguards the network from the inefficient use of bandwidth, and minimizes the overhead of broadcast traffic, allowing for greater throughput of application traffic.

As many designers migrate their networks toward switching architectures, they begin to lose the firewalls and the safeguards that routers provide. By not placing any routers between the switches, broadcasts (Layer 2 transmissions) are sent to every switched port. This is commonly referred to as a "flat" network, in which one broadcast domain exists across the entire network. The advantage of a flat switched network is that it provides very low latency and high throughput performance; the disadvantage is that it increases the susceptibility to broadcast traffic across all switches, ports, backbone links, and users.

Similar to routers, VLANs offer an effective mechanism for setting up multiple independent broadcast domains within a switch fabric and protecting the network against potentially dangerous broadcast problems. Additionally, VLANs maintain all the performance benefits of switching. These multiple independent broadcast domains are accomplished by assigning switch ports or users to specific VLAN groups, both within single switches and across multiple connected switches. Broadcast traffic within one VLAN is not transmitted outside the VLAN. Conversely, adjacent ports do not receive any of the broadcast traffic generated from other VLANs. This type of configuration substantially reduces the overall broadcast traffic, frees bandwidth for real user traffic, and lowers the overall vulnerability of the network to broadcast storms (see Figure 3-13).

Network managers can easily control the size of the broadcast domain by regulating the overall size of their VLANs, restricting the number of switch ports within a VLAN and the number of users residing on these ports. The smaller the VLAN group, the less effect broadcast traffic activity within the VLAN group has on everyone else within the network. Additionally, VLAN groups can be assigned based on the type of applications used and the amount of broadcasts these applications create. Users sharing a broadcast-intensive application are placed in the same VLAN group, while at the same time allowing the network manager to distribute the application across the campus.

Figure 3-13   *Configuration to Effectively Control Broadcast Activity*

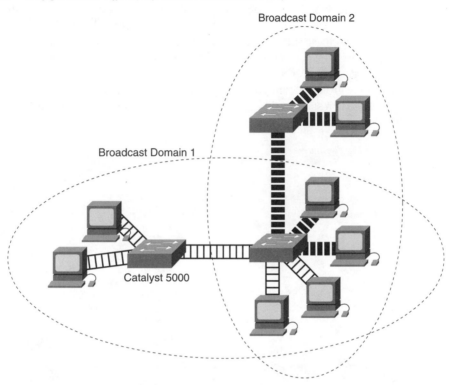

Enhanced Network Security

Over the past five years, the use of LANs has increased exponentially. As a result, LANs often have confidential, mission-critical data moving across them. Confidential data requires security through access restriction. One of the inherent shortcomings of shared LANs is that they are relatively easy to penetrate. By plugging into a live port, an intrusive user has access to all broadcasts within the segment. The larger the broadcast group, the greater the access unless security control functions are present in the switch.

One of the most cost-effective and easiest administrative techniques to increase security is to segment the network into distinct broadcast groups. Additionally, this enables the network manager to restrict the number of users in a VLAN group and to disallow another user from joining without first receiving approval from the VLAN network management application. VLANs thus provide security, restrict individual user access, flag any unwanted intrusion to a network manager, and control the size and composition of the group.

Implementing this type of segmentation is relatively straightforward. Switch ports are grouped together based on the type of applications and access privileges. Restricted applications and resources are commonly placed in a secured VLAN group. Any users trying to tap into these secured VLANs are flagged by the network management software. Further security enhancements can be added using router access lists. These are especially useful when communicating between VLANs. On the secured VLAN, the router restricts access into the group as configured on both the switches and the routers. Restrictions can be placed based on station addresses, application types, protocols types, or even by time of day (see Figure 3-14).

Figure 3-14   *Added Security of Routers*

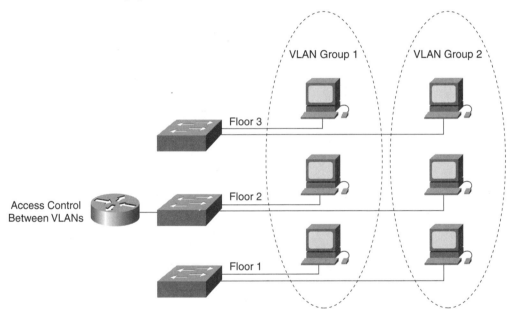

Leveraging Legacy Hub Investments

Since 1994, network administrators have installed a significant number of shared-hub chassis, modules, and stackable devices. Although many of these devices are being replaced with newer switching technologies as network applications require more dedicated bandwidth and performance directly to the desktop, these concentrators still perform useful functions in many existing installations. Network managers are leveraging their investments by connecting switches to the backplanes of the hubs. In the context of this discussion, a backplane hub connection defines any shared-media hub connection into a a network backbone; stackable hubs, hub chassis, and even hub modules provide some form of this connection. The connections between the shared hubs and the switches provide opportunities for VLAN segmentation. The greater the number of hub connections, the greater the opportunities for VLAN segmentation down to individual users.

Each hub segment (as defined within individual hub architectures) connected to a switch port can be assigned to a VLAN. Stations that share a hub segment are all assigned to the same VLAN group.

If an individual station needs to be reassigned to another VLAN, the station will be relocated to the appropriate corresponding hub module. The interconnected switch fabric handles the communication between the switching ports and automatically determines the appropriate receiving segments. The more the shared hub can be broken into smaller groups, the greater the microsegmentation and the greater the VLAN flexibility for assigning individual users to VLAN groups.

This furthers the migration to a high-performance switching architecture within enterprise LANs. With this approach, network managers can configure their shared hubs as part of the VLAN architecture and can share traffic and network resources that directly attach to switching ports with VLAN designations.

Centralized Administration Control

Controlling network broadcasts; planning moves, adds, and changes; and establishing access privileges to the network and secured resources are common functions of the central planning and administration group. VLAN communications facilitate this type of planning by providing effective VLAN management applications that can be centrally configured, managed, and monitored.

From a centralized VLAN management application, network managers can determine VLAN groups, assign specific users and switch ports to these groups, set security levels, limit the size of the broadcast domains, load-distribute traffic across redundant links, configure the communication of VLANs across the switch fabric, and monitor traffic flow and bandwidth utilization of these VLANs across critical hot spots within their network. These capabilities substantially increase the amount of control, flexibility, and monitoring functions of network management applications, reducing the cost of switch management and increasing overall services from centralized management operations. VLAN network management applications will play a larger role in configuring and managing the network as users evolve to a switched LAN architecture.

Token Ring VLANs

CLSC Objectives Covered in This Section

22	Describe Token Ring VLANs.

Because a VLAN is essentially a broadcast domain, a Token Ring VLAN is slightly more complex than an Ethernet VLAN. In transparent bridging, there is only one type of broadcast frame and therefore only one level of broadcast domain. In source routing, however, there are multiple types of broadcast frames that fall into two categories:

- Those that are confined to a single ring

- Those that traverse the bridged domain

These two categories of broadcast frames result in a broadcast domain that is hierarchical in nature, as a local ring domain can exist only within a domain of all the interconnected rings. In a Token Ring VLAN, logical ring domains are formed by defining groups of ports that have the same ring number. The IEEE calls such a port group a Concentrator Relay Function (CRF). On Catalyst switches, such a grouping of Token Ring ports is called a Token Ring CRF (TrCRF).

The domain of interconnected rings is formed using an internal multiport bridge function that the IEEE calls a Bridge Relay Function (BRF). On Catalyst switches, such a grouping of logical rings is called a Token Ring BRF (TrBRF).

TrCRFs

A TrCRF is a logical grouping of ports. Within the TrCRF, source-route switching is used for forwarding based on either MAC addresses or route descriptors. Frames can be switched between ports within a single TrCRF. A TrCRF has two global parameters: a ring number and a parent TrBRF identifier. On the Catalyst 3900, the ring number of the TrCRF can be defined or learned from external bridges. On the Catalyst 5000, the ring number must be defined.

As a rule, a TrCRF is limited to the Token Ring ports of a single Catalyst 5000 series switch, the ports of a single Catalyst 3900, or the ports within a stack of Catalyst 3900 switches. This type of TrCRF is called an *undistributed* TrCRF. However, if your switches are connected via ISL, the Cisco Duplicate Ring Protocol (DRiP) enables two types of TrCRFs in which the ports of a single TrCRF can exist on different switches. These types of TrCRFs are the *default* and the *backup* TrCRF.

Undistributed TrCRF

The undistributed TrCRF is the standard type of TrCRF in the Catalyst 5000 series switch. The undistributed TrCRF is located on one switch and has a logical ring number associated with it. Multiple undistributed TrCRFs located on the same or separate switches can be associated with a single parent TrBRF. The parent TrBRF acts as a multiport bridge, forwarding traffic between the undistributed TrCRFs.

Default TrCRF

As a rule, TrCRFs cannot span different switches. One exception exists: the default TrCRF (1003). The default TrCRF can contain ports that are located on multiple switches. It is associated with the default TrBRF (1005), which can span switches via ISL. The default TrCRF is the only TrCRF that can be associated with the default TrBRF; the default TrBRF does not perform any bridging functions, but it uses source-route switching to forward traffic between the ports of the TrCRF.

Backup TrCRF

The backup TrCRF enables you to configure an alternate route for traffic between undistributed TrCRFs located on separate switches that are connected by a TrBRF. The backup TrCRF is used only if the ISL connection between the switches becomes inactive.

Although a TrBRF can contain multiple TrCRFs, it can contain only one TrCRF that is configured as a backup TrCRF. The backup TrCRF can contain only one port from each related switch. If you have more than one TrBRF defined on a switch, you can have more than one backup TrCRF defined on a switch (one defined for each TrBRF).

To create a backup TrCRF, create the TrCRF, assign it to the TrBRF that traverses the switches, mark it as a backup TrCRF, and then assign one port on each switch to the backup TrCRF.

CAUTION   If the backup TrCRF port is attached to a Token Ring MAU, it will not provide a backup path unless the ring speed and port mode are set by another device. Therefore, we recommend that you manually configure the ring speed and port mode for the port assigned to the backup TrCRF.

Under normal circumstances, only one port in the backup TrCRF is active. The active port is the port with the lowest MAC address. If the ISL connection between the switches becomes inactive, the port that is a part of the backup TrCRF on each affected switch will automatically become active and will reroute traffic between the undistributed TrCRFs through the backup TrCRF. When the ISL connection is reestablished, all but one port in the backup TrCRF will be disabled.

TrBRFs

A TrBRF is a logical grouping of TrCRFs. The TrBRF is used to join different TrCRFs contained within a single Catalyst 3900, a stack of Catalyst 3900s, or the Token Ring modules of a single Catalyst 5000 switch. In addition, the TrBRF can be extended across a network of switches via high-speed uplinks between the switches to join TrCRFs contained in different switches.

A TrBRF has two global parameters: a bridge number and a bridge type. The bridge number is used to identify the logical distributed SRB, which interconnects all logical rings that have the same parent TrBRF.

A TrBRF can function as an SRB or SRT bridge running either the IBM or IEEE Spanning-Tree Protocol. If SRB is used, duplicate MAC addresses can be defined on different logical rings.

To accommodate SNA traffic, you can use a combination of SRT and SRB modes. In a mixed mode, the TrBRF considers some ports (internal ports connected to TrCRFs) to be operating in SRB mode while others are operating in SRT mode.

Q&A

As mentioned in Chapter 1, "The Cisco LAN Switch Configuration (CLSC) Exam Overview," the questions and scenarios are more difficult than what you should experience on the actual exam. The questions do not attempt to cover more breadth or depth than the exam; however, the questions are designed to make sure you know the answers. Rather than allowing you to derive the answer from clues hidden inside the question itself, the questions will challenge your understanding and recall of the subject. Questions from the "Do I Know This Already?" quiz from the beginning of the chapter are repeated here to ensure that you have mastered the chapter's topic areas. Hopefully, these questions will help limit the number of exam questions on which you narrow your choices to two options and then guess!

1 Broadcast frequency depends on the types of _____, the type of _____, the amount of logical _____, and how the network resources are used.

2 Frame filtering creates a filtering table for each _____.

3 Frame identification is supported on the _____ and _____ Catalyst series switches.

4 Users can be assigned to VLANs using several different configuration options that include _____, _____, and _____.

5 An ISL port is considered a _____ port.

6 Stations that share a hub segment are all assigned to the _____ VLAN group.

7 What are the five components of VLAN implementation?

8 Network managers can group users into VLANs by what categories?

9 What is the advantage of a flat switched network?

10 What is the disadvantage of a flat switched network?

Source Material

Some content in this chapter is based on the following sources:

- Understanding VLANs

  http://www.cisco.com/univercd/cc/td/doc/product/rtrmgmt/sw_ntman/vlandir/vdir1gsg/overvw.htm

- Designing Switched LAN Internetworks

  http://www.cisco.com/univercd/cc/td/doc/cisintwk/idg4/nd2012.htm#14487

- Token Ring VLANs and Related Protocols

  http://www.cisco.com/univercd/cc/td/doc/product/lan/trsrb/vlan.htm#xtocid295930

  http://www.cisco.com/univercd/cc/td/doc/product/lan/trsrb/vlan.htm#xtocid295931

The objectives of the Cisco LAN Switch Configuration (CLSC) exam are taken from the Cisco web site, at the Cisco career certification and training area. The following table shows the exam objectives covered in this chapter:

Objective	Description
3	Place the Catalyst series switches in a network for optimal performance benefit.
24	Describe demand nodes and resource nodes.
25	Describe configuration rules for demand nodes and resource nodes.
26	Describe local resources and remote resources.
27	Describe configuration rules for local resources and remote resources.
28	Name five applications for Catalyst 5000 series switches.

CHAPTER 4

Placing Catalyst 5000 Series Switches in Your Network

These objectives are very important to understand due to the number of switches that are being implemented in today's networks. Most network designers are beginning to integrate switching devices into their existing shared-media networks to achieve the following goals:

- Increase the bandwidth that is available to each user, thereby alleviating congestion in their shared-media networks.

- Employ the manageability of VLANs by organizing network users into logical workgroups that are independent of the physical topology of wiring closet hubs. This, in turn, can reduce the cost of moves, adds, and changes while increasing the flexibility of the network.

- Deploy emerging multimedia applications across different switching platforms and technologies, making them available to a variety of users.

- Provide a smooth evolution path to high-performance switching solutions, such as Fast Ethernet and ATM.

How to Best Use This Chapter

By taking the following steps, you can make better use of your study time:

- Keep your notes and the answers for all your work with this book in one place, for easy reference.

- Take the quiz, and write down your answers. Studies show that retention is significantly increased through writing down facts and concepts, even if you never look at the information again.

- Use the diagram in Figure 4-1 to guide you to the next step.

Figure 4-1 *How to Best Use This Chapter in Preparation for the CLSC Exam*

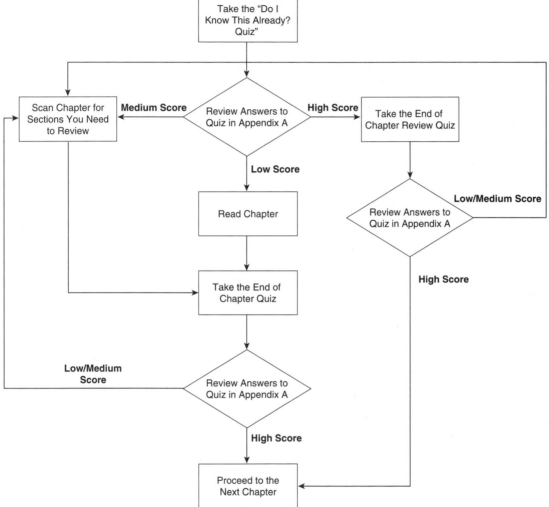

Do I Know This Already? Quiz

You can find the answers to this quiz in Appendix A, "Answers to 'Do I Know This Already?' Quizzes and Q & A Sections." Review the answers, grade your quiz, and choose an appropriate next step in this chapter based on the suggestions diagramed in Figure 4-1.

1 Demand nodes include:

a. Servers

b. Network backbone devices

c. PCs

d. Mainframe hosts

2 Resource nodes include:

a. Workstations

b. Terminal servers

c. PCs

d. Servers

3 Local resources should be placed on segments with users who access those resources most.

a. True

b. False

4 Global resources should be placed on the same shared segment as high-end demand nodes.

a. True

b. False

5 The Catalyst 5000 is intended to be used:

a. As a backbone switch.

b. To connect clusters of servers.

c. To provide desktop switched Fast Ethernet.

d. All of the above.

6 A successful switched internetworking solution must combine the benefits of both routers and switches.

a. True

b. False

7 LAN switches provide excellent performance for individual users by allocating dedicated bandwidth to each switch port (for example, each network segment). This technique is known as _____.

  a. Micro-segmenting

  b. Segmenting

  c. Super netting

  d. Network partitioning

8 When designing a network, the basic design rules that should be followed are:

  a. Examine single points of failure carefully.

  b. Characterize application and protocol traffic.

  c. Analyze bandwidth availability.

  d. A, B

  e. A, C

  f. C, B

  g. A, B, C

9 The core layer of the network should not perform any packet manipulation access lists and filtering.

  a. True

  b. False

10 The distribution layer of the network is the demarcation point between the access and core layers and helps to define and differentiate the core.

  a. True

  b. False

Using the answer key in Appendix A, grade your answers.

- **5 or less correct**—Read this chapter.

- **6, 7, or 8 correct**—Review this chapter, looking at the charts and diagrams that summarize most of the concepts and facts within it.

- **9 or more correct**—If you want more review on these topics, skip to the Q&A section at the end of this chapter. If you do not want more review on these topics, skip this chapter.

Foundation Topics

Switched LAN Network Designs

The material presented here is intended to help the reader understand switched LAN network design features; however, it is not directly related to one of the objectives.

A successful switched internetworking solution must combine the benefits of both routers and switches in every part of the network and must offer a flexible evolution path from shared-media networking to switched internetworks.

In general, incorporating switches in campus network designs results in the following benefits:

- Easy configuration
- High bandwidth
- Low cost
- Quality of service (QoS)

If you need advanced internetworking services, however, routers are necessary. Routers offer the following services:

- Broadcast firewalling
- Communication between mixed-media LANs
- Fast convergence
- Hierarchical addressing
- Multimedia group membership
- Policy routing
- QoS routing
- Redundancy and load balancing
- Security
- Traffic flow management

Some of these router services will be offered by switches in the future. For example, support for multimedia often requires a protocol, such as Internet Group Management Protocol (IGMP), which enables workstations to join a group that receives multimedia multicast packets. In the future, Cisco will enable switches to participate in this process by using the Cisco Group Management Protocol (CGMP). One router will still be necessary, but you will not need a router in each department because CGMP switches can communicate with the router to determine whether any of their attached users are part of a multicast group.

Switching and bridging sometimes can result in non-optimal routing of packets. This is because every packet must go through the root bridge of the spanning tree. When routers are used, the routing of packets can be controlled and designed for optimal paths. Cisco now provides support for improved routing and redundancy in switched environments by supporting one instance of the spanning tree per VLAN.

When designing switched LAN networks, you should consider the following:

- Comparison of LAN switches and routers

- Benefits of LAN switches (Layer 2 services)

- Benefits of routers (Layer 3 services)

- General network design principles

- Switched LAN network design principles

Comparison of LAN Switches and Routers

The material presented here is intended to help the reader understand the differences and similarities between LAN switches and routers; however, it is not directly related to one of the objectives.

The fundamental difference between a LAN switch and a router is that the LAN switch operates at Layer 2 of the OSI model, and the router operates at Layer 3. This difference affects the way that LAN switches and routers respond to network traffic. This section compares LAN switches and routers with regard to the following network design issues:

- Broadcasts

- Convergence

- Loops

- Media dependence

- Security

- Subnetworking

NOTE   Because routers implement Layer 2 functionality and because switches are beginning to implement Layer 3 functionality, the functions of a LAN switch and a router are merging.

Loops

Switched LAN topologies are susceptible to loops, as shown in Figure 4-2.

Figure 4-2   *Switched LAN Topology with Loops*

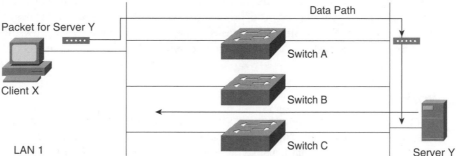

In Figure 4-2, it is possible for packets from Client X to be switched by Switch A, and then for Switch B to put the same packets back onto LAN 1. In this situation, packets loop and undergo multiple replications. To prevent looping and replication, topologies that may contain loops need to run the Spanning-Tree Protocol. The Spanning-Tree Protocol uses the spanning-tree algorithm to construct topologies that do not contain any loops. Because the spanning-tree algorithm places certain connections in blocking mode, only a subset of the network topology is used for forwarding data. In contrast, routers provide freedom from loops and make use of optimal paths.

Convergence

In transparent switching, neighboring switches make topology decisions locally based on the exchange of Bridge Protocol Data Units (BPDUs). This method of making topology decisions means that convergence on an alternative path can take an order of magnitude longer than in a routed environment.

In a routed environment, sophisticated routing protocols, such as Open Shortest Path First (OSPF) and Enhanced Interior Gateway Routing Protocol (Enhanced IGRP), maintain concurrent topological databases of the network and allow the network to converge quickly.

Broadcasts

LAN switches do not filter broadcasts, multicasts, or unknown address frames. The lack of filtering can be a serious problem in modern distributed networks in which broadcast messages are used to resolve addresses and dynamically discover network resources such as file servers. Broadcasts originating from each segment are received by every computer in the switched internetwork. Most devices discard broadcasts because they are irrelevant, which means that large amounts of bandwidth are wasted by the transmission of broadcasts.

In some cases, the circulation of broadcasts can saturate the network so that no bandwidth is left for application data. In this case, new network connections cannot be established, and existing connections may be dropped (a situation known as a *broadcast storm*). The probability of broadcast storms increases as the switched internetwork grows. Routers do not forward broadcasts, and, therefore, routed networks are not subject to broadcast storms.

Subnetworking

Transparently switched internetworks are composed of physically separate segments but are logically considered to be one large network (for example, one IP subnet). This behavior is inherent to the way that LAN switches work—they operate at OSI Layer 2 and must provide connectivity to hosts as if each host were on the same cable. Layer 2 addressing assumes a flat address space with universally unique addresses.

Routers operate at OSI Layer 3 and thus can formulate and adhere to a hierarchical addressing structure. Routed networks can associate a logical addressing structure to a physical infrastructure so that each network segment has, for example, a TCP/IP subnet or an IPX network. Traffic flow on routed networks is inherently different from traffic flow on switched networks. Routed networks have more flexible traffic flow because they can use the hierarchy to determine optimal paths, depending on dynamic factors such as network congestion.

Security

Information is available to routers and switches that can be used to create more secure networks. LAN switches may use custom filters to provide access control based on destination address, source address, protocol type, packet length, and offset bits within the frame. Routers can filter on logical network addresses and provide control based on options available in Layer 3 protocols. For example, routers can permit or deny traffic based on specific TCP/IP socket information for a range of network addresses.

Media Dependence

Two factors need to be considered with regard to mixed-media internetworks. First, the maximum transfer unit (MTU) differs for various network media. Table 4-1 lists the maximum frame size for various network media.

Table 4-1   *MTUs for Various Network Media*

Media	Minimum Valid Frame	Maximum Valid Size
Ethernet	64 bytes	1518 bytes
Token Ring	32 bytes	16 KB theoretical, 4 KB normal
Fast Ethernet	64 bytes	1518 bytes
FDDI	32 bytes	4400 bytes
ATM LANE	64 bytes	1518 bytes
ATM Classical IP	64 bytes	9180 bytes
Serial HDLC	14 bytes	No limit, 4.5 KB normal

When LANs of dissimilar media are switched, hosts must use the MTU that is the lowest common denominator of all the switched LANs that make up the internetwork. This requirement limits throughput and can seriously compromise performance over a relatively fast link, such as FDDI or ATM. Most Layer 3 protocols can fragment and reassemble packets that are too large for a particular subnetwork, so routed networks can accommodate different MTUs, which maximizes throughput.

Second, because they operate at Layer 2, switches must use a translation function to switch between dissimilar media. The translation function can result in serious problems, such as non-canonical versus canonical conversion from Token Ring to Ethernet MAC format. One issue with moving data from a Token Ring to an Ethernet network is Layer 2 addressing. Token Ring devices read the Layer 2 MAC address with the most significant bit starting from left to right. Ethernet devices read the Layer 2 MAC address with the most significant bit starting from right to left.

By working at Layer 3, routers are essentially independent of the properties of any physical media and can use a simple address resolution algorithm (such as *Novell-node-address = MAC-address*) or a protocol, such as the Address Resolution Protocol (ARP) to resolve differences between Layer 2 and Layer 3 addresses.

Benefits of LAN Switches (Layer 2 Services)

An individual Layer 2 switch might offer some or all of the following benefits:

- *Bandwidth*—LAN switches provide excellent performance for individual users by allocating dedicated bandwidth to each switch port (for example, each network segment). This technique is known as *microsegmenting*.

- *VLANs*—LAN switches can group individual ports into logical switched workgroups called VLANs, thereby restricting the broadcast domain to designated VLAN member ports. VLANs are also known as switched domains and autonomous switching domains. Communication between VLANs requires a router.

- *Automated packet recognition and translation*—Cisco's unique Automatic Packet Recognition and Translation (APaRT) technology recognizes and converts a variety of Ethernet protocol formats into industry-standard CDDI/FDDI formats. With no changes needed in either client or server end stations, the Catalyst solution can provide an easy migration to 100 Mbps server access while preserving the user's investment in existing shared 10BaseT LANs.

Benefits of Routers (Layer 3 Services)

Because routers use Layer 3 addresses, which typically have structure, routers can use techniques such as address summarization to build networks that maintain performance and responsiveness as they grow in size. By imposing structure (usually hierarchically) on a network, routers can effectively use redundant paths and determine optimal routes even in a dynamically changing network. This section describes the router functions that are vital in switched LAN designs:

- Broadcast and multicast control

- Broadcast segmentation

- Media transition

Broadcast and Multicast Control

Routers control broadcasts and multicasts in the following ways:

- *By caching the addresses of remote hosts*—When a host sends a broadcast packet to obtain the address of a remote host that the router already knows, the router responds on behalf of the remote host and drops the broadcast packet (sparing hosts from having to respond to it).

- *By caching advertised network services*—When a router learns of a new network service, it caches the necessary information and does not forward broadcasts related to it. When a client of that network service sends a broadcast to locate that service, the router responds on behalf of that service and drops the broadcast packet (sparing hosts from having to respond to it). For example, Novell clients use broadcasts to find local services. In a network without a router, every server responds to every client broadcast by multicasting its list of services. Routers manage Novell broadcasts by collecting services not local to the switch and sending out periodic updates that describe the services offered on the entire network. Each router sends out one frame for every seven services on the network.

- *By providing special protocols, such as the IGMP and Protocol Independent Multicast (PIM)*—These new protocols enable a multicasting application to "negotiate" with routers, switches, and clients to determine the devices that belong to a multicast group. This negotiation helps limit the scope and impact of the multicast stream on the network as a whole.

Successful network designs contain a mix of appropriately scaled switching and routing. Given the effects of broadcast radiation on CPU performance, well-managed switched LAN designs must include routers for broadcast and multicast management.

Broadcast Segmentation

In addition to preventing broadcasts from radiating throughout the network, routers are also responsible for generating services to each LAN segment. The following are examples of services that the router provides to the network for a variety of protocols:

- *AppleTalk*—ZIP table updates
- *IP*—Proxy ARP and Internet Control Message Protocol (ICMP)
- *IPX*—SAP table updates
- *Network management*—SNMP queries

In a flat virtual network, a single router would be bombarded by a myriad of requests needing replies, severely taxing its processor. Therefore, the network designer needs to consider the number of routers that can provide reliable services to a given subset of VLANs. Some type of hierarchical design needs to be considered.

Media Transition

In the past, routers have been used to connect networks of different media types, taking care of the OSI Layer 3 address translations and fragmentation requirements. Routers continue to perform this function in switched LAN designs. Most switching is done within like media (such as Ethernet, Token Ring, and FDDI switches) with some capability of connecting to another media type. However, if a requirement for a switched campus network design is to provide high-speed connectivity between unlike media, routers play a significant part in the design.

General Network Design Principles

The material presented here is intended to help the reader understand general network design principles; however, it is not directly related to one of the objectives.

Good network design is based on many concepts that are summarized by the following key principles:

- *Examine single points of failure carefully*—Redundancy should exist in the network so that a single failure does not isolate any portion of the network. Two aspects of redundancy need to be considered: backup and load balancing. In the event of a failure in the network, there should be an alternative or backup path. Load balancing occurs when two or more paths to a destination exist and can be utilized, depending on the network load. The level of redundancy required in a particular network varies from network to network.

- *Characterize application and protocol traffic*—For example, the flow of application data will profile client-server interaction and is crucial for efficient resource allocation, such as the number of clients using a particular server or the number of client workstations on a segment.

- *Analyze bandwidth availability*—For example, there should not be an order of magnitude difference between the different layers of the hierarchical model. It is important to remember that the hierarchical model refers to conceptual layers that provide functionality. The actual demarcation between layers does not have to be a physical link—it can be the backplane of a particular device.

- *Build networks using a hierarchical or modular model*—The hierarchy enables autonomous segments to be internetworked.

Figure 4-3 shows a high-level view of the various aspects of a hierarchical network design. A hierarchical network design presents three layers—core, distribution, and access—with each layer providing different functionality.

The core layer is a high-speed switching backbone and should be designed to switch packets as quickly as possible. This layer of the network should not perform any packet manipulation access lists and filtering that would slow down the switching of packets.

The distribution layer of the network is the demarcation point between the access and core layers and helps to define and differentiate the core. The purpose of this layer is to provide boundary definition, and this is the place at which packet manipulation can take place. In the campus environment, the distribution layer can include several functions, such as the following:

- Address or area aggregation

- Any media transitions that need to occur

- Broadcast/multicast domain definition

- Departmental or workgroup access

- Security

- VLAN routing

Figure 4-3   *Hierarchical Network Design Model*

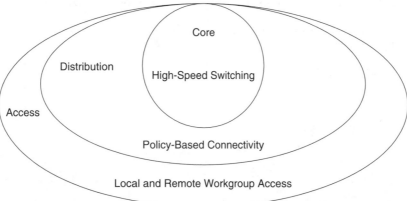

In the non-campus environment, the distribution layer can be a redistribution point between routing domains or the demarcation between static and dynamic routing protocols. It can also be the point at which remote sites access the corporate network. The distribution layer can be summarized as the layer that provides policy-based connectivity.

The access layer is the point at which local end users are allowed into the network. This layer may also use access lists or filters to further optimize the needs of a particular set of users. In the campus environment, access-layer functions can include the following:

- Shared bandwidth
- Switched bandwidth
- MAC-layer filtering
- Microsegmentation

In the non-campus environment, the access layer can give remote sites access to the corporate network via some wide-area technology, such as Frame Relay, ISDN, or leased lines.

It is sometimes mistakenly thought that the three layers (core, distribution, and access) must exist in clear and distinct physical entities, but this does not have to be the case. The layers are defined to aid successful network design and to represent functionality that must exist in a network. The instantiation of each layer can be in distinct routers or switches, can be represented by a physical media, can be combined in a single device, or can be omitted altogether. The way the layers are implemented depends on the needs of the network being designed. Note, however, that for a network to function optimally, hierarchy must be maintained.

With respect to the hierarchical model, traditional campus LANs have followed one of two designs: single router or distributed backbone, as shown in Figure 4-4.

Figure 4-4   *Traditional Campus Design*

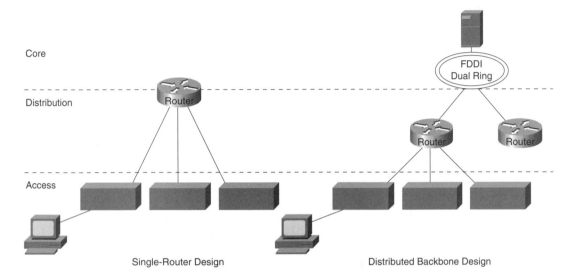

In the single-router design, the core and distribution layers are present in a single entity: the router. Core functionality is represented by the backplane of the router, and distribution is represented by the router. Access for end users is through individual- or chassis-based hubs. This design suffers from scalability constraints because the router can be in only one physical location, so all segments end at the same location: the router. The single router is responsible for all distribution functionality, which can cause CPU overload.

The distributed backbone design uses a high-speed backbone media—typically FDDI—to spread routing functionality among several routers. This also enables the backbone to traverse floors, a building, or a campus.

Switched LAN Network Design Principles

The material presented here is intended to help the reader understand switched LAN network design principles; however, it is not directly related to one of the objectives.

Despite improvements in equipment performance and media capabilities, internetwork design is becoming more difficult. The trend is toward increasingly complex environments involving multiple media, multiple protocols, and interconnection to networks outside any single organization's dominion of control. Carefully designing internetworks can reduce the hardships associated with growth as a networking environment evolves. When designing switched LAN campus networks, the following factors must be considered:

- *Broadcast radiation*—Broadcast radiation can become fatal—that is, 100 percent of host CPU cycles can be consumed by processing broadcast and multicast packets. Because of delays inherent in carrier sense multiple access collision detect (CMSA/CD) technologies, such as Ethernet, any more than a small amount of broadcast traffic will adversely affect the operation of devices attached to a switch. Although VLANs reduce the effect of broadcast radiation on all LANs, there is still a scaling issue as to how many hosts should reside on a given VLAN. A router provides for larger network designs because a VLAN can be subsegmented, depending on traffic patterns. However, in a nonoptimal network design, a single router can be burdened with large amounts of traffic.

- *Well-behaved VLANs*—A well-behaved VLAN is a VLAN in which 80 percent or more of the traffic is local to that VLAN. In an example in which the Marketing, MIS, and Engineering departments each have an individual VLAN segment, the 80 percent rule is violated when a user in the Marketing VLAN reads mail from the MIS VLAN, mounts servers from the Engineering VLAN, and sends e-mail to members of the Engineering VLAN.

- *Available bandwidth to access routing functionality*—Inter-VLAN traffic must be routed, so the network design must allocate enough bandwidth to move inter-VLAN traffic from the source, through the device that provides routing functionality, and to the destination.

- *Appropriate placement of administrative boundaries*—Switching has the effect of flattening networks, and the deployment of switching outside your administrative boundary can adversely affect the network within your administrative boundary.

Campus network designs are evolving rapidly with the deployment of switching at all levels of the network, from the desktop to the backbone. Three topologies have emerged as generic network designs:

- Scaled switching
- Large switching/minimal routing
- Distributed routing/switching

Scaled Switching

The scaled switching design shown in Figure 4-5 deploys switching at all levels of the network without the use of routers. In this design, each layer consists of switches, with switches in the access layer providing 10 Mbps Ethernet or 16 Mbps Token Ring to end users.

Figure 4-5 *Scaled Switching Design*

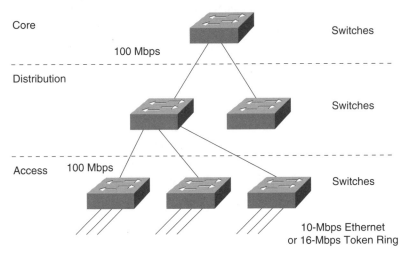

Scaled switching is a low-cost and easy-to-install solution for a small campus network. It does not require knowledge of address structure, is easy to manage, and enables all users to communicate with one another. However, this network comprises a single broadcast domain. If a scaled switched network needs to grow beyond the broadcast domain, it can use VLANs to create multiple broadcast domains. Note that when VLANs are used, end users in one VLAN cannot communicate with end users in another VLAN unless routers are deployed.

Large Switched/Minimal Routing

The large switched/minimal routing design deploys switching at the access layer of the network, either ATM switching or LAN switching at the distribution layer of the network, and ATM/LAN switching at the core. Figure 4-6 shows an example of this network design.

Figure 4-6   *Large Switched/Minimal Routing Design*

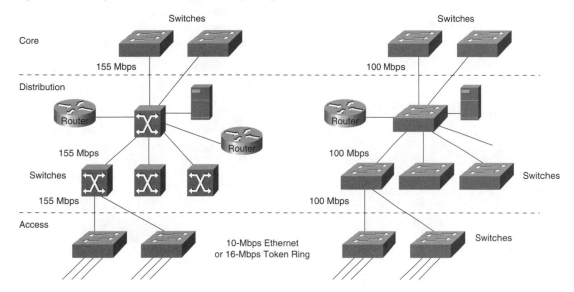

In the case of ATM in the distribution layer, the following key issues are relevant:

- LANE support on routers and switches

- Support for UNI 3.X signaling (including point-to-multipoint)

- The mesh as a single point of failure, if redundancy is provided by a virtual PVC or SVC mesh

In the case of LAN switching in the distribution layer, the following key issues are relevant:

- Support for VLAN trunking technology is enabled in each device.

- The switches in the distribution layer must run the Spanning-Tree Protocol to prevent loops, which means that some connections will be blocked and load balancing cannot occur.

To scale the large switched/minimal routing design, a logical hierarchy must be imposed. The logical hierarchy consists of VLANs and routers that enable inter-VLAN communication. In this topology, routing is used in only the distribution layer, and the access layer depends on bandwidth through the distribution layer to gain access to high-speed switching functionality in the core layer.

The large switched/minimal routing design scales well when VLANs are designed so that the majority of resources are available in the VLAN. Therefore, if this topology can be designed so that 80 percent of traffic is intra-VLAN and only 20 percent of traffic is inter-VLAN, the bandwidth needed for inter-VLAN routing is not a concern. However, if inter-VLAN traffic is greater than 20 percent, access to routing in the core becomes a scalability issue. For optimal network operation, scalable routing content is needed at the distribution layer of the network.

Distributed Routing/Switching

The distributed routing/switching design deploys switching in the access layer, routing in the distribution layer, and some form of high-speed switching in the core layer, as shown in Figure 4-7.

Figure 4-7   *Distributed Routing/Switching Design*

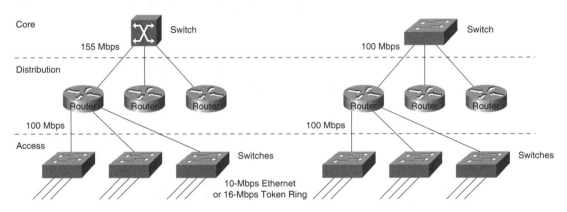

The distributed routing/switching design follows the classic hierarchical network model both physically and logically. Because it provides high bandwidth for access to routing functionality, this design scales very well. This design is optimized for networks that do not have the 80/20 pattern rule. If servers are centralized, most traffic is inter-VLAN; therefore, high routing content is needed.

Demand Nodes and Resource Nodes

CLSC Objectives Covered in This Section

24	Describe demand nodes and resource nodes.
25	Describe configuration rules for demand nodes and resource nodes.
26	Describe local resources and remote resources.
27	Describe configuration rules for local resources and remote resources.

Planning is extremely important when the decision is made to segment a network. The usual reasons for segmentation are to relieve network congestion and to provide additional bandwidth needed to satisfy the types of information the network is to carry. A review of current and planned network devices, the type of traffic the existing network facilitates, the user access needed to contain network resources, the number of users on the network, security needs, the applications used, and a host of other considerations must be made to ensure effective network performance. With these needs in mind, we will now examine some factors relevant to effective network segmentation.

Node Types

A network can be viewed as providing connectivity for two basic device types. These device types ask for services or act as a reservoir or provider of services, and are called demand nodes and resource nodes, respectively. Figure 4-8 illustrates a demand node and a resource node.

Figure 4-8   *Example of Demand and Resource Nodes*

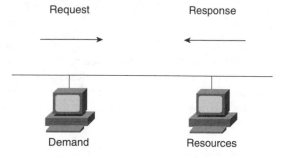

Demand nodes include the following:

- Workstations

- Personal computers

- Client applications

- Terminal servers

Resource nodes include the following:

- Minicomputers or mainframe hosts

- Servers

- WAN routers

Resource Types

Segmentation of an Ethernet LAN creates multiple collision domains. Each segment supports simultaneous communication between same-segment nodes, resulting in multiple conversations. Communication can still take place between stations located on different segments. Intersegment communication creates two resource types:

- *Local resource*—A resource node in the same collision domain as that of the demand node.

- *Remote resources*—A resource node located in a different collision domain.

Multiple conversations do not cause collisions in themselves; the frames that constitute them simply sit in the buffers of the switch. Collisions affect the workstations trying to reach the same resource in addition to other conversations on that segment.

Local Resource Capacity

Segmentation of an Ethernet LAN results in a capacity increase on the LAN because each segment supports a separate conversation. Switched multiple segments enable local conversations between nodes in the same collision domain. The capacity of a segmented network is measured as the number of segments (collision domains) that can carry on simultaneous local conversations, multiplied by the speed of the medium in each segment.

Remote Resources

A remote conversation takes place between a demand node and a resource node located in different collision domains. *Throughput* is a measurement of activity during a network conversation. The most common measurement of throughput is in bits per second. Effective throughput is the number of bits that can be transmitted within a given period of time. A measurement of throughput in remote conversation is the maximum number of simultaneous remote conversations that can take place.

Placing Local and Global Resources

To maximize throughput for the network, certain rules for configuration should be observed:

- Local resources should be placed on segments with users who access those resources most.

- Global resources (those requiring equal access by network users) should be on their own dedicated segment to guarantee a minimum of 10 Mbps throughput. Servers should be 100 Mbps, preferably operating in full-duplex mode.

Buffer Overflow Condition

Configuring three or more demand segments to communicate with one resource segment can cause multiple ports to transmit continuously to a single port. The consequence of this sort of bottleneck can result in the following error conditions (see Figure 4-9):

- Buffer overflow condition on the switch

- Dropped frames, resulting in retransmissions

Figure 4-9   *Buffer Overflow Condition*

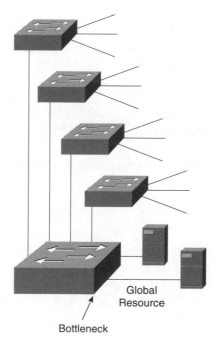

Remedies for these conditions include:

- Increasing the size of the switch buffers

- Increasing the size of the link to the servers

- Creating multiple links

- Setting higher priority for ports attached to the servers

- Using a packet retry mechanism

Configuration: Demand and Resource Nodes

A cardinal rule for segmented network configuration is to never configure a network so that the demands exceed the resources. The result of configuration for a five-segment network with four demand segments and one response segment at the same speed would make the switched network no more effective than putting all nodes on the same segment. Instead, allocate plenty of bandwidth for your resource nodes so that they can have access to adequate bandwidth to respond to the demand nodes. This means you should:

- Place resource nodes on dedicated, not shared links.

- Use Fast Ethernet, where appropriate.

- Use full duplex, where appropriate.

Additionally, you should place your local resource nodes close to their associated demand nodes to reduce the amount of traffic that must cross the network and that could cause bottlenecks on the backbone.

Five Switch Applications

CLSC Objectives Covered in This Section

3	Place the Catalyst series switches in a network for optimal performance benefit.
28	Name five applications for Catalyst 5000 series switches.

The proliferation of bandwidth-hungry intranet applications is changing the requirements for enterprise networks. The random browsing and the any-to-any communications that these applications encourage have changed the traditional traffic model, which assumes a high degree of locality within subnets and lower forwarding rates between them. The 80/20 rule is inverting. To create an effective switched network design to meet these requirements, the following five switching applications must be utilized in your network:

- Improved network performance
- Backbone switch
- Server cluster
- 10/100 Mbps workgroups
- Desktop switched Fast Ethernet

The following sections will define the five switch applications in detail.

Application 1: Improved Network Performance

Figure 4-10   *Application 1: Improved Network Performance*

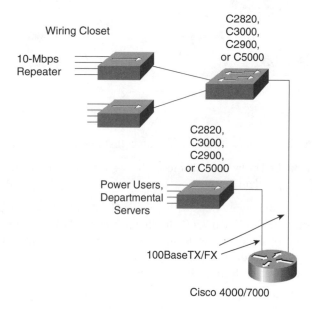

In the first application, the objective is to enhance the performance of an existing network.

- Remove bottlenecks at the server and backbone with the use of switched Fast Ethernet for server connections and for backbone connections.
- Catalyst 5000 series 10/100BaseTX capabilities enable connectivity of 10 Mbps Ethernet or 100 Mbps Ethernet for easy migration to 100 Mbps Ethernet.

- The embedded traffic-management capabilities of the Catalyst 5000 series switches enable you to manage the switched internetwork.

An engineering firm that is experiencing problems on its shared-hub network typifies the need for improved network performance. Its problems include the following (see Figure 4-11):

Figure 4-11 *Engineering Firm Example Network*

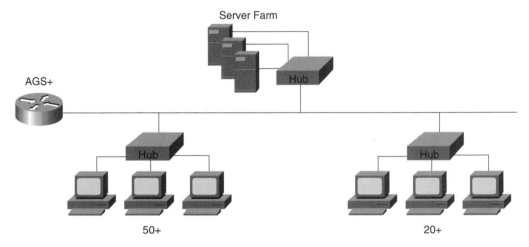

- Sluggish network response and high collision rates due to inadequate bandwidth

- Uncontrolled broadcasts that result from a large broadcast domain and compound the collision problem

After replacing the shared hubs with a single Catalyst 5000 switch and the AGS+ router with a more powerful Cisco 7500, the sluggish network response and high collision rates are eliminated by the micro-segmentation of the network (shown in Figure 4-12). Now, each server is on a dedicated 100 Mbps Ethernet connection, and each workstation is attached to dedicated 10 Mbps Ethernet ports.

Figure 4-12   *New Network Design of Engineering Firm*

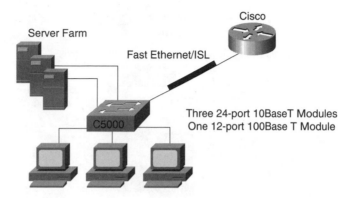

The previously uncontrolled broadcasts are now controlled by the use of virtual LANs. Now, broadcast messages are confined to the VLAN of the source node.

Application 2: Backbone Switch

In this second application, a Catalyst 5000 is used to connect wiring closet switches to create a core backbone. The core layer is a high-speed switching backbone and should be designed to switch packets as quickly as possible. This layer of the network should not perform any packet manipulation, such as access lists and filtering, that would slow down the switching of packets. See Figure 4-13.

Figure 4-13 *Backbone Switch*

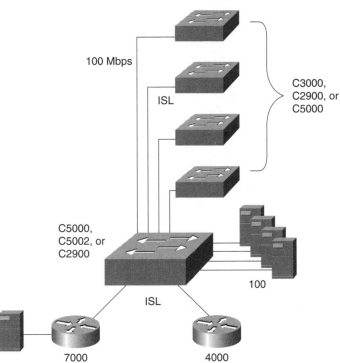

Fast Ethernet Backbone

The Catalyst 5000 series of switches are well suited for Fast Ethernet backbone applications, including collapsed backbones with Fast Ethernet switching at the center or distributed backbones with Fast Ethernet switching in several locations.

In addition, the Catalyst 5000 switch has uplinks to FDDI and ATM for those types of backbones.

Benefits for backbone applications are high-performance throughput, a complete VLAN solution, and traffic management.

Long-Distance Connections

The Catalyst 5000 100BaseFX multimode fiber (MMF) module and the Catalyst 2902 each provide 12 100BaseFX interfaces for connection to existing multimode fiber backbones. Full duplex operation enables distance runs of up to 2 km.

Fault Tolerance

The use of a spanning tree per port and per VLAN enables redundant network connections for fault tolerance in the data center and in mission-critical applications. Load sharing across ISL trunk links improves throughput capacity and fault tolerance.

Application 3: Server Cluster

Figure 4-14 is basically the same as Figure 4-13. The main difference is in the emphasis on the Catalyst 5000 switch's usefulness in connecting servers in addition to being a backbone switch.

Figure 4-14   *Server Cluster*

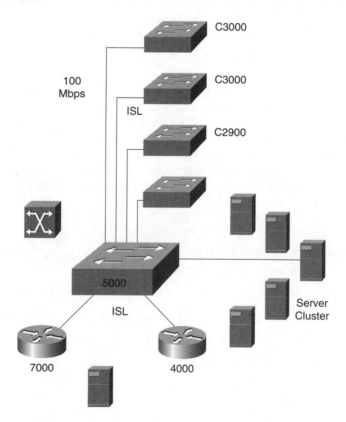

Easy Migration

Fast Ethernet is well suited for server cluster connections because of the low cost and easy migration from 10 Mbps to 100 Mbps. The Catalyst 5000 and Catalyst 2901 switches have 10/100 auto-negotiating and auto-sensing for connectivity to 10/100 server network interface cards, which enables you to easily migrate servers from 10 Mbps to 100 Mbps.

Fast Throughput

The Catalyst 5000 series switches provide high-performance servers with enough throughput to handle data-intensive client/server applications. They handle bursty and overload traffic well. The low latency and high per-port throughput are well suited for client/server applications. Server-to-server communication is increased when full duplex is used.

VLANs

A VLAN consists of a single broadcast domain and solves the scalability problems of large flat networks by breaking a single broadcast domain into several smaller broadcast domains or VLANs. Virtual LANs offer easier moves and changes in a network design than traditional networks. LAN switches can be used to segment networks into logically defined virtual workgroups. This logical segmentation, commonly referred to as VLAN communication, offers a fundamental change in how LANs are designed, administered, and managed. The following is a list of key benefits that are provided by VLANs in an enterprise network environment:

- VLANs used here simplify adds, moves, and changes.

- Workgroups with high traffic can be managed with broadcast, multicast, and unicast control within each VLAN workgroup.

- VlanDirector provides point-and-click administration of VLANs.

- ISL-aware servers can communicate with clients on multiple VLANs.

Figure 4-15 shows a more complex solution implementing the previous two applications within a single network.

Figure 4-15   *Backbone and Server Cluster Switch*

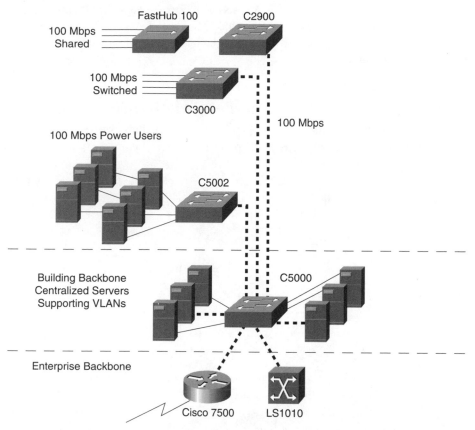

The network design shown in Figure 4-15 provides a switched backbone topology with a server cluster for high-speed application access. The design is made possible by utilizing the following:

- 10/100BaseT Ethernet LAN switching is used to connect servers in the data center and at central wiring closet locations.

- 100BaseFX is used for backbone distances of up to 2 km.

- Fast Ethernet repeaters, such as the FastHub 100, provide 100 Mbps shared Ethernet segments for desktop connections.

- VLANs are overlaid on the switched internetwork to improve management and to define logical workgroups. VLANs can be extended to ATM networks using the Catalyst 5000 ATM LAN Emulation Module. VLANs can also be extended to FDDI networks using the IEEE 802.10, which is supported on the Catalyst 5000 FDDI/ CDDI modules.

Application 4: 10/100 Mbps Ethernet Switching

In this fourth application, 10/100 Mbps Ethernet switching is extended to the workgroup. An example of 10/100 Mbps Workgroups is shown in Figure 4-16.

Figure 4-16   *10/100 Mbps Workgroups*

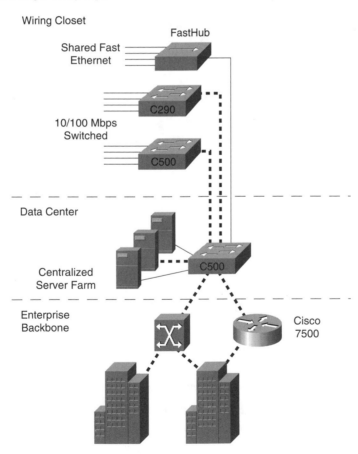

High-performance workgroups require dedicated 100 Mbps connections. CiscoPro FastHub100 repeaters can be used for connection of smaller workgroups with lower-performance demands. In the data center, the Catalyst 5000 acts as a collapsed backbone Fast Ethernet switch for connection of centralized servers.

Easy Migration

The Catalyst 2901, like the Catalyst 5000 10/100 Ethernet switching module, has 10/100 auto-sensing for connectivity to 10/100 server network interface cards, which enables you to easily migrate workstations from 10 Mbps to 100 Mbps.

Fast Throughput

The Catalyst 5000 series of switches provides high-performance workgroups with enough throughput to handle demanding desktop applications. They offer low latency and high per-port throughput without losing frames under bursty or overload traffic conditions. Throughput is 200 Mbps when full duplex is used.

VLANs

VLANs simplify moves, adds, and changes. Desktops with high traffic are easily managed with broadcast, multicast, and unicast control within each VLAN workgroup. VlanDirector provides point-and-click administration of VLANs.

Manageable

The Catalyst 5000 series switches' embedded traffic management capabilities enable management of the switched internetwork and include embedded RMON.

Application 5: Switched Fast Ethernet

In the fifth application, switched Fast Ethernet is extended to the desktop for maximum end-node performance. The difference between Figure 4-17 and the previous figure is that the FastHub 100 repeater is replaced by a switch so that all end nodes are on dedicated, switched segments.

Figure 4-17 *Desktop Switched Fast Ethernet*

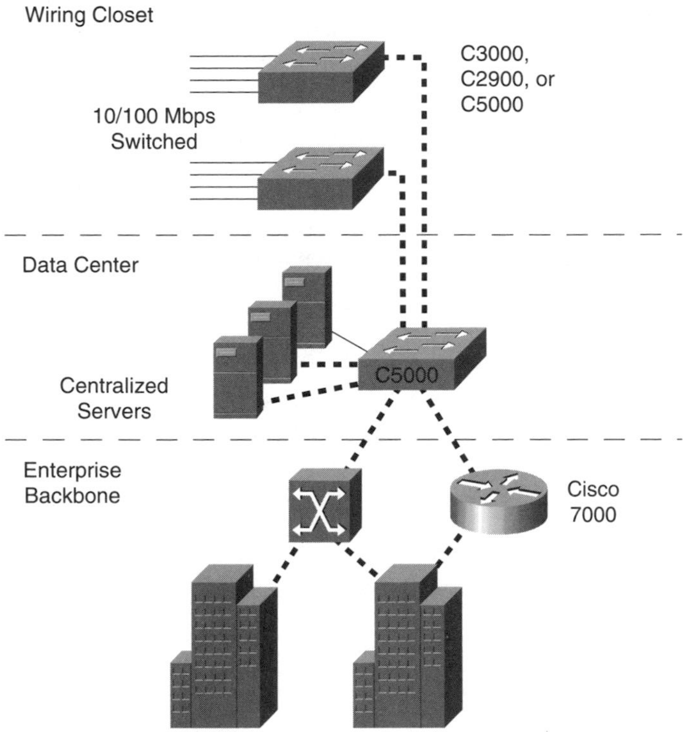

The Catalyst 2900 is effective for small groups of desktops, and the Catalyst 5000 is effective for larger numbers of desktops requiring larger-density Fast Ethernet switching.

VLANs are implemented to create virtual workgroups that can span the enterprise. The VLAN implementation can include Fast Ethernet, FDDI, and ATM LANE.

The entire switched internetwork is managed with switched internetwork management applications.

Q&A

As mentioned in Chapter 1, "The Cisco LAN Switch Configuration (CLSC) Exam Overview," the questions and scenarios are more difficult than what you should experience on the actual exam. The questions do not attempt to cover more breadth or depth than the exam; however, the questions are designed to make sure you know the answers. Rather than allowing you to derive the answer from clues hidden inside the question itself, the questions will challenge your understanding and recall of the subject. Hopefully, these questions will help limit the number of exam questions on which you narrow your choices to two options and then guess!

1   Remedies for Buffer Overflow Condition include: _____.

2   A remote conversation takes place between a demand node and a resource node located in different _____.

3   Switched multiple segments enable local conversations between nodes in the same _____.

4   Define *local resource*.

5   Define *remote resource*.

6   Demand nodes include what type of nodes?

7   Resource nodes include what type of nodes?

8   The large switched/minimal routing design scales well when VLANs are designed so that the majority of resources are available in the VLAN. Therefore, if this topology can be designed so that _____ percent of traffic is intra-VLAN and only _____ percent of traffic is inter-VLAN, the bandwidth needed for inter-VLAN routing is not a concern.

9   In a hierarchical network design, distribution layer can be summarized as the layer that provides _____ connectivity.

10 In the campus environment, access-layer functions can include _____.

Source Material

Some content in this chapter is based on the following sources:

- Designing Switched LAN Internetworks

  http://www.cisco.com/univercd/cc/td/doc/cisintwk/idg4/nd2012.htm#14487

- Designing Internetworks for Multimedia

  http://www.cisco.com/univercd/cc/td/doc/cisintwk/idg4/nd2013.htm

The objectives of the Cisco LAN Switch Configuration (CLSC) exam are taken from the Cisco web site, at the Cisco career certification and training area. The following table shows the exam objectives covered in this chapter:

Objective	Description
2	Describe the architecture and functions of the major components of the Catalyst switches.
33	Describe the architecture and function of major components of the Catalyst 5000 series switch:
	• Processors: NMP, MCP, and LCP
	• Logic Units: LTL, CBL, Arbiter, and EARL
	• ASICs: SAINT, SAGE, SAMBA, and Phoenix
34	Trace a frame's progress through a Catalyst 5000 series switch.

CHAPTER **5**

Catalyst 5000 Series Switch Architecture

The range of media support in the Catalyst 5000 series enables network managers to deliver high-performance backbone access to accommodate Web browser-based traffic across the intranet. A growing number of interface modules operate in any Catalyst 5000 series switch to deliver dedicated bandwidth to users through the following:

- High-density group switched and switched 10BaseT or 100BaseT Ethernet

- Flexible 10/100BaseT Ethernet, fiber-based Fast Ethernet, and Fast EtherChannel

- Token Ring

- CDDI/FDDI

- ATM LAN Emulation (LANE)

- The Route/Switch module (based on the Route/Switch Processor for the Cisco 7500 router series)

- The future Gigabit Ethernet

Unique to the Catalyst 5500 platform are the ATM Switch Processor and ATM switch interface modules and port adapters. This chapter will cover the hardware architecture of the Catalyst 5000 series switch.

How to Best Use This Chapter

By taking the following steps, you can make better use of your study time:

- Keep your notes and the answers for all your work with this book in one place, for easy reference.

- Take the quiz, and write down your answers. Studies show that retention is significantly increased through writing down facts and concepts, even if you never look at the information again.

- Use the diagram in Figure 5-1 to guide you to the next step.

Figure 5-1   *How to Best Use This Chapter in Preparation for the CLSC Exam*

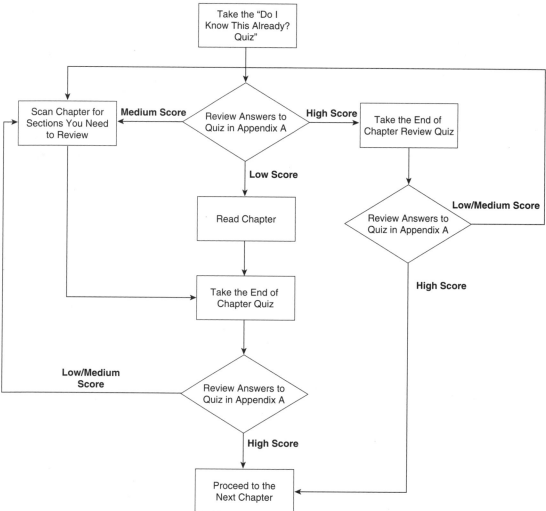

Do I Know This Already? Quiz

The answers to this quiz are found in Appendix A, "Answers to 'Do I Know This Already?' Quizzes and Q & A Sections." Review the answers, grade your quiz, and choose an appropriate next step in this chapter based on the suggestions diagramed in Figure 5-1.

1 The architecture of the Catalyst 5000 series switch supports which of the following media types?

a. Ethernet

b. Fast Ethernet

c. Token Ring

d. ATM

e. FDDI

f. PPP

2 The Catalyst 5000 series switch architecture uses a store-and-forward model for input and output.

a. True

b. False

3 The Management Bus carries configuration information from the _____ to each module and statistical information from each module to the NMP.

a. SAINT

b. EARL

c. NMP

d. CAL

4 Using the Bus Arbiter, the bus supports a two-level priority request scheme.

a. True

b. False

5 The switching bus is _____ bits wide and operates at 25 MHz.

a. 48

b. 64

c. 256

d. 512

6 Each dedicated Ethernet and Fast Ethernet switch port has its own SAINT ASIC and
_____ KB of dedicated frame buffer.

a. 64

b. 128

c. 192

d. 256

7 As a frame is received from the network and stored in the port's frame buffer, ASICs
on each port encapsulate Ethernet frames with _____ bytes of information to indicate
VLAN ID.

a. 12

a. 24

a. 48

a. 64

8 You can also configure static entries in the EARL table. The EARL stores up to _____
addresses.

a. 16,000

b. 32,000

c. 64,000

d. 128,000

9 The Catalyst 5000 series switch architecture enables media-rate performance not only
for unicast traffic, but also for broadcast and multicast traffic.

a. True

b. False

10 The SNMP agent executes in the _____.

a. EARL

b. CAL

c. NMP

d. SAINT

Using the answer key in Appendix A, grade your answers.

- **5 or less correct**—Read this chapter.

- **6, 7, or 8 correct**—Review this chapter, looking at the charts and diagrams that
summarize most of the concepts and facts in this chapter.

- **9 or more correct**—If you want more review on these topics, skip to the Q&A section at
the end of this chapter. If you do not want more review on these topics, skip this chapter.

Foundation Topics

Catalyst 5000 Overview

CLSC Objectives Covered in This Section	
2	Describe the architecture and functions of the major components of the Catalyst switches.
33	Describe the architecture and function of major components of the Catalyst 5000 series switch: • Processors: NMP, MCP, and LCP • Logic Units: LTL, CBL, Arbiter, and EARL • ASICs: SAINT, SAGE, SAMBA, and Phoenix

Figure 5-2 shows the hardware components of the Catalyst 5000 chassis. This chapter will cover the architecture and function of major components of the Catalyst 5000 series switch:

Figure 5-2   *Catalyst 5000 Overview*

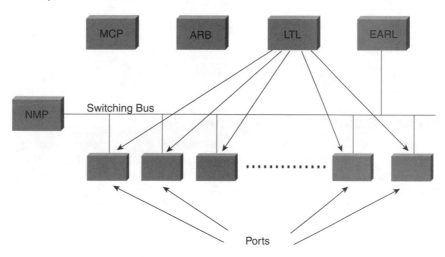

Processors: NMP, MCP, and LCP

Logic units: LTL, CBL, Arbiter, and EARL

ASICs: SAINT, SAGE, SAMBA, and Phoenix

The following terms are used in Figure 5-2 and throughout the chapter:

• NMP: Network Management Processor.

- MCP: Master Control Processor.

- LCP: Line Module Communication Processor.

- SCP: Serial Communication Protocol.

- SAINT: Synergy Advanced Interface and Network Termination.

- SAGE: Synergy Advanced Gate Array Engine; equivalent to SAINT without Ethernet MAC.

- EARL: Encoded Address Recognition Logic used for learning network addresses. Uses SAINT and SAGE application-specific integrated circuits (ASICs).

- LTL: Local Target Logic. Used to select which port or ports on the switching bus are to receive the current packet on the bus.

- CBL: Color Blocking Logic. Blocks VLAN traffic going out of a port or coming in from a port.

- ARB: One arbiter is located on each line card and on each Supervisor engine.

- Control arbitration for each bus.

- Low, high, and system (critical) priorities.

- Low and high priorities that can be set by the user.

- Phoenix: A gate array ASIC used to connect the switching buses.

- SAMBA: Synergy Advanced Multipurpose Bus Arbiter.

Catalyst 5000 Backplane Architecture

The range of media support in the Catalyst 5000 Family enables network managers to deliver high-performance backbone access to accommodate Web browser-based traffic across the intranet. Unique to the Catalyst 5500 Series are the ATM Switch Processor and ATM switch interface modules and port adapters. See Figure 5-3.

Figure 5-3   *Catalyst 5000 Backplane Architecture*

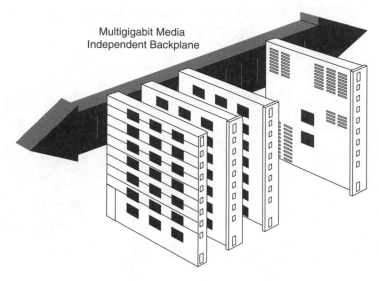

Multigigabit Media
Independent Backplane

The Catalyst 5000 series switch is media-independent and supports both ATM cells or Ethernet frames.

The Catalyst 5500 series switches provide support for standards-based ATM switching and routing:

- ATM Forum ABR congestion control
- ATM PNNI routing
- ATM Forum ILMI support
- Autosensing of UNI/NNI interface
- ATM access lists

The benefits of the Catalyst 5000 series are listed here:

- Ensures investment protection with Catalyst 5000/5002/5500
- Ensures long-term migration
- Provides seamless integration for all media types, with no translational overhead across backplane
- Provides features and functionality of Cisco IOS software
- Offers guaranteed application integrity

Catalyst 5000 1.2 Gbps Architecture

The Catalyst 5000 series switch architecture shown in Figure 5-4 uses a store-and-forward model for input and output. Each switch port maintains its own frame buffer memory. Each frame is stored in a frame buffer before it is forwarded.

Figure 5-4 *Catalyst 5000 1.2 Gbps Architecture*

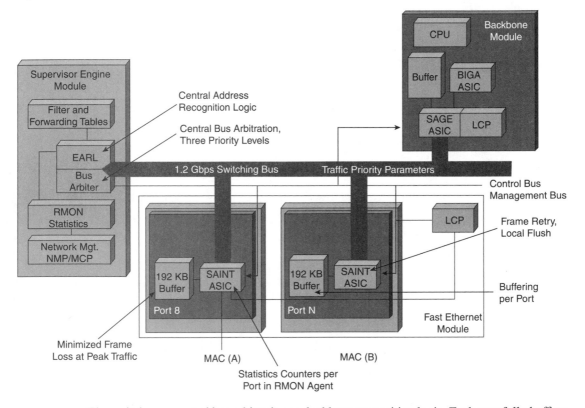

The switch uses central bus arbitration and address recognition logic. Each port fully buffers each frame received from the network before issuing a request to the switch's central bus arbiter to access the switching bus to transmit its stored frames. When given the go-ahead, the port forwards the frame across the backplane. The switch's central EARL determines the destination port(s) and instructs each port to either flush or keep the frame, as appropriate.

Frame copies are not required for high-speed broadcast and multicast frame forwarding. The 1.2 Gbps switching bus resides on the backplane. Each module port has direct access to the bus through the 192-pin Future Bus connector of each backplane slot. In addition, the bus arbiter maintains three priority queues in the system. It enables each port to perform a local flush, and it maintains a frame retry mechanism for outbound port congestion.

The Catalyst 5000 series switch architecture is based on a high-speed switching fabric that uses an output/input queuing model. This architecture gives the most efficient switching fabric for both unicast applications today and multicast applications tomorrow. In addition to the backbone switching bus, the Catalyst maintains the management bus and the Index Bus.

The management bus carries configuration information from the NMP to each module and carries statistical information from each module to the NMP. The Index Bus carries port-select information from the central EARL to the ports. This information determines which ports forward the packet and which flush it from the buffer.

The Catalyst 5000 series architecture shown in Figure 5-5 has three basic components: the bus arbiter and EARL, the Port Interface, and the NMP. The bus arbiter and EARL (shared by all ports) govern access to the data-switching bus and control packet transfer destinations. Each Ethernet Port Interface comprises a custom ASIC (application-specific integrated circuits) and a SAINT that has an integrated 10/100 Mbps Ethernet MAC controller. Other media ports make use of a second custom ASIC and a SAGE that does not have an integrated MAC controller.

Figure 5-5   *Catalyst 5500 3.6 Gbps Architecture*

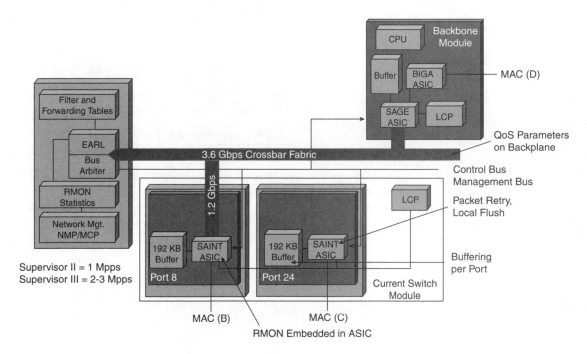

Each frame traversing the switching bus may be destined to a single port or to multiple ports, which provides for high-speed multicast forwarding without the need for frame copies. Frames cross the backplane just one time, thereby optimizing performance. The switching bus operates at 1.2 Gbps and resides on the backplane with interfaces to each line module.

Using the bus arbiter, the bus supports a three-level priority request scheme.

The bus also enables each port to perform a local flush and maintains a packet retry mechanism used during outbound port congestion. The Catalyst 5000 architecture enables media-rate performance for all traffic types (unicast, broadcast, and multicast).

NOTE   Supervisor II can forward up to 1 Mpps (with feature card 1 or 2), and Supervisor III can forward up to 2 to 3 Mpps.

The following are the major differences between the Catalyst 5000 and 5500 switches:

Catalyst 5000	Catalyst 5500
5 slots	13 slots
1 Supervisor engine (slot 1)	2 Supervisor engines (slots 1 and 2)
No redundancy (Supervisor engine)	Redundancy (Supervisor engine in slot 2)
No chassis slot for LS1010 module	LS1010 module shares chassis slot (ASP in slot 13)
No support for ATM switching modules	Slots 9–12 support ATM switching modules
1.2 Gbps support (1 bus)	3.6 Gbps support with Supervisor III (3 buses)

The Catalyst 5000 series switches provide wire-speed, single-stream 10 Mbps or 100 Mbps Ethernet performance for any frame size, from 64-byte to 1500-byte frames (see Figure 5-6). In addition, the Catalyst 5000 supports wire-speed, multiple-stream 10 Mbps Ethernet traffic throughput with no frame loss when 100 pairs of interfaces are configured.

Figure 5-6   *Media Rate Performance*

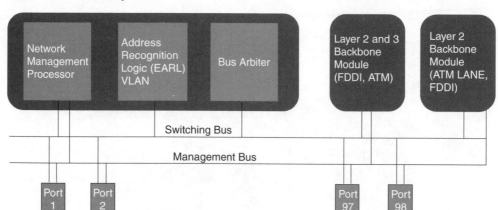

It is theoretically possible to oversubscribe the backplane when the chassis is populated with 100 Mbps ports. Real-world networks, however, seldom provide continuous media-rate data streams simultaneously to all ports. Independent benchmarking has proven that even in oversubscribed conditions, the Catalyst 5000 is capable of maintaining throughput with minimal frame loss.

The Catalyst 5000 series switch architecture enables media-rate performance not only for unicast traffic, but also for broadcast and multicast traffic. This performance becomes important in environments with high volumes of multicast traffic, such as those using multimedia or continuous point-to-multipoint information delivery applications.

Latency between any ports in the Catalyst 5000—as measured by Scott Bradner of Harvard University and based on the LIFO (last in, first out) basis—has been found to be in the order of 10 microseconds plus the length of the frame between Ethernet, Fast Ethernet, and ATM. Ethernet-to-FDDI latency is approximately 100 microseconds plus the length of the frame.

The Supervisor engine uses separate hardware for switching and network management, which means that the EARL ASIC and the NMP can each focus on their specialized tasks. The Catalyst 5000 series switch is designed to provide for maximum network uptime and availability. The completely passive backplane has no active components that can fail. The Catalyst 5000 series switch provides superior buffering, including increased system-level buffering (see Figure 5-7):

Figure 5-7 *Buffering and Congestion Control*

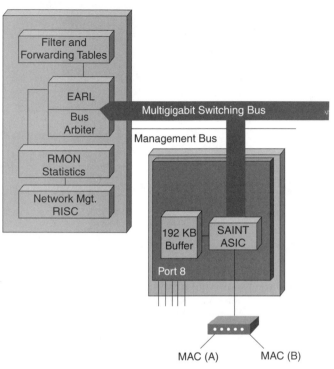

- Embedded per-port buffering: 192 KB
- System-level buffer capacity: 100 MB (fully configured Catalyst 5500)

The active congestion control feature includes the following:

- Per-port priority across the backplane.
- Higher priorities for ports automatically as required.
- Sustained throughput under congestive conditions.
- No head-of-line blocking. If 11 ports of a 12-port module are fully congested, the 12th port will continue to forward at media rates.
- Broadcast suppression (hardware or software).

Switching Components

The NMP uses system software that governs the general control of the hardware, its configuration, and diagnostic routines, including the loading of run-time code to the line modules.

The system executes separate instances of the Spanning-Tree Protocol per virtual LAN by executing a single instance of the protocol software against a set of parameters specified per VLAN.

The SNMP agent also executes in the NMP. It is accessible via either the CLI, Telnet, or an SNMP-based network management station.

The primary function of the master communication processor (MCP) on the Supervisor engine is to communicate information between the NMP and the line module communication processors (LCPs) distributed on Catalyst 5000 line modules. This intermodule communication occurs across the management bus, which is a serial bus operating at 761 kbps.

Other functions of the MCP include the following:

- Test and configuration of local ports
- Control of local ports using local target logic (LTL) and color blocking logic (CBL)
- Local diagnostics of onboard RAM, SAINT ASICs, LTL, and CBL
- Support for download of run-time code

The MCP includes the following hardware:

- 8051 processor with built-in universal asynchronous receiver/transmitter (UART) interface
- 32 KB EPROM
- 64 KB code SRAM
- 32 KB data SRAM
- 32 KB I/O space

As with the MCP, each line module LCP is an 8051 processor that processes information sent to it by the MCP across the management bus. The Serial Communication Protocol (SCP) is an internal communications protocol used for this communication between modules.

The line module boot process consists of the following steps:

- On power-up or reset, the line module LCP executes boot code residing in local ROM.

- The LCP runs diagnostics on all the local module hardware and prepares an information package called *resetack*, which contains module type information and diagnostic results.

- The LCP raises a flag to the MCP when the package is ready. The MCP retrieves the resetack over the serial bus and transfers it to the NMP. The NMP stores this information and begins using it.

The switching bus illustrated in Figure 5-8 is 48 bits wide and operates at 25 MHz. If you multiply 48 bits by 25 MHz, you arrive at a data transfer rate of 1.2 Gbps. A bus access arbitration scheme is implemented on the Supervisor engine. All line modules and the Supervisor engine have access to the switching bus.

Figure 5-8   *Switching Bus Throughput*

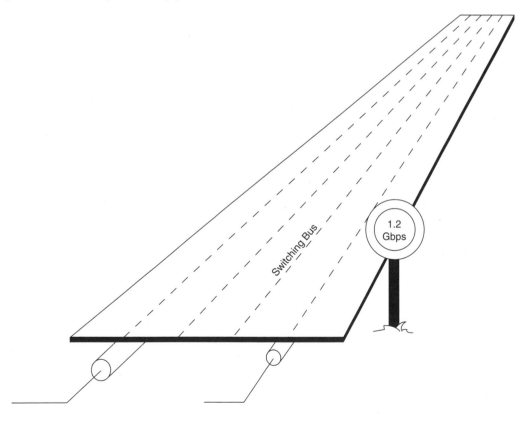

Both the SAINT and the SAGE ASICs are used to perform the encapsulation of the Ethernet frames before they cross the switching bus. Each dedicated Ethernet and Fast Ethernet switch port has its own SAINT ASIC and 192 KB of dedicated frame buffer. ATM and FDDI MAC layers are not IEEE 802.3-compliant, so these interfaces use the SAGE (non-Ethernet) ASIC and 1 MB to 2 MB (ATM has 2 MB) of additional buffering. The only line module that has ports that are not dedicated is the group switching module, which uses four SAINTs. All other Ethernet and Fast Ethernet modules have one SAINT for each port.

The first ASIC that performs the encapsulation of the Ethernet frames before they cross the switching bus is called the SAINT. The SAINT is part of the port interface that also includes a dual-channel direct memory access (DMA) controller for getting packets in and out of the buffer and onto and off of the switching backplane, an Ethernet MAC, a CPU interface, and frame buffers.

The SAINT is a highly integrated, high-performance, custom 10/100 Ethernet MAC (802.3)-compliant ASIC. It has built-in support for 10 Mbps Ethernet, 4B/5B Fast Ethernet, and the MII interface. It permits the use of half- and full-duplex Ethernet and two priority request levels. (A third priority, which is hardware-initiated, is reserved to prevent per-port buffer overflow conditions.) SAINT also performs Inter-Switch Link (ISL) encapsulation and de-encapsulation on frames outbound from ports configured as ISL trunks.

SAINT

The SAINT gate array, shown in Figure 5-9, is a 10/100 Mbps Ethernet MAC with built-in DMA and statistics interface. The DMA provides buffer management of the local packet buffer as well as an interface to the switching bus. The SAINT provides a low-cost, high-performance 10/100 Mbps Ethernet port interface for the switching product.

Figure 5-9   *SAINT ASIC*

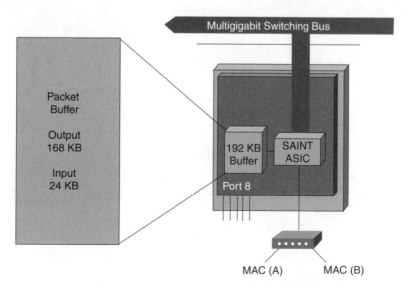

In addition to providing the MAC and DMA functions required for the Ethernet port, the SAINT provides support for VLANs in hardware, support for transferring VLAN information between Catalyst 5000 switches and other ISL-compliant devices, port monitoring features, and external CPU access to diagnostic modes and RMON counters.

Performance is wire speed, full-duplex at both 10 and 100 Mbps. The overall system performance of the Catalyst 5000 switch depends on external logic functions as well as the SAINT.

Packet Buffer

The external packet buffer stores data coming from the network before it is forwarded to the switching bus. Likewise, this packet buffer is used to store data coming from the switching bus before it is forwarded to the network.

The packet buffer is divided into two sections. One is used for packets going to the network and is called the output (transmit) buffer. The other is used for packets going to the switching bus and is called the input (receive) buffer. The dividing line between the two sections is set by the PBDIV register in the SAINT ASIC. The switching bus is very efficient in processing the incoming packets. Therefore, the output buffer is larger in size than the input buffer because the switch more likely will need more output buffer than input buffer.

As a frame is received from the network and stored in the port's frame buffer, ASICs on each port encapsulate Ethernet frames with 12 bytes of information to indicate VLAN ID (color), the port of origin for the frame, and a frame check sequence (FCS) (this is shown in Figure 5-10). This FCS is checked at the port that receives the frame from the switching bus.

Figure 5-10   *Ethernet Frame Encapsulation*

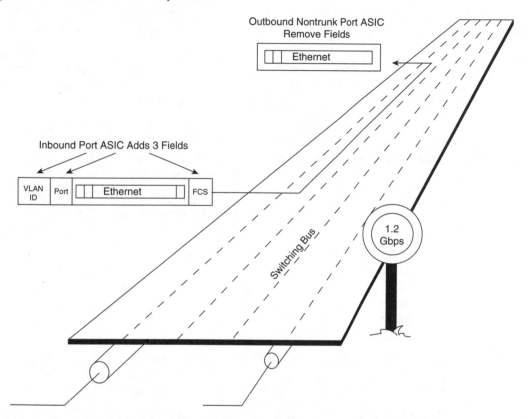

The same ASIC on each port also strips off that encapsulated information and extracts the Ethernet frame before sending it out destination ports.

NOTE   This encapsulation is different from the 30-byte ISL encapsulation discussed in the "Catalyst 5000 Series Switch Software Overview" module.

Ports configured as ISL trunks also strip off the 12-byte encapsulation used across the Catalyst 5000 series switch backplane before forwarding the frame to the network. In addition, these ports add a 30-byte header on the outbound frame. Because this frame encapsulation for VLAN is done in hardware, it requires negligible additional processing.

The SAGE ASIC design is similar to that of the SAINT, but without the SAINT's 10/100 Mbps Ethernet MAC-layer functionality. This design is used for non-Ethernet applications, such as the FDDI module, ATM LANE module, Token Ring, and the NMP on the Supervisor engine.

The SAMBA ASIC, located on both line modules and the Supervisor engines, provides arbitration to the switching bus both among the ports and among the line modules in the chassis. Its dual usage is accomplished by strapping on external device pins.

The SAMBA can be strapped in either master mode or slave mode. SAMBA in master mode is located on the Supervisor engine, and SAMBA in slave mode is on the line module and the Fast Ethernet ports on the Supervisor engine. A master can support up to 13 line cards, and a slave can support up to 48 ports on a single device.

An arbitration process starts with ports on the line cards requesting access to the bus through the slave SAMBA, which forwards the requests to the master SAMBA on the Supervisor engine. The slave SAMBA then waits for permission from the master SAMBA before issuing grants to the ports.

Broadcast/multicast suppression capability is available when SAMBA is in slave mode. This capability enables SAMBA to monitor the number of broadcast packets going through every port on the line card, and removes the entire broadcast packet if the total number of broadcast packet words reaches a threshold within a given time period. The threshold number and the time period are both initialized by the CPU.

Counters are set up to gather statistics in either slave or master mode. A slave SAMBA counts the number of grants received for each level. The same counter is used in master mode to keep track of the total number of grants issued for each level.

The EARL is a custom Catalyst 5000 series switch component that is similar in function to the learning bridges or content addressable memory (CAM) used on other systems. The EARL automatically learns source MAC addresses and associated VLANs and saves them in a RAM address table with VLAN and port information. You can also configure static entries in the EARL table, which stores up to 128,000 addresses.

The EARL then uses the learned entries to perform lookup operations on destination addresses (DAs) to get VLAN and port information to be used to direct the frame. It stores these addresses for 300 seconds (5 minutes) by default, or 60 to 1200 seconds (1 to 20 minutes), if so configured by the user.

Local target logic (LTL), illustrated in Figure 5-11, on each line module helps the EARL find the destination port(s) for each frame. Index values generated by the EARL can select a single port, multiple ports, or all ports in a VLAN. LTL memory is segmented to support unicast, multicast, and flood cases.

Figure 5-11   *Making the Forward or Filter Decision—LTL and CBL*

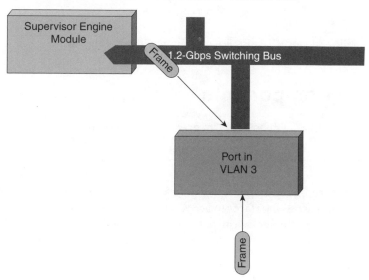

Color blocking logic (CBL) performs the following three functions:

- It blocks traffic coming into a port that is part of a VLAN.

- It blocks traffic going out of a port that is part of a VLAN.

- It assists the spanning tree in blocking ports to prevent loops.

The PHOENIX gate array enables you to continue to use all the Catalyst 5000 switch modules, and it also provides a migration path to switching modules that are capable of 3.6 Gbps switching.

PHOENIX does this by connecting two switching buses and providing intelligent forwarding of packet data from one bus to another. The gate array also has a host processor interface to enable DMA to packet buffer by the CPU, and an interface to the 1 Gbps Ethernet MAC device.

The performance of the device will be full-duplex at 1 Gbps. This gate array will provide support for transferring forwarding information (that is, destination index value, source color information, and trap information) between switching buses.

This design enables the Catalyst 5500 switch to increase the bandwidth support to 3.6 Gbps by interconnecting three 1.2 Gbps switching buses.

The PHOENIX ASIC supports the following features:

- 3.6-Gbps crossbar fabric

- Enhanced MIPS 4700 processor (a tenfold increase in performance over Supervisor I)

- Layer 3 switching support with EARL II
- Cisco IOS software support
- Modular uplink support (Fast Ethernet or future Gigabit Ethernet)

Operation of Bus Components

CLSC Objectives Covered in This Section

34	Trace a frame's progress through a Catalyst 5000 series switch.

The Catalyst 5000 bus arbitration shown in Figure 5-12 uses a hierarchical two-tier design to distribute permission to all interfaces to access and send data across the switching bus. This design is useful for such time-sensitive traffic as voice or video, and for ensuring that more important nodes, such as servers, are given higher priority to the switching bus.

Figure 5-12 *Two-Tier Arbitration Scheme*

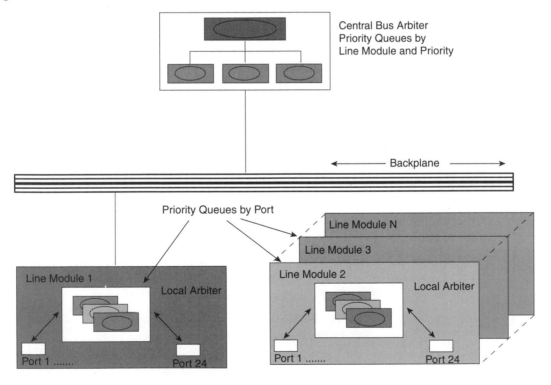

First Tier

The first tier resides on each switching module, where all interfaces send their individual requests to their module's local bus arbiter. Each local bus arbiter maintains separate queues to handle each priority level. Normal and high priority levels are user-configurable, but the critical priority level can be set only by hardware to prevent buffer overflow. The buffer overflow would likely occur only during peak traffic conditions, as a port buffer starts to get full.

The local bus arbiter issues independent requests at the normal, high, and critical priority levels to the central bus arbiter.

Second Tier

The central bus arbiter, which resides on the Supervisor engine, receives the requests from all the modules in the system and uses a round-robin scheme within each priority level to determine access to the switching bus. When a local arbiter sends a request at the critical level, the central bus arbiter services only critical priority requests. If more than one port has traffic with critical priority, the ports take turns sending one frame at a time. When all critical requests have been granted, the central bus arbiter then services high-priority frames for five cycles for every one cycle of normal priority frames. During each cycle, each local arbiter will post one frame from each port with traffic at the critical, high, or normal priority level, whichever is currently being serviced. By using this scheme, the Catalyst 5000 reduces average latency on selected ports while minimizing potential packet loss during peak bursts.

To understand how the major components that comprise the architecture of the Catalyst 5000 series of switches work, we will follow the path of a frame through the switch. When an Ethernet frame arrives at a port, illustrated in Figure 5-13, the port's DMA controller stores it in its receive buffer. The port fully receives, buffers, and checks the frame's FCS, adds the 12-byte frame header containing the port number and VLAN number, and increments the Ethernet MIB and RMON counters before storing the frame in the frame buffer and requesting access to the switching bus to forward the frame.

Figure 5-13   *Frame Flow, Phase 1*

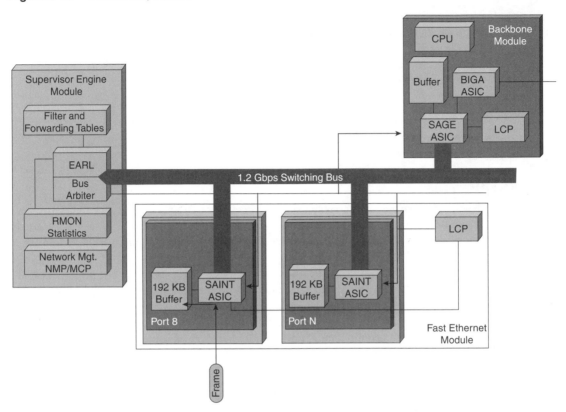

When the entire frame is received and stored in the frame buffer, the SAINT ASIC posts a request to the bus arbiter to transmit the frame across the high-speed switching bus illustrated in Figure 5-14. The Supervisor engine performs the necessary bus arbitration and grants bus access to the line module as soon as it becomes available using a round-robin method. The local arbiter on the line module then uses a round-robin method to grant each port permission to transmit one frame at the priority level being serviced.

Figure 5-14   *Frame Flow, Phase 2*

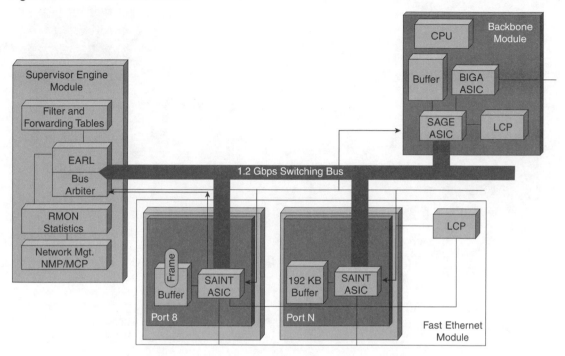

The bus arbiter issues a grant to the local arbiter, which, at the appropriate time, signals the SAINT ASIC to initiate the data transfer illustrated in Figure 5-15. The frame that is stored in the buffer is then transmitted across the high-speed switching backplane by the DMA controller.

Figure 5-15 *Frame Flow, Phase 3*

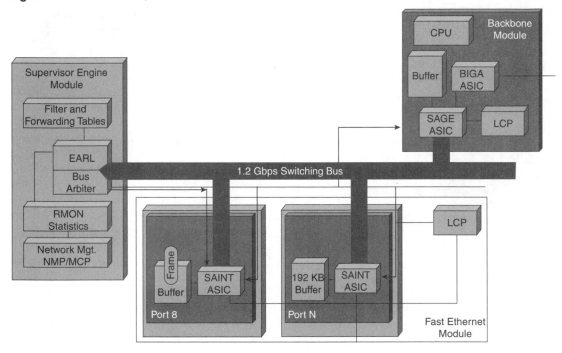

As the frame is transmitted across the switching backplane, all ports receive the frame and store it in their frame input buffers, as illustrated in Figure 5-16. As with all bus architectures, there is no need for multiple copies of broadcast and multicast frames because all ports on the bus receive the frame.

Figure 5-16   *Frame Flow, Phase 4*

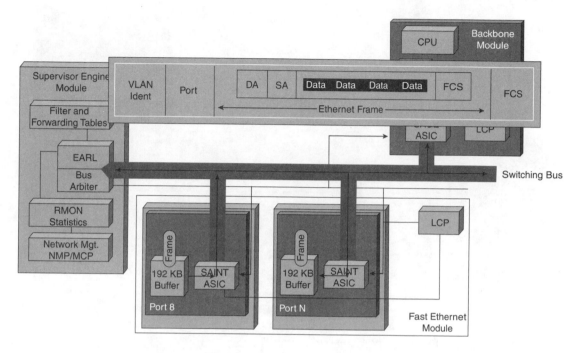

The last step in the frame flow process, shown in Figure 5-17, varies depending on the following factors:

Figure 5-17 *Frame Flow, Phase 5*

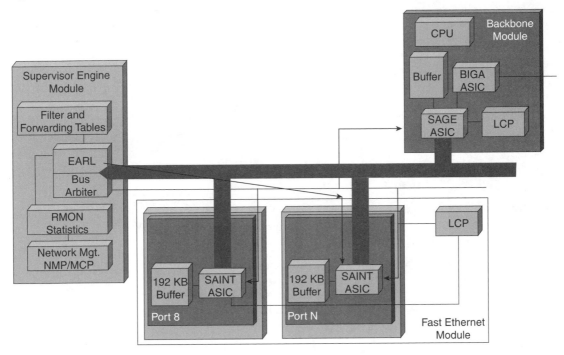

Unicast and Multicast

When the EARL, in conjunction with LTL and CBL, identifies a specific port or set of ports as the destination, it instructs the SAINT ASICs on the destination ports via the control bus to continue to receive the frame and subsequently transmit it out its port. The SAINT ASICs on the other ports will flush their buffers.

Broadcasts and Unknown Destination Addresses

If the destination address is unknown to the EARL or is a broadcast or multicast address, then the frames are forwarded to all ports on the same VLAN as the source address.

Local Port

If the EARL determines that the frame does not require switching into the system, it issues a flush to terminate frame transfer on the bus from the source interface and causes all ports to flush their buffers. However, only a few bits of the packet are stored in each buffer before the EARL orders the flush. The EARL then flushes the buffer of only that packet.

Buffers Full

If the destination interface has no buffer to accommodate a frame, it issues a retry to the source. The source terminates the frame transfer and retries the frame at a later time.

Token Ring Module Architecture

The Encoded Address Recognition Logic Plus (EARL+) is based on the original EARL used for Ethernet switching. The "Plus" part of EARL is the added logic required to perform Token Ring switching in the Catalyst 5000. These EARL changes are required by ISL for Token Ring and for the Token Ring card for the Catalyst 5000.

As data traverses the switching bus of the Catalyst 5000 backplane, the EARL+ monitors the type field of the switching bus header. If the packet is not of type B0001, then EARL performs its current Ethernet switching function. If the packet type is B0001, then the EARL+ latches data from an additional switching bus header word (48 bits) added for Token Ring.

The SAGE and SAINT ASICs take the 48-bit MAC address along with the 10 bits of VLAN information and encode them into 15 bits. The 15 bits are presented to the EARL and used to access a lookup table that contains the actual MAC address and its associated port index and VLAN information. The EARL+ is not capable of using the SAGE/SAINT hash because the effective destination or source address may not be the MAC address of the frame.

Although Token Ring addresses are noncanonical and Ethernet addresses are canonical, a match conflict will never occur within the EARL+ lookup tables because a Token Ring address will never have the same VLAN ID as an Ethernet address. The VLAN ID acts as an additional qualifier for the EARL+ lookup/compare.

Q&A

As mentioned in Chapter 1, "The Cisco LAN Switch Configuration (CLSC) Exam Overview," the questions and scenarios are more difficult than what you should experience on the actual exam. The questions do not attempt to cover more breadth or depth than the exam; however, the questions are designed to make sure you know the answers. Rather than allowing you to derive the answer from clues hidden inside the question itself, the questions will challenge your understanding and recall of the subject. Questions from the "Do I Know This Already?" quiz from the beginning of the chapter are repeated here to ensure that you have mastered the chapter's topic areas. Hopefully, these questions will help limit the number of exam questions on which you narrow your choices to two options and then guess!

1 The Catalyst 5000 series architecture has three basic components: the _____ and _____, the _____ , and the _____.

2 Supervisor II can forward up to _____ Mpps (with feature card 1 or 2), and the Supervisor III can forward up to _____ to _____ Mpps.

3 It is theoretically possible to oversubscribe the backplane when the chassis is populated with 100 Mbps ports.

   a. True

   b. False

4 This intermodule communication occurs across the management bus, which is a serial bus operating at _____ kbps.

5 The EARL automatically learns source MAC addresses and associated _____ and saves them in a RAM address table with VLAN and port information.

6 The EARL stores learned addresses for 300 seconds (5 minutes) by default, or _____ to _____ seconds if so configured by the user.

   a. 20—100

   b. 60—300

   c. 60—600

   d. 60—1200

7 When an Ethernet frame arrives at a port on the Fast Ethernet module, the port's _____ controller stores it in its receive buffer.

   a. EARL

   b. DMA

   c. SAINT

   d. CAL

8 When the entire frame is received and stored in the frame buffer, the SAINT ASIC posts a request to the _____ to transmit the frame across the high-speed switching bus.

9 On power-up or reset, the line module LCP executes boot code residing in _____.

10 A bus access arbitration scheme is implemented on the _____.

Source Material

Some content in this chapter is based on material in the *CLSC Course Book*.

The objectives of the Cisco LAN Switch Configuration (CLSC) exam are taken from the Cisco web site, at the Cisco career certification and training area. The following table shows the exam objectives covered in this chapter:

Objective	Description
1	Describe the major features of the Catalyst switches.
29	Describe Catalyst 5000 series product evolution.
30	Describe Catalyst 5000 product features.
31	Describe Catalyst 5002 product features.
32	Describe Catalyst 5500 product features.
35	Describe the hardware features, functions, and benefits of Catalyst 5000 series switches.
36	Describe the hardware features and functions of the Supervisor Engine.
37	Describe the hardware features and functions of the modules in the Catalyst 5000 series switches.

CHAPTER 6

Catalyst 5000 Series Switch Hardware

With integrated frame and cell switching, full support for Cisco IOS-based routing, and full support for Fast EtherChannel, Gigabit EtherChannel, and ATM, the Catalyst 5000 Family is well positioned to evolve as campus bandwidth needs grow. Furthermore, the Catalyst 5000 Family supports data communication between any type of media. The media-independent architecture supports all legacy LAN and Asynchronous Transfer Mode (ATM) switching technologies through a wide range of Ethernet, Fast Ethernet, Gigabit Ethernet, Fiber Distributed Data Interface (FDDI), Token Ring, and ATM switch modules.

How to Best Use This Chapter

By taking the following steps, you can make better use of your study time:

- Keep your notes and the answers for all your work with this book in one place, for easy reference.

- Take the quiz, and write down your answers. Studies show that retention is significantly increased through writing down facts and concepts, even if you never look at the information again.

- Use the diagram in Figure 6-1 to guide you to the next step.

Figure 6-1   *How to Best Use This Chapter in Preparation for the CLSC Exam*

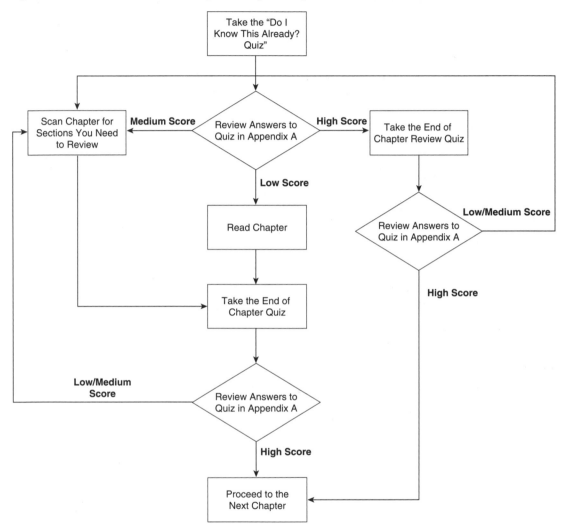

Do I Know This Already? Quiz

You can find the answers to this quiz in Appendix A, "Answers to 'Do I Know This Already?' Quizzes and Q & A Sections." Review the answers, grade your quiz, and choose an appropriate next step in this chapter based on the suggestions diagramed in Figure 6-1.

1 Which one of the following is an option currently available on the Supervisor Engine?

   a. Two 100BaseTX ports with SC connectors

   b. Two SMF ports with RJ-45 connectors

   c. Two multimode fiber ports with RJ-45 connectors

   d. Two multimode fiber ports with SC connectors

2 The Catalyst 5000 series switch has environmental monitoring and reporting functions.

   a. True

   b. False

3 Online insertion and removal are supported on the Catalyst 5000 series switch for:

   a. The fan trays only

   b. The fan trays and redundant power supplies only

   c. The fan trays and all switching modules only

   d. The fan trays, redundant power supplies, and all switching modules

4 On the Catalyst 5000 switch, the Supervisor Engine:

   a. Must be installed in slot 1.

   b. May be installed in either slot 1 or slot 2.

   c. May be installed in slots 1, 2, or 3.

   d. May be installed in any slot.

5 On the Catalyst 5500 switch, the Supervisor Engine:

   a. Must be installed in slot 1.

   b. May be installed in either slot 1 or slot 2.

   c. May be installed in slots 1, 2, or 3.

   d. May be installed in any slot.

6 The Catalyst 5000 series switch 10/100 Mbps Ethernet module:

   a. Controls data access to the switching backplane.

   b. Uses RJ-45 connectors to attach to Category 5 cable.

   c. Determines the destination of frames.

   d. Provides system processing and memory.

7 The Catalyst 5000 series switch Supervisor Engine Status LED is red:

   a. During system boot.

   b. If the module is disabled.

   c. If the redundant power supply is installed but not turned on.

   d. All of the above.

8 The Catalyst 5000 series switch Supervisor Engine allows:

   a. Two 100 Mbps Ethernet connections

   b. Four 100 Mbps Ethernet connections

   c. Two 10/100 Mbps Ethernet connections

   d. Four 10/100 Mbps Ethernet connections

9 Maximum station-to-station cabling distances for the Catalyst 5000 series Ethernet switching modules are:

   a. 100 m for 100BaseTX half-duplex, and 200 m for 100BaseTX full-duplex

   b. 400 m for 10BaseFL half-duplex, and 200 m for 10BaseFL full-duplex

   c. 400 m for MMF 100BaseFX half-duplex, and 2 km for MMF 100BaseFX full-duplex

   d. 2000 m for SMF 100BaseFX half-duplex, and 2000 m for SMF 100BaseFX full-duplex

10 The Catalyst 5002 supports:

   a. One Supervisor Engine and one switching module

   b. Two Supervisor Engines and one switching module

   c. One LS1010 module and one ATM LAN Emulation module

   d. One Supervisor engine and one LS1010 module

Using the answer key in Appendix A, grade your answers.

- **5 or less correct**—Read this chapter.
- **6, 7, or 8 correct**—Review this chapter, looking at the charts and diagrams that summarize most of the concepts and facts in this chapter.

- **9 or more correct**—If you want more review on these topics, skip to the Q&A section at the end of this chapter. If you do not want more review on these topics, skip this chapter.

Foundation Topics

Catalyst 5000 Family Features

CLSC Objectives Covered in This Section	
1	Describe the major features of the Catalyst switches.
29	Describe Catalyst 5000 series product evolution.
30	Describe Catalyst 5000 product features.
31	Describe Catalyst 5002 product features.
32	Describe Catalyst 5500 product features.

Cisco's Catalyst 5000 Family features five modular chassis: one 2-slot model, two 5-slot models (the 5000 and the 5505), one 9-slot model, and one 13-slot model. All five chassis share the same set of interface modules and software features, providing scalability while also maintaining interoperability and investment protection across all chassis.

The Cisco Catalyst 5000 Family consists of the following multilayer switching systems:

- Catalyst 5000

  The Catalyst 5000 platform is a five-slot chassis that will continue to serve as a platform supporting both wiring closet and data center applications. The five module slots support the required Supervisor Engine and four additional interface modules. The Catalyst 5000 supports all Supervisor Engines and will support all new line cards as part of a complete solution.

  High-speed connectivity between switches, switches and routers, and switches and servers is provided using standard 100/1000 Ethernet, FDDI, or ATM interfaces. Fast EtherChannel is supported on Supervisor Engine II ports and on Fast EtherChannel-capable line cards on which Sup II and Sup III users can group up to four Fast Ethernet ports; this provides up to 800 Mbps (full-duplex) of load-sharing, redundant, point-to-point connections among Catalyst 5500, 5509, 5505, 5002, and 5000 switches. For higher bandwidth applications, users can deploy Gigabit EtherChannel, which supports up to 8 Gbps (full-duplex) of interswitch bandwidth. Gigabit EtherChannel is also supported across the entire Catalyst 5500/5000 series. Users can choose dual AC or DC power supplies for fault tolerance.

- Catalyst 5002

  The Catalyst 5002 is a two-slot chassis where one slot is used by the Supervisor Engine (supporting two built-in Fast Ethernet ports), and the second slot is used for any Catalyst 5000 family module for Ethernet, Fast Ethernet, Token Ring, FDDI, or ATM. The 5002 also supports all Supervisor Engines and the Route Switch module.

  The chassis has two built-in, redundant power supplies and is designed to address the needs of smaller environments requiring Catalyst 5000 features and performance.

- Catalyst 5500

  The Catalyst 5500, the 13-slot member of the Catalyst 5000 family, serves as the high-end modular switching platform. With a Gigabit Ethernet-ready architecture that scales to more than 50 Gbps and throughput of tens of millions of packets or cells per second (pps), the Catalyst 5500 provides the scalability, flexibility, and redundancy required for building large, switched intranets; it can be used in both wiring closet and backbone applications.

  At the same time, the Catalyst 5500 protects your investment in current Cisco products by seamlessly integrating existing Catalyst 5000 and Catalyst 8510 interface modules and features, as well as LightStream 1010 interface modules and features into the 5500 chassis.

  With its support for hot-swappable modules, power supplies, and fans, the Catalyst 5500 delivers high availability for production networks.

- Catalyst 5505

  The Catalyst 5505 is a high-performance, five-slot chassis for the evolving Catalyst 5500 series. The Catalyst 5505 combines the size of the original Catalyst 5000 with the performance boost and added features of the Catalyst 5500. The Catalyst 5505 is ideal for high-performance wiring closet and data applications.

  The Catalyst 5505 protects customers' Catalyst 5500 series investments by seamlessly integrating existing Catalyst 5000 interface modules and features into a high-performance chassis. Customers who desire a performance boost for existing Catalyst 5000 chassis can redeploy all Catalyst 5500 series line cards in the five-slot Catalyst 5505. Supervisor Engines II or III can also be used in a Catalyst 5505. The Catalyst 5505 can be configured for backbone applications with feature-rich, scalable 100/1000 Ethernet, ATM, and FDDI, as well as optional redundant Supervisor Engines and power supplies. In the wiring closet, switched 10/100 Ethernet, Token Ring, and ATM modules provide high-performance connectivity.

- Catalyst 5509

  The Catalyst 5509 is the nine-slot member of the Catalyst 5500 Series that is ideally suited for both wiring closet and backbone applications. As a low-cost wiring closet solution, the Catalyst 5509 supports high-density, dedicated Token Ring or 10/100/1000 Ethernet switching. The Catalyst 5509 can support high-density switching with only a 15 amp circuit requirement, allowing for easy installation in most wiring closet environments. The Catalyst 5509 also supports all of Cisco's advanced features for the wiring closet, such as automatic protocol broadcast filtering to conserve valuable bandwidth, intelligent multicast forwarding to handle multimedia traffic, and load balancing over redundant links.

  For Gigabit Ethernet backbone applications, the Catalyst 5509 supports up to 38 ports of Gigabit Ethernet, the highest port density available today for the Catalyst 5500 series. This capability can be combined with Cisco's Gigabit EtherChannel technology. Gigabit EtherChannel technology enables multiple Gigabit Ethernet links to be treated as one logical link, for up to 8 Gbps (full-duplex) of device-to-device throughput. Used in such a configuration, the Catalyst 5509 creates an industry-leading Gigabit Ethernet backbone solution to meet the requirements of today's demanding and fast-growing enterprise intranets.

  With its support for hot-swappable modules, power supplies, and fans, the Catalyst 5509 chassis delivers high availability for production networks. Dual redundant switching engines, power supplies, and a passive backplane design ensure full system redundancy for mission-critical environments. The Catalyst 5509 chassis fits into a standard 19-inch rack, and all system components are accessible from the same side of the chassis. Only one power supply is required to run a fully configured system.

The Supervisor Engine

CLSC Objectives Covered in This Section

36	Describe the hardware features and functions of the Supervisor Engine.

Supervisor I is the original Supervisor Engine used in the Catalyst 5000 series switches (except the Catalyst 5500). You cannot use it in the Catalyst 5500 chassis because it will not provide the full functionality of the Supervisor II.

The Supervisor II module is used in the Catalyst 5500 switch and supports the following features:

- Two 100 MB links

- Fast EtherChannel

- Same switching performance as the Supervisor

- Ships with all the Catalyst 5000 series switches

- Only 1.2 Gbps bandwidth on the 3.6 Gbps backplane

- Includes a daughter card (feature card)

The Supervisor III module uses an enhanced NMP RISC processor and supports the following features:

- 10 times NMP performance improvement (as compared to Supervisor)

- All Catalyst 5000 series switch chassis except the Catalyst 2900 switch

- High-end backbone/wiring closet

- Layer 3 switching

- Same form factor feature card as Supervisor II

- 3.6 Gbps switch fabric

- Fast EtherChannel feature to provide a 400 Mbps (800 Mbps in full-duplex mode) link between two Catalyst 5000 series switches

- Gigabit Fast EtherChannel

Supervisor Engine Overview

The Supervisor Engine (see Figure 6-2) is the main system processor in the switch. It contains the Layer 2 switching engine, the network management processor for the system software, and the system memory components. The Supervisor Engine controls data access to the switching backplane, determines the destination of packets, and provides additional system processing and memory for supporting standard MIBs (Ethernet MIB, FDDI MIB, Bridge MIB, MIB II, and Catalyst MIB extensions).

Figure 6-2   *Supervisor Engine*

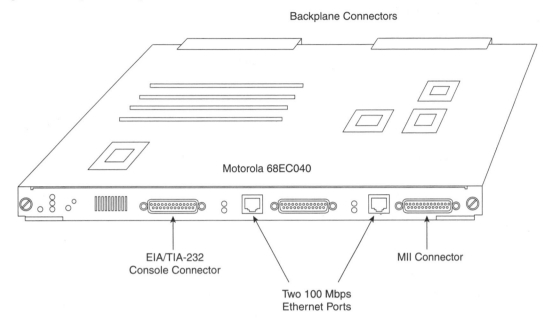

The Supervisor Engine module must be installed in the top slot (slot 1). The Supervisor Engine has the following features:

- A 1.2 Gbps switching bus that provides the data path and that is capable of handling more than 1 million packets per second (pps).

- Bridge address table for up to 16,000 active MAC addresses and associated VLANs dynamically allocated between active ports.

- 25 MHz Motorola MC68EC040 NMP that can process approximately 25 million to 30 million instructions per second (MIPS).

- MAC-layer switching engine that controls all switching.

- Two integrated Fast Ethernet interfaces that can support redundancy using the spanning-tree algorithm, or load sharing when used with VLANs and the Spanning-Tree Protocol.

- One version of the Supervisor Engine that has two RJ-45 connectors and media-independent interface (MII) connectors. The other Supervisor Engine has two fiber connectors.

- Hardware support for 1000 VLANs, with a current practical limitation of 255. (Implementations of more than 100 VLANs are very rare.)

- Memory components, including up to 16 MB of DRAM components that store the default (run-time) system software, 8 MB of Flash memory for downloading the system software, and 256 KB NVRAM for storing the configuration file.

- Air-temperature sensors for environmental monitoring.

- Capability of monitoring interface and environmental status.

- SNMP management capability and the console/Telnet interface.

Supervisor Engine Module LEDs

The LEDs on the Supervisor Engine, shown in Figure 6-3, indicate the system status. The system includes the fan assembly, power supply or supplies, and the Supervisor Engine. The PS1 and PS2 LEDs on the Supervisor Engine go on when the power supply is receiving AC source power and providing DC power to the internal system components. The power supply monitors its own temperature and internal voltages.

Figure 6-3   *Supervisor Engine Module LEDs*

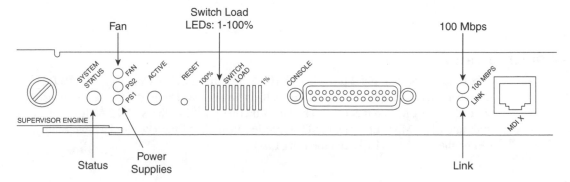

NOTE	The Supervisor Engine status light is red if the redundant power supply is installed but not turned on.

Supervisor Engine with 100BaseTX RJ-45 Connectors

The Supervisor Engine Fast Ethernet operates in full- or half-duplex mode. The ports use RJ-45 connectors with 100BaseTX Category 5 UTP cabling. The Fast Ethernet ports of the Supervisor Engine provide only 100 Mbps operation.

Reset Switch

Access to the reset switch located behind the faceplate of the Supervisor Engine is through a small hole to the right of the Supervisor module LEDs.

Console Port

The console port is the local (out-of-band) console terminal connection (DCE) to the switch, a DB-25 female connector. The console port, which is discussed further in the "Managing the Catalyst 5000 Series Switch" module, enables you to use the command-line interface to perform the following functions:

- Configure the switch.

- Monitor network statistics and errors.

- Configure SNMP agent parameters.

- Download software updates to the switch.

- Distribute software images in Flash memory to other devices remotely using network ports.

Fast Ethernet Ports

Fast Ethernet ports 1 and 2 provide two 100 Mbps (100BaseTX Category 5 UTP) Fast Ethernet interfaces operating in full- or half-duplex mode. The Fast Ethernet ports use either RJ-45 or MII connections. The Fast Ethernet ports use the SAINT ASIC with an integrated 100 Mbps Ethernet MAC controller. Each Fast Ethernet port has two Status LEDs: the 100 Mbps LED and the Link LED.

Dual MMF Supervisor Engine

The multimode fiber-optic (MMF) (WS-X5006) Supervisor Engines shown in Figure 6-4 provide two half- and full-duplex Fast Ethernet multimode fiber interfaces with SC connectors for connection distances up to 400 meters for half-duplex and up to 2 kilometers for full-duplex. This Supervisor Engine requires NMP software version 2.1 or later.

Figure 6-4   *Dual MMF Supervisor Engine*

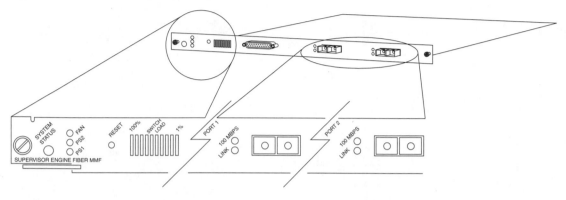

Dual SMF Supervisor Engine

The single-mode fiber-optic (SMF) (WS-X5005) Supervisor Engines shown in Figure 6-5 provide two half- and full-duplex Fast Ethernet single-mode fiber interfaces with SC connectors for connection distances up to 10 km. This Supervisor Engine requires NMP software version 2.1 or later.

Figure 6-5   *Dual SMF Supervisor Engine*

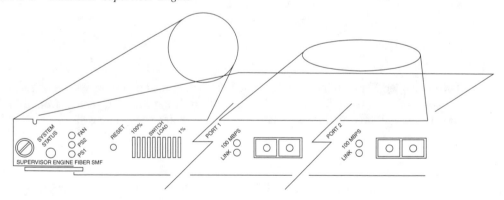

MMF and SMF SC Connectors

Figure 6-6 provides a close look at the SC connectors used on both fiber versions of the Supervisor Engine on the 100BaseFX line modules and on the ATM LANE module.

Figure 6-6   *MMF and SMF SC Connectors*

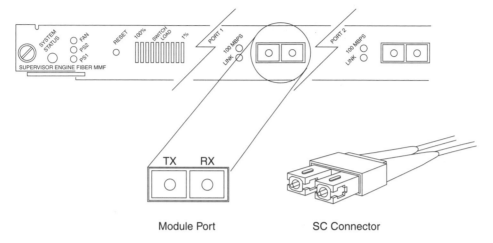

Supervisor Engine Memory

The Supervisor Engine onboard memory consists of dynamic random-access memory (DRAM) for the default system software, Flash memory for downloading the system software, and NVRAM for the configuration file.

Flash Memory

The embedded Flash memory enables you to remotely load and store system software images. You can download a new software image over the network, such as from a TFTP server, and add the new image to Flash memory or replace an existing file.

EPROM

An erasable programmable read-only memory (EPROM) component on the Supervisor Engine stores module-specific information such as the module serial number, part number, controller type, hardware revision, and other details unique to each module. In addition to this standard information, the Supervisor Engine EPROM also contains an address allocator, which is a bank of 1024 hardware or MAC-level addresses, one for each possible VLAN in the system. On the Catalyst 5500 switch, the EPROM is located on the backplane. On the Catalyst 5000 and 5002 switches, it is located on the Supervisor Engine.

Additional Memory

The Supervisor Engine also uses up to 16 MB of DRAM to store the run-time software and 256 KB of NVRAM to store configuration information.

Redundant Supervisor Module (Catalyst 5500 Only)

Redundancy is accomplished by using two Supervisor II NMPs residing on the Catalyst 5500 backplane simultaneously and by providing a separate redundant clock generation module.

On startup (on boot), initial-level diagnostics are performed on both active and standby Supervisor Engines. Under normal operation, if two Supervisor Engines are installed in the switch, the Supervisor module in slot 1 is in active (primary) mode and the Supervisor Engine in slot 2 is on standby status.

The active Supervisor Engine updates the standby Supervisor Engine software and NVRAM configuration. In the current release, only warm standby is supported, meaning that the system resets during switchover.

Slot 2 supports either a second Supervisor Engine or a line module. However, if only one Supervisor Engine is installed in the switch, slot 1 must contain the Supervisor Engine. The Ethernet ports on the standby Supervisor Engine are inactive, and the standby console port is also inactive.

The dynamic NVRAM updates the configuration of the standby Supervisor module as a result of a set command issued to the active Supervisor Engine. The Flash code synchronization goes from the active Supervisor Engine to the standby Supervisor Engine.

A hardware failure on the active Supervisor Engine forces the failover to the standby Supervisor Engine. If the ports on the standby Supervisor module are connected to a transceiver that has two 100BaseT incoming connections, the standby link becomes active when the active link goes down. Similarly, if the console ports on each Supervisor Engine are connected to a communications server, the standby console connection becomes active when the active link goes down. Active and standby status are indicated by front panel LEDs.

Supervisor Engine Overview

The Supervisor Engine is the main system processor. An overview of the Supervisor Engine in shown in Figure 6-7. It contains the Layer 2 switching engine and NMP for the system software and most of the system components. Each Supervisor Engine stores all interface configurations in NVRAM.

Figure 6-7 *Supervisor Engine Overview*

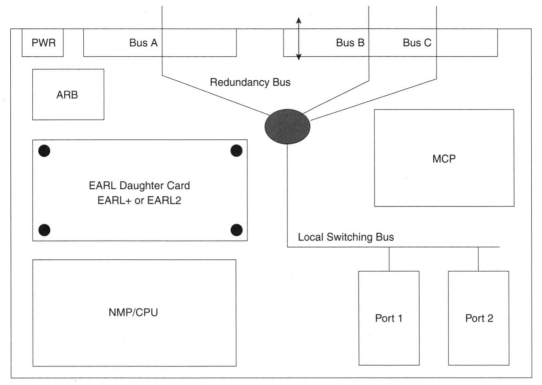

Three module versions are available on the Catalyst 5000 series Supervisor Engine:

- Dual Fast Ethernet RJ-45 and media-independent interface (MII) connector interfaces
- Dual Fast Ethernet MMF connector interfaces
- Dual Fast Ethernet SMF SC interfaces

The following hardware components are part of the Supervisor Engine operation:

- NMP/CPU ties into the local switching bus
- ARB— Arbiter
- Redundancy bus—A, B, and C (Supervisor II and III only)
- EARL daughter card—EARL+, EARL2 (Supervisor II and III only)
- MCP—Management control processor

- NMP/CPU—Network management processor

- Port-1 and Port-2—100 Mbps Fast Ethernet or fiber ports

- Local switching bus—Local ports to the bus

Ethernet and Fast Ethernet Modules

CLSC Objectives Covered in This Section

37	Describe the hardware features and functions of the modules in the Catalyst 5000 series switches.

All the Ethernet and Fast Ethernet switching modules share the following features:

- Wire-speed packet transfer at the port

- Media-rate performance across the 1.2 Gbps backplane

- Half- or full-duplex operation on dedicated switch ports

- 192 KB buffers on each interface to accommodate bursty traffic

- Connectivity from switched Ethernet and Fast Ethernet to Fast Ethernet, FDDI, and ATM backbones

- Online insertion and removal

- Three levels of prioritization per port

The Ethernet and Fast Ethernet modules support dedicated ASICs on each port with embedded RMON and standard Ethernet MIBs. As ports are added to the switch, each additional ASIC becomes a new collection engine for RMON information for that segment.

Ethernet and Fast Ethernet modules are as follows:

- Ethernet Switching Module—10BaseT 24 port, Telco 50 (WS-X5010)

- Ethernet Switching Module—10BaseT 24 port, RJ-45 (WS-X5013)

- Ethernet Switching Module—10BaseFL 12 port (WS-X5011)

- 10/100 Mbps Fast Ethernet Switching Module—10/100BaseTX 12 port (WS-X5213A)

- Fast Ethernet Switching Module—100BaseFX 12 port Multimode Fiber Module (WS-X5111)

- Fast Ethernet Switching Single-Mode/Multimode Fiber Module—100BaseFX 12 port (WS-X5114)

- Group Switching Fast Ethernet Module—100BaseTX 24 port (WS-X5223)

- Group Switching Ethernet Module—10BaseT 48 port (WS-X5020)

Ethernet Switching Module (10BaseT 24 Port, Telco)

The 24-port 10BaseT Ethernet Switching Module shown in Figure 6-8 uses two telco connectors to attach to Category 3, 4, or 5 UTP cable. Telco connectors now support Category 3 or Category 5 cable. You can connect a telco connector to a patch panel. From the patch panel, you can connect to Category 3 or Category 5 cable. Each port can be individually assigned to a different virtual LAN.

Figure 6-8 *Ethernet Switching Module (10BaseT 24 Port, Telco)*

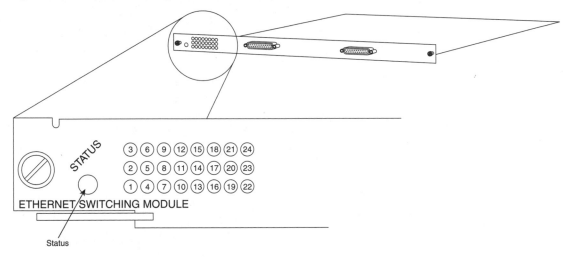

The module indicators for this and all the Ethernet and Fast Ethernet switching modules include the following:

- Module status

  — Green (operational)

  — Red (faulty)

  — Orange (minor fault or manually disabled)

- Link

  — Green (good)

— Orange (disabled by software)

— Orange flashing (link is bad and has been disabled)

— Off (not connected)

Ethernet Switching Module (10BaseT 24 Port, RJ-45)

The 24-port 10BaseT Ethernet Switching Module shown in Figure 6-9 uses Category 3 cable to connect Ethernet devices to the 24 RJ-45 connectors. The ports support full- or half-duplex operation. The Ethernet Switching Module (10BaseT 24 Port, RJ-45) requires NMP software Release 2.2(1) or later.

Figure 6-9   *Ethernet Switching Module (10BaseT 24 Port, RJ-45)*

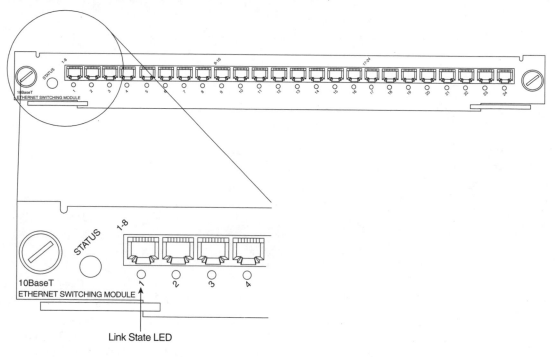

Ethernet Switching Module (10BaseFL 12 Port)

The 12-port switched 10BaseFL Ethernet Switching Module shown in Figure 6-10 uses ST connectors to attach to multimode fiber. The Ethernet Switching Module (10BaseFL 12 Port) requires NMP software Release 1.2 or later. Each port can be assigned to a different virtual LAN.

Figure 6-10   *Ethernet Switching Module (10BaseFL 12 Port)*

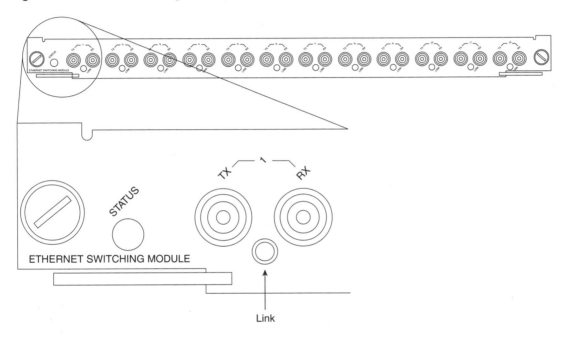

10/100 Mbps Fast Ethernet Switching Module (10/100BaseTX 12 Port)

The 12-port 10/100BaseTX Fast Ethernet Switching Module shown in Figure 6-11 uses RJ-45 connectors to attach to Category 5 UTP cable. It supports the IEEE 802.3u auto-negotiation process that allows the switch to negotiate speed (10 or 100 Mbps) and duplex mode (half- or full-duplex) with an attached device. If the attached device does not negotiate, the switching module configures the port for half-duplex and 10 Mbps by default.

The 10/100 Mbps Fast Ethernet Switching Module (10/100BaseTX 12 Port) requires NMP software Release 2.1(7) or later. Each port can be configured as follows:

Figure 6-11   *10/100 Mbps Fast Ethernet Switching Module (10/100BaseTX 12 Port)*

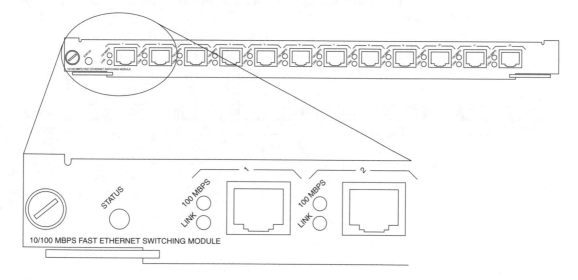

- To a different virtual LAN
- As a trunk port running dynamic ISL

The indicators for this module include the usual for Ethernet and Fast Ethernet switching modules and add the following:

- 100 Mbps

  — Green (indicates that the port is operating at 100 Mbps)

  — Off (indicates that the port is operating at 10 Mbps)

NOTE   This new module (WS-X5213A) replaces the earlier version of this module (WS-X5213).

Fast Ethernet Switching (Module 100BaseFX 12 Port)

The 12-port 100BaseFX Fast Ethernet Switching Module shown in Figure 6-12 uses SC connectors to attach to 62.5/125-micron multimode fiber. The Fast Ethernet Switching Module (100BaseFX 12 Port) requires NMP software Release 1.4 or later. Each port can be configured as follows:

Figure 6-12 *Fast Ethernet Switching (Module 100BaseFX 12 Port)*

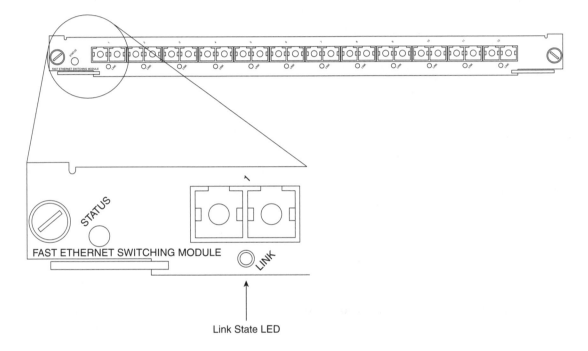

Link State LED

- To a different virtual LAN
- As a trunk port running dynamic ISL

Fast Ethernet Switching SMG/MMF Module (100BaseFX 12 Port)

The 12-port Fast Ethernet Switching Module (SMF/MMF) shown in Figure 6-13 provides six single-mode and six multimode SC fiber-optic connectors to attach to 62.5/125-micron multimode fiber or 8/125 single-mode fiber. The ports provide half- or full-duplex operation. The Fast Ethernet Switching Module SMF/MMF requires NMP software Release 2.1(5) or greater. Each port can be configured as follows:

Figure 6-13   *Fast Ethernet Switching Module (100BaseFX 12 Port)*

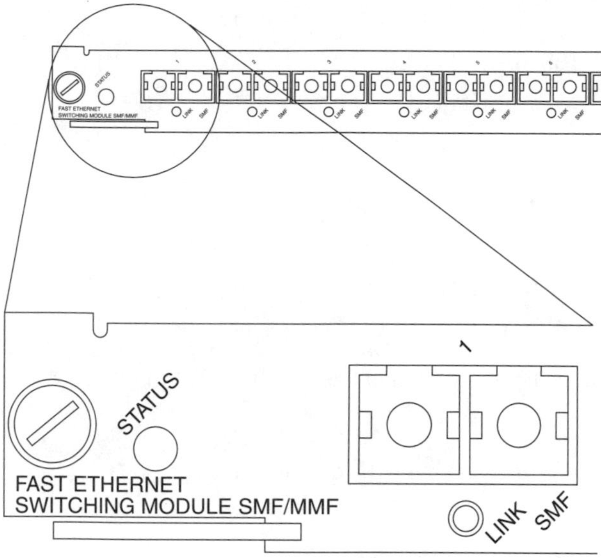

- To a different virtual LAN
- As a trunk port running dynamic ISL

Distance Limitations

Maximum station-to-station cabling distances for the Catalyst 5000 Ethernet switching modules are shown in Table 6-1:

Table 6-1   *Distance Limitations*

	Module Type	Half-Duplex	Full-Duplex
Copper	10BaseT	100 m	100 m
	100BaseTX	100 m	100 m
MMF	10BaseFL	2 km	2 km
	100BaseFX	400 m	2 km
SMF	100BaseFX	10 km	10 km

- 10BaseT Ethernet:

    — Category 3-5 UTP: 100 m

    — 100-ohm shielded UTP: 100 m

- 10/100BaseTX and 100BaseTX Fast Ethernet

    — Category 5 UTP: 100 m

    — 100-ohm shielded UTP: 100 m

- 10BaseFL Ethernet:

    — 62.5/125 micron multimode fiber: 2 km

- 100BaseFX Fast Ethernet:

    — 62.5/125 micron multimode fiber: 400 m half-duplex, 2 km full-duplex

- 100BaseFX Fast Ethernet:

    — 8.7/125 micron single-mode fiber: 10 km half- or full-duplex

Ethernet and Fast Ethernet Group Switching Modules

Group Switching Ethernet Module (10BaseT 48 Port, Telco)

The 48-port 10BaseT Group Switching Ethernet uses four telco connectors to attach to Category 3, 4, or 5 UTP cable. Each group of 12 ports can be assigned to a different virtual LAN. The module supports up to four VLANs. The Group Switching Ethernet Module requires NMP software Release 2.1(1) or later.

Group Switching Fast Ethernet Module (100BaseTX 24 Port)

The 24-port Group Switching Fast Ethernet Module shown in Figure 6-14 provides connection to 24 100 Mbps (100BaseTX) half-duplex Fast Ethernet ports in three switched segments of eight repeated ports each. The module uses RJ-45 connectors for attaching Ethernet devices. The Group Switching Fast Ethernet Module (100BaseTX 24 Port) requires NMP software Release 2.2(2) or later. Each group can be configured to a different virtual LAN.

Figure 6-14 *Group Switching Fast Ethernet Module (100BaseTX 24 Port)*

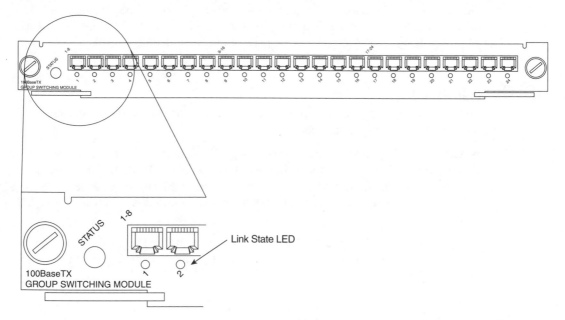

Token Ring Switching Module

The Catalyst 5000 Series Token Ring module is a switching module that can be used with any of the Catalyst 5000 series switches. The Token Ring module is available in fiber or copper. The copper Token Ring module provides 16 RJ-45 ports. The fiber Token Ring module provides 16 ST-type ports. On all Catalyst 5000 series switches, interface slot 1 is reserved for the Supervisor Engine module. The maximum number of Token Ring ports varies, depending on the model of Catalyst 5000 switch, as follows:

- Catalyst 5002 contains two slots, allowing a maximum configuration of 16 Token Ring ports.

- Catalyst 5000 contains five slots, allowing a maximum configuration of 64 Token Ring ports.

- Catalyst 5500 contains 13 slots, but slot 13 is reserved for the ATM Switch Processor (ASP) module. Therefore, the maximum configuration of Token Ring ports is 176.

As in the Catalyst 3900, an ASIC design results in low-latency, wire-speed switching of unicast, multicast, and broadcast frames at either half- or full-duplex speeds, regardless of whether they are source-route bridged, source-route transparently bridged, or source-route switched.

Like the Catalyst 3900, the Catalyst 5000 Series Token Ring module supports IEEE 802.5r, which defines standards for the direct attachment of end stations to the switch as well as for the transmission of data at half-duplex (4/16 Mbps) and full-duplex (32 Mbps) speeds. The fiber Token Ring module also allows the ports to operate in RI/RO mode.

FDDI/CDDI Modules

The LEDs on the Catalyst 5000 series switch FDDI module provide status information for each module and each port connection.

The CDDI module provides a single- (SAS) or dual-attachment station (DAS) connection to two (Category 5 UTP) 100 Mbps CDDI interfaces using two RJ-45 female connections. The FDDI MMF provides a SAS or DAS connection to the FDDI backbone network using multimode media interface connector (MIC) fiber-optic connections. It connects to 62.5/125-micron multimode fiber.

The FDDI module SMF provides a SAS or DAS connection to the FDDI backbone network using two single-mode ST fiber-optic connections. It connects to 8/125-micron single-mode fiber.

ATM LAN Emulation Dual PHY Modules

Three models of the ATM LAN Emulation Dual PHY Module exist. The ATM LAN Emulation Dual PHY Module (UTP) provides two direct connections between an ATM network and the Catalyst 5000 series switch. The module supports two RJ-45 connectors.

The ATM LAN Emulation Dual PHY Module (UTP) module supports the following features:

- Reassembly of up to 256 buffers simultaneously; each buffer represents a packet.
- Support for up to 4096 virtual circuits.
- Support for AAL5.

The ATM LAN Emulation Dual PHY Module (MMF) provides an active and a standby connection between an ATM network and the Catalyst 5000 series switch. The module supports two multimode SC fiber-optic connectors.

The ATM LAN Emulation Dual PHY Module (SMF) provides an active and a standby connection between an ATM network and the Catalyst 5000 series switch. The module supports two single-mode SC fiber-optic connectors.

In addition to the features supported by the UTP module mentioned, the MMF and SMF modules support ATM LANE 1.0, including LAN Emulation Client (LEC), LAN Emulation Server (LES), Broadcast and Unknown Server (BUS), and LAN Emulation Configuration Server (LECS).

The ATM LAN Emulation Dual PHY Modules have the following LEDs: Status, TX, RX, Link, and Active. The LEDs provide the following status indications:

- Status LED:
    - Green (operational)
    - Red (failed port test)
    - Orange (boot, self-test, or disabled)
- RX LED:
    - Green (port is receiving a cell)
    - Off (idle)
- TX (transmit) LED:
    - Green (port is transmitting a cell)
    - Off (idle)
- Link LED:
    - Green (link integrity is good)
    - Blinking green (detected a collision)
- Active LED:
    - Green (port is in active mode)
    - Off (port is in standby mode)

Route Switching Module

The Route Switching Module (RSM) is a router module running normal Cisco IOS router software that directly plugs into the Catalyst switch backplane. The RSM is configured to do multiprotocol routing for the Catalyst switch Ethernet interfaces.

The PCMCIA slots are for additional PCMCIA-based Flash memory. You can use this Flash memory to store and run Cisco IOS software images, or as a file server for other routers to access as clients.

You can use the console port to connect a terminal to the RSM for configuration and monitoring. You can use the auxiliary port to connect a modem for remote access to the RSM.

The Reset button causes a nonmaskable interrupt (NMI) and places the RSM in ROM monitor mode. The RSM module provides the following LEDs to display status:

- Status LED: green (operational), orange (module in boot, test, or disabled status), and red (power-up diagnostics failure or module not operational).
- CPU Halt and Enabled LEDs: CPU Halt LED is on during normal operation; CPU halt LED is off if the system detects a processor hardware failure.

- The Enabled LED: This LED is on when the IP microcode is loaded and the RSM is operational.

- PCMCIA Slot 1 and Slot 0 LEDs: The LEDs light when their respective slot 1 and slot 0 PCMCIA devices are accessed by the RSM.

- Channel 0 and Channel 1 LEDs: The RSM has two channels that transfer packet data between the Catalyst 5500 backplane and the network VLANs. The channel 0 (VLAN 0) and channel 1 (VLAN 1) transmit (TX) and receive (RX) LEDs indicate transmit and receive activity for each channel.

- MAC addresses: VLAN 0 (channel 0) is assigned the MAC address of a PROM on the RSM line communication processor (LCP). This MAC address is used for diagnostics and identification of the RSM physical slot. Note that VLAN 0 is not accessible to the user.

VLAN 1 and additional VLANs are assigned the base MAC address from a MAC address PROM on the RSM that contains 512 MAC addresses. All routing interfaces (except VLAN 0) use the base MAC address. You can override this address and use one of the other block addresses by using the **interface mac-address** command or the **mac-address configuration** command. The other block addresses are determined as follows: base MAC address plus 1, base MAC address plus 2, and so on.

NOTE   Normally, no need exists to override the default MAC address.

NOTE   The ICRC and ACRC courses provide training for configuring a Cisco router.

Chassis and Backplane

CLSC Objectives Covered in This Section

35	Describe the hardware features, functions, and benefits of Catalyst 5000 series switches.

The Catalyst 5000 series switches enable you to scale from 10/100 Mbps switching for small workgroups and backbones with the Catalyst 2900 and the Catalyst 5002 to wiring closet or backbone applications with the Catalyst 5000.

The Catalyst 5000 series switches share a common hardware, software, and feature set to provide scalability and flexibility needed in large switched networks. The needs of the enterprise network are addressed by the Catalyst 5000 with embedded Cisco IOS software support and a range of switched and backbone modules.

The modularity of the system enables the Catalyst 5000 series switches to function as a desktop, workgroup, wiring closet, or backbone switch.

Each of the five slots in the Catalyst 5000 chassis contains a 192-pin FutureBus connector to the backplane. The top slot also contains a 48-pin connector used for clock and arbitration signals on the Supervisor Engine. Having the pins on the chassis instead of on the module makes it less likely that the pins will bend when the module is outside the chassis.

The chassis provides for power distribution to and control of the modules contained in each slot. It also enables you to use the Supervisor Engine to remotely disable a line module. In addition, you can reset individual modules or perform a global reset on the chassis. The passive backplane has no active components that could fail.

Online insertions and removals are supported by the use of four different pin lengths. Backplane operation is briefly suspended during an online insertion or removal to ensure that packets are not corrupted across the backplane during the insertion and removal process.

The frame switching bus is the bus over which the data passes. The frame switching bus, the management, and the index bus (also called the control bus) are all discussed in more detail in Chapter 5, "Catalyst 5000 Series Switch Architecture."

Catalyst 2900 Overview

The Catalyst 2900 is a 14-port, fixed-configuration Fast Ethernet switch. It contains the equivalent of a Catalyst 5000 Supervisor Engine and a 10/100BaseTX or 100BaseFX Ethernet module. Therefore, the Catalyst 2900 has essentially the same hardware architecture and the same software functionality as the Catalyst 5000, including support for up to 1000 virtual LANs and at least 16,000 learned or user-defined MAC addresses. (As noted previously, there is currently a practical limitation of 255 VLANs on Catalyst 5000 series switches.)

Catalyst 2900 Configurations

The Catalyst 2900 is available in the following two configurations:

- 10/100BaseTX (Catalyst 2901)
- 100BaseFX (Catalyst 2902)

The Catalyst 2900 has a single, fixed power supply.

Catalyst 5002 Switch

The Catalyst 5002 can be configured with any of the current or future Catalyst 5000 family modules. Slot 1 is reserved for the Supervisor Engine, which provides Layer 2 switching and network management. The Supervisor Engine includes two full-duplex Fast Ethernet uplinks for redundant connections to switches, routers, and servers. Users can choose dual 100BaseTX, dual-multimode 100BaseFX, or dual single-mode 100BaseFX uplinks. Furthermore, with Cisco Fast EtherChannel technology, the two ports can be configured as a single 400 Mbps fault-tolerant connection.

The Catalyst 5002 chassis fits into a standard 19-inch rack, and all system components are accessible from the same side of the chassis. The chassis includes dual load-sharing, redundant power supplies. A single supply can support any configuration, making the system highly reliable. The Catalyst 5002 complements the Catalyst 5000 family, which grants users the benefit of common hardware, software, and spares from the data center to network periphery.

The port densities for the two-slot Catalyst 5002 switch are as follows:

- Up to 48 group-switched Ethernet interfaces
- Up to 48 switched Ethernet interfaces
- Up to 12 switched fiber-optic Ethernet interfaces
- Up to 24 10/100 Mbps switched Fast Ethernet interfaces
- Up to 24 group-switched Fast Ethernet interfaces
- Up to 12 switched 10/100 Ethernet interfaces
- Up to 12 switched fiber-optic Fast Ethernet interfaces
- One ATM module
- One CDDI or FDDI module
- One Route Switching Module (RSM)

Catalyst 5000 Overview

The Catalyst 5000 uses a media-independent backplane that is capable of supporting all types of LAN traffic. It is even possible to switch cells directly across this backplane, which supports data transmission at speeds up to 1.2 Gbps.

The modular design of the Catalyst 5000 series switch accommodates up to these limitations:

- 192 switched Ethernet connections
- 192 group-switched Ethernet connections

- 96 10/100-Mbps Ethernet connections, plus 2 Fast Ethernet connections on the Supervisor Engine

These connections can be made to existing LAN segments or to high-performance workstations and servers using the following cabling:

- UTP and shielded UTP (100 ohm)
- Fiber-optic cable

These various interface modules provide flexibility to accommodate the bandwidth demands of future applications.

Backbone connections to Fast Ethernet, CDDI/FDDI, and ATM are available.

The Catalyst 5000 also supports the creation of up to 1000 virtual LANs and at least 16,000 learned or user-defined MAC addresses.

Catalyst 5000 Chassis Features

The Supervisor Engine enables switching and controls data flow across the switch backplane. The Supervisor Engine must be installed in the top slot of the Catalyst 5000 series switch for the system to operate. The other four slots can accommodate any combination of other Catalyst 5000 modules, except four ATM modules. Unlike the Catalyst 5500 switch, the Catalyst 5000 does not have ATM switching capabilities.

The front panel of the switch provides access to the switch backplane. All switching modules, the fan trays, and the dual, fault-tolerant power supplies are rear-mounted and support online insertion and removal. Online insertion and removal enables you to add, replace, or remove components without interrupting the system or entering any console commands. Only the functions performed by the removed component are affected.

Environmental monitoring and reporting functions enable you to maintain normal system operation by resolving adverse environmental conditions prior to loss of operation. If conditions reach critical thresholds, the system may shut down to avoid damage to equipment from excessive heat or electrical current.

Fast, reliable system upgrades are possible because downloadable software and Flash code enable you to load new images into Flash memory remotely, without having to physically access the switch.

A rack-mount kit is included for mounting the chassis in an EIA-310-C standard 19-inch equipment rack. You can mount the switch in a standard 19-inch two- or four-post equipment rack, enclosed cabinet, or two- or four-post telco rack, with either the front panel or back panel facing out. Mounting the Catalyst 5000 series switch with the back facing out provides easy access to all system components, cables, network connections, diagnostic LEDs, and power connections.

Redundant Power Supplies

The Catalyst 5000 switch is fully powered by one 376W, AC-input power supply. An optional second redundant AC power supply is also available for fault-tolerant power. When two power supplies are installed and both are turned on, each provides about half the required power to the system. If one power supply fails, the second power supply immediately begins operating at full power to maintain uninterrupted system operation indefinitely, without any software configuration. A second power supply can be installed or replaced without interrupting system operation.

Each power supply is 3.3V ready for future use and provides the following:

- +5 V at 70 A

- +12 V at 2 A

- +24 V at 120 mA (used by hot insertion circuitry)

Separate AC Power Sources

Each power supply should be connected to a separate AC source so that, in case of an input power line or power supply failure, the second power supply maintains uninterrupted system power.

Catalyst 5500 Overview

The Catalyst 5500 is a 13-slot chassis with two dedicated slots: slots 1 and 13. Slot 1 is dedicated for the Supervisor Engine that monitors all system components and is responsible for all frame-switching and forwarding functions in the switch. Supervisor Engine II or Supervisor III is required for operation of the Catalyst 5500. A Supervisor II is a 1.2 Gbps switch fabric. A Supervisor III is a 3.6 Gbps crossbar switching fabric. Slot 13 is the second dedicated slot and is reserved for the LS1010 ATM SwitchProcessor (ASP) module.

The Catalyst 5500 architecture is based on a combination of two high-capacity switching fabrics integrated into a single platform. This architecture ensures optimal performance whether the Catalyst 5500 is used as a high-density cell or a frame switch. All Catalyst 5000 family interface modules can be used in slots 2 to 12, whereas LightStream 1010 or Catalyst 8510 modules can be used in slots 9 to 12. Slot 2 is a dual-purpose slot that can be used for either a redundant Supervisor Engine or any Catalyst 5000 family interface module.

With its support for hot-swappable modules, power supplies, and fans, the Catalyst 5500 chassis delivers high availability for production networks. Dual redundant switching engines, power supplies, and a passive backplane design ensure full system redundancy for mission-critical environments. The Catalyst 5500 chassis fits into a standard 19-inch rack, and all system components are accessible from the same side of the chassis. Only one power supply is required to run a fully configured system.

Supervisor Redundancy

As discussed earlier, the Catalyst 5500 chassis supports redundant Supervisor Engines. The redundant Supervisor Engine is installed in slot 2.

Clock Redundancy

The Catalyst 5500 switch has two clocks on the backplane. Both the clocks continuously monitor each other. If the active clock fails, the standby clock takes over.

You can view the clock status with the **show log** command.

Power Supply Redundancy

The Catalyst 5500 switch supports two power supply modules. Each power supply can power a fully populated chassis. Each power supply can be inserted or removed online. When two power supplies are installed and both are turned on, each provides about half the required power to the system.

Catalyst 5500 Chassis

The Catalyst 5500 chassis is based on the Catalyst 5000 five-slot chassis, with the line modules still organized horizontally. Cooling is provided by a hot-swappable fan tray pulling air from side to side.

The chassis facilitates 19-inch and telco rack-mount installation, and this mounting hardware is shipped with every unit. The total height of the chassis is 25 inches, or about 15U (rack units). Its total weight without power supplies and switching modules is 60 pounds. A fully loaded system with two power supplies and 13 modules is 176 pounds.

Two cable organizers are available: One is mounted vertically on either side of the unit on the rack, and the other can be mounted horizontally above or below the unit on the rack. The purpose of the cable organizers is to ease the installation and facilitate routing, bundling, and dressing of the multiple cables coming from the front panel. Both cable organizers are shipped with every unit.

The chassis has small feet mounted on its underside for use in free-standing applications. Each chassis can bear the weight of another fully loaded chassis while in a free-standing configuration. Two shelf brackets support the weight of the chassis in the rack. Remove the power supply (or supplies) and the modules before attempting to lift the Catalyst 5500 chassis.

WARNING   Two people are required to lift the chassis. Grasp the chassis underneath the lower edge, and lift with both hands. To minimize the chance of injury, keep your back straight and lift with your legs, not your back.

To prevent damage to the chassis and components, never attempt to lift the chassis with the handles on the power supplies or on the interface processors, or by the plastic panels on the front of the chassis. These handles were not designed to support the weight of the chassis.

Catalyst 5500 Backplane Features

The Catalyst 5500 can use the Supervisor II or Supervisor III. If a Supervisor III is replaced with a Supervisor II, the added features and capabilities of the Supervisor III are not available.

The Catalyst 5500 has two clocks mounted on the back of the backplane. A Supervisor module installed in the Catalyst 5500 chassis utilizes this external clock on the backplane. A Supervisor module installed in the Catalyst 5000 chassis utilizes the onboard clock. A total of 1024 MAC addresses are available from an EPROM mounted on the backplane. Connection between the LS1010 and frame fabrics is external.

Catalyst 5500 Status Monitoring

The Catalyst 5500 switch enables you to monitor the status of the power supply, voltage, temperature, and fan module. The power supply monitor is used to monitor the power supply type and status.

The voltage monitor is used to monitor the 5 V, 12 V, and 24 V levels. The temperature monitor is used to monitor the equipment temperature and has a two-stage response to elevated temperatures:

- 50 C: Major alarm

- 75 C: Shutdown with warning

The fan module monitor is used to monitor all nine fans in the fan module. Failure of any fan causes a major alarm indicated by a red Status LED.

Catalyst 5500 Power Supplies

The Catalyst 5500 operates with either one or two power supplies. Both AC input and DC (48 VDC) input power supplies are available. A single supply is capable of powering a fully configured chassis, with no configuration restrictions. Each power supply can deliver

1100 W. Each slot can use up to 16 A on the +5 V (80 W) power supply. The same chassis and backplane are used for both the single supply and redundant supply configurations.

In the two-supply configuration, power is load-shared. In the event of a power supply failure, the other power supply can support the load of the entire box. The power supplies can handle live insertion so that a failed supply can be replaced without powering down the box. The supply being inserted or removed must be turned off. A safety latch is engaged when the power switch is in the ON position.

The power supplies have built-in thermal shutdown and overcurrent protection. Each power supply has Status LEDs on the front panel.

Each AC power supply has an IEC receptacle for the main input power. The receptacles are rated at 20 A, 100–240 VAC. The following are the power supply specifications:

- 200 A at 5 V
- 6 A at 12 V
- 120 mA at 24 V
- Built-in cooling fan
- Front-to-back airflow

The Catalyst 5500 switch power supplies are very similar to Cisco 7513 routers, but they produce a lower amperage output. Power supplies from Cisco 7513 routers can be used in Catalyst 5500 switches, but Catalyst 5500 power supplies cannot be used in Cisco 7513 routers.

Catalyst Fan Module

The hot-swappable fan tray is easily replaced by loosening the two thumbscrews on its front panel. The fan module has nine 5-inch fans, running at full speed, powered by the system +12 V. The fan module does not have air filters.

The operation of each fan is monitored by an active circuit, and results are reported to the Supervisor modules; a missing module is also reported. The system can run momentarily without the fan module. However, based on the amount of system load, the chassis may go into the overtemperature limit and shut down. Both overtemperature and shut-down are reported by the Supervisor modules.

Catalyst 5500 Backplane

The Catalyst 5500 backplane, shown in Figure 6-15, implements three 1.2 Gbps buses identical to the single bus used in the Catalyst 5000, for a total of 3.6 Gbps of available bandwidth. The white connectors are 1.2 Gbps, and the black connectors (used for ATM cell switching) are 5 Gbps. The original Catalyst 5000 line modules can access one of three buses, based on position.

Figure 6-15 *Catalyst 5500 Backplane*

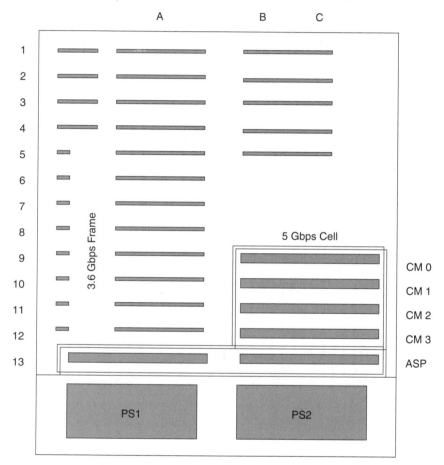

The Supervisor module designed for the Catalyst 5000 is not forward-compatible with the Catalyst 5500 chassis. However, the Supervisor II is backward-compatible with the current Catalyst 5000 switch.

Slot 1 is reserved for the Supervisor II Engine, and slot 13 is reserved for the ASP module. Slots 2 through 12 can accommodate existing Catalyst 5000 line modules; slot 2 can also support a second Supervisor Engine module. Slots 9 through 12 support LS1010 line modules. Slots 9 through 13 can accommodate a complete LS1010 switch inside the Catalyst 5500 chassis.

Existing switching modules cannot choose the switching bus to which they connect; the switching bus is assigned by the slot number it occupies. Second-generation modules are capable of selecting the switching bus to be used through the CLI, Telnet, or SNMP, or by automatic load-balancing software.

Clocks for the entire system are provided by a separate module mounted on the backplane. This architecture for the Catalyst 5500 provides improved clock distribution, noise margin, system support, and Supervisor redundancy operations. The module has redundant circuits and drivers. Clock status is sent to the Supervisor modules, and two identical clock modules are provided to enhance system redundancy. Replacement of the clock module(s) is accomplished by removing the chassis front panel. Clock modules are *not* hot-swappable—as a result, clock replacement requires a system halt.

NOTE   A software clock switchover causes a system reset.

Catalyst 5500 Slot Usage

The Catalyst 5500 chassis slots (see Figure 6-16) can be configured as follows:

Figure 6-16   *Catalyst 5000 Slot Usage*

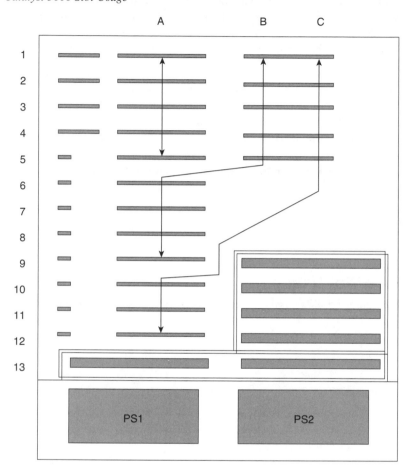

- Slot 1 for the primary Supervisor II or III only
- Slot 2 for a redundant Supervisor II or III or a line module
- Slots 2 through 12 for any line module
- Slots 9 through 12 for the LS1010 line modules
- Slot 13 for one ASP module (ATM cell switching) only

The backplane provides access to the three switching buses (A, B, and C). Slots 1 through 5 access all three buses. Slots 6 through 9 access the B switching bus, and slots 10 through 12 access the C switching bus. The A switching bus is fully compatible with all Catalyst 5000 line modules. The B and C switching buses allow the additional 2.4 Gbps throughput of the Catalyst 5500 switch's 3.6 Gbps crossbar matrix. This design provides for full backward-compatibility with all Catalyst 5000 line modules.

LS1010 Modules

You can install an ATM Switch Processor (ASP) module and other LS1010 modules in the bottom slots of a Catalyst 5500 switch. The ASP module must be installed in slot 13. The LS1010 modules must be installed in slots 9 through 12.

This design essentially combines a Catalyst 5000 switch and an LS1010 switch within the Catalyst 5500 chassis. The LS1010 switch and the ATM modules share only the chassis and the power supply with the Catalyst switch. There is no integration of these two different switches on the backplane of the Catalyst 5500 switch.

You can install the following ATM modules in a Catalyst 5500 switch:

- 25 Mbps Port Adapter Module

- 155 Mbps Port Adapter Modules

  — 155 MM Port Adapter Module

  — 155 SM Port Adapter Module

  — 155 Mixed Port Adapter Module

  — 155 UTP Port Adapter Module

- 622 Mbps Port Adapter Modules

  — 622 MM Port Adapter Module

  — 622 SM Port Adapter Module

  — 622 SM Long-Reach Port Adapter Module

- CES Port Adapter Modules

  — CES T1 Twisted-Pair Port Adapter Module

  — CES E1 Twisted-Pair Port Adapter Module

  — CES E1 BNC Port Adapter Modules

- DS-3/E3 Port Adapter Modules

  — E3 Port Adapter Module

  — Quad DS-3 CES T1 Twisted-pair Port Adapter Module

NOTE   The details about the installation and configuration of the ASP module and the LS1010 modules are covered in the Cisco ATM Solutions course.

Hot Plug ASP

Some critical differences exist between the LS1010 ASP and the ASP that installs in the Catalyst 5500:

- The Catalyst 5500 version recognizes that it is in a Catalyst 5500 chassis using data provided by a backplane ID PROM containing the model number. This version is programmed to show the module mounted in a Catalyst 5500 chassis.

- The LS1010 modules are arranged differently in the LS1010, as compared to the Catalyst 5500 arrangement. Slot identification is different in the two chassis.

- The LS1010 is renumbered in the Catalyst 5500 chassis so that it understands the slot configuration.

CAUTION The ASP module that is new for the Catalyst 5500 switch is hot-swappable, whereas the ASP module is not hot-swappable in the LS1010 switch. Attempting to hot-swap a previous version of the ASP will severely damage the ASP.

A fabric bridge card will serve as a 622 Mbps pipe between the frame and cell fabrics. This card performs all the LAN Emulation functions from the frame to the cell backplane. You can use CiscoView to manage the LS1010 modules in the Catalyst 5500 switch.

NOTE Catalyst 5500 ATM modules, including the ASP, do not communicate across the backplane with the Supervisor Engine or line modules on the Catalyst 5500 switch. Connectivity between the frame-switching modules and the ATM modules on the Catalyst 5500 switch uses external Ethernet cabling.

ATM Slot Numbers

The slots on the Catalyst 5500 and LS1010 switches are numbered as shown in Figure 6-17.

Figure 6-17   *Catalyst 5500 ATM Slot Numbers*

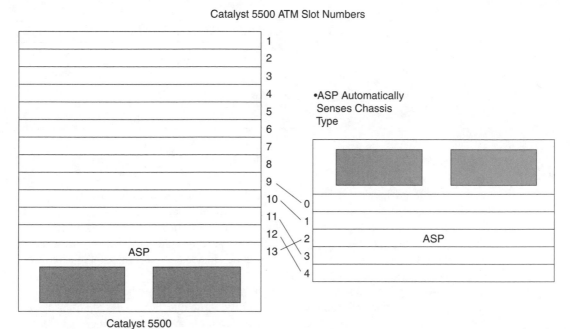

Catalyst 5500 ATM Slot Numbers

Catalyst 5500

When you connect to the serial port of the ASP to configure ATM modules in either a Catalyst 5500 or an LS1010 switch, the ASP automatically senses in which chassis it is installed. This sensing enables you to use the slot numbers of the chassis in which the modules are installed, without having to be concerned with the slot numbers of the other chassis type.

Switch Summary Table

Table 6-2 summarizes the hardware features of the Catalyst 5000 series switches.

Table 6-2   *Switch Summary Table*

Product	Slots	PS	Fixed PS	Modular	Sups	LS1010
2900	2	1	Y	N	1	N
5002	2	2	Y	Y	1	N
5000	5	2	N	Y	1	N
5500	13	2	N	Y	2	Y

Q&A

As mentioned in Chapter 1, "The Cisco LAN Switch Configuration (CLSC) Exam Overview," the questions and scenarios are more difficult than what you should experience on the actual exam. The questions do not attempt to cover more breadth or depth than the exam; however, the questions are designed to make sure you know the answers. Rather than allowing you to derive the answer from clues hidden inside the question itself, the questions will challenge your understanding and recall of the subject. Questions from the "Do I Know This Already?" quiz from the beginning of the chapter are repeated here to ensure that you have mastered the chapter's topic areas. Hopefully, these questions will help limit the number of exam questions on which you narrow your choices to two options and then guess!

1 The ASP module must be installed in slot _____.

2 The Catalyst 5500 backplane implements _____ 1.2 Gbps buses identical to the single bus used in the Catalyst 5000.

3 There are _____ MAC addresses available from an EPROM mounted on the backplane.

4 The Catalyst 5000 supports the creation of up to _____ virtual LANs.

5 The Catalyst 5002 switch is a Catalyst 5000 series switch with _____ slots.

6 The Catalyst 2900 is a _____ port, fixed-configuration Fast Ethernet switch.

7 The Group Switching Fast Ethernet Module (100BaseTX 24 Port) requires NMP software Release _____ or later.

8 The 12-port 100BaseFX Fast Ethernet Switching Module uses _____ connectors to attach to 62.5/125-micron multimode fiber.

9 The multimode fiber-optic (MMF) (WS-X5006) Supervisor Engines provide two half- and full-duplex Fast Ethernet, multimode fiber interfaces with SC connectors for connection distances up to _____ meters for half-duplex, and up to _____ kilometers for full duplex.

10 The Supervisor Engine is the main system processor in the switch. It contains the Layer _____ switching engine, the network management processor for the system software, and the system memory components.

Source Material

Some content in this chapter is based on material in the *CLSC Course Book*.

The objectives of the Cisco LAN Switch Configuration (CLSC) exam are taken from the Cisco web site, at the Cisco career certification and training area. The following table shows the exam objectives covered in this chapter:

Objective	Description
4	Use the command-line menu or menu-driven interface to configure the Catalyst series switches and their switching modules.
5	Use the command-line menu or menu-driven interface to configure trunks, virtual LANs, and ATM LAN Emulation.
38	Prepare network connections.
39	Establish a serial connection.
40	Use the Catalyst 5000 switch CLI to: • Enter privileged mode. • Set system information. • Configure interface types.

CHAPTER 7

Configuring the Catalyst 5000 Series Switches

This chapter discusses the initial configuration of the Catalyst 5000 series switch and describes how you configure such functions as IP addressing, system configuration, and SNMP management.

How to Best Use This Chapter

By taking the following steps, you can make better use of your study time:

- Keep your notes and the answers for all your work with this book in one place, for easy reference.

- Take the quiz, and write down your answers. Studies show that retention is significantly increased through writing down facts and concepts, even if you never look at the information again.

- Use the diagram in Figure 7-1 to guide you to the next step.

Figure 7-1 *How to Best Use This Chapter in Preparation for the CLSC Exam*

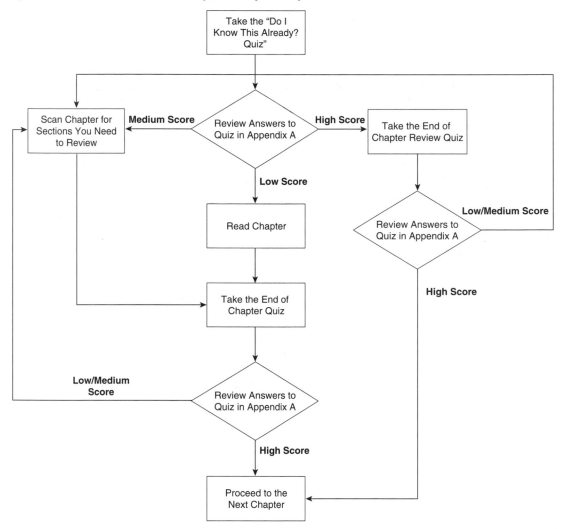

Do I Know This Already? Quiz

You can find the answers to this quiz in Appendix A, "Answers to 'Do I Know This Already?' Quizzes and Q & A Sections ." Review the answers, grade your quiz, and choose an appropriate next step in this chapter based on the suggestions diagramed in Figure 7-1.

1 The SLIP connection *must* use the _____.

   a. IP address 127.0.0.1

   b. Console port

   c. IP address of the administrator's PC as a default gateway

   d. MAC address of the RSM

2 The system initiates a BOOTP or Reverse Address Resolution Protocol (RARP) request:

   a. At the end of every system boot.

   b. When the TFTP server IP address is set to 0.0.0.0.0.

   c. When the sc0 interface IP address is set to 0.0.0.0.

   d. All of the above.

3 Match each of the following commands with its description.

   ___**set**

   ___**show**

   ___**clear**

   a. Used to overwrite or erase a parameter

   b. Used to establish switch parameters

   c. Used to verify a configuration

4 Match each of the following command element descriptions with the syntax used to depict them.

   Command element descriptions:
   ___Commands and keywords
   ___Prompt that indicates user level
   ___Prompt that indicates privileged level
   ___Arguments for which you supply values
   ___Indicator for optional parameter
   ___Separator for alternative but required keywords
   ___Sample console screen display
   ___Indicator for text you enter
   ___Indicator for nonprinting characters, such as passwords

Syntax:

a. Console>

b. Screen font

c. *Italic* font

d. **Boldface** font

e. Elements in square brackets ([ ])

f. Console >(enable)

g. Angle brackets (< >)

h. **Boldface screen** font

i. Vertical bars (|)

5 The **set interface** command:

   a. Can be used to configure static routes on the Catalyst 5000.

   b. Must be used to bring the sc0 interface up before you can use the serial console port after using the **clear config all** command.

   c. Can be used to enable SLIP.

   d. Can be used to assign network addresses and subnet masks for SLIP interfaces.

6 Which command is used to copy a switch configuration to a file on a host?

   a. write terminal

   b. write network

   c. write config

   d. upload config

7 The default setting for port speed on a 10/100 Mbps Ethernet port is:

   a. 10 Mbps

   b. 100 Mbps

   c. Auto

   d. Desirable

8 The default setting for port speed on Token Ring switching ports is:

   a. Half-duplex

   b. Full-duplex

   c. Auto

   d. Desirable

9 The default setting for port mode on 10/100 Mbps Ethernet ports and Token Ring switching ports is:

   a. Half-duplex

   b. Full-duplex

   c. Auto

   d. Desirable

10 The default setting for port mode on 10 Mbps Ethernet ports and 100 Mbps Fast Ethernet is:

   a. Half-duplex

   b. Full-duplex

   c. Auto

   d. Desirable

Using the answer key in Appendix A, grade your answers.

- **5 or less correct**—Read this chapter.

- **6, 7, or 8 correct**—Review this chapter, looking at the charts and diagrams that summarize most of the concepts and facts in this chapter.

- **9 or more correct**—If you want more review on these topics, skip to the Q&A section at the end of this chapter. If you do not want more review on these topics, skip this chapter.

Foundation Topics

Configuring the Software

CLSC Objectives Covered in This Section

38	Prepare network connections.
39	Establish a serial connection.
40	Use the Catalyst 5000 switch CLI to:
	• Enter privileged mode.
	• Set system information.
	• Configure interface types.

This chapter discusses the initial configuration of the Catalyst 5000 series switch and describes how you configure such functions as IP addressing and SNMP management. An IP address must be assigned if you need to use Telnet to connect to the switch or use SNMP network management for the switch. Up to eight simultaneous Telnet sessions are possible. If your Telnet station or SNMP network management workstation is on a different network from the switch, a static routing table entry must also be added to the routing table. Use the **set ip route** command to set the static routing table entry.

NOTE   For definitions of all commands discussed in this chapter, refer to the "Command Reference" chapter of the publication *Catalyst 5000 Series Configuration Guide and Command Reference.*

Default Configuration

The Catalyst 5000 features you can customize have default values that will most likely suit your environment, and you will probably not need to change them. The default values of these features are set as follows:

* The command-line connection is set to normal mode.

* The system information defaults are set as follows:

    — No defaults exist for the system contact, location string, system name, system clock time, or password for accessing the command-line in normal mode or privileged mode.

    — The system prompt is set to **Console>**.

- The interface type defaults are set as follows:
  - sc0, sl0, IP address, netmask, and broadcast are set to 0.0.0.0.
  - The destination address for sl0 is 0.0.0.0.
  - The sc0 interface is assigned to VLAN 1.
  - The default gateway is 0.0.0.0, with a metric of 0.
- The Serial Line Interface Protocol (SLIP) for the command line is set to **detach** and is not active.
- Remote Monitoring (RMON) support is not enabled.
- Simple Network Management Protocol (SNMP) defaults are set with the following SNMP community defaults:
  - Read-Only: Public
  - Read-Write: Private
  - Read-Write-All: Secret
  - No SNMP traps enabled
- The Virtual Trunking Protocol (VTP) interval is 5 minutes. No domain name is specified. The mode of operation is server. No VTP password exists.
- All VLANs are allowed for trunking; trunking is set to auto mode for Fast Ethernet ports and to nontrunking for FDDI ports.
- No Ethernet-FDDI mapping is provided; no trunk traffic is forwarded.
- The native VLAN (internal Ethernet VLAN that translates to native FDDI packets) is 1.
- The trunk configuration, Ethernet-FDDI VLAN mapping, and the native VLAN are stored in the supervisor engine module NVRAM and are sent to the FDDI module after a module reset, for configuration purposes.
- All trunk-capable ports are set to auto mode for trunking.

Customizing the Configuration

The steps listed here describe how to initially configure the Catalyst 5000 series switch:

- Establish the console port connection
- Set the system information
- Set port speeds and transmission type
- Set the interface type
- Configure SLIP on the console port

- Create a BOOTP server

- Configure SNMP management

- Set up remote monitoring (RMON)

- Set virtual LANs (VLANs)

- Set trunks

- Test the configuration

You configure the switch through the command line using three basic types of commands: **set**, **show**, and **clear**. Use the **set** commands to establish switch parameters. After each **set** command, use the **show** command to verify that you have entered the correct values and configured the switch correctly. If you make errors, use the **set** or **clear** command to overwrite or erase the parameter.

For a list of available commands, type **set help**, **show help**, or **clear help**. To display the command usage, type the command and the word **help**, as the following example shows:

```
Console> (enable) set spantree hello help
Usage: set spantree hello <interval> [vlan]
       (interval = 1..10, vlan = 1..1000)
```

These materials use the following conventions for command descriptions:

- Examples that contain system prompts denote interactive sessions, indicating the commands that you should enter at the prompt. The system prompt indicates the current level of the EXEC command interpreter. For example, the prompt Console> indicates that you should be at the user level, and the prompt Console> (enable) indicates that you should be at the privileged level.

- Commands and keywords are in **boldface** font.

- Arguments for which you supply values are in *italic* font.

- Elements in square brackets ([ ]) are optional.

- Alternative but required keywords are separated by vertical bars (|).

Command examples use these conventions:

- Terminal sessions and sample console screen displays are in `screen` font.

- Information you enter is in **`boldface screen`** font.

- Nonprinting characters, such as passwords, are in angle brackets (< >).

- Default responses to system prompts are in square brackets ([ ]).

- Exclamation points (!) at the beginning of a line indicate a comment line.

- **Caution** means "reader be careful." In this situation, you might do something that could result in equipment damage or loss of data.

- **Note** means "reader take note." Notes contain helpful suggestions.

Getting Ready to Install

CLSC Objectives Covered in This Section

4	Use the command-line menu or menu-driven interface to configure the Catalyst series switches and their switching modules.
5	Use the command-line menu or menu-driven interface to configure trunks, virtual LANs, and ATM LAN Emulation.

Before you begin your configuration, you will need the following information:

- Interface type
  - sc0: Use this interface type when assigning the Catalyst 5000 series switch IP address.
  - sl0: Use this interface type when configuring a Serial Line Internet Protocol (SLIP) connection on the switch.

NOTE	After SLIP is enabled and attached on the console port, an EIA/TIA-232 terminal cannot access the Catalyst 5000 series switch through this port.

- IP address
- Netmask address
- Broadcast address (optional)

Establishing the Console Port Connection

After installing and connecting the switch, perform the following steps to start up and access the switch.

Task	Command
Turn on the power to the switch and the console terminal. The information shown in Example 7-1 appears on the screen.	None
Access the console port using the console terminal.	None
At the Enter password prompt, press Return.	None
Enter privileged mode.	**enable**
At the Enter password prompt, press Return.	None

Example 7-1   *Initial Bootup Example*

```
ATE0
ATS0=1


Catalyst 5000 Power Up Diagnostics


Init NVRAM Log
LED Test
ROM CHKSUM
DUAL PORT RAM r/w
RAM r/w
RAM address test
Byte/Word Enable test
RAM r/w 55aa
RAM r/w aa55
EARL test
BOOTROM Version 1.4, Dated Dec  5 1995 16:49:40
BOOT date: 00/00/00 BOOT time: 03:18:57
SIMM RAM address test
SIMM Ram r/w 55aa
SIMM Ram r/w aa55
Start to Uncompress Image ...
IP address for Catalyst not configured
BOOTP will commence after the ports are online
Ports are coming online ...
Cisco Systems Console
Enter password:
Thu Mar 21 1996  03:20:41    Module 1 is online


Enter Password:
Thu Mar 21 1996  03:20:41    Module 2 is online


Enter Password:
Sending RARP request with address 00:40:0b:6c:2b:ff
Sending bootp request with address: 00:40:0b:6c:2b:ff
Sending RARP request with address 00:40:0b:6c:2b:ff
Sending bootp request with address: 00:40:0b:6c:2b:ff
Sending RARP request with address 00:40:0b:6c:2b:ff
Sending bootp request with address: 00:40:0b:6c:2b:ff
Sending RARP request with address 00:40:0b:6c:2b:ff
Sending bootp request with address: 00:40:0b:6c:2b:ff
Sending RARP request with address 00:40:0b:6c:2b:ff
Sending bootp request with address: 00:40:0b:6c:2b:ff
Sending RARP request with address 00:40:0b:6c:2b:ff
Sending bootp request with address: 00:40:0b:6c:2b:ff
Sending RARP request with address 00:40:0b:6c:2b:ff
Sending bootp request with address: 00:40:0b:6c:2b:ff
Sending RARP request with address 00:40:0b:6c:2b:ff
Sending bootp request with address: 00:40:0b:6c:2b:ff
Sending RARP request with address 00:40:0b:6c:2b:ff
Sending bootp request with address: 00:40:0b:6c:2b:ff
Sending RARP request with address 00:40:0b:6c:2b:ff
```

Example 7-1 *Initial Bootup Example (Continued)*

```
Sending bootp request with address: 00:40:0b:6c:2b:ff
Console>
Console> enable
Enter password:
Console> (enable)
```

NOTE   The system only initiates a BOOTP or RARP request when the sc0 interface is set to 0.0.0.0, or when you use the command **clear config all**.

Setting the System Information

Although not required, several system parameters should be set as part of the initial system setup. To set the system parameters, perform the following steps in privileged mode:

Task	Command
Set the system contact.	**set system contact** *contact_string*
Set the system location string.	**set system location** *location_string*
Set the system name.	**set system name** *name_string*
Set the system clock.	**set time** *day_of_week mm/dd/yy hh:mm:ss*
Set the system prompt.	**set prompt** *prompt_string*
Set password protection for accessing the command line in normal mode.	**set password**
Set password protection for accessing the command line in privileged mode.	**set enablepass**

Setting Port Speed and Transmission Type

This section describes the procedure used to configure the port speed and transmission type for the Ethernet switching module using the command-line interface. The features you can customize have default values that will most likely suit your environment and will probably need not be changed. The default values of these features are set as follows:

- All ports enabled
- No port names

- Normal priority level

- All 4/16 and 10/100 Mbps ports set to auto

- All Token Ring, Ethernet, and Fast Ethernet ports set to half-duplex

Setting the Port Speed

Task	Command
Configure the 10/100 port speed.	**set port speed** *mod_num/port_num* **10	100	auto**
Configure the Token Ring port speed.	**set port speed** *mod_num/port_num* **4	16	auto**
Verify the port name.	**show port** *mod_num/port_num*

By default, 4/16 Token Ring Switching Modules is set to auto. Interfaces set to auto automatically configure themselves to operate at the proper speed and transmission type (half- or full-duplex). However, you can configure the speed to be 10 Mbps or 100 Mbps.

Examples of the **set port speed** command follow:

```
Console> (enable) set port speed 2/1 auto
Port 2/1 speed set to auto-sensing mode.
Console> (enable) set port speed 2/2 10
Port 2/2 speed set to 10 Mbps.
Console> (enable) set port speed 2/3 100
Port 2/3 speed set to 100 Mbps.
Console>
```

Setting the Port Transmission Type

The ports on the Catalyst switch may be set to operate in full- or half-duplex modes. To set the transmission type to full- or half-duplex for the ports that will be used, perform the following steps in privileged mode:

Task	Command
Set the port.	**set port duplex** *mod_num/port_num* **full	half	auto**
Verify the port transmission type.	**show port** *mod_num/ port_num*

The features you can customize when setting the Port Transmission Type have default values that will most likely suit your environment and will probably need not be changed. The default values of these features are set as follows:

- Default for 10 Mbps and 100 Mbps modules is half-duplex.

- Default for 10/100 Mbps modules is auto.

You can set the transmission type to full- or half-duplex for these:

- 100 Mbps Fast Ethernet ports on the Supervisor engine
- 10 Mbps ports

You can set the transmission type for 10/100 Mbps modules and Token Ring Switching Modules to auto, full-, or half-duplex. The default configuration for all ports on 10 Mbps modules and 100 Mbps ports on the Supervisor engine is set to half-duplex. The default configuration for 10/100 Mbps modules and Token Ring Switching Modules has all ports set to auto.

Two examples of the **set port duplex** command follow:

```
Console> (enable) set port duplex 2/1 half
Port 2/1 set to half-duplex.
Console> (enable) set port duplex 2/2 full
Port 2/2 set to full-duplex.
```

Setting the Interface Type

To set the interface type, perform the following steps in privileged mode:

Task	Command
If you are using a local network connection to the console port, set the logical port to sc0. Assign the Catalyst 5000 IP address to a VLAN. See Example 7-2 for an example.	**set interface sc0 up**
	set interface sc0 *ip_address [netmask [broadcast]]*
	set interface sc0 *vlan_num ip_address*
If you are using a SLIP connection to the console port, set the slip port to sl0. See Example 7-3 for an example.	**set interface sl0 up**
	set interface *slip_address dest_address*
Configure static routes. For example, you need to configure static routes if your Telnet station or SNMP network management workstation is on a different network from the switch.	**set ip route** *destination gateway* [**metric**]
Configure a default route, if desired. See Example 7-2 for an example.	**set ip route default** *gateway metric*
Check the status of the configuration of the switch. See Example 7-3 for an example.	**show interface**
Display the route table entries of the configuration. See Example 7-4 for an example.	**show ip route**

Example 7-2 *set interface and set ip route Commands Example*

```
Console> (enable) set interface sc0 up
Interface sc0 administratively up.
Console> (enable) set interface sc0 192.200.11.44 255.255.255.0 192.200.11.255
Interface sc0 IP address and netmask set.
Console> (enable) set interface sl0 up
Interface sl0 administratively up.
Console> (enable) set interface sl0 192.200.10.45 192.200.10.103
Interface sl0 SLIP and destination address set.
Console> (enable) set interface sc0 1
Interface sc0 vlan set.
Console> (enable) set ip route default 192.122.173.42
Route added.
```

The default configuration is as follows:

Example 7-3 *show interface Command Examples*

```
Console> (enable) show interface
sl0:   flags=10<DOWN,POINTOPOINT>
          vlan1 inet 0.0.0.0 netmask 0.0.0.0 broadcast 0.0.0.0
sc0:   flags=863<UP,BROADCAST,RUNNING>
          inet 0.0.0.0 netmask 0.0.0.0 broadcast 0.0.0.0
Console> (enable)
```

After the **set interface** command has been executed, the **show interface** command shows
the following configuration:

```
Console> (enable) show interface
sl0:   flags=10<DOWN,POINTOPOINT>
          inet 192.200.10.45 netmask 192.200.10.103 broadcast 192.200.10.103
sc0:   flags=863<UP,BROADCAST,RUNNING>
          inet 192.200.11.44 netmask 255.255.255.0 broadcast 192.200.11.255
Console> (enable)
```

Example 7-4 *show route Command Example*

```
Console> (enable) show ip route
Redirect
--------
enabled
Destination      Gateway          Flags   Use        Interface
--------------- --------------- ------- ---------- ---------
default          192.22.74.102    UG          59444  sc0
192.22.74.0      192.22.74.223    U               5  sc0
Console> (enable)
```

Configuring SLIP on the Console Port

To configure the console port for SLIP, perform the following steps:

Task	Command
Access the switch from a remote host with Telnet.	None
Set the IP address of the console port.	**set interface** *slip_address dest_address*
Enable the SLIP for the console port.	**slip attach**

CAUTION The SLIP connection *must* use the console port; while this connection is active, it will cause you to lose your console port connection. If you are connected to the command line through the console port and you enter the **slip attach** command, you will lose the console port connection. In that case, use Telnet to access the command line, enter privileged mode, and type slip detach to restore the console port connection, or reset the switch.

NOTE The command line is not accessible from a direct local terminal. You must use the SLIP to access it.

Creating a BOOTP Server

IP address information can be set using BOOTP protocol. You can configure a BOOTP server with the MAC and IP addresses of the switch. When the switch boots, it automatically retrieves the IP address from the BOOTP server.

The switch performs a BOOTP request *only* if the current IP address is set to 0.0.0.0. (This is the default for a new switch or a switch that has had its configuration file cleared using the **clear config all** command.)

To configure a workstation as a BOOTP server, you must determine the MAC address of the switch and add that MAC address to the BOOTP configuration file on the server. The following table provides an example of creating a BOOTP server on a Sun workstation:

Task	Command
Install the BOOTP server code on the workstation, if it is not already installed.	None
Obtain the first address in the MAC address range for module 1 (the supervisor module). Example 7-5 shows an example of the **show config** command output. In this example, the first MAC address shown for module 1 is 00-04-0b-90-b5-00.	**show module**
Add an entry in the BOOTP configuration file (usually */usr/etc/bootptab*) for each Catalyst 5000 series switch. Press Return after each entry to create a blank line between each entry. In the example in Example 7-6, *ht* is hardware type, *ha* is hardware address (use the first address in the MAC address range), *sm* is the network subnet mask, and *ip* is IP address.	None

Example 7-5 *show module Command Example*

```
Console> (enable) show module
Mod Module-Name     Ports  Model    Serial-Num Hw     Fw     Sw    Status
--- --------------- ------ -------- ---------- ------ ------ ----- ------
1                   2      WS-X5009 000102691  1.40   1.12   1.12  ok
2                   24     WS-X5010 000095702  1.302  1.12   1.12  ok
3                   24     WS-X5010 000124907  1.304  1.12   1.12  ok
Mod MAC-Address(es)
--- ----------------------------------------
1   00-40-0b-90-b5-00 thru 00-40-0b-90-b7-ff
2   00-40-0b-30-04-f8 thru 00-40-0b-30-05-0f
3   00-40-0b-30-04-08 thru 00-40-0b-30-04-1f
Console> (enable)
```

Example 7-6 *BOOTP Tab File on a Sun Workstation Example*

```
catalyst-1:\

ht=ether:\

ha=0040b90b500:\

sm=255.255.255.0:\

ip=197.22.74.223
```

Configuring SNMP Management

Simple Network Management Protocol (SNMP), an application-layer protocol, facilitates the exchange of management information bases (MIBs) between network devices. SNMP community strings authenticate access to the MIB and function as embedded passwords.

For an SNMP message to be processed, the community string must match one of following three community-string modes configured in the switch:

- *Read-only*—This mode gives read access to all objects in the MIB except the community strings, but it does not allow write access.

- *Read-write*—This mode gives read and write access to all objects in the MIB, but it doesn't allow access to the community strings.

- *Read-write all*—This mode gives read and write access to all objects in the MIB, including the community strings.

The switch sends a trap to the receiver (such as an SNMP manager or workstation) under the following conditions:

- When a port or module goes up or down

- When temperature limitations are exceeded

- When spanning-tree topology changes occur

- When authentication failures occur

- When power supply errors occur

The **set snmp trap** command enters the IP address of the receiving station into the trap receiver table, which can hold up to 10 addresses. When you enter addresses in the table, you must specify the community string that will appear in the trap message. You can control whether the switch issues a trap by using the **set snmp trap enable** or **set snmp trap disable** command.

To configure the switch to be managed using an SNMP network management workstation, perform the following steps:

Task	Command
Configure the SNMP community strings. See Example 7-7 for an example.	**set snmp community read-only | read-write | read-write-all** *community_string*
Assign a trap receiver address and community. If you enter incorrect information, use the **clear snmp trap** command to delete the entry. Then re-enter the **set snmp trap** command again.	**set snmp trap** *rcvr_address rcvr_community*
If desired, configure the switch so that it issues an authentication trap.	**set snmp trap enable**
Check the SNMP settings using the **show snmp** command. See Example 7-8 for an example.	**show snmp**

Example 7-7 *set snmp* *Command Example*

```
Console> (enable) set snmp community read-only public
SNMP read-only community string set.
Console> (enable) set snmp community read-write private
SNMP read-write community string set.
Console> (enable) set snmp community read-write-all secret
SNMP read-write-all community string set.
To enable RMON on the Catalyst please use the following command:
Console> (enable) set snmp rmon enable
SNMP RMON support enabled.
Console> (enable) set snmp
Set snmp commands:

-----------------------------------------------------------------
set snmp community      Set SNMP community string
set snmp help           Show this message
set snmp rmon           Set SNMP RMON
set snmp trap           Set SNMP trap information
Console> (enable) set snmp trap
Usage:
set snmp trap <enable|disable> [all|module|chassis|bridge|repeater|auth|vtp]
set snmp trap <rcvr_address> <rcvr_community>
    (rcvr_address is ipalias or IP address, rcvr_community is string)
Console> (enable) set snmp trap enable all
All SNMP traps enabled.
Console> (enable)
```

Example 7-8 *show snmp* *Command Example*

```
Console> show snmp
RMON: Enabled
Traps Enabled: Chassis
Port Traps Enabled: None
Community-Access      Community-String
----------------      --------------------
read-only             public
Trap-Rec-Address      Trap-Rec-Community
----------------      --------------------
192.122.173.42        public
Console>
```

Setting Up Remote Monitoring

To configure the switch for Remote Monitoring (RMON) perform the following steps:

Task	Command
Activate SNMP remote monitoring support. See Example 7-9 for an example.	**set snmp rmon enable**
Check the SNMP settings using the **show snmp** command. Refer to Example 7-10 for an example.	**show snmp**

NOTE   For a detailed explanation of the RMON feature, refer to the section "Setting Up Remote Monitoring (RMON)."

Example 7-9 *set snmp rmon Command Example*

```
Console> (enable) set snmp rmon enable
SNMP RMON support enabled.
```

Example 7-10 *show snmp Command Example*

```
Console> show snmp
RMON: Enabled
Traps Enabled: Chassis
Port Traps Enabled: None
Community-Access      Community-String
----------------      -------------------
read-only             public
Trap-Rec-Address      Trap-Rec-Community
----------------      -------------------
192.122.173.42        public
Console>
```

Setting Virtual LANs

Virtual LANs (VLANs) enable ports on the same or different switches to be grouped so that traffic is confined to members of that group only. This feature restricts broadcast, unicast, and multicast traffic (flooding) to only ports included in a certain VLAN. You can set up VLANs for an entire management domain from a single Catalyst 5000 series switch. A maximum of 250 VLANs can be active at any time.

Setting up VLANs for a management domain requires two tasks, as follows:

- Creating VLANs in a management domain
- Grouping switch ports to VLANs

Creating VLANs in a Management Domain

The **set vtp** and **set vlan** commands use Virtual Trunk Protocol (VTP) to set up VLANs across an entire management domain. The default configuration has all switched Ethernet ports and Ethernet repeater ports grouped as VLAN 1.

By default, Catalyst 5000 switches are in a no-management domain state. They remain in this state until they are configured with a management domain or receive an advertisement for a domain. If a switch receives an advertisement, it inherits the management domain name and configuration revision number; it ignores advertisements with a different management domain or a smaller configuration revision number and checks all received advertisements with the same domain for consistency. While a Catalyst 5000 series switch is in the no-management domain state, it is a VTP server that learns from received advertisements.

The **set vtp** command sets up the management domain. It establishes a management domain name, the VLAN trunk protocol mode of operation (server, client, or transparent), the interval between VLAN advertisements, and the password value. No default domain name exists (the value is set to null). The default advertisement interval is 5 minutes. The default VLAN trunk protocol mode of operation is set to server.

By default, management domains are set to non-secure mode without a password; adding a password sets the management domain to secure mode. A password must be configured on each Catalyst 5000 series switch in the management domain to use secure mode.

CAUTION   A management domain does not function properly if the management domain password is not assigned from each Catalyst 5000 series switch in the domain.

The **set vlan** command uses the following parameters to create a VLAN in the management domain:

- The VLAN number
- A VLAN name
- The VLAN type (Ethernet, FDDI, Token Ring, FDDI NET, or TR NET)
- The maximum transmission unit (packet size, in bytes) that the VLAN can use
- A security association identifier (SAID)
- The state of the VLAN (active or suspended)
- The ring number for FDDI and Token Ring VLANs
- A bridge identification number

- A parent VLAN number

- A Spanning Tree Protocol (STP) type

- The VLAN number to use for translation when translating from one VLAN type to another

The Catalyst 5000 uses the security association identifier (SAID) parameter of the **set vlan** command to identify each VLAN. The default SAID for VLAN 1 is 100001, for VLAN 2 is 100002, for VLAN 3 is 100003, and so on. The default maximum transmission unit (MTU) is 1500 bytes. The default state is active on an 802.10 trunk.

When translating from one VLAN type (Ethernet, FDDI, Token Ring, FDDI NET, or TR NET) to another, the Catalyst 5000 series switch requires a different VLAN number for each media type.

To create a VLAN across a networking domain, perform the following steps in privileged mode:

Task	Command
Define the VLAN management domain, indicating the domain name, VLAN trunk protocol mode of operation, interval between VLAN advertisements, and password value. Example 7-11 shows an example of the **set vtp** command.	**set vtp** [**domain** *name*] [**mode** *mode*] [**interval** *interval*] [**passwd** *passwd*]
Verify that the VLAN management domain configuration is correct. Example 7-12 shows a sample display of the **show vtp domain** command.	**show vtp domain**
Define the VLAN, indicating the parameters described previously: VLAN number, name, type, maximum transmission unit, SAID, state, ring number, bridge identification number, and number to indicate whether source routing should be set to transparent or bridging. A maximum of 250 VLANs can be active at any time. Example 7-13 shows an example of the **set vlan** command. Figure 7-2 shows a diagram of the established VLANs, illustrating how VTP can traverse trunk connections using the ISL and 802.10 protocols and ATM LAN emulation (LANE). In Example 7-14, Ethernet VLAN 1 is translated to FDDI VLAN 4 on the FDDI module, Ethernet VLAN 2 is translated to FDDI VLAN 5, and so on.	**set vlan** *vlan_num* [**name** *name*] [**type** *type*] [**mtu** *mtu*] [**said** *said*] [**state** *state*] [**ring** *ring_number*] [**bridge** *bridge_number*] [**parent** *vlan_num*] [**stp** *stp_type*] [**translation** *vlan_num*]
Verify that the VLAN configuration is correct. Example 7-14 shows a sample display of the **show vlan** command.	**show vlan**

Example 7-11 *set vtp Command Example*

```
Console (enable) set vtp
Usage:
set vtp [domain <name>][mode <mode>][interval <interval>]
[passwd <passwd>]
(name: 1-32 characters, mode = (client, server, transparent),
interval = 120-600 sec, passwd : 0-64 characters)
Console> (enable) set vtp domain engineering mode client interval 160
VTP: domain engineering modified
Console> (enable)
```

Example 7-12 *show vtp domain Command Example*

```
Console> show vtp domain
Domain Name                        Domain Index VTP Version Local Mode
-----------------------------      ------------ ----------- -----------
engineering                             1            1          client
Last Updater    Vlan-count Max-vlan-storage Config Revision Notifications
--------------  ---------- ---------------- --------------- -------------
172.20.25.130   5          256                    0             disabled
```

Example 7-13 *set vlan Command Example*

```
Console> (enable) set vlan
Usage:
set vlan <vlan_num> <mod/ports...>
set vlan <vlan_num> [name <name>][type <type>][mtu <mtu>][said <said>]
          [state <state>] [ring <ring_number>]
          [bridge <bridge_number>] [parent <vlan_num>]
          [stp <stp_type>] [translation <vlan_num>]
          (An example of mod/ports is 1/1,2/1-12,3/1-2,4/1-12
           type = (ethernet, fddi, token_ring, fddi_net, tr_net)
           name = 1..32 characters, status = (active, suspend)
           vlan_num = 1..1005)
Console> (enable) set vlan 3 name engineering type ethernet
VTP: vlan addition successful
Console> (enable)
```

Figure 7-2   *VLAN Configuration across a Management Domain*

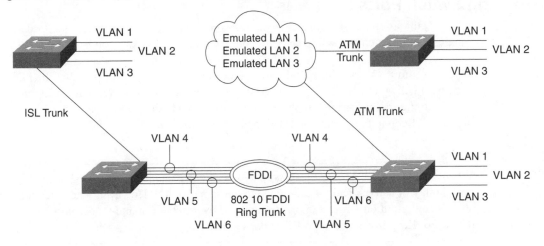

Example 7-14 *show vlan Command Display Sample*

```
Console> (enable) show vlan

VLAN Name                         Type  Status    Mod/Ports
---- ------------------------     ----- --------- ----------------
1    default                      enet  active    2/1-24
                                                  3/1-12
                                                  4/13-48
3    vlan3                        enet  active
55   vlan55                       enet  active
66   vlan66                       fddi  active
88   vlan88                       tring active
99   vlan99                       fddi  active
1002 fddi-default                 fddi  active
1003 token-ring-default           tring active
1004 fddinet-default              fdnet active
1005 trnet-default                trnet active
VLAN SAID       MTU   RingNo BridgeNo StpNo Parent Trans1 Trans2
---- ---------- ----- ------ -------- ----- ------ ------ ------
1    100001     1500  0      0        0     0      0      0
3    100003     1500  0      0        0     0      0      0
55   100055     1500  0      0        0     0      0      0
66   100066     4500  5000   0        0     5000   0      0
88   100088     1500  0      0        0     0      0      0
99   100099     1500  0      0        0     0      0      0
1002 101002     4500  0      0        0     0      1      1003
1003 101003     4500  0      0        0     0      1      1002
1004 101004     4500  0      1004     0     0      0      0
1005 101005     4500  0      1005     0     0      0      0
```

Grouping Switch Ports to VLANs

A VLAN that is created in a management domain remains unused until it is mapped to Catalyst 5000 switch ports. The **set vlan** command maps VLANs to ports.

When assigning a VLAN for FDDI ports, you can designate port 1 or port 2 of the FDDI port; both will automatically be assigned to the same VLAN. However, when viewing the VLAN configuration—for example, using the **show port** command—only port 1 is displayed. Keep in mind that port 2 belongs to the same VLAN.

NOTE   When assigning a VLAN for FDDI ports, you can designate port 1 or port 2 of the FDDI port; both will automatically be assigned to the same VLAN. However, when viewing the VLAN configuration—for example, using the **show port** command—only port 1 is displayed. Keep in mind that port 2 belongs to the same VLAN.

The default configuration has all Ethernet ports on VLAN 1. However, you can enter groups of ports as individual entries, as in 2/1,3/3,3/4,3/5. You can also use a hyphenated format, such as 2/1,3/3-5.

To create a VLAN, perform the following steps in privileged mode:

Task	Command
Define the VLAN and indicate the included ports. Example 7-15 shows an example of the **set vlan** command. Example 7-16 shows a diagram of the established VLANs. In the example in Example 7-16, VLAN 10, the engineering department, includes module 2, Ethernet ports 1 through 4. VLAN 20, the accounting department, includes module 2, Ethernet ports 5 through 24. The accounting and engineering departments are totally isolated from each other in this configuration.	**set vlan** *vlan_num* *mod/port*s
Verify that the VLAN configuration is correct. Example 7-16 shows a sample display of the **show vlan** command.	**show vlan**

Example 7-15   *set vlan Command Example*

```
system1> (enable) set vlan 10 2/1-4
VLAN 10 modified.
VLAN 1 modified.
VLAN    Mod/Ports
10      2/1-4
system1> (enable) set vlan 20 2/5-24
VLAN 20 modified.
VLAN 1 modified.
VLAN    Mod/Ports
20      2/5-24
```

Figure 7-3   *Local VLAN Configuration*

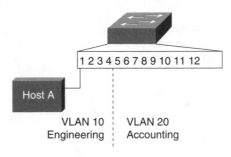

Example 7-16 *show vlan Command Display Sample*

```
system1> (enable) show vlan

VLAN    Mod/Ports
----    ----------------------------------------------------------------
1       1/1-2
10      2/1-4
20      2/5-24
system1> (enable)
```

Setting Trunks

Use the **set trunk** command to configure trunks on ports and to configure the mode for the trunk: on, off, desirable, or auto. To establish a trunk, the port on each Catalyst 5000 series switch must be configured as a trunk port. To establish trunks, perform the following steps in privileged mode:

Task	Command
Establish trunks on specific ports. Set the trunk to on to make it a trunk port, to off to make it a non-trunk port, to desirable to make it a trunk port if the port to which it is connected allows trunking, or to auto to make it a trunk port if the port to which it is connected becomes set for trunking. Example 7-17 shows an example of the **set trunk** command. Port 1 on module 1 is configured as a trunk.	**set trunk** *mod_num/port_num* [**on** | **off** | **desirable** | **auto**] [*vlans*]
Verify that the trunk configuration is correct. Example 7-18 shows a sample display of the **show trunk** command.	**show trunk**

Example 7-17 *set trunk* *Command Example*

```
Console> (enable) set trunk 1/2 5
Port 1/2 allowed vlans modified to 1-5.
Console> (enable) set trunk 1/1 desirable
Port 1/1 mode set to desirable.
Port 1/1 has become a trunk.
```

Example 7-18 *show trunk* *Command Display Sample*

```
Console> (enable) show trunk
Port      Mode        Status
-------   ---------   ------------
1/1       desirable   trunking
1/2       auto        not-trunking
3/1       auto        not-trunking
3/2       auto        not-trunking
3/3       auto        not-trunking
3/4       auto        not-trunking
3/5       auto        not-trunking
3/6       auto        not-trunking
3/7       auto        not-trunking
3/8       auto        not-trunking
3/9       auto        not-trunking
3/10      auto        not-trunking
3/11      auto        not-trunking
3/12      auto        not-trunking
Port      Vlans allowed
-------   ----------------------------------------------------------------
1/1       1-1000
1/2       1-5
3/1       1-1000
3/2       1-1000
3/3       1-1000
3/4       1-1000
3/5       1-1000
3/6       1-1000
3/7       1-1000
3/8       1-1000
3/9       1-1000
3/10      1-1000
3/11      1-1000
3/12      1-1000
Port      Vlans active
-------   ----------------------------------------------------------------
1/1       1,55
1/2       1
3/1       1
3/2       1
3/3       1
3/4       1
3/5       1
3/6       1
3/7       1
```

Example 7-18 *show trunk Command Display Sample (Continued)*

```
3/8       1
3/9       1
3/10      1
3/11      1
3/12      1
Console> (enable)
```

Testing the Configuration

After you have configured the IP address(es), test for connectivity between the switch and a host. The host can reside anywhere in your network. To test for connectivity, perform the following steps:

Task	Command
Test the configuration using the **ping** command. The **ping** command sends an echo request to the host specified in the command line.	**ping** *host*
If necessary, reset the configuration to its default values and re-enter the configuration information.	**clear config**

NOTE   The host must be connected to a port with an address on the same IP network, or you must configure a static route entry to reach the host network. Refer to the **set ip route** command in the "Command Reference" chapter of the publication *Catalyst 5000 Series Configuration Guide and Command Reference*.

For example, to test connectivity from the switch to a workstation with an IP address of 192.34.56.5, enter the command **ping 192.34.56.5**. If the switch receives a response, the following message is displayed:

```
192.34.56.5 is alive
```

NOTE   Parameters set using the command line remain set even if you disconnect power to the switch. The **clear config all** command returns all parameters to their default values.

Configuration Files and Software Image Management

The following steps outline the backing up and downloading of configuration files to the Catalyst platform:

* Backing up the configuration file
* Downloading a saved configuration
* Downloading and uploading software images

Backing Up the Configuration File

Use the **write** command in the privileged command mode to upload the current configuration to a host (typically in the *tftpboot* directory) or to display it on the terminal.

The **write terminal** command is exactly the same as the **show config** command. The **write** *host filename* command is a shorthand version of the **write network** command.

You cannot use the **write network** command to upload software to the ATM module. The **write network** command requires a Layer 3 network address; the ATM module operates at Layer 2 and does not support Layer 3 services.

The following example shows how to upload the *system5.cfg* configuration file from the *VFR* host using the **write network** command:

```
Console> (enable) write network
IP address or name of host? VFR
Name of configuration file to write? system5.cfg
Upload configuration to system5.cfg on VFR (y/n) [y]? y
..........................................
Done. Finished Network Upload. (9003 bytes)
Following is a sample configuration file:
begin
show time
set ip alias conc7 192.133.219.207
set ip alias montreux 192.133.119.42
set ip alias cres 192.122.174.42
set prompt system5>
set password
#empty string old password
end
```

Each line contains a command, except lines that begin with "!" or "#."

Downloading a Saved Configuration

Use the **configure network** command to download a configuration file from the network and execute each command in that file.

The following example shows how to download the configuration file called *system5.cfg* from the 192.122.174.42 host:

```
Console> (enable) configure network 192.122.174.42 system5.cfg
Configure using system5.cfg from cres (y/n) [n]? y
/
Done. Finished Network Download. (446 bytes)
>> show time
Wed Feb 22 1995, 17:42:50
>> set ip alias squaw_valley 192.133.219.207
IP alias added.
>> set ip alias pensacola 192.133.219.40
IP alias added.
>> set ip alias destin 192.122.174.42
IP alias added.
>> set prompt system5>
>> set password
Enter old password:
Enter new password: toomuchfun
Retype new password: toomuchfun
Password changed.
system5> (enable)
```

Downloading and Uploading Software Images

Use the **upload** command to copy a software image from a designated module to a specified host. The Catalyst 5000 switch supports two ways to download and upload new code: TFTP network connections through any network port, and Kermit serial transfer through the EIA/TIA-232 console port. Only the first method applies to the ATM module.

The **download** command downloads code to the module's flash memory. Catalyst 5000 software will reject an image if it is not a valid image for the module. When downloading to the ATM module, the Supervisor module acts as a TFTP gateway, forwarding TFTP packets to the ATM module through an in-band interprocessor communication (IPC) method.

If a module number is not specified for either of these commands, the default is module 1, the Supervisor engine.

The following example shows a download of the *c5000_2152.cbi* file from the *buell* host to the Supervisor NMP:

```
Console> (enable) download buell c5000_2152.cbi
Download image c5000_2152.cbi from buell to module 1 FLASH (y/n) [n]? y
Done. Finished Network Download. (100604 bytes)
```

The following example shows an upload of the *fddi_223.cbi* code to the *buell* host:

```
Console> (enable) upload buell fddi_223.cbi 4
Upload Module 4 image to fddi_223.cbi on buell (y/n) [n]? y
Done. Finished network upload. (1064876 bytes)
```

Q&A

As mentioned in Chapter 1, "The Cisco LAN Switch Configuration (CLSC) Exam Overview," the questions and scenarios are more difficult than what you should experience on the actual exam. The questions do not attempt to cover more breadth or depth than the exam; however, the questions are designed to make sure you know the answers. Rather than allowing you to derive the answer from clues hidden inside the question itself, the questions will challenge your understanding and recall of the subject. Questions from the "Do I Know This Already?" quiz from the beginning of the chapter are repeated here to ensure that you have mastered the chapter's topic areas. Hopefully, these questions will help limit the number of exam questions on which you narrow your choices to two options and then guess!

1 The default IP address of sc0 is _____.

2 The default sc0 interface is assigned to VLAN _____.

3 The default gateway on Catalyst switch is set to _____.

4 The Virtual Trunking Protocol (VTP) interval is ____ minutes.

5 All trunk-capable ports are set to _____ mode for trunking.

6 SNMP community defaults are set to these parameters:

   Read-Only: _____

   Read-Write: _____

   Read-Write-All: _____

7 The command-line connection is set to _____ mode.

8 If you are connected to the command line through the console port and you enter the **slip attach** command, you will lose the console port connection.

   a. True

   b. False

9 You can configure a BOOTP server with the MAC and IP addresses of the switch.

   a. True

   b. False

10 The *read only* SNMP community string gives what access?

Source Material

Some content in this chapter is based on the following sources:

- Configuring the Software

  http://www.cisco.com/univercd/cc/td/doc/product/lan/cat5000/rel_2_1/
  c5k_ig/config.htm#17471

The objectives of the Cisco LAN Switch Configuration (CLSC) exam are taken from the Cisco web site, at the Cisco career certification and training area. The following table shows the exam objectives covered in this chapter:

Objective	Description
4	Use the command-line or menu-driven interface to configure the Catalyst series switches and their switching modules.

CHAPTER 8

Catalyst 5000 Series Switch Software

This chapter describes how to create a virtual local-area network (VLAN) and how the VLANs work.

A VLAN is a group of end stations, independent of physical location, with a common set of requirements. For example, several end stations might be grouped as a department, such as the engineering or accounting departments. If the end stations are located close to one another, they can be grouped into a LAN segment. If any of the end stations are on a different LAN segment, such as different buildings or locations, they can be grouped into a VLAN that has all the same attributes as a LAN even though the end stations are not all on the same LAN segment. The information identifying a packet as part of a specific VLAN is preserved across a Catalyst 5000 series switch connection to a router or other switch.

How to Best Use This Chapter

By taking the following steps, you can make better use of your study time:

- Keep your notes and the answers for all your work with this book in one place, for easy reference.

- Take the quiz, and write down your answers. Studies show that retention is significantly increased through writing down facts and concepts, even if you never look at the information again.

- Use the diagram in Figure 8-1 to guide you to the next step.

Figure 8-1   *How to Best Use This Chapter in Preparation for the CLSC Exam*

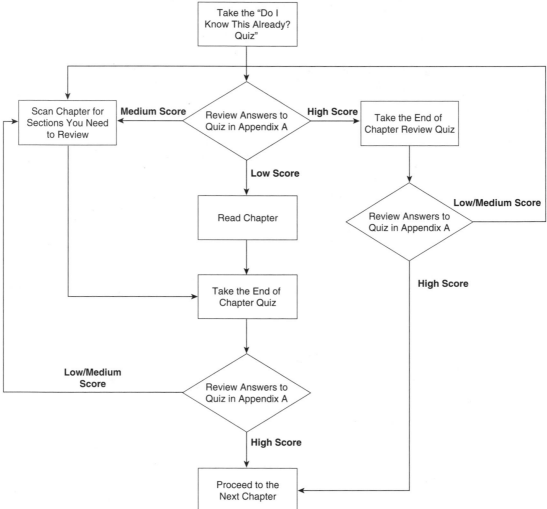

Do I Know This Already? Quiz

You can find the answers to this quiz in Appendix A, "Answers to 'Do I Know This Already?' Quizzes and Q & A Sections." Review the answers, grade your quiz, and choose an appropriate next step in this chapter based on the suggestions in Figure 8-1.

1 ISL tagging:

    a. Is performed by the NMP software.

    b. Is performed by the client stations.

    c. Is performed by the network devices or server with ISL intelligence.

    d. Is effective between Catalyst 5000 switches only.

2 VLAN Trunk Protocol:

    a. Synchronizes the configuration of two connected Catalyst 5000s from nontrunk to trunk.

    b. Supports four RMON groups on all Ethernet and Fast Ethernet ports.

    c. Advertises on Catalyst 5000 trunk ports VLAN information to other Catalyst 5000s in the same management domain.

    d. Uses a data-link protocol with a multicast destination address of 01-00-0CC-CC-CC.

3 Hardware and software-based broadcast/multicast packet suppression is available in the software release 2.2.

    a. True

    b. False

4 CGMP is:

    a. A messaging format for routers to download MAC tables to enable Layer 2 switching in the router.

    b. A protocol that provides dynamic configuration, forwarding multicast traffic to only those ports that have IP multicast clients attached.

    c. A serial protocol for communications between routers and switches.

    d. An alternative protocol that can be used instead of SNMP to manage groups of routers or switches.

5 Multicast traffic in the Catalyst 5000 switch is:

   a. Handled by the EARL learning broadcast or multicast addresses.

   b. Flooded out each port within the VLAN if the destination address is unknown.

   c. Handled by the EARL if it is dynamically programmed by the SAGE ASIC.

   d. Routed by the IGMP protocol.

6 The **set vtp** command sets up the management domain.

   a. True

   b. False

7 All switches in the same VTP domain will automatically share VLAN information using VTP if configured correctly.

   a. True

   b. False

8 An ISL trunk port must be:

   a. On the Supervisor module.

   b. An FDDI or CDDI connection.

   c. A Fast Ethernet port.

   d. Capable of maintaining several instances of the Spanning-Tree Protocol.

9 Fast EtherChannel:

   a. Uses two line modules that act as a single module.

   b. Is configured as separate instances of spanning tree per link.

   c. Treats two links as a single spanning tree.

   d. Uses Gigabit Ethernet.

10 To verify that the VLAN configuration is correct, enter the _____ command.

   a. show vtp

   b. show vlan trunk

   c. show vlan

   d. show domain

Using the answer key in Appendix A, grade your answers.

- **5 or less correct**—Read this chapter.

- **6, 7, or 8 correct**—Review this chapter, looking at the charts and diagrams that summarize most of the concepts and facts in this chapter.

- **9 or more correct**—If you want more review on these topics, skip to the Q&A section at the end of this chapter. If you do not want more review on these topics, skip this chapter.

Foundation Topics

Creating a VLAN Across a Domain

CLSC Objectives Covered in This Section

4	Use the command-line or menu-driven interface to configure the Catalyst series switches and their switching modules.

To define the VLAN, indicate the VLAN number, name, type, maximum transmission unit, security association identifier (SAID), state, ring number, bridge identification number, and number to indicate whether source routing should be set to transparent or bridging. For more information on the commands for creating VLANs, refer to the *Catalyst 5000 Series Command Reference* publication.

Procedure

To create a VLAN across a networking domain, perform these steps in privileged mode:

Task		Command
Step 1	Define the VLAN management domain.	**set vtp** [**domain** *name*] [**mode** *mode*] [**passwd** *passwd*] [**pruning** {**enable** | **disable**}] [**v2** {**enable** | **disable**}]
Step 2	Define the VLAN.	**set vlan** *vlan_num* [**name** *name*] [**type** *type*] [**state** *state*] [**said** *said*] [**mtu** *mtu*] [**ring** *ring_number*] [**bridge** *bridge_number*] [**parent** *vlan_num*] [**mode** *bridge_mode*] [**stp** *stp_type*] [**translation** *vlan_num*] [**backupcrf** {**off** | **on**}] [**aremaxhop** *hopcount*] [**stemaxhop** *hopcount*]

Verification

To verify that the VLAN management domain configuration is correct, enter the **show vtp domain** command. After entering this command, you see the display shown in Example 8-1.

Example 8-1 Output from the *show vtp domain* command

```
Console> (enable) show vtp domain
Domain Name                      Domain Index VTP Version Local Mode  Password
-------------------------------- ------------ ----------- ----------- ----------
Engineering                      1            2           server      -
Vlan-count Max-vlan-storage Config Revision Notifications
---------- ---------------- --------------- -------------
16         1023             0               enabled
Last Updater    V2 Mode    Pruning   PruneEligible on Vlans
--------------- ---------- --------- ----------------------
172.20.52.10    disabled   enabled   2-1000
c5k_1> (enable)
```

Verification

To verify that the VLAN configuration is correct, enter the **show vlan** command.

Grouping Switch Ports to VLANs

A VLAN created in a management domain remains unused until it is mapped to Catalyst 5000 series switch ports. The **set vlan** command maps VLANs to ports. The default configuration has all switched Ethernet ports on VLAN 1. However, you can enter groups of ports as individual entries—for example, 2/1, 3/3, 3/4, 3/5. You can also use a hyphenated format—for example, 2/1, 3/3-5. Figure 8-2 shows a local VLAN configuration that groups switch ports into VLAN 10 and VLAN 20.

Figure 8-2   *Local VLAN Configuration*

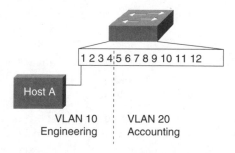

Procedure

To create a VLAN, perform the following task in privileged mode:

Task	Command
Define the VLAN and indicate the included ports.	**set vlan** *vlan_num mod_num/port_num*

NOTE   When assigning a VLAN for Fiber Distributed Data Interface (FDDI) ports, you can designate Port 1 or Port 2 of the FDDI port; both are automatically assigned the same VLAN. However, if you view the VLAN configuration by entering the **show port** command, only Port 1 is displayed. Recall that Port 2 belongs to the same VLAN.

After entering the **set vlan** command, you see this display:

```
system1> (enable) set vlan 10 2/1-4
VLAN 10 modified.
VLAN 1 modified.
VLAN    Mod/Ports
10      2/1-4
system1> (enable) set vlan 20 2/5-12
VLAN 20 modified.
VLAN 1 modified.
VLAN    Mod/Ports
2/5-12
```

Verification

To verify that the VLAN configuration is correct, enter the **show vlan** command.

Configuring VLAN Trunks

A trunk physically links two Catalyst 5000 series switches or Catalyst 5000 series switches and routers. Trunks carry the traffic of multiple VLANs and enable you to extend VLANs from one Catalyst 5000 switch to another.

Enter the **set trunk** command to configure trunks on ports or to configure the mode for the trunk: on, off, desirable, or auto. Set the trunk to on to make the port a trunk port, and set the trunk to off to make the port a nontrunk port. Set the trunk to desirable to make the port a trunk port if the port to which it is connecting enables trunking. Set the trunk to auto to make the port a trunk port if the port to which it is connected becomes set for trunking. Port 1 on module 1 is configured as a trunk.

NOTE   Catalyst 5000 series switches ship with trunking-capable ports in nontrunking mode and DISL in the auto state. In this state, if a port sees a DISL ON or a DISL DESIRED frame, it will transition into trunking mode. DISL is a point-to-point protocol, but some internetworking devices may forward DISL frames. To avoid problems associated with loss of connectivity—which may be caused by the Catalyst 5000 series switch acting on these forwarded frames—you should do two things: 1) Use the **set trunk** *mod_num/port_num* **off** command to configure trunk-capable Catalyst 5000 series ports to off for ports connected to non-Catalyst 5000 series devices where trunking is not currently being used. 2) When manually enabling trunking on a link to a Cisco router, use the **set trunk** *mod_num/ port_num* **nonegotiate** command. The **nonegotiate** parameter, available in Catalyst 5000 series software release 2.4(3) and later, transitions a link into ISL trunking without sending DISL frames.

To establish a trunk, you must configure the port on each Catalyst 5000 series switch as a trunk port. For more information, refer to the *Catalyst 5000 Series Command Reference* publication.

Procedure

To establish trunks, perform these steps in privileged mode:

Task	Command
Step 1 Establish trunks on specific ports.	**set trunk** *mod_num/port_num* [**on** | **off** | **desirable** | **auto** | **nonegotiate**] [*vlans*]
Step 2 Verify that the trunk configuration is correct.	**show trunk**

After entering the **set trunk** command, you see the following display:

```
Console> (enable) set trunk 1/2 5
Port 1/2 allowed vlans modified to 1-5.
Console> (enable) set trunk 1/1 desirable
Port 1/1 mode set to desirable.
Port 1/1 has become a trunk.
```

Verification

To verify the VLAN trunk configuration, enter the **show trunk** command.

How VLAN Trunks Work

With VLAN trunks, you can connect switches to each other and to routers via high-speed interfaces. The Catalyst 5000 series switch can multiplex up to 1000 VLANs between switches and routers by using Inter-Switch Link (ISL) on Fast Ethernet, LAN emulation on Asynchronous Transfer Mode (ATM), or 802.10 on FDDI. You can use any combination of these trunk technologies to form enterprise-wide VLANs and choose between low-cost copper and long-distance fiber connections for your trunks.

Load sharing enables VLAN traffic on parallel Fast Ethernet ISL trunks to split between multiple trunks. By setting Spanning-Tree Protocol parameters on a VLAN basis, you can define which VLANs have priority access to a trunk and which use the trunk as a backup when another trunk fails.

In Spanning-Tree Protocol, low integer values have the highest priority. Therefore, when you assign spanning-tree port priorities lower than the default value of 32 to VLANs, the traffic of those VLANs travels on the trunk with the lowest integer value. You must set the spanning-tree port priority to the same value at both ends of each trunk on each Catalyst 5000 series switch.

Figure 8-3 illustrates two trunks that connect to the ports of Supervisor engine modules on two Catalyst 5000 series switches. The port cost of carrying VLAN traffic across these trunks is equal.

- VLANs 8 through 10 are assigned a port priority of 1 on trunk 1.

- VLANs 3 through 6 retain the default port priority of 32 on trunk 1.

- VLANs 3 through 6 are assigned a port priority of 1 on trunk 2.

- VLANs 8 through 10 retain the default port priority of 32 on trunk 2.

This splits VLAN traffic between the two trunks and increases the throughput capacity and fault tolerance between Catalyst 5000 series switches; trunk 1 carries traffic for VLANs 8 through 10, and trunk 2 carries traffic for VLANs 3 through 6. If either trunk fails, the remaining trunk carries the traffic for all the VLANs.

CAUTION   The port cost of a VLAN must be equal on all parallel trunks when setting port priority for load sharing.

Figure 8-3   *Spanning-Tree Load-Sharing VLAN Trunks*

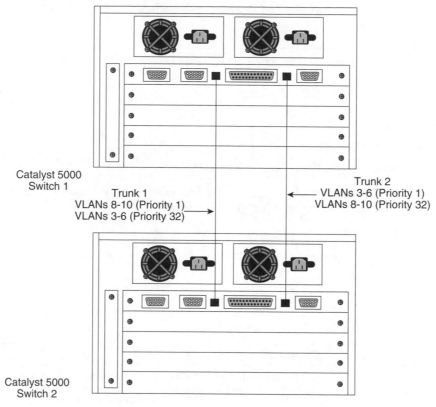

Catalyst 5000
Switch 1

Trunk 1
VLANs 8-10 (Priority 1)
VLANs 3-6 (Priority 32)

Trunk 2
VLANs 3-6 (Priority 1)
VLANs 8-10 (Priority 32)

Catalyst 5000
Switch 2

Configuring VLAN Trunk Protocol

The material presented here is intended to help the reader understand VLAN Trunk
Protocol configuration; however, it is not directly related to one of the objectives.

VLAN Trunk Protocol (VTP) is a Layer 2 messaging protocol that maintains VLAN
configuration consistency throughout the network. VTP manages the addition, deletion, and
renaming of VLANs at the system level. This protocol enables you to manage VLANs on
a network-wide basis and make central changes that are automatically communicated to all
the other switches in the network without requiring manual intervention at each switch.
In addition, VTP minimizes possible configuration inconsistencies that arise when
inappropriate changes are made. These inconsistencies can result in security violations
because VLANs cross-connect when duplicate names are used and internally disconnect
when VLANs are incorrectly mapped between one LAN type and another.

VTP is disabled by default on the Catalyst 5000 series switch and must be explicitly
enabled. VTP works only with the Catalyst 5000 series Supervisor engine software release

2.1 or later and ATM software release 3.1 or later. For more information, refer to the *Catalyst 5000 Series Command Reference* publication.

NOTE   This section refers to VTP version 1, except where noted.

Prerequisites

The following prerequisites apply when configuring VTP:

- Verify that the server is in server mode.
- Verify that the server has a VTP domain so that the VTP VLAN information that is created can be sent to other VTP switches in the VTP domain.
- Verify that VTP is enabled.

Use the **show vtp domain** command to verify these prerequisites.

Procedure

To configure VTP, perform this task:

Task	Command
Define a VLAN management domain.	**set vtp** [**domain** *name*] [**mode** *mode*] [**passwd** *passwd*] [**pruning** {**enable** | **disable**}] [**v2** {**enable** | **disable**}]

After entering the **set vtp** command, you see this example display:

```
Console (enable) set vtp
Usage: set vtp [domain <name>] [mode <mode>] [passwd <passwd>]
               [pruning <enable|disable>] [v2 <enable|disable>
       (mode = client|server|transparent
        Use passwd '0' to clear vtp password)
Console> (enable) set vtp domain catbox mode client interval 160
VTP: domain catbox modified
   Console> (enable)
```

To disable VTP, enter the **set vtp domain** *domain_name* **mode transparent** command. This disables VTP from the domain but does not remove the domain from the router. Use the **clear config all** command to remove the domain from the router.

Verification

Enter these commands to verify your VTP configuration:

- To find your current mode and domain, enter the **show vtp domain** command.

- To see VLANs learned through VTP on a switch, enter the **show vlan** command.

- To see the result of VTP-activating trunks with a newly created VTP VLAN, enter the **show trunk** command.

For more information, refer to the *Catalyst 5000 Series Command Reference* publication.

VTP Version 2

Catalyst 5000 series software release 3.1 supports VTP version 2, an extension to VTP that supports Token Ring LAN switching, unrecognized Type-Length-Value (TLV) propagation, version-dependent transparent mode, and consistency checks. The following sections describe these features.

CAUTION   VTP version 1 and VTP version 2 are not interoperable on switches in the same VTP domain. See the section "Configuration Guidelines" later in this chapter for details on configuring VTP version 2.

Token Ring

VTP version 2 must be enabled to support Token Ring switching. VTP version 2 differs from VTP version 1 in the following ways:

- Two new types of Token Ring VLANs are defined: Token Ring Concentrator Relay Function (TrCRF) and Token Ring Bridge Relay Function (TrBRF).

- The name for the default TrCRF (VLAN number 1003) is changed to trcrf-default.

- The name for the default TRBTF (VLAN number 1005) is changed to trbrf-default.

- The default maximum transmission unit (MTU) for both TrCRF and TRBTF is 4472 bytes.

Table 8-1 lists and describes the supported TrCRF parameters.

Table 8-1   *Supported TrCRF Parameters*

Parameter	Description
Parent	TrCRF must be a child of a parent TrBRF. One TrCRF can have only one parent, but one TrBRF may have multiple TrCRFs. The default TrBRF can be the parent of default TrCRF only.
Ring Number	1 through 0xFFF
Bridge Mode	SRT[1] or SRB[2] (default)
ARE[3] Max. Hops	1 through 14 (default 7)
STE[4] Max. Hops	1 through 14 (default 7)
Backup CRF[5]	For the same parent TrBRF, only one child TrCRF can be the backup (default OFF).

[1] SRT = source-route transparent bridging
[2] SRB = source-route bridging
[3] ARE = All Route Explorer
[4] STE = Spanning-Tree Explorer
[5] CRF = Concentrator Relay Function

Table 8-2 lists and describes the supported TrBRF parameters.

Table 8-2   *Supported TrBRF Parameters*

Parameter	Description
Bridge Number	1 through 0xF
Spanning-Tree Protocol	Auto, IEEE, or IBM (default)

Unrecognized TLV Support

A VTP server or client will propagate configuration changes to its other trunks, even for TLVs it is not capable of parsing. The unrecognized TLV will be saved in NVRAM.

Version-Dependent Transparent Mode

In VTP version 1, the transparent mode inspects VTP messages for the domain name and version, and forwards a message only if the version and domain name match. Because only one domain is supported in Catalyst 5000 series, VTP version 2 forwards VTP messages in transparent mode, without checking the version.

Consistency Checks

In VTP version 2, VLAN consistency checks (such as VLAN names and values) are done only when new information is entered through SNMP or the CLI. These consistency checks are not done when new information is obtained from a VTP message, nor when information is read from NVRAM. If the digest on a received VTP message is correct, its information will be accepted without consistency checks.

Configuration Guidelines

VTP version 1 and VTP version 2 are not interoperable on switches in the same VTP domain. The following guidelines apply to switches within the same VTP domain:

- All switches in a VTP domain must be running the same version of VTP.

- A switch must be running software release 3.1(1) or later to be a VTP version 2-capable switch.

- If any switch in a domain is capable only of running VTP version 1, all the switches in the domain must be running VTP version 1.

- By default, VTP version 2 is disabled.

- A switch that is capable of running VTP version 2 can operate in the same domain as a switch running VTP version 1 *if* VTP version 2 remains disabled on the VTP version 2-capable switch.

- If all switches in a domain are capable of running VTP version 2, you need to enable VTP version 2 on only one switch (using the **set vtp v2 enable** command); the version number will then be propagated to the other VTP version 2-capable switches in the VTP domain.

Configuring VTP Version 2

VTP version 2 is disabled by default. You must manually enable VTP version 2 using the **set vtp v2** {**enable** | **disable**} command. After it is enabled, the configuration is updated and propagated to the other switches by a higher VTP-advertisement revision number.

NOTE	VTP implementations do not transition from version 2 to version 1 automatically. You must manually configure this transition.

To configure VTP version 2, perform these steps:

Task		Command
Step 1	Enable VTP version 2.	**set vtp v2** {**enable** | **disable**}
Step 2	Set VTP version 2 parameters.	**set vtp** [**domain** *name*] [**mode** *mode*] [**passwd** *passwd*] [**pruning** {**enable** | **disable**}] [**v2** {**enable** | **disable**}]

To verify that VTP version 2 is enabled and configured, enter the **show vtp domain** command.

How VTP Works

Using VTP, each Catalyst 5000 series switch advertises its management domain on its trunk ports, its configuration revision number, and its known VLANs and their specific parameters. A VTP domain is made up of one or more interconnected devices that share the same VTP domain name. A switch can be configured to be in one and only one VTP domain.

VTP servers and clients maintain all VLANs everywhere within the VTP domain. A VTP domain defines the boundary of the specified VLAN. Servers and clients also transmit information through trunks to other attached switches and receive updates from those trunks.

VTP servers either maintain information in nonvolatile memory or access it using Trivial File Transfer Protocol (TFTP). Using VTP servers, you can modify the global VLAN information with either the VTP Management Information Base (MIB) or the command-line interface (CLI). When VLANs are added and advertised, both servers and clients are notified that they should be prepared to receive traffic on their trunk ports. A VTP server can also instruct a switch to delete a VLAN and disable all ports assigned to it.

Advertisement frames are sent to a multicast address so that they can be received by all neighboring devices, but they are not forwarded by normal bridging procedures. All devices in the same management domain learn about any new VLANs configured in the transmitting device. Because of this process, you need to configure a new VLAN only on one device in the management domain. All other devices in the same management domain automatically learn the configured information. VTP is transmitted on all trunk connections, including ISL, 802.10, and LAN Emulation (LANE).

A new VLAN is indicated by a VTP advertisement received by a device running VTP. Devices then accept the traffic of the new VLAN and propagate it to their trunks after adding the VTP-learned VLANs to their trunks. The VTP pruning protocol (see "Configuring VTP Pruning," later in this chapter) limits the extent of this forwarding to areas of the network where the VLAN extends, based on VLAN membership resident within the switch.

Using periodic advertisements, VTP tracks configuration changes and communicates them to other switches in the network. When a new switch is added to the network, the added devices receive updates from VTP and automatically configure existing VLANs within the network. VTP also dynamically maps VLANs across multiple LAN types with unique names and internal index associations. Mapping eliminates excessive device administration required from network administrators.

VTP establishes global configuration values and distributes the following global configuration information:

- VLAN IDs (ISL)

- Emulated LAN names (ATM LAN Emulation)

- 802.10 SAID values (FDDI)

- Maximum transmission unit (MTU) size for a VLAN

- Frame format

The VTP MIB provides the Simple Network Management Protocol (SNMP) instrumentation for the VTP, which governs the reading and setting of specific VTP parameters.

Configuring VTP Pruning

VTP pruning enhances network bandwidth use by reducing unnecessary flooded traffic, which includes broadcast, multicast, unknown, and flooded unicast packets. This feature restricts flooded traffic to only those trunk links that the traffic must use to access the appropriate network devices, thus increasing available bandwidth.

By default, VTP pruning is disabled in a management domain; make sure that all devices in the management domain support VTP pruning before enabling it. VTP pruning is supported in software release 2.3 and later.

Even if enabled, VTP pruning does not take effect on a VLAN that is not pruning-eligible. By default, VLAN 1 is not pruning-eligible, but VLANs 2 through 1000 *are* pruning-eligible. To enable pruning eligibility, enter the **set vtp pruneeligible** command. To disable pruning eligibility, enter the **clear vtp pruneeligible** command. You can invoke these commands independently of the pruning mode. Pruning eligibility resides on the local device only.

You can set the **pruning enable** or **pruning disable** option at any VTP server, and propagation takes effect on all devices in the same management domain. After enabling pruning, you must assign a domain name for VTP pruning to take effect. For information on assigning a domain name, refer to the "Configuring VLAN Trunk Protocol" section earlier in this chapter.

VTP pruning takes effect several seconds after configuration. To configure VTP pruning, you must enter the **pruning enable** option of the **set vtp** command.

Procedure

To configure VTP pruning, perform these steps:

Task		Command
Step 1	Enable the VTP pruning option.	**set vtp** [**domain** *name*] [**mode** *mode*] [**passwd** *passwd*] **pruning enable** [**v2** {**enable** | **disable**}]
Step 2	Disable the VLAN pruning eligibility.	**clear vtp pruneeligible** *vlan_range*
Step 3	Enable VTP pruning eligibility.	**set vtp pruneeligible** *vlan_range*
Step 4	Disable the VTP pruning option.	**set vtp** [**domain** *name*] [**mode** *mode*] [**passwd** *passwd*] **pruning disable** [**v2** {**enable** | **disable**}]

- The **pruning enable** option of the **set vtp** command enables pruning in the entire management domain and asks for confirmation.

- The **pruning disable** option of the **set vtp** command disables pruning in the entire management domain and asks for confirmation.

- The **clear vtp pruneeligible** command turns off the VLAN pruning eligibility for the device only. For example, after entering this command for VLANs 2 and 3, VLANs 6 through 8, and VLANs 100 through 200, you see the following display:

```
Console> (enable) clear vtp pruneeligible 2,3,6-8,100-200
```

As a result, VLANs 1 through 3, 6 through 8, and 100 through 200 will not be pruned on this device.

- The **set vtp pruneeligible** command configures VLAN pruning eligibility for the device only. For example, after entering the **set vtp pruneeligible** command for VLANs 120 and 150, you see the following display:

```
Console> (enable) set vtp pruneeligible 120,150
```

This command specifies that VLANs 120 and 150 are eligible for pruning. It also displays all pruning-eligible VLANs.

Verification

To verify the pruning mode for the management domain, enter the **show vtp domain** command.

To show the VLAN status for specified trunk ports on the device, enter the **show trunk** command.

To display VTP statistics and VTP pruning statistics, enter the **show vtp statistics** command.

How VTP Pruning Works

VTP pruning enables you to forward traffic only on those trunks necessary for access to the appropriate network devices. (Refer to Figure 8-4 and Figure 8-5.) The Catalyst 5000 series switches are connected by trunks that also are spanning-tree forwarding paths.

Figure 8-4   *Nonoptimal Flooding Traffic Without VTP Pruning*

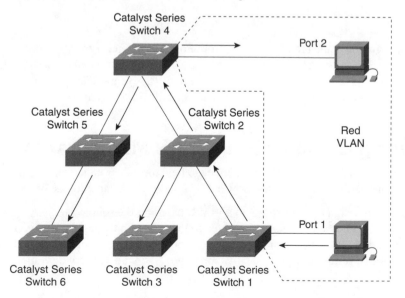

In Figure 8-4, VTP pruning is not configured. The switch fabric consists of six Catalyst 5000 series switches, shown as Switches 1 through 6. Port 1 on Switch 1 and Port 2 on Switch 4 are associated with the Red VLAN. The flooded traffic from Port 1 on Switch 1 to Port 2 on Switch 4 is forwarded to all switches, even though Switches 3, 5, and 6 have no ports on the Red VLAN.

In Figure 8-5, VTP pruning is enabled.

Figure 8-5 *Optimized Flooding Traffic with VTP Pruning*

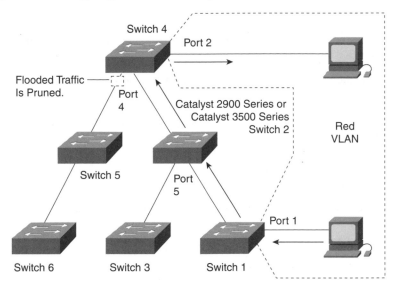

In Figure 8-5, the broadcast traffic from Port 1 on Switch 1 to Port 2 on Switch 4 is not forwarded to Switches 3, 5, and 6, because the traffic is pruned on the specified ports. Switches 3, 5, and 6 have no ports on the Red VLAN, and VTP pruning has reduced unnecessary flooding to switches not associated with the Red VLAN.

Configuring Dynamic Port VLAN Membership

The material presented here is intended to help the reader understand dynamic port VLAN membership configuration; however, it is not directly related to one of the objectives.

You can assign dynamic ports to a VLAN based on the source Media Access Control (MAC) address of the hosts connected to that port. On dynamic ports, you can move a connection from a port on one switch to a port on another switch in the network. This section describes how to set up dynamic ports, including the configuration of the VLAN

Membership Policy Server (VMPS), which has a database of MAC address-to-VLAN mappings necessary for setting up dynamic ports.

To configure dynamic port VLAN membership, complete the following tasks in this section:

- Configure the VLAN Membership Policy Server.

- Configure dynamic ports on clients.

Configuring the VLAN Membership Policy Server

The database of MAC address-to-VLAN mappings enables your workstation to be placed into the correct VLAN. You must configure the VLAN Membership Policy Server (VMPS) before configuring a port as dynamic.

Prerequisites

Before configuring the VMPS, you must perform the following tasks:

- Determine the MAC address-to-VLAN mapping by entering the **show cam** command.

- Use the information obtained by displaying the dynamic content-addressable memory (CAM) entries to build an ASCII file on your workstation or PC.

- Move the ASCII file to the TFTP server so that it can be downloaded to the Catalyst 5000 series switch.

Procedure

When you enable the VMPS, it begins to download the configuration information from the TFTP server. After a successful download, the VMPS task is started, and it accepts the VMPS requests. To enable the VMPS, use the following procedure:

Task	Command
Step 1 Configure the IP address of the TFTP server on which the ASCII file resides.	**set vmps tftpserver** *ip_addr* [*filename*]
Step 2 Enable VMPS.	**set vmps state** {**enable**	**disable**}

The **set vmps tftpserver** *ip_addr* [*filename*] command specifies the VMPS database location. The *filename* is the name of the ASCII VMPS file.

After entering the **set vmps state enable** command, you see this display:

```
Console> (enable) set vmps state enable
```

VLAN Membership Policy Server enable is in progress.

The **set vmps state enable** command sets the VMPS state in nonvolatile RAM (NVRAM) to enable. If it is previously disabled, this command initiates a background task to begin the database download. After a successful database download, this command sets the operational status to active.

You can also enter the following VMPS-related commands:

- To download VMPS database information or change the VMPS database, enter the **download vmps** command.

  Enter this command if you want to change the VMPS database or if a previous download failed.

- To disable VMPS, enter the **set vmps state disable** command.

  When you disable the VMPS, tasks are removed and all configuration information is flushed. You see the following display:

```
Console> (enable) set vmps state disable
    All the VMPS configuration information will be lost and the resources
    released on disable.
    Do you want to continue (y/n[n]): yes
    Vlan Membership Policy Server disabled.
```

  For more information, refer to the *Catalyst 5000 Series Command Reference* publication.

Verification

Enter the following commands to verify the status of port VLAN membership:

- To show current VMPS configuration information, enter the **show vmps** command. You also can enter this command to verify the operational status.

- To display MAC address-to-VLAN mapping, enter the **show vmps mac** [*mac_address*] command. You can also enter the **show vmps vlan** *vlan_name* command.

- To display ports belonging to a restricted VLAN, enter the **show vmps vlanports** *vlan_name* command.

- To display VMPS statistics, enter the **show vmps statistics** command.

- To clear VMPS statistics, enter the **clear vmps statistics** command.

For more information, refer to the *Catalyst 5000 Series Command Reference* publication.

Error Messages

Table 8-3 shows sample error messages and the actions you need to take after entering the **set vmps state** {**enable** | **disable**} command.

Table 8-3   *Error Messages for **set vmps state enable** Command*

Error Message	Recommended Action
TFTP server IP address is not configured.	Enter the **set vmps tftpserver** *ip_addr* [*filename*] command, and configure the TFTP server address.
Unable to contact the TFTP server 198.4.254.222.	Enter the **set route** command to reach the TFTP server.
File "vmps_configuration.db" not found on the TFTP server 198.4.254.222.	Create a configuration file in the file server.
Enable failed due to insufficient resources.	The Catalyst 5000 series switch does not have sufficient resources to run the database. You can fix this problem by increasing the dynamic random-access memory (DRAM).

Table 8-4 shows sample error messages and the actions you need to take after entering the **download vmps** command.

Table 8-4   *Error Messages for **download vmps** Command*

Error Message	Recommended Action
TFTP server IP address is not configured.	Enter the **set vmps tftpserver** *ip_addr* [*filename*] command, and configure the TFTP server address.
Unable to contact the TFTP server 198.4.254.222.	Enter the **set route** command to reach the TFTP server. This message is printed to the syslog server.
File "vmps_configuration.db" not found on the TFTP server 198.4.254.222.	Create a configuration file in the file server. This message is printed to the syslog server.

VMPS File

The following list describes the parameters in the configuration file. A sample VMPS configuration file is shown in the next section, "Example VMPS Configuration File."

- The VMPS domain must be defined in the file. This domain corresponds to the VTP domain name of the switch. The mode defines the VMPS to be in either open or secure mode. The fallback VLAN is assigned to the MAC addresses not defined in the database.

- MAC Addresses defines the MAC address and the corresponding VLAN table. The keyword NONE specifies that the MAC address should be denied connectivity. A port is identified by the IP address of the switch and the module/port number of the port, in the form *mod_num/port_num*.

- Port Group defines a logical group of ports. The keyword all-ports specifies all the ports in the specified switch.

- VLAN Group defines a logical group of VLANs. These logical groups define the VLAN port policies in the following section.

- VLAN Port Policies defines the ports associated with a restricted VLAN. You can configure a restricted VLAN by defining the set of dynamic ports on which it can exist.

- The VMPS parser is a line-based parser. Each entry in the file must be started on a new line. Ranges are not allowed for the port numbers.

Example VMPS Configuration File

The following example provides an overview of the syntax required to enable VMPS support on a Catalyst switch:

```
!vmps domain <domain-name>
! The VMPS domain must be defined.
!vmps mode { open|secure }
! The default mode is open.
!vmps fallback <vlan-name>
!vmps no-domain-req { allow|deny }
!
! The default value is allow.
vmps domain WBU
vmps mode open
vmps fallback default
vmps no-domain-req deny
!
!
!MAC Addresses
!
vmps-mac-addrs
!
```

```
! address <addr> vlan-name <vlan_name>
!
address 0012.2233.4455 vlan-name hardware
address 0000.6509.a080 vlan-name hardware
address aabb.ccdd.eeff vlan-name Green
address 1223.5678.9abc vlan-name ExecStaff
address fedc.ba98.7654 vlan-name --NONE--
address fedc.ba23.1245 vlan-name Purple
!
!
!Port Groups
!
!vmps-port-group <group-name>
! device <device-id> { port <port-name>|all-ports }
!
vmps-port-group WiringCloset1
 device 198.92.30.32 port 3/2
 device 172.20.26.141 port 2/8
vmps-port-group "Executive Row"
 device 198.4.254.222 port 1/2
 device 198.4.254.222 port 1/3
 device 198.4.254.223 all-ports
!
!
!VLAN groups
!
!vmps-vlan-group <group-name>
! vlan-name <vlan-name>
!
vmps-vlan-group Engineering
vlan-name hardware
vlan-name software
!
!
!VLAN port Policies
!
!vmps-port-policies {vlan-name <vlan_name>|vlan-group <group-name> }
! { port-group <group-name>|device <device-id> port <port-name> }
!
vmps-port-policies vlan-group Engineering
 port-group WiringCloset1
vmps-port-policies vlan-name Green
 device 198.92.30.32 port 4/8
vmps-port-policies vlan-name Purple
 device 198.4.254.22 port 1/2
 port-group "Executive Row"
```

How the VMPS Works

After you enable VMPS by entering the **set vmps state** {**enable** | **disable**} command, the configuration information is downloaded from a TFTP server, and the VMPS begins to accept requests from clients. Upon subsequent resets of the Catalyst 5000 series switch, the configuration information is downloaded automatically from a TFTP server, and the VMPS is enabled.

The VMPS opens a User Datagram Protocol (UDP) socket to communicate with clients and listen to client requests. Upon receiving a valid request from a client, the VMPS searches its database for a MAC address-to-VLAN mapping. If the assigned VLAN is restricted to a group of ports, the VMPS verifies the requesting port against this group. If the VLAN is legal on this port, the VLAN name is passed in the response. If the VLAN is illegal on that port and the VMPS is not in secure mode, it sends an *access denied* response. If the VMPS is in secure mode, it sends a *port shutdown* response.

If the VLAN from the table does not match the current VLAN on the port and there are active hosts on the port, the VMPS sends an *access denied* or a *port shutdown* response, based on the secure mode of the VMPS.

You can configure a fallback VLAN name into the VMPS. If the requested MAC address is not in the table, the VMPS sends the fallback VLAN name in response. If you do not configure a fallback VLAN and the MAC address does not exist in the table, the VMPS sends an *access denied* response. If the VMPS is in secure mode, it sends a *port shutdown* response. You can also make an explicit entry in the configuration table to deny access to specific MAC addresses for security reasons by specifying a NONE keyword for the VLAN name. In this case, the VMPS sends an *access denied* or *port shutdown* response.

Troubleshooting

After the VMPS successfully downloads the ASCII configuration file, it parses the file and builds a database. The VMPS outputs the statistics about the total number of lines parsed and the number of parsing errors. Set the syslog level for VMPS to 3 to obtain more information on the errors.

Configuring Dynamic Ports on Clients

To configure dynamic port VLAN membership on a client, use the procedure shown in the following sections.

Prerequisites

The following prerequisites apply when configuring dynamic ports:

- You must configure the VMPS before configuring dynamic ports.
- The VMPS must be active and accessible to the Catalyst 5000 series switch.

Procedure

To configure dynamic ports on clients, perform the following steps:

Task	Command
Step 1 Configure the VMPS IP address to be queried on the client.	**set vmps server** *ip_addr* [**primary**]
Step 2 Configure the VLAN membership assignment to a port.	**set port membership** *mod_num /port_num* {**dynamic	static**}

Verification

To verify the status of the VMPS IP address, enter the following commands.

Enter the **show vmps server** command to display the VMPS addresses after clearing a VMPS. After entering the **show vmps server** command, you see the following display:

```
Console> (enable) show vmps server
VMPS domain server       VMPS Status
----------------------------------------
192.0.0.6
192.0.0.1        primary
192.0.0.9
```

Enter the **clear vmps server** *ip_addr* command to clear the VMPS IP address.

To verify the status of port VLAN membership, enter the following commands:

- To display the port status, enter the **show port** command. If a dynamic port is shut down, its status on the display is shown as shutdown. The default port membership setting is static.

```
Console> (enable) set port membership help
Usage: set port membership < mod_num / port_num..> < dynamic|static >
Console> (enable) set port membership 3/1-3 dynamic
Ports 3/1-3 vlan assignment set to dynamic.
Spantree port fast start option enabled for ports 3/1-3.
Console> (enable) set port membership 1/2 dynamic
Trunking port 1/2 vlan assignment cannot be set to dynamic.
Console> (enable) set port membership 2/1 dynamic
ATM LANE port 2/1 vlan assignment can not be set to dynamic.
```

- To reconfirm the current dynamic port VLAN membership with VMPS, enter the **reconfirm vmps** command. The VMPS database changes are not automatically conveyed to dynamic port entities. After making a VMPS database change, you can apply the change to the dynamic port entity on a device. After entering the command, you see the following display:

```
Console> (enable) reconfirm vmps
    reconfirm process started
    Use 'show dvlan statistics' to see reconfirm status
    Console> (enable)
```

Troubleshooting

A port may shut down under the following circumstances:

- The VMPS is in secure mode, and it is illegal for the host to be on the port. The port shuts down to remove the host.

- More than 50 active hosts reside on a dynamic port.

If a dynamic port shuts down, enter the **set port enable** *mod_num/port_num* to re-enable the port.

Example Configuration Assumptions

Refer to Figure 8-5. For this example, the following assumptions apply:

- You can configure the VMPS and the client on separate switches.

- The Catalyst 5000 series Switch 1 is the primary VMPS server.

- The Catalyst 5000 series Switch 3 and Switch 10 are the secondary VMPS servers.

- End stations are connected to the following clients:

  — Catalyst 5000 series Switch 2

  — Catalyst 5000 series Switch 9

- The database file is called *Bldg-G.db*, which resides in TFTP server 172.20.22.7.

Dynamic Port Configuration

Figure 8-6 shows an example of a dynamic port configuration.

Figure 8-6   *Dynamic Port VLAN Membership Configuration*

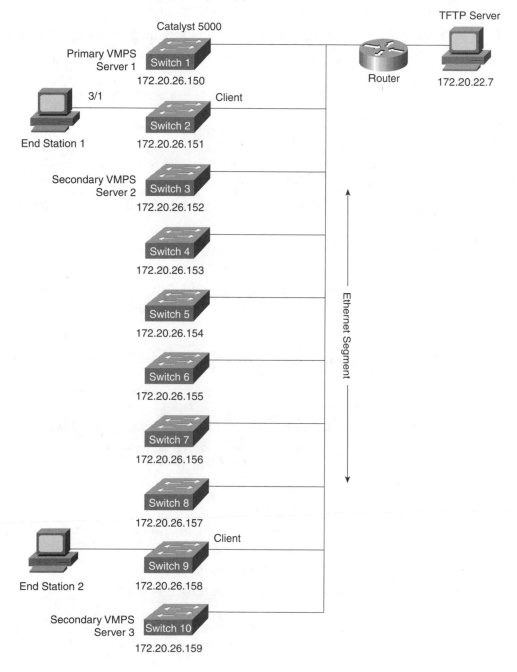

Example Configuration Procedure

Use the following procedure to configure the VMPS and dynamic ports:

1 Configure Switch 1 as the primary VMPS, by performing these tasks on Switch 1:

a. Configure the IP address of the FTP server on which the ASCII file resides, as follows:

```
Console> (enable) set vmps tftpserver 172.20.22.7 Bldg-G.db
```

b. Enable the VMPS, as follows:

```
Console> (enable) set vmps enable
```

After entering these commands, the file *Bldg-G.db* is downloaded to Switch 1, and Switch 1 becomes the VMPS server.

2 Configure dynamic ports on the clients, Switch 2, and Switch 9, by performing the following tasks:

a. Configure the primary VMPS IP address on Switch 2, as follows:

```
Console> (enable) set vmps server 172.20.26.150 primary
```

Entering this command on Switch 2 designates the VMPS switch to be queried. The primary switch option configures Switch 1 as the primary VMPS.

NOTE   Even if the local switch is to be used as the VMPS server, the IP address of the local switch should be configured as the VMPS server.

---

b. Configure the secondary VMPS IP addresses on Switch 2, as follows:

```
Console> (enable) set vmps server 172.20.26.152
Console> (enable) set vmps server 172.20.26.159
```

c. Verify the VMPS IP addresses, as follows:

```
Console> (enable) show vmps server
```

Switches 1, 3, and 10 are configured as VMPSs. Switch 1 is the primary VMPS. Switches 3 and 10 are secondary servers. All the switches are clients.

d. Configure port 3/1 on Switch 2 as dynamic, as follows:

```
Console> (enable) set port membership 3/1 dynamic
```

Suppose you connect End Station 2 on port 3/1. When End Station 2 sends a packet, Switch 2 sends a query to the primary VMPS, Switch 1. Switch 1 responds with a VLAN that is assigned to port 3/1. Because Spanning-Tree Protocol (Portfast mode) is enabled by default for dynamic ports, port 3/1 is immediately connected and enters forwarding mode. Spanning-Tree PortFast causes a spanning-tree port to enter the forwarding state immediately, bypassing the listening and learning states. You can use PortFast on switch ports connected to a single workstation or server to enable those devices to connect to the network immediately, rather than waiting for spanning tree to converge.

3 Configure dynamic ports on Switch 9 by repeating Step 2 for Switch 9.

How Dynamic Port VLAN Membership Works

Dynamic ports work in conjunction with the VMPS, which holds a database of MAC address-to-VLAN mappings.

On the current Catalyst 5000 series switch hardware platform, a dynamic (nontrunking) port can belong to only one VLAN at a time. Upon link-up, a dynamic port is isolated from its static VLAN. The source MAC address from the first packet of a new host on the dynamic port is sent to the VMPS, which provides the VLAN number to which this port must be assigned. When a new host sends a packet on a dynamic port, the packet is detected by the Network Management Processor (NMP). Using status information from the host packet, the NMP sends a query to the VMPS, and then the VMPS responds with options. For example, suppose the NMP sends a query to the VMPS, and the VMPS response is "Place port in VLAN X." The port is then placed in VLAN X if the response is valid. At this point, the host is connected to VLAN X through the switch fabric.

Multiple hosts (MAC addresses) can be active on a dynamic port, provided that they are all in the same VLAN. Upon link-down, a dynamic port is moved back to a state in which it is isolated from other VLANs, and the port ends in its initial state. Any hosts that come online through this port are detected by the NMP and then checked with the VMPS before these hosts are allowed network VLAN connectivity.

Dynamic port VLAN membership interacts with the following features:

- *Spanning–tree mode*—When a port becomes dynamic, spanning-tree portfast mode is automatically enabled for that port. Portfast-enabled dynamic ports that are moved to a new VLAN are placed in forwarding mode and participate in spanning-tree mode. Automatic enabling of spanning-tree mode enables you to connect to the network quickly. In addition, spanning-tree mode prevents applications on the host from timing out and entering loops caused by incorrect configurations. If desired, you can disable spanning-tree portfast mode on a dynamic port.

- *Static ports*—A host can move from a dynamic port to a static port on the same VLAN. When a host moves from a static port to an operational dynamic port on the same VLAN in less than 5 minutes, it immediately connects to that VLAN. When the NMP detects this event at a later time, it checks with the VMPS about the legality of the specific host on the dynamic port.

- *Static secure ports*—Static secure ports cannot become dynamic ports. You must turn off security on the static secure port before it can become dynamic.

- *Trunk ports*—Static ports that are trunking cannot become dynamic ports. You must first turn off trunking on the trunk port before changing it from static to dynamic.

NOTE   The management domain and the management VLAN of the client and the server must be the same.

How VLANs Work

The material presented here is intended to help the reader understand how VLANs work; however, it is not directly related to one of the objectives.

The VLANs on a Catalyst 5000 series switch simplify adding and moving end stations on a network. For example, when an end station is physically moved to a new location, its attributes can be reassigned from a network management station via SNMP or the CLI. When an end station is moved within the same VLAN, it retains its previously assigned attributes in its new location. When an end station is moved to a different VLAN, the attributes of the new VLAN are applied to the end station, according to the security levels in place.

The IP address of a Catalyst 5000 series switch supervisor engine module can be assigned to any VLAN. This mobility enables a network management station and workstations on any Catalyst 5000 VLAN to directly access another Catalyst 5000 series switch on the same VLAN without a router. Only one IP address can be assigned to a Catalyst 5000 series switch; if the IP address is reassigned to a different VLAN, the previous IP address assignment to a VLAN is invalid.

VLANs enable ports on the same or different switches to be grouped so that traffic is confined to members of that group only. This feature restricts broadcast, unicast, and multicast traffic (flooding) to ports included in only a certain VLAN. You can set up VLANs for an entire management domain from a single Catalyst 5000 series switch. A maximum of 250 VLANs can be active at any time.

Figure 8-7 shows an example of VLANs segmented into logically defined networks.

Figure 8-7   *VLANs as Logically Defined Networks*

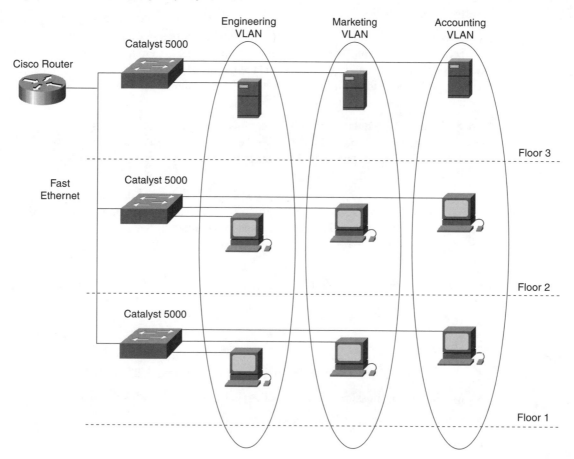

VLANs in a Management Domain

The **set vtp** and **set vlan** commands use VTP to set up VLANs across an entire management domain. The default configuration group, defined as VLAN 1, includes all switched Ethernet ports and Ethernet repeater ports.

By default, the Catalyst 5000 series switch is in the no-management domain state until it is configured with a management domain or receives an advertisement for a domain. If a switch receives an advertisement, it inherits the management domain name and configuration revision number. The switch ignores advertisements with a different management domain or an earlier configuration revision number, and checks all received advertisements with the same domain for consistency. While a Catalyst 5000 series switch is in the no-management domain state, it is a VTP server; that is, it learns from received advertisements.

The **set vtp** command sets up the management domain, including establishing the management domain name, the VTP mode of operation (server, client, or transparent), the interval between VLAN advertisements, and the password value. No default domain name exists (the value is set to null). The default advertisement interval is 5 minutes. The default VTP mode of operation is set to **server**.

By default, the management domain is set to nonsecure mode without a password; a password sets the management domain to secure mode. You must configure a password on each Catalyst 5000 series switch in the management domain when in secure mode.

CAUTION   A management domain does not function properly if the management domain password is not assigned to each Catalyst 5000 series switch in the domain.

The **set vlan** command uses the following parameters to create a VLAN in the management domain:

- VLAN number

- VLAN name

- VLAN type (Ethernet, FDDI, FDDI network entity title [NET], or TR NET)

- Maximum transmission unit (packet size, in bytes) that the VLAN can use

- Security association identifier (SAID)

- State of the VLAN (active or suspended)

- Ring number for FDDI and Token Ring VLANs

- Bridge identification number

- Parent VLAN number

- Spanning-Tree Protocol type

- VLAN number to use when translating from one VLAN type to another

The Catalyst 5000 series switch uses the SAID parameter of the **set vlan** command to identify each VLAN on an 802.10 trunk. The default SAID for VLAN 1 is 100001, for VLAN 2 is 100002, for VLAN 3 is 100003, and so on. The default MTU is 1500 bytes. The default state is active on an 802.10 trunk.

When translating from one VLAN type (Ethernet, FDDI, FDDI NET, or TR NET) to another, the Catalyst 5000 series switch requires a different VLAN number for each media type.

VLAN Components

VLANs consist of the following components:

- *Switches that logically segment connected end stations*—Switches are the entry point for end-station devices into the switched fabric and provide the intelligence to group users, ports, or logical addresses into common communities of interest. LAN switches also increase performance and dedicated bandwidth across the network.

  You can group ports and users into communities using a single switch or connected switches. By grouping ports and users together across multiple switches, VLANs can span single-building infrastructures, interconnected buildings, or campus networks. Each switch has the intelligence to make filtering and forwarding decisions by packet and to communicate this information to other switches and routers within the network.

  Frame identification or tagging is one approach for logically grouping users into administratively defined VLANs. Tagging places a unique identifier in the header of each frame as it is forwarded throughout the switch fabric. The identifier is understood and examined by each switch prior to any broadcasts or transmissions to other switches, routers, or end-station devices. When the frame exits the switch fabric, the switch removes the identifier before the frame is transmitted to the target end station. Based on rules defined by the administrator, tagging determines where the frame is to be sent or broadcast.

- *Routers that extend VLAN communications between workgroups*—Routers provide policy-based control, broadcast management, and route processing and distribution. They also provide the communication between VLANs and VLAN access to shared resources such as servers and hosts. Routers connect to other parts of the network that either are logically segmented into subnets or that require access to remote sites across wide-area links. Consolidating the overall number of physical router ports required for communication between VLANs, routers use high-speed backbone connections over Fast Ethernet, FDDI, or ATM for higher throughput between switches and routers.

- *Interoperability with previously installed LAN systems*—VLANs provide system compatibility with previously installed systems, such as shared hubs and stackable devices. While many of these devices are being replaced with newer switching technologies, previously installed concentrators still perform useful functions. With

VLANs, you can configure devices such as shared hubs as a part of the VLAN architecture and can share traffic and network resources that directly attach to switching ports with VLAN designations.

- *Transport protocols that carry VLAN traffic across shared LAN and ATM backbones*—The VLAN transport enables information exchange between interconnected switches and routers residing on the corporate backbone. Transport capabilities remove physical boundaries, increase flexibility of a VLAN solution, and provide mechanisms for interoperability between backbone system components.

  The backbone acts as the aggregation point for large volumes of traffic. It also carries end user VLAN information and identification between switches, routers, and directly attached servers. Within the backbone, high-bandwidth, high-capacity links carry the traffic throughout the enterprise. Three high-bandwidth options include Fast Ethernet, FDDI/CDDI, and ATM.

- *VLAN management*—Network management solutions offer centralized control, configuration, and traffic management functions.

VLAN Technologies

Because switches and routers directly attach to the backbone, they must be capable of transporting VLAN information and interoperating with other network components. In response to these requirements, several different transport mechanisms are used for communicating VLAN information across high-performance backbones. Among them are the LANE standard that has been approved by the ATM Forum, ISL for Fast Ethernet, and the IEEE 802.10 protocol, which provides VLAN communication across shared FDDI backbones. These different yet interoperable VLAN technologies are supported on the Catalyst 5000 series switch. Each allows a single link to carry information from multiple VLANs.

VLAN Examples

This section contains examples of VLAN configurations for ISLs on Fast Ethernet ports, multiple Catalyst 5000 series switches using Spanning-Tree Protocol, and 802.10 protocol on FDDI ports.

Inter-Switch Links on Fast Ethernet Ports

Any Fast Ethernet port can be configured as a trunk. Trunks use ISL to support multiple VLANs. An ISL trunk is like a continuation of the switching backplane—it enables the Catalyst 5000 series switch to multiplex up to 1000 VLANs between switches and routers.

The Dynamic ISL (DISL) protocol dynamically configures trunk ports between Catalyst 5000 series switches; it synchronizes two interconnected Fast Ethernet interfaces into becoming ISL trunks and minimizes VLAN trunk configuration procedures because only one end of a link must be configured as a trunk or nontrunk.

Figure 8-8 shows an example of a Fast Ethernet ISL configuration.

Figure 8-8 *Fast Ethernet ISL Configuration*

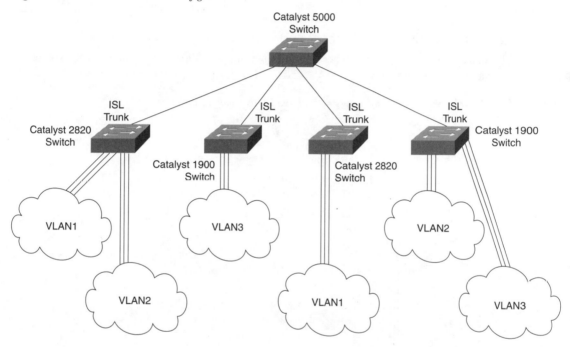

Fast EtherChannel

Fast EtherChannel is similar to the EtherChannel in the Catalyst 3000 series products. Fast EtherChannel provides an interim step to Gigabit Ethernet and treats two links as a single spanning tree. These links need to be configured in a bundle of two or four links that will enable two links on the same module to load-balance on two Fast Ethernet links. Fast EtherChannel is available on Supervisor II.

If two or more links are configured as a Fast EtherChannel, an immediate switchover to the surviving link(s) occurs if one link fails. 400 Mbps throughput can be obtained with two links configured for full-duplex; 800 Mbps throughput can be obtained with four links configured for full-duplex.

Fast EtherChannel is supported on the newer 12-port Fast Ethernet Line Module. This module enables up to six groups of two links or two groups of four links. Fast EtherChannel is available in switch-to-switch, switch-to-router, and switch-to-server implementations. A number of vendors have announced their support of the Fast EtherChannel technology. Because Fast EtherChannel utilizes the standard Fast Ethernet signaling, sufficient standards exist to ensure device interoperability. The ISL VLAN trunking protocol can carry multiple VLANs across a Fast EtherChannel.

Multiple Switch Spanning-Tree Protocol and VLAN Configuration

VLAN groups can be set up across multiple Catalyst 5000 series switches if the switches have any two ports of the same VLAN connected, as shown in Figure 8-9.

Figure 8-9 *Multiple Switch Spanning-Tree Protocol and VLAN Configuration*

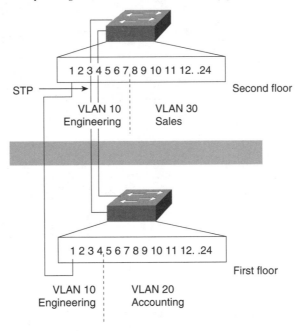

The trunks and VLANs for the Catalyst 5000 series Switch 1 on the first floor were configured as shown in Example 8-2:

Example 8-2   *Configuration of the Trunks and VLANs*

```
System1> (enable) set vtp domain abc
VTP: domain abc modified
System1> (enable) set vlan 10
VTP: vlan addition successful
System1> (enable) set vlan 10 2/1-4
VLAN 10 modified.
VLAN 1 modified.
VLAN  Mod/Ports
----  ----------------------
10    1/1-4
System1> (enable) set vlan 20
VTP: vlan addition successful
System1> (enable) set vlan 20 2/5-24
VLAN 20 modified.
VLAN 1 modified.
VLAN  Mod/Ports
----  ----------------------
20    2/5-24
System1> (enable) set trunk 1/1-2 on
Port 1/1 mode set to on.
Port 1/2 mode set to on.
System1> (enable)
Mon May 6 1996, 18:22:07  Port 1/1 and 1/2 has become trunk.
System1> (enable) show trunk
Port     Mode        Status
-------  ---------   -----------
1/1
1/2      on          trunking
Port     Vlans allowed
-------  --------------------------------------------------- ----------------
1/1      1-1000
1/2      1-1000
4/1-2    1-1000
Port     Vlans active
-------  ----------------------------------------------------------------
1/1      1
1/2      1,10,20
4/1-2    1
System1> (enable) show port
Port Name           Status      Vlan      Level  Duplex Speed Type
---- ------------   ----------  --------- ------ ------ ----- -----------
1/1                 connected   trunk     normal half   100   100BaseTX
1/2                 connected   trunk     normal half   100   100BaseTX
2/1                 notconnect  10        normal half   10    10BaseT
2/2                 notconnect  10        normal half   10    10BaseT
2/3                 notconnect  10        normal half   10    10BaseT
2/4                 connected   10        normal half   10    10BaseT
.
.
```

Example 8-2 *Configuration of the Trunks and VLANs (Continued)*

```
  .
  2/23                notconnect 20        normal half  10    10BaseT
  2/24                notconnect 20        normal half  10    10BaseT
  Port Align-Err  FCS-Err     Xmit-Err    Rcv-Err
  ----  ----------- ----------- ----------- -----------
  1/1        0           0           0           0
  1/2        0           0           0           0
  2/1        0           0           0           0
  2/2        0           0           0           0
  2/3        0           0           0           0
  2/4        0           0           0           0
  .
  .
  .
  2/22       0           0           0           0
  2/23       0           0           0           0
  2/24       0           0           0           0
  Port Single-Col Multi-Coll Late-Coll Excess-Col Carri-Sens Runts Giants
  ----  ----------- ----------- --------- ----------- ----------- ----- -------
  1/1        0           0          0          0          0        0      -
  1/2        0           0          0          0          0        0      -
  2/1        0           0          0          0          0        0      0
  2/2        0           0          0          0          0        0      0
  2/3        0           0          0          0          0        0      0
  2/4        0           0          0          0          0        0      0
  .
  .
  .
  2/22       0           0          0          0          0        0      0
  2/23       0           0          0          0          0        0      0
  2/24       0           0          0          0          0        0      0
  Port CE-State ConnState Type Neig Con Est Alm Cut Lem-Ct Lem-Rej-Ct Tl-Min
  ----  -------- --------- ---- ---- --------------- ------- ---------- ------
  Last-Time-Cleared
  -------------------------
  Mon May 6 1996, 17:59:45
```

The trunks and VLANs for the Catalyst 5000 series Switch 2 on the second floor were configured as shown in Example 8-3:

NOTE   Switch 2 is automatically configured with a trunk when the trunk is set on Switch 1. Switch 2 learns about the VLANs set on Switch 1 through VTP.

Example 8-3 *Trunks and VLANs on the Second Floor*

```
System2> (enable)
Mon May 6 1996, 16:35:47  Port 1/2 has become trunk.
System2> (enable) show trunk
Port    Mode        Status
-------  ---------   -----------
1/1     auto trunking
1/2     auto trunking
Port    Vlans allowed
-------  ---------------------------------------------------------------
1/1     1-1000
1/2     1-1000
Port    Vlans active
-------  ---------------------------------------------------------------
1/1     1,10,20,30
1/2     1,10,20,30
System2> (enable) show port
Port Name          Status      Vlan        Level  Duplex Speed Type
---- -----------   ----------  ----------  ------ ------ ----- ----------
1/1                connected   trunk       normal half   100   100BaseTX
1/2                connected   trunk       normal half   100   100BaseTX
2/1                notconnect  10          normal half   10    10BaseT
2/2                notconnect  10          normal half   10    10BaseT
2/3                notconnect  10          normal half   10    10BaseT
2/4                connected   10          normal half   10    10BaseT
.
.
.
2/21               notconnect  20          normal half   10    10BaseT
2/22               notconnect  20          normal half   10    10BaseT
2/23               notconnect  20          normal half   10    10BaseT
2/24               notconnect  20          normal half   10    10BaseT
Port Align-Err  FCS-Err    Xmit-Err    Rcv-Err
---- ----------  ---------- ----------- -----------
1/1       0          0          0           0
1/2       0          0          0           0
2/1       0          0          0           0
2/2       0          0          0           0
2/3       0          0          0           0
2/4       0          0          0           0
.
.
2/19      0          0          0           0           0         0         0
2/20      0          0          0           0           0         0         0
2/21      0          0          0           0           0         0         0
2/22      0          0          0           0           0         0         0
2/23      0          0          0           0           0         0         0
2/24      0          0          0           0           0         0         0
Last-Time-Cleared
-------------------------
Mon May 6 1996, 16:04:07
System2> (enable) show port
```

Example 8-3   *Trunks and VLANs on the Second Floor (Continued)*

```
Port Name            Status     Vlan        Level  Duplex Speed Type
---- ------------    ---------- ----------  ------ ------ ----- -----------
1/1                  connected  trunk       normal full   100   100BaseTX
1/2                  connected  trunk       normal full   100   100BaseTX
2/1                  notconnect 10          normal half   10    10BaseT
2/2                  notconnect 10          normal half   10    10BaseT
2/3                  notconnect 10          normal half   10    10BaseT
2/4                  connected  10          normal half   10    10BaseT
.
.

.
2/21                 notconnect 20          normal half     10 10BaseT
2/22                 notconnect 20          normal half     10 10BaseT
2/23                 notconnect 20          normal half     10 10BaseT
2/24                 notconnect 20          normal half     10 10BaseT
Port Align-Err  FCS-Err   Xmit-Err    Rcv-Err
---- ---------- --------- ----------- ----------
1/1      0          0          0         0
1/2      0          0          0         0
2/1      0          0          0         0
2/2      0          0          0         0
2/3      0          0          0         0
2/4      0          0          0         0
.
.

.
2/19     0          0          0         0         0         0         0
2/20     0          0          0         0         0         0         0
2/21     0          0          0         0         0         0         0
2/22     0          0          0         0         0         0         0
2/23     0          0          0         0         0         0         0
2/24     0          0          0         0         0         0         0
Last-Time-Cleared
-------------------------
Mon May 6 1996, 16:04:07
```

802.10 Protocol on FDDI Ports

VLANs can extend across an FDDI network by multiplexing switched packets over a
CDDI/FDDI interface using the 802.10 protocol. Using 802.10, Catalyst 5000 series CDDI/
FDDI interface links can operate as interswitch trunks that provide broadcast control
between configured VLANs. The 802.10 protocol encapsulates a VLAN identifier and
packet data according to the IEEE 802.10 specification. CDDI/FDDI interfaces that support
802.10 make selective forwarding decisions within a network domain based upon the
VLAN identifier.

The VLAN identifier is a user-configurable 4-byte SAID. The SAID identifies traffic as
belonging to a particular VLAN, and it determines to which VLAN each packet is switched.

Refer to Figure 8-10 for an example of configuring FDDI trunks. In this example, the SAID ensures that packets destined for VLAN 1 reach VLAN 1 only after they are transmitted across the FDDI trunks. Refer to Figure 8-11 for an example of an FDDI 802.10 VLAN network configuration.

Figure 8-10   *FDDI Trunks Configuration*

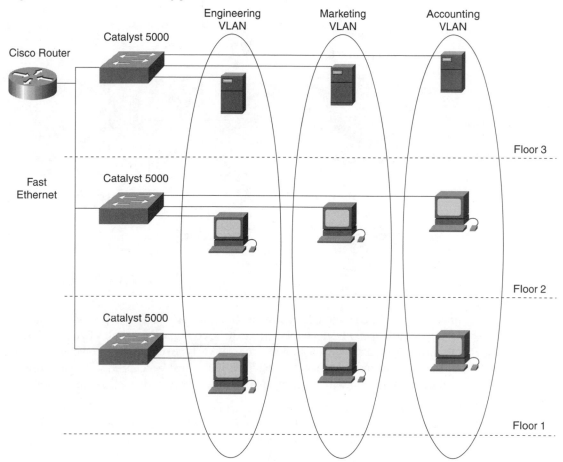

Figure 8-11 *FDDI 802.10 VLAN Network Configuration*

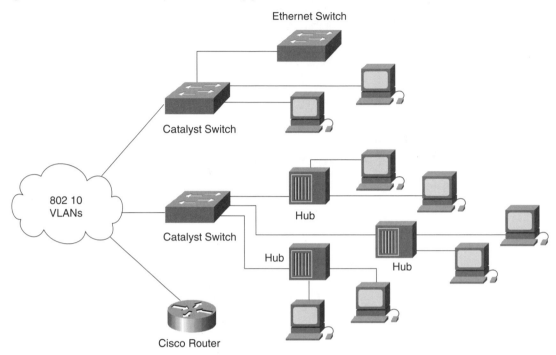

VTP provides CDDI/FDDI module configuration for 802.10-based VLANs. VTP requires a protocol type (Ethernet, FDDI, or Token Ring) to be configured for each VLAN. A VLAN can have only one type associated with it. Each VLAN type must have its own unique identifier, and translations between different identifiers must be mapped. VTP advertises VLAN translation mappings to all Catalyst 5000 series switches in a management domain.

FDDI/CDDI modules integrate switched Ethernet and Fast Ethernet LANs into the FDDI network. To map an 802.10 FDDI VLAN to an Ethernet VLAN, you must map the 802.10 VLAN SAID to an Ethernet VLAN by mapping an Ethernet VLAN to an FDDI VLAN and assigning a SAID value to the FDDI VLAN.

If a CDDI/FDDI module receives a packet containing a VLAN SAID that maps to a locally supported Ethernet VLAN on the Catalyst 5000 series switch, the CDDI/FDDI module translates the packet into Ethernet format and forwards it across the switch backplane to the Ethernet module. CDDI/FDDI modules filter the packets they receive from reaching the backplane if the VLAN SAIDs in the packets do not map to a locally supported VLAN.

Figure 8-12 illustrates the configuration for forwarding a packet from the Ethernet module Port 1 in Slot 2 to the FDDI module Port 1 in Slot 5. For this example, you would specify the translation of Ethernet VLAN 2 to FDDI VLAN 22. FDDI VLAN 22 is then automatically translated to Ethernet VLAN 2. The VLAN SAID must be identical on both FDDI modules. Because 802.10 CDDI/FDDI interface links can operate as interswitch trunks, you can configure multiple VLAN translations over a link.

Figure 8-12   *VLAN Identifiers for an FDDI 802.10 Configuration*

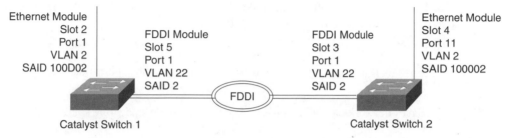

CDDI/FDDI modules also support one native (nontrunk) VLAN, which handles all non-802.10 encapsulated FDDI traffic. A translation number does not need to be configured for the native VLAN because packets that are forwarded to the native VLAN do not contain VLAN identifiers. To map an Ethernet VLAN to an FDDI native VLAN, you must configure the FDDI port to be on the Ethernet VLAN. To do this, configure the Ethernet VLAN with the module number and port number of the FDDI-native VLAN.

Configuring Multicast Services

The material presented here is intended to help the reader understand multicast services configuration; however, it is not directly related to one of the objectives.

This section describes how to configure multicast services on Catalyst 5000 series switches.

Multicast Services Overview

Interactive applications such as video conferencing, delivery of live stock quotes, and shared whiteboard applications rely on multicast traffic, both within intranets and on the Internet. Multicasting saves bandwidth by forcing the network to replicate packets only when necessary. In addition, multicasting enables hosts to dynamically join and leave groups at any time, unrestricted by the number of members in the group or by the location of the group within the network.

This section describes the following multicast services:

- Cisco Group Management Protocol (CGMP)

- Broadcast/multicast suppression

Cisco Group Management Protocol

Cisco Group Management Protocol (CGMP) manages multicast traffic in Catalyst 5000 series switches by providing directed switching of IP multicast traffic within a network at rates greater than 1 million packets per second.

CGMP requires only a software upgrade on the Catalyst 5000 series switch and at least one Cisco router running software release 11.1(3) or later.

CGMP offers the following benefits:

- Enables IP multicast packets to be switched only to those ports that have IP multicast clients.

- Saves network bandwidth on user segments by not propagating spurious IP multicast traffic.

- Does not require changes to the end host systems.

- Does not incur the overhead of creating a separate VLAN for each multicast group in the switched network.

Prerequisites

CGMP filtering requires a network connection from the Catalyst 5000 series switch to a router running CGMP.

Procedure

By default, CGMP is disabled, and no multicast routers are configured.

To configure CGMP, perform the following steps:

Task	Command
Step 1 Enable CGMP on a device.	**set cgmp enable**
Step 2 Configure multicast router ports.	**set multicast router** *mod_num/port_num*

In the **set multicast router** command, *mod_num* is the number of the module, and *port_num* is the number of the port on that module to which the CGMP-capable router is attached.

NOTE   When CGMP is enabled, it automatically identifies the ports to which the CGMP-capable router is attached. The **set multicast router** command enables you to statically configure multicast router ports.

CGMP fast-leave-processing enables the switch to detect IGMP V.2 leave messages sent to the all-routers multicast address by hosts on any of the Supervisor engine module ports. When the Supervisor engine module receives a leave message, it starts a query-response timer. If this timer expires before a CGMP join message is received, the port is pruned from the multicast tree for the multicast group specified in the original leave message. Fast-leave processing ensures optimal bandwidth management for all hosts on a switched network, even when multiple multicast groups are in use simultaneously. To enable CGMP leave processing, enter the following command:

Task	Command
Enable CGMP leave processing on a device.	**set cgmp leave enable**

To disable CGMP leave processing, enter the following command:

Task	Command
Disable CGMP leave processing on a device.	**set cgmp leave disable**

To disable all CGMP router ports, enter the following command:

```
console> (enable) clear multicast router all
```

To disable specific CGMP router ports, enter the following command:

```
console> (enable) clear multicast router mod_num/port_num
```

Verification

To verify the CGMP configuration, enter the **show multicast router**, **show multicast group**, and **show cgmp statistics** commands, as follows:

```
console> (enable) show multicast router [cgmp] [mod_num/port_num] [vlan_id]
console> (enable) show multicast group [cgmp] [mac_addr] [vlan_id]
console> (enable) show cgmp statistics [vlan_id]
```

The Examples section contains complete output for the **show multicast router**, **show multicast group**, **show cgmp leave**, and **show cgmp statistics** commands.

CGMP Configuration Examples

This section contains examples of the commands used to configure CGMP.

Enabling CGMP

To enable CGMP on the Catalyst 5000 series switch, enter the following command:

```
console> (enable) set cgmp enable
CGMP support for IP multicast enabled.
```

Assigning Ports to the Multicast Router Port List

To specify which ports have CGMP-capable routers attached—either directly or indirectly—to them, enter the following command:

```
console> (enable) set multicast router 3/1
Port 3/1 added to multicast router port list.
```

This example associates a CGMP-capable router to module 3, port 1.

Displaying CGMP Configuration on Particular Modules and Ports

To display the CGMP configuration for module 4, port 9, enter the following command:

```
console> (enable) show multicast router 4/9
CGMP enabled
Port        Vlan
------      -----------
4/9         1,5,200-203
Total Number of Entries = 1
```

This example shows that multicast router module 4, port 9, is in VLAN 1, VLAN 5, and VLANs 200 through 203.

Displaying CGMP Configuration for Ports in Particular VLANs

To display the CGMP configuration for all ports on VLAN 5, enter the following command:

```
console> (enable) show multicast router 5
CGMP enabled
Port        Vlan
------      -----------
3/1         5
4/9         5
Total Number of Entries = 2
```

This example shows that VLAN 5 contains two CGMP ports: one on module 3, port 1, and one on module 4, port 9.

Displaying Multicast Router Information

To display only the multicast router information that has been learned automatically through CGMP, enter the **show multicast router** command with the **cgmp** keyword, as follows:

```
console> (enable) show multicast router cgmp 5
CGMP enabled
Port       Vlan
------     -----------
4/9        5
```

This example shows that module 4, port 9, on VLAN 5 has been automatically configured by CGMP to be a multicast router port. By entering the cgmp keyword, you can distinguish between information that has been learned automatically through CGMP and information that has been entered manually.

Displaying Learned CGMP Information

To display only the information that has been learned automatically through CGMP, enter the **show multicast group** command with the **cgmp** keyword, as follows:

```
console> (enable) show multicast group cgmp 5
CGMP enabled
Vlan       Destination MAC        Destination Ports of VC's
------     ----------------       -------------------------
5          01-00-5E-00-00-5C      3/1, 3/9
5          01-00-5E-00-00-FF      3/7, 3/9
```

This example shows two multicast groups automatically defined for VLAN 5 (media access controller [MAC] addresses 01-00-5E-00-00-5C and 01-00-5E-00-00-FF) and the ports associated with those groups.

Displaying Multicast Group Information by MAC Address

To display information for the multicast group at MAC address 01-00-5E-00-00-5C on VLAN 5, enter the following command:

```
console> (enable) show multicast group 01-00-5E-00-00-5C 5
CGMP enabled
Vlan       Destination MAC        Destination Ports of VC's
------     ----------------       -------------------------
5          01-00-5E-00-00-5C      3/1, 3/9
```

This example shows that the multicast group at MAC address 01-00-5E-00-00-5C on VLAN 5 is associated with module 3, port 1; and module 3, port 9.

Displaying CGMP Statistics

This example shows that module 4, port 9, on VLAN 5 has been automatically configured. To display CGMP statistics for VLAN 2, enter the following command:

```
console> (enable) show cgmp statistics 2
CGMP enabled
CGMP statistics for vlan 2:
No of valid rx pkts rcvd: 20
No of invalid rx pkts rcvd: 0
No of valid join msgs rcvd: 15
No of valid leave msgs rcvd: 5
No of failures to add  to EARL: 0
No of topology notifications rcvd: 0
Console> (enable>
```

To enable CGMP leave processing and verify its status, enter the following commands:

```
Console> (enable) set cgmp leave enable
CGMP leave processing enabled.
Console> (enable)
Console> (enable) show cgmp leave
CGMP:        enabled
CGMP leave: enabled
Console> (enable)
```

To disable CGMP leave processing and verify its status, enter the following commands:

```
Console> (enable) set cgmp leave disable
CGMP leave processing disabled.
Console> (enable)
Console> (enable) show cgmp leave
CGMP:        enabled
CGMP leave: disabled
Console> (enable)
```

How CGMP Works

CGMP works with Internet Group Management Protocol (IGMP) messages to dynamically configure Catalyst 5000 series switch ports so that IP multicast traffic is forwarded only to those ports associated with IP multicast hosts.

NOTE   For information on IP multicast (including IGMP), refer to RFC 1112.

CGMP software components run on both the router and the Catalyst 5000 series switch. A CGMP-capable IP multicast router sees all IGMP packets and can inform the Catalyst 5000 series switch when specific hosts join or leave IP multicast groups. When the CGMP-capable router receives an IGMP control packet, it creates a CGMP packet that contains the request type (either join or leave), the multicast group address, and the actual MAC address of the host. The router then sends the CGMP packet to a well-known address to which all Catalyst 5000 series switches listen. When a switch receives the CGMP packet, the supervisor engine module interprets the packet and modifies the Encoded Address Recognition Logic (EARL) forwarding table automatically, without user intervention.

You can explicitly set up multicast groups by entering the **set cam static** command. User-specified multicast group settings are static, whereas multicast groups learned through CGMP are dynamic. If you specify group membership for a multicast group address, your static setting supersedes any automatic manipulation by CGMP. Multicast group membership lists can consist of both user-defined and CGMP-learned settings.

If a spanning-tree VLAN topology changes, the CGMP-learned multicast groups on the VLAN are purged and the CGMP-capable router generates new multicast group information.

If a CGMP-learned port link is disabled for any reason, CGMP removes that port from any multicast group memberships.

Joining a Multicast Group

When a host wants to join an IP multicast group, it sends an IGMP join message specifying its MAC address and which IP multicast group it wants to join. The CGMP-capable router then builds a CGMP join message and multicasts the join message to the well-known address to which the Catalyst 5000 series switches listen. Upon receipt of the join message, each Catalyst 5000 series switch searches its EARL table to determine if it contains the MAC address of the host asking to join the multicast group. If a switch finds the host's MAC address in its EARL table associating the MAC address with a nontrunking port, the switch creates a multicast forwarding entry in the EARL forwarding table. The host associated with that port then receives multicast traffic for that multicast group. In this way, the EARL automatically learns the MAC addresses and port numbers of the IP multicast hosts.

Leaving a Multicast Group

The CGMP-capable router sends periodic multicast-group queries. If a host wants to remain in a multicast group, it responds to the query from the router. In this case, the router does nothing. If a host does not want to remain in the multicast group, it does not respond to the router query. If after a number of queries, the router receives no reports from any host in a multicast group, the router sends a CGMP command to the Catalyst 5000 series switch, telling it to remove the multicast group from its forwarding tables.

NOTE   If other hosts are present in the same multicast group and they *do* respond to the multicast-group query, the router does not tell the switch to remove the group from its forwarding tables. The router does not remove a multicast group from the switch's forwarding tables until all the hosts in the group have asked to leave the group.

The CGMP fast-leave-processing feature enables the Catalyst 5000 series Supervisor engine module to detect IGMP V.2 leave messages sent on the all-routers multicast address by hosts on any of the Supervisor engine module ports. When the Supervisor engine module receives a leave message, it starts a query-response timer. If this timer expires before a join message (an IGMP membership report) is received, then the port is pruned from the multicast tree for the multicast group specified in the original leave message. Fast-leave processing ensures optimal bandwidth management for all hosts on a switched network, even when multiple multicast groups are in use simultaneously.

Broadcast/Multicast Suppression

Broadcast/multicast suppression prevents switched ports on a LAN from being disrupted by a broadcast storm on one of the ports. A LAN broadcast storm occurs when broadcast or multicast packets flood the LAN, creating excessive traffic and degrading network performance. Because switched LANs act as a single LAN, a broadcast storm on one port can adversely affect the entire LAN. Errors in the protocol-stack implementation or in the network configuration cause a broadcast storm.

Because Catalyst 5000 series LAN switches operate at Layer 2, broadcast/multicast suppression is a critical element for preventing network performance degradation.

Procedure

By default, broadcast/multicast suppression is disabled.

To configure broadcast/multicast suppression, perform the following task:

Task	Command
Set the broadcast/multicast suppression threshold for one or more ports.	**set port broadcast** *mod_num/port_num threshold* [%]

In the **set port broadcast** command, *mod_num* is the module number, and *port_num* is the number of the port on the module.

The *threshold* setting in the **set port broadcast** command can be defined in two ways:

- As a percentage of total bandwidth that can be used by broadcast/multicast traffic. Bandwidth-based broadcast/multicast suppression affects all ports on a device.

- As the number of broadcast/multicast packets that can be sent during a specified time period. Packet-based broadcast/multicast suppression can be targeted to specific ports on a device.

When specifying a bandwidth-based threshold, you must include the percent (%) sign. When specifying a packets-per-second-based threshold, do not include the percent sign.

To disable broadcast/multicast suppression for one or more ports, enter the following command:

```
Console> (enable) clear port broadcast mod_num/port_num
```

Verification

To verify the broadcast/multicast suppression configuration for all ports on module 3, use the **show port broadcast 3** command. After entering this command, you see the following display:

```
Console> (enable) show port broadcast 3
Port     Broadcast-Limit  Broadcast-Drop
------   ---------------  --------------
3/1                30 %                0
3/2                30 %                0
3/3                30 %                0
3/4                30 %                0
3/5                30 %                0
3/6                30 %                0
3/7                30 %                0
3/8                30 %                0
3/9                30 %                0
3/10               30 %                0
3/11               30 %                0
3/12               30 %                0
```

This display shows that all ports on module 3 are configured for bandwidth-based broadcast/multicast suppression, that the broadcast limit is set to 30 percent, and that 0 packets have been dropped due to broadcast/multicast suppression.

To verify the broadcast/multicast suppression configuration for port 1 on module 2, use the **show port broadcast 2/1** command. After entering this command, you see the following display:

```
Console> (enable) show port broadcast 2/1
Port     Broadcast-Limit  Broadcast-Drop
------   ---------------  --------------
2/1              100 p/s  259
```

This display shows that Port 1 on module 2 is configured for packet-based broadcast/
multicast suppression, that the broadcast limit is set to 100 packets per second, and that 259
packets have been dropped due to broadcast/multicast suppression.

Configuration Example for Broadcast/Multicast Suppression

This section provides examples for setting the broadcast/multicast suppression threshold
for one or more ports.

- To display the syntax for the **set port broadcast** command, enter the command with
  no arguments. You see the following display:

```
Console> (enable) set port broadcast
Usage: set port broadcast <mod_num/port_num> <threshold>[%]
       (threshold = 0..150000 packets/second or 0-100 percent
        0 pps or 100% unlimits broadcast traffic)
```

- To limit broadcast/multicast traffic on ports 2/1 through 3/24 to 500 packets per
  second, enter the following command:

```
Console> (enable) set port broadcast 2/1-3/24 500
Ports 2/1-3/24 broadcast traffic limited to 500 packets.
```

- To limit broadcast/multicast traffic to all the ports on module 4 to 20 percent, enter the
  following command:

```
Console> (enable) set port broadcast 4/3 20%
Ports 4/1-24 broadcast traffic limited to 20%.
```

NOTE   Although bandwidth-based broadcast/multicast suppression applies to all ports on a
module, you must still specify a port number according to the syntax rules of the **set port
broadcast** *mod_num/port_num threshold* [%] command. The following example specifies
Port 3 on module 4 (4/3). You can specify any port number between 1 and 24.

- To allow unlimited broadcast/multicast traffic to all ports on module 4 using
  bandwidth-based broadcast/multicast suppression, enter the following command:

```
Console> (enable) set port broadcast 4/3 100%
Ports 4/1-24 broadcast traffic unlimited.
```

- To allow unlimited broadcast/multicast traffic to ports 10 through 12 on module 3
  using packet-based broadcast/multicast suppression, enter the following command:

```
Console> (enable) set port broadcast 3/10-12 0
Ports 3/10-12 broadcast traffic unlimited.
```

How Broadcast/Multicast Suppression Works

Broadcast/multicast suppression works by measuring broadcast/multicast activity on a LAN. Broadcast/multicast activity can be measured in two ways:

- By the amount of network bandwidth used over a 1-second time period, called bandwidth-based broadcast/multicast suppression

- By the number of broadcast/multicast packets detected over a 1-second time period, called packet-based broadcast/multicast suppression

Because the packet size varies, bandwidth-based measurement is more accurate and effective than packet-based measurement.

Broadcast/multicast suppression uses filtering that measures broadcast/multicast activity on a LAN over a 1-second time period and compares the measurement with a predefined threshold. If the threshold is reached, further broadcast activity is suppressed for the duration of the time period.

Figure 8-13 provides an example in which broadcast/multicast suppression occurred between time intervals T1 and T2 and between T4 and T5.

Figure 8-13   *Broadcast/Multicast Suppression*

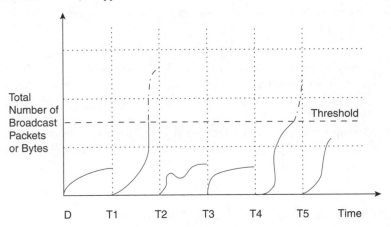

The broadcast suppression threshold numbers and the time interval combination make the broadcast/multicast suppression algorithm work with different levels of granularity. A higher threshold allows more broadcast/multicast packets to pass through.

Broadcast/multicast suppression is implemented in either hardware or software. Hardware broadcast/multicast suppression uses the bandwidth-based method. Software broadcast/multicast suppression uses the packet-based method.

Hardware Broadcast/Multicast Suppression

Hardware broadcast/multicast suppression circuitry in Catalyst 5000 series switches monitors packets passing from a port to the Catalyst 5000 switching bus. Using the Individual/Group bit in the packet destination address, the broadcast/multicast suppression circuitry determines whether the packet is a unicast or broadcast/multicast packet. It keeps track of the current count of broadcast/multicast words within the 1-second time interval; when a threshold is reached, it filters out subsequent broadcast/multicast packets.

Hardware broadcast/multicast suppression uses a bandwidth-based method of measuring broadcast/multicast activity, so the most significant implementation factor is setting the percentage of total available bandwidth that can be used by broadcast/multicast traffic. A threshold value of 100 percent means that no limit is placed on broadcast traffic. A threshold value of 0 percent means that broadcast/multicast suppression is disabled (the default). The set port broadcast command enables you to set up the broadcast suppression threshold value. You enable broadcast/multicast suppression by setting the threshold to a value greater than 0 percent.

Because packets do not arrive at uniform intervals, the 1-second time interval during which broadcast/multicast activity is measured can affect the behavior of broadcast/multicast suppression.

The following Catalyst 5000 series switching modules support hardware broadcast/ multicast suppression:

> Ethernet Switching Module (10BaseT 48 Port)—WS-X5012
> Ethernet Switching Module (10BaseT 24 Port, RJ-45)—WS-X5013
> Fast EtherChannel Switching Module (100BaseFX 12 Port)—WS-X5201
> 10/100 Mbps Fast EtherChannel Switching Module (10/100BaseTX 12 Port)—WS-X5203
> Group Switching Fast Ethernet Module (100BaseTX 24 Port)—WS-X5223
> 10/100 Mbps Workgroup Fast Ethernet Switching Module (10/100BaseTX 24 Port)—WS-X5224

Software Broadcast/Multicast Suppression

Software broadcast/multicast suppression is supported in all Ethernet line cards that support hardware broadcast/multicast suppression (see the previous section "Hardware Broadcast/Multicast Suppression"); it is not available for use with ATM or FDDI cards.

Software broadcast/multicast suppression uses a packet-based method of measuring broadcast/multicast activity, so the most significant implementation factor is setting a threshold value for the number of broadcast packets per second allowed. If the threshold number is set as 0 packets per second, no broadcast/multicast packets are suppressed.

NOTE   Validation of command-line interface (CLI) and Simple Network Management Protocol (SNMP) commands by the Supervisor engine module occurs only if a line card has the broadcast/multicast suppression feature. Hardware broadcast/multicast suppression takes precedence over software broadcast/multicast suppression unless the hardware broadcast/multicast suppression feature is disabled (that is, when the threshold value is set to 100 percent).

Q&A

As mentioned in Chapter 1, "The Cisco LAN Switch Configuration (CLSC) Exam Overview," the questions and scenarios are more difficult than what you should experience on the actual exam. The questions do not attempt to cover more breadth or depth than the exam; however, the questions are designed to make sure you know the answers. Rather than allowing you to derive the answer from clues hidden inside the question itself, the questions will challenge your understanding and recall of the subject. Questions from the "Do I Know This Already?" quiz from the beginning of the chapter are repeated here to ensure that you have mastered the chapter's topic areas. Hopefully, these questions will help limit the number of exam questions on which you narrow your choices to two options and then guess!

1 VTP version 1 and VTP version 2 are interoperable on switches in the same VTP domain.

   a. True

   b. False

2 In VTP version 1, the transparent mode inspects VTP messages for the domain name and version, and forwards a message only if _____.

3 VTP is transmitted on all trunk connections, including _____, _____, and _____.

4 Determine the MAC address-to-VLAN mapping by entering the _____ command.

5 VLANs can extend across an FDDI network by multiplexing switched packets over a CDDI/FDDI interface using the _____ protocol.

6 CDDI/FDDI modules also support one _____ VLAN, which handles all non-802.10 encapsulated FDDI traffic.

7 By default, broadcast/multicast suppression is _____.

8 Using the _____ bit in the packet destination address, the broadcast/multicast suppression circuitry determines whether the packet is a unicast or broadcast/multicast packet.

9 Because software broadcast/multicast suppression uses a packet-based method of measuring broadcast/multicast activity, the most significant implementation factor is setting a threshold value for the number of _____ allowed.

10 CGMP manages multicast traffic in Catalyst 5000 series switches by enabling directed switching of IP multicast traffic within a network at rates greater than 1 million packets per second.

   a. True

   b. False

Source Material

Some content in this chapter is based on the following sources:

- Configuring VLANs

  http://www.cisco.com/univercd/cc/td/doc/product/lan/cat5000/c5k3_1/c5kcg3_1/09vlans.htm

- Configuring Multicast Services

  http://www.cisco.com/univercd/cc/td/doc/product/lan/cat5000/c5k3_1/c5kcg3_1/10multi.htm#31735

- Understanding VLAN Trunk Protocol

  http://www.cisco.com/univercd/cc/td/doc/product/rtrmgmt/sw_ntman/cwsimain/cwsi2/cwsiug2/vlan2/vtpapp.htm

- Configuring Routing Between VLANs with ISL Encapsulation

  http://www.cisco.com/univercd/cc/td/doc/product/software/ios120/12cgcr/switch_c/xcprt7/xcisl.htm#15621

The objectives of the Cisco LAN Switch Configuration (CLSC) exam are taken from the Cisco web site, at the Cisco career certification and training area. The following table shows the exam objectives covered in this chapter:

Objective	Description
41	Upon completion of this module, you will be able to describe the different ways of managing the Catalyst 5000 series switch, including: • Out-of-band management (console port) • In-band management (network connection using SNMP) • RMON • SPAN • CWSI

CHAPTER **9**

Managing the Catalyst 5000 Series Switch Family

You can manage your Catalyst 5000 series switch through a console port using either the command-line interface (CLI) or other methods for performing network management functions, such as Cisco Discovery Protocol (CDP), Embedded Remote Monitoring (RMON), or Switched Port Analyzer (SPAN). The console port is an EIA/TIA-232 DCE interface to which you can connect a console terminal or modem.

Through the console port, you can directly access the CLI or configure a Serial Line Internet Protocol (SLIP) interface to access network management functions, such as Telnet, ping, and the Simple Network Protocol (SNMP). You can assign the IP address for the Catalyst 5000 to any VLAN. You can direct Telnet to access the IP address of the Catalyst 5000 to reach the CLI. You can also use the IP address of the switch to access an SNMP agent.

NOTE   EIA/TIA-232 was known as recommended standard RS-232 before its acceptance as a standard by the Electronics Industry Association (EIA) and the Telecommunications Industry Association (TIA).

How to Best Use This Chapter

By taking the following steps, you can make better use of your study time:

- Keep your notes and the answers for all your work with this book in one place, for easy reference.

- Take the quiz, and write down your answers. Studies show that retention is significantly increased through writing down facts and concepts, even if you never look at the information again.

- Use the diagram in Figure 9-1 to guide you to the next step.

Figure 9-1   *How to Best Use This Chapter in Preparation for the CLSC Exam*

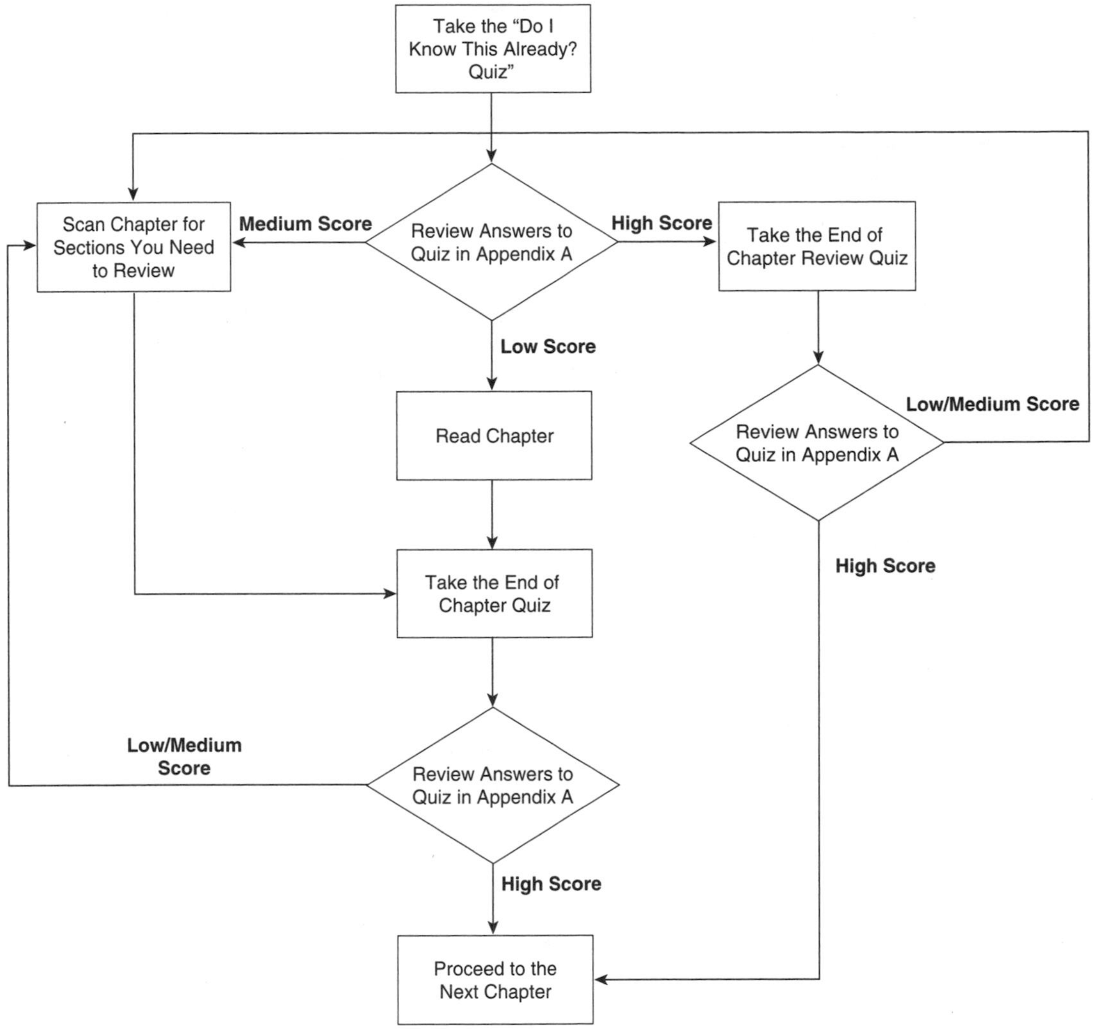

Do I Know This Already? Quiz

You can find the answers to this quiz in Appendix A, "Answers to 'Do I Know This Already?' Quizzes and Q & A Sections." Review the answers, grade your quiz, and choose an appropriate next step in this chapter based on the suggestions in Figure 9-1.

1 You can manage the Catalyst 5000 via which of the following?

  a. Via the command-line interface through a terminal attached to the console port

  b. By attaching a modem and using the Point-to-Point Protocol (PPP)

  c. By attaching a terminal to the console port and using the Cisco Discovery Protocol (CDP)

  d. Via the command-line interface through a terminal attached to the parallel port on the Supervisor engine front panel

2 Which of the following is true of the Telnet capability on the Catalyst 5000?

  a. Telnet capability on the Catalyst 5000 is not supported.

  b. Telnet capability on the Catalyst 5000 is supported, but it does not allow any outgoing Telnet.

  c. Telnet capability on the Catalyst 5000 is supported and allows up to three outgoing Telnet connections.

  d. Telnet capability on the Catalyst 5000 is supported and allows up to eight outgoing Telnet connections.

3 Which of the following is true of the Embedded RMON feature on the Catalyst 5000?

  a. The Embedded RMON feature on the Catalyst 5000 requires the use of a dedicated RMON probe or network analyzer.

  b. The Embedded RMON feature on the Catalyst 5000 supports four RMON groups: Statistics, History, Alarms, and Events.

  c. The Embedded RMON feature on the Catalyst 5000 is contained in the EARL ASIC.

  d. The Embedded RMON feature on the Catalyst 5000 enables you to monitor traffic from across a VLAN to a single port, for analysis.

4 Which of the following items accurately completes the statement: "Switched Port Analyzer (SPAN) lets you monitor traffic ____"?

   a. For analysis by a network analyzer.

   b. For analysis by an RMON probe.

   c. From across a VLAN (multiple ports) to a single port, for analysis.

   d. All of the above

5 Which of the following items accurately completes the statement: "The Fast Ethernet SwitchProbe _____"?

   a. Collects statistics on four RMON groups: Statistics, History, Alarms, and Events.

   b. Works with VlanDirector to provide a view of switched internetwork traffic.

   c. Collects RMON2 statistics on all seven protocol layers.

   d. Can communicate with the network management station across the SPAN port while monitoring traffic on the same interface.

6 Which of the following items accurately completes the statement: "The Cisco Discovery Protocol (CDP) _____"?

   a. Uses the network layer.

   b. Allows network management applications to discover Cisco devices.

   c. Is media-dependent.

   d. Is media- and protocol-independent.

7 Match the following network management application to its description:

   CiscoWorks Switched Internetwork Solutions (CWSI)_____

   CiscoView_____

   VlanDirector_____

   TrafficDirector_____

   a. Enables you to graphically display traffic levels.

   b. Graphically represents Cisco products with IP addresses.

   c. Includes three network management applications.

   d. Enables you to use the GUI representation of switches to drag the appropriate ports into the desired VLAN.

8 To establish an out-of-band connection on a Catalyst 5000 series switch, a 100 percent Hayes-compatible modem, a _____ cable, is used between the modem and the switch.

   a. Straight-through

   b. Cross-over

   c. Parallel cable

   d. A straight-through cable with a 9 pin D-type connector

9 Which of the following items accurately completes the statement: "The console port of the Catalyst 5000 is an _____"?

   a. EIA/TIA-232 DCE

   b. EIA/TIA-232 DTE

   c. EIA/TIA-256 DCE

   d. EIA/TIA-256 DTE

10 Which of the following items provides the correct syntax to enable support for RMON on a 5000 series switch?

   a. set snmp rmon

   b. set rmon enable

   c. set snmp rmon enable

   d. set snmp rmon enable sc0

Using the answer key in Appendix A, grade your answers.

- **5 or less correct**—Read this chapter.

- **6, 7, or 8 correct**—Review this chapter, looking at the charts and diagrams that summarize most of the concepts and facts in this chapter.

- **9 or more correct**—If you want more review on these topics, skip to the Q&A section at the end of this chapter. If you do not want more review on these topics, skip this chapter.

Foundation Topics

Out-of-Band Management

The material presented here is intended to help the reader understand out-of-band management features; however, it is not directly related to one of the objectives.

Out-of-band management access for the Catalyst 5000 series switches is performed via the following methods:

- Console port connection
- SLIP

Console Port Connection

The console port is the local (out-of-band) console terminal connection to the switch—a DB-25 female connector shown in Figure 9-2.

Figure 9-2   *The Catalyst 5000 Console Port*

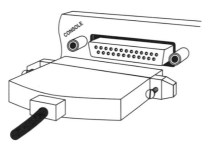

To use the console port, connect via a straight-through cable, an EIA/TIA-232 terminal (configured for 9600 baud, no parity, 8 data bits, and 1 stop bit), modem, or network management workstation, as shown in Figure 9-3.

Figure 9-3   *Attaching to the Catalyst 5000 Console Port*

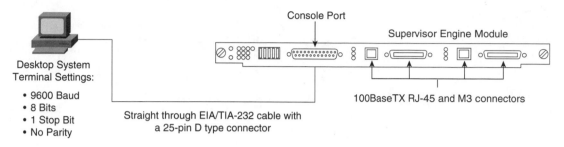

The console port enables you to perform the following functions:

- Configure the switch with a command-line interface.

- Monitor network statistics and errors.

- Configure SNMP agent parameters.

- Download software updates to the switch, or distribute software images residing in flash memory to attached devices.

Serial Line Internet Protocol

You can access the Catalyst 5000 series switch command line using Serial Line Internet Protocol (SLIP). This protocol is a version of Internet Protocol (IP) that runs over serial links, allowing IP communications through the console port.

Configuring SLIP on the Console Port

The Catalyst 5000 series switch supports out-of-band management through the use of a modem attached to the console port. This out-of-band connection works in conjunction with SLIP. The out-of-band connection can be used to perform these functions:

- Establish a Telnet session that provides access to the Catalyst 5000 series switch CLI.

- Use the Telnet Server feature.

- Establish an SNMP management session that provides the capability to use an SNMP-based management platform such as CWSI solutions.

To establish an out-of-band connection on a Catalyst 5000 series switch, connect a 100-percent Hayes-compatible modem by means of a straight-through cable with a 25-pin D-type connector, as shown in Figure 9-4. The modem should be configured for auto answer mode.

Figure 9-4   *Out-of-band Management Using SLIP*

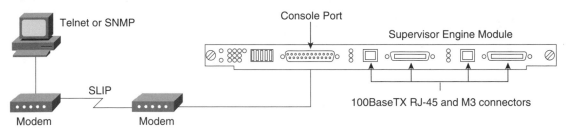

Use the SLIP (sl0) interface for point-to-point SLIP connections between the switch and an IP host.

WARNING   You *must* use the console port for the SLIP connection. When the SLIP connection is enabled and SLIP is attached on the console port, an EIA/TIA-232 terminal cannot connect via the console port. If you are connected to the switch CLI through the console port and you enter the **slip attach** command, you will lose the console port connection. Use Telnet to access the switch, enter privileged mode, and enter the **slip detach** command to restore the console port connection.

To enable and attach SLIP on the console port, perform the following sequence of tasks:

Step 1   Access the switch from a remote host with Telnet via the **telnet** {*host_name* | *ip_addr*} command.

Step 2   Enter privileged mode on the switch via the **enable** command.

Step 3   Set the console port SLIP address and the destination address of the attached host via the **set interface sl0** *slip_addr dest_addr* command.

Step 4   Enable SLIP for the console port via the **slip attach** command.

Step 5   Verify the SLIP interface configuration via the **show interface** command.

Example 9-1 shows how to configure SLIP on the console port and then verify the configuration:

Example 9-1 *Configuring SLIP on the Console Port and Verifying the Configuration*

```
sparc20% telnet 172.20.52.71
Trying 172.20.52.71 ...
Connected to 172.20.52.71.
Escape character is '^]'.

Cisco Systems Console
Enter password:
Console> enable
Enter password:
Console> (enable) set interface sl0 10.1.1.1 10.1.1.2
Interface sl0 slip and destination address set.
Console> (enable) slip attach
Console Port now running SLIP.
Console> (enable) show interface
sl0: flags=51<UP,POINTOPOINT,RUNNING>
        slip 10.1.1.1 dest 10.1.1.2
sc0: flags=63<UP,BROADCAST,RUNNING>
        vlan 523 inet 172.20.52.71 netmask 255.255.255.224 broadcast 172.20.52.95
Console> (enable)
```

In-Band Management

The material presented here is intended to help the reader understand in-band management features; however, it is not directly related to one of the objectives.

The following protocols are used to perform in-band management of the Catalyst 5000 series switches:

- Simple Network Management Protocol (SNMP)
- Telnet
- Ping
- IP Traceroute
- Cisco Discovery Protocol (CDP)

SNMP

Simple Network Management Protocol (SNMP) is an application-layer protocol designed to facilitate the exchange of management information between network devices. The SNMP system consists of three parts: SNMP manager, SNMP agent, and Management Information Base (MIB).

Instead of defining a large set of commands, SNMP places all operations in a get-request, get-next-request, and set-request format. For example, an SNMP manager can get a value from an SNMP agent or can store a value in that SNMP agent. The SNMP manager can act a part of a network management system (NMS), and the SNMP agent can reside on a networking device such as a switch. The SNMP agent can respond to MIB-related queries sent by the NMS.

The following list details the basic functions supported by SNMP agents:

- *Accessing a MIB variable using the get-request or get-next-request format.* This function is initiated by the SNMP agent as a result of a request for the value of a MIB variable from a network management station. The SNMP agent gets the value of a MIB variable by accessing information stored in the MIB, and it then responds.

- *Setting a MIB variable.* This function is also initiated by the SNMP agent as a result of a message from a network management station. The SNMP agent requests that the value of a MIB variable be changed.

- *Setting an SNMP trap.* This function is used to notify a network management station that an extraordinary event has occurred at an agent. When a trap condition occurs, the SNMP agent sends an SNMP agent trap message to each of the network management stations, as specified in the trap receiver table.

To configure SNMP on your switch, perform the following steps:

Step 1   Configure the SNMP community strings via the **set snmp community** {**read-only** | **read-write** | **read-write-all**} *community_string* command.

Step 2   Assign a trap receiver address and community via the **set snmp trap** *rcvr_address rcvr_community* command. If you enter incorrect information, enter the **clear snmp trap** command to delete the entry. Then reenter the **set snmp trap** command.

Step 3   If desired, configure the switch so that it issues an authentication trap via the **set snmp trap enable** command.

The **set snmp** Command Options

The syntax for the **set snmp community** command, used to configure SNMP community strings, is as follows:

`set snmp community {read-only | read-write | read-write-all} [community_string]`

The keywords for the **set snmp community** command are as follows:

- **read-only**—Keyword to assign read-only access to the specified SNMP community.

- **read-write**—Keyword to assign read-write access to the specified SNMP community.

- **read-write-all**—Keyword to assign read-write access to the specified SNMP community.

- *community_string*—(optional) Name of the SNMP community. The default SNMP community strings are listed here:

  — **read-only**—Public

  — **read-write**—Private

  — **read-write-all**—Secret

After entering the **set snmp community** command, you see these displays:

```
Console> (enable) set snmp community read-only public
SNMP read-only community string set.

Console> (enable) set snmp community read-write private
SNMP read-write community string set.

Console> (enable) set snmp community read-write-all secret
SNMP read-write-all community string set.
```

To view the options of the **set snmp** command, enter the command at the CLI in enable mode:

```
Console> (enable) set snmp

Set snmp commands:
----------------------------------------------------------------
set snmp community    Set SNMP community string
set snmp help         Show this message
set snmp rmon         Set SNMP RMON
set snmp trap         Set SNMP trap information
```

An IP permit trap is sent when unauthorized access based on the IP permit list is attempted. The **set snmp trap** command is a privileged mode switch command used to enable or disable the different SNMP traps on the system or to add an entry into the SNMP authentication trap receiver table. The default configuration has SNMP traps disabled. Use the **show snmp** command to verify that the appropriate traps were configured. The syntax for the **set snmp trap** command is as follows:

```
set snmp trap {enable | disable} [all | module | chassis | bridge | repeater | auth
| vtp | ippermit | vmps | config | entity | stpx]
set snmp trap rcvr_addr rcvr_community
```

The keywords and arguments for the **set snmp trap** command are listed here:

- **enable**—Keyword to activate SNMP traps

- **disable**—Keyword to deactivate SNMP traps

- **all**—Optional keyword to specify all trap types

- **module**—Optional keyword to specify the moduleUp and moduleDown traps from the CISCO-STACK-MIB

- **chassis**—Optional keyword to specify the ciscoSyslogMIB trap from the CISCO-SYSLOG-MIB

- **bridge**—Optional keyword to specify the newRoot and topologyChange traps from RFC 1493 (the BRIDGE-MIB)

- **repeater**—Optional keyword to specify the rptrHealth, rptrGroupChange, and rptrResetEvent traps from RFC 1516 (the SNMP-REPEATER-MIB)

- **auth**—Optional keyword to specify the authenticationFailure trap from RFC 1157

- **vtp**—Optional keyword to specify the VTP from the CISCO-VTP-MIB

- **ippermit**—Optional keyword to specify the IP Permit Denied access from the CISCO-STACK-MIB

- **vmps**—(Optional) Keyword to specify the vmVmpsChange trap from the CISCO-VLAN-MEMBERSHIP-MIB

- **config**—Optional keyword to specify the sysConfigChange trap from the CISCO-STACK-MIB

- **entity**—Optional keyword to specify the entityMIB trap from the ENTITY-MIB

- **stpx**—Optional keyword to specify the STPX trap

- *rcvr_addr*—IP address or IP alias of the system to receive SNMP traps

- *rcvr_community*—Community string to use when sending authentication traps

Example 9-2 shows how to enable SNMP chassis traps:

Example 9-2 *Enabling SNMP Chassis Traps*

```
Console> (enable) set snmp trap enable chassis
SNMP chassis alarm traps enabled.
Console> (enable)
```

Example 9-3 shows how to enable all SNMP traps:

Example 9-3 *Enabling All SNMP Traps*

```
Console> (enable) set snmp trap enable
All SNMP traps enabled.
Console> (enable)
```

Example 9-4 shows how to disable SNMP chassis traps:

Example 9-4 *Disabling SNMP Chassis Traps*

```
Console> (enable) set snmp trap disable chassis
SNMP chassis alarm traps disabled.
Console> (enable)
```

Example 9-5 shows how to add an entry in the SNMP trap receiver table:

Example 9-5 *Adding an Entry in the SNMP Trap Receiver Table*

```
Console> (enable) set snmp trap 192.122.173.42 public
SNMP trap receiver added.
Console> (enable)
```

SNMP Verification

To verify SNMP settings, enter the **show snmp** command. After entering this command, you will see the output in Example 9-6:

Example 9-6 *show snmp Command Output*

```
Console> show snmp
RMON: Enabled
Traps Enabled: Chassis
Port Traps Enabled: None
Community-Access      Community-String
----------------      -------------------
read-only             public
Trap-Rec-Address      Trap-Rec-Community
----------------      -------------------
192.122.173.42        public
Console>
```

Telnet Client Access

Remote, in-band SNMP management is possible through any LAN or ATM interface that is assigned to the same VLAN as the Supervisor module's NMP IP address. (In 1.X versions of the Catalyst 5000 series switch software, the NMP address was hard-coded to VLAN 1.) In-band connections can be used to establish Telnet sessions to the Catalyst 5000 series CLI, or to establish SNMP management sessions on an SNMP-based management platform, such as CWSI solutions.

The Catalyst 5000 series switch provides outgoing Telnet functionality from the command-line interface; this feature enables a network manager to use Telnet from the command-line interface of the switch to other devices on the network. Moreover, using Telnet, a network manager can maintain a connection to a Catalyst 5000 series switch while also connecting to another switch or router. The Catalyst 5000 series switch supports up to eight simultaneous Telnet sessions. Telnet sessions disconnect automatically after remaining idle for a configurable time period. To access the switch through a Telnet session, you must first set the IP address for the switch.

To access the switch from a remote host with Telnet, perform these steps:

Step 1   From the remote host, enter the **telnet** command and the name or IP address of the switch you want to access. The syntax for this command is: **telnet** {*hostname* | *ip_addr*}.

Step 2   At the prompt, enter the *<password>* for the CLI. If no password has been configured, press Return.

Step 3   Enter the necessary commands to complete your desired tasks.

Step 4   When finished, exit the Telnet session via the **quit** command.

After entering the **telnet** command, you will see the display in Example 9-7.

Example 9-7   *telnet Command Output*

```
host% telnet cat5000-1.cisco.com
Trying 172.16.44.30 ...
Connected to cat5000-1.
Escape character is '^]'.
Cisco Systems Console
Enter password: <password>
Console>
```

Cisco Discovery Protocol

Cisco Discovery Protocol (CDP) is media- and protocol-independent and runs on all Cisco-manufactured equipment, including routers, bridges, access and communication servers, and switches. With CDP, network management applications can retrieve the device type and SNMP-agent address of neighboring devices (see Figure 9-5). This enables applications to send SNMP queries to neighboring devices.

Figure 9-5 *A Typical Cisco Network Environment with CDP Enabled*

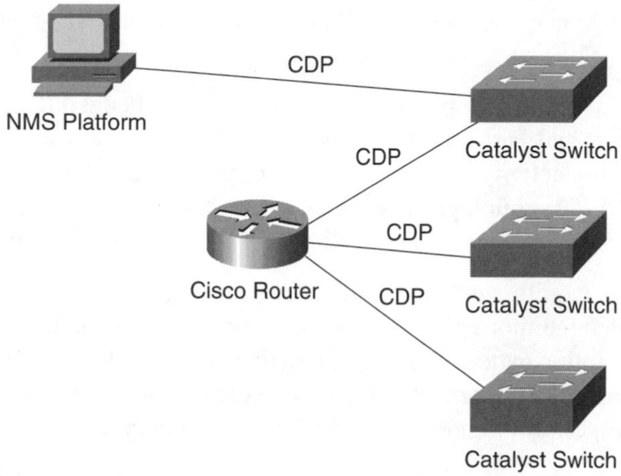

CDP meets a need created by the existence of lower-level, virtually transparent protocols. CDP enables network management applications to dynamically discover Cisco devices that are neighbors of already known devices—in particular, neighbors running lower-layer, transparent protocols. CDP runs on all media that support the Subnetwork Access Protocol (SNAP). CDP runs over the data link layer only, not the network layer. Therefore, two systems that support different network-layer protocols can learn about each other. Cached CDP information is available to network management applications. Cisco devices never forward a CDP packet; when new information is received, old information is discarded.

Example 9-8 shows how to display CDP information about neighboring systems:

Example 9-8 *Displaying CDP Information about Neighboring Systems*

```
Console> show cdp neighbor 4
Capability Codes: R - Router, T - Trans Bridge, B - Source Route Bridge
                  S - Switch, H - Host, I - IGMP, r - Repeater
Port     Device-ID               Port-ID            Platform     Capability
-------  ----------------------  ----------------   -----------  ----------
4/1      001905905               4/1                WS-C5000         TS
4/1      062000101(CAT3)         9                  WS-C1201         SI
4/1      069000022               8/1                WS-C5500         TS
4/1      069000040               4/2                WS-C5500         TS
Console>
```

Embedded Remote Monitoring

The material presented here is intended to help the reader understand embedded remote monitoring features; however, it is not directly related to one of the objectives.

The Catalyst 5000 series switch provides support for the Embedded Remote Monitoring (RMON) of Ethernet and Fast Ethernet ports. Embedded RMON provides you with visibility into network activity. It enables you to access and remotely monitor the RMON specification RFC 1757 groupings of statistics, historical information, alarms, and events for any port, through SNMP or the TrafficDirector Management application.

The RMON feature monitors network traffic at the link layer of the OSI model without requiring a dedicated monitoring probe or network analyzer. It enables a network manager to analyze network traffic patterns, to set up proactive alarms to detect problems before they affect users, to identify heavy network users as candidates to move to dedicated or higher-speed ports, and to perform trend analysis for long-term planning.

The statistics group of the RMON specification maintains utilization and error statistics for the switch that is monitored. Statistics include information about collisions; cyclic redundancy checks (CRC) and alignment; undersized or oversized packets; jabber; fragments; broadcast, multicast, and unicast messages; and bandwidth utilization.

The history group takes periodic samples from the statistics section and stores them for later retrieval. This includes information such as utilization, error counts, and packet counts.

A system network administrator uses the alarm group to set a sampling interval and threshold for any RMON-recorded item. Examples of alarm settings include absolute or relative values, rising or falling thresholds of utilization, packet counts, and CRC errors.

The event group enables events (generated traps) to be logged, printed, and provided to a network manager. The time and date is recorded with each logged event. Network managers use the event group to create customized reports based on alarm types.

Extended RMON capabilities are provided through the use of a Cisco SwitchProbe connected to the switch's SPAN port. Refer to the section "Switched Port Analyzer" for additional information.

To configure the Catalyst 5000 series switch for RMON, activate SNMP remote monitoring support via the **set snmp rmon enable** command. After entering the **set snmp rmon enable** command, you will see the display in Example 9-9:

Example 9-9 *set snmp rmon enable Command Output*

```
Console> (enable) set snmp rmon enable
SNMP RMON support enabled.
```

Switched Port Analyzer

The material presented here is intended to help the reader understand the features of the Switched Port Analyzer; however, it is not directly related to one of the objectives.

The Catalyst 5000 series Switched Port Analyzer (SPAN) feature enables you to monitor traffic on any port for analysis by a network analyzer device or RMON probe, and it provides RMON2 statistics on all nine RMON groups and all seven layers of the OSI model. Enhanced SPAN (E-SPAN) enables you to monitor traffic from multiple ports with the same VLAN to a port for analysis. The SPAN redirects traffic from an Ethernet, Fast Ethernet, or Fiber Distributed Data Interface (FDDI) port or VLAN to an Ethernet or Fast Ethernet monitor port for analysis and troubleshooting. You can monitor a single port or VLAN using a dedicated analyzer, such as a Network General Sniffer, or an RMON probe, such as a Cisco SwitchProbe. Figure 9-6 shows an example of the SPAN feature on the Catalyst 5000 series switch.

Figure 9-6   *SPAN Configuration on the Catalyst 5000 Series Switch*

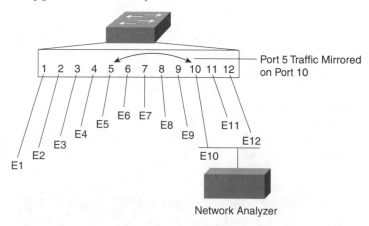

In this configuration, all traffic on Ethernet port 5 is mirrored onto the configured SPAN port Ethernet 10. The network analyzer located on Ethernet 10 can see network traffic on Ethernet 5 without being physically attached to it.

Example 9-10 shows how to display SPAN information:

Example 9-10   *Displaying SPAN Information*

```
Console> show span
Status      : enabled
Admin Source: VLAN 1
Oper Source : None
Destination : Port 1/1
Direction   : transmit/receive
Console>
```

The following list defines the **show span** command output fields in Example 9-10.

- *Admin Source*—Source port or VLAN for SPAN information

- *Open Source*—Operator port or VLAN for SPAN information

- *Destination*—Destination port for SPAN information

- *Direction*—Status of whether transmit, receive, or transmit/receive information is monitored

- *Status*—Status of whether SPAN is enabled or disabled

CiscoWorks for Switched Internetworks

The material presented here is intended to help the reader understand the features of CiscoWorks for Switched Internetworks; however, it is not directly related to one of the objectives.

CiscoWorks for Switched Internetworks (CWSI) provides network administrators with all the tools they need to manage their growing switched internetworks comprising Catalyst switches (the Cisco Management applications are outlined in Figure 9-7). The suite includes management applications for critical services such as autodiscovery and topology, VLAN management, and performance management, all integrated with Cisco's CiscoView graphical device management application. CWSI can be integrated with popular SNMP management platforms such as SunNet Manager or HP OpenView for seamless management of complex internetworks. Additionally, CWSI solutions can be used independently of these SNMP management applications and do not require these services to be fully functional.

Figure 9-7   *Switched Management Applications*

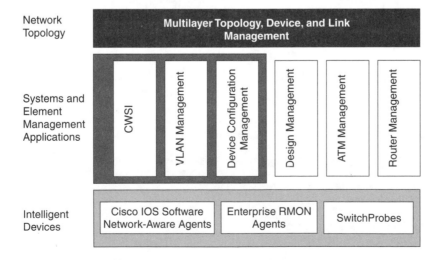

The following list defines the various features of CWSI in greater detail:

- *AtmDirector*—Discovers Asynchronous Transfer Mode (ATM) switches, physical links, and permanent and switched virtual circuits. It provides performance monitoring of ATM switches and links within the ATM network, and provides traffic analysis of RMON-enabled ATM links. It also enables you to display and monitor ATM-VLANs and Private Network-to-Network Interface (PNNI) components and to display their status in the network.

- *CiscoView*—Displays a graphical representation of a device and enables you to configure and monitor device chassis, port, and interface information. It also provides color-coded indicators to monitor port status.

- *Network Map*—Provides a map of the physical devices and links in your discovered network. It enables you to locate a specific device or link in the network and then to view and understand how the devices are linked together. It also enables you to view the virtual topology of your virtual LAN (VLAN) configuration in relation to the physical topology.

- *TrafficDirector*—Provides RMON and protocol analysis, as well as troubleshooting of protocol-related problems.

- *UserTracking*—Simplifies moves within VLANs and tracks mover and end user information. It provides information about end stations and user IDs easily, and enables you to verify and look up end station changes in the UserTracking database. If an end station is moved and plugged into another port, UserTracking provides configuration information from the Media Access Control (MAC)-VLAN mapping that enables the device to remain on the same VLAN as before without manual reconfiguration.

- *VlanDirector*—A VLAN configuration and management tool that enables you to display, configure, modify, and manage VLANs. It also enables you to display reports on VLAN status and membership.

Q&A

As mentioned in Chapter 1, "The Cisco LAN Switch Configuration (CLSC) Exam Overview," the questions and scenarios are more difficult than what you should experience on the actual exam. The questions do not attempt to cover more breadth or depth than the exam; however, the questions are designed to make sure you know the answers. Rather than allowing you to derive the answer from clues hidden inside the question itself, the questions will challenge your understanding and recall of the subject. Hopefully, these questions will help limit the number of exam questions on which you narrow your choices to two options and then guess!

1 What is the default value for the read-only community string?

2 What is the default value for the read-write community string?

3 What is the default value for the read-write-all community string?

4 What is the syntax to enable SNMP on a Catalyst 5000 switch?

5 What is the syntax to enable RMON on a Catalyst 5000 switch?

6 The Catalyst 5000 series switch console port is what type of interface?

7 What is the command to verify that RMON is enabled on the switch?

8 What is the command to display CDP information about neighboring systems?

9 The Catalyst 5000 series switch supports how many simultaneous Telnet sessions?

10 CDP operates at what layer of the OSI model?

Source Material

Some content in this chapter is based on the following sources on the Cisco web site:

- Configuring Software

  http://www.cisco.com/univercd/cc/td/doc/product/lan/cat5000/rel_2_1/ c5k_ig/config.htm#xtocid40720

- Administering the Switch

  http://www.cisco.com/univercd/cc/td/doc/product/lan/cat5000/rel_4_3/ config/admin.htm#23750

The objectives of the Cisco LAN Switch Configuration (CLSC) exam are taken from the Cisco web site, at the Cisco career certification and training area. The following table shows the exam objectives covered in this chapter:

Objective	Description
6	Maintain Catalyst series switches and perform basic troubleshooting
42	Upon completion of this module, you will be able to:

- Describe the approach for troubleshooting Catalyst switches.
- Describe the physical-layer problem areas.
- Use the **show** command to troubleshoot problems.
- Describe the switch hardware status.
- Describe the network test equipment.

CHAPTER 10

Troubleshooting the Catalyst 5000

Failures in internetworks are characterized by certain symptoms, either general (such as clients being unable to access specific servers) or specific (such as routers not residing in a routing table). Each symptom can be traced to one or more problems or causes by using specific troubleshooting tools and techniques. After a problem is identified, it can be remedied by implementing a solution consisting of a series of actions.

This chapter describes how to define symptoms, identify problems, and implement solutions in generic environments. You should always apply the specific context in which you are troubleshooting to determine how to detect symptoms and diagnose problems for your specific environment.

How to Best Use This Chapter

By taking the following steps, you can make better use of your study time:

- Keep your notes and the answers for all your work with this book in one place, for easy reference.

- Take the quiz, and write down your answers. Studies show that retention is significantly increased through writing down facts and concepts, even if you never look at the information again.

- Use the diagram in Figure 10-1 to guide you to the next step.

Figure 10-1 *How to Best Use This Chapter in Preparation for the CLSC Exam*

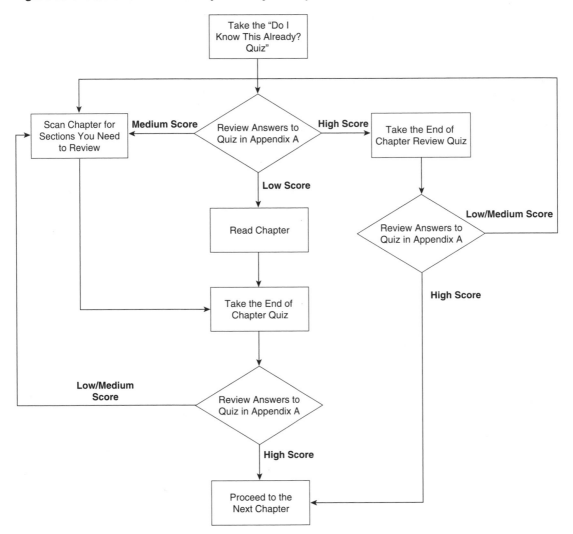

Do I Know This Already? Quiz

You can find the answers to this quiz in Appendix A, "Answers to 'Do I Know This Already?' Quizzes and Q & A Sections." Review the answers, grade your quiz, and choose an appropriate next step in this chapter based on the suggestions diagramed in Figure 10-1.

1 A red PS2 LED indication on the Supervisor indicates:

   a. The power supply in slot 2 is not installed.

   b. The power supply in slot 1 is not installed.

   c. The power supply is in a load-sharing mode.

   d. The power supply in slot 2 has failed.

2 The most common UTP cable problems are:

   a. Broken wire at the punch-down block.

   b. Broken wire in the patch cable connector.

   c. Straight-through instead of crossover cable.

   d. a, b, c

   e. a, b

   f. b, c

   g. c, a

3 Which of the following is true about the Fan LED on the Supervisor module?

   a. It indicates whether the fan is operational.

   b. If the fan is operational, the fan LED is green.

   c. If the fan is not operational, the fan LED is red.

   d. All of the above.

4 The **show log** command can be used to display errors.

   a. True

   b. False

5 The console connection can be used to display testing status during boot process.

   a. True

   b. False

6 The AC OK (or DC OK) is _____ if input is supplied and power is on.

   a. Red

   b. Green

   c. Yellow

   d. Orange

7 The fan OK LED is _____ when the power supply fan is operating properly.

   a. Red

   b. Green

   c. Yellow

   d. Orange

8 The Output Failed LED is _____ if the power supply is not within the normal regulated limits.

   a. Red

   b. Green

   c. Yellow

   d. Orange

9 The **sh trunk** command displays the encapsulation information, including trunking status (trunking/nontrunking).

   a. True

   b. False

10 The **sh vlan** command displays the virtual LAN type, status, and assigned modules/ports.

   a. True

   b. False

Using the answer key in Appendix A, grade your answers.

- **5 or less correct**—Read this chapter.

- **6, 7, or 8 correct**—Review this chapter, looking at the charts and diagrams that summarize most of the concepts and facts in this chapter.

- **9 or more correct**—If you want more review on these topics, skip to the Q&A section at the end of this chapter. If you do not want more review on these topics, skip this chapter.

Foundation Topics

General Problem-Solving Model

CLSC Objectives Covered in This Section

6	Maintain Catalyst series switches and perform basic troubleshooting:
42	Upon completion of this module, you will be able to:
	• Describe the approach for troubleshooting Catalyst switches.
	• Describe the physical-layer problem areas.
	• Use the **show** command to troubleshoot problems.
	• Describe the switch hardware status.
	• Describe the network test equipment.

When you're troubleshooting a network environment, a systematic approach works best. Define the specific symptoms, identify all potential problems that could be causing the symptoms, and then systematically eliminate each potential problem (from most likely to least likely) until the symptoms disappear.

Figure 10-2 illustrates the process flow for the general problem-solving model. This process flow is not a rigid outline for troubleshooting an internetwork; it is a foundation from which you can build a problem-solving process to suit your particular environment.

Figure 10-2 *General Problem-Solving Model*

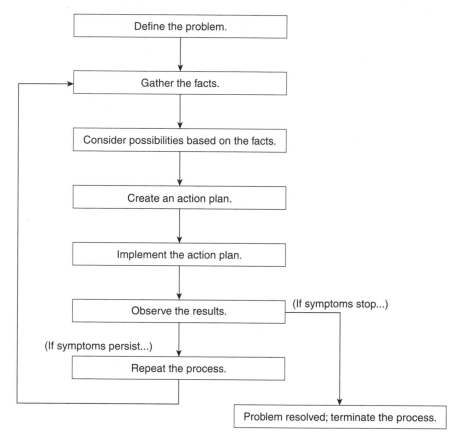

The following steps detail the problem-solving process outlined in Figure 10-2:

1 When analyzing a network problem, make a clear problem statement. You should define the problem in terms of a set of symptoms and potential causes. To do this, identify the general symptoms and then ascertain what kinds of problems (causes) could result in these symptoms. For example, hosts might not be responding to service requests from clients (a symptom). Possible causes might be a misconfigured host, bad interface cards, or missing router configuration commands.

2 Gather the facts you need to help isolate possible causes. Ask questions of affected users, network administrators, managers, and other key people. Collect information from sources such as network management systems, protocol analyzer traces, output from router diagnostic commands, or software release notes.

3   Consider possible problems based on the facts you gathered. Using those facts, you can eliminate potential problems from your list. For example, depending on the data, you might be able to eliminate hardware as a problem, allowing you to focus on software problems. At every opportunity, try to narrow the number of potential problems so you can create an efficient plan of action.

4   Create an action plan based on the remaining potential problems. Begin with the most likely problem and devise a plan in which only *one* variable is manipulated. This approach enables you to reproduce a given solution to a specific problem. If you alter more than one variable simultaneously, you might solve the problem, but identifying the specific change that eliminated the symptom becomes more difficult.

5   Implement the action plan, performing each step carefully while testing to see if the symptom disappears.

6   Whenever you change a variable, be sure to gather results. Generally, you should use the same method of gathering facts that you used in Step 2. Analyze the results to determine whether the problem has been resolved. If it has, then the process is complete.

7   If the problem has not been resolved, you must create an action plan based on the next most likely problem in your list. Return to Step 4, and repeat the process until the problem is solved. Make sure to undo any "fixes" you made in implementing your action plan. Remember that you want to change only one variable at a time.

Troubleshooting the Catalyst 5000 Series Switch Platform

The material presented here is intended to help the reader understand Catalyst 5000 series switch platforms; however, it is not directly related to one of the objectives.

Failures in internetworks are characterized by certain symptoms, either general (such as clients being unable to access specific servers) or more specific (such as routes not residing in a routing table). Each symptom can be traced to one or more problems or causes by using specific troubleshooting tools and techniques. After a problem is identified, it can be remedied by implementing a solution consisting of a series of actions.

Troubleshooting a Catalyst switch LAN can be performed utilizing and observing the following:

* Module Status LEDs
* Troubleshooting hardware

- Network layer

- Troubleshooting flowchart

- Problem solving with subsystems

- Identifying startup problems

Each of these is discussed in the following sections.

Module Status LEDs

This section describes the LEDs used to confirm and troubleshoot operation of the Catalyst 5000 series modules. The LEDs on the Supervisor engine module indicate the system power, processor, and interface status; LEDs on the switching modules indicate the status of the individual switching module and their interfaces.

The status LEDs on the Supervisor engine module and switching modules go on to indicate that the modules are powered up. When on, however, they do not necessarily mean that the interface ports are functional or enabled. Additionally, although the LEDs for many interface types go on at the initial system startup, they do not indicate an accurate status until the interface is configured. All status LEDs go on when the module receives power. The color of the LED indicates the actual status of the ports and modules. The following sections contain details about the meanings of each color.

Supervisor Engine Module LEDs

The LEDs on the Supervisor engine module indicate the system status; the system includes the fan assembly, power supply (or supplies), and the Supervisor engine module. The PS1 and PS2 LEDs on the Supervisor engine module are lit when the power supply is receiving AC source power and providing DC power to the internal system components. The power supply monitors its own temperature and internal voltages. Tables 10-1, 10-2, and 10-3 show the LEDs for the following Supervisor cards:

- Supervisor Engine Module with RJ-45 and Media-Independent Interface (MII) Connectors

- Multimode Fiber-Optic Supervisor Engine Module

- Single-Mode Fiber-Optic Supervisor Engine Module

Table 10-1 *Supervisor Engine Module LEDs*

LED	Description
Status	The switch performs a series of self-tests and diagnostic tests. If all the tests pass, the Status LED is green. If any test fails, the Status LED is red. During system boot or if the module is disabled, the LED is orange. If the redundant power supply is installed but not turned on or receiving AC input, the status LED is red. If the fan module fails, the status is red.
Fan	This LED indicates whether the fan is operational. If the fan is operational, the fan LED is green. If the fan is not operational, the fan LED is red.
PS1, left bay	If the power supply in the left bay is operational, the PS1 LED is green. If the power supply in the left bay is not operational, is switched off, or is not receiving AC input, the PS1 LED is red. If the left bay power supply is off or is not installed, the PS1 LED is red.
PS2, right bay	If the power supply in the right bay is operational, the PS2 LED is green. If the power supply in the right bay is not operational, is switched off, or is not receiving AC input, the PS2 LED is red. If the right bay power supply is off or is not installed, the PS2 LED is red.
100 Mbps	If the port is operating at 100 Mbps, the LED is green.
Link	If the port is operational, the LED is green. If the link has been disabled by software, the LED is orange. If the link is bad and has been disabled due to a hardware failure, the LED flashes orange. If no signal is detected, the LED is off.

The switch load-meter LEDs provide a visual indication (as an approximate percentage) of the current traffic load over the backplane (see Figure 10-3).

Figure 10-3 *Switch Load LED*

Switch Load	Load %
▮▮▮▮▮▮▮▮▮▮	90-100
▯▮▮▮▮▮▮▮▮▮	80-89
▯▯▮▮▮▮▮▮▮▮	70-79
▯▯▯▮▮▮▮▮▮▮	60-69
▯▯▯▯▮▮▮▮▮▮	50-59
▯▯▯▯▯▮▮▮▮▮	40-49
▯▯▯▯▯▯▮▮▮▮	30-39
▯▯▯▯▯▯▯▮▮▮	20-29
▯▯▯▯▯▯▯▯▮▮	10-19
▯▯▯▯▯▯▯▯▯▮	1-9

Group Switching Ethernet Module (10BaseT 48 Port) LEDs

The LEDs provide status information for the module and individual 10BaseT Ethernet port connections. The LEDs are described in Table 10-2.

Table 10-2 *Group Switching Ethernet Module LED Descriptions*

LED	Description
Status	The switch performs a series of self-tests and diagnostic tests.
	If all the tests pass, the status LED is green.
	If a test other than an individual port test fails, the status LED is red.
	During system boot or if the module is disabled, the LED is orange.
	During self-test diagnostics, the LED is orange.
	If the module is disabled, the LED is orange.
Link	If the port is operational (a signal is detected), the LED is green.
	If the link has been disabled by software, the LED is orange.
	If the link is bad and has been disabled due to a hardware failure, the LED flashes orange.
	If no signal is detected, the LED is off.

Ethernet Switching Module (10BaseT 24 Port) LEDs

The LEDs provide status information for the module and individual 10BaseT Ethernet port connections. These LEDs are described in Table 10-3.

Table 10-3 *Ethernet Switching Module (10BaseT 24 Port) LED Descriptions*

LED	Description
Status	The switch performs a series of self-tests and diagnostic tests.
	If all the tests pass, the status LED is green.
	If a test other than an individual port test fails, the status LED is red.
	During system boot or if the module is disabled, the LED is orange.
	During self-test diagnostics, the LED is orange.
	If the module is disabled, the LED is orange.
Link	If the port is operational (a signal is detected), the LED is green.
	If the link has been disabled by software, the LED is orange.
	If the link is bad and has been disabled due to a hardware failure, the LED flashes orange.
	If no signal is detected, the LED is off.

Problem Solving with Subsystems

The key to problem solving the system is to try to isolate the problem to a specific subsystem. The first step in solving startup problems is to compare what the system *is doing* to what it *should be doing*. A startup problem can usually be attributed to a single component, so it is more efficient to first isolate the problem to a subsystem rather than troubleshoot each separate component in the system.

The switch consists of the following subsystems:

- *Power subsystem*—Includes the power supplies and power supply fans.

- *Cooling subsystem*—The chassis fan assembly should be operating whenever system power is on. It usually continues to operate even when the environmental monitor shuts down the system because of an overtemperature or overvoltage condition (although it will shut down in the event of a power supply shutdown). You should be able to hear the fan assembly to determine whether it is operating. If the fan LED is red and you determine that the fan assembly is not operating, you should immediately contact a customer service representative. The fan assembly is located in the interior of the chassis, and there are no installation adjustments that you should make if it does not function properly at initial startup.

- *Processors subsystem*—The Supervisor engine module contains the system operating software, so check here if you have trouble with the system software.

- *Status LED*—The status LED on the Supervisor engine module and each switching module indicates whether the Supervisor engine module is capable of initializing the card. Remember that a switching module that is partially installed in the backplane causes the system to halt.

Identifying Startup Problems

This section contains a more detailed description of the normal startup sequence and describes what to do if the system does *not* perform the sequence as expected. With the exception of the system fan assembly, LEDs indicate all system states in the startup sequence. By checking the state of the LEDs, you can determine when and where the system failed in the startup sequence. When you turn on the power supply switch(es) to start the system, the following should occur:

- You should immediately hear the system fan assembly operating. If not, proceed to the next section, "Troubleshooting the Power Subsystem." If you determine that the power supplies are functioning normally and that the fan assembly is faulty, contact a customer service representative.

- If the system fan assembly does not function properly at initial startup, there are no installation adjustments that you should make.

- The power supply LEDs on the Supervisor engine module at the left of the chassis should go on as follows:

  — The PS1 or PS2 LED on the Supervisor engine module should turn green immediately when you turn the power supply switch on (l), and should remain on during normal system operation.

  — If the PS1 or PS2 LEDs do not go on, proceed to the following section, "Troubleshooting the Power Subsystem."

- The LEDs on the Supervisor engine module should go on as follows:

  — The status LED flashes orange once and then stays orange during diagnostic boot tests. It turns green when the module is operational (online). If the system software is unable to start up, this LED will remain red.

  — Each link LED flashes orange once and then stays orange during diagnostic boot tests. It turns green when it is operational (online). Note that this LED turns off if no signal is detected, and it blinks orange if the port is bad.

  — The fan LED should always remain green. This LED shows red only if the system detects a fan failure.

  — If any LEDs on the Supervisor engine module faceplate are red, proceed to the "Troubleshooting Suggestions" section, later in this chapter.

  — The status LED on the Supervisor engine module and on each switching module is green when the Supervisor engine module has completed initialization for operation. This LED indicates that the Supervisor engine module or switching modules are receiving power, have been recognized by the Supervisor engine module, and contain a valid Flashcode version; however, this LED does not indicate the state of the individual interfaces on the switching modules. If a status LED is red or orange, proceed to the section "Troubleshooting Suggestions," later in this chapter.

Troubleshooting the Power Subsystem

Check the following to help isolate a power subsystem problem:

- On the Supervisor engine module, are the PS1 and/or PS2 LEDs on?

  — If yes, the AC source is good and the power supply is functional.

  — If no, first ensure that the power supply is flush with the back of the chassis. Tighten the captive installation screws, and then turn the power switch to the on (l) position.

- If the PS1 or PS2 LEDs both remain off, there might be a problem with the AC source or the power cable.

  — Turn off the power to the switch, connect the power cord to another power source if one is available, and turn the power back on.

  — If the LED then goes on, the problem is the first power source.

- If the LED fails to go on after you connect the power supply to a new power source, replace the power cord and turn the switch back on.

  If the PS1 or PS2 LEDs then go on, return the first power cord for replacement.

NOTE   This unit might have more than one power cord. Repeat this previous step for each power supply.

- If the LED still fails to go on when the switch is connected to a different power source with a new power cord, the power supply is probably faulty.

  If a second power supply is available, install it in the second power supply bay and contact a customer service representative for further instructions.

- If the PS LED is not on for the second (redundant) power supply, repeat these procedures for the second power supply.

If you are unable to resolve the problem, or if you determine that either a power supply or a chassis connector is faulty, contact a customer service representative for instructions.

Troubleshooting the Fan Assembly Subsystem

Check the following items to help isolate a fan assembly problem:

- If the fan LED on the Supervisor engine module is not green, refer to the section "Problem Solving with Subsystems," earlier in this chapter, to determine whether the power subsystem is functioning properly.

- If it is red, suspect that the fan assembly is not seated in the backplane or that it has malfunctioned.

- If the fan LED is still red, the system has detected a fan assembly failure. Contact a customer service representative for instructions.

Troubleshooting Suggestions

Check the following to help isolate a Supervisor engine module or switching module problem:

- Are all status LEDs on?

- Are any status LEDs on the Supervisor engine module or any switching modules red or orange?

  If yes, the module might have shifted out of its slot.

  Reseat the module until both ejector levers are at a 90° orientation to the rear of the chassis. Tighten the captive installation screws at the left and right of the module faceplate, and restart the system.

- If the status LED on a switching module is orange, the module might be busy or disabled. Refer to the *Catalyst 5000 Series Configuration Guide and Command Reference* to configure or enable the interfaces. After the system reinitializes the interfaces, the status LED on the module should be green.

Command-Line Interface

The material presented here is intended to help the reader understand command-line interface; however, it is not directly related to one of the objectives.

Using the show system Command

Enter the **show system** command to display the power supply, fan, temperature alarm, system, and modem status; the number of days, hours, minutes, and seconds since the last system restart; the baud rate; the MAC address range; and the system name, location, and contact.

In the following example, the system status and other information is displayed:

```
Console> show system
PS-Status Fan-Status Temp-Alarm Sys-Status Uptime d,h:m:s
--------- ---------- ---------- ---------- --------------
ok        ok         off        ok         27,17:05:50
Modem     Baud  MAC-Address-Range
--------  ----- --------------------------------------
disabled  9600  00-04-0b-a0-04-1f to 00-04-0b-a0-05-56
System Name              System Location          System Contact
----------------------   ----------------------   ---------------------
WBU-Catalyst-5000 5      Closet 202 1/F           Luis x5529
```

The following **show** commands can assist in troubleshooting hardware, configuration, or network problems in a switched network environment:

- **sh arp**—Displays the contents of the ARP table and aging time.

- **sh atm**—Displays the ATM interfaces, traffic, VC and VLAN information and status.

- **sh cam**—Displays the CAM table.

- **sh config**—Displays the current system configuration.

- **sh fddi**—Displays the settings of the FDDI/CDDI module.

- **sh flash**—Displays the flash code names, version numbers, and sizes.

- **sh int**—Displays the Supervisor module network interface information.

- **sh ip route**—Displays the IP route information.

- **sh log**—Displays the system or module error log.

- **sh mac**—Displays the MAC counters for all the installed modules.

- **sh module**—Displays module status and information (hardware/firmware/software).

- **sh netstat**—Displays statistics for the various TCP/IP stack protocols and the state of active network connections.

- **sh port**—Displays the port status and counters for all installed modules.

- **sh spantree**—Displays the spanning-tree information for the VLANs, including port states.

- **sh system**—Displays the status of the power supply, fan, temperature alarm, system, and uptime.

- **sh test**—Displays the results of diagnostic tests on the specified modules.

- **sh trunk**—Displays the ISL information including trunking status (**trunking/ nontrunking**).

- **sh vlan**—Displays the virtual LAN type, status, and assigned modules/ports.

Physical Layer Troubleshooting

The material presented here is intended to help the reader understand physical layer troubleshooting; however, it is not directly related to one of the objectives.

The most common network problems can be traced to cable problems. The following questions will help determine whether there is a UTP cable problem.

- Are the cables the correct type for this installation?

  — *Category 3*—Category 3 cabling can only support 10BaseT. Was a Category 3 cable installed instead of a Category 5 cable?

    — *Category 5*—Was the cable installed correctly? Severe bends in a Category 5 cable can cause a 10/100 Mbps interface to run at 10 Mbps. Some devices do not handle auto negotiation correctly. Check whether a 10/100 Mbps connection is connected at 10 Mbps instead of 100 Mbps.

- Is the cable a crossover or straight-through? Which type should it be? Compare the RJ-45 connector wiring at both ends of the cable, including all wiring closet connections.

- Is the punchdown wiring correct? Are there missing, loose, or broken wires on the punch-down block?

- One of the first ways to determine whether a cable is installed correctly is to check the devices' port link integrity LED on both ends of the cable. Each device transmits a link integrity pulse to the other device.

    — If the link LED is not on, try another port.

    — Is the other device powered up? Is the link LED lit on the other device?

- Is there a broken wire at either end of the cable?

    — Cables that are installed too tightly with a tie wrap may have broken wires in the connectors.

    — Cables that are pulled through plenum can have broken wires and exhibit intermittent open circuit conditions.

Troubleshooting Ethernet

This section provides troubleshooting procedures for common Ethernet media problems. Table 10-4 outlines problems commonly encountered on Ethernet networks and offers general guidelines for solving those problems.

Table 10-4 *Media Problems: Ethernet*

Media Problem	Suggested Actions
Excessive noise	**Step 1** Use the **show interfaces ethernet** EXEC command to determine the status of the router's Ethernet interfaces. The presence of many CRC errors but not many collisions is an indication of excessive noise. **Step 2** Check cables to determine whether any are damaged. **Step 3** Look for badly spaced taps causing reflections. **Step 4** If you are using 100BaseTX, make sure you are using Category 5 cabling and not another type, such as Category 3.
Excessive collisions	**Step 1** Use the **show interfaces ethernet** command to check the rate of collisions. The total number of collisions with respect to the total number of output packets should be around 0.1 percent or less. **Step 2** Use a TDR[1] to find any unterminated Ethernet cables. **Step 3** Look for a jabbering transceiver attached to a host. (This might require host-by-host inspection or the use of a protocol analyzer.)
Excessive runt frames	In a shared Ethernet environment, runt frames are almost always caused by collisions. If the collision rate is high, refer to the problem of excessive collisions, earlier in this table. If runt frames occur when collisions are not high or in a switched Ethernet environment, then they are the result of underruns or bad software on a network interface card. Use a protocol analyzer to try to determine the source address of the runt frames.
Late collisions[2]	**Step 1** Use a protocol analyzer to check for late collisions. Late collisions should never occur in a properly designed Ethernet network. They usually occur when Ethernet cables are too long or when there are too many repeaters in the network. **Step 2** Check the diameter of the network, and make sure it is within specification.
No link integrity on 10BaseT, 100BaseT4, or 100BaseTX	**Step 1** Make sure you are not using 100BaseT4 when only two pairs of wire are available. 100BaseT4 requires four pairs. **Step 2** Check for 10BaseT, 100BaseT4, or 100BaseTX mismatch (for example, a card different than the port on a hub). **Step 3** Determine whether there is cross-connect (for example, be sure straight-through cables are not being used between a station and the hub). **Step 4** Check for excessive noise (earlier in this table).

[1] TDR = time domain reflectometer
[2] A late collision is a collision that occurs beyond the first 64 bytes of an Ethernet frame.

Networking Testing

One of the most useful and most important troubleshooting aids when performing network testing is the **ping** command. Enter the **ping** command to send Internet Control Message Protocol (ICMP) echo request packets to another node on the network to confirm the connection to that node. Enter **Ctrl-C** to stop pinging.

```
ping -s host [packet_size] [packet_count]
```

The syntax descriptions for each parameter are as follows:

-s	Causes **ping** to send one datagram per second, printing one line of output for every response received. The **ping** command does not return any output when no response is received.
host	Gives the IP address or IP alias of the host.
packet_size	(Optional) Determines the number of bytes in a packet, from 1 byte to 2000 bytes, with a default of 56 bytes. The actual packet size is 8 bytes larger because the switch adds header information.
packet_count	(Optional) Gives the number of packets to send.

Following are sample results of the **ping** command:

- *Normal response*—The normal response occurs in 1 to 10 seconds, depending on network traffic.

- *Destination does not respond*—If the host does not respond, a no answer message appears in 10 seconds.

- *Destination unreachable*—The gateway given in the route table for this destination indicates that the destination is unreachable.

- *Network or host unreachable*—The switch found no corresponding entry in the route table.

In the following **ping** command example, a host with IP alias *elvis* is pinged a single time and then is pinged once per second until **Ctrl-C** is entered to stop pinging:

```
Console> ping elvis
elvis is alive
Console> ping -s elvis
ping elvis: 56 data bytes
64 bytes from elvis: icmp_seq=0. time=11 ms
64 bytes from elvis: icmp_seq=1. time=8 ms
64 bytes from elvis: icmp_seq=2. time=8 ms
64 bytes from elvis: icmp_seq=3. time=7 ms
64 bytes from elvis: icmp_seq=4. time=11 ms
64 bytes from elvis: icmp_seq=5. time=7 ms
```

```
64 bytes from elvis: icmp_seq=6. time=7 ms
^C
----elvis PING Statistics----
7 packets transmitted, 7 packets received, 0% packet loss
round-trip (ms)  min/avg/max = 7/8/11
Console>
```

If when using the **ping** command you do not get a response, the following items should be evaluated:

- Is there a cable problem?

- Can the testing terminal (or workstation) communicate with any other devices?

- Can any other devices communicate with the switch?

- Are there port errors on the switch? (Check with the **sh port** command.)

- Is there normal port traffic? (Check with the **sh mac** command.)

- Are the port and interface sc0 in the same VLAN? (Check with the **sh port** and **sh int** commands.)

Network Test Equipment

In many situations, third-party diagnostic tools can be more useful than commands that are integrated into the router. For example, enabling a processor-intensive **debug** command can be disastrous in an environment experiencing excessively high traffic levels. However, attaching a network analyzer to the suspect network is less intrusive and is more likely to yield useful information without interrupting the operation of the router.

The following are some typical third-party troubleshooting tools used for troubleshooting internetworks:

- Volt-ohm meters, digital multimeters, and cable testers

- TDRs and OTDRs

- Breakout boxes, fox boxes, and BERTs/BLERTs

- Network monitors

- Network analyzers

Each of these is discussed in the following sections.

Volt-Ohm Meters, Digital Multimeters, and Cable Testers

Volt-ohm meters and digital multimeters come in at the lower end of the spectrum of cable testing tools. These devices measure parameters such as AC and DC voltage, current, resistance, capacitance, and cable continuity. They are used to check physical connectivity.

Cable testers (scanners) also enable you to check physical connectivity. Cable testers are available for shielded twisted-pair (STP), unshielded twisted-pair (UTP), 10BaseT, and coaxial and twinax cables. A given cable tester might be capable of performing any of the following functions:

- Test and report on cable conditions, including near-end crosstalk (NEXT), attenuation, and noise.

- Perform time domain reflectometer (TDR), traffic monitoring, and wire map functions.

- Display MAC-layer information about LAN traffic, provide statistics such as network utilization and packet error rates, and perform limited protocol testing (for example, TCP/IP tests such as **ping**).

Similar testing equipment is available for fiber-optic cable. Due to the relatively high cost of fiber cable and its installation, however, fiber-optic cable should be tested both before installation (on-the-reel testing) and after installation. Continuity testing of the fiber requires either a visible light source or a reflectometer. Light sources capable of providing light at the three predominant wavelengths—850 nanometers (nm), 1300 nm, and 1550 nm—are used with power meters that can measure the same wavelengths and test attenuation and then return loss in the fiber.

TDRs and OTDRs

At the top end of the cable testing spectrum are time domain reflectometers (TDRs). These devices can quickly locate open and short circuits, crimps, kinks, sharp bends, impedance mismatches, and other defects in metallic cables.

A TDR works by bouncing a signal off the end of the cable. Opens, shorts, and other problems reflect the signal back at different amplitudes, depending on the problem. A TDR measures how much time it takes for the signal to reflect and calculates the distance to a fault in the cable. TDRs can also be used to measure the length of a cable, and some can calculate the propagation rate based on a configured cable length.

Fiber-optic measurement is performed by an optical time domain reflectometer (OTDR). OTDRs can accurately measure the length of the fiber, locate cable breaks, measure the fiber attenuation, and measure splice or connector losses. An OTDR can be used to take the "signature" of a particular installation, noting attenuation and splice losses. This baseline measurement can then be compared with future signatures when a problem in the system is suspected.

Breakout Boxes, Fox Boxes, and BERTs/BLERTs

Breakout boxes, fox boxes, and bit/block error rate testers (BERTs/BLERTs) are digital interface testing tools used to measure the digital signals present at PCs, printers, modems, and CSU/DSUs, and other peripheral interfaces. These devices can monitor data line conditions, analyze and trap data, and diagnose problems common to data communication systems. Traffic from data terminal equipment (DTE) through data communications equipment (DCE) can be examined to help isolate problems, identify bit patterns, and ensure that the proper cabling has been installed. These devices cannot test media signals such as Ethernet, Token Ring, or FDDI.

Network Monitors

Network monitors continuously track packets crossing a network, providing an accurate picture of network activity at any moment or crafting a historical record of network activity over a period of time. They do not decode the contents of frames. Monitors are useful for baselining, in which the activity on a network is sampled over a period of time to establish a normal performance profile, or baseline.

Monitors collect information such as packet sizes, the number of packets, error packets, overall usage of a connection, the number of hosts and their MAC addresses, and details about communications between hosts and other devices. This data can be used to create profiles of LAN traffic as well as assist in locating traffic overloads, planning for network expansion, detecting intruders, establishing baseline performance, and distributing traffic more efficiently.

Network Analyzers

A network analyzer (also called a protocol analyzer) decodes the various protocol layers in a recorded frame and presents them as readable abbreviations or summaries, detailing which layer is involved (physical, data link, and so forth) and what function each byte or byte content serves.

Most network analyzers can perform many of the following functions:

- Filter traffic that meets certain criteria so that, for example, all traffic to and from a particular device can be captured.
- Time-stamp captured data.
- Present protocol layers in an easily readable form.
- Generate frames and transmit them onto the network.
- Incorporate an "expert" system in which the analyzer uses a set of rules, combined with information about the network configuration and operation, to diagnose and solve, or offer potential solutions to network problems.

Q&A

As mentioned in Chapter 1, "The Cisco LAN Switch Configuration (CLSC) Exam Overview," the questions and scenarios are more difficult than what you should experience on the actual exam. The questions do not attempt to cover more breadth or depth than the exam; however, the questions are designed to make sure you know the answers. Rather than allowing you to derive the answer from clues hidden inside the question itself, the questions will challenge your understanding and recall of the subject. Questions from the "Do I Know This Already?" quiz from the beginning of the chapter are repeated here to ensure that you have mastered the chapter's topic areas. Hopefully, these questions will help limit the number of exam questions on which you narrow your choices to two options and then guess!

1 Explain the function of the **sh arp** command.

2 Explain the function of the **sh atm** command.

3 Explain the function of the **sh cam** command.

4 Explain the function of the **sh config** command.

5 Explain the function of the **sh fddi** command.

6 Explain the function of the **sh flash** command.

7 Explain the function of the **sh int** command.

8 Explain the function of the **sh ip route** command.

9 Explain the function of the **sh log** command.

10 Explain the function of the **sh mac** command.

11 Explain the function of the **sh module** command.

12 Explain the function of the **sh netstat** command.

13 Explain the function of the **sh port** command.

14 Explain the function of the **sh spantree** command.

Source Materials

Some content in this chapter is based on the following sources:

- Troubleshooting the Installation

  http://www.cisco.com/univercd/cc/td/doc/product/lan/cat5000/rel_2_1/
  c5k_ig/trblsh.htm

- Troubleshooting Overview

  http://www.cisco.com/univercd/cc/td/doc/cisintwk/itg_v1/
  itg_intr.htm#xtocid293640

- Troubleshooting Tools

  http://www.cisco.com/univercd/cc/td/doc/cisintwk/itg_v1/
  itg_tool.htm#xtocid60390

The objectives of the Cisco LAN Switch Configuration (CLSC) exam are taken from the Cisco web site, at the Cisco career certification and training area. The following table shows the exam objectives covered in this chapter:

Objective	Description
43	Describe the major features and functions of the Catalyst 5000 FDDI/CDDI Module.
44	Describe IEEE 802.10 VLANs.
45	Configure the Catalyst 5000 FDDI/CDDI Module.

CHAPTER 11

Catalyst 5000 Series Switch FDDI Module

This chapter is a discussion of the FDDI/CDDI Module. For those who don't already know it, FDDI stands for *Fiber Data Distributed Interface*. CDDI stands for *Copper Data Distributed Interface*.

FDDI is a LAN standard, which is defined by ANSI X3T9.5, specifying a 100 Mbps token-passing network using fiber-optic cable with dual counter-rotating rings.

You might have already guessed that CDDI is the implementation of FDDI protocols over STP and UTP cabling. CDDI is based on the ANSI twisted-pair physical medium dependent (TP-PMD) standard. CDDI transmits over relatively short distances (up to 100 meters), providing data rates of 100 Mbps and also employing a dual-ring architecture for the sake of redundancy.

How to Best Use This Chapter

By taking the following steps, you can make better use of your study time:

- Keep your notes and the answers for all your work with this book in one place, for easy reference.

- Take the quiz, and write down your answers. Studies show that retention is significantly increased through writing down facts and concepts, even if you never look at the information again.

- Use the diagram in Figure 11-1 to guide you to the next step.

Figure 11-1   *How to Best Use This Chapter in Preparation for the CLSC Exam*

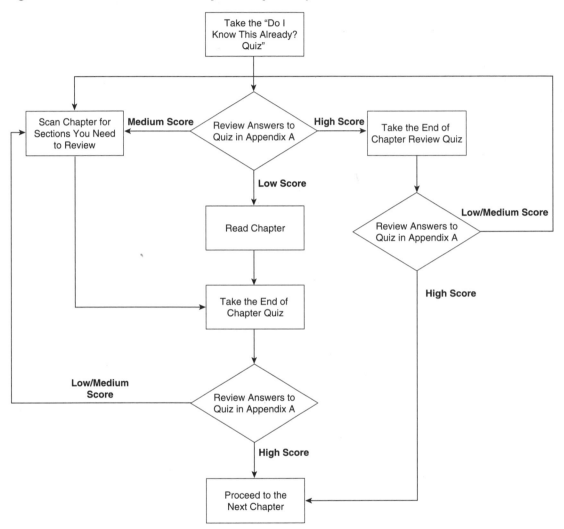

Do I Know This Already? Quiz

You can find the answers to this quiz in Appendix A, "Answers to 'Do I Know This Already?' Quizzes and Q & A Sections." Review the answers, grade your quiz, and choose an appropriate next step in this chapter based on the suggestions diagramed in Figure 11-1.

1   What is APaRT, and what is its function?

2   What media/connectors are supported in the FDDI/CDDI cards?

3   What is the distance limitation on a CDDI module?

4   What is the distance limitation on an FDDI SMF Module?

5   What is the protocol that is used to create FDDI VLANs?

6   What would the value of the SAID be (default) if you typed the command *set vlan 100* (while in enable mode)?

7 What is the command to translate an Ethernet VLAN to an FDDI VLAN?

8 If you disable APaRT, what happens to fddicheck?

9 In what environment might you consider disabling APaRT?

Using the answer key in Appendix A, grade your answers.

- **4 or less correct**—Read this chapter.

- **5, 6, or 7 correct**—Review this chapter, looking at the charts and diagrams that summarize most of the concepts and facts in this chapter.

- **8 or more correct**—If you want more review on these topics, skip to the Q&A section at the end of this chapter. If you do not want more review on these topics, skip this chapter.

Foundation Topics

Catalyst 5000 FDDI/CDDI Features

CLSC Objectives Covered in This Section

43	Describe the major features and functions of the Catalyst 5000 FDDI/CDDI Module.

The following list describes the major features of the Catalyst 5000 CDDI/FDDI Module:

- 85,000 packets per second (pps) translational bridging between FDDI and Ethernet
- 1000 IEEE 802.10 protocol-based VLANs
- Spanning-tree algorithm (IEEE 802.1d), CDP, VTP, and IEEE 802.10 support
- 4000 active MAC addresses
- MTU discovery, APaRT, and fddicheck

Applications of FDDI can be varied, but FDDI solutions in switching platforms can be categorized into three general groups:

- FDDI concentration, where port density is the concern
- FDDI translational switching, where the major function is to provide a 100 Mbps translational link connecting Ethernet, Token Ring, ATM, and Fast Ethernet LANs
- Pure FDDI switching, where packets are switched in FDDI format between FDDI ports

The FDDI and CDDI modules are available in three types of media: Category 5 UTP with RJ-45 connector, multimode fiber with MIC connector, and single-mode fiber with ST connector.

The Catalyst 5000 FDDI Module supports a feature called maximum transmission unit (MTU) discovery. The MTU discovery protocol automatically determines the maximum packet size allowed by each module with which it converses.

APaRT

APaRT, short for Automated Packet Recognition and Translation, uses content-addressable memory (CAM) table entries on the Catalyst 5000 FDDI or CDDI module to associate a specific Layer 2 frame type with each MAC address. When frames are transferred between FDDI/CDDI and Ethernet, APaRT translates them into the destination device's native frame format, such as Ethernet 802.3, FDDI_802.2, Ethernet II, Raw, FDDI_SNAP, or Ethernet_SNAP.

APaRT eliminates the need to reconfigure applications or network protocols.

You can also manually configure the FDDI module to translate to the frame format of your choice using the **set bridge** command.

fddicheck

Before we start with this section, let's get one thing out of the way—no, I don't know why fddicheck is always lowercase. If you find out, let me know—it makes for interesting trivia while teaching classes.

The fddicheck feature was created to fix a problem. Unfortunately, it introduces new problems while trying to fix an old one.

The Catalyst 5000 FDDI/CDDI Module behaves according to the FDDI specification, which is to wait until it receives the FDDI token before forwarding frames onto the FDDI ring from the Ethernet side (assuming that we have an Ethernet side). Immediately following each data frame that it forwards onto the ring, it sends two void frames, also in accordance with the FDDI specification. Because the FDDI module maintains control of the token, it expects all other FDDI nodes to refrain from transmitting. Therefore, it strips any spurious frames off the ring until it sees a void frame.

Occasionally, some older FDDI devices have been known to violate the FDDI specification, which is why we have fddicheck. These devices release void frames onto an FDDI ring, even when they do not have the token. When the Catalyst 5000 FDDI/CDDI Module receives the void frame, it assumes compliance with the FDDI specification. Accordingly, it interprets the void frame's arrival as its signal to stop removing frames off the ring, even though its own data frame has not yet completely circled the ring. Then, when the data frame that it previously sent arrives after completely circling the ring, it erroneously interprets it as a new data frame, sourced by a device attached on the FDDI side. It reads the frame's source address and then forwards the frame back onto the ring (again).

This presents a new problem. Each source node in FDDI is responsible for removing from the ring each frame that it forwards onto the ring. However, in this scenario, the source node is not attached to the ring. Therefore, the unclaimed frame continues to circulate around the ring indefinitely, creating useless background traffic and consuming valuable bandwidth.

A second problem is also created. In this case, the FDDI/CDDI Module determines from the frame's source address that the node has moved to an Ethernet segment attached to the FDDI ring, and it updates its CAM table accordingly. Then, traffic from any FDDI-attached device is discarded by the module because it interprets the traffic from the Ethernet segment as being on the same ring as other FDDI-attached devices.

To prevent the loss of connectivity as discussed, the Catalyst 5000 FDDI/CDDI Module's fddicheck feature prevents the module from updating its CAM with the address of a device based on the source address of frames seen on the FDDI ring if the frame's source address was previously learned on the Ethernet side.

If APaRT is disabled, fddicheck is automatically disabled.

CDDI Module

The CDDI module provides a single attachment (SAS) or dual-attachment (DAS) connection to two Category 5 UTP 100 Mbps CDDI interfaces using two RJ-45 female connections.

NOTE   The maximum distance supported is 100 meters.

The LEDs provide status information for the module and each port connection. Table 11-1 discusses each LED and provides a description of their functions.

Table 11-1   *FDDI/CDDI Module LED Information*

LED	Description
Status	The switch performs a series of self-tests and diagnostic tests.
	If all tests pass, the Status LED is green.
	If a test other than an individual port test fails, the LED is red.
	During system boot, or if the module is disabled, the LED is orange.
	During self-test diagnostics, the LED is orange.
	If the module is disabled, the LED is orange.
RingOp	Indicates whether the ring is operational.
	If the ring is operational, the RingOp LED is green.
	If the ring is not operational, the LED is off.
Thru	If the FDDI/CDDI A and B ports are connected to the primary and secondary rings, the Thru LED is green; otherwise, it is off.
Wrap A	If the FDDI/CDDI A port is connected to the ring and the B port is isolated, the Wrap A LED is green; otherwise, it is off.
Wrap B	If the FDDI/CDDI B port is connected to the ring and the A port is isolated, the Wrap B LED is green; otherwise, it is off.
A Port Status	If the A port is connected to the ring, the A port LED is green.
	If the A port receives a signal but fails to connect, or if a dual homing condition exists, the A port LED is orange.
	The LED is turned off if no receive signal is detected.
B Port Status	If the B port is connected to the ring, the B port LED is green.
	If the B port receives a signal but fails to connect, or if a dual homing condition exists, the B port LED is orange.
	The LED is turned off if no receive signal is detected.

FDDI MMF Module

The FDDI multimode fiber (MMF) module also provides an SAS or DAS connection to the FDDI backbone using MMF media interface connector (MIC) connections. It connects to a 62.5/125 micron MMF. The LEDs provided on this module are the same as the CDDI, with the notable exception of the In LED, which is related to the Optical Bypass Switch. When the LED is on, the bypass switch is activated and is in Thru mode (the line module is attached to the dual ring).

Fiber-Optic Bypass Switch Connector

As FDDI networks grow, the probability of multiple ring failures increases. When two ring failures occur, the ring will be wrapped in both cases, effectively segmenting the ring into two separate rings that cannot communicate with each other. Subsequent failures cause additional ring segmentation. Optical bypass switches can be used to prevent ring segmentation by eliminating failed stations from the ring.

The six-pin mini-DIN connector connects an external optical bypass switch to the module. An activated bypass switch keeps the module inserted into the ring, even though it is powered off.

If you install or remove an optical bypass switch, you must reset the FDDI module for the change to take effect.

NOTE   The maximum distance supported is 2 km.

FDDI SMF Module

The single-mode fiber (SMF) provides an SAS or DAS connection to the FDDI backbone network using two single-mode (ST) fiber-optic connections. It connects to 8/125-micron single mode fiber. As with the MMF Module, the FDDI SMF Module comes with an optical bypass switch connector.

NOTE   The maximum distance supported by the FDDI module CAS is 32 km.

Applications

FDDI is generally implemented as some kind of backbone in a network. Prior to the advent of 100 Mbps Ethernet and ATM, FDDI was the only way to carry traffic at 100 Mbps and provide redundancy. Consequently, FDDI is a legacy network technology, and you should expect to see it in older networks.

This section discusses two implementations of FDDI using Catalyst switches.

The most basic use of FDDI is shown in Figure 11-2, implementing a shared FDDI backbone connecting multiple Ethernet segments. The two features of the FDDI module used here are APaRT and IP fragmentation, where frames larger than the maximum frame size for Ethernet are fragmented into properly sized frames.

Figure 11-2   *Shared FDDI Backbone*

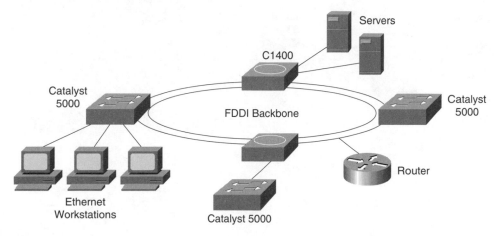

FDDI can also be used in a heterogeneous topology, as shown in Figure 11-3. This topology includes ATM, Fast Ethernet, FDDI, and Ethernet. As you can see, the Catalyst 5000 supports multiple FDDI links in one chassis. Using the 802.10 protocol support, VLANs can be supported across the network fabric using FDDI.

Figure 11-3 *Heterogeneous Network*

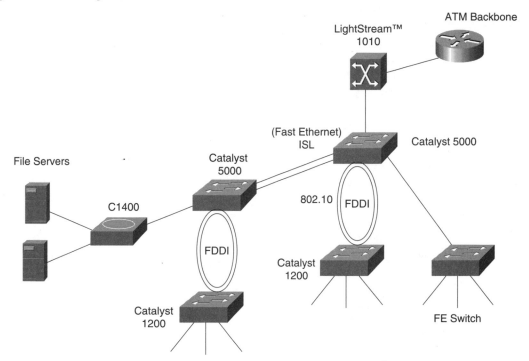

FDDI VLANs

CLSC Objectives Covered in This Section

44	Describe IEEE 802.10 VLANs.

FDDI networks can be integrated into an enterprise-wide VLAN architecture by using the 802.10 protocol on Cisco routers and switches. By using Cisco's VLAN network management software and VLAN Trunk Protocol (VTP), you can map ISL, ATM ELANs, and 802.10 VLANs to provide a method for VLAN propagation across a variety of media types.

The IEEE 802.10 Header

The 802.10 protocol incorporates a mechanism whereby LAN traffic can carry a VLAN identifier, thus enabling selective switching of packets with this identifier. The protocol is the IEEE 802.10 Interoperable LAN/MAN Security (SLS) standard, ratified in late 1992. This specification was originally conceived to address the growing need for security with shared LAN/metropolitan-area network (MAN) environments, and it incorporates authentication and encryption techniques to ensure data confidentiality and integrity throughout the network. Additionally, the SLS standard functions at Layer 2 of the OSI reference model, making it well-suited to high-throughput, low latency switching environments.

The 802.10 standard defines a single protocol data unit, known as a Secure Data Exchange (SDE) PDU. This is a MAC-layer frame with an 802.10 header inserted between the MAC header and the frame's data. As shown in Figure 11-4, the 802.10 header consists of an inner and an outer header, known respectively as the Clear Header and the Protected Header portions.

Figure 11-4   *IEEE 802.10 Header*

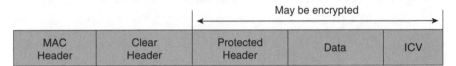

The Protected Header replicates the source address contained in the MAC header to provide for address validation, which prevents another station from being identified as the real source.

The Integrity Check Value (ICV) safeguards against unauthorized internal data modification using a security algorithm.

Support for each portion of the 802.10 header, including encryption, is optional. When used to fully secure data transfer across shared media, the protocol can be used in conjunction with a Security Management Information Base (SMIB), which provides the SAID and encryption keys used by LAN devices to exchange data within the same secured community.

The Security Association Identifier

The 802.10 frame's Clear Header includes a Security Association Identifier (SAID) and an optional Management-Defined Field (MDF), which can carry information to facilitate PDU processing.

When the IEEE 802.10 protocol is used to effect a VLAN topology, VLAN ID is the essential piece of required header information. The 802.10 SAID field is used as the VLAN ID. This field identifies traffic as belonging to a particular 802.10 VLAN. Internetworking devices with VLAN intelligence, such as the Catalyst 5000, can then make forwarding decisions based on which ports are configured for which VLANs.

Therefore, where the goal is to establish logical VLAN topologies across a physical network (rather than encrypting the actual data and thereby incurring performance reduction caused by applying security algorithms), high-throughput devices must minimally support only the Clear Header portion of the 802.10 packet format. In this case, only the SDE Designator (IEEE 802.2 LSAP, indicating an 802.10 VLAN frame) and the actual VLAN ID (SAID field) must be carried, which adds the advantage of low processing overhead. These two fields total 7 bytes.

The 4-byte SAID provides for 4.29 billion (2^{32}) distinct VLANs, making it possible to configure ports for multiple VLANs and, in the future, extend the criteria for VLAN membership to interface and protocol, for example.

Associating 802.10 VLANs with Ethernet VLANs

FDDI 802.10 SAIDs are associated by the Catalyst 5000 with Ethernet VLANs to create a single broadcast domain.

Native frames that originate from stations assigned Ethernet VLANs and whose destination address is on an 802.10 FDDI ring acquire an 802.10 header that contains the appropriate VLAN ID (SAID) as the packets are forwarded onto the FDDI backbone. Networking devices on the backbone, such as the Catalyst 5000 FDDI Module, perform a VLAN ID match to keep the propagation of such packets within the VLAN. Received 802.10 frames that bear an ID not supported on any of a device's ports are filtered. Frames that match are stripped of the 802.10 frames that bear an ID not supported on any of a device's ports. Frames that match are stripped of the 802.10 portion and switched out the corresponding ports in native Ethernet format.

The VLAN matching process relies on the VLAN-to-SAID mapping that you configure using the **translation** parameter in the **set vlan** command, detailed later in this chapter. The VLAN numbers and the SAID numbers are completely independent of one another. You can choose any number from 1 to 1000 for VLAN numbers, and you can choose any number from 1 to 4.29 billion for SAID numbers. Furthermore, you can map any VLAN number to any SAID number. Because 802.10 VLAN packets are valid MAC frames, they are handled transparently by non-802.10-compatible devices. Therefore, the VLAN multiplexing/demultiplexing function must be applied only at the boundary device that connects a VLAN subnet to the common backbone.

The VLAN Trunk Protocol (VTP) provides CDDI/FDDI module configuration for 802.10-based VLANs. Cisco employs the 802.10 protocol within both switching and routing products. The interchange of 802.10 across the backbone provides broadcast control between configured VLANs.

Using a VLAN Numbering Scheme

When you create a new Ethernet VLAN, the Catalyst 5000 software automatically creates a default SAID unless you specifically override it with one of your own creation. The Catalyst 5000 adds 100,000 to the Ethernet VLAN ID to create the default SAID value. However, unless you configure a router interface with SDE encapsulation, you do not need to track this SAID value. Only the FDDI VLAN number that you create and subsequently map to it will join its broadcast domain.

In practice, you can effectively ignore the system-assigned SAID; instead, you may find it easier to deal only with VLAN numbers.

Mapping Ethernet and FDDI VLANs

The user-configurable 4-byte SAID identifies traffic as belonging to a particular VLAN. The Catalyst 5000 that receives the packets from the trunk decodes the 802.10 format using the SAID value and internally translates the FDDI VLAN packets into Ethernet VLAN packets.

VLANs can be extended across an FDDI network by multiplexing switched packets over a CDDI/FDDI interface using the 802.10 protocol. Using 802.10, Catalyst 5000 CDDI/FDDI interface links can operate as interswitch trunks that provide broadcast control between configured VLANs. The 802.10 protocol encapsulates a VLAN identifier and packet data according to the IEEE 802.10 specification. CDDI/FDDI interfaces that support 802.10 make selective forwarding decisions within a network domain based on the VLAN identifier.

In Figure 11-5, 802.10 VLANs are mapped to Ethernet VLANs; Ethernet VLAN 20 is mapped to 620, Ethernet VLAN 30 is mapped to 630, and Ethernet VLAN 40 is mapped to 640. The FDDI ring in this diagram is acting as a trunk, integrating 10/100 Ethernet LANs with FDDI.

Figure 11-5 *Mapping Ethernet and FDDI VLANs*

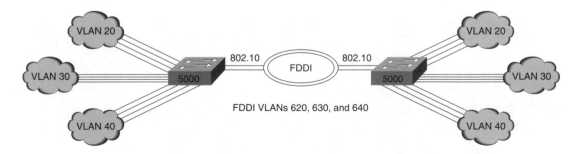

The SAID ensures that packets destined for VLAN 20 reach VLAN 20 only after they traverse the FDDI trunks.

CDDI/FDDI modules also support one native (nontrunk) VLAN, which handles all non-802.10 encapsulated FDDI traffic. A translation number does not need to be configured for the native VLAN because frames forwarded to the native VLAN do not contain VLAN identifiers.

To map an Ethernet VLAN to an FDDI native VLAN, you must configure the Ethernet VLAN with the VLAN identifier and the module number and port number of the FDDI native VLAN.

Managing the FDDI Module

CLSC Objectives Covered in This Section

45	Configure the Catalyst 5000 FDDI/CDDI Module.

The FDDI module, which can be managed using CiscoView, has the following network management-related features:

- Cisco Discovery Protocol (CDP) support for easy network discovery of Cisco devices.

- Flash download capability to simplify software updates.

- Support for industry-standard MIBs, including the Cisco Workgroup MIB, the Simple Network Management Protocol (SNMP) standard network management tools, and station management (SMT) version 7.3.

- Password-protected admin interface that enables out-of-band local network management, remote access via dial-up modem, or remote in-band access via Telnet. The admin interface can also be used to download new software locally or across the network.

- Power-up diagnostic support for easy module status diagnosis.

Configuring the FDDI/CDDI Module

Most features that you need to run the FDDI/CDDI Module are configured right out of the box, as default. The more important features are listed here:

- Default IPX protocol translations are set.

  — FDDI SNAP to Ethernet 802.3 RAW

  — FDDI 802.2 to Ethernet 802.3

  — Ethernet 802.3 RAW to FDDI SNAP

- IP fragmentation is enabled.

- ICMP unreachable messages are enabled.

Setting the Port Name

Setting the port name requires the steps in this table to be executed in enable or privileged mode.

Task	Command
Set the port name	**set port name** *mod_num/port_num* [*name_string*]
Verify the port name	**show port** *mod_num/port_num*

As an example, this code shows the setting of port names for ports 2/1 and 2/2 and illustrates the process for verifying that information using the **show port** command.

```
Console> (enable) set port name 2/1 FDDI A
Console> (enable) set port name 2/2 FDDI A
Console> (enable) show port 2
Port Name                  Status    Vlan        Level  Duplex Speed Type
---- -------------------- --------- ---------- ------ ------ ----- -----
2/1  FDDI A                connect   1                  half   100   FDDI
2/2  FDDI B                standby   1                  half   100   FDDI

Port CE-State Conn-State Type Neig Con Est Alm Cut Lem-Ct Lem-Rej-Ct T1-Min
---- -------- ---------- ---- ---- --- --- ------- ------ ---------- -------
4/1  isolated active     A    U    yes 9   10  11      0            0 40
4/2  isolated standby    B    U    yes 9   10  11      0            0 134000

Last-Time-Cleared
-------------------------
Sat Mar 13, 1999, 23:11
```

Setting Up an FDDI 802.10 Configuration

Two tasks are involved in setting up an FDDI 802.10 configuration. The first is to set up a VTP domain. While the Catalyst 5000 comes with a default set up as a VTP server, the domain name must be filled in by the user.

The second task is to configure trunks between two switches, using FDDI. In the example shown in Figure 11-6, an Ethernet VLAN 20 exists on two switches, connected by the trunks of FDDI VLAN 7. The configuration is set up with the FDDI VLAN 7 having an SAID value of 20 and Ethernet VLAN 20 with a translation to FDDI VLAN 7. Switches 1 and 2 are set up to enable Ethernet VLAN 20 on the FDDI trunk.

Figure 11-6 *An FDDI 802.10 Configuration*

Creating an FDDI VLAN

The **set vlan** command creates the VLAN but does not assign it to a port. VTP advertises the VLAN to all available trunks of all types (such as Ethernet or FDDI) that are set to on, and to all Catalyst 5000 series switches in the same VTP domain. This command enables you to set the MTU, but there is no advantage to setting the MTU higher than 1500 because all FDDI traffic is translationally bridged to Ethernet before crossing the backplane. This command also enables you to set a SAID manually, instead of taking the default.

Task	Command
Create a FDDI VLAN	**set vlan** *vlan_num* **type** *fddi* **mtu** *mtu* **said** *said*

Take a look at this example:

```
Console> (enable) set vlan 300 type fddi said 300
VTP: vlan addition successful
```

This command has created FDDI VLAN 300, with a SAID that happens to match the FDDI VLAN number. This simplifies your administration.

Assigning a VLAN to a Port

The **set vlan** command can be used to set up the native FDDI VLAN. The following mini-table shows the syntax:

Task	Command
Assign VLAN to a port	**set vlan** *vlan_num mod_num/port_num*

Take a look at this example:

```
Console> (enable) set vlan 300 2/1
VLAN 300 modified.
VLAN 1 modified.
VLAN Mod/Ports
---- -----------------------
2/1
```

The FDDI port 2/1 has been changed from the default VLAN 1 to VLAN 300. The output of the command shows all ports included in the VLAN (only one at this point).

Multiswitch VLAN Configuration Without Trunking Example

A VLAN group can be set up across multiple Catalyst 5000 switches without trunking if the switches have any two ports of the same VLAN connected, as shown in Figure 11-7. You need to configure the VLANs individually for both switches using the **set vlan** command.

Figure 11-7   *Multiswitch VLAN Configuration Without Trunking*

Verifying Your Results

The VLAN configuration results can be viewed either by individual VLAN number or by all VLANs. An example of both can be viewed here:

```
Console> (enable) show vlan 10
VLAN Name                        Type  Status    Mod/Ports
---- -------------------------- ----- --------- ---------------
10   VLAN0010                    enet  active    4/1-2

VLAN SAID       MTU   RingNo BridgeNo StpNo Parent Trans1 Trans2
---- ---------- ----- ------ -------- ----- ------ ------ -----
10   100010     1500  0      0        0     0      0      0
```

Mapping VLANs

You can map VLANs in two different ways, either mapping Ethernet to FDDI, or vice versa. The result is the same.

The syntax for both mappings is shown here.

```
Set vlan ether_vlan_num translation fddi_vlan_num
```

or

```
set vlan fddi_vlan_num translation ether_vlan_num
```

Let's take a closer look at this process. In the following code, we will translate the Ethernet VLAN 10 to the FDDI VLAN 300, using the first version of the syntax shown previously.

```
Console> (enable) set vlan 10 translation 300

VTP:  vlan modification successful
```

In this case, we translated the Ethernet VLAN 10 to the FDDI VLAN 300.

Setting Trunks

As with the Ethernet modules, the **set trunk** command is used to configure trunk ports and to turn the trunk on or off on the FDDI module. Unlike the Ethernet modules, no desirable or auto settings exist on the FDDI module. The syntax is shown here:

```
Set trunk mod_num/port_num [on|off][vlan range]
```

In the following example, trunking is turned on for port 2/1.

```
Console> (enable) set trunk 2/1 on

Port 2/1 mode set to on
```

To verify a trunk, use the command **show trunk**.

NOTE   The trunk must be set to on at both ends of a link.

Displaying VLAN Information

Although most of this information was previously covered in the configuration section of the Catalyst Ethernet modules, we will show the display here for review. As you can see, there are some new entries. The syntax is **show vlan**.

```
Console> (enable) show vlan
VLAN Name                         Type  Status    Mod/Ports
---- -------------------------- ----- --------- ---------------
1    default                      enet  active    1/1
                                                  2/1-10
10   VLAN0010                     enet  active    2/11-20
20   VLAN0020                     enet  active    2/22-23
30   VLAN0030                     enet  active    2/21,2/24
200  VLAN0200                     fddi  active
300  VLAN0300                     fddi  active
1002 fddi-default                 fddi  active
```

```
1004 fddinet-default              fdnet active

VLAN SAID        MTU   RingNo BrdgeNo StpNo Parent Trans1 Trans2
---- ----------- ----- ------ ------- ----- ------ ------ -----
1    100001      1500  0      0       0     0      0      0
10   100010      1500  0      0       0     0      0      0
20   100020      1500  0      0       0     0      200    0
30   100030      1500  0      0       0     0      300    0
200  100200      1500  0      0       0     0      20     0
610  10          1500  0      0       0     0      30     0
1002 101002      1500  0      0       0     0      0      0
1004 101004      1500  0      0       0     0      0      0
```

Disabling APaRT?

To disable or not to disable? That is the question. It's not a question for Shakespeare to ponder, but you might want to. APaRT is enabled by default; some advantages to disabling APaRT include these:

- Throughput is increased by 5000 pps to 10,000 pps.

- The EARL will continue to provide packet-forwarding information.

Now for the disadvantages:

- Only the default IPX translations can be used.

- All traffic from the FDDI ring is translated and forwarded to the Catalyst backplane.

- Disabling APaRT also disables fddicheck.

To generalize, you might want to disable APaRT if you have an IP-only network. The syntax for disabling APaRT is shown here:

```
set bridge apart disable
```

Here's an example of the syntax to disable APaRT:

```
Console> (enable) set bridge apart disable

APaRT disabled
```

The command to verify your results is the **show bridge** command.

Here's an example:

```
Console> (enable) show bridge

APaRT disabled
FDDICHECK Disabled
IP fragmentation Enabled
Default IPX translation:
    FDDI SNAP to Ethernet      8023raw
    FDDI 802.2 to Ethernet     8023
Ethernet 802.3 Raw to FDDI snap
```

Disabling fddicheck?

As mentioned before, fddicheck is disabled by default. If your FDDI network is operating smoothly and is not prone to frequent losses of connectivity and high levels of background traffic, you can stay with the default setting. The default setting maximizes the performance of your FDDI/CDDI module by bypassing this lookup for each FDDI packet.

However, if your FDDI network is prone to frequent losses of connectivity and high levels of background traffic, you can use the **show cam mod_num/port_num** command to determine whether the MAC address of Ethernet-attached devices is registered as being attached on the FDDI side. If this is the case, then fddicheck can serve as a useful fix.

To summarize, fddicheck should be left off unless needed because it requires APaRT to be disabled and it increases latency. However, it can prevent loss of connectivity.

Q&A

As mentioned in Chapter 1, "The Cisco LAN Switch Configuration (CLSC) Exam Overview," the questions and scenarios are more difficult than what you should experience on the actual exam. The questions do not attempt to cover more breadth or depth than the exam; however, the questions are designed to make sure you know the answers. Rather than allowing you to derive the answer from clues hidden inside the question itself, the questions challenge your understanding and recall of the subject. Questions from the "Do I Know This Already?" quiz from the beginning of the chapter are repeated here to ensure that you have mastered the chapter's topic areas.

  1 The 4-byte SAID field allows for:

   a. 255 VLANs

   b. 1000 VLANs

   c. 2.32 billion VLANs

   d. 4.29 billion VLANs

  2 What is APaRT, and what is its function?

  3 When creating FDDI VLANs, it is important to configure the SAID values.

   a. True

   b. False

  4 What media/connectors are supported in the FDDI/CDDI cards?

  5 What is the distance limitation on a CDDI module?

  6 What would be the value of the SAID (default) if you typed the command *set vlan 100* (while in enable mode)?

   7 What is the command to translate an Ethernet VLAN to an FDDI VLAN?

   8 If you disable APaRT, what happens to fddicheck?

   9 In what environment might you consider disabling APaRT?

  10 The FDDI module's implementation of the IEEE 802.10 protocol:

     a. Uses the ICV field of the IEEE 802.10 frame.

     b. Uses the SAID field of the Protected Header in the IEEE 802.10 frame.

     c. Uses the SAID field of the Clear Header in the IEEE 802.10 frame.

     d. All of the above.

Source Material

Some content in this chapter is based on the following sources:

- *Cisco LAN Switching Student Guide*, Chapter 12

- Catalyst 5000 Series FDDI and CDDI Switching Modules Configuration Note

  http://www.cisco.com/univercd/cc/td/doc/product/lan/cat5000/cnfg_nts/
  5013fddi.htm

- Configuring the CDDI/FDDI Module

  http://www.cisco.com/univercd/cc/td/doc/product/lan/cat5000/rel_2_2/
  c5kcg2_2/06fddi.htm

The objectives of the Cisco LAN Switch Configuration (CLSC) exam are taken from the Cisco web site, at the Cisco career certification and training area. The following table shows the exam objectives covered in this chapter:

Objective	Description
46	Define LAN Emulation.
47	Describe the LAN Emulation components.
48	Describe the start-up procedure of a LAN Emulation Client.
49	Describe how one LEC establishes communications with another LEC.
50	Discuss how internetworking is achieved in a LANE environment.
51	List the features of the Catalyst 5000 LANE module.
52	Outline the performance ratings for the ATM bus and the switching bus.
53	Describe how to access the CLI for the LANE Module.
54	Describe the Simple Server Redundancy Protocol (SSRP).
55	Explain ATM address structure.
56	Describe how ATM addresses are automatically assigned.
57	Describe the rules for assigning ATM components to interfaces.
58	Configure LANE components on a Catalyst 5000 switch.

CHAPTER 12

Introduction to ATM Networking

Following the chapter opener information and quiz is an introduction to Asynchronous Transfer Mode (ATM) networking, presented for a clearer understanding of ATM. Some of the material is covered later in the chapter. You will not be tested on the introductory material in this section—it is intended to introduce you to ATM in case you need such an introduction. If you just want to see the material on which you will be tested, jump ahead to the section "Introduction to LAN Emulation" (page 376).

How to Best Use This Chapter

By taking the following steps, you can make better use of your study time:

- Keep your notes and the answers for all your work with this book in one place, for easy reference.

- Take the quiz, and write down your answers. Studies show that retention is significantly increased through writing down facts and concepts, even if you never look at the information again.

- Use the diagram in Figure 12-1 to guide you to the next step.

Figure 12-1 *How to Best Use This Chapter in Preparation for the CLSC Exam*

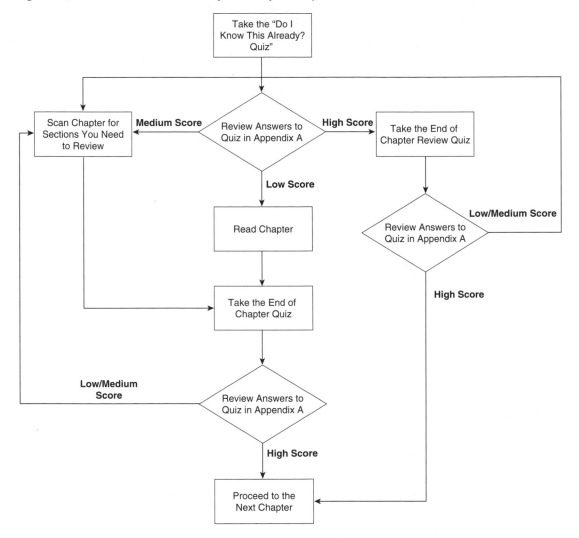

Do I Know This Already? Quiz

You can find the answers to this quiz in Appendix A, "Answers to 'Do I Know This Already?' Quizzes and Q & A Sections." Review the answers, grade your quiz, and choose an appropriate next step in this chapter based on the suggestions diagramed in Figure 12-1.

1 What is an LECS, and what is it used for?

2 What devices can be LAN Emulation Clients (LECs)? Which devices can be LAN Emulation Servers (LESs)?

3 In the ATM address structure, what is an ESI?

4 What command is used from the Catalyst to access the LANE module?

5 What is the maximum distance that can be achieved using an MMF ATM LANE Module?

6 What are the performance characteristics of the ATM LANE module with respect to throughput?

7 What media types are available using LANE?

8 What is the configuration command to enable an LES? What component of ATM LANE does this also enable?

Using the answer key in Appendix A, grade your answers.

- **3 or less correct**—Read this chapter.

- **4, 5, or 6 correct**—Review this chapter, looking at the charts and diagrams that summarize most of the concepts and facts in this chapter.

- **7 or more correct**—If you want more review on these topics, skip to the Q&A section at the end of this chapter. If you do not want more review on these topics, skip this chapter.

Foundation Topics

Introduction to Asynchronous Transfer Mode Switching

The material presented here is intended to help the reader understand Asynchronous Transfer Mode (ATM) features; however, it is not directly related to one of the objectives.

ATM is an International Telecommunication Union Telecommunication Standardization Sector (ITU-T) standard for cell relay wherein information for multiple service types (such as voice, video, or data) is conveyed in small, fixed-size cells. ATM networks are connection-oriented. This chapter provides summaries of ATM protocols, services, and operation. Figure 12-2 illustrates a private ATM network and a public ATM network carrying voice, video, and data traffic.

Figure 12-2   *A Private ATM Network and a Public ATM Network Both Carrying Voice, Video, and Data Traffic*

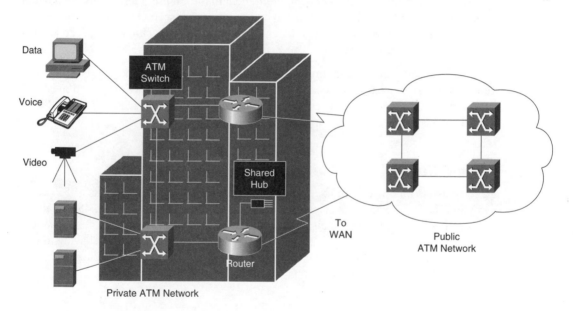

Standards

ATM is based on the efforts of the ITU-T Broadband Integrated Services Digital Network (BISDN) standard. It originally was conceived as a high-speed transfer technology for voice, video, and data over public networks. The ATM Forum extended the ITU-T's vision of ATM for use over public and private networks. The ATM Forum has released work on the following specifications:

- User-to-Network Interface (UNI) 2.0
- UNI 3.0
- UNI 3.1
- Public-Network Node Interface (P-NNI)
- LAN Emulation (LANE)

ATM Devices and Network Environment

ATM is a cell-switching and multiplexing technology that combines the benefits of circuit switching (guaranteed capacity and constant transmission delay) with those of packet switching (flexibility and efficiency for intermittent traffic). It provides scalable bandwidth from a few megabits per second (Mbps) to many gigabits per second (Gbps). Because of its asynchronous nature, ATM is more efficient than synchronous technologies, such as time-division multiplexing (TDM).

With TDM, users are assigned time slots in which other stations cannot send during that time slot. If a station has more data to send than can be sent during a time slot, it must wait until its next time slot arrives, even if other time slots are not used. Unlike TDM, ATM is asynchronous and time slots are available on demand.

ATM Cell Basic Format

ATM transfers information in fixed-size units called cells. Each cell consists of 53 octets, or bytes. The first 5 bytes contain cell-header information, and the remaining 48 contain the *payload* (user information). Small fixed-length cells are well-suited to transferring voice and video traffic because such traffic is intolerant of delays that result from having to wait for large variable-length data packets to be routed through a conventional internetwork. Figure 12-3 illustrates the basic format of an ATM cell.

Figure 12-3 *An ATM Cell*

ATM Devices

An ATM network is made up of an ATM switch and ATM endpoints. An ATM switch is responsible for cell transit through an ATM network. The job of an ATM switch is well-defined: It accepts the incoming cell from an ATM endpoint or another ATM switch. It then reads and updates the cell-header information and quickly switches the cell to an output interface toward its destination. An ATM endpoint (or end system) contains an ATM network interface adapter. Examples of ATM endpoints are workstations, routers, data-service units (DSUs), LAN switches, and video coder-decoders (CODECs). Figure 12-4 illustrates an ATM network made up of ATM switches and ATM endpoints.

Figure 12-4   *An ATM Network, Comprised of ATM Switches and Endpoints*

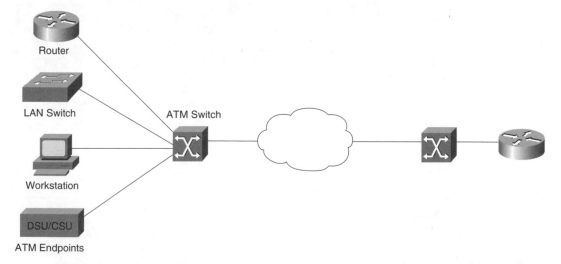

ATM Network Interfaces

An ATM network consists of a set of ATM switches interconnected by point-to-point ATM links or interfaces.

ATM switches support two primary types of interfaces: user-network interface (UNI) and network-node interface (NNI). The UNI connects ATM end systems (such as hosts and routers) to an ATM switch. The NNI connects two ATM switches.

Depending on whether the switch is owned and located at the customer's premises or is publicly owned and operated by the telephone company, UNI and NNI can be further subdivided into public and private UNIs and NNIs. A private UNI connects an ATM endpoint and a private ATM switch. Its public counterpart connects an ATM endpoint or private switch to a public switch. A private NNI connects two ATM switches within the same private organization. A public NNI connects two ATM switches within the same public organization.

An additional specification, the Broadband Interexchange Carrier Interconnect (B-ICI), connects two public switches from different service providers.

ATM Cell-Header Format

An ATM cell header can be one of two formats: UNI or NNI. The UNI header is used for communication between ATM endpoints and ATM switches in private ATM networks. The NNI header is used for communication between ATM switches. Figure 12-5 depicts the basic ATM cell format, the ATM UNI cell-header format, and the ATM NNI cell-header format.

Figure 12-5 *An ATM Cell, ATM UNI Cell, and ATM NNI Cell Header, Each Containing 48 Bytes of Payload*

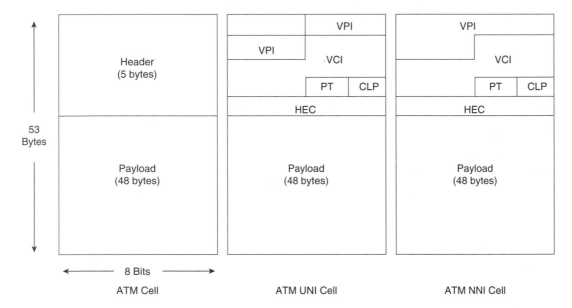

Unlike the UNI, the NNI header does not include the Generic Flow Control (GFC) field. Instead, the NNI header uses the same bits that the UNI assigns to the GFC to expand the Virtual Path Identifier (VPI) field, giving the VPI 4 additional bits for a total of 12 bits. This provides for larger trunks between ATM switches.

ATM Cell-Header Fields

In addition to the GFC and VPI header fields, several others are used in ATM cell-header fields. The following descriptions summarize the ATM cell-header fields illustrated in Figure 12-5.

- *Generic Flow Control (GFC)*—Provides local functions, such as identifying multiple stations that share a single ATM interface. This field is typically not used and is set to its default value.

- *Virtual Path Identifier (VPI)*—In conjunction with the VCI, identifies the next destination of a cell as it passes through a series of ATM switches on the way to its destination.

- *Virtual Channel Identifier (VCI)*—In conjunction with the VPI, identifies the next destination of a cell as it passes through a series of ATM switches on the way to its destination.

- *Payload Type (PT)*—Indicates in the first bit whether the cell contains user data or control data. If the cell contains user data, the second bit indicates congestion, and the third bit indicates whether the cell is the last in a series of cells that represent a single AAL5 frame.

- *Congestion Loss Priority (CLP)*—Indicates whether the cell should be discarded if it encounters extreme congestion as it moves through the network. If the CLP bit equals 1, the cell should be discarded in preference to cells with the CLP bit equal to 0.

- *Header Error Control (HEC)*—Calculates the checksum only on the header itself.

ATM Services

Three types of ATM services exist: permanent virtual connections (PVC), switched virtual connections (SVC), and connectionless service (which is similar to SMDS).

A PVC provides direct connectivity between sites; in this way, a PVC is similar to a leased line. Among its advantages, a PVC guarantees availability of a connection and does not require call setup procedures between switches. Disadvantages of PVCs include static connectivity and manual setup.

An SVC is created and released dynamically and remains in use only as long as data is being transferred. In this sense, it is similar to a telephone call. Dynamic call control requires a signaling protocol between the ATM endpoint and the ATM switch. The advantages of SVCs include connection flexibility and call setup that can be handled automatically by a networking device. Disadvantages include the extra time and overhead required to set up the connection.

ATM Virtual Connections

ATM networks are fundamentally connection-oriented, which means that a virtual channel (VC) must be set up across the ATM network prior to any data transfer. (A VC is roughly equivalent to a virtual circuit.)

Two types of ATM connections exist: virtual paths, which are identified by virtual path identifiers (VPIs); and virtual channels, which are identified by the combination of a VPI and a virtual channel identifier (VCI).

A virtual path is a bundle of VCs, all of which are switched transparently across the ATM network on the basis of the common VPI. All VCIs and VPIs, however, have only local significance across a particular link and are remapped, as appropriate, at each switch.

A transmission path is a bundle of VPs. Figure 12-6 illustrates how VCs concatenate to create VPs, which in turn, concatenate to create a transmission path.

Figure 12-6 *VCs Concatenating to Create VPs*

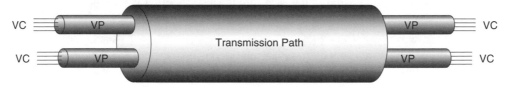

ATM Switching Operation

The basic operation of an ATM switch is straightforward: The cell is received across a link on a known VCI or VPI value. The switch looks up the connection value in a local translation table to determine the outgoing port (or ports) of the connection and the new VPI/VCI value of the connection on that link. The switch then retransmits the cell on that outgoing link with the appropriate connection identifiers. Because all VCIs and VPIs have only local significance across a particular link, these values are remapped, as necessary, at each switch.

ATM Reference Model

The ATM architecture uses a logical model to describe the functionality it supports. ATM functionality corresponds to the physical layer and part of the data link layer of the OSI reference model.

The ATM reference model is composed of the following planes, which span all layers:

- *Control*—This plane is responsible for generating and managing signaling requests.

- *User*—This plane is responsible for managing the transfer of data.

- *Management*—This plane contains two components:

    — Layer management manages layer-specific functions, such as the detection of failures and protocol problems.

    — Plane management manages and coordinates functions related to the complete system.

The ATM reference model is composed of the following ATM layers:

- *Physical layer*—Analogous to the physical layer of the OSI reference model, the ATM physical layer manages the medium-dependent transmission.

- *ATM layer*—Combined with the ATM adaptation layer, the ATM layer is roughly analogous to the data link layer of the OSI reference model. The ATM layer is responsible for establishing connections and passing cells through the ATM network. To do this, it uses information in the header of each ATM cell.

- *ATM Adaptation Layer (AAL)*—Combined with the ATM layer, the AAL is roughly analogous to the data link layer of the OSI model. The AAL is responsible for isolating higher-layer protocols from the details of the ATM processes.

Finally, the higher layers residing above the AAL accept user data, arrange it into packets, and hand it to the AAL. Figure 12-7 illustrates the ATM reference model.

Figure 12-7   *The ATM Reference Model, Which Relates to the Lowest Two Layers of the OSI Reference Model*

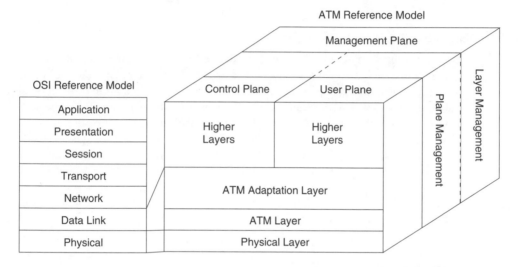

ATM Physical Layer

The ATM physical layer has four functions: bits are converted into cells; the transmission and receipt of bits on the physical medium are controlled; ATM cell boundaries are tracked; and cells are packaged into the appropriate type of frame for the physical medium.

The ATM physical layer is divided into two parts: the physical medium-dependent (PMD) sublayer and the transmission-convergence (TC) sublayer.

The PMD sublayer provides two key functions. First, it synchronizes transmission and reception by sending and receiving a continuous flow of bits with associated timing information. Second, it specifies the physical media for the physical medium used, including connector types and cable. Examples of physical medium standards for ATM include Synchronous Optical Network/Synchronous Digital Hierarchy (SONET/SDH), DS-3/E3, 155 Mbps over multimode fiber (MMF) using the 8B/10B encoding scheme, and 155 Mbps 8B/10B over shielded twisted-pair (STP) cabling.

The TC sublayer has four functions: cell delineation, header error-control (HEC) sequence generation and verification, cell-rate decoupling, and transmission-frame adaptation. The cell delineation function maintains ATM cell boundaries, enabling devices to locate cells within a stream of bits. HEC sequence generation and verification generates and checks the header error-control code to ensure valid data. Cell-rate decoupling maintains synchronization and inserts or suppresses idle (unassigned) ATM cells to adapt the rate of valid ATM cells to the payload capacity of the transmission system. Transmission-frame adaptation packages ATM cells into frames acceptable to the particular physical-layer implementation.

ATM Adaptation Layers: AAL1

AAL1, a connection-oriented service, is suitable for handling circuit-emulation applications, such as voice and video conferencing. Circuit-emulation service also accommodates the attachment of equipment currently using leased lines to an ATM backbone network. AAL1 requires timing synchronization between the source and destination. For this reason, AAL1 depends on a medium, such as SONET, that supports clocking. The AAL1 process prepares a cell for transmission in three steps. First, synchronous samples (for example, 1 byte of data at a sampling rate of 125 microseconds) are inserted into the Payload field. Second, Sequence Number (SN) and Sequence Number Protection (SNP) fields are added to provide information that the receiving AAL1 uses to verify that it has received cells in the correct order. Third, the remainder of the Payload field is filled with enough single bytes to equal 48 bytes.

ATM Adaptation Layers: AAL2

AAL2 is used for connection-oriented services that support a variable bit rate, such as some isochronous video and voice traffic. The AAL2 specification is largely unfinished at this point.

ATM Adaptation Layers: AAL3/4

AAL3/4 supports both connection-oriented and connectionless data. It was designed for network service providers and is closely aligned with Switched Multimegabit Data Service (SMDS). AAL3/4 will be used to transmit SMDS packets over an ATM network.

AAL3/4 prepares a cell for transmission in four steps. First, the convergence sublayer (CS) creates a protocol data unit (PDU) by prepending a beginning/end tag header to the frame and appending a length field as a trailer.

Second, the segmentation and reassembly (SAR) sublayer fragments the PDU and prepends a header to it. Then, the SAR sublayer appends a CRC-10 trailer to each PDU fragment for error control. Finally, the completed SAR PDU becomes the Payload field of an ATM cell, to which the ATM layer prepends the standard ATM header.

An AAL 3/4 SAR PDU header consists of type, sequence number, and multiplexing identifier fields. Type fields identify whether a cell is the beginning, continuation, or end of a message. Sequence number fields identify the order in which cells should be reassembled. The multiplexing identifier determines which cells from different traffic sources are interleaved on the same VCC so that the correct cells are reassembled at the destination.

ATM Adaptation Layers: AAL5

AAL5 is the primary AAL for data and supports both connection-oriented and connectionless data. It is used to transfer most non-SMDS data, such as classical IP, over ATM and LAN Emulation (LANE). AAL5 also is known as the simple and efficient adaptation layer (SEAL) because the SAR sublayer simply accepts the CS-PDU and segments it into 48-octet SAR-PDUs without adding any additional fields.

AAL5 prepares a cell for transmission in three steps. First, the CS sublayer appends a variable-length pad and an 8-byte trailer to a frame. The pad ensures that the resulting PDU falls on the 48-byte boundary of an ATM cell. The trailer includes the length of the frame and a 32-bit cyclic redundancy check (CRC) computed across the entire PDU. This enables the AAL5 receiving process to detect bit errors, lost cells, or cells that are out of sequence. Second, the SAR sublayer segments the CS PDU into 48-byte blocks. A header and trailer are not added (as in AAL3/4), so messages cannot be interleaved. Finally, the ATM layer places each block into the Payload field of an ATM cell. For all cells except the last, a bit in the Payload Type (PT) field is set to zero to indicate that the cell is not the last cell in a series that represents a single frame. For the last cell, the bit in the PT field is set to 1.

ATM Addressing

The ITU-T standard is based upon the use of E.164 addresses (similar to telephone numbers) for public ATM (BISDN) networks. The ATM Forum extended ATM addressing to include private networks. It decided upon the subnetwork or overlay model of addressing, in which the ATM layer is responsible for mapping network-layer addresses to ATM addresses. This subnetwork model is an alternative to using network-layer protocol addresses (such as IP and IPX) and existing routing protocols (such as IGRP and RIP). The ATM Forum defined an address format based on the structure of the OSI network service access point (NSAP) addresses.

Subnetwork Model of Addressing

The subnetwork model of addressing decouples the ATM layer from any existing higher-layer protocols, such as IP or IPX. As such, it requires an entirely new addressing scheme and routing protocol. All ATM systems must be assigned an ATM address, in addition to any higher-layer protocol addresses. This requires an ATM address resolution protocol (ATM_ARP) to map higher-layer addresses to their corresponding ATM addresses.

NSAP Format ATM Addresses

The 20-byte NSAP format ATM addresses are designed for use within private ATM networks, while public networks typically use E.164 addresses, which are formatted as defined by ITU-T. The ATM Forum did specify an NSAP encoding for E.164 addresses, which will be used for encoding E.164 addresses within public networks, but this address also can be used by some private networks.

Such private networks can base their own (NSAP format) addressing on the E.164 address of the public user-network interface (UNI) to which they are connected and can take the address prefix from the E.164 number, identifying local nodes by the lower-order bits.

All NSAP format ATM addresses consist of three components: the Authority and Format Identifier (AFI), the Initial Domain Identifier (IDI), and the domain-specific part (DSP). The AFI identifies the type and format of the IDI, which in turn identifies the address allocation and administrative authority. The DSP contains actual routing information.

Three formats of private ATM addressing differ by the nature of the AFI and IDI. In the NSAP-encoded E.164 format, the IDI is an E.164 number. In the DCC format, the IDI is a Data Country Code (DCC), which identifies particular countries as specified in ISO 3166. Such addresses are administered by the ISO National Member Body in each country. In the ICD format, the IDI is an International Code Designator (ICD), which is allocated by the ISO 6523 registration authority (the British Standards Institute). ICD codes identify particular international organizations.

The ATM Forum recommends that organizations or private network service providers use either the DCC or ICD formats to form their own numbering plan.

Figure 12-8 illustrates the three formats of ATM addresses used for private networks.

Figure 12-8   *Three Formats of ATM Addresses*

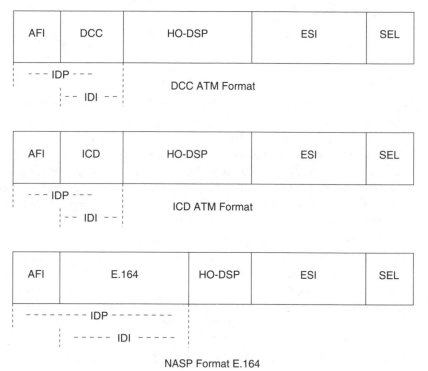

ATM Address Fields

ATM Address Fields

The following descriptions summarize the fields illustrated in Figure 12-8:

- *Authority and Format Identifier (AFI)*—Identifies the type and format of the address (E.164, ICD, or DCC).

- *Data Country Code (DCC)*—Identifies particular countries.

- *High-Order Domain-Specific Part (HO-DSP)*—Combines the Routing Domain (RD) and Area Identifier (AREA) of the NSAP addresses. The ATM Forum combined these fields to support a flexible, multilevel addressing hierarchy for prefix-based routing protocols.

- *End System Identifier (ESI)*—Specifies the 48-bit MAC address, as administered by the Institute of Electrical and Electronic Engineers (IEEE).

- *Selector (SEL)*—Used for local multiplexing within end stations; has no network significance.

- *International Code Designator (ICD)*—Identifies particular international organizations.

- *E.164*—Indicates the BISDN E.164 address.

ATM Connections

ATM supports two types of connections: point-to-point and point-to-multipoint.

Point-to-point connects two ATM end systems and can be unidirectional (one-way communication) or bidirectional (two-way communication). Point-to-multipoint connects a single-source end system (known as the root node) to multiple destination end systems (known as leaves). Such connections are unidirectional only; root nodes can transmit to leaves, but leaves cannot transmit to the root or each other on the same connection. Cell replication is done within the ATM network by the ATM switches, where the connection splits into two or more branches.

It would be desirable in ATM networks to have bidirectional multipoint-to-multipoint connections. Such connections are analogous to the broadcasting or multicasting capabilities of shared-medium LANs, such as Ethernet and Token Ring. A broadcasting capability is easy to implement in shared-medium LANs, where all nodes on a single LAN segment must process all packets sent on that segment. Unfortunately, a multipoint-to-multipoint capability cannot be implemented by using AAL5, which is the most common ATM adaptation layer (AAL) to transmit data across an ATM network.

Unlike AAL3/4, with its Message Identifier (MID) field, AAL5 does not provide a way within its cell format to interleave cells from different AAL5 packets on a single connection. This means that all AAL5 packets sent to a particular destination across a particular connection must be received in sequence; otherwise, the destination reassembly process will be unable to reconstruct the packets. This is why ATM AAL5 point-to-multipoint connections can be only unidirectional. If a leaf node were to transmit an AAL5 packet onto the connection, for example, it would be received by both the root node and all other leaf nodes. At these nodes, the packet sent by the leaf could be interleaved with packets sent by the root and possibly other leaf nodes, precluding the reassembly of any of the interleaved packets.

ATM and Multicasting

ATM requires some form of multicast capability. AAL5 (which is the most common AAL for data) currently does not support interleaving packets, so it does not support multicasting.

If a leaf node transmitted a packet onto an AAL5 connection, the packet could get intermixed with other packets and could be improperly reassembled. Three methods have been proposed for solving this problem: VP multicasting, multicast server, and overlaid point-to-multipoint connection.

Under the first solution, a multipoint-to-multipoint VP links all nodes in the multicast group, and each node is given a unique virtual channel identifier (VCI) value within the VP. Interleaved packets hence can be identified by the unique VCI value of the source. Unfortunately, this mechanism would require a protocol to uniquely allocate VCI values to nodes, and such a protocol mechanism currently does not exist. It is also unclear whether current segmentation and reassembly (SAR) devices could easily support such a mode of operation.

A multicast server is another potential solution to the problem of multicasting over an ATM network. In this scenario, all nodes wanting to transmit onto a multicast group set up a point-to-point connection with an external device known as a multicast server (perhaps better described as a resequencer, or serializer). The multicast server, in turn, is connected to all nodes wanting to receive the multicast packets through a point-to-multipoint connection. The multicast server receives packets across the point-to-point connections and then retransmits them across the point-to-multipoint connection—but only after ensuring that the packets are serialized (that is, one packet is fully transmitted prior to the next being sent). In this way, cell interleaving is precluded.

An overlaid point-to-multipoint connection is the third potential solution to the problem of multicasting over an ATM network. In this scenario, all nodes in the multicast group establish a point-to-multipoint connection with each other node in the group and, in turn, become a leaf in the equivalent connections of all other nodes. Hence, all nodes can both transmit to and receive from all other nodes. This solution requires each node to maintain a connection for each transmitting member of the group, while the multicast server mechanism requires only two connections. This type of connection also would require a registration process for informing the nodes that join a group of the other nodes in the group so that the new nodes can form the point-to-multipoint connection. The other nodes also must know about the new node so that they can add the new node to their own point-to-multipoint connections. The multicast-server mechanism is more scalable in terms of connection resources but has the problem of requiring a centralized resequencer, which is both a potential bottleneck and a single point of failure.

ATM Quality of Service

ATM supports quality of service (QoS) guarantees comprised of traffic contract, traffic shaping, and traffic policing.

A traffic contract specifies an envelope that describes the intended data flow. This envelope specifies values for peak bandwidth, average sustained bandwidth, and burst size, among others. When an ATM end system connects to an ATM network, it enters a contract with the network based on QoS parameters.

Traffic shaping is the use of queues to constrain data bursts, limit peak data rate, and smooth jitters so that traffic will fit within the promised envelope. ATM devices are responsible for adhering to the contract by means of traffic shaping. ATM switches can use traffic policing to enforce the contract. The switch can measure the actual traffic flow and compare it against the agreed-upon traffic envelope. If the switch finds that traffic is outside the agreed-upon parameters, it can set the cell-loss priority (CLP) bit of the offending cells. Setting the CLP bit makes the cell *discard-eligible*, which means that any switch handling the cell is allowed to drop the cell during periods of congestion.

ATM Signaling and Connection Establishment

When an ATM device wants to establish a connection with another ATM device, it sends a signaling-request packet to its directly connected ATM switch. This request contains the ATM address of the desired ATM endpoint, as well as any QoS parameters required for the connection.

ATM signaling protocols vary by the type of ATM link and can be either User-Network Interface (UNI) signals or Network Node Interface (NNI) signals. UNI is used between an ATM end system and ATM switch across ATM UNI, while NNI is used across NNI links.

The ATM Forum UNI 3.1 specification is the current standard for ATM UNI signaling. The UNI 3.1 specification is based on the Q.2931 public network signaling protocol developed by the ITU-T. UNI signaling requests are carried in a well-known default connection: VPI = 0, VPI = 5.

Standards currently exist only for ATM UNI signaling, but standardization work is continuing on NNI signaling.

ATM Connection-Establishment Process

ATM signaling uses the one-pass method of connection setup that is used in all modern telecommunication networks, including telephone networks. An ATM connection setup proceeds in the following manner. First, the source end system sends a connection-signaling request. The connection request is propagated through the network. As a result, connections are set up through the network. The connection request reaches the final destination, which either accepts or rejects the connection request.

Connection-Request Routing and Negotiation

Routing of the connection request is governed by an ATM routing protocol (which routes connections based upon destination and source addresses), traffic, and the QoS parameters requested by the source end system.

Negotiating a connection request that is rejected by the destination is limited because call routing is based on parameters of initial connection; changing parameters might, in turn, affect the connection routing.

ATM Connection-Management Messages

A number of connection management message types—including Setup, Call Proceeding, Connect, and Release—are used to establish and tear down an ATM connection. The source end-system sends a Setup message (including the destination end system address and any traffic QoS parameters) when it wants to set up a connection. The ingress switch sends a Call Proceeding message back to the source in response to the Setup message. The destination end system next sends a Connect message if the connection is accepted. The destination end system sends a Release message back to the source end system if the connection is rejected, thereby clearing the connection.

Connection-management messages are used to establish an ATM connection in the following manner. First, a source end system sends a Setup message, which is forwarded to the first ATM switch (ingress switch) in the network. This switch sends a Call Proceeding message and invokes an ATM routing protocol. The signaling request is propagated across the network. The exit switch (called the egress switch) that is attached to the destination end system receives the Setup message. The egress switch forwards the Setup message to the end system across its UNI, and the ATM end system sends a Connect message if the connection is accepted. The Connect message traverses back through the network along the same path to the source end system, which sends a Connect Acknowledge message back to the destination to acknowledge the connection. Data transfer then can begin.

LAN Emulation

LAN Emulation (LANE) is a standard defined by the ATM Forum that provides to stations attached via ATM the same capabilities they normally obtain from legacy LANs, such as Ethernet and Token Ring. As the name suggests, the function of the LANE protocol is to emulate a LAN on top of an ATM network. Specifically, the LANE protocol defines mechanisms for emulating either an IEEE 802.3 Ethernet or an 802.5 Token Ring LAN. The current LANE protocol does not define a separate encapsulation for FDDI. (FDDI packets must be mapped into either Ethernet or Token Ring emulated LANs [ELANs] by using existing translational bridging techniques.) Fast Ethernet (100BaseT) and IEEE 802.12 (100VG-AnyLAN) both can be mapped unchanged because they use the same packet formats. Figure 12-9 compares a physical LAN and an ELAN.

Figure 12-9   *ATM Network Emulating a Physical LAN*

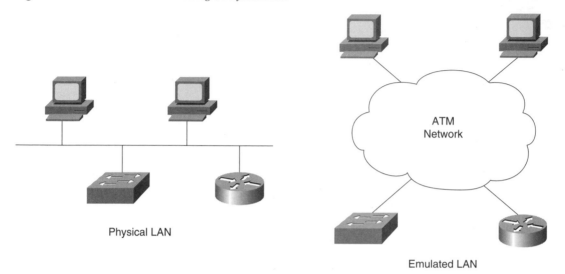

The LANE protocol defines a service interface for higher-layer (that is, network-layer) protocols that is identical to that of existing LANs. Data sent across the ATM network is encapsulated in the appropriate LAN MAC packet format. Simply put, the LANE protocols make an ATM network look and behave like an Ethernet or Token Ring LAN—albeit one that takes full advantage of available ATM bandwidth.

It is important to note that LANE does not attempt to emulate the actual MAC protocol of the specific LAN concerned (that is, CSMA/CD for Ethernet, or token passing for IEEE 802.5). LANE requires no modifications to higher-layer protocols to enable operation over an ATM network. Because the LANE service presents the same service interface of existing MAC protocols to network-layer drivers (such as an NDIS- or ODI-like driver interface), no changes are required in those drivers.

LANE Protocol Architecture

The basic function of the LANE protocol is to resolve MAC addresses to ATM addresses. The goal is to resolve such address mappings so that LANE end systems can set up direct connections between themselves and then can forward data. The LANE protocol will be deployed in two types of ATM-attached equipment: ATM network interface cards (NIC), and internetworking and LAN switching equipment.

ATM NICs will implement the LANE protocol and interface to the ATM network but will present the current LAN service interface to the higher-level protocol drivers within the attached end system. The network-layer protocols on the end system will continue to communicate as if they were on a known LAN, by using known procedures.

They will, however, be capable of using the vastly greater bandwidth of ATM networks.

The second class of network gear that will implement LANE consists of ATM-attached LAN switches and routers.

These devices, together with directly attached ATM hosts equipped with ATM NICs, will be used to provide a virtual LAN service in which ports on the LAN switches will be assigned to particular virtual LANs independent of physical location. Figure 12-10 shows the LANE protocol architecture implemented in ATM network devices.

Figure 12-10   *LANE Protocol Architecture*

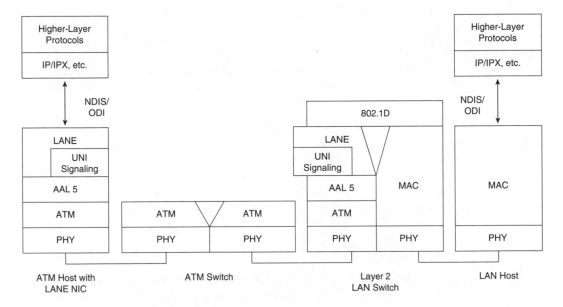

Note that the LANE protocol does not directly impact ATM switches. As with most of the other ATM internetworking protocols, LANE builds upon the overlay model. As such, the LANE protocols operate transparently over and through ATM switches, using only standard ATM signaling procedures.

LANE Components

The LANE protocol defines the operation of a single emulated LAN (ELAN). (An ELAN is equivalent to a virtual LAN [VLAN].) Although multiple ELANs can simultaneously exist on a single ATM network, an ELAN emulates either an Ethernet or a Token Ring and consists of the following components:

- *LAN Emulation Client (LEC)*—The LEC is an entity in an end system that performs data forwarding, address resolution, and registration of MAC addresses with the LAN Emulation Server (LES). The LEC also provides a standard LAN interface to higher-level protocols on legacy LANs. An ATM end system that connects to multiple ELANs will have one LEC per ELAN.

- *LAN Emulation Server (LES)*—The LES provides a central control point for LECs to forward registration and control information. (Only one LES exists per ELAN.)

- *Broadcast and Unknown Server (BUS)*—The BUS is a multicast server that is used to flood unknown destination address traffic and to forward multicast and broadcast traffic to clients within a particular ELAN. Each LEC is associated with only one BUS per ELAN.

- *LAN Emulation Configuration Server (LECS)*—The LECS maintains a database of LECs and the ELANs to which they belong. This server accepts queries from LECs and responds with the appropriate ELAN identifier, namely the ATM address of the LES that serves the appropriate ELAN. One LECS per administrative domain serves all ELANs within that domain.

LANE Connection Types

The Phase 1 LANE entities communicate with each other by using a series of ATM virtual circuit connections (VCCs). LECs maintain separate connections for data transmission and control traffic. The LANE data connections are Data-Direct VCC, Multicast Send VCC, and Multicast Forward VCC.

Data-Direct VCC is a bidirectional point-to-point VCC set up between two LECs that want to exchange data.

Two LECs typically use the same data-direct VCC to carry all packets between them rather than opening a new VCC for each MAC address pair. This technique conserves connection resources and connection setup latency.

Multicast Send VCC is a bidirectional point-to-point VCC set up by the LEC to the BUS.

Multicast Forward VCC is a unidirectional VCC set up to the LEC from the BUS. It typically is a point-to-multipoint connection, with each LEC as a leaf.

Figure 12-11 shows the LANE data connections.

Figure 12-11 *LANE Data Connections*

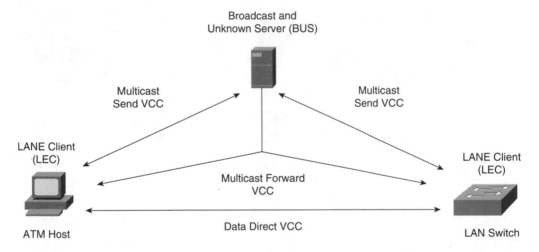

Control connections include Configuration-Direct VCC, Control-Direct VCC, and Control-Distribute VCC. Configuration-Direct VCC is a bidirectional point-to-point VCC set up by the LEC to the LECS. Control-Direct VCC is a bidirectional VCC set up by the LEC to the LES. Control-Distribute VCC is a unidirectional VCC set up from the LES back to the LEC (typically a point-to-multipoint connection). Figure 12-12 illustrates LANE control connections.

Figure 12-12 *LANE Control Connections*

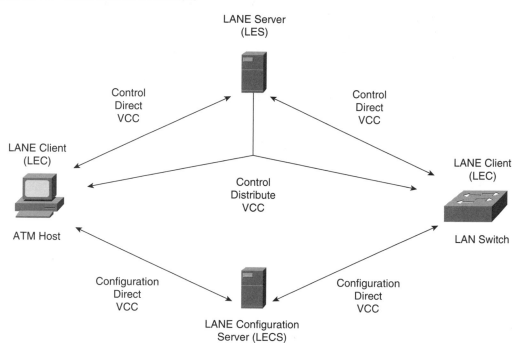

LANE Operation

The operation of a LANE system and components is best understood by examining these stages of LEC operation: initialization and configuration; joining and registering with the LES; finding and joining the BUS; and data transfer.

Initialization and Configuration

Upon initialization, an LEC finds the LECS to obtain required configuration information. It begins this process when the LEC obtains its own ATM address, which typically occurs through address registration.

The LEC then must determine the location of the LECS. To do this, the LEC first must locate the LECS by one of the following methods: by using a defined ILMI procedure to determine the LECS address, by using a well-known LECS address, or by using a well-known permanent connection to the LECS (VPI = 0, VCI = 16).

When the LECS is found, the LEC sets up a configuration-direct VCC to the LECS and sends an LE_CONFIGURE_REQUEST. If a matching entry is found, the LECS returns an

LE_CONFIGURE_RESPONSE to the LEC with the configuration information it requires to connect to its target ELAN. This information includes the ATM address of the LES, the type of LAN being emulated, the maximum packet size on the ELAN, and the ELAN name (a text string for display purposes).

Joining and Registering with the LES

When an LEC joins the LES and registers its own ATM and MAC addresses, it does so by following three steps.

1 After the LEC obtains the LES address, the LEC optionally clears the connection to the LECS, sets up the control-direct VCC to the LES, and sends an LE_JOIN_REQUEST on that VCC. This enables the LEC to register its own MAC and ATM addresses with the LES and (optionally) any other MAC addresses for which it is proxying. This information is maintained so that no two LECs will register the same MAC or ATM address.

2 After receipt of the LE_JOIN_REQUEST, the LES checks with the LECS via its open connection, verifies the request, and confirms the client's membership.

3 Upon successful verification, the LES adds the LEC as a leaf of its point-to-multipoint control-distribute VCC and issues the LEC a successful LE_JOIN_RESPONSE that contains a unique LAN Emulation Client ID (LECID). The LECID is used by the LEC to filter its own broadcasts from the BUS.

Finding and Joining the BUS

Now that the LEC has successfully joined the LECS, its first task is to find the BUS's ATM address to join the broadcast group and become a member of the emulated LAN.

First, the LEC creates an LE_ARP_REQUEST packet with the MAC address 0xFFFFFFFF. Then, the LEC sends this special LE_ARP packet on the control-direct VCC to the LES. The LES recognizes that the LEC is looking for the BUS and responds with the BUS's ATM address on the control-distribute VCC.

When the LEC has the BUS's ATM address, it joins the BUS by first creating a signaling packet with the BUS's ATM address and setting up a multicast-send VCC with the BUS. Upon receipt of the signaling request, the BUS adds the LEC as a leaf on its point-to-multipoint Multicast Forward VCC. The LEC is now a member of the ELAN and is ready for data transfer.

Data Transfer

The final state, data transfer, involves resolving the ATM address of the destination LEC and actual data transfer, which might include the flush procedure.

When a LEC has a data packet to send to an unknown-destination MAC address, it must discover the ATM address of the destination LEC through which the particular address can be reached. To accomplish this, the LEC first sends the data frame to the BUS (via the multicast-send VCC) for distribution to all LECs on the ELAN via the multicast-forward VCC. This is done because resolving the ATM address might take some time, and many network protocols are intolerant of delays.

The LEC then sends a LAN Emulation Address Resolution Protocol Request (LE_ARP_REQUEST) control frame to the LES via a control-direct VCC.

If the LES knows the answer, it responds with the ATM address of the LEC that owns the MAC address in question. If the LES does not know the answer, it floods the LE_ARP_REQUEST to some or all LECs (under rules that parallel the BUS's flooding of the actual data frame, but over control-direct and control-distribute VCCs instead of the multicast-send or multicast-forward VCCs used by the BUS). If bridge/switching devices with LEC software participating in the ELAN exist, they translate and forward the ARP on their LAN interfaces.

In the case of actual data transfer, if an LE_ARP is received, the LEC sets up a data-direct VCC to the destination node and uses this for data transfer rather than the BUS path. Before it can do this, however, the LEC might need to use the LANE flush procedure.

The LANE flush procedure ensures that all packets previously sent to the BUS were delivered to the destination prior to the use of the data-direct VCC. In the flush procedure, a control cell is sent down the first transmission path following the last packet. The LEC then waits until the destination acknowledges receipt of the flush packet before using the second path to send packets.

Introduction to LAN Emulation

CLSC Objectives Covered in This Section

46	Define LAN Emulation.
47	Describe the LAN Emulation components.
48	Describe the start-up procedure of a LAN Emulation Client.
49	Describe how one LEC establishes communication with another LEC.
50	Discuss how internetworking is achieved in a LANE environment.

This section covers an introduction to LAN Emulation. Topics covered include the definition of LANE, the components that make up LANE, and overall operation of LANE clients.

What Is LAN Emulation?

Developed in 1994, LAN Emulation (LANE) is an ATM Forum standard used to connect legacy Ethernet and Token Ring networks to an ATM network.

The LANE specification hides the ATM network from the users and enables the ATM network to look like a legacy Ethernet or Token Ring LAN. It works by making the ATM network emulate a Media Access Control (MAC) network. This enables all endpoints to transparently send MAC-based packets to each other.

LAN Emulation enables upper-layer protocols that expect connectionless service to use connection-oriented ATM switches. It requires software in clients as well as a LAN emulation service.

ATM Forum LAN Emulation Sub-Working group has approved version 1.0. Cisco is a leading member of the ATM Forum (and, in fact, was one of the four original founding partners of the Forum).

Emulated LANs

An emulated LAN (ELAN) is a group of ATM-attached devices, including legacy shared-media devices and fully ATM-attached devices. An ELAN is treated as an independent broadcast domain and can be thought of as a single Ethernet segment or independent token ring.

A broadcast frame that originates from a particular ELAN is sent only to members of the same ELAN. For members of different ELANs to communicate, they must use a router.

LANE Architecture

LAN Emulation is equivalent to a data link layer protocol, operating at the MAC sublayer and below. The LANE protocol sits directly on top of the ATM and ATM Adaptation Layer protocols.

The LAN Emulation specification defines the following LANE interfaces:

> *Between the LANE entity and higher layers*—Used for transmitting and receiving user data frames
>
> *Between the LANE entity and AAL 5*—Used for transmitting and receiving AAL 5 frames
>
> *Between the LANE entity and the UNI Signaling entity*— Used for requesting the setup and release of virtual connects for both SVCs and PVCs

The UNI Signaling entity is also known as the connection management entity.

LANE Components

LAN Emulation defines two components: the LAN Emulation Client and LAN Emulation Services. LAN Emulation Services are made up of the LAN Emulation Configuration Server (LECS), the LAN Emulation Server (LES), and the Broadcast and Unknown Server (BUS).

The LANE Services can all be located in the same device or can be distributed among one, two, or three devices. The LAN Emulation Client can be located in the same device(s) as the LAN Emulation Services.

In the Cisco implementation, the LES and the BUS must be located in the same device.

LAN Emulation Client

The LAN Emulation Client (LEC) implements the LANE protocol via software. The LEC software must reside on every ATM end device participating in the LANE network, and on all edge devices that provide LANE services to legacy end systems.

An edge device is an intermediate system (router, switch, or bridge) that provides LANE connection services for stations on the Ethernet or Token Ring legacy network.

The LEC is responsible for the following four functions:

- Data forwarding
- Address resolution
- Control functions
- MAC-level emulated Ethernet/IEEE 802.3 or IEEE 802.5 service interface to upper-layer protocols

The LEC registers its MAC and ATM addresses with the LES.

LAN Emulation Configuration Server

The LAN Emulation Configuration Server (LECS) contains configuration information for all ELANs in the administrative domain. It is responsible for assigning each LEC to an emulated LAN. It does this by providing the LEC with the ATM address of the LAN Emulation Server assigned to the ELAN.

One LECS exists per administrative domain. An administrative domain may be a company or a campus.

Moving a station to a different ELAN means altering the tables contained in the LECS.

LAN Emulation Server

The LAN Emulation Server (LES) manages the stations that make up the ELAN. It registers and resolves all MAC addresses to ATM addresses using the LAN Emulation Address Resolution Protocol (LE-ARP). LECs register all MAC addresses with the LES.

When a device on the ELAN has data to send to another device on the ELAN, the sending station requests the ATM address of the destination station from the LES.

Each ELAN has its own LES. The standards do not forbid the use of more than one LES for an ELAN, but until the LNNI standard is produced, it is not at all clear as to how the many LESs should interact. The LNNI standard is being worked on as part of the next release (version 2.0) of the LANE Specification.

Broadcast and Unknown Server

All LANs are broadcast systems. It is necessary that LANE emulate broadcast capabilities of legacy LAN systems.

The Broadcast and Unknown Server (BUS) is responsible for handling both broadcasts and multicasts. When a broadcast frame is sent to the BUS, the BUS forwards the frame to all stations in the ELAN, using a point-to-multipoint virtual channel connection (VCC).

Currently, one BUS is allowed per ELAN. Future revisions of the LANE Specification will include the details on using redundant BUS implementations.

Each LES can have only a single BUS associated with it.

ILMI

The Interim Local Management Interface (ILMI) provides the exchange of management information between ATM systems that are managed entities in SNMP.

ILMI communicates using SNMP. Both the ATM end stations (such as the Catalyst 5000) and the ATM switches (such as the Cisco LightStream 1010) maintain a management information base (MIB). ATM end stations and switches can communicate using ILMI.

ILMI is used by LAN Emulation clients to initially locate the LECS.

LAN Emulation Client Startup

To join an ELAN, an LEC first must contact the LECS. The LECS provides the ATM address of the LES for the ELAN.

The LEC contacts the LECS via one of the following four methods (in this order):

- Using a preconfigured address for the LECS
- Using the ILMI protocol

- Using the well-known address of the configuration service

- Using the well-known PVC (VPI = 0, VCI = 16)

The LEC and LECS communicate using a Configuration Direct VCC.

When the LEC has obtained the LES address from the LECS, the LEC contacts the LES using a bidirectional Control Direct VCC.

The LES has the option of checking with the LECS prior to allowing the LEC to join the ELAN.

If the LEC has permission to join the ELAN, the LES adds the address of the LEC to its Control Distribute VCC. The Control Distribute VCC is a point-to-multipoint VCC used by the LES to send information to all the LECs in the ELAN.

After the LES allows the LEC to join the ELAN, the LEC must learn the address of the BUS. The LEC does this by sending an LE-ARP request to the broadcast address. The LES responds to the LE-ARP request with the ATM address of the BUS.

The LEC then sets up a Multicast Send VCC with the BUS.

The BUS forwards the address of the LEC to its Multicast Forward VCC. The Multicast Forward VCC is a point-to-multipoint VCC used by the BUS to broadcast data to all LECs in the ELAN.

As the number of LECs in the ELAN climbs, the number of control VCCs needed to service all the LECs increases linearly. This raises issues about the scalability of LAN Emulation in a single ELAN and the number of LECs that can easily be supported in an ELAN.

Figure 12-13 shows Client A, which has information to send to Client B.

Figure 12-13 *ATM LANE Client Behavior, Part 1*

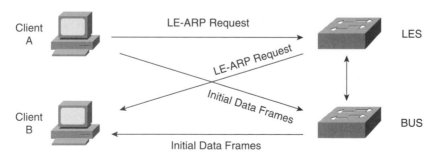

The order of transactions that occur so that Client A can forward information to Client B is detailed here:

Step 1   Client A knows the MAC address of Client B but needs to learn the ATM address of Client B. It sends an LE-ARP request to the LES.

Step 2   Simultaneously with Step 1, Client A begins forwarding data frames to the BUS.

Step 3   The LES checks its LE-ARP table for the ATM address of Client B. If this address is in the table, the LES sends it to Client A. If the ATM address is not in the LE-ARP table, the LES forwards the LE-ARP request to all the LECs using the Control Distribute VCC (point-to-multipoint). Note that if the LEC is a bridge, the ATM address will not be in the table.

Step 4   Simultaneously with Step 3, the BUS forwards the initial frames to all stations using the Multicast Forward VCC (point-to-multipoint).

Now that the first half of the conversation is over, let's continue with the second half. The activity is shown in Figure 12-14.

Figure 12-14   *ATM LANE Client Behavior, Part 2*

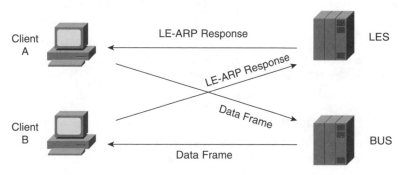

Step 1   Client B responds to the LE-ARP sent by the LES.

Step 2   The LES relays the LE-ARP response (containing the ATM address of Client B) to Client A.

Step 3   Client A sets up a Data Direct VCC with Client B.

Step 4   Client A sends a Flush message to the BUS. The Flush message tells the BUS to stop forwarding any remaining frames that have not yet been sent.

Step 5   Client A uses the Data Direct VCC to communicate with Client B.

LANE Internetworking

When two end systems need to communicate within the same ELAN, their data transmissions are handled by the various switches in the ELAN.

If the two end systems reside in different ELANs, a Layer 3 router or switch must be used to interconnect the ELANs. This is true even if the two end systems are physically connected to the same edge device.

If the ELAN contains devices using IP as the network-layer protocol, all devices in the ELAN must be part of the same IP subnet. Conversely, devices on different IP subnets cannot be members of the same ELAN because they must use a router to communicate.

The ATM LANE Module

CLSC Objectives Covered in This Section

51	List the features of the Catalyst 5000 LANE module.
52	Outline the performance ratings for the ATM bus and the switching bus.
53	Describe how to access the CLI for the LANE module.
54	Describe the Simple Server Redundancy Protocol (SSRP).

This section outlines the hardware aspects of the LANE module. Also covered are Cisco's SSRP, a proprietary redundancy feature, and information on how to access the command-line interface (CLI) for the LANE Module.

LANE Module Features

The Catalyst 5000 LANE Module supports SONET/SDH OC3 at speeds of 155 Mbps. It can be ordered with one of three different interfaces:

- Multimode fiber (MMF)
- Single-mode fiber (SMF)
- Unshielded twisted-pair (UTP)

In addition, the ATM LAN Emulation Module offers the following hardware options:

- Dual single mode
- Dual multimode
- Dual unshielded twisted-pair (UTP)

Note that in the ATM LAN Emulation Module, dual PHY provides redundancy only of the physical connection. Only one ATM interface can be active at any time.

In release 2.1 of the LANE software, the LANE module has full LANE functionality. It can be configured as one of the following:

- LAN Emulation Client (LEC)
- LAN Emulation Configuration Server (LECS)
- LAN Emulation Server (LES)
- LAN Emulation Broadcast and Unknown Server (BUS)

Note that all ATM information resides on the LANE module and does not appear in NVRAM when the **show config** command is issued. To see the information, establish a Telnet session to the LANE module.

Multimode Fiber Module

The ATM LANE Module provides a direct connection between the 155 Mbps ATM network and the Catalyst 5000 switch using a single or multimode fiber-optic connector.

The LEDs provide status information for the module and individual port connections. The physical layer interface module (PLIM) on the ATM LAN Emulation module determines the type of ATM connection.

No restrictions are imposed on slot locations or sequence; an ATM LAN Emulation Module can be installed in any available slot. Dual PHY LAN Emulation modules are available for all module types.

The optical source on the multimode module is LED, and the distance limitation is 2 km.

Single-Mode Fiber Module

The single-mode fiber version of the ATM LANE Module is identical to the multimode module, but it takes advantage of the single-mode fiber and expands its distance limitation to 10 km.

UTP Module

The UTP version of the ATM LANE Module is based on the same technology as the fiber modules. Because we're talking about UTP here, the cabling is Category 5 and the connector is RJ-45. As always with Category 5 UTP, the distance limitation is 100 meters, or 328 feet.

LANE Module LEDs

The LANE Module has four LEDs present. The LEDs and their function are listed here:

- Status

    — Green—All tests pass.

    — Red—One or more tests failed.

    — Orange—System is booting, or the module is disabled.

- TX (Transmit)—Port is transmitting a cell.

- RX (Receive)—Port is receiving a cell.

- Link—Green—The link integrity is good.

LANE Module SAR

The LANE module has a chip called the SAR chip, which stands for Segmentation and Reassembly. This is the function of the ATM Adaptation Layer. The ATM LANE Module functions at ATM Adaptation Layer 5 (AAL5), per the LAN Emulation specification.

To provide 155 Mbps throughput, two ATMizer chips are used: one for transmitting (segmentation) and one for receiving (reassembly).

The default number of virtual circuits is set at 1024 but is expandable to 4096, depending upon memory and other requirements.

Traffic shaping is provided by a single rate queue. Traffic shaping is used to spread out the bursty traffic normally produced by a LAN. Bursty traffic may come off a conventional LAN, but it must be managed within ATM networks. Traffic shaping is the mechanism to manage the bursts.

Simple Server Redundancy Protocol

Simple Server Redundancy Protocol (SSRP) for LAN Emulation is new in Cisco IOS 11.2. This feature adds a measure of fault tolerance to the standard LAN Emulation described in RFC 1577, "Classical IP over ATM."

The LANE protocol does not specify where any of the ELAN server entities should be located, but by placing these components in Cisco ATM switches and routers, performance and reliability can be assured.

With Phase 1 LANE, only one LECS is capable of serving multiple ELANs, and only one LES/BUS per ELAN could exist for an ATM switch cloud. The Phase 1 LANE protocol did not provide for multiple LES/BUSs within an ELAN, so these components represented single points of failure for LANE service.

LANE with SSRP corrects these limitations by providing for backup LECS and LES/BUSs for an ELAN. Offered in Catalyst 5000 ATM release 3.1 or higher, LANE simple server redundancy is always enabled. An administrator uses this redundancy feature by configuring for multiple servers.

This server redundancy does not overcome other points of failure beyond the router ports. However, additional redundancy on the LAN side or in the ATM switch cloud is not a part of the SSRP for LAN Emulation feature.

This redundancy feature works only with Cisco LECS and LES/BUS combinations. Third-party LANE components continue to interoperate with the LECS and LES/BUS function of Cisco routers, but they cannot take advantage of SSRP.

The LANE with SSRP feature improves LANE fault tolerance using standard LANE protocols and mechanisms. If a failure occurs on the hardware running the LECS or on the LES/BUS, the ELAN can continue to operate using the services of a backup LECS or LES/BUS on different hardware.

Redundant LECSs are defined by configuring one or more LECS addresses—obtained through the ILMI—on the ATM switch.

The LECS controls LES/BUS redundancy by using its database to accommodate more than a single LES ATM address for a particular ELAN.

To enable this feature, the ATM switch must support multiple LECS addresses. This mechanism is specified in the LANE standard. The LECS and LES/BUS establish and maintain a standard control circuit that enables the LANE server redundancy to operate.

LANE with SSRP comes ready to operate with Cisco IOS Release 11.2 software. To activate the feature, add entries for the hierarchical list of servers that will support the given ELAN. All database modifications for the ELAN must be identical on all LECS servers.

Older LANE configuration files continue to work with this new software. LANE configurations that link with non-Cisco ATM equipment continue to work as well, but the non-Cisco ATM equipment does not participate in the SSRP for LANE.

LANE Module Network Management

The LANE module uses a command-line interface (CLI) for configuration and maintenance. The CLI is provided on the card itself and is not part of the Supervisor module code.

Access to the ATM configuration software is via the Supervisor CLI through the use of the **session** command. Unlike other modules, the ATM LANE module contains no console port.

The CLI used for the LANE module is based on Cisco's Internetwork Operating System (IOS) CLI. Unlike the Catalyst 5000 flat syntax structure, the LANE CLI has multiple hierarchies that must be traversed for configuration, just as with a Cisco router.

SNMP software runs on the module. The following MIBs are supported:

- MIB II
- AToM MIB
- LANE MIB
- ILMI MIB

ATM ELAN Network Designs

This section reviews several network designs that you may be called upon in the test to consider. Mostly, these designs are used to illustrate how the different LANE components can be distributed. Later in this chapter, we will discuss the rules for assigning LANE components.

Figure 12-15 is an example of a single-ELAN network design. This is perhaps the simplest LANE scenario.

Figure 12-15   *Single ELAN Network Design*

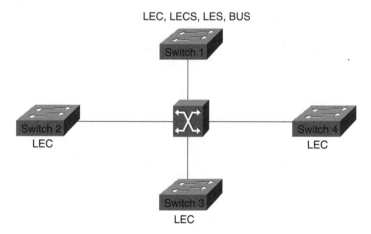

The LANE components in Figure 12-15 have been assigned as follows:

- Switch 1 includes:

    — LECS (one per LANE administrative domain)

    — LEC, LES, and BUS, for this particular ELAN

- Switch 2 includes:

    — LEC for the ELAN

- Switch 3 includes:

    — LEC for the ELAN

- Switch 4 includes:

    — LEC for the ELAN

A more complex network design is shown in Figure 12-16. In this case, there are multiple ELANs and multiple LES/BUS servers, but still only one administrative domain. Many other iterations of this design use other components. For instance, the ATM switch itself could be the LECS or LES/BUS pair, or there could be a Cisco router that can also implement all four LANE components. However, in all these designs, Cisco recommends that the ATM LANE Module be used to host these services for performance reasons.

Figure 12-16 *Multiple ELAN Network Design*

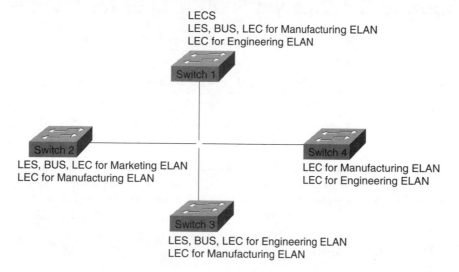

LECS
LES, BUS, LEC for Manufacturing ELAN
LEC for Engineering ELAN

Switch 1

Switch 2

LES, BUS, LEC for Marketing ELAN
LEC for Manufacturing ELAN

Switch 4

LEC for Manufacturing ELAN
LEC for Engineering ELAN

Switch 3

LES, BUS, LEC for Engineering ELAN
LEC for Manufacturing ELAN

In this multiple ELAN scenario, a single LECS is assigned to the entire ATM switch network because it is one administrative domain. One LES and one BUS are assigned per ELAN. A single Catalyst 5000 could run the LES and BUS for more than one ELAN, but each ELAN must have an independent instance of the LES and BUS software.

In this diagram, three ELANs have been configured on the four switches, as follows:

- Switch 1 includes:

    — LECS

    — LES, BUS, and LEC for the manufacturing ELAN

    — LEC for the engineering ELAN

- Switch 2 includes:

  — LES, BUS, and LEC for the marketing ELAN

  — LEC for the manufacturing ELAN

- Switch 3 includes:

  — LES, BUS, and LEC for the engineering ELAN

  — LEC for the manufacturing ELAN

- Switch 4 includes:

  — LECs for the manufacturing ELAN and the marketing ELAN

Configuring the Catalyst 5000 ATM LANE Module

CLSC Objectives Covered in This Section

55	Explain ATM address structure.
56	Describe how ATM addresses are automatically assigned.
57	Describe the rules for assigning ATM components to interfaces.
58	Configure LANE components on a Catalyst 5000 switch.

This section delineates the ATM address structure and tells how addresses are assigned. Also covered are the rules for assigning ATM components to interfaces. Last, but not least, this section covers how to configure LANE components on a Catalyst 5000.

LANE ATM Addressing

The following establishes some of the rules for ATM addressing:

- All ATM addresses must be unique.

- Every LEC must have a MAC address.

- The MAC address is used as the end system identifier (ESI) part of the ATM address.

- All LECs on the same ATM interface have the same automatically assigned MAC address.

- Every LANE component (LECS, LES, BUS, LEC) must have a unique ATM address.

ATM Address Formats

ATM routing protocols operate on ATM private network, NSAP format addresses. Prefixes of such addresses identify individual switches and collections of switches within peer groups. Switches also supply these prefixes to attached end systems, using the ILMI protocol. ATM private network address prefixes can be obtained either from ATM service providers or directly from the various national authorities designated by the International Standards Organization (ISO) to allocate the NSAP address space. The mechanisms for administering such addresses are not yet well understood by the industry, however, and there are few ATM service providers from whom customers may obtain their addresses.

ATM addresses have a substructure defined in the UNI specification. Three types of ATM addresses exist, shown in Figure 12-17. These are identified by the first byte, called the AFI (Authority and Format Identifier):

Figure 12-17 *ATM Address Formats*

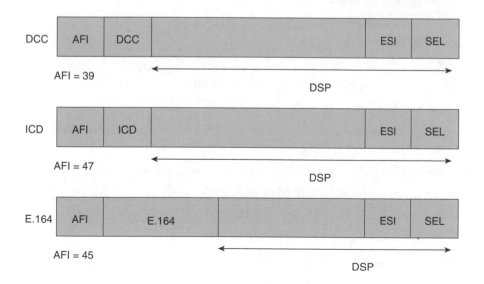

AFI	Authority and Format Identifier
DCC	Data Country Code
DSP	Domain Specific Part
E.164	ISDN (Telephone) Number
ESI	End System Identifier (IEEE)
HO-DSP	High Order Part of DSP
ICD	International Code Designator
IDI	Initial Domain Identifier
SEL	NSAP Selector

- Data Country Code (DCC), AFI = 39. The DCC code is assigned by the ISO.

- International Code Designator (ICD), AFI = 47. The ICD is assigned by the British Standards Institute.

- E.164, AFI = 45

The remaining portion of the address is domain-specific. The domain-specific part (DSP) contains the ESI and the selector byte. The prefix of the domain-specific part can be further subdivided to create the appropriate hierarchy that the user needs to operate an ATM network. The ESI is a 6-byte field, and the selector is a 1-byte field.

Automatically Assigned ATM Addresses

Each ATM LANE Module has a pool of MAC addresses assigned automatically. Each pool has a total of 16 consecutive MAC addresses.

NOTE   The pool of addresses can be seen from the Catalyst 5000 CLI (not the ATM LANE Module CLI) by typing the **show module** command.

The MAC addresses are assigned to LANE components as follows:

- Prefix fields are identical for all the LANE components, which identifies the switch.

- The first ESI in the pool is assigned to every LEC on the interface.

- The second ESI is assigned to every LES on the interface.

- The third ESI is assigned to every BUS on the interface.

- The fourth ESI is assigned to LECS.

The selector field value is set to the subinterface number of the LANE component, with the notable exception of the LECS, which always has the selector field of 00.

Let's give an example here.

Suppose you typed **show module** and saw that the LANE card in slot 4 had MAC addresses 0800.2000.1000 through 0800.2000.100f.

The ESI part of ATM addresses would be assigned to LANE components as follows:

- Any LEC would have the ESI of 0800.2000.1000.

- Any LES would have the ESI of 0800.2000.1001.

- Any BUS would have the ESI of 0800.2000.1002.

- The LECS would have the ESI of 0800.2000.1003.

Rules for Assigning LANE Components to Interfaces

The following rules apply for assigning LANE components to interfaces when configuring LANE:

- The LECS is always assigned to the major interface (such as ATM 0).
- The LES and LEC of the same ELAN can be configured on the same subinterface (such as ATM 0.1).
- LECs of two different ELANs cannot be configured on the same subinterface.
- LESs of two different ELANs cannot be configured on the same subinterface.
- The LEC and LES of two different ELANs cannot be configured on the same subinterface.

LANE Configuration Tasks

The following tasks should be performed when configuring LANE:

1 Create a LANE plan and worksheet.
2 Configure the LECS, BUS, LES, and LEC addresses, or use the auto-address configuration.
3 Configure LES, BUS, and LEC.
4 Set up the LECS database.
5 Enable the LECS ATM address.
6 Configure the server ATM address on a LightStream 1010.

In creating the LANE plan and worksheet, it would be beneficial to draw up a configuration that would determine the location of the LES and BUS for each ELAN, the location of each LEC for each ELAN, the location of LECS, and the name of the default ELAN in LECS (optional).

Configuring from the Terminal

To configure the LANE Module, you must first **session** to the LANE Module from the Catalyst 5000 CLI. After you're in the ATM Module, the prompt will be as follows:

```
ATM>
```

To enter the privileged exec mode, enter the **enable** command, as shown here:

```
ATM>enable
```

The system will then prompt you for the password. Enter the password, and press Return. The prompt will then show a "#" sign at the end, to designate privileged mode.

At this point, you must enter configuration mode by typing **configure terminal** at the prompt, as shown here:

```
ATM>#configure terminal
ATM>#(config)
```

The various configuration commands will be shown later in this chapter.

When you finish configuring, type **end** or **Ctrl-Z**, and then type **write memory** to save the configuration file to NVRAM.

Setting Up Only an LEC on a Subinterface

In interface configuration mode, perform these tasks:

Task	Command
Specify the subinterface for an ELAN on this switch.	**interface atm 0.**subinterface-number
Enable a LEC for the first ELAN.	**lane client ethernet** vlan# elan-name

Setting Up the LECS Database

The tasks for setting up the LECS database are listed here:

* Set up a database for the default ELAN.

* Set up a database for unrestricted-membership ELANs.

* Set up a database for restricted-membership ELANs.

Setting Up the Default ELAN

When you configure a Catalyst 5000 switch as the LECS for one default ELAN, you provide a name for the database, the ATM address of the LES for the ELAN, and a default name for the ELAN. In addition, you indicate that the LECS ATM address is to be computed automatically.

If your database has only default and/or unrestricted ELANs, you need not specify where the LANE LECs are located. That is, when you set up the LECS database for a single default ELAN, you need not provide any database entries that link the ATM addresses of any LECs with the ELAN name.

The tasks for setting up the default VLAN are listed here. In global configuration mode, perform these tasks:

Task	Command
Create a named database for the LANE configuration LECS.	**lane database** *database-name*
Bind the ELAN name to its LES ATM address.	**name** *elan-name* **server-atm-address** *atm-address*
Provide a default ELAN name.	**default-name** *elan-name*
Exit from database configuration mode.	**exit**

Unrestricted-Membership ELANs

When you set up a database for unrestricted ELANs, you create database entries that link the name of each ELAN to the ATM address of its LES.

However, you may choose not to specify where the LECs are located. That is, when you set up the LECS database, you do not have to provide any database entries that link the ATM addresses or MAC addresses of any LECs with the ELAN name.

The tasks to configure unrestricted-membership ELANs are shown here. In global configuration mode, perform these tasks:

Task	Command
Create a named database.	**lane database** *database-name*
Bind the first ELAN to its LES ATM address.	**name** *elan-name1* **server-atm-address** *atm-address*
Bind the second ELAN to its LES ATM address. (Repeat for each ELAN.)	**name** *elan-name2* **server-atm-address** *atm-address*
(Optional) Specify a default ELAN for LECs not explicitly bound to an ELAN.	**default name** *elan-name*
Exit.	**exit**

Restricted-Membership ELANs

When you set up the database for restricted-membership ELANs, you create database entries that link the name of each ELAN to the ATM address of its LES.

However, you also must specify where the LECs are located. That is, for each restricted-membership ELAN, you provide a database entry that explicitly links the ATM address or MAC address of each LEC on that ELAN with the name of that ELAN.

Those LEC database entries specify the LECs that are permitted to join the ELAN. When an LEC requests that the LECS indicate which ELAN it is to join, the LECS consults its database and then responds as configured.

When LECs for the same restricted-membership ELAN are located in multiple Catalyst 5000 ATM modules, each LEC ATM address or MAC address must be linked explicitly with the name of the ELAN. As a result, you must configure as many LEC entries as you have LECs for ELANs in all the ATM modules of the Catalyst 5000 switches. Of course, each LEC will have a different ATM address in the database entries.

The tasks for setting up Restricted-Membership ELANs are shown here. In global configuration mode, perform these tasks:

Task	Command
Create a named database.	**lane database** *database-name*
Bind the first ELAN name to the LES ATM address.	**name** *elan-name1* **server-atm-address** *atm-address* **restricted**
Bind the second ELAN name to its LES ATM address. (Repeat for all ELANs.)	**name** *elan-name2* **server-atm-address** *atm-address* [**restricted**]
(Optional) Specify a default ELAN for LECs not bound to an ELAN.	**default name** *elan-name*
Associate a specific LEC ATM address with a specific restricted membership ELAN. (Repeat for all LECs in ELAN.)	**client-atm-address** *atm-address* **name** -*elan-name*
Exit.	**exit**

Enabling the LECS ATM Address

After you have created the database entries as appropriate to the type and the membership conditions of the ELANs, you can enable the LECS on the selected ATM interface and Catalyst 5000 ATM module. Then, you can display its ATM address.

Make a note of the LECS ATM address so that you can configure it on each ATM subinterface where an LES and BUS are configured.

The tasks associated with enabling the LECS ATM address are as follows:

Task	Command
Specify the major ATM interface where the LECS is located.	**interface atm 0**
Link the database name to the interface, and enable the LECS.	**lane config** *database-name*
Specify that the LECS ATM address will be computed automatically.	**lane auto-config-atm-address**
Exit interface configuration mode.	**exit**
Return to EXEC mode.	**Ctrl-Z**
Display the LECS ATM address.	**show lane config**

Configuring the Server ATM Address

You must enter the LECS ATM address into a Cisco LS1010 ATM switch and save it to NVRAM so that the value will not be lost when the ATM switch is reset or powered off.

The tasks to be performed are shown here. On the Cisco LS1010 ATM Switch, perform these tasks:

Task	Command
Enter configuration mode.	**configure terminal**
Enter the address of the LEC.	**atm lecs-address <atm-address>**
Verify the address entered.	**show atm ilmi-configuration**

NOTE   You must specify the full 40-digit ATM address of the LECS.

Monitoring and Maintaining LANE Components

The following commands are used in monitoring and maintaining LANE Components.

In EXEC mode, perform these tasks:

Task	Command
Display global and per-VCC LANE.	**show lane** [**interface atm 0** [.*subinterface-* **LANE** information *number*]|**name** *elan-name*] [**brief**]
Display global and per-VCC BUS information.	**show lane bus** [**interface atm 0** – [.*subinterfacenumber*]|**name** *elan-name*] [**brief**]
Display global and per-VCC LEC information.	**show lane client** [**interface atm 0** [.*subinterfacenumber*]|**name** *elan-name*] [**brief**]
Display global and per-VCC LECS information.	**show lane config** [**interface atm 0**]
Display the LECS database.	**show lane database** [*database-name*]

Q&A

As mentioned in Chapter 1, "The Cisco LAN Switch Configuration (CLSC) Exam Overview," the questions and scenarios are more difficult than what you should experience on the actual exam. The questions do not attempt to cover more breadth or depth than the exam; however, the questions are designed to make sure you know the answers. Rather than allowing you to derive the answer from clues hidden inside the question itself, the questions will challenge your understanding and recall of the subject. Questions from the "Do I Know This Already?" quiz from the beginning of the chapter are repeated here to ensure that you have mastered the chapter's topic areas.

1 The LANE protocol is implemented in what layer of the OSI model?

2 ILMI is used for what purpose?

3 Transmission to unknown stations is performed by which component of LANE?

4 What is an LECS, and what is it used for?

5 ATM LANE uses which ATM Adaptation Layer?

6 What devices can be a LANE Client (LEC)? What devices can be an LES?

7 In the ATM address structure, what is an ESI?

8 What command is used from the Catalyst to access the LANE module?

9 What is the maximum distance that can be achieved using an MMF ATM LANE Module?

10 What is SSRP, and what is it used for?

11 What are the performance characteristics of the ATM LANE module with respect to throughput?

12 The command-line interface (CLI) for the LANE Module is similar to what other interface?

13 On a dual-PHY LANE module, can both interfaces be active at the same time?

14 How many ATM LANE Modules can be installed in a Catalyst 5000 switch?

15 What LANE component gets the first MAC address of the pool?

16 How many LECSs are needed for each individual administrative domain?

17 How many MAC addresses are assigned to an individual ATM LANE Module?

18 What function does SAR perform?

19 What media types are available using LANE?

Source Material

Some content in this chapter is based on the following sources:

- Cisco LAN Switching Student Guide, Chapters 13, 14, 15

- Asynchronous Transfer Mode Switching

  http://www.cisco.com/univercd/cc/td/doc/cisintwk/ito_doc/55755.htm

- Configuring the ATM Module

  http://www.cisco.com/univercd/cc/td/doc/product/lan/cat5000/rel_2_2/c5kcg2_2/05atm.htm

- Catalyst 5000 Series ATM Switching Modules Configuration Note

  http://www.cisco.com/univercd/cc/td/doc/product/lan/cat5000/cnfg_nts/5012atm.htm

The following CLSC exam objectives are reviewed in this chapter. The numbers shown correspond to the master list of objectives found in Chapter 1, "The Cisco LAN Switch Configuration (CLSC) Exam Overview."

Objective	Description
59	Describe the major features and benefits of the Catalyst 1900 and Catalyst 2820 switches.
60	Describe the hardware components and their functions of the Catalyst 1900 and Catalyst 2820 switches.
61	Describe the architecture and operation of the Catalyst 1900 and Catalyst 2820 switches.
62	Describe the following key features and applications of the Catalyst 1900 and Catalyst 2820 switches: • Switching modes • Virtual LANs • Multicast packet filtering and registration • Management support, CDP, and CGMP
63	Trace a frame's progress through a Catalyst 1900 or Catalyst 2820 switch.
64	Use the Catalyst 1900 and Catalyst 2820 switch menus for configuration.
65	Configure IP addresses and ports on the Catalyst 1900 and Catalyst 2820 switches.
66	Configure VLANs on the Catalyst 1900 and Catalyst 2820 switches.
67	View the Catalyst 1900 and Catalyst 2820 switch reports and summaries.
68	Configure the ATM LANE module on the Catalyst 2820 switch.
78	Describe the POST and diagnostic messages on the Catalyst 1900 and Catalyst 2820 switches.
79	Describe the cabling guidelines for the Catalyst 1900 and 2820 switches.
80	Use the statistics and reports to maintain on the Catalyst 1900 and 2820 switches.
81	Describe the firmware upgrade procedures for the Catalyst 1900 and 2820 switches.

CHAPTER 13

Catalyst 1900 and Catalyst 2820 Switches

This chapter focuses on the Catalyst 1900 and 2820 switches, which share the same user interface and many of the same features. We will discuss hardware specifics and configuration of the switches.

How to Best Use This Chapter

By taking the following steps, you can make better use of your study time:

- Keep your notes and the answers for all your work with this book in one place, for easy reference.

- Take the quiz, and write down your answers. Studies show that retention is significantly increased through writing down facts and concepts, even if you never look at the information again.

- Use the diagram in Figure 13-1 to guide you to the next step.

Figure 13-1   *How to Best Use This Chapter in Preparation for the CLSC Exam*

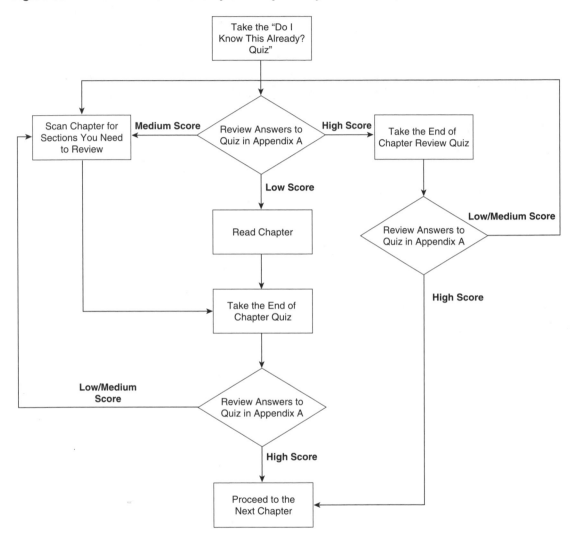

Do I Know This Already? Quiz

You can find the answers to this quiz in Appendix A, "Answers to 'Do I Know This Already?' Quizzes and Q & A Sections." Review the answers, grade your quiz, and choose an appropriate next step in this chapter based on the suggestions diagramed in Figure 13-1.

1 How many MAC addresses are supported on the Catalyst 1900 switch?

2 Name three features that are common to both the Catalyst 1900 and the Catalyst 2820 switches.

3 What three types of modules are available for the Catalyst 2820 expansion slots?

4 Where is the EIA/TIA-232 located on the Catalyst 1900, and what is it used for?

5 Name three features that are implemented in the Embedded Control Unit (ECU).

6 What mode of switching would you use if you were experiencing FCS or alignment errors?

7 When implementing Port Security, what is the maximum number of addresses that can be associated with a secure port?

8 Assume that you have configured a broadcast threshold of 500. What happens to broadcasts if you choose the block option and the threshold is exceeded?

9 What does the hold time mean when configuring CDP?

10 How many VLANs can be configured on a Catalyst 2820 switch?

11 Can the ATM LANE module be configured from the menus directly?

12 What command verifies the LANE configuration?

Using the answer key in Appendix A, grade your answers

- **5 or less correct**—Read this chapter.

- **6, 7, or 8 correct**—Review this chapter, looking at the charts and diagrams that summarize most of the concepts and facts in this chapter.

- **9 or more correct**—If you want more review on these topics, skip to the exercises at the end of this chapter. If you do not want more review on these topics, skip this chapter.

Catalyst 1900 and 2820 Switch Family: Features, Benefits, Hardware, and Architecture

CLSC Objectives Covered in This Section

59	Describe the major features and benefits of the Catalyst 1900 and Catalyst 2820 switches.
60	Describe the hardware components and their functions of the Catalyst 1900 and Catalyst 2820 switches.
61	Describe the architecture and operation of the Catalyst 1900 and Catalyst 2820 switches.

The Catalyst 1900 and 2820 switches serve the low-cost small office marketplace. These switches are considered standalone switches, compared to the more flexible, higher-cost 5000 series switches.

The Catalyst 1900 switch offers the following features:

- 12 or 24 switched 10BaseT ports

- One or two fixed 100BaseT ports

- Support for 1024 MAC addresses

- Cut-through or store-and-forward switching

- CiscoView and Telnet management

The Catalyst 2820 switch offers the following features:

- 24 switched 10BaseT ports

- Two expansion slots for high-speed modules

- 100BaseT, FDDI, and ATM modules

- Support for 2048 or 8192 MAC addresses

- Cut-through or store-and-forward switching

- CiscoView and Telnet management

Both switches offer the following common features:

- AUI port on back of switch

- IEEE 802.1 STP support

- Shared memory architecture
- Connection to a redundant power system
- Up to four VLANs, allowing ports to be grouped into separate logical networks
- Cisco Group Membership Protocol (CGMP)
- Port Security
- Flooding and broadcast control
- Cisco Discovery Protocol
- Embedded RMON support
- SNMP support

Catalyst 1900 and 2820 Switch LEDs

The Catalyst 1900 and 2820 switches share a common set of LEDs on the front of the switch. See Figure 13-2 for an illustration.

Figure 13-2   *Catalyst 1900 and 2820 LEDs*

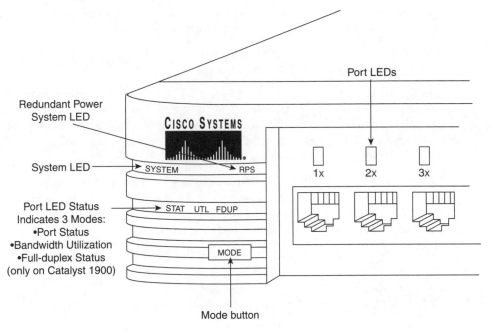

In general, as with most devices, a green LED indicates a proper functioning of the device or feature. If the LED is not lit, the feature or device is off or disabled. An amber LED indicates a problem or malfunction of the device or feature.

- *System LED*—This LED is green during normal operation, amber when the switch fails the POST, and off when the system is powered off.

- *Redundant Power System (RPS) LED*—This LED is green when the RPS is operational and local power supply is unplugged, alternating green/off when the RPS is operational and local power supply is plugged in, amber when an RPS is installed but not operational, and off, when an RPS is not installed.

- *Expansion Slot Status LED (2820 only)*—This LED is green when the expansion slot module is operational, alternating green/off when the module is running POST, amber when the module fails POST, and off when the module is not installed.

- *Port LEDs*—Both the Catalyst 1900 and 2820 switches have port LEDs that operate in three different modes: Port Status (STAT), Bandwidth Utilization (UTL), and Full-Duplex Status (FDUP). You can select each mode individually by pressing the Mode button until you receive the mode you desire; then, release the button.

When the STAT mode is deployed, the STAT LED is green when a link status is present, flashing green/off when transmitting or receiving data, alternating green/amber when a link fault occurs due to error conditions (such as an excessive number of collisions and CRC errors), and off when there is no link. The STAT mode is the default mode for both switches.

When the FDUP mode (1900 only) is deployed, the LED is green during full-duplex operation and off during half-duplex operation.

When the UTL mode is deployed, the group of LEDs displays the current and peak utilization of the switch. The peak utilization is recorded in the current bandwidth capture interval. Current bandwidth is shown by way of a series of illuminated LEDs topped by one rapidly blinking LED. The furthest right green LED provides a visual indication of the peak utilization recorded in the current bandwidth capture interval.

The switch uses the port LEDs to establish a scale showing the utilization in Mbps. Utilization LEDs show the current and peak bandwidth utilization of the switch. The peak utilization is recorded in the bandwidth-capture interval. The default setting for this interval is 24 hours; it is recorded each night at midnight.

The bandwidth utilization scale for the Catalyst 2820 and 1900 switches with 24 10BaseT ports is shown here:

Port LEDs	Mbps
1–8	0.1–< 6
9–16	6–< 120
17–24	120–280

The bandwidth utilization scale for the Catalyst 1900 version with 12 10BaseT ports is shown here:

Port LEDs	Mbps
1–4	0.1–< 1.5
5–8	1.5–< 20
9–12	20–140

Switch Rear Panels

This section describes those features available on the rear panel of the Catalyst 1900 and 2820 switches. The EIA/TIA-232 port, the Reset Switch, Switch Management, and AUI port are all covered in detail.

EIA/TIA-232 (RS-232) Port

The Electronics Industries Association (EIA) and the Telecommunications Industry Association's (TIA) standard EIA/TIA-232 (RS-232) port is used to connect a modem or terminal to the switch. The Catalyst 2820 or 1900 switches ship with a null modem cable. If you are using a terminal or a program such as Hyperterm, which is part of Windows 95, you must use a null modem cable to connect to the management console.

Switch Management

You can use Telnet, an ASCII terminal, or a terminal emulation program such as Hyperterm to run the management console. You can configure and manage the Catalyst 2820 and Catalyst 1900 switches using an SNMP-compatible management station, or with the Catalyst switch management console using the EIA/TIA-232 port and an ASCII terminal or terminal emulator program.

Reset Switch

The reset switch must be used only if the Catalyst 2820 or 1900 switch does not respond to network management, or if it stopped forwarding packets. Resetting the switch has the same effect as turning the power off and on. Use a sharp pointed object, such as a paper clip or a pen, to reach through the hole and reset the switch.

AUI Port

The AUI port (25th port) connector on the back panel supports a 10 Mbps connection to thick coaxial, thin coaxial, UTP, or a fiber media through a transceiver connection.

Catalyst 2820 Modules

The Catalyst 2820 switch supports the following four types of optional high-speed expansion modules:

- Four types of Catalyst 2820 100BaseT (Fast Ethernet) modules; UTP with one port switched or eight shared ports

- Any fiber with one port switched or four shared ports

- Three types of Catalyst 2820 FDDI modules; fiber with dual-attachment station (DAS), single-attachment station (SAS), and UTP single-attachment station (SAS) (CDDI)

- Two types of Catalyst 2820 ATM modules; OC-3 multimode fiber and OC-3 UTP

Catalyst 2820 100BaseT Modules

The Catalyst 2820 switch supports four types of 100BaseT modules:

- 100BaseTX modules that are compatible with the IEEE 802.3u-standard. The modules have RJ-45 connectors and use two-pair Category 5 UTP cabling. Two port configurations are available:

    — 100BaseTX/1: One switched 100BaseTX port

    — 100BaseTX/8: Eight shared 100BaseTX ports (repeater)

- 100BaseFX modules that are compatible with the IEEE 802.3u-standard. The modules have ST connectors and use 50/125 or 62.5/100 micron multimode fiber-optic cabling. The following port configurations are available:

    — 100BaseFX/1: One switched 100BaseFX port

    — 100BaseFX/8: Four shared 100BaseFX ports (repeater)

These modules are hot-swappable, which means that they can be installed while power is on, without interruption of the network. All modules plug into the expansion ports using thumbscrews. The Catalyst 2820 automatically senses the presence of the module and verifies the operation.

100BaseT Module LEDs

The 100BaseT modules have individual Port and Group Status LEDs, and the single-port modules have a Full Duplex LED.

- *Port Status LEDs*—Three status LEDs are included for each individual 100BaseT port: Link Integrity, Network Activity, or Receive and Disabled.

- *Link*—The Link LED indicates that the port is properly connected to a power-up device. The LED is on when the link integrity test passes and is off when the link integrity test fails. The Link LED blinks when a packet with an error condition is received at a port.

- *Activity*—The Activity LED for switched 100BaseT ports blinks when the corresponding port is transmitting or receiving data. If the traffic level is high, the LED is on continuously. If there is no activity, the LED is off.

- *Receive (shared 100BaseT ports only)*—The Receive LED for shared 100BaseT ports blinks when the corresponding port is receiving data. If the traffic level is high, the LED is on continuously. If there is no activity, the LED is off.

- *Disabled*—This LED is on when the port is disabled or suspended (either by a network connection error or a secure address violation), or if the port is manually disabled or suspended using the Catalyst 2820 management console.

  If a shared 100BaseT port is automatically disabled due to a jabber or auto-partition error, the LED blinks.

- *Full Duplex LED (switched 100BaseT ports only)*—Indicates when a switched 100BaseT port has been set to operate in full-duplex mode. The LED is on when the port is operating in full-duplex mode and is off when operating in half-duplex mode.

- *Group Status LEDs (shared 100BaseT ports only)*—Two Group Status LEDs are included for the shared 100BaseT modules. The Group Activity LED blinks when the corresponding shared 100BaseT ports are transmitting or receiving data. If the traffic level is high, the LED is on continuously. If there is no activity, the LED is off. The Group Collision LED blinks when the corresponding shared 100BaseT ports detect a packet collision. If no packet collisions are detected, the LED is off.

Catalyst 2820 FDDI Modules

The Catalyst 2820 switch supports the following three types of FDDI modules:

- *Fiber DAS Module*—This module has a dual-attachment station compatible with the ANSI X3T12 standard. It has two MIC connectors and uses 50/125 or 62.5/125 micron multimode fiber-optic cabling. It also has a six-pin mini-DIN connector to connect to an optical bypass switch.

- *Fiber SAS Module*—This module has a single-attachment station (SAS) compatible with the ANSI X3T12 standard. It has one MIC connector and uses 50/125 or 62.5/125 micron multimode fiber-optic cabling.

- *UTP SAS Module*—This module has a single-attachment station (SAS) compatible with the ANSI X3T12 standard. It has an RJ-45 connector and uses two-pair Category 5 UTP cabling.

FDDI Module LEDs

The following three LEDs on the front panel indicate the operating status of the FDDI module.

- *Connected*—This LED is lit when the module is connected to an operational FDDI ring. It is off when not connected to the FDDI ring.

- *Activity*—This LED blinks when the corresponding port is transmitting or receiving data. A rapid blink indicates the traffic level is high. The LED is off when there is no activity.

- *Disabled*—This LED is lit when the port has been disabled by administrative intervention or by a secure address violation. You can disable a port with the Catalyst 2820 Out-of-Band Management console.

The LEDs also indicate the type of failure when the module does not pass the POST.

Catalyst 2820 ATM Modules

The Catalyst 2820 supports two types of ATM modules: the ATM 155 multimode fiber module with one SC style connector, and the ATM 155 UTP module with one RJ-45 connector. Each is a physical-layer interface between an ATM module and an ATM switch. You can use the ATM module to connect workstations, hubs, and other switches to the following ATM devices:

- ATM switch, such as the Cisco LightStream 1010

- Multilayer LAN switch (such as the Catalyst 5000 series) with an installed ATM LANE card

- Router with an ATM interface, such as a Cisco 7000 series

Both the ATM modules discussed previously include the following features:

- Full-duplex operation

- 155.52 Mbps data transfer rate

- Store-and-forward packet relay

- LAN Emulation Client (LEC) for emulated LANs, and ATM Adaptation Layer 5 (AAL5) for LAN Emulation (LANE) data transfer

- User-Network Interface (UNI) 3.0 and 3.1 for switched virtual connections (SVCs) and permanent virtual connections (PVCs)

Each ATM module supports the following ATM management features:

- Integrated Link Management Interface (ILMI) for ATM UNI 3.0 and 3.1 MIBs

- Operation, administration, and maintenance (OAM)

Each model of the ATM module complies with the following standards:

- LANE 1.0 for LANE client (LEC) only
- Synchronous Optical Network (SONET) and Synchronous Transport Signal level 3 (STS-3c) physical layer
- SONET Digital Hierarchy (SDH) STM-1

Architecture

The material presented here is intended to help the reader understand switch features; however, it is not directly related to one of the objectives.

The ClearChannel architecture shown in Figure 13-3 is made up of the following components: packet exchange bus (X-bus), forwarding engine, embedded control unit (ECU), management interface, shared buffer memory, and switched ports. The Catalyst 2820 and 1900 switches employ shared memory buffering with a 3 MB memory capacity. The ClearChannel architecture uses a 1 Gbps packet exchange bus.

Figure 13-3   *ClearChannel Architecture*

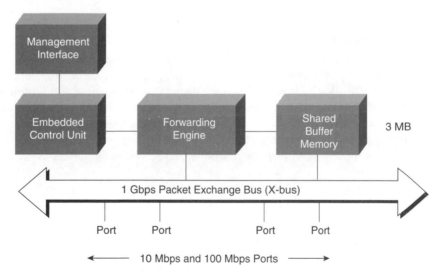

X-bus bandwidth = 1 Gbps (53 bit wide x 20 MHz)

Within the switch, data is transferred through the bus, so the bus sees all the traffic passing through the switch. Access to the bus is prioritized because several components could attempt to place data on the bus concurrently. Access is sequenced according to transaction priority and time of arrival.

Transaction requests have different priorities. A transaction requesting buffer memory for a packet, for example, has higher priority than one sending status at the end of a transmission. The X-bus is also used to transmit signals between switch components for initiating transactions associated with receiving and transmitting packets. Access to the bus is controlled by a separate master scheduler.

Transactions are scheduled by a combination of time of arrival, transaction priority, and port priority. Each port tells the forwarding engine it has a packet engine and grabs packets based on priority. Port 1 has the lowest priority, and port 27 has the highest priority; however, the bus runs fast enough that no user will be able to see a difference. The packet exchange bus sees all the traffic going through the switch.

The X-bus is a 53-bit-wide bus running at 20 MHz. This high bandwidth (1 Gbps packet) enables the switch to be completely nonblocking—that is, it is capable of handling wire speed on all ports concurrently. Also, the 25 10 Mbps and 2 100 Mbps ports require less than half of available bandwidth.

Port access to the packet exchange bus is pipelined to prevent loss of bandwidth. The Catalyst 1900 and 2820 switches each provide 27 switched ports consuming 450 Mbps of bandwidth, which is less than half the 1 Gbps available switch bandwidth.

Forwarding Engine

The forwarding engine is the heart of the switch. It is responsible for the central function of the switch: examining packets from incoming ports, allocating packet buffers, looking up the destination address, and queuing them to the appropriate port for transmission. A diagram of the forwarding engine is shown in Figure 13-4. The forwarding engine of the Catalyst 2820 and 1900 switches is implemented entirely in hardware (ASIC) to ensure low latency and higher throughput through the switch. The implementation also serves to reduce complexity and increase reliability, and consequently lowers the switch cost.

Figure 13-4   *Forwarding Engine*

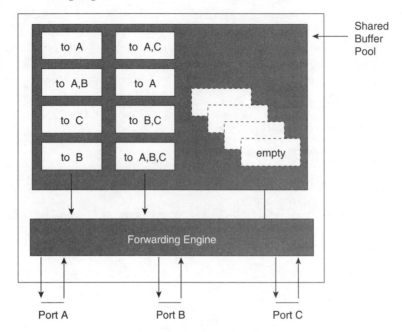

In addition to packet processing, the engine also collects and maintains switch statistics. By monitoring the packet exchange bus, it is capable of counting packet lengths, throughput, crrors, and exceptions. This data is collected by network management stations to construct switch statistic tables and monitor traffic patterns on the network that in turn can be sued to design efficient network architectures.

When the forwarding engine determines that a packet is to be forwarded, it waits until it receives the number of bytes associated with the configured switching mode and then initiates forwarding to the appropriate ports.

As shown in the example in Figure 13-4, a packet can be queued for transmission to many ports, such as ports A, B, and C, without negatively affecting the performance of the switch.

NOTE   The shared buffer implementation in the Catalyst 2820 or Catalyst 1900 switch prevents the head-of-line blocking of packets, a common problem in switches using individual port buffers.

Embedded Control Unit

Most of the per-packet processing in the switch is done in the hardware; both network management and related activities are handled by the software in the Embedded Control Unit (ECU) subsystem. This clear demarcation provides for regular switch-forwarding functions to be performed at wire speed with minimal latency in hardware, leaving the ECU to handle more complicated scenarios. The ECU subsystem comprises the modules shown in Figure 13-5.

Some of the management and related activities are detailed in the following list.

- Configuration and supervision
- Interface for in-band and out-of-band management
- Statistics reporting
- Diagnostics and error handling
- Control of the front panel display
- Control of STP
- Embedded RMON

Figure 13-5   *Embedded Control Unit (ECU)*

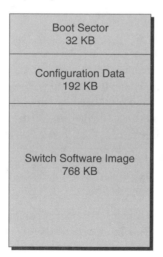

- Embedded CPU
- 512 KB DRAM (for CPU)
- 2 MB Flash for firmware, configuration data, and statistics

The Flash memory on the Catalyst 2820 and 1900 switches is partitioned into three areas:

- Switch software image (768 KB)
- Switch configuration data (192 KB)
- Boot sector (32 KB)

Most of the CPU Flash is used to store the switch software image. This is also the area that changes during software upgrades. The area above this in Flash stores the switch configuration data. Whenever a new switch configuration is written, data in this section of the Flash changes.

The boot sector is located at the top of the Flash and is write-protected. The Flash would not be consistent if a power failure resulted during the upgrade process before a complete image was written to Flash. The write-protected boot sector ensures that at least one section of the Flash always retains its data integrity, allowing the switch to boot up correctly every time. The boot sector contains the diagnostic console that is used to recover from a failed upgrade.

The ECU subsystem is responsible for diagnostics and error handling, switch configuration, STP, in-band and out-of-band management, statistics reporting, and control of front panel display. The ECU also contains an embedded RMON software agent that provides enhanced manageability, monitoring, and traffic analysis to a network management station.

Both the Catalyst 2820 and 1900 switches use the Intel 80486 CPU.

Shared Buffer Memory

The Catalyst 2820 and 1900 switches employ a shared memory buffering scheme using 3 MB of DRAM. Because each packet buffer is 1.5 KB, the 3 MB of DRAM supports 2048-packet buffers, which provides a large packet buffer as a shared system resource for dynamic allocation of packet buffer memory to individual ports.

Using a memory allocation mechanism, incoming packets are deposited into empty buffers that are kept in a common pool available to all ports. They are then dynamically linked into the appropriate transmit queues and are transmitted when allowed by the destination ports. These are logical queues that are associated with each port. Packets are never copied or moved to another memory location.

In the cut-through switching mode (described in the switch features section), leading bytes of a packet are fetched and transmitted before the entire packet is received into the buffer.

Shared memory architecture used in the Catalyst 2820 and 1900 switches completely eliminates a problem found in port-based buffering architectures known as head-of-line blocking that can lead to under-utilization of a switch. Shared memory switches do not have receive queues and are not subject to head-of-line blocking.

To prevent one single port from monopolizing all available buffers and starving out other ports, the switch enforces a 1.5 MB limit on the amount of packet buffer memory that may be queued for any one port at any instance. The 1.5 MB limit assures that, at most, half the available buffer pool may be utilized by any one port, regardless of circumstances.

Features and Applications

CLSC Objectives Covered in This Section

62	Describe the following key features and applications of the Catalyst 1900 and 2820 switches:
	• Switching modes.
	• Virtual LANs.
	• Multicast packet filtering and registration.
	• Broadcast storm control.
	• Management support, CDP, and CGMP.
63	Trace a frame's progress through a Catalyst 1900 or Catalyst 2820 switch.

Switching Modes

The Catalyst 1900 and Catalyst 2820 switches support three switching modes: FastForward, FragmentFree (cut-through), and Store-and-Forward. The switching mode used determines how quickly the switch can forward a packet; this, in turn, directly affects the latency that a packet experiences. The switching mode that you choose is applied to the entire switch and is applied to traffic flowing between all ports, with the following exceptions:

- *FastForward*—The FastForward switching mode uses a cut-through technique to offer the lowest level of latency by immediately forwarding a packet after receiving the destination address. Because FastForward starts forwarding before the entire packet is received, there can be times when packets are relayed with errors. Using the FragmentFree option can reduce the number of packets forwarded with errors. In FastForward mode, latency is measured first-bit-received to first-bit-transmitted, or FIFO. The FastForward mode is normally used on ports connected to single nodes.

- *FragmentFree*— The FragmentFree switching mode also uses the cut-through technique to filter out collision fragments—the majority of packet errors—before forwarding begins. If your network experiences a significant number of collisions, you can use FragmentFree to eliminate the chance of forwarding collision fragments. FragmentFree switching waits until the received packet has been determined not to be a collision fragment before forwarding the packet. In FragmentFree mode, latency is measured as FIFO.

- *Store-and-Forward*—The traditional Store-and-Forward mode stores the entire packet and checks for errors prior to transmission. Store-and-Forward is always used for transfers from 10 Mbps to 100 Mbps ports. Store-and-Forward is optional for multicast packets and is always used for broadcast packets. Store-and-Forward mode is usually used on ports connected to hubs.

If you are experiencing FCS or alignment errors, Store-and-Forward switching mode can be used to ensure that packets with errors are filtered and are not propagated to the rest of the network. Store-and-Forward is the most error-free form of switching. All broadcasts are sent store-and-forward, and all multicast packets are sent either via store-and-forward or via selected switch mode.

The switching mode is set in the System Configuration menu.

Latency Comparison

The forwarding latency of the Store-and-Forward mode is higher than either of the two cut-through modes. In Store-and-Forward mode, latency is measured last-bit-received to first-bit-transmitted, or LIFO. This LIFO method does not include the time it takes to receive the entire packet, which can vary according to packet size from 65 microseconds to 1.3 milliseconds.

The Store-and-Forward latency shown in (7 microseconds) is slower than that of the FastForward or FragmentFree switching modes because the time it takes to receive the entire packet in the Store-and-Forward mode is not included in the 7 microseconds.

Table 13-1   *Catalyst 2820 and Catalyst 1900 Switching Latencies*

Switching Mode	10 Mbps➔100 Mbps	100 Mbps➔100 Mbps
FastForward (FIFO)	31 microseconds	7 microseconds
FragmentFree (FIFO)	70 microseconds	9 microseconds
Store-and-Forward (LIFO)	7 microseconds	3 microseconds

The Full-Duplex Support feature is only available on 100BaseT ports and is used for switch-to-switch, switch-to-router, and switch-to-server connections. The CollisionFree feature of the Catalyst 2820 and 1900 switches provides full-duplex operation on the 100BaseT ports, delivering up to 200 Mbps of bandwidth and extended cable distance using fiber.

A common configuration is to connect the full-duplex port of a Catalyst switch to a server with a 100BaseT adapter in full-duplex mode, or to another Catalyst switch configured for full-duplex operation.

Full-duplex operation requires that each end of the link connect to a single device, such as a workstation or a switched port.

When configuring a switch port for full-duplex mode, you must configure both ends of the link for full-duplex mode.

Repeaters may not be connected to a switch configured as full-duplex.

FDDI Support (Catalyst 2820)

Starting with software version 1.14, the Catalyst 2820 FDDI module supports Path MTU Discovery to recover when it encounters an FDDI packet that needs to be fragmented but that has the "Don't Fragment" bit set. The module returns a "Destination Unreachable" message to the source host. The module also indicates the size of the MTU as 1500 bytes in the same message. Having determined the size of the MTU for the next hop, the source can then suitably break up the packet and retransmit.

APaRT for IPX and AppleTalk

APaRT stands for Automatic Packet Recognition and Translation. APaRT eliminates the need for reconfiguration of common packet formats for Ethernet devices in IPX networks, and it enables AppleTalk Phase I and Phase II devices to coexist on the network.

ATM Support (Catalyst 2820)

The Catalyst 2820 ATM module supports the following features:

- Full-duplex operation
- 155.52 Mbps data transfer rate
- Store-and-forward packet relay
- LAN Emulation Client (LEC) for ELANs
- ATM Adaptation Layer 5 (AAL5) for LANE data transfer
- User-Network Interface (UNI) 3.0 and 3.1 for switched virtual circuits (SVCs) and permanent virtual circuits (PVCs)

The ATM modules support the following ATM management features:

- Integrated Local Management Interface (ILMI) for ATM UNI 3.0 and 3.1 MIBs
- Operation, administration, and maintenance (OAM)

The ATM modules comply with the following standards:

- LANE 1.0 for LANE client only
- Synchronous Optical Network (SONET) and Synchronous Transport Signal level 3 (STS-3c) physical layer
- Synchronous Digital Hierarchy (SDH) STM-1

Network Port

The Network Port option specifies the destination port for all packets with unknown unicast addresses. You can designate any port on the switch to be the Network Port. Addresses are not learned on this port, and unknown unicast frames are forwarded out this port instead of being flooded.

When a Catalyst 2820 or 1900 receives a unicast packet with a destination address that it has not learned, the default is to flood it to all ports. However, on ports with only statically assigned addresses or with single stations attached, no unknown destinations exist, and flooding would serve no purpose. You can disable flooding in this case on a per-port basis.

You can also assign a single port, referred to as the Network Port, to act as the destination for all packets with unknown unicast addresses. Packets with unknown unicast addresses are always flooded to the Network Port. A secured port cannot be the Network Port, and the Network Port does not learn addresses. If you select a secure port to act as the Network Port, you are prompted to disable the security feature before continuing.

When using a Network Port, it must be the only switch port connected to a backbone. If you are using a Network Port and you connect more than one port to a backbone, the switch might lose communication with the network. You can connect several ports to other multi-address devices if you are not using a Network Port.

Port Security

Secured ports restrict the use of a port to a user-defined group of stations. The maximum number of devices on a secured port is 132. The addresses for the devices on a secure port are statically assigned by an administrator or are obtained through sticky learning. Sticky learning takes place when the address table for a port set as secured does not contain a full complement of static addresses. The port dynamically learns the source address of incoming packets and automatically assigns them as static addresses.

Secured ports generate address-security violations under the following conditions:

- When the address table of a secured port is full and the address of an incoming packet is not found in the table

- When an incoming packet has a source address statically assigned to another port

When a security violation occurs, the port can be suspended or disabled, and SNMP traps can be generated. You can also choose to ignore the violation and keep the port enabled.

The action taken by the Catalyst 2820 or 1900 switch is defined by the administrator through an SNMP-compatible workstation or by using the Management Console menu.

NOTE   Fully securing the port requires disabling flooding to the port.

Many reasons exist as to why you may want to use secure ports. If you define a port's address table to contain only one address, the workstation or server attached to that port is guaranteed the full bandwidth of the port. This type of configuration is referred to as the private Ethernet configuration.

Address security can also be used to ensure that only members of a particular workgroup have access to the switch on a given port. By assigning static addresses to a secure port, the switch does not forward packets with source addresses outside the group. Secured ports used in conjunction with VLANs allow for a completely secure switch.

Virtual LANs

The Catalyst 2820 and 1900 switches support up to four VLANs per switch. This capability enables ports on the switch to be grouped into separate logical networks. Unicast, broadcast, and multicast packets are forwarded (and flooded) only to those stations within a VLAN.

The default management VLAN is VLAN 1.

Each VLAN contains its own bridge MIB information and supports its own implementation of some of the features described in this chapter, including Spanning-Tree Protocol (STP).

Communication between VLANs requires a router connection for each VLAN.

VLANs are configured through the Virtual LAN Configuration menu.

SPAN (Port Monitoring)

SPAN stands for Switch Port ANalyzer and is a single port that is capable of monitoring one, all, or any group of other switch ports. The SPAN function monitors traffic that is seen on the switch bus only. A common use for a configured SPAN port is to connect a protocol analyzer or dedicated RMON probe. Because each port is dedicated bandwidth, just connecting a protocol analyzer on any switch port will not enable you to see traffic on other ports, thus the reason for SPAN.

Multicast Address Packet Filtering

The Catalyst 2820 and 1900 switches incorporate multicast Address Packet Filtering. As a result, the switches can handle both IP-based multicast and MAC address-based multicast protocols in the network.

Multicast filtering can be further combined with source port filtering, a type of packet forwarding using both the destination address and the source port, to achieve load balancing across servers. The switches also incorporate broadcast storm control, a Cisco IOS software feature, to filter out broadcast traffic from a port that is receiving unacceptable levels of broadcast packets without affecting unicast and multicast traffic.

With increasing use of audio/video conferencing packages and video servers that use broadcast and multicast traffic, even high-capacity networks encounter bandwidth congestion. Switches that proliferate network traffic without intelligent filtering can seriously degrade network performance.

The Catalyst 2820 and 1900 switches prevent multicast flooding by interoperating with intelligent routing software to restrict transmission to only ports interested in receiving a particular multicast by communicating with routers through Cisco Group Management Protocol (CGMP). CGMP is a Layer 3 enhancement that provides value-added functionality and tighter integration between the switches and traditional router-based Cisco IOS software components.

Multicast Registration

The multicast registration feature enables you to register multicast addresses with a list of ports to which packets are forwarded. When the Catalyst 2820 or 1900 switch receives a multicast or broadcast packet, the default is to flood it to all ports. You can use the management console or SNMP to register multicast addresses and list the ports to which these packets should be forwarded. You can also disable the normal flooding of unregistered multicast packets on a per-port basis.

You can use this feature in conjunction with source port filtering for load balancing the traffic. Besides reducing unnecessary traffic, these features open up the possibility of using multicast packets for dedicated groupcast applications, such as broadcast video.

Cisco Group Multicast Protocol

CGMP reduces unnecessary flooding of the IP multicast packets. The Catalyst 2820 or 1900 switch receives data from a Cisco router identifying clients that should receive certain IP multicast packets. These clients constitute the group serviced by CGMP. With this information, the switch limits the transmission of the IP multicast packets to the users in the group.

Broadcast Storm Control

A broadcast storm is an increase in the number of broadcast packets coming from a given port. Forwarding these packets can cause significant network degradation. To avoid this condition, the broadcast storm control feature enables you to set a threshold for the number of broadcast packets that can be received from a port before forwarding is blocked. A second threshold is defined to determine when to reenable the normal forwarding of broadcast packets.

The broadcast storm control (default is off) feature is implemented at the port level but is configured at the switch level. This feature does not reduce the number of broadcasts to a certain level. Broadcasts are shut off until their number drops below a specified packets-per-second (pps) threshold. Broadcast forwarding is resumed when the port falls below the re-enable pps threshold.

It must be noted that the broadcast storm control feature does not eliminate broadcasts. Another important note is that it always uses store-and-forward mode.

Spanning-Tree Protocol

The Catalyst 2820 and 1900 switches conform to the IEEE 802.1d Spanning-Tree Protocol (STP) specification. Spanning-Tree Protocol is implemented between switches to detect and remove redundant paths from the network. All Catalyst ports are included in STP support, and management of STP goes through the standard bridge MIB. One instance of STP exists for each VLAN that has been created.

NOTE   Two excellent books that discuss Spanning-Tree Protocol in detail are *Cisco Lan Switching* by Kennedy Clark and Kevin Hamilton (Cisco Press, ISBN 1-57870-094-9) and *Interconnections*, Second Edition, by Radia Perlman (Addison-Wesley, ISBN 0201634481).

Dynamic addresses are aged and dropped from the address table after a configurable period of time. In the case of the Catalyst 2820 and 1900 switches, the default for aging dynamic addresses is 5 minutes. A reconfiguration of the spanning tree, however, can cause many station locations to change. Because this could mean that many stations are unreachable for 5 minutes or more, the address-aging time is accelerated so that station addresses can be dropped from the address table and then relearned. The accelerated aging is the same as the forward-delay value when STP reconfigures.

The forward-delay parameter is used to configure the time interval in seconds spent waiting to change a port from its STP learning and listening states to a forwarding state. Because STP conforms to the IEEE 802.1d specification, the spanning tree will interoperate with other vendors' bridges and switches.

Management Support

You can use an SNMP-compatible management station to fully manage the Catalyst 2820 and 1900 switches. The switches support all pertinent SNMP MIB II variables, as well as a comprehensive set of Cisco MIB extensions designed for maximum support of the hub and switching capabilities of the switches.

NOTE   The Catalyst 2820 and Catalyst 1900 SNMP MIB objects are documented in a separate manual from Cisco, called *Catalyst 2820 and Catalyst 1900 MIB Reference Manual.*

In traditional Ethernet implementations that used shared media, such as thinnet or thicknet coaxial cabling, network management was relatively easy. A protocol analyzer could be attached to the segment, and all traffic on the segment could be observed.

In a switched network environment, a protocol analyzer can see information only on the port or VLAN that it has been mirrored to (see the section on SPAN, earlier in this chapter). The protocol analyzer cannot see traffic on other ports on the switch. To do that, network management tools use Simple Network Management Protocol (SNMP) to communicate and collate information among managed elements of a network. SNMP messages can be sent and received only by SNMP-enabled devices. The information used in this communication is stored in a MIB.

Remote Monitoring (RMON) is a MIB agent specification (RFC 1271) that defines functions for the remote monitoring of network devices. RMON-MIB was developed by the Internet Engineering Task Force (IETF) and became a standard in 1991. RMON organized monitoring functions into nine groups to support Ethernet technologies.

Using an RMON MIB, a network management tool can monitor traffic coming into and going out of distant ports. An RMON MIB defines nine groups containing information pertinent to managing a switched network. An RMON-based network management application can graphically display statistics and event generation based on information stored in groups of the RMON MIB.

An embedded RMON agent built into the Catalyst 2820 and 1900 switches provides optional MIB specification support used by TrafficDirector. The agent provides visibility into network activity and enables remote access to Statistics, History, Alarms, and Events RMON groups for any port through SNMP or TrafficDirector management applications, without requiring a dedicated probe or network analyzer.

Cisco Discovery Protocol

Cisco Discovery Protocol (CDP) is a Cisco proprietary protocol that defines a protocol to exchange information between devices in the network. Cisco IOS software uses the CDP to obtain and maintain a comprehensive understanding of the network topology. The CDP management agent is part of the Cisco IOS software and functions as a lower-layer protocol that interrogates adjacent devices for information.

NOTE   CDP only collects information about adjacent devices; CDP frames are never forwarded as with a routing protocol.

The CDP agent gathers information about the type of devices in the network, configuration information about the links connecting those devices, and the number of interfaces within each device. A network management application, such as VlanDirector, imports data provided through CDP and uses that to construct a low-level connectivity model of the network and a graphical topology map.

TrafficDirector is a GUI-based network management application tool for monitoring and managing network traffic and troubleshooting network problems. TrafficDirector works with Cisco devices with embedded RMON agents or with RMON probes such as Cisco's SwitchProbe. An RMON probe is a network device used for monitoring any segment, ring, or switch link in an enterprise network.

Frame Processing

When the Catalyst 2820 or 1900 switch receives a packet, the following two processes take place simultaneously:

- *Forwarding decision*—The destination address is examined and a forwarding decision is made based on that address, VLAN configuration, port monitoring, and the source port information.

- *Address learning*—The source address is examined and a learning process occurs based on whether the address is in the source address table.

Forwarding Packets

When a packet is received, the switch first checks the availability of buffers. If a buffer is available, the switch continues to process the packet; otherwise, the packet is dropped and a No Buffer Discard error is recorded for that port. After allocating a buffer to the packet, the forwarding engine checks the status of the source port.

Buffer Allocation

An incoming frame is stored in an empty packet buffer. If no more empty buffers are available, a No Buffer Discard error is generated for the port, and the packet is dropped. The condition should never occur under normal switch operation. To look for this condition, check the Port Statistics Report. The No Buffer Discard entry indicates whether you are running out of buffer locations. This error count is tabulated on a per-port basis.

Source Status Check

The forwarding engine next checks the source port status. This port can be in one of three states: active, suspended, or disabled. An active port is in a ready state to receive packets; this is the normal state for the port. A port can get suspended by STP to break a topology loop in the network, by address violation caused by a secure port receiving a packet from an unauthorized station, or through management control.

Packets from a disabled or suspended port do not get forwarded to any port except the monitor port, if enabled. If the monitor port is not enabled, the switch drops the packet. If the port is suspended or disabled for any reason, the process does the monitoring check instead of forwarding.

Port Status

As previously mentioned, the port can be in one of three conditions: active, suspended, or disabled. The active mode indicates that the port is enabled and is transmitting packets. The suspended mode means the port is not active but will be automatically returned to the enable status when the condition causing the suspension is removed. Disabled indicates that the port is inactive and must be manually returned to the enable state.

Although a suspended port does not forward the packet, it is monitored by the ECU subsystem for diagnostic purposes. A suspended port gets reenabled by STP or by encountering a valid packet after an address violation. A port enters a disabled state on encountering an address violation or by management control. A disabled port can be reenabled only through management intervention.

Unicast Filtering

When a Catalyst 2820 or Catalyst 1900 switch receives a unicast packet with a destination address that has not been learned, the default is to flood it to all ports. However, on ports with only statically assigned addresses or a single station attached, these ports have no unknown destinations; therefore, flooding would serve no purpose. You can disable flooding, in this case, on a per-port basis.

Source Port Filtering

Source port filtering provides additional security to devices connected to designated restricted addresses on a Catalyst 2820 or 1900 switch. You can designate restricted static addresses for which you want packets forwarded only if the packets are received on specified ports. Packets to restricted static addresses received on other ports are filtered. This feature provides for load balancing of traffic, such as video, by using the same multicast address for streams sent from servers on different ports.

By default, all multicast frames are forwarded to all ports in a VLAN. However, you can register multicast addresses so that they are sent to only the ports you define. Because these packets are then not forwarded to other ports, the amount of flooding performed by the switch is reduced. This current form of filtering must be manually set. The decision for multicast address filtering happens during the CAM matching process.

NOTE   The broadcast address cannot be used as a registered multicast address.

Destination Address Matching

The forwarding engine next looks up the destination address in the CAM table, which maintains an association between MAC addresses and ports. The CAM table contains the address and the port through which the address can be reached. If the address is found in the CAM, the packet is flagged for delivery to the corresponding ports. The CAM entries are obtained through dynamic source address learning and management configuration of static addresses. During the source address learning process, an entry for the address and port is added to the CAM table.

If the destination address of a packet resides on the same port as the source address, the packet is dropped (filtered) and is not forwarded to the destination port. If the address is not found in the CAM table, the packet is flagged for delivery to all ports except the source port. This process, called flooding, happens every time the switch receives a packet for an address it is unaware of. Flooding of both unknown unicast and unregistered multicast can be disabled on a per-port basis. Flooding control prevents ports from receiving unicast traffic destined for unknown addresses and is configurable on a per-port basis because it is useful for ports with single or statically assigned addresses. The default is to flood to all ports.

VLAN Matching

The Catalyst 2820 and 1900 switches address the scalability issues and network management complexities associated with flat switched network topologies through port-based VLANs. The Catalyst 2820 or 1900 switches support four port-based VLANs per switch. Each VLAN has its own bridge MIB and spanning tree. After obtaining the list of destination ports from the CAM table, the forwarding engine uses the VLAN map at this point to further prune the list of ports on which this packet would be forwarded.

In the case of a unicast packet, if the destination port is outside the source port's VLAN, the packet is treated as an unknown unicast within that VLAN. The ports belonging to the source address VLAN are flooded with the packet. Flooded packets (unicast, broadcast, and multicast) also stay within the same VLAN.

Destination Status

The switch maintains a map of destination ports for each packet in buffer memory. Because a packet cannot be forwarded out a suspended or disabled port, the switch checks each destination port mapped to the packet and removes it from the map before forwarding the packet.

If any destination port is in a suspended or disabled state, it does not receive the packet and is removed from the map. If all destination ports are suspended or disabled, the switch drops the packets and frees the buffer.

Port Monitoring

The last check before the packet can be queued for transmission is to determine whether the destination or source port is being monitored. If so, the switch adds the monitoring port—called the Switched Port Analyzer, or SPAN, port—to the map of ports associated with the packet. Usually the network manager configures one of the high-speed ports as a SPAN port.

To analyze the functioning of a switch, an administrator can configure any port in the switch to be a monitoring port. This port can be set up to see traffic destined for any port or group of ports in the switch. An RMON probe or protocol analyzer can attach to a monitoring port to analyze network traffic.

The switch does not mirror broadcast packets or spanning-tree packets because spanning-tree packets are used to spread information about network topology. This action ensures that the monitoring port does not see duplicate broadcast packets or control packets that do not originate from a host in the network. The SPAN port provides a powerful and flexible way to monitor switch performance.

Packet Queuing

The packet is now forwarded to each destination port in the map, starting with the port with the highest priority. To ensure that no single port occupies all available shared memory, the switch imposes a 1.5 MB limit on each destination port. If a destination port already has more than this amount of buffer memory allocated to it, a Queue Full Discard error is generated and the buffer is freed. After the packet is successfully transmitted through all destination ports, the buffer is freed.

The packet queue has a limit of 1024 packets. If the packet queue of a destination port is full, the packet will be dropped, the buffer will be freed, and the Queue Full Discard error will be generated for the receiving port.

If the address is not found in the CAM table, the packet is forwarded (flooded) to all the ports except the source port. As you have learned previously, flooding for both unknown unicast and unregistered multicast can be disabled on a per-port basis.

Source Address Processing

The material presented here is intended to help the reader understand switch features; however, it is not directly related to one of the objectives.

This section covers how a source address is processed through the switch, including error checking. Also addressed is the topic of port security and how this feature works.

Packet Error Check

Whereas the forwarding processing occurs as soon as the destination address (DA) is read, the source address (SA) processing begins as soon as the source Ethernet address is read from the incoming packet. The packet then is checked for errors. In case an error is found in the packet, the switch does not learn information about the SA.

Because forwarding in cut-through mode begins as soon as the DA is read, the errored packet continues through the switch like a regular packet. In Store-and-Forward mode, the switch drops the packet if it encounters an error. Even in FastForward mode, the packet is checked for errors; if the packet is an errored packet, no learning takes place and the appropriate error counter is incremented on the port.

Source Address Lookup

If the packet is error-free, the CAM is examined to check whether the source port already exists in it. This checking would happen if the switch has previously learned this address. The CAM table is the same table in which the DA is looked up during frame processing. If the address is not found in the CAM, the switch goes through the address learning process. First, though, it must check whether port security has been enabled. After the address has been found in the CAM, the switch checks whether addressing security has been set for that source port.

Port Security

Port security can be set to prevent unauthorized users from accessing the network. Each port can have an individual address or a group of addresses representing stations permitted on that port. A secure port is allowed to have a maximum of 132 addresses associated with it. If the address in question does appear in the CAM but is associated with a different port than the one it has originated from, it is called a duplicate address violation.

If the address does not appear in the CAM, it is added to the list of secure addresses associated with that port. In a case when the per-port limit of secure addresses is reached (defaults to 132), the address is not added and a mismatch violation is generated. The administrator can specify the appropriate action on detecting a violation: to disable or suspend a port, to issue a trap, or to ignore the violation.

If port security is not enabled, then the packet goes from the CAM lookup straight into address learning. Address security is set on a per-port basis. A secure port is allowed to have only up to 132 addresses associated with it.

Unauthorized packets may get into the switch because software cannot make administrative decisions as quickly as hardware can forward packets.

Address Violations

Two types of address violations exist:

- *Mismatch*—The address table is full, and a new unknown address appears on the port.
- *Duplicate*—The address that appears in a port's table shows up on a different port.

When an address violation occurs, you can choose to ignore the violation or choose one of two options:

- *Disable*—Turns off the port; must be manually enabled
- *Suspend*—Turns off the port; as soon as a valid address is seen, turns the port back on

Address Learning

Addresses are dynamically learned and stored in the CAM table. If an SA is not found in the CAM table, it is learned (stored) for future reference. A time stamp is recorded with the address that allows the address to age. When a predetermined age is reached, the address expires and is erased from the CAM. Each time an address is referenced, its time stamp is updated, which restarts the aging process. In a case in which the address exists in the CAM table but causes a mismatch address violation, the time stamp is not updated. Address aging in the Catalyst 2820 and 1900 switches conforms to the IEEE 802.1d specification.

If the space limitation of the CAM is reached—which is 1024 addresses for the Catalyst 1900 switch, and 2048 or 8096 addresses for the Catalyst 2820—the switch skips the address learning process for an incoming packet. The number of nodes in the network can be greater than the size of the CAM. If a switch with a CAM space of 1024 is placed in a network with a larger number of nodes and the CAM becomes full despite address aging, the switch will continue to forward the packets correctly but will resort to flooding to forward packets it cannot match in the CAM tables; this results in some performance degradation. Address aging ensures that the switch uses the CAM most efficiently, retaining only addresses that have been active over a certain time period. This completes the SA learning process.

If addressing security is enabled, then the switch determines whether the SA is a member of the address table for that port. If the address is not a member of that port's address table, an address violation is generated. Depending on the switch configuration, a trap and some action may occur. This type of address violation is called a duplicate address found. The address is not learned on this port, and the address violation parameters are set in the System Configuration menu.

When the packet has been determined to be valid, another CAM lookup is done using source address. If the SA is found in the CAM table, the switch checks whether security has been set for that source port. A secure port can support up to 132 addresses. If address security is enabled, the switch determines whether the source address is a member of the address table for that port.

If the address is not a member of the port's address table, an address violation (duplicate address found) is generated. Also, if a trap has been configured, a trap alert is sent to the trap management station. In the case of this type of violation, the SA is not learned on this port.

If the SA is not found in the CAM table and the address security is enabled, the switch determines whether the secure address table is full. If the address table is full, the source address is not learned and a mismatch address violation error is generated. If the address security is disabled or the secure address table is not full, the address is learned for this port and a time stamp is created for this address.

Static Addresses

A network administrator can manually enter addresses into the address table. These are static addresses that do not age and that remain in the CAM table until manually removed.

Time-Stamp Update

The switch updates the time stamp for that SA and uses this information for aging addresses that are not current. The address aging time (default is 5 minutes) is configured in the System Configuration menu.

Applications

The material presented here is intended to help the reader understand switch features; however, it is not directly related to one of the objectives.

You can connect a Catalyst 2820 or 1900 switch directly to a 10BaseT repeater or individual node to boost network performance for workgroup applications. This cost-effective design preserves customer investment in network equipment such as hubs and adapters while improving overall network performance.

Workgroups utilizing client/server applications will benefit by using the Catalyst switches because the network performance will be significantly improved. Two examples show how you could use the Catalyst 1900 or Catalyst 2820 to configure high-performance client/ server network configurations.

In this configuration example, a Catalyst 2820 or 1900 switch supports up to 25 switched (dedicated) Ethernet connections to workstations or 10BaseT hubs. Each workstation or hub directly connected to a port on the Catalyst switch has a dedicated bandwidth of 10 Mbps. However, all the workstations connected to the 10BaseT hub or repeater share the 10 Mbps of bandwidth.

In the example shown in Figure 13-6, two 100 Mbps servers are connected to the 100BaseTX modules on the Catalyst 2820 (or the 100BaseTX ports on the Catalyst 1900). These servers are accessible to all the users in the workgroup. As a result, this configuration could significantly improve the performance of the client/server applications.

Figure 13-6   *Single-Switch Client/Server Workgroup Configuration*

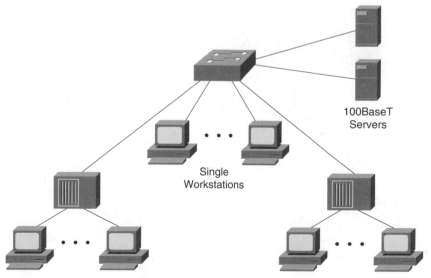

100BaseT
Servers

Single
Workstations

10BaseT Hub-Attached Workstations

This configuration uses multiple Catalyst 2820 or 1900 switches connected to each other with 100 Mbps ports. In the example shown in Figure 13-7, a Catalyst 2820 switch with an eight-port 100BaseTX module is used to connect two Catalyst 1900 (or Catalyst 2820) switches via shared Fast Ethernet (shown in Figure 13-8).

Figure 13-7   *Multiswitch Client/Server Workgroup Configuration*

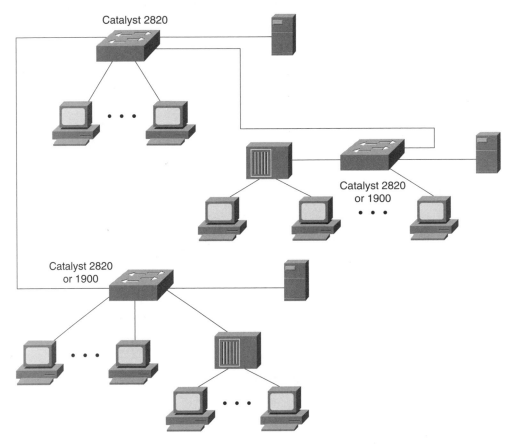

Figure 13-8   *100BaseT Collapsed Backbone Configuration*

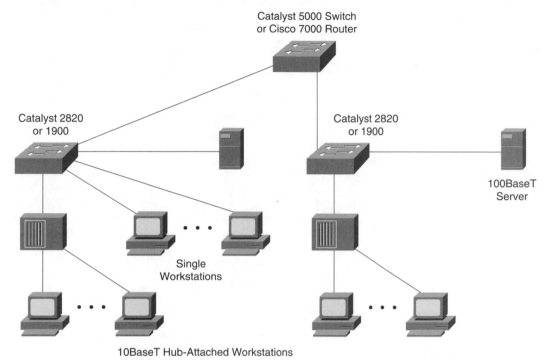

Collapsed Backbone

The Catalyst 2820 and 1900 switches can be used to create collapsed backbone networks. A collapsed backbone is a nondistributed backbone in which all network segments are interconnected through an internetworking device. By definition, collapsed backbones are created using centrally located switches or routers.

100BaseT Collapsed Backbone Configuration

You can create a collapsed backbone by connecting Catalyst 2820 and 1900 switches to a 100BaseT backbone switch or router. In Figure 13-7, shown previously, two Catalyst 2820 switches are connected to a Catalyst 5000 switch or Cisco 7000 router. The Catalyst 1900 and 2820 switches are connected to the Catalyst 5000 switch or Cisco 7000 router via 100BaseT ports in CollisionFree full-duplex operation mode. This configuration enables the link to support up to 200 Mbps of bandwidth using the full-duplex operation mode and a fiber cabling distance of up to 2 km.

Configuring Catalyst 1900 and Catalyst 2820 Switches

CLSC Objectives Covered in This Section

64	Use the Catalyst 1900 and Catalyst 2820 switch menus for configuration.
65	Configure IP addresses and ports on the Catalyst 1900 and Catalyst 2820 switches.
66	Configure VLANs on the Catalyst 1900 and Catalyst 2820 switches.
67	View the Catalyst 1900 and Catalyst 2820 switch reports and summaries.
68	Configure the ATM LANE module on the Catalyst 2820 switch.
80	Use the statistics and reports to maintain the Catalyst 1900 and Catalyst 2820 switches.

This section covers the configuration of the Catalyst 1900 and 2820 switches. Configuration is done using menus that are largely straightforward; however, the trick is knowing which menu to use. Also covered are the 2820 ATM module and how to obtain statistics and reports on the Catalyst 1900 and 2820 switches.

Configuring Switch Parameters

The Catalyst 2820 and 1900 switches can be managed by either in-band or out-of-band management.

- Out-of-band management
    - Terminal connected to the console port
    - Modem
- In-band management
    - SNMP-compatible workstation
    - Telnet

Management Console

You can connect a terminal (or a PC with a terminal emulator) to the console port of a Catalyst 2820 or 1900 switch to use the management console menus. When connected to a terminal or modem, the Catalyst 2820 or 1900 must be configured to the same baud rate and character format as the terminal or modem.

Although the Match Baud Rate option matches the baud rate when the switch is answering an incoming call, the Catalyst 2820 and 1900 switches do not change from their configured rate. When they complete a call and disconnect, the switch always returns to the last configured baud rate.

The default EIA/TIA-232 settings for the Catalyst 2820 and 1900 switches are 9600 baud, 8 data bits, 1 stop bit, and no parity.

First, make sure that the switch is turned on, connect a terminal to the management console port, and turn on the terminal power. When you see the Management Console Logon menu, press Return or Enter to display the Main Menu. Although you can assign a password to limit access to the management console, it is not required.

Catalyst Switch Menus

This section covers the Catalyst 2820 and 1900 switch menus. Most of them are straightforward in nature. We will be illustrating them by using screen shots from actual menus. In general, menus are the same between the 1900 and 2820 platforms. Most differences are related to the 2820's use of expansion ports. Please familiarize yourself with the overall layout of the menus for the most effective use of this text.

Example 13-1 *Catalyst 2820 Main Menu*

```
        [C] Console Password
        [S] System
        [N] Network Management
        [P] Port Configuration
        [A] Port Addressing
        [D] Port Statistics Detail
        [M] Monitoring
        [V] Virtual LAN
        [R] Multicast Registration
        [F] Firmware
        [I] RS-232 Interface
        [U] Usage Summaries
        [H] Help


        [X] Exit Management Console

 Enter Selection:
```

As you can see in Example 13-1, the management console is a menu-driven system with the following characteristics:

- To select a menu, enter the letter in square brackets that precedes or follows the selection. The selected menu is displayed immediately.

- Press Return after entering any parameters. When pressed at the beginning of a parameter entry, Return cancels the attempt, and the menu redisplays.

- Enter an **X** to return to the previous menu. Enter an **X** at the Main Menu to exit the management console and return to the command prompt.

- Certain menus, such as the RS-232 Interface Configuration Menu, enable activation of the given parameters as a group.

- Menus display the current values used by the switch, except when entered as a descriptive string that preserves case.

- The Backspace key works as expected; it erases the character previously entered. When pressed at the beginning of a parameter entry, Backspace causes the entry to be cleared.

NOTE   Parameter changes take effect immediately. However, changed parameters may not be written to NVRAM for up to 30 seconds. If you turn off the switch before the new parameters are written to NVRAM, they will be lost.

Configuring RS-232 Interface

The RS-232 Interface Configuration menu is accessed by selecting option [I] from the Main menu. See Example 13-2.

Example 13-2 *Catalyst 2820 RS-232 Configuration Menu*

```
Catalyst 2820: RS-232 Interface Configuration

           -------------------- Group Settings ----------
           [B] Baud rate                              9600 baud
           [D] Data bits                              8 bit(s)
           [S] Stop bits                              1 bit(s)
           [P] Parity setting                         None


           -------------------- Settings ---------------
           [M] Match remote baud rate (auto baud)     Enabled
           [A] Auto answer                            Enabled
           [N] Number for dial-out connection
           [T] Time delay between dial attempts       300
           [I] Initialization string for modem


           ----------------- Actions -------------------
           [C] Cancel and restore previous group settings
           [G] Activate group settings

           [X] Exit to Main Menu

Enter Selection:
```

This menu is used to define the EIA/TIA-232 (RS-232) port's physical characteristics as well as call features. The menu should be self-explanatory with the exception of the group settings. Any group settings that you make are not invoked until you press the **G** key. Press **C** to cancel the session and return to the previous settings.

Setting Console Password

The Console Password menu is accessed by selecting option [C] from the Main menu, shown in Example 13-3.

Example 13-3 *Catalyst 2820 Console Password Menu*

```
Catalyst 2820: Console Password

     -------------------- Settings ---------------
     [P] Password intrusion threshold              3 attempt(s)
     [S] Silent time upon intrusion detection      None

     -------------------- Actions ----------------
     [M] Modify password

     [X] Exit to Main Menu

Enter Selection:
```

The Console Password menu is used to configure the management console parameters.

- The password intrusion threshold enables you to set the number of failed logon attempts before the console is shut down for the silent time configuration (discussed in the next section).

- The silent time is the amount of minutes the management console will be unavailable after the password intrusion threshold has been reached.

- The modify password option enables you to change your logon password.

Configuring System Parameters

The System Configuration menu is accessed by selecting option [S] from the Main menu, shown in Example 13-4.

Example 13-4 *Catalyst 2820 System Configuration Menu*

```
Catalyst 2820: System Configuration

      System Revision:  1   Address Capacity:  8192
      System Last Reset:    Sat Feb 27 16:10:59 1999

    -------------------- Settings -------------
    [N] Name of system
    [C] Contact name
    [L] Location
    [D] Date/time                               Sat Feb 27 16:15:24 1999
    [S] Switching mode                          FragmentFree
    [U] Use of store-and-forward for multicast  Enabled
    [A] Action upon address violation           Disable
    [G] Generate alert on address violation     Disabled
    [M] Management Console inactivity timeout    60000 second(s)
    [I] Address aging time                      5000 second(s)
    [P] Network port                            None


    -------------------- Actions --------------
    [R] Reset system                   [F] Reset to factory defaults

    -------------------- Related Menus ---------
    [B] Broadcast storm control        [X] Exit to Main Menu

Enter Selection:
```

Besides setting the time and date, the System menu controls a number of other key functions:

- Governs switching mode

- Enables the store-and-forward mode for multicast frames

- Defines the action taken upon address violation

- Generates an alert based upon address violation

- Sets the management console inactivity timeout

- Sets the dynamic address aging time in the CAM

- Defines the network port

You can also reset the system from this menu and reset to factory defaults.

We've discussed the function of most of the other selections in this chapter, but the Network Port is worthy of some coverage here.

The Network Port option specifies the destination port for all packets with unknown unicast addresses. The Network Port configuration applies to a switch that uses the Network Port as the only connection to the network. This is commonly known as an *uplink* on other devices, such as the Catalyst 5000.

NOTE   When using the Network Port, this port must be the only connection to a backbone.

Configuring Broadcast Control

The Broadcast Storm Control menu is accessed by selecting option [B] from the System Configuration menu, shown in Example 13-5.

Example 13-5   *Catalyst 2820 Broadcast Storm Control Menu*

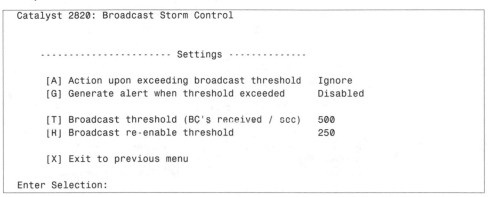

```
Catalyst 2820: Broadcast Storm Control


        -------------------- Settings ------------

    [A] Action upon exceeding broadcast threshold    Ignore
    [G] Generate alert when threshold exceeded       Disabled

    [T] Broadcast threshold (BC's received / sec)    500
    [R] Broadcast re-enable threshold                250

    [X] Exit to previous menu

Enter Selection:
```

If the broadcast rate for a port exceeds the specified threshold, the switch can be set to ignore the broadcast storm or to block the storm by blocking broadcast packets received from the port until the rate drops below the re-enable threshold. Broadcast storm control serves to monitor the number of broadcast packets received per second from each port.

The broadcast rate is measured by the number of broadcast packets received from a port in a single second.

Independent of the action the switch takes on a port, the switch can be set to generate an SNMP alert (trap) to a management station if broadcast storm control is enabled and the broadcast threshold is exceeded on a port.

The broadcast rate is the number of broadcast packets received from a port in a single second. If the broadcast rate exceeds the specified threshold and broadcast storm control is enabled, the switch may generate an alert or block broadcast packets received from the port.

When a port has been blocked, the number of broadcast packets received per second from the port must drop below the reenable threshold before broadcast packet forwarding for the port is automatically reenabled.

The reenable threshold is relevant only if the user has chosen to block broadcast forwarding to control broadcast storms.

Configuring Port Parameters

You can view the configuration of an individual port by entering the port number in the Port Configuration menu, shown in Example 13-6.

Example 13-6 *Catalyst 2820 Port Configuration Menu*

```
Catalyst 2820: Port 1 Configuration

        Built-in 10Base-T
   802.1d STP State: Forwarding     Forward Transitions:  1


       -------------------Settings--------------------
      [D] Description/name of port
      [S] Status of port 1                          Enabled
      [I] VTP pruning mode                          128 (80 hex)
      [C] Port cost (spanning tree)                 100
      [H] Port fast mode (spanning tree)            Enabled
       ----------------Related Menus------------------
      [A] Port addressing           [V] View port statistics
      [N] Next port                 [G] Goto port
      [P] Previous port             [X] Exit to Main Menu

   Enter Selection:
```

Configuring port parameters requires selecting each port individually. In this example, we've selected port 1.

Using the Port Configuration, you can assign a name to a port, view the status of a port, assign STP path cost, assign STP port priority, and view port statistics.

The Port Fast option is a way to bypass the normal STP behavior and put the port into forwarding right away. This is recommended for ports attached to end user computers and servers with only one NIC card. Port Fast occurs on a per-port basis.

Configuring FDDI Port Parameters

You can display the FDDI Port Configuration menu by entering **P** on the Main menu and then the letter of an expansion slot (A1 or B1) containing a Catalyst 2820 switch FDDI module. See Example 13-7.

Example 13-7   *Catalyst 2820 Expansion Port Configuration Menu*

```
Catalyst 2820: Port A1 Configuration (Left Slot)

    Module Name:  FDDI (Fiber SAS Model), Version 00
    Description:  Single Attach Station   Ring Status:  Operational
    802.1d STP State:  Forwarding     Forward Transitions: 1


    ------------------Settings------------------
    [D] Description/name of port
    ----------------Module Settings-------------

    [M] Module Status                         Enabled
    [I] Port priority (spanning tree)         128 (80 hex)
    [C] Path cost (spanning tree)             10
    [L] Novell SNAP frame translation         Automatic
    [U] Unmatched SNAP frame destination      All


    ------------------Actions-------------------
    [R] Reset FDDI module        [F] Reset FDDI with factory defaults
    ----------------Related Menus---------------
    [1] Basic FDDI settings      [2] Secondary FDDI settings
    [A] Port addressing          [V] View port statistics
    [N] Next port                [G] Goto port
    [P] Previous port            [X] Exit to Main Menu

  Enter Selection:
```

The menu for FDDI configuration will be accessible only if you have the FDDI module installed in the switch.

The following options are available for FDDI modules and are in addition to the other port configuration menu options discussed in the Port Configuration menu section.

Ring Status, shown at the right of the menu, indicates whether the module is successfully attached to the ring. The two possible values are operational and nonoperational.

- *[L] Novell SNAP frame translation*—Use this option to define how you want to translate Novell FDDI SNAP frames. Enter the number associated with your choice at the prompt, and press Return.

- *[U] Unmatched SNAP frame destination*—This option appears only when you have selected Automatic as the SNAP translation format. You use it to select which FDDI-to-Ethernet translation to use for packets whose destinations cannot be determined from the Novell SNAP translation table. Enter the number associated with your choice at the prompt, and press Return.

Catalyst 2820 FDDI Bridging

When an FDDI module is installed in the expansion slot of a Catalyst 2820 switch and is connected to network devices, the switch learns the packet format type from the incoming packets and keeps a table that maps the source addresses with the packet format.

The Catalyst 2820 and 1900 switches keep a table that maps the source address with the packet format type learned from incoming packets. If the format type has not been learned for a source address, all three packet format types are broadcast. You can override this default and manually enter a format type.

Table 13-2 shows the IPX packet format types that are converted when FDDI bridging is used.

Table 13-2   *Catalyst 2820 FDDI Bridging*

Ethernet Packet Format	FDDI Packet Format
Ethernet II	FDDI SNAP
Ethernet SNAP	FDDI SNAP
Ethernet 802.3 RAW	FDDI SNAP
Ethernet 802.2	FDDI 802.2
FDDI Packet Format	**Ethernet Packet Format**
FDDI SNAP	Ethernet II
FDDI SNAP	Ethernet SNAP
FDDI SNAP	Ethernet 802.3 RAW
FDDI 802.2	Ethernet 802.2

Catalyst 2820 FDDI bridging also allows AppleTalk to run over FDDI and be converted. AppleTalk Phase I and Phase II networks can coexist in the network. This is covered under IEEE 802.1H, known as bridge tunneling.

Table 13-1 shows the AppleTalk packet format types that are converted when FDDI bridging is used.

Table 13-3   *Catalyst 2820 FDDI Bridging—AppleTalk Packet Formats*

AppleTalk	Ethernet Format	FDDI Format
Phase 1	Ethernet II	Bridge Tunnel Frame
Phase 2	Ethernet SNAP	FDDI Snap
	FDDI Format	**Ethernet Format**
	FDDI SNAP	Ethernet SNAP
	Bridge Tunnel Frame	Ethernet II

Configuring VLANs

The Virtual LAN Configuration menu is accessed by selecting option [V] from the Main menu, shown in Example 13-8.

Example 13-8   *Catalyst 1900 VLAN Configuration Menu*

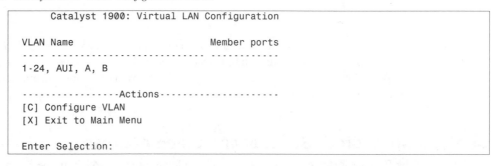

```
        Catalyst 1900: Virtual LAN Configuration

VLAN Name                       Member ports
---- ------------------------- -----------
1-24, AUI, A, B

----------------Actions--------------------
[C] Configure VLAN
[X] Exit to Main Menu

Enter Selection:
```

You can configure up to four separate VLANs in a Catalyst 2280 or 1900 switch. Every port belongs to one—and only one—VLAN. The switch is shipped factory default with all ports belonging to VLAN1. To add ports to a VLAN, move the port from VLAN1.

VLAN1 is usually used as the Management VLAN; there should be at least one port in VLAN1.

NOTE   If you are using CGMP, all ports must belong to the same VLAN.

Configuring SPAN

The Monitoring Configuration menu is accessed by selecting option [M] from the Main menu. See Example 13-9.

Example 13-9 *Catalyst 1900 Monitoring Configuration Menu*

```
Catalyst 1900: Monitoring Configuration

      --------------------- Settings -------------
      [C] Capturing frames to the Monitor          Disabled
      [M] Monitor port assignment                  None
      Current capture list:  No ports in list


      --------------------- Actions --------------
      [A] Add ports to capture list
      [D] Delete ports from capture list

      [X] Exit to Main Menu

Enter Selection:
```

SPAN is used to monitor traffic occurring on other ports. This menu is used to define what ports you're going to capture to the SPAN port and to define which port will act as the SPAN port. The SPAN port must be enabled to use it. If you want to resume normal use of the port, you must disable SPAN monitoring.

Configuring Address Security and Static Address

The Port Addressing menu is accessed by selecting option [A] from the Main menu and then entering the port number, as shown in Example 13-10.

Example 13-10 *Catalyst 2820 Port Addressing Menu*

```
    Catalyst 2820: Port B Addressing (Right Slot)

    --------------------Settings----------------
    [T] Address table size                   Unrestricted
    [S] Addressing security                  Disabled
    [U] Flood unknown unicasts               Enabled
    [M] Flood unregistered multicasts        Enabled

    --------------------Actions-----------------
    [A] Add a static address
    [D] Define restricted static address
    [L] List address
    [E] Erase an address
    [R] Remove all addresses
```

Example 13-10 *Catalyst 2820 Port Addressing Menu (Continued)*

```
        [C] Configure port          [V] View port statistics
        [N] Next port               [G] Goto port
        [P] Previous port           [X] Exit to Main menu

   Enter Selection:
```

You can use this menu to configure address security of a port and to define static unicast addresses. Static addresses and port security are added by entering a device's MAC address. This menu can also be used to specify how a port filters and forwards unmatched unicast addresses and nonregistered multicast addresses.

Although multicast address registrations are configured elsewhere, you can use this menu to specify additional source-port filtering on the multicast addresses.

Registering Multicast Addresses

The Multicast Registration menu is accessed by selecting option [R] from the Main menu. See Example 13-11.

Example 13-11 *Catalyst 1900 Multicast Registration Menu*

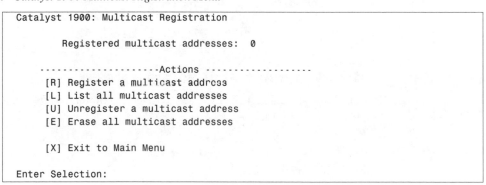

```
   Catalyst 1900: Multicast Registration

          Registered multicast addresses:  0

          -------------------Actions -----------------
      [R] Register a multicast address
      [L] List all multicast addresses
      [U] Unregister a multicast address
      [E] Erase all multicast addresses

      [X] Exit to Main Menu

   Enter Selection:
```

By default, all multicast frames are forwarded to all ports in a VLAN. You can, however, register multicast addresses so that they are sent to only the ports you define. Because these packets are then not forwarded to other ports, the amount of flooding performed by the switch is reduced. Registering a multicast address prompts you for the address and the ports for which frames destined for this address are to be forwarded.

Displaying Port Statistics

The Port Statistics Detail menu is accessed by selecting option [D] from the Main menu. See Example 13-12.

Example 13-12 *Catalyst 2820 Port Statistics Detail Menu*

```
Catalyst 2820: Port B (Right Slot)
      Receive Statistics                   Transmit Statistics
----------------------------------   ----------------------------------
Total good frames             8   Total Frames                 9
Total octets                512   Total Octets               926
Broadcast/multicast frames    0   Broadcast/multicast frames   0
Broadcast/multicast octets    0   Broadcast/multicast octets   0
Good frames forwarded         8   Deferrals                    0
Frames filtered               0   Single collisions            0
Runt frames                   0   Multiple collisions          0
No buffer discards            0   Excessive collisions         0
                                  Queue full discards          0
Errors:                           Errors:
  FCS errors                  0     Late collisions            0
  Alignment errors            0     Excessive deferrals        0
  Giant frames                0     Jabber errors              0
  Address violations          0     Other transmit errors      0

Select [A] Port addressing, [C] Configure port,
       [N] Next port, [P] Previous port, [G] Goto port,
                 [R] Reset port statistics, or [X] Exit to Main Menu:
```

Configuring Network Management Parameters

The Network Management menu is accessed by selecting option [N] from the Main menu, as shown in Example 13-13.

Example 13-13 *Catalyst 1900 Network Management Menu*

```
Catalyst 1900: Network Management

     [I] IP Configuration
     [S] SNMP Management
     [B] Bridge - Spanning Tree
     [C] Cisco Discovery Protocol
     [G] Cisco Group Management Protocol
     [X] Exit to Main Menu

Enter Selection:
```

This section is self-explanatory. We will take each submenu as an individual item.

Configuring IP Parameters

The IP Configuration menu is accessed by selecting option [I] from the Network management menu. See Example 13-14.

Example 13-14 *Catalyst 1900 IP Configuration Menu*

```
Catalyst 1900: IP Configuration

      Ethernet Address:  00-C0-1D-79-CE-00

    --------------------- Settings -------------
    [I] IP address                          172.16.99.71
    [S] Subnet mask                         255.255.255.0
    [G] Default gateway                     172.16.99.1
    [V] Management VLAN
                        1
    [X] Exit to previous menu


Enter Selection:
```

This menu enables the user to select the IP address, subnet mask, default gateway, and the management VLAN. This information is used for in-band management.

SNMP Management

The Network Management (SNMP) Configuration menu is accessed by selecting option [S] from the Network Management menu. See Example 13-15.

Example 13-15 *Catalyst 1900 SNMP Configuration Menu*

```
Catalyst 1900: Network Management (SNMP) Configuration

    --------------------- Settings -------------
    [R] READ  community string
    [W] WRITE community string
    [1] 1st WRITE manager name or IP address    0.0.0.0
    [2] 2nd WRITE manager name or IP address    0.0.0.0
    [3] 3rd WRITE manager name or IP address    0.0.0.0
    [4] 4th WRITE manager name or IP address    0.0.0.0

    [F] First  TRAP community string
    [A] First  TRAP manager name or IP address  172.16.100.254
    [S] Second TRAP community string
    [B] Second TRAP manager name or IP address  0.0.0.0
    [T] Third  TRAP community string
    [C] Third  TRAP manager name or IP address  0.0.0.0
```

continues

Example 13-15 *Catalyst 1900 SNMP Configuration Menu (Continued)*

```
       [U] Authentication trap generation           Enabled
       [L] LinkUp/LinkDown trap generation          Enabled


       --------------------- Actions --------------
       [X] Exit to previous menu


 Enter Selecttion:
```

This menu enables you to define network management stations to receive traps that have been configured. You can define the READ and WRITE community strings that are used to manage the switch. Four WRITE managers can be assigned by entering their IP addresses where indicated.

Three TRAP managers can be assigned as well.

Configuring STP Parameters

The Spanning Tree Configuration menu is accessed by selecting option [C] from the Network Management menu. See Example 13-16.

Example 13-16 *Catalyst 1900 Spanning Tree Configuration Menu*

```
 Catalyst 1900: VLAN 1 Spanning Tree Configuration
     Bridge ID:  8000 00-C0-1D-79-CE-00


     ----------------- Information ---------------
 Designated root 8000 00-C0-1D-79-CE-00
 Number of member ports     27   Root port              N/A
 Max age (sec)              20   Root path cost          0
 Forward Delay (sec)        15   Hello time (sec)        2
 Topology changes            0   Last TopChange   0d00h00m00s
 ------------------Settings-------------------
 [S] Spanning Tree Algorithm & Protocol         Enabled
 [B] Bridge priority                            32768 (8000 hex)
 [M] Max age when operating as root             20 second(s)
 [H] Hello time when operating as root          2 second(s)
 [F] Forward delay when operating as root       15 second(s)


     ------------------Actions-------------------
 [N] Next VLAN bridge         [G] Goto VLAN bridge
 [P] Previous VLAN bridge     [X] Exit to previous menu


 Enter Selection:
```

The STP Parameters menu is used to display and configure Spanning Tree settings defined for the switch. A VLAN must be entered to display the menu. If no VLANs have been configured, all ports belong to VLAN1.

You can use the STP Parameters menu to do the following:

- Enable or disable STP.

- Select a bridge as the root bridge or as a designated bridge.

- Define the maximum age interval when this bridge becomes the root bridge.

- Define the hello-time interval when this bridge becomes the root bridge.

- Define the forward-delay interval when this bridge becomes the root bridge. STP uses this value to accelerate aging when the spanning tree is reconfigured.

Configuring CDP Parameters

The CDP/Configuration/Status menu is accessed by selecting option [C] from the Network Management menu. See Example 13-17.

Example 13-17 *Catalyst 1900 CDP Configuration/Status Menu*

```
Catalyst 1900: CDP Configuration/Status

    CDP enabled on: 1-24, AUI, A, B

---------------------- Settings ------------------

[H] Hold Time (secs)                      180
[T] Transmission Interval (secs)           60

---------------------- Actions -------------------

[E] Enable CDP on Port(s)
[D] Disable CDP on Port(s)
[S] Show Neighbor
[X] Exit to previous menu

Enter Selection:
```

The Cisco Discovery Protocol (CDP) Configuration/Status menu allows you to enable CDP on some or all of the switch ports. This menu can also be used to set the transmission interval between CDP messages and to determine the hold time, which defines how long the CDP information is retained.

The **show cdp neighbor** command is useful in troubleshooting, as it displays all neighbor devices that have CDP enabled on them.

Configuring CGMP Parameters

A router supporting IP multicasting can use CGMP to distribute membership of each IP multicast group to switches. CGMP-capable switches such as the Catalyst 2820 or 1900 can automatically restrict the forwarding of IP multicast packets to only those ports belonging to a specific group.

The Router Hold Time is used to configure the amount of time the switch holds multicast-group information. CGMP can also be enabled or disabled on this menu, and you can list the IP multicast addresses being handled by CGMP.

Upgrading Firmware

The Firmware menu is accessed by selecting option [F] from the Main menu. See Example 13-18.

Example 13-18 *Catalyst 2820 Firmware Configuration Menu*

```
Catalyst 2820: Firmware Configuration

      ---------------System Information------------
      FLASH:  1024K bytes
      V5.33    :
      Upgrade status:
      No upgrade currently in progress.

      ---------------Module Information------------
      Slot A v1.14 written 12-27-98 192.009.200.213: valid

      ------------------Settings------------------
      [S] Server:  IP address of TFTP server        0.0.0.0
      [F] Filename for firmware upgrades
      [A] Accept upgrade transfer from other hosts     Enabled

      ------------------Actions-------------------
      [1] FDDI (A) XMODEM upgrade    [2] FDDI (B) XMODEM upgrade
      [3] FDDI (A) TFTP upgrade      [4] FDDI (B) TFTP upgrade
      [U] System XMODEM upgrade      [D] Download test subsystem (XMODEM)
      [T] System TFTP upgrade        [X] Exit to Main Menu

 Enter Selection:
```

Use the Firmware Configuration menu to display the firmware version used by the switch and to perform firmware upgrades. You can use this menu to upgrade the firmware for Catalyst 2820 FDDI and ATM modules and to download diagnostic software for use by customer support.

Displaying Summaries Reports

The Usage Summaries menu is accessed by selecting option [U] from the Main menu. See Example 13-19.

Example 13-19 *Catalyst 2820 Usage Summaries Menu*

```
Catalyst 2820: Usage Summaries

     [P] Port Status Report
     [M] Module Status Report
     [A] Port Addressing Report
     [E] Exception Statistics Report
     [U] Utilization Statistics Report
     [B] Bandwidth Usage Report

     [X] Exit to Main Menu

Enter Selection:
```

This menu is fairly self-explanatory. The port status of all the ports is displayed under the Port Status report; the same goes for the Module Status report. This would apply only for the Catalyst 2820 because the 1900 does not have modules. The Port Addressing report lists the port's address mode, tells whether the address is static or dynamic, and tells how many addresses have been assigned to the port. The Exception Statistics report displays receive errors, transmit errors, and security violations for each port. The Utilization report lists frame-count statistics for each port. The Bandwidth Usage report displays the bandwidth of the network during a given period of time.

Configuring the ATM LANE Module

You learned the basic details about the ATM concepts and ATM operation in Chapter 12, "Introduction to ATM Networking."

Here, let's review the basics of ATM LANE before we proceed with the configuration of the Catalyst 2820 ATM LANE module.

The four components of LANE are listed here:

- *LANE Client (LEC)*—The LANE client is a device that would like to communicate using LANE across the ATM network. The Catalyst 2820 can implement only the LEC in the ATM Module.

- *LANE Configuration Server (LECS)*—This is a database server of sorts that assigns a LANE client to particular Emulated LANs (ELANs) by directing them to the LES that corresponds to the ELAN. One LECS is permitted for each administrative domain.

- *LANE Server (LES)*—The LANE server implements the control function for an ELAN. Only one LES exists for each particular ELAN, and it has a unique address within the domain.

- *LANE Broadcast and Unknown Server (BUS)*—The BUS is a multicast server that floods traffic addressed to an unknown destination in ELANs. It also forwards multicast and broadcast traffic to the appropriate clients. The Cisco LightStream 1010 implements both the LES and the BUS as a pair.

To use the ATM Module in the Catalyst 2820, there must be existing devices in the ATM network running the other components of LANE. These devices could be other switches, routers, or an ATM switch. A LANE configuration is shown in Figure 13-9. For purposes of the rest of this section, the Cisco LightStream 1010 will be the ATM Switch referred to.

Figure 13-9   *LANE Configuration Example*

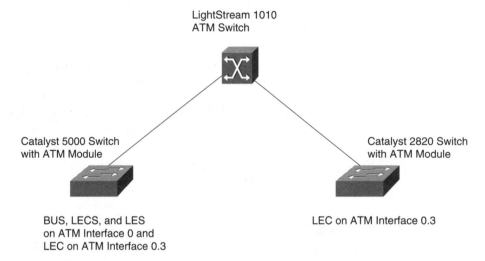

LightStream 1010
ATM Switch

Catalyst 5000 Switch
with ATM Module

Catalyst 2820 Switch
with ATM Module

BUS, LECS, and LES
on ATM Interface 0 and
LEC on ATM Interface 0.3

LEC on ATM Interface 0.3

LANE Configuration Example

The following assumptions apply to the LANE configuration example:

- The LightStream 1010 ATM switch default ATM Network Service Access Point (NSAP) prefix is 47.0091.8100.0000.0000.0ca7.ce01.

- The Catalyst 5000 switch has an ATM module installed in slot 3.

- The Catalyst 5000 switch runs the LECS, LES, BUS on ATM interface 0.

- The Catalyst 5000 switch runs the LEC on ATM interface 0.3.

- The Catalyst 2820 switch has the ATM module installed in slot A.

- The Catalyst 2820 switch runs the LEC on ATM interface 0.1.

- The ELAN name used in the example is the default.

Accessing the ATM LANE Client CLI

To access the Catalyst 2820 CLI, you must enter through the Port Configuration selection from the Main Menu and select option [K] from the ATM Port Configuration menu. That takes you to the menu shown in Example 13-20.

Example 13-20 *Catalyst 2820 ATM Module Configuration Menu*

```
Catalyst 2820: Port A Configuration (Left Slot)

        Module Name:  ATM 155 MM Fiber, Version 01
        Description:  Multimode Fiber
        ATM Network Status: Operational
        802.1d STP State:  Forwarding     Forwarding Transitions: 9


        -------------------Settings---------------------
        [D] Description/name of port
        ------------------Module Settings----------------
        [M] Module status                           Enabled
        [I] Port priority (spanning tree)           128
        [C] Path cost (spanning tree)               10
        [H] Port fast mode (spanning tree)          Enabled


        -------------------Actions---------------------
        [R] Reset module            [F] Reset module with factory defaults
        -----------------Related Menus------------------
        [K] Command Line Interface   [L] ATM and LANE status
        [A] Port addressing          [V] View port statistics
        [N] Next port                [G] Goto port
        [P] Previous port            [X] Exit to Main Menu

Enter Selection:
```

In this menu, slot A is known as interface 1. Select the command-line interface from the Port Configuration menu. The CLI screen is displayed. To end the CLI session, enter **Ctrl-G**.

The command-line interface used on the ATM module is Cisco IOS, which is similar to that used in Cisco router configurations.

The ATM module is installed in slot A (interface 0), the VLAN number is 1, and the ELAN name is Marketing.

The following steps are necessary to configure the ATM module as shown in the example:

1 Enter privileged EXEC mode by entering the **enable** command:

— ATM>enable

— ATM>#

NOTE   The "# "indicates enable or privileged mode. You must be in this mode to make any changes to the configuration.

---

2 Enter global configuration mode by entering the **configure terminal** command:

— ATM#configure terminal

— Enter configuration command, one per line. End with **Ctrl-Z**.

— ATM(config)#

3 Enter interface configuration mode by entering the **interface type_number.subif** command:

— ATM(config)#interface atm0.1

— ATM(config-if)#

4 Configure the LEC by entering the **lane client ethernet vlan_number elan_name** command:

— ATM(config-if)#lane client ethernet 1 elan1

— ATM(config_if)#

5 Exit interface configuration mode, and return to EXEC mode by pressing **Ctrl-Z**:

— ATM(config-if)#^Z

— ATM#

6 (Optional) From EXEC mode, save the configuration to nonvolatile RAM (NVRAM) by entering the **write memory** command:

— ATM#write memory

— ATM#

7 To end the CLI session, enter **Ctrl-G**.

Catalyst 2820 ATM Module-Specific Commands

The ATM Module has two specific commands that are needed when configuring ATM LANE. Both are generated from this command:

```
atm pvc vcd vpi vci {ilmi ¦ qsaal}
```

The default configuration is listed here:

```
atm pvc 2 0 16 ilmi
atm pvc 1 0 5 qsaal
```

While these are already configured for you, a discussion of them is helpful.

- *VCD*—Virtual circuit descriptor. This is a unique number per ATM module that identifies to the ATM module which virtual path identifier/virtual channel identifier (VPI/VCI) to use for a particular packet. Valid values range from 1 to 1023. The ATM module requires this feature to manage packet transmission. The VCD is not associated with VPI/VCI used for the ATM network cells.

- *VPI*—ATM network VPI of this PVC. On the Catalyst 2820 ATM module, this value must be 0. The VPI is an 8-bit field in the header of the ATM cell. The VPI value is unique only on a single link, not throughout the ATM network (it has local significance only). The VPI value must match that of the switch.

- *VCI*—ATM network VPI for this PVC, in the range of 1 to 1023. The VCI value is unique only on a single link, not throughout the ATM network (it has local significance only).

- *ILMI*—Interim Local Management Interface (ILMI). The default VPI and VCI values are 0 and 16.

- *QSAAL*—Configures or removes switched virtual connections (SVCs). The default VPI and VCI values are 0 and 5, respectively. Q.2931 is the standard for the ATM signaling message. SAAL, which stands for Signaling ATM Adaptation Layer, resides between the ATM layer and Q.2931. The purpose of the SAAL is to provide reliable transport of Q.2931 between peer Q.2931 entities.

Verifying LANE Configuration

The ATM LANE configuration can be verified by using the **show lane** command. This command verifies that the LANE client is operational and displays the ATM NSAP address of the LANE configuration. See Example 13-21.

Example 13-21   *Output of a **show lane** command*

```
ATM>show lane
LE Client ATM1.1 ELAN name: marketing Admin: up State: operational
Client ID: 2                    LEC up for 6 minutes, 14 seconds
Join Attempt: 2
HW Address  00c0.1dfc.a2fc  Type: ethernet            Max Frame Size: 1516
        VLANID: 1
ATM Address: 47.00918100000000000ca7ce01.00C01DFCA2FC.00

VCD   rxFrames   txFrames   Type       ATM Address
  0          0          0   configure  47.00918100000000000ca7ce01.00605C28DA23.00
  4          0          2   direct     47.00918100000000000ca7ce01.00605C28DA21.01
  5          0          0   distribute 47.00918100000000000ca7ce01.00605C28DA21.01
  6          0         20   send       47.00918100000000000ca7ce01.00605C28DA22.01
 13          0          0   forward    47.00918100000000000ca7ce01.00605C28DA22.01
  8         58         55   data       47.00918100000000000ca7ce01.00605C28DA20.01


ATM>
```

Viewing LANE Module Status

The LANE Module status also can be viewed by exiting the CLI and going back into the
Catalyst 2820 Main Menu. Select [P] for Port Configuration, and select the port that the
ATM module is in. Then select [L] to view the ATM and LANE status. See Example 13-22.

Example 13-22   *Catalyst 2820 LANE Module Status Menu*

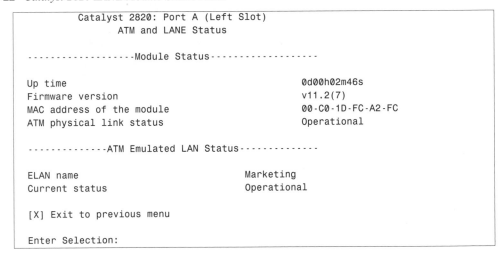

```
              Catalyst 2820: Port A (Left Slot)
                    ATM and LANE Status


        ------------------Module Status------------------

Up time                               0d00h02m46s
Firmware version                      v11.2(7)
MAC address of the module             00-C0-1D-FC-A2-FC
ATM physical link status              Operational


        --------------ATM Emulated LAN Status--------------

ELAN name                         Marketing
Current status                    Operational

[X] Exit to previous menu

Enter Selection:
```

ATM Port Statistics

ATM Port statistics can also be viewed using the **show interface** from the CLI, or you can use the menu system by selecting [V] from the ATM Port Configuration menu. See Example 13-23.

Example 13-23 *Catalyst 2820 ATM Module Port Statistics Menu*

```
Catalyst 2820: Port A (Left Slot)

     Receive Statistics                    Transmit Statistics
-----------------------------------   -----------------------------------
Good AAL5 frames              0  Good AAL5 frames                1
Good ATM cells                0  Good ATM cells                  3
Broadcast/multicast frames    0  Broadcast/multicast frames      0
Good frames forwarded         0  Queue full discards             0
Frames filtered               0
Runt frames                   0
No buffer discards            0
Other discards                0

Errors:
    CRC errors                0
    Cell HEC errors           0
    Giant frames              0
```

Maintaining the Catalyst 1900 and 2820 Switches

CLSC Objectives Covered in This Section

78	Describe the POST and diagnostic messages on the Catalyst 1900 and Catalyst 2820 switches.
79	Describe the cabling guidelines for the Catalyst 1900 and 2820 switches.
81	Describe the firmware upgrade procedures for the Catalyst 1900 and 2820 switches.

This section describes diagnostic features available on the Catalyst 1900 and 2820 switches. Also covered are cabling guidelines and firmware upgrade procedures.

Power-On-Self-Test (POST)

When the Catalyst 2820 or 1900 is first turned on and the switch begins its POST, the system and port LEDs are green. As each of 13 separate tests are performed, the port LEDs turn off, starting with 16. (Because there are only 13 tests, LEDs 15, 14, and 13 are unaffected.)

After the POST completes successfully, the port LEDs turn green, indicating that the switch is operational. If a test fails, the associated port LED stays off, and the system LED turns amber.

All POST failures except the real-time clock test (number 5) are fatal. If the real-time clock fails POST, the switch begins forwarding packets, but the system LED turns amber and a POST-failure message is displayed on the console.

NOTE   When the POST completes successfully, Spanning Tree Protocol (assuming it's enabled) immediately turns the port LEDs amber while it discovers the network's topology. Spanning-tree discovery takes approximately 30 seconds to complete, and no packet forwarding takes place during this time.

The following is a list of the tests performed during POST:

Port #	Test Type
1	Port test (Loopback)
2	Ethernet address PROM
3	CAM
4	RS-232 port
5	Real-time clock
6	CAM SRAM
7	Timer interrupt
8	Port control/status
9	Flag DRAM
10	Buffer DRAM
11	Forwarding engine SRAM
12	Forwarding engine
13	ECU DRAM

Diagnostic Console

The material presented here is intended to help the reader understand switch features; however, it is not directly related to one of the objectives.

The diagnostic console is displayed when the switch firmware has been corrupted or when the current switch configuration prevents the firmware from operating correctly. See Example 13-24.

Example 13-24 *Catalyst 2820 System Diagnostic Console*

```
Cisco System Diagnostic Console
Copyright © Cisco Systems, Inc. 1996
All rights reserved.

Ethernet Address: 00-C0-1D-77-21-AB
-------------------------------------------------

Press enter to continue
```

If you have configured a password for the switch, you are prompted to enter the password. If you have forgotten the password, you can obtain one by calling Cisco TAC and providing the Ethernet address displayed on the screen, as shown in Example 13-23. If no password exists, press Enter to display the diagnostic console.

If there is a problem with the configuration and you need to bring up the diagnostic console, use the following procedure:

Step 1   Attach a terminal to the management console.

Step 2   Disconnect power from the switch.

Step 3   Press and hold the LED Mode button on the front panel.

Step 4   While continuing to hold the LED Mode button, reapply the power.

Step 5   The diagnostic console menu should appear now. See Example 13-25.

Example 13-25 *Catalyst 2820 Diagnostic Console System Engineering Menu*

```
Diagnostic Console: Systems Engineering

        Operation firmware version:  5.10     Status: valid
      Boot firmware version:  1.06

    [C] Continue with standard system start up
    [U] Upgrade operation firmware (XMODEM)
    [S] System Debug Interface

Enter Selection:
```

This is the second screen you will see. If the firmware were corrupted or is incapable of running, the status would be invalid and the [C] option would not be displayed. If necessary, you would upgrade your firmware using the [U] option and a modem using XMODEM. We will not cover the procedure for doing this here.

The other menu option here is the System Debug Interface. The submenu is shown in Example 13-26:

Example 13-26 *Catalyst 2820 Diagnostic Console System Debug Menu*

```
Diagnostic Console: System Debug Interface


        [G] Generic I/O
        [M] Memory (CPU) I/O
        [F] Return system to factory defaults
        [R] Reset main console RS232 interface to 9600,8,1,N

        [X] Exit to Previous Menu

  Enter Selection:
```

You can use the System Debug Interface to reset the RS-232 interface to factory default or return the entire switch to factory defaults.

NOTE   Choosing item [F] will completely erase any configuration you may have programmed.

Cabling Guidelines

Certain guidelines must be followed when working with 100BaseT networks. Category 5 UTP cabling is a requirement for a 100BaseT copper wiring network, and the distance limitation on a 100BaseT copper network is 100 meters.

As you know, 100BaseFX is a fiber-optic cabling equivalent to 100BaseT. This cabling can be either 50/125 or 62.5/125 multimode fiber. Fiber-optic cabling provides a much greater distance with 412 meters for half-duplex operation and 2 kilometers for full-duplex operation.

Upgrading Switch Firmware

Three methods of upgrading the switch firmware exist:

- *In-band TFTP server*—Before the upgrade can proceed, the name of the TFTP server and the name of the upgrade file must be entered. The upgrade can be initiated through the management console or through an SNMP management station. The switch will then download the upgrade file from the server via TFTP.

- *In-band TFTP client*—A TFTP client can download the firmware upgrade into the switch.

- *Serial via XMODEM*—Attach a terminal to the RS-232 port at the back of the switch to transfer the firmware via the XMODEM protocol.

NOTE   The switch will appear to freeze while the new firmware file is written into flash memory. *Do not power off the switch while this is happening, or you risk corrupting the firmware.* It may take longer than 1 minute to complete the upgrade.

Upgrading FDDI Firmware is different than the main switch in that you must select which expansion port the FDDI module is in. After that, the upgrade procedure is the same as that for the switch firmware upgrade.

Q&A

As mentioned in Chapter 1, the questions and scenarios are more difficult than what you should experience on the actual exam. The questions do not attempt to cover more breadth or depth than the exam; however, the questions are designed to make sure you know the answers. Rather than allowing you to derive the answer from clues hidden inside the question itself, the questions will challenge your understanding and recall of the subject. Questions from the "Do I Know This Already?" quiz from the beginning of the chapter are repeated here to ensure that you have mastered the chapter's topic areas.

1 How many expansion slots are available on the Catalyst 2820 switch?

2 What is the maximum amount of 100BaseTX ports that the Catalyst 1900 switch can provide?

3 When the System LED on a Catalyst 1900 switch is amber, what does this indicate?

4 What does a rapidly blinking activity LED on the Catalyst 2820 FDDI Module indicate?

5   What three modes can be indicated by the Port LEDs using the Mode button on the front of a Catalyst 1900?

6   To initially configure the Catalyst 1900 switch, you must connect a terminal to which port?

7   If the destination address of a packet resides on the same port as the source address, what happens to the packet?

8   What are the maximum instances of Spanning Tree Protocol that can run in a Catalyst 2820 switch?

9   You could create a collapsed backbone network with a Catalyst 1900 by doing what?

10 By default, the broadcasts and multicasts in a Catalyst 2820 switch's VLAN are forwarded where?

11 The source port filtering feature on a Catalyst 2820 or 1900 switch is used to do what?

12 What mode of switching would you use if you were experiencing FCS or alignment errors?

13 Under which menu option do you find the information about the switching mode of a Catalyst 2820 or 1900 switch?

14 What is the out-of-band management connector called?

15 What methods can be used for in-band management of the Catalyst 2820 and 1900?

16 What must be done before you can use in-band management with the Catalyst 2820 or 1900 switch?

17 Which menu enables you to configure the read and write community strings?

18 What is the main task that is performed using the Multicast Registration menu on a Catalyst 2820 or 1900 switch?

19 What does SPAN stand for, and what function does it provide?

20 How many MAC addresses are supported on the Catalyst 1900 switch?

21 Which LANE component can be configured on a Catalyst 2820 ATM LANE module?

22 What command is used to display the status of the ATM LANE module in a Catalyst 2820 switch?

23 What is the ATM address commonly known as?

24 What is the theoretical effect of configuring full-duplex on a 100BaseT link to a server also running in full-duplex mode?

25 What three types of modules are available for the Catalyst 2820 expansion slots?

26 When implementing Port Security, what is the maximum number of addresses that can be associated with a secure port?

27 What does the hold time mean when configuring CDP?

Source Material

Some content in this chapter is based on the following sources.

- Catalyst 2820/1900 Installation and Configuration Guide

  http://www.cisco.com/univercd/cc/td/doc/product/lan/28201900/1928v5x/icg5x/index.htm

- Catalyst 2820 ATM Modules Installation and Configuration Guide

  http://www.cisco.com/univercd/cc/td/doc/product/lan/28201900/28module/28atmmod/index.htm

The objectives of the Cisco LAN Switch Configuration (CLSC) exam are taken from the Cisco web site, at the Cisco career certification and training area. The following table shows the exam objectives covered in this chapter:

Objective	Description
69	Describe Catalyst 3000 series LAN switch products.
70	Describe Catalyst 3000 series LAN switch product differences.
71	Describe the Catalyst Stack System.
72	Perform initial setup of a Catalyst 3000 series switch.
73	Configure the switch for management.
74	Configure port parameters.
75	Configure VLANs and trunk links.
76	Configure the ATM LANE module.
77	Perform basic router module configuration.
82	Troubleshoot the Catalyst 3000 series switch subsystems.
83	Troubleshoot the Catalyst 3000 series switch network interfaces and connections.
84	Use the switch LEDs to isolate problems.
85	Isolate network segment problems.

CHAPTER 14

Catalyst 3000 Series Switches

The Catalyst 3000 switch system is designed to incorporate the advantages of stacked systems for growth; expansion capability for mixed resource delivery; and modular, pay-as-you go cost effectiveness. Used in conjunction with the Catalyst Matrix, the Catalyst 3000 series switch provides up to 224 switched ports in a mixed 10 Mbps, 100 Mbps, and 155 Mbps environment.

The Advanced Feature Set is available to facilitate VLANs, EtherChannel, and full-duplex port operation. The following example shows the features of the Catalyst 3000, Catalyst Matrix, and Catalyst Stack System.

```
Cisco Catalyst Manager
©Copyright ciscoSystems Inc., 1995—All Rights Reserved.

MAC Address: 00 80 24 04 23 A0
System Contact: instructor@cisco.com
Type Password, then press <Return>

--No password has been set, press <Return to continue.>--
```

How to Best Use This Chapter

By taking the following steps, you can make better use of your study time:

- Keep your notes and the answers for all your work with this book in one place, for easy reference.

- Take the quiz and write down your answers. Studies show that retention is significantly increased through writing down facts and concepts, even if you never look at the information again.

- Use the diagram in Figure 14-1 to guide you to the next step.

Figure 14-1   *How to Best Use This Chapter in Preparation for the CLSC Exam*

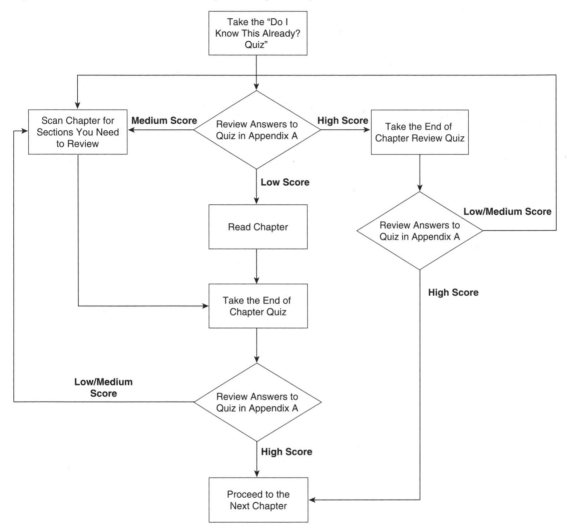

Do I Know This Already? Quiz

You can find the answers to this quiz in Appendix A, "Answers to 'Do I Know This Already?' Quizzes and Q & A Sections." Review the answers, grade your quiz, and choose an appropriate next step in this chapter based on the suggestions diagramed in Figure 14-1.

1 What size is the buffer space on a 10 Mbps port on the Catalyst 3000 switch?

2 How many MAC addresses per port are supported on the Catalyst 3000 switch?

3 Which switch in the Catalyst 3000 series has seven expansion slots?

4 The Catalyst Matrix has how many SCSI ports?

5 What is the name of the switching bus in the Catalyst 3000 architecture, and how much switching bandwidth does it support?

6 What is the PFPA, and what purpose does it serve?

7 What is the name of the switching mode that enables the switch to monitor errors and change from cut-through to store-and-forward and back?

8 Which takes precedence regarding port duplex mode, hardware control or software control?

9 What is the name of the menu that enables you to view VLAN configuration information?

10 How many filter types are available?

11 What is the meaning of the Broadcast Water Mark when configuring Broadcast Suppression?

Using the answer key in Appendix A, grade your answers.

- **5 or less correct**—Read this chapter.

- **6, 7, or 8 correct**—Review this chapter, looking at the charts and diagrams that summarize most of the concepts and facts in this chapter.

- **9 or more correct**—If you want more review on these topics, skip to the Q&A section at the end of this chapter. If you do not want more review on these topics, skip this chapter.

Foundation Topics

The Catalyst 3000 Series

CLSC Objectives Covered in This Section

69	Describe Catalyst 3000 series LAN switch products.

The Catalyst 3000 series of LAN switches consists of the Catalyst 3000, Catalyst 3100, and Catalyst 3200 switches. Basic features of the switches are listed in the following example. For purposes of this example, switch capacity and throughput measurements are calculated as follows:

- Switch capacity equals the number of simultaneous conversations possible on each port multiplied by the speed of the port.

- Switch throughput is the number of simultaneous interport conversations possible multiplied by the speed of the port.

```
Main Menu
Configuration...
Statistics...
Download...
Reset...
Exit Console

Display the Configuration Menu
Use cursor keys to choose item. Press <RETURN> to confirm choice.
Press <CTRL><P> to exit console.
```

The Catalyst 3000 is a 16- to 24-port switch. The standard configuration includes 16 10BaseT ports, 4 MB of memory (all models now ship with 8 MB of memory), 1 MB of Flash memory, real-time clock, console port, SwitchProbe port, AUI port, and the following:

- Two expansion slots
- 4 port 10BaseT
- 1 port 100BaseT/F
- 2 port 100VG-AnyLAN
- 3 port 10BaseFL

- 1 port 155-Mbps ATM

- 3 port 10Base2 Thinwire

- 2 port 100BaseT/ISL

- 2 port 100BaseF/ISL

- Switch-controlled half-duplex and full-duplex capability on all ports

- User-selectable cut-through or store-and-forward switching

- User-selectable thresholds for error-free cut-through and runt-free operation

- Demand aging for port and master address tables

- EtherChannel and VLAN support

- Port 1 auto-selectable between 10BaseT and AUI

- Port 16 selectable between MDI and MDIX

- Security, destination, and source address filtering

- Optional additional 4 MB of system memory

- 1700 addresses per port, 6000 addresses per system (10,000 addresses per system with optional 4 MB memory expansion)

- EtherChannel connectivity for certain models of Cisco and Kalpana switches

- Catalyst Stack system for connecting up to eight Catalyst 3000 series switches in a stack

Hardware features and specifications are shown here.

```
Return to Previous Menu              Configuration
Switch/Stack Information...           SwitchProbe...
VLAN/VTP Configuration...             EtherChannel...
IP Configuration...                   MAC Filter & Port Security...
SNMP Configuration...                 Learn and Lock...
Spanning Tree…                        Address Aging...
Port Configuration...                 Port Switching Mode...
CDP Configuration...                  Broadcast Suppression...
Module Information...                 Password...
100VG Port Information...             Console Configuration...
ISL Port Configuration...             ATM Configuration...
RMON Configuration...                 Router Configuration...
Display the Main Menu
Use cursor keys to choose item. Press <RETURN> to confirm choice.
Press <CTRL><P> to return to Main Menu.
```

Catalyst 3000 Architecture

The material presented here is intended to help the reader understand switch features; however, it is not directly related to one of the objectives.

The Catalyst 3000 switch bus is called the AXIS bus. 10 Mbps-to-10 Mbps ports use the LAN module ASIC (LMA) to perform port switching. High-speed ports (all above 10 Mbps) use a Proprietary Fat Pipe ASIC (PFPA) for switching operations. All switching ASICs, the Arbiter, and CPU ASIC connect directly to the AXIS bus. All ports have sufficient buffer space to prevent congestion.

The AXIS Bus

The AXIS bus is a partially asynchronous time-division multiplexed (TDM) bus used for switching packets between LMAs and PFPAs. The bandwidth is allocated by the central bus arbiter on a cycle-by-cycle basis in 52 10 Mbps slots. The AXIS bus supports multiple packet transfers at 10 Mbps and 170 Mbps simultaneously. The 170 Mbps bandwidth prevents overflow when insufficient bandwidth is available.

Two priorities are available:

- *Priority 1*—An LMA requests a priority.

- *Low priority*—A low priority request might not be handled in the same sync period if there is insufficient bandwidth.

The bus priority assignments are listed here:

- 10 Mbps LMAs request priority 1 cycles on a 10 Mbps-to-10 Mbps transfer.

- 10 Mbps LMAs request low-priority cycles on a 10 Mbps-to-fat pipe transfer.

- High-speed PFPAs request low-priority cycles on a fat pipe-to-fat pipe transfer.

- High-speed PFPAs request low-priority cycles on a fat pipe-to-10 Mbps transfer.

Time slots are assigned by the Arbiter on a cycle-by-cycle basis. Each cycle is called a *sync period* and is divided into 48 time slots. The Arbiter allocates time slots to 10 Mbps-to-10 Mbps transfers first, followed by all other requests. All ports are granted access during a sync period. Allocation takes place in a round-robin fashion.

Broadcasts are given a Priority 1, but only after all 10 Mbps-to-10 Mbps transfers have taken place. The Arbiter waits until all ports are quiet before sending broadcasts to the bus. While a broadcast is in progress, the Arbiter does not grant access to other ports.

The LAN Module

Each port on the switch contains a LAN Module. As stated earlier, two types of LAN Modules exist: the 10 Mbps LAN modules and the high-speed LAN Module. For the purposes of this discussion, we will refer to the 10 Mbps LAN Module.

Each LAN Module consists of the LMA, the port address table, and 256 KB of VRAM. Of this 256 KB of VRAM, 192 KB is allocated for packet buffering. The buffering is dynamic and is allocated by pages, a much more effective way of utilizing buffering than with fixed buffers. In a fixed buffer, packets are stored in 1518-byte buffers, regardless of size. Dynamic buffers use only the space necessary.

The LMA is responsible for transferring and receiving packets from the AXIS bus. In addition, it is responsible for signaling the Arbiter to request time slot(s) for data transfer.

The port table records up to 1700 addresses, enabling the port to make switching decisions for learned addresses locally. The port table is updated on an as-needed basis by the CPU and sends a packet to the CPU only when the source or destination address is unknown.

The LAN Module ASIC

This section covers the behavior of the LAN Module ASIC (LMA).

When receiving a packet from the LAN, the receiving port LMA requests access to the destination port. If the destination port is not busy, the LMA drives the data onto the AXIS bus. If the media of the destination port is available, the packet is forwarded by the destination port LMA. If the media of the destination port is busy, the packet is buffered in the output buffer of the destination port LMA, and the packet is forwarded as soon as the media is no longer busy.

If the destination port is busy, access to the destination port is refused and the receiving LMA stores the packet in its input buffer. As soon as the destination port is available, the packet is forwarded to the destination port. If the destination address is unknown, the receiving port LMA forwards the packet to the CPU to facilitate packet broadcast to all ports except the receiving port and address learning.

When a port is not busy and receives an access request to accept traffic from a source port over the AXIS bus, the receiving port LMA grants access to the port requesting the access and receives the packet. If the port media is busy, the packet is buffered in the output buffer of the port receiving traffic from the AXIS bus. When the media is available, the packet is forwarded.

Proprietary Fat Pipe ASIC

The Fat Pipe ASIC is the interface between the AXIS bus and high-speed LANs, and it performs the same function as the LMA. The Fat Pipe ASIC provides for connection of heterogeneous topologies to the AXIS bus. Each high-speed expansion module—such as the 100BaseT, ATM, or the StackPort—implements a Proprietary Fat Pipe ASIC (PFPA).

Like the LAN Module, the high-speed LAN Module consists of the PFPA, an ASIC specific to the technology, port memory, and a physical interface. The PFPA is also used in the StackPort, which enables the connection of multiple Catalyst 3000 series switches to the Catalyst Matrix.

The PFPA is embedded in the following modules:

- *100BaseX*—Interface between Standard ASIC and AXIS bus

- *ATM*—Interface between SAR and AXIS bus

- *ISL*—Interface between ISL ASIC and AXIS bus

- *StackPort*—280 Mbps interface for the Catalyst Matrix

Central Processor Unit

The Central Processor Unit (CPU) is an Intel i960SA 16.25 MHz processor that contains interfaces to the AXIS bus and Arbiter, the CPU bus for address learning, the buffer manager, the network, and the CPU memory. It also contains a master address table for the Catalyst Stack and ATM module(s).

The CPU has four major components, as follows:

- The CPU ASIC (CPA) defines how access to the CPU is granted for various tasks, such as address filtering, aging, and learning.

- The main memory is the area where the system code resides and is used at system bootup.

- The network memory is the master address table for the Catalyst 3000 series switch. A packet with an unknown destination is sent to the network memory, which sends an interrupt to the CPU and begins address learning.

- The Intel i960SA is the core of the CPU.

All packets are seen by the network memory but are not taken into the CPU unless a packet is destined for it. All packets with an unknown source or destination address are sent to the CPU for address learning.

A packet taken into the CPU causes an interrupt to be sent into the Packet Demux (PD). The PD contains a queuing table that matches the packet type (Ethernet, multicast, 802.3) to the task it is attempting to perform. This queue is then accessed by the task queues to perform the individual tasks (such as SNMP and Spanning Tree). In addition to the type, a bit is turned on if the packet is unknown, which queues the packet for the address-learning task within the CPU.

The Catalyst 3000 series switch can be configured as a single standalone unit or as a logical combination of up to eight units. The logical combination of units is called a Catalyst Stack.

This section describes how the Catalyst 3000 series switch operates as a single standalone unit. The Catalyst 3000 series switch contains four main elements:

- *AXIS bus*—This bus establishes switched connections between two segments. Each connection lasts only for the duration of the packet transmission.

- *10BaseT ports*—Sixteen 10BaseT ports are provided in the basic configuration, enabling multiple conversations. Users running basic applications are able to share bandwidth, and users running bandwidth-intensive applications can receive their own dedicated 10 Mbps port. With the optional enhanced version of the Catalyst 3000 series switch, each 10BaseT port can be set to full-duplex mode, providing a theoretical 20 Mbps per port.

- *AUI connector*—The AUI connector can be attached to an external transceiver for connection to another media type, such as 10BaseFL.

- *High-speed expansion slots*—The Catalyst 3000 series switch supports two optional high-speed modules that can be mounted in the chassis front panel. These modules provide connectivity to servers or backbones:

  — *100BaseT*—100 Mbps Fast Ethernet

  — *100VG-AnyLAN*—100 Mbps deterministic Ethernet media access scheme using demand priority

  — *100BaseF*—Fiber-based 100 Mbps technology

  — *ATM*—155 Mbps cell-switching technology

Cut-Through Switching

The Catalyst 3000 series switch provides extremely fast packet-switching capability. If the packet needs to be switched to another LAN segment, its data begins flowing through the destination port before the entire packet has been received. This concept enables packets to arrive at the output port 40 microseconds after entering the input port. By minimizing delay, the Catalyst 3000 series switch can move more packets freely throughout the LAN without degrading performance.

Store-and-Forward Switching

The Catalyst 3000 series switch can be set to full-time store-and-forward operation to ensure that every packet is checked for errors before forwarding. In store-and-forward mode, all packets are buffered, checked for errors, and, if error-free, forwarded to the destination port. If the destination port is busy, the receiving port buffers the packet. If the port is available, and the media is busy, the destination port buffers the packet.

Filtering Capabilities

The Catalyst 3000 series switch supports the configuration of MAC-layer filters on a per-port basis. This flexibility enables network managers to specify client access only to designated resources, for security purposes. Filters can be for source or destination addresses, which enables the network manager to restrict access to certain servers or MAC addresses, or to specify that an end user can communicate with only one server.

Catalyst 3000 series switch filters are established on MAC addresses and are defined by way of SNMP or through the console port in a specific VLAN. Filters must be individually configured per MAC address.

A maximum of 100 filters can be configured on the Catalyst 3000. These filters work within the switch, not between boxes over the stack. Only one address filter, or static route, can be configured over the stack.

Address Filter Applications—Multicast

The advantage of address filtering is increased access control and network segmentation. For example, a switch port is connected to a server containing confidential information from the engineering group. You can prevent access to the server by setting up filters for the addresses of workgroups other than engineering. In reality, this is an example of the following two types of filters:

- Source address filters enabling a source address from the engineering group.

- Source address filters blocking a source address from workgroups other than engineering.

Examples of different types of filters are listed here:

- Allowing, forcing, or blocking packets from a source address

- Allowing, forcing, or blocking packets to a destination address

The following guidelines should be used when setting up address filters:

- Use the Port Configuration menu to create port filters.

- Filters are port-specific and should be applied to an incoming port only.

You can create up to 100 filters for each Catalyst 3000 series switch. The filters must be applied to specific ports on a specified Catalyst 3000 series switch. A filter is a combination of a MAC address and a type of filter. For example, if a MAC address is configured as a source type on a port and is also configured as a destination type, it would count as two filters toward the maximum number of 100 filters.

You can apply these filters to any combination of ports as long as there is a maximum of 100 filters. Because more than one port can be a part of a filter, use the following examples as a guide to filtering:

- Filter A (MAC 00000ABC0010, source type) can be applied to ports 1, 3, 5, 7, 9, or to all 16 ports.

- Filter B (MAC 00000ABC0023, destination type) can be applied to the same ports, different ports, or to all 16 ports.

- Filter C (MAC 00000ABC003E, source type) can be applied to any combination of ports until a maximum of 100 filters are created.

Address Filter Applications—Host Access

Unauthorized access to host systems is prevented by first entering the MAC address of the host in the MAC address field of the MAC address filter table, and then applying the filter to the desired ports.

Buffering

If the destination port is receiving a packet from another Catalyst 3000 series switch port, or if the output segment is busy, the switch stores the packet in one of its internal buffers. Each Catalyst 3000 series switch buffer can hold up to 384 packets in each direction (incoming and outgoing). This amount of buffer space helps balance throughput when networks are operating near peak load and more than one packet may be directed to the same port at the same time.

Catalyst 3000 Enhanced Feature Set

The material presented here is intended to help the reader understand switch features; however, it is not directly related to one of the objectives.

The Catalyst 3000 series switch provides three options as part of the Enhanced Feature Set: full-duplex communications, EtherChannel technology, and VLANs.

- *Full-duplex communications*—You can select half-duplex or full-duplex communications for all module ports except the 100VG-AnyLAN and the 10Base2 modules. This capability doubles throughput capacity for ports operating in full-duplex mode. The advantage of using full-duplex is that packets can flow in both directions at the same time, while eliminating collisions from the equation. Full-duplex communications should be enabled at both ends of a link.

- *EtherChannel*—EtherChannel provides a way of bundling multiple Ethernet links to offer a high-bandwidth connection between two switches. Using the EtherChannel feature, you can connect the Catalyst 3000 series switch to other Catalyst 3000 series units or to Kalpana Ethernet switches. Each EtherChannel comprises two to seven ports, for up to 140 Mbps bandwidth in full-duplex mode. By connecting three cables between two Catalyst 3000 series switch devices, for example, you increase EtherChannel throughput to 30 Mbps in half-duplex mode, or 60 Mbps in full-duplex mode. Network managers can connect multiple 10 Mbps ports (up to three) to create a single fat pipe. Existing Catalyst units can gain access to high-speed servers, routers, and backbones connected to the Fast Ethernet ports through EtherChannel connections to a Catalyst 3000 series switch.

- *VLANs*—Using the Catalyst VLAN feature, you can partition a single Catalyst 3000 series switch into VLANs (also referred to as Catalyst VLANs), with each containing its own set of ports. Packets are forwarded between ports belonging to same VLAN only. The benefit of Catalyst VLAN is to restrict access from one segment to another for security purposes or to reduce intersegment traffic.

Spanning Tree, Load Balancing, and Redundancy

The material presented here is intended to help the reader understand switch features; however, it is not directly related to one of the objectives.

The Catalyst 3000 series switch supports the IEEE 802.1d Spanning-Tree Protocol. One instance of spanning tree is implemented in each VLAN, and all five states of spanning tree are supported. In addition, the Fast Mode feature is supported, which bypasses the usual calculation and puts a port into forwarding mode immediately. Path redundancy and load balancing are achieved by using a separate spanning tree per VLAN. If multiple paths exist between two switches, the Spanning-Tree Protocol will prune the path to the minimal connection. In the event of a failure, the protocol will recalculate and provide redundancy.

VLAN Trunk Protocol

The VLAN Trunk Protocol (VTP) is used to set up and manage VLANs across an entire management domain. When new VLANs are added to a Catalyst switch in a management domain, VTP can be used to automatically distribute the information to other trunks of all the devices in the management domain. This distribution enables VLAN naming consistency and connectivity between all devices in the domain. The VTP is transmitted on all trunk connections, including ISL and 802.10, and ATM LANE. On bootup, a Catalyst 3000 series switch sends out periodic requests for VTP configuration on all its trunks until it receives a summary advertisement from a neighbor. It uses that summary advertisement to determine whether its currently stored configuration is obsolete; if it is, the switch requests all VTP information from the neighbor.

VTP defines VLANs for the switch and the Stack. Although the VTP supports 1024 VLANs, the Catalyst 3000 series switch supports a maximum of 64 active VLANs.

The Catalyst switch transmits VTP frames on its trunk ports, advertising its management domain name, configuration revision number, and VLAN information that it has learned. Other Catalyst switches in the domain use these advertisements to learn about any new VLANs that are configured in the transmitting switch. This process of advertising and learning enables a new VLAN to be created and configured on only one switch in the management domain. This information is then learned automatically by all the other devices in the domain.

A Catalyst switch can operate in three different VTP modes, as follows:

- *Server*—Server mode permits changes to the domain's VLAN configuration. Redundancy can be achieved by having more than one server in the domain.

- *Client*—Client mode accepts changes from other devices in the domain, such as servers.

- *Transparent*—Transparent mode accepts and stores changes to the local VLAN configuration database, but it never propagates them. Transparent mode essentially means not using VTP, as the configuration is relevant only to the local configuration.

Broadcast Suppression

Broadcast suppression is a feature that prevents broadcast packets from flooding the switching fabric. This function is set on a per-port basis at the Broadcast Suppression screen. If this function is set to enable, a user-defined threshold is implemented. When the threshold is achieved over a 5-second window, broadcast packets will be dropped until broadcasts drop below the threshold.

Address Aging

Address aging is configured both on a per-port basis and through the master table. The default setting is 15 minutes. The Catalyst 3000 implements a feature called demand aging, which enables the user to set a threshold to which the address table will decrease when it reaches full capacity. On a Catalyst 3000, full capacity is 1700 addresses. When the CPU attempts to learn and send the 1701st address to the port address table, the full table condition triggers the address aging algorithm, and the port table is aged to the user-defined or default value.

The Catalyst 3000 Series Switch Optional Modules

The material presented here is intended to help the reader understand switch features; however, it is not directly related to one of the objectives.

- *Single-Port 100BaseT Module*—The WS-X3001 is a single-port 100BaseTX expansion module that has an RJ-45 connector and that uses Category 5 UTP cabling. This module has DIP switches on the front panel to enable full-duplex mode when port switching has been set to hardware control.

- *Four-Port 10BaseT Module*—The WS-X3002 is a four-port 10BaseT expansion module. The module has four RJ-45 connectors and supports Category 3 UTP cabling. This module has DIP switches on the front panel to enable full-duplex mode when port switching has been set to hardware control.

- *Three-Port 10BaseF Module*—The WS-X3003 is a three-port 10BaseF expansion module. The module has three ST fiber connectors and supports 50/125 and 65/125 micron multimode fiber-optic cabling. As with the previous modules, it has dip switches on the front panel to enable full-duplex mode when the port switching has been set to hardware control. Full-duplex operation is supported up to 2 km.

- *Single-Port 100BaseF Module*—The WS-X3005 is a single-port 100BaseF expansion module. The module has a single ST connector and supports 50/125 and 65/125 micron multimode fiber-optic cabling. It also has DIP switches on the front panel for full-duplex mode, and full-duplex is supported up to 2 km.

- *ATM Expansion Module*—The WS-X3006A is a single-port ATM expansion module used to establish a high-speed 155 Mbps ATM connection between the Catalyst 3000 series switch and ATM networks. A maximum of two ATM modules per Catalyst 3000 may be configured.

- *StackPort Module*—The WS-X3004 module is a single-port expansion module with a special 50-pin connector. The Catalyst StackPort is a high-speed module containing a PFPA-facilitating connection between two directly connected Catalyst 3000 series switches, or between three to eight Catalyst 3000 series switches connected through a Catalyst matrix. The cable link and connectors are standard SCSI-2 with proprietary signaling. The module bandwidth is 280 Mbps in the default full-duplex mode of operation.

- *100VG-AnyLAN Modules*—Two models of the 100VG-AnyLAN modules are available. The WS-X3007 is a two-port expansion module supporting 100VG-AnyLAN that uses RJ-45 connectors and supports Category 3 or Category 5 UTP cabling. The WS-X3008 is a two-port expansion module supporting 100VG-AnyLAN that uses ST connectors and supports 100BaseFX media.

NOTE   Catalyst 3000 series expansion modules are *not* hot-swappable.

- *Dual Fast Ethernet with ISL Modules*—Two models of the Dual Fast Ethernet modules also exist. The WS-X3009 modules is a dual-port SC connector module supporting 100 Mbps Fast Ethernet and ISL. The WS-X3010 module is a dual-port RJ-45 connector module supporting 100 Mbps Fast Ethernet and ISL.

- *10Base2 Ethernet Module*—The WS-X3013 expansion module is used to interconnect up to three segments of 10Base2 Ethernet using BNC-style connectors. 10Base2 is commonly known as Thinnet because of the thin, jacketed coaxial cable.

The Catalyst 3000 Series Switches

CLSC Objectives Covered in This Section

70	Describe Catalyst 3000 series LAN switch product differences.
71	Describe the Catalyst Stack System.

The Catalyst 3100 switch provides 24 dedicated 10BaseT ports and a FlexSlot for use with the Cisco 3011 WAN access module, or a Catalyst 3000 series expansion module. The 3100 has a double-wide FlexSlot and can be used in conjunction with the Cisco 3011 WAN access module to provide a Catalyst 3100 or Catalyst 3200, or an entire stack, with connectivity to the WAN. The Cisco 3011 is based on the Cisco 2503 router, which provides two serial ports, an ISDN BRI port, and an auxiliary port.

The two serial ports operate in either DCE and DTE mode at speeds up to 2.048 Mbps. These ports can be configured to operate in either synchronous or asynchronous mode, which provides support for both dedicated leased lines and dial-up lines. The serial port connectors have a universal design common to the Cisco 2500 series and Cisco 7000 Fast Serial Interface Processor (FSIP) card. This feature enables easy transition to any of the common physical interfaces, including V.35, EIA/TIA-232, EIA/TIA-449, EIA/TIA-530, and X.121.

In addition to the two serial interfaces, the AUX port can be configured to provide an additional dialup line for asynchronous routing. The ISDN BRI removes the requirement for an external ISDN terminal adapter. The BRI S/T interface provides two 64 kbps B channels and one 16 kbps D channel for ISDN signaling for user data access to the ISDN network.

The Cisco 3011 WAN module provides no external Ethernet or AUI ports. Packets are routed on the Cisco 3011 WAN module through the Catalyst 3100 or Catalyst 3200 AXIS bus. Each Cisco 3011 module provides WAN connectivity to any one VLAN or network segment within a Catalyst 3000 series stacked hub.

Catalyst 3200 is a modular version of the Catalyst 3000 series switch. Seven slots are present for Catalyst 3000 series media modules. No fixed slots exist for 10BaseT ports. All ports are provided on expansion modules. The 3200 has redundant power supplies.

Table 14-1 is a configuration guide that lists the nonblocking maximum number of ports allowed for a single media type and the number of slots available for other media.

Table 14-1   *Catalyst 3200 Port Configurations*

Media	No. of Cards	Ports	Total Ports	Unused Slots
10BaseT	7	4	28	0
10BaseF	7	3	21	0
100BaseT	7	1	7	0
100BaseF	7	1	7	0
100BaseT/ISL	4	2	8	3
100BaseF/ISL	4	2	8	3
100BaseVG-T	4	2	8	3
100BaseVG-F	4	2	8	3
ATM/155	2	1	2	5
3011 WAN	1	3	3	6

The Catalyst Matrix is an eight-port Cross-Point Matrix switch used to connect from three to eight Catalyst 3000 switches to create a single-stack entity. When the switches are connected using the Matrix (depending upon the switch model used), the stack supports up to 224 switched 10BaseT Ethernet ports. The Catalyst matrix accepts an optional redundant module, which includes both logic and a power supply to enable truly fault-tolerant switching.

The Catalyst Matrix supports up to eight 280 Mbps connections for Catalyst 3000 series switches in a managed stack. It provides the cross-point switching architecture that delivers 4.8 Gbps of bandwidth, ensuring bottleneck-free traffic flow.

Eight SCSI-2 connections are located on the rear panel of the Catalyst Matrix. The rear panel also has eight LEDs located in the top-right corner to display whether a port is connected to a Catalyst 3000 series switch. The Catalyst Matrix is a cross-point matrix switch designed for high output. The switch performs arbitration in a round-robin fashion. Each switch operates independently and in parallel, except for multicast packets.

The Catalyst matrix contains two slots for switch modules: a primary and an optional secondary module. When both modules are installed, they operate in a one-to-one redundant configuration, with one module online. Each module contains a switch matrix and power supply, and each can be hot-swapped. When both modules are installed, the secondary module becomes operational in less than 1 second after a failure is detected in the primary. When repair or replacement of the primary module is affected, the primary module must be forced to resume active primary operation by depressing its Activate switch. This manual intervention requirement prevents module-swap oscillations that could take place under automated operation. Switchover can be user-requested from SNMP (when only one module is installed, switchover requests are ignored). Module failure detection and control of automatic switchover are exercised by the attached Catalyst 3000 series switches. There is no intelligence in the Catalyst Matrix to enable primary-to-secondary module switchover.

The Catalyst 3000 Series Stack System

A PFPA link between two Catalyst 3000 series switches, or between three to eight switches, provides a data path supplying 140 Mbps in each direction. The PFPA operates in full-duplex mode, yielding 280 Mbps bandwidth. The optional module providing this connectivity is the StackPort module (WS-X3004), which can be inserted in the rear panel of the Catalyst 3000 series switch.

Catalyst Stack Using the StackPort and Stack Matrix

The cable used to make the connection between Catalyst 3000 series switches, or between a switch and a Catalyst Matrix, is a 1-meter-long standard SCSI-2 cable with male connectors at each end. Most of the cable wires are swapped between the two cable ends, which permits Catalyst 3000-to-Catalyst 3000 series switch as well as Catalyst 3000-to-Catalyst Matrix connections with the same cable. Connectivity using the StackPort and Catalyst Matrix options offers the availability of up to 224 10BaseT switched ports.

Catalyst 3000 Family Software Architecture

The material presented here is intended to help the reader understand switch features; however, it is not directly related to one of the objectives.

The Catalyst 3000 series switch software is responsible for the following:

- Maintaining and distributing address tables throughout the stack.

- Learning the location of end stations.

- Performing address filtering, port security, or static route switching.

- Enabling creation and maintenance of the stack.

Address Tables

The Catalyst 3000 series switch uses two different types of address tables: the master table and the port table. The master table is maintained in the network memory and contains all the current addresses on the network. The master table is also responsible for updating the port tables when a new address is learned. The addresses in the master table are constant across the stack and are also updated on other boxes in the stack. The port table resides at each port and is updated by the master table on an as-needed basis. The port address table has a capacity of 1700 addresses.

Address Learning

At system power-up, the switch address tables are empty. When a switch receives a packet with an unknown source or destination address, it masks the port of entry and sends the packet to the system module for processing. The switch learns the location of the new source, makes an appropriate entry in the receiving ports address table, and sends the packet to all its output ports if the destination address is unknown. When the response packet is received, the switch learns the address of the destination station and the port associated with it, and makes the appropriate entry in the address tables. Subsequent packets exchanged between these two stations are switched without system module intervention, resulting in faster transmission.

Stack Packet-Switching Software

The stack software is an integral part of forming a Catalyst 3000 series switch stack. The five areas that the stack software is responsible for are listed here:

- *Heartbeat message*—Each Catalyst 3000 series switch broadcasts a heartbeat message to its neighbors. The heartbeat message consists of the stack ID, the source's MAC address, and the box number of the source.

- *Matrix switchover*—If a switch fails to see five consecutive heartbeats from its neighbor, a loopback is sent through the matrix. If the loopback is received, then the neighbor has left the stack. If the loopback is not received, then the matrix failed.

- *Stack formation*—A stack is formed either when two switches are connected back-to-back via a StackPort module, or when three or more are connected to a Matrix.

- *Addition/removal of units to or from a stack*

- *Stack address learning*

Configuring the Catalyst 3000 Series Switches

CLSC Objectives Covered in This Section

72	Perform initial setup of a Catalyst 3000 series switch.

The Catalyst 3000 series switch uses a menu-based system for configuration that is configured via the console port. A dumb terminal or a PC can be used to connect to the console port. Repeatedly pressing the Return key will autobaud the terminal and then display the Catalyst Manager screen. The Catalyst Manager is the first screen displayed and is used to enter and display System Contact and password information.

Upon entry of either the password or Return, if there is no password entry, the Main Menu is displayed.

The Main Menu offers five options:

- *Configuration Menu*—All configuration changes can be made or viewed from this menu.

- *Statistics Menu*—This displays the statistics menu for the Catalyst 3000 for use in monitoring switch and network performance.

- *Download Menu*—This menu is used to load system images to Flash memory via two methods: either TFTP or Serial Link Download.

- *Reset Menu*—Reset options are listed here.

- *Exit Console*—This option exits the menu.

Most of the focus of this section will be spent on the Configuration Menu because this is where virtually all the test objectives for this chapter are listed. There are a large number of options, but we will focus on the options that are most important.

After configuring the initial setup on the Catalyst 3000, the next testing objective is to configure the switch for management.

Configuring for Management

73	Configure the switch for management.

The tasks for configuring the Catalyst 3000 series switch for management are listed here:

- Configuring IP parameters
- Configuring SNMP parameters
- Configuring RMON
- Configuring SwitchProbe
- Configuring Cisco Discovery Protocol (CDP)

Configuring IP parameters requires selecting the IP Configuration menu selection. The options include the following:

- *IP Address*—Displays the IP address. To change the IP address, highlight it and enter in a new address.
- *Default Gateway*—Displays the current gateway address.
- *Subnet Mask*—Displays the current subnet mask.
- *IP State*—Select from IP Disabled, BOOTP When Needed, or BOOTP Always by highlighting IP State and pressing Return, highlighting one of the choices, and pressing Return. The default is BOOTP When Needed.
- *IP Packet Type*—Displays the type of Ethernet packet being presented.
- *Send PING*—Prompts for an IP address to be entered, and then sends a ping to that address.

Configuring SNMP Parameters requires selecting the SNMP Configuration menu selection. The options include the following:

- *Send Authentication Traps*—Indicates whether SNMP should issue traps to the trap receivers. The default is yes.
- *Community Strings*—Displays and sets the community strings for the Catalyst 3000.
- *Trap Receivers*—Displays and sets the trap receivers to which traps are sent.

The configuration for Community Strings requires entering the string name and determining whether it is a read or a read/write string. The Trap Receiver's configuration requires entering the trap receiver's IP address, the associated community string, and the VLAN in which the trap is sent out. Up to 20 trap receivers can be entered.

Configuring RMON is a one-entry screen. Enable RMON is either a yes or a no option.

Configuring SwitchProbe is almost as easy. You must select which port you want to use as a SwitchProbe Port. Entering a 0 will disable the function. The other option is to select the Traffic to Probe function. The selections are None, Half-Duplex, and Full-Duplex.

Configuring CDP is done on a port-by-port basis. Entry of a port number prompts the following options:

- *Ena/Dis*—Enables or disables CDP on the selected port.

- *Trans Freq*—Enables entry of the transmission frequency for discovery frames.

- *Time-to-live*—Enables entry of discovery time to live.

Configuring Port Parameters

CLSC Objectives Covered in This Section

74	Configure port parameters.

Configuring port parameters requires selection of the following individual configuration items under the Configuration Menu:

- Port Switching Mode
- Broadcast Suppression
- EtherChannel
- MAC Filter & Port Security
- Learn and Lock

The Port Switching Mode screen shows the status of the switching error-handling modes available on the Catalyst 3000 switch. Three error-handling switching modes are displayed:

- *Auto*—Automatically converts error-handling from cut-through to store-and-forward. The user sets a percentage threshold, referred to as Error Water Mark, on the Port Switching Mode screen. When set to automatic (auto), the error handling is normally in cut-through mode. If the error rate exceeds the Error Water Mark, error-handling is automatically converted to store-and-forward. If the error rate once again falls below the Error Water Mark, the error-handling automatically reverts to cut-through. This process continues as long as this mode is selected.

- *Cut-through*—This mode forces error-handling in the cut-through mode only. Cut-through mode reduces latency times by reading only the beginning of the packet and immediately routing the packet to its destination.

- *Store-and-forward*—This mode forces error-handling in the store-and-forward mode only. The complete incoming packet is read, stored, and then forwarded to its destination.

To change the switching mode, highlight Change and press Return. You are prompted to select the mode, the high water percentage (if Auto mode is selected), and the setting for runtless mode. Make your selections as follows:

- *Error Water Mark*—If Auto mode is selected for that port, set the percentage level of errors that the Catalyst 3000 will switch from cut-through to store-and-forward.

- *Runtless Mode*—The last item screen displays the setting of the runtless mode. This mode is set to either on or off. If on, incomplete packets (less than 64 bytes) are discarded, and a runt packet error is logged and displayed in the Statistics menus. If off, runt packets are forwarded.

Broadcast Suppression

This feature is used to suppress broadcast packets and is set on a per-port basis on the Broadcast Suppression screen. If set to on, that port is set to a percentage threshold level (Broadcast Water Mark) based on total traffic at which broadcast packets are suppressed. If the broadcast level on a specific port exceeds the set threshold, all broadcasts originating from that port are blocked until the broadcast level drops below that mark.

The three fields displayed are listed here:

- *Port*—Indicates the port number selected.

- *Broadcast Suppression*—Displays whether broadcast suppression is enabled or disabled for that specific port.

- *Broadcast Water Mark*—Displays a user-defined percentage level based on broadcast traffic compared to the total traffic on that port. If broadcast traffic exceeds this level, packets are suppressed until they fall below that level.

EtherChannel

Use the EtherChannel Configuration menu to add, delete, or change EtherChannels. Before creating an EtherChannel, determine which ports are to be designated as EtherChannel ports. The EtherChannel may consist of two to seven ports.

The EtherChannel selection from the Configuration menu brings up a submenu called EtherChannel Configuration. The EtherChannel menu is then displayed. EtherChannels must be manually added to the configuration. The following procedure must be followed to set up an EtherChannel:

1 Disconnect the ports you want to add to the EtherChannel, or disable them using the Port Configuration menu.

2 For one Catalyst 3000, select the EtherChannel menu, and then choose Add Entry from the menu bar at the bottom of the screen.

3 Enter the ports (Port 1 is not recommended for EtherChannel use) for the EtherChannel column, separated by spaces.

4 Choose Exit, and press Return.

Repeat Steps 1 through 4 for the other Catalyst 3000 devices.

Set the Address Aging Time to the same value for the Catalyst 3000 series switch.

If you disconnected the ports in the EtherChannel, reconnect them. If you disabled them using the Port Configuration menu, use the menu to reenable them.

Use the EtherChannel Configuration menu to add, delete, or change EtherChannels. Before creating an EtherChannel, determine which ports are to be designated as EtherChannel ports. The EtherChannel may consist of two to seven ports.

The EtherChannel Configuration menu offers the following options:

- *EtherChannel*—Lists the different EtherChannel setups.

- *Ports*—Lists the ports within that specific EtherChannel.

- *Add Entry*—This option and the following four options are displayed at the bottom of the EtherChannel Configuration screen. They prompt you to enter port numbers in the EtherChannel. Enter at least two ports (but no more than seven ports), from lowest number to highest, separated by spaces. Do not use 10BaseT port 1 for EtherChannel.

- *Delete Entry*—Asks whether you want to remove the entry, and then deletes the selected EtherChannel.

- *Change Entry*—Prompts you to reenter the port numbers in the selected EtherChannel, from lowest to highest, separated by spaces.

- *Clear Table*—Deletes all EtherChannel definitions. The table is displayed to show all EtherChannels with no port entries.

MAC Filter and Port Security

The MAC Filter and Port Security option is selected under the Configuration menu. The options under this menu are listed here:

- *Configure Filters*—Establishes specific filtering of addresses.
- *Configure Port Security Mode*—Establishes address security at specific ports.
- *View Port Filters*—Displays filters setup for specific ports.

To configure a new MAC address filter, select the Configure Filters option in the MAC Filter and Port Security screen. The screen displays the Configure Filters screen.

Six selectable options are displayed at the bottom of the screen:

- *Return*—Returns the previously displayed screen.
- *Zoom*—Enables a display of additional information on a selected filter.
- *More*—Enables a display of additional filter table entries.
- *Add Entry*—Prompts for entry of the MAC address you want to filter and the ports that will not be capable of forwarding to this address. To create the filter on all ports, press Return. The terminal displays the following prompts:
  — MAC address (XX:XX:XX:XX:XX:XX)
  — Enter port mask (ZZZZZZZZ)
- *Delete Entry*—Prompts you to enter the index number of the filter to be removed. The index number appears in the left column of the table display.
- *Clear Table*—Clears all filters in the table.

When the Add Entry option is selected, the screen displays the available filter functions.

Choose the filter type you desire from the Configure Filters menu. An explanation of each type of filter follows.

Selections are made by highlighting and then pressing Return. The display prompts for entry of the necessary parameters.

The following four filter selections are available:

- *Block any packet with Source Address*—All packets from that source address are blocked from the specified port(s).
- *Block any packet with Destination Address*—All packets with the specified destination address are blocked at the specified port(s).
- *Allow any packet with Designated Source Address to port(s)*—Packets received from a specific address are allowed to go to the specified port(s).
- *Force any packet with the Designated Destination Address to port(s)*—Packets with a specific address must go to specified port(s).

The Port Security section of the MAC Filter and Port Security menu establishes secure address levels for specific ports.

NOTE   This function disables the address-learning capability of the Catalyst 3000 series switch and totally blocks (secures) specific addresses at specified ports.

Selecting the Configure Port Security Mode option in the MAC Filter and Port Security screen displays the Configure Port Security Mode screen.

The following four address security choices are available:

- *Normal*—Forwards all packets.
- *Send the specified source address*—Blocks all other addresses.
- *Send the specified destination address*—Blocks all other addresses.
- *Send the specified source and destination addresses*—Blocks all other addresses.

Learn and Lock

The Learn and Lock feature provides added security by monitoring and controlling switch port access. When enabled, a port is set up to learn a single MAC address and to lock out input from any address other than that learned address.

Learn and Lock, also known as MAC Address Port Security, enables an Ethernet port in a Catalyst 3000 series switch to block input to an Ethernet or Fast Ethernet port when the MAC address of a station attempting to access the port is different from the MAC address learned on or configured for that port. When a Catalyst 3000 switch receives a packet, the switch compares the source address of that packet to the secure source address learned by or configured for that port. When a source MAC address other than that learned by or configured for a port is detected, the port is disabled and an SNMP trap is sent.

NOTE   Learn and Lock is not applicable to trunk ports.

Follow these steps to enable Learn and Lock at a specific port:

1 Select the Learn and Lock option in the Configuration menu.

2 Select the Learn and Lock Variables heading. Use this menu to enable or disable Learn and Lock.

The Learn and Lock Variables screen displays the following options:

- *Enable/Disable Learn and Lock*—Enables or disables the Learn and Lock feature.

- *Disable Port*—If Yes, the port is disabled when an unauthorized MAC address accesses the port.

- *Learning Time (minutes)*—User-settable time for learning addresses dynamically.

When Learn and Lock is enabled, port-learning options can be configured from the Static Address Learning menu.

NOTE   After an address is determined through Learn and Lock on a port and that same address is used on another port, the address for the first port will not be automatically deleted. The first address must be deleted manually.

Configure VLANs and Trunk Links

CLSC Objectives Covered in This Section

75	Configure VLANs and trunk links.

Configuring VLANs and VTP is a menu under the Configuration menu. The options on this menu are listed here:

- *Local VLAN Port Configuration*—Displays the port configuration menu that you use to assign ports to VLANs.

- *VTP Administrative Configuration*—Enables you to examine details of a domain (VLAN) and make administrative changes, if required.

- *VTP VLAN Configuration*—Displays the assigned name of the VLANs. The names can be changed by using the prompts displayed on the screen.

- *Local Preferred VLANs Configuration*—Displays all VLANs in the system that currently transit the Catalyst Stack.

- *Reassign Ports in Local VLAN*—Enables reassignment of ports in VLANs.

The Local VLAN Port Configuration screen displays current VLAN port assignments. You can make changes to VLAN port assignments by using the cursor control keys to select Change. You will be prompted for changes to be entered. If more than 14 ports are assigned, you must select More to display the additional ports.

The VTP Administrative Configuration screen enables display of VLAN descriptive information. The following fields are displayed:

- *Domain Name*—Displays the administrative domain the device is participating in (accepts updates from and propagates configuration changes).

- *Local Mode*—Displays the operating mode of a domain. The choice of modes includes server, client, or transparent.

  Server mode permits configuration changes from the local device. (All devices in server mode must be capable of storing configurations for all VLANs in the administrative domain. The switch will not permit the user to configure VLANs in excess of 68. If this number is exceeded, the switch will automatically enter client mode.)

  Client mode accepts configuration changes from other devices only.

  Transparent mode passes VTP packets received. Transparent mode also accepts and stores changes to the local VLAN configuration database. Database changes are not propagated to other devices.

- *Domain Password*—Is a password of up to 64 characters. This password is common to all devices in the administrative domain. A configuration will not pass between two devices with passwords that do not match, even if they are configured with the same administrative domain name.

- *Configuration Storage*—Indicates NVRAM or TFTP server (display only).

- *Configuration TFTP Server*—Indicates the TFTP server containing the configuration storage file (display only).

- *Server VLAN*—Indicates the resident VLAN of the TFTP server containing the configuration storage file (display only).

- *Configuration File Directory*—Is the directory on the TFTP server where the configuration storage file is located.

- *Domain Revision Number*—Indicates the revision number of the current configuration database implemented on this device.

- *Time of Last Revision Change*—Indicates the time revision that the current configuration database implemented on this device was created.

- *Last Updater*—Indicates the IP address of the server providing the revision of the current configuration database implemented on this device.

The VTP VLAN Configuration menu is displayed when chosen under the VLAN and VTP Configuration menu. When the switch is in server mode, the following options are available:

- Return
- More
- Change
- Add
- Delete

Selecting the Add or Change options causes display of the following action item:

- Enter VLAN ID for the VLAN to be added (or changed).
- Enter a VLAN ID and press Return to display the VLAN Configuration menu.

When the switch is in client mode, the following options are displayed below the VLAN Name parameters (display-only options):

- Return
- More
- Examine

The VLAN Configuration menu provides the following options:

- *VLAN ID*—The numeric VTP ID. Synonymous with the VLANs ISL ID-associated VLAN packets on ISL trunks. The permissible range is 1 to 1005.
- *VLAN Name*—The name associated with the VLAN. The name is synonymous with the VLANs ELAN name on LAN Emulation trunks. The name can be a maximum of 32 characters.
- *State*—The state of the VLAN can be operational or suspended. Packets are passed when the state is operational. Packets are not passed while in the suspended state.
- *Type*—Identifier for the VLAN type: Ethernet, FDDI, Token Ring, FDDI-net, or Token Ring-net.
- *MTU*—The maximum transmission unit of the VLAN.
- *SAID*—The SAID associated with the VLAN. This SAID is the same as the VLAN's ID on FDDI trunks.
- *Ring Number*—The ring number of the VLAN. This number is settable for FDDI and Token Ring VLANs only.

- *Bridge Number*—The bridge number of the VLAN. This number is settable for FDDI-net and Token Ring-net VLANs only.

- *Spanning Tree Type*—The spanning tree type implemented for the VLAN. This type can be IEEE 802.1 or IBM. This option can be set for FDDI-net and Token Ring-net VLANs only.

- *Parent VLAN*—The VLAN ID of the parent ring associated with the VLAN. This option can be set for FDDI or Token Ring VLANs only.

- *TB VLAN 1 and TB VLAN 2*—The VLAN ID of VLANs translationally bridged to this VLAN.

Select the VLAN VTP Configuration option from the VTP and VLAN Configuration menu. To display a description of a particular VLAN, enter the VLAN ID for the VLAN to be examined. Entering a VLAN ID and pressing Return displays a description of that VLAN.

The Local Preferred VLANs option displays all VLANs in the system that currently transit the Catalyst Stack when selected from the VLAN and VTP Configuration menu. The maximum number of Preferred VLANs is 64. VLANs denoted by asterisks are those selected as Preferred VLANs. Other VLANs displayed are those automatically selected for transit because they are the lowest-numbered Ethernet VLANs in the global VTP configuration.

The options on this menu are listed here:

- *Return*—Returns to the previously displayed screen.

- *More*—Displays additional Preferred VLANs.

- *Add*—Displays the screen shown on the next page. You can select preferred VLANs.

- *Delete*—Enables removal of a VLAN from the preferred list.

Configure the ATM LANE Module

CLSC Objectives Covered in This Section

76	Configure the ATM LANE module.

We've covered the basics of ATM in other chapters, so we'll skip over that and go straight into the configuration of ATM LANE on the Catalyst 3000.

The configuration of LANE on the ATM Module is fairly straightforward. The ATM Module can function as any of the four components of LANE: LECS, LES, BUS, and LEC. The ATM Configuration is an option under the Configuration menu, which has four options available:

- ATM LANE Global Configuration
- LANE Client Configuration
- LANE Server Configuration
- LANE Configuration Server

The ATM LANE Global Configuration option from the ATM Configuration menu displays the ATM LANE Global Configuration by ATM module port number. The following information is listed:

- *Operation Mode*—Client or server
- *Configuration Type*—Address registration sent to ATM switch
- *ATM NSAP Prefix*—The ATM prefix, LECS ESI address, and a selector byte value of FF, to form the ATM address for LECS

The other menus are straightforward and are easy to follow from the configuration menus. Just know what menu selection is used to configure the ATM portion of the 3000 switch.

Perform Basic Router Module Configuration

CLSC Objectives Covered in This Section

77	Perform basic router module configuration.

Some parameters for the router module are configurable from the switch Main menu. The parameters govern the boot-up process, router reset, and router flow control, and they provide access to the router command-line interface (CLI). Selecting the Router Configuration option from the Configuration menu displays just the one option.

- *Enter a Port Number*—Enter the port number of the router module (if in a stack, you must also identify the box number).

Upon entering the port number (and box number, if required), the screen will display the Router Configuration menu.

The options on the Router Configuration menu are listed here:

- *Boot Up Console Selects*—Displays two boot-up choices: switch and router. You can set the default boot-up console to be either the switch Main menu or the router CLI.
- *Switch to Router Console*—Provides access to the router CLI. This option functions the same as pressing Ctrl-R. To return to the switch menus from the router CLI, press Ctrl-R.

- *Router Reset*—Resets the router card without resetting the switch.

- *Board Information*—Displays information about the board.

- *Net Addr*—Displays the IP address of the Ethernet port (e0) that connects the router card to the switch.

- *Op State*—Displays the operational state of the router card.

- *Router Boot Option*—Displays the Router Boot Option screen.

- *Router Flow Control*—Displays the Router Flow Control screen.

The Router Boot Option screen displays two choices for the default boot-up procedure, as follows:

- *With Switch*—This selection forces the router card to reboot whenever the switch is rebooted.

- *Leave Alone*—This selection sets the router card to remain in running mode when the switch is rebooted.

The Router Flow Control screen displays the following two options:

- *None*—No flow control. This is the default flow control for the router.

- *Software Flow Control*—If characters are not displayed correctly on the router CLI, change the router flow control to software flow control

Troubleshooting the Catalyst 3000 Series Switches

CLSC Objectives Covered in This Section

82	Troubleshoot the Catalyst 3000 series switch subsystems.
83	Troubleshoot network interfaces and connections.
84	Use the switch LEDs to isolate problems.
85	Isolate network segment problems.

Troubleshooting requires tracing a problem to a specific area and then attempting to isolate a specific component associated with the problem. Comparing what the system is doing to what it should be doing will usually identify the cause and help solve the problem.

First, determine which of the following Catalyst 3000 subsystems has a problem:

- *Power system*—This category includes input power, AC power cable, and power supply.
- *Cooling system*—The fans should go on when power is applied.
- *System cables*—This includes all the interface cables that connect the equipment to the network.

Troubleshooting the Power and Cooling Systems

For the following problems, refer to the accompanying instructions to help isolate and determine the possible causes.

Unit Will Not Power-Up

- The Catalyst 3000 should power up when the AC power cord is attached to the unit and plugged into a proper AC outlet.
- Verify that the PWR LED is on. If it is not on and both of the fans are not running:
  — Check the AC power cord.
  — Check power at the AC outlet itself.

If input power and the power cord are good, then contact the Cisco Technical Assistance Center (TAC).

If the FAULT LED comes on after power up or after the unit has been running for a while, cycle the power to the unit. If the FAULT LED continues to come on, contact the Cisco TAC.

Unit Powers Off After Running

If the system successfully powers on, but loses power after a short period of time, take these actions:

- Verify that there are no loose power connections.
- Check power outlet for power losses or surges.
- Suspect an internal power supply problem.
- Suspect a thermal-induced shutdown.

Make certain that the two fans are running, that the chassis intake vents and exhaust ports are clear, and that the area around them is unobstructed. If no visible external problems exist, use the console connection to see whether a temperature error has occurred. If you continue to experience problems powering down, or if temperature errors are reported to the console and you cannot isolate a specific cause and correct it, contact the Cisco TAC.

Troubleshooting the Network Interface and Connections

Check for the following symptoms when troubleshooting the network interface:

- A network interface is not recognized by the system:

  — Check the interface cable and connection.

  — Check the LED that corresponds to the network interface.

- A network interface is recognized, but it will not communicate properly.

  — Check the interface cable and connections.

- System boots, but the console is frozen:

  — Check the external console connection.

  — Verify the console setup procedures.

If the system will not boot properly or intermittently reboots, the processor may be faulty or the hardware/software setup may be wrong.

The LEDs on the Catalyst 3000 and expansion modules indicate the operating state of the equipment. If you are experiencing problems, the following table may help you find the cause. If these basic checks do not resolve the problem, contact the Cisco TAC.

LED	Status	What to do
PWR	Off	If the PWR LED is off and both the fans are not running, check for power to the switch.
DIAG	Remains on	The DIAG LED is on during self-test.
FAULT	On	The FAULT LED should remain off during normal operation. If it is on, an error has occurred. Cycle the power on the switch. The FAULT LED should not come back on.
LNK/FDX	Off	Check all port connections. Check the cables and all cable connections. Recheck the sytem configuration.
XMIT/RCV	Not blinking	The XMIT and RCV LEDs should blink as packets are forwarded to other ports. If the LEDs do not blink, verify that the physical network configuration is correct. Check the console for proper configuration and operation.

For problem isolation using the diagnostic LEDs, follow these instructions:

- If all LEDs are off during POST, DIAG has failed.
- If an LED remains on after POST, the associated LMA or HSPA has failed.

- If an LED turns on during normal switch operations, the associated LMA or HSPA has failed.

- If all LEDs turn on during operations, the power supply has failed.

Excessive broadcast traffic can be diagnosed as follows:

- The RCV and XMIT LEDs on one port, and the XMIT LED on all other ports are flashing.

- The RCV LED is on steady or is constantly flashing at a high rate; heavy utilization or a high number of collisions are probable problem causes.

Checking Network Operation and Setup

If any problems exist with the actual networking operation of the Catalyst 3000 series switch, verify through the console connection that there are no errors reported, that setups are still correct, and that operations are normal.

Checking Segment Communications

Check that devices on the same segment can communicate. If the segment has a server, try sending some network traffic to it. If the segment does not have a server, use available applications to exchange packets with other stations.

In a TCP/IP environment, try issuing a "ping" to another station on the segment. If the workstation does not receive the signal, check the connections and verify that you are using the appropriate network software and hardware.

Verifying Ethernet Segment Operations

Verify that all segments belong to the same logical network:

- All segments should have the same IP subnet.

- All segments must have the same network number.

Then, send data to the local network devices:

- Attach to the local server to send and retrieve data.

- If there is no server, use diagnostic utilites to exchange data with other workstations (such as the UNIX **ping** command).

Check the switch LEDs for performance:

- Verify that the DIAG LED is on after power is applied to the switch while POST is run. After POST, the DIAG LED is off.

- If the switch has network connectivity, verify that the RCV, XMIT, and FWD LEDs are active.

Use a cable tester, Time Domain Reflectometer (TDR), or a similar device to verify that the segment lengths attached to the Catalyst 3000 series switch meet Ethernet/IEEE 802.3 specifications.

NOTE   Be sure to use a cable tester or TDR. Do not rely on the physical measurement of cables between stations and wiring closets, because cables are often routed through ceiling areas.

If you discover a cable segment that exceeds the specified length, replace it with a cable of the appropriate length or add a repeater, being sure to use no more than four repeaters.

Using a TDR or other such cable-checking device, verify that the cable has no open or short circuits.

For 10BaseT connections from the Catalyst 3000, verify that the FDX/LNK status LED is illuminated. If not, verify that the following are true:

- The cables are good.
- You are using the correct type of cable: straight or crossover.

Make sure that both ends of the connection are set to the same communication mode:

- Half-duplex or full-duplex
- Check cable impedance

Verify that cable impedance is within the following ranges:

- UTP—85–110 ohms.
- Thick/Thin Ethernet—50 ohms (+/– 2 ohms)

NOTE   Impedance cannot be measured with a Digital Multimeter (DMM). Verify the impedance with a TDR device or by reviewing the cable manufacturer's specifications.

To verify that transceivers are operating correctly, check the following:

- Make sure the PWR LED is illuminated. If the network device is powered on and the power LED on the transceiver is not lit, try replacing the transceiver with one that you know is good.
- When changing a transceiver, always disable the SQE signal.

- If the Catalyst 3000 is connected to a 10BaseT transceiver, verify that the FDX/LNK LED is lit. This indicates a good connection with the transceiver at the other end. If the LED is not lit, there may be a connection problem or a transceiver problem. Verify that the correct cable is being used. If so, try replacing the transceiver to see if you can establish a good connection.

- Verify that the XMIT and RCV LEDs blink when data is sent through a port. Try sending data to devices to which these transceivers are attached, and observe the transmit and receive LEDs. Both LEDs should blink on both transceivers during an exchange. If not, a transceiver may be faulty. Try replacing each transceiver with a known good one.

Q&A

As mentioned in Chapter 1, "The Cisco LAN Switch Configuration (CLSC) Exam Overview," the questions and scenarios are more difficult than what you should experience on the actual exam. The questions do not attempt to cover more breadth or depth than the exam; however, the questions are designed to make sure you know the answers. Rather than allowing you to derive the answer from clues hidden inside the question itself, the questions will challenge your understanding and recall of the subject. Questions from the "Do I Know This Already?" quiz from the beginning of the chapter are repeated here to ensure that you have mastered the chapter's topic areas.

1 The port duplex mode is set from which configuration menu?

2 Does the Router Configuration menu provide for rebooting the router module without resetting the switch?

3 Which switch in the Catalyst 3000 series has seven expansion slots?

4 What is the maximum number of ports that can be used for EtherChannel?

5 What is the name of the switching bus in the Catalyst 3000 architecture, and how much switching bandwidth does it support?

6 The Catalyst 3200 supports a range of how much capacity, where capacity equals the number of simultaneous conversations possible on each port times the speed of the port?

7 What size is the packet buffer on a 100 Mbps port on a Catalyst 3000?

8 What is the name of the switching mode that enables the switch to monitor errors and change from cut-through to store-and-forward and back?

9 A single Catalyst 3000 supports how many switched ports without using expansion slots?

10 What is the maximum bandwidth provided by the Catalyst StackPort module?

11 What is the maximum length of the SCSI-2 cable used to interconnect Catalyst 3000 switches to the Matrix?

12 What is the name of the menu that enables you to view VLAN configuration information?

13 How many filter types are available?

14 If a Catalyst 3000 had 8 MB of memory, how many MAC addresses would be supported?

Source Material

Some content in this chapter is based on the following sources:

- *Catalyst 3000 Series Switches (3000, 3100)*

  http://www.cisco.com/univercd/cc/td/doc/product/lan/cat3ks/index.htm

- *Catalyst 3200 Installation and Configuration Guide*

  http://www.cisco.com/univercd/cc/td/doc/product/lan/cat3200/3200/index.htm

This chapter is designed to assist you in final preparation for the CLSC exam. It presents a case study and its solution involving the move from a traditional collapsed backbone to a flatter, switched network using Catalyst switches and ATM LANE modules. Interspersed throughout this chapter are questions that test your knowledge of the material. In addition, we provide some configurations and the results of some **show** commands related to this network. Keep in mind that although the Cisco LAN Switch Configuration (CLSC) exam contains no scenarios of this type, the real-world applicability and skill used when analyzing this case study will strengthen your knowledge base.

As we just mentioned, this is the final preparation phase before you take your exam. If you want even more final preparation, you can read through the many practice questions located in each chapter and on the CD-ROM. You can find the answers to all pre-chapter quiz and chapter-ending questions in Appendix A, "Answers to 'Do I Know This Already?' Quizzes and Q & A Sections." You can read and review these conveniently located questions and their explanations quickly. In addition, the CD-ROM has testing software, as well as many additional questions in the multiple-choice format of the CLSC exam. These questions should be a valuable resource when performing final preparations.

CHAPTER 15

Final Network Scenario

How to Best Use This Chapter

These scenarios focus on easily forgotten items, the first of which involves the **show** commands. The options of these commands are often ignored, mainly because we can get online help about the correct option easily when using the Cisco CLI. However, questions about the exact command options used to see a particular piece of information are scattered throughout the exam. Take care to review the output of the commands in these scenarios.

This chapter also focuses on a review of command-line tricks and acronym trivia. Like it or not, part of the preparation involves memorization; hopefully, these reminders will save you a question or two on the exam!

Finally, more configurations are shown for almost all options already covered in the book. If you can configure these options without online help, you should feel confident that you can choose the correct command from a list of five options in a multiple-choice question.

Many of you will read this chapter as your final review before taking the exam; let us take this opportunity to wish you success. We hope that you will be relaxed and confident for your exam, and we trust that this book has helped you build your knowledge and confidence.

The Scenario

Our scenario is set in a large campus environment with the traditional collapsed backbone connecting large numbers of Ethernet hubs to large routers. The routers are then attached via ATM and FDDI to other buildings and routers. Note the diagram in Figure 15-1.

Figure 15-1 *Legacy FDDI Routed Backbone with Ethernet Hubs*

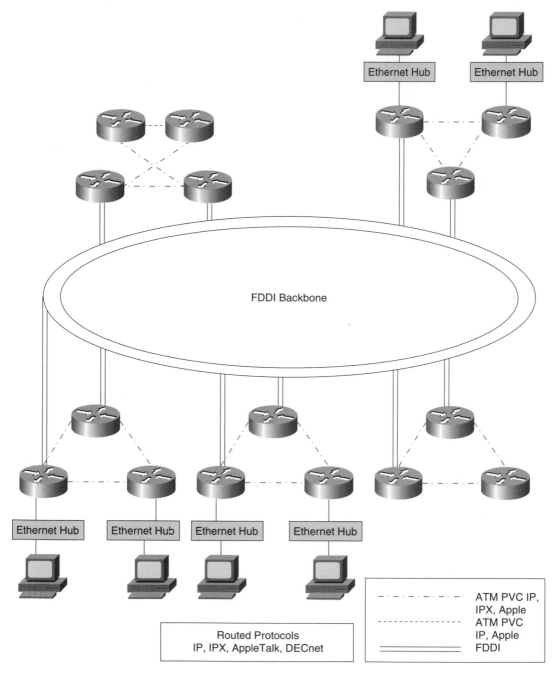

We've done the design work for you, by turning a legacy FDDI routed network into a switched network using Cisco Catalyst switches and ATM LANE modules. This before and after information is provided just so the user can see a typical redesign project. See the final product in Figure 15-2.

Figure 15-2   *Switched Catalyst Network with ATM LANE*

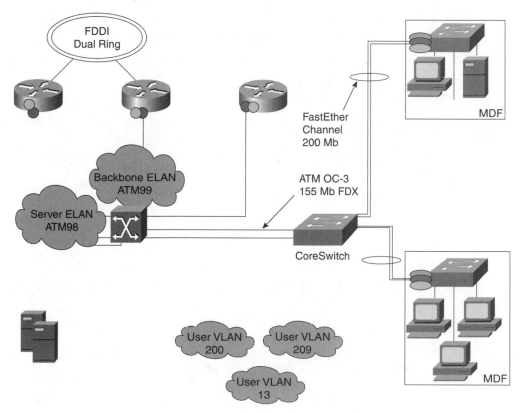

We have provided for you the before and after network diagrams. Based on the ending diagram, we will quiz you with some questions related to the diagram. Following that, we will provide some **show** commands and configurations and test you on various aspects of those.

Questions on Figure 15-2

1 How many physical connections exist from CoreSwitch to Cat1?

2 Let's assume for a moment that we have turned off the FastEtherChannel between Cat1 and CoreSwitch. With Spanning Tree turned on, what would be the state of the connections between the switches?

3 Let's assume for a moment that the connections between CoreSwitch and Cat1 are multimode fiber. What's the maximum distance that can used?

Shown here are the results of a particular **show** command. Let's examine this in detail.

```
Switch1> (enable) sh cam dyn 200
VLAN  Dest MAC/Route Des  Destination Ports or VCs
----  ------------------  -------------------------------------------------
200   00-20-af-a7-61-6b   1/2
200   00-a0-24-b4-f2-4d   1/1
200   00-c0-4f-d5-b2-dd   3/8
200   00-20-af-e8-de-54   3/15
200   00-80-5f-54-5d-9b   1/1
200   00-a0-24-53-68-61   3/10
200   00-c0-4f-ac-c6-f0   3/14
200   00-20-af-6f-b1-06   1/2
200   00-20-af-6f-b1-28   1/2
```

4 What exactly is the function of the command, and what is it showing?

5 Look at MAC address 00-20-af-e8-de-54. What is the significance of the 3/15 noted to the side?

6 Notice that multiple ports have 1/1 to the side. What is the significance of this?

Shown here are the results of another **show** command. The command has been abbreviated, as would normally be the case when someone performs this.

```
Cat 2> (enable) sh cdp nei
Capability Codes: R - Router, T - Trans Bridge, B - Source Route Bridge
                  S - Switch, H - Host, I - IGMP, r - Repeater

Port    Device-ID              Port-ID           Platform              Capability
------- ---------------------- ----------------- --------------------- ----------
1/1     076018000(CoreSwitch)  4/5               WS-C5500              T S
1/2     076018000(CoreSwitch)  4/6               WS-C5500              T S
```

7 What is the significance of the port 1/1 and port-id 4/5?

Shown here are the results of the **show module** command on the switch named CoreSwitch.

```
CoreSwitch> (enable) sh mod
Mod Module-Name         Ports Module-Type           Model     Serial-Num Status
--- ------------------- ----- --------------------- --------- ---------- -------
1   CoreSwitch      2   100BaseFX MM Supervis WS-X5506  007431646 ok
2                   12    100BaseFX MM Ethernet WS-X5201  006492549 ok
3                   12    100BaseFX MM Ethernet WS-X5201  006522436 ok
4                   12    100BaseFX MM Ethernet WS-X5201  006690116 ok
5                   12    100BaseFX MM Ethernet WS-X5201  006496570 ok
6   CoreSW_RSM      1     Route Switch          WS-X5302  006506737 ok
7                   2     MM OC-3 Dual-Phy ATM  WS-X5158  005912297 ok
10                  24    10BaseT Ethernet      WS-X5013  006786528 ok
11                  24    10BaseT Ethernet      WS-X5013  006786791 ok
12                  24    10BaseT Ethernet      WS-X5013  006783605 ok

Mod MAC-Address(es)                          Hw     Fw      Sw
--- ---------------------------------------- ------ ------- -----------------
1   00-10-29-50-05-00 thru 00-10-29-50-08-ff 2.1    2.4(1)  3.1(1)
2   00-e0-1e-b6-48-28 thru 00-e0-1e-b6-48-33 1.1    2.3(2)  3.1(1)
3   00-e0-1e-82-d5-84 thru 00-e0-1e-82-d5-8f 1.1    2.3(2)  3.1(1)
4   00-e0-1e-83-bc-6c thru 00-e0-1e-83-bc-77 1.1    2.3(2)  3.1(1)
5   00-e0-1e-92-cb-40 thru 00-e0-1e-92-cb-4b 1.1    2.3(2)  3.1(1)
6   00-e0-1e-91-af-2c thru 00-e0-1e-91-af-2d 3.0    20.4    11.2(11)P
7   00-60-2f-45-0d-d0 thru 00-60-2f-45-0d-df 2.0    1.3     3.2(6)
10  00-e0-14-a2-81-f8 thru 00-e0-14-a2-82-0f 1.1    2.3(1)  3.1(1)
11  00-e0-1e-47-b0-20 thru 00-e0-1e-47-b0-37 1.1    2.3(1)  3.1(1)
12  00-e0-14-a2-65-18 thru 00-e0-14-a2-65-2f 1.1    2.3(1)  3.1(1)
```

8 Based only on the information presented here, what model of switch is this?

9 What kind of uplink does the Supervisor have, and how many Supervisor cards are there?

10 Note the bottom half of the display, where the MAC addresses are shown. What is the significance of the 3.2(6) on line 7, and why is it different from most of the other modules?

11 Following Question 12 is the output of a show command. From where was the command performed?

12 How many LANE clients are there, based on the output shown here?

```
CoreSW_ATM#show lane

LE Server ATM0.99  ELAN name: atm99  Admin: up  State: operational
type: ethernet        Max Frame Size: 1516
ATM address: 47.000580FFFD0081CB23050101.001029500561.63
LECS used: 47.000580FFFD0081CB23050101.001029500563.00 connected, vcd 329
control distribute: vcd 341, 4 members, 218953 packets

proxy/ (ST: Init, Conn, Waiting, Adding, Joined, Operational, Reject, Term)

lecid ST vcd    pkts Hardware Addr  ATM Address
```

```
1P O  333   193876  0010.2950.0560  47.000580FFFD0081CB23050101.001029500560.63
2  O  334     8369  0000.0c4d.5c00  47.000580FFFD0081CB23050101.00000C4D5C00.63
3  O  355     8356  0060.47c7.cf00  47.000580FFFD0081CB23050101.006047C7CF00.63
4  O  379     8356  0060.47f3.ef00  47.000580FFFD0081CB23050102.006047F3EF00.63
```

The following is a configuration from an ATM LANE Module. Examine it in detail, and then answer the following questions.

13 What LANE components are implemented under interface ATM0.99?

14 What is the name of the ELAN under interface ATM0.99?

Example 15-1 *ATM LANE Module Configuration*

```
 lane database LECS-DB
 name atm99 server-atm-address 47.000580FFFD0081CB23050101.001029500561.63
 name atm01 server-atm-address 47.000580FFFD0081CB23050101.001029500561.62
 !
interface ATM0
 atm preferred phy A
 atm pvc 1 0 5 qsaal
 atm pvc 2 0 16 ilmi
 atm ilmi-keepalive 3
 lane config fixed-config-atm-address
 lane config auto-config-atm-address
 lane config database LECS-DB
 !
interface ATM0.99 multipoint
 description Backbone ELAN
 lane config-atm-address 47.000580FFFD0081CB23050101.001029500563.00
 lane server-bus ethernet atm99
 lane client ethernet 99 atm99
```

The following is a Route Switch Module (RSM) configuration, shown here so that you know what one looks like. No material on the CLSC exam relates to the RSM, but it is interesting to see how all the pieces fit together. If you are familiar with Cisco routers, you will notice that much is the same. The major difference is that the interfaces are no longer physical, such as Serial0, but are virtual; they are created at the time you configure the RSM. This is how VLAN traffic is routed between each other and to other devices.

Example 15-2 *Route Switch Module Configuration*

```
int vlan 99
description Backbone ELAN
ip address 192.168.10.1 255.255.255.0
ipx network 101
appletalk zone Backbone
appletalk cable-range 101-101
int vlan 98
description Server ELAN
ip address 192.168.11.1 255.255.255.0
appletalk cable-range 111-111
appletalk zone Server
ipx network 111
ipx delay 3
int vlan 1
description Management VLAN
ip address 192.168.20.1 255.255.255.0
int vlan 207
description Marketing segment
ip address 192.168.21.1 255.255.255.0
appletalk cable-range 211-211
appletalk zone Mktg
ipx network 211
ipx delay 4
router eigrp 9975
distribute-list 93 out vlan 98
access-list 93 deny 0.0.0.0 255.255.255.255
```

Finally, we will look at some excerpts from a switch that has a connection to the upstream switch CoreSwitch.

15 What is the significance of the "1" in the following first statement?

16 What would happen if the route statement (line 3) were not present?

Example 15-3 *Cat1 Configuration*

```
set interface sc0 1 192.168.10.3 255.255.255.0 192.168.10.255
set ip redirect    disable
set ip route 0.0.0.0 192.168.10.1  1
set prompt Cat1>
set system name  Cat1
set system contact I.M. Notworthy
set system location "1st Floor Wiring Closet
set port duplex    1/1-2  full
set cdp enable   1/1-2
set trunk 1/1  on 1-1000
```

continues

Example 15-3 *Cat1 Configuration (Continued)*

```
set trunk 1/2  on 1-1000
set port enable    1/1-2
set port channel 1/1-2 on
set vtp domain YourBldg
set vtp mode client
set vtp passwd
set spantree portfast    2/1-24 enable
set spantree portfast    3/1-24 enable
set spantree portfast    4/1-24 enable
set spantree portfast    5/1-24 enable
set spantree portfast    6/1-24 enable
set spantree portfast    7/1-24 enable
set spantree portfast    8/1-24 enable
set spantree portfast    9/1-24 enable
set spantree portfast    10/1-24 enable
set spantree portfast    11/1-24 enable
set spantree portfast    12/1-24 enable
set snmp community read-only       flighty
set snmp community read-write      caveinrock
set snmp community read-write-all secret
set snmp rmon enable
set snmp trap enable  all
set ip dns server 192.168.11.250 primary
set ip dns enable
set cgmp enable
set logging console enable
set logging server 192.168.11.190
set logging level all 7 default
set ntp broadcastclient enable
set ntp broadcastdelay 3000
set ntp client enable
set ntp server 192.168.11.180
clear timezone
set summertime disable
set cam agingtime 1-1005 300
```

Answers to the Questions

1 Based on the information given, the drawing shows a 200 MB connection from Cat1 to the CoreSwitch. The only possible conclusion would be that there are two physical connections because all uplinks are 100 MB.

2 Turning off EtherChannel would leave you with two trunks. When Spanning Tree has become a steady state, one trunk would be in forwarding mode and the second trunk would be in blocking or standby mode.

3 This question takes you back to the section on hardware. The correct answer is 2 km for multimode fiber.

4 The command is **show cam dynamic** in its full form. The command as shown here displays the contents of the CAM table for just those in VLAN 200.

5 The 3/15 listed to the side of the output means that the MAC address listed was learned on Module 3, Port 15.

6 Generally, multiple MAC addresses under one port number indicate that they were learned on a trunk port, which would be carrying multiple MAC addresses and VLANs. However, it could be that the port in question has a legacy hub attached, which would have similar results. In this case, however, we're talking about a trunk link.

7 This command is **show cdp neighbors** in its full form. Remember that CDP is never forwarded, so all you will see is the nearest attached devices. In this case, we are connected with two links to CoreSwitch. The 1/1 indicates which port this switch (Cat2) is using to connect to CoreSwitch, and 4/5 indicates which port on CoreSwitch connects back to Cat2.

8 Notice that 12 modules are actively being used. This rules out all platforms *except* the Catalyst 5500, which has 13 slots.

9 Module 1 has interfaces shown as "100 Mb FX MM," which indicates Multimode Fiber Fast Ethernet. Only one Supervisor module exists.

10 Module 7 is an ATM LANE Module, and it runs separate code from the other modules. The majority of the cards are Ethernet line cards and will share the same code level as the Supervisor card.

11 Two things are key to note here. First, the prompt contains a # sign, which is a clue that the card is something other than switch CLI. The # sign indicates privileged EXEC mode or enable mode. Switch CLI displays (*enable*) at the prompt. The other indicator is the command itself: We've limited our discussion to a Catalyst, so the only module that could execute this command is the ATM LANE Module.

12 Based on the fact that four different ATM addresses are listed at the bottom, there are four LANE clients.

13 The LANE components implemented under interface ATM0.99 are LES, the BUS, and a LEC.

14 The name of the ELAN is atm99.

15 The 1 indicates that the interface is in VLAN 1.

16 If not default route statement were present, no communication would take place outside of the VLAN. In other words, it would be a standalone segment.

Conclusion

This exercise explored certain areas of knowledge of the Catalyst 5000, primarily knowledge of configuration commands. The exam is not heavy on the configuration commands, but you never know which one you might be quizzed on. Good luck!

Answers to "Do I Know This Already" Quizzes and Q&A Sections

Answers to the Chapter 2 "Do I Know This Already?" Quiz

1　An advantage to LAN segmentation is:

　a. It places more internetworking devices between clients and servers.

　b. It provides more bandwidth per user.

　c. It reduces WAN costs.

　d. It increases the number of dumb terminals on the network.

　B. It provides more bandwidth per user.

2　Segmenting LANs with bridges:

　a. Occurs at OSI Layer 3.

　b. Reduces the propagation of multicast and broadcast frames.

　c. Provides fewer users per segment.

　d. Uses address tables that associate segment end stations with protocol types.

　C. Provides fewer users per segment.

3　Segmenting LANs with routers (configured as routers):

　a. Occurs at OSI Layer 2.

　b. Has no effect on the propagation of multicast and broadcast frames.

　c. Typically costs less per port than using bridges or switches.

　d. Allows multiple active paths.

　D. Allows multiple active paths.

4 Segmenting LANs with switches:

   a. Enables multiple high-speed data exchanges.

   b. Increases the number of users per segment.

   c. Occurs at OSI Layer 3.

   d. Requires replacing 802.3-compliant NICs and cabling.

   A. Enables multiple high-speed data exchanges.

5 A switch that receives a frame completely before forwarding it uses what switching technology?

   a. Cut-through

   b. In and out

   c. Receive-and-send

   d. Store-and-forward

   D. Store-and-forward

6 Using full-duplex Ethernet:

   a. Requires the attached node to be directly attached to a repeater hub.

   b. Requires the attached node to have an installed network interface card that supports full-duplex Ethernet.

   c. Provides the same performance as half-duplex Ethernet.

   d. Increases contention on Ethernet point-to-point links.

   B. Requires the attached node to have an installed network interface card that supports full-duplex Ethernet.

7 Full-duplex port connections can use which of the following media types to provide point-to-point links between switches or end nodes:

   a. 10BaseT

   b. 10BaseFL

   c. 100BaseTX

   d. 100BaseFX

   e. ATM

   f. Token Ring

   A, B, C, D, and E

8 To implement full-duplex Ethernet, which of the following are required?

   a. Two 10 Mbps or 100 Mbps data paths

   b. Full-duplex Ethernet controllers, or an Ethernet controller for each path

   c. Loopback and collision detection disabled

   d. Software network interface drivers supporting two simultaneous data paths

   e. All of the above

   E. All of the above

9 Cut-through switching is supported on which of the following Catalyst platforms:

   a. 1900

   b. 2820

   c. 3000

   d. 5000

   e. 5500

   A, B, and C

10 Store-and-forward switching is supported on which of the following Catalyst platforms:

   a. 1900

   b. 2820

   c. 3000

   d. 5000

   e. 5500

   A, B, C, D, and E

Answers to the Chapter 2 Q&A Section

1 Name the three main methods for segmenting an Ethernet LAN to increase available bandwidth.

Segmentation with bridges; segmentation with routers; segmentation with switches

2 What are the two primary operational modes used to handle frame switching?

Store-and-forward and cut-through

3 What Catalyst switch platforms support cut-through switching?

Catalyst 1900, 2820, and 3000 series

4 What Catalyst switch platforms support store-and-forward switching?

Catalyst 1900, 2820, 3000, and 5000 series

5 Name at least two benefits of implementing Ethernet switching.

Number of collisions are reduced; simultaneous, multiple communications; high-speed uplinks; improved network response

6 At which layer of the OSI model do routers operate?

Layer 3, the network layer

7 At which layer of the OSI model do bridges operate?

Layer 2, the data link layer

8 At which layer of the OSI model do switches operate?

Layer 2, the data link layer

9 What are the four types of bridging?

Transparent bridging, source-route bridging, source-route transparent bridging, source-route transparent translational bridging

10 Using full-duplex Ethernet requires the attached node to be directly attached to a repeater hub. (True/False)

False

11 Define the link layer of the OSI model.

The link layer (formally referred to as the data link layer) provides reliable transit of data across a physical link. In so doing, the link layer is concerned with *physical* (as opposed to *network*, or *logical*) addressing, network topology, line discipline (how end systems will use the network link), error notification, ordered delivery of frames, and flow control.

12 Define the network layer of the OSI model.

The network layer is a complex layer that provides connectivity and path selection between two end systems that may be located on geographically diverse *subnetworks*. A subnetwork, in this instance, is essentially a single network cable (sometimes called a *segment*).

Because a substantial geographic distance and many subnetworks can separate two end systems desiring communication, the network layer is the domain of routing. Routing protocols select optimal paths through the series of interconnected subnetworks. Traditional network-layer protocols then move information along these paths.

13 What LAN segmentation device can be utilized to control broadcast?

Router

14 What LAN segmentation device makes forwarding decisions based on Layer 3 information?

Router

15 What LAN segmentation device(s) makes forwarding decisions based on layer 2 information?

LAN Switches and Bridges

Answers to the Chapter 3 "Do I Know This Already?" Quiz

1 A virtual LAN:

a. Is a group of ports or users in the same collision domain.

b. Is a group of ports or users in the same broadcast domain.

c. Is defined at the application layer (OSI Layer 7).

d. None of the above.

B. Is a group of ports or users in the same broadcast domain.

2 Virtual LANs:

a. Complicate moves, adds, and changes.

b. Increase administrative costs.

c. Loosen network security.

d. Reduce the propagation of broadcast frames.

D. Reduce the propagation of broadcast frames.

3 Frame filtering:

a. Is used by the Catalyst 5000 series.

b. Was developed specifically for multi-VLAN, interswitch communications.

c. Involves comparing frames with table entries.

d. Places a unique identifier in the header of each frame.

C. Involves comparing frames with table entries.

4 Frame tagging:

   a. Is used by the Catalyst 5000 series.

   b. Uses a filtering table developed by each switch.

   c. Involves comparing frames with table entries.

   d. Is a technique that is very similar to that used by bridges and routers.

   A. Is used by the Catalyst 5000 series.

5 Multisegment hubs:

   a. Are basically useless in a switched network.

   b. Must have all segments attached to the same VLAN.

   c. May have each segment attached to a separate VLAN.

   d. Are useful for establishing inter-VLAN communication.

   C. May have each segment attached to a separate VLAN.

6 Static VLANs:

   a. Use a VLAN configuration server.

   b. Require less configuration in the wiring closet than do dynamic VLANs.

   c. Provide for automatic notification of a new network user.

   d. Are typically assigned by port.

   D. Are typically assigned by port.

7 Dynamic VLANs:

   a. Remain configured on a port until the port's configuration is changed.

   b. Typically use a VLAN configuration server.

   c. Are typically assigned by port.

   d. Require more configuration in the wiring closet than static VLANs.

   B. Typically use a VLAN configuration server.

8 ISL is the VLAN transport protocol used across which type of trunk link?

   a. Fast Ethernet

   b. Token Ring

   c. FDDI

   d. ATM

   A. Fast Ethernet

9 IEEE 802.10 is the VLAN transport protocol used across which type of trunk link?

   a. Fast Ethernet

   b. Token Ring

   c. FDDI

   d. ATM

   C. FDDI

10 LAN Emulation is the VLAN transport protocol used across which type of trunk link?

   a. Fast Ethernet

   b. Token Ring

   c. FDDI

   d. ATM

   D. ATM

11 How many instances of spanning tree are supported per VLAN in Cisco's VLAN implementation?

   a. 1 per switch

   b. 1 per VLAN

   c. 64

   d. 255

   B. 1 per VLAN

Answers to the Chapter 3 Q&A Section

1 Broadcast frequency depends on the types of _____, the type of _____, the amount of logical _____, and how the network resources are used.

   Application, servers, and segmentation

2 Frame filtering creates a filtering table for each _____.

   Switch

3 Frame identification is supported on the _____ and ____ Catalyst series switches.

   3000 and 5000

4 Users can be assigned to VLANs using several different configuration options that include _____, _____, and _____.

Static port assignments, dynamic port assignments, and multi-VLAN port assignments

5 An ISL port is considered a ____ port.

Trunk

6 Stations that share a hub segment are all assigned to the ____ VLAN group.

Same

7 The five components of VLAN implementation are:

Switches, Routers, Interoperability, VLAN Management, and Transport Protocols

8 Network managers can group users into VLANs by what categories?

MAC Address, network layer protocol type, and application type

9 The advantage of a flat switched network is:

It provides very low latency and high throughput performance.

10 The disadvantage of a flat switched network is:

It increases the susceptibility to broadcast traffic across all switches, ports, backbone links, and users.

Answers to the Chapter 4 "Do I Know This Already?" Quiz

1 Demand nodes include:

a. Servers

b. Network backbone devices

c. PCs

d. Mainframe hosts

C. PCs

2 Resource nodes include:

a. Workstations

b. Terminal servers

c. PCs

d. Servers

D. Servers

3 Local resources should be placed on segments with users who access those resources most.

   a. True

   b. False

   A. True

4 Global resources should be placed on the same shared segment as high-end demand nodes.

   a. True

   b. False

   B. False

5 The Catalyst 5000 is intended to be used:

   a. As a backbone switch.

   b. To connect clusters of servers.

   c. To provide desktop switched Fast Ethernet.

   d. All of the above.

   D. All of the above.

6 A successful switched internetworking solution must combine the benefits of both routers and switches.

   a. True

   b. False

   A. True

7 LAN switches provide excellent performance for individual users by allocating dedicated bandwidth to each switch port (for example, each network segment). This technique is known as _____.

   a. Micro-segmenting

   b. Segmenting

   c. Super netting

   d. Network partitioning

   A. Micro-segmenting

8 When designing a network, the basic design rules that should be followed are:

a. Examine single points of failure carefully.

b. Characterize application and protocol traffic.

c. Analyze bandwidth availability.

d. A, B

e. A, C

f. C, B

g. A, B, C

G. A, B, C

9 The core layer of the network should not perform any packet manipulation access lists and filtering.

a. True

b. False

A. True

10 The distribution layer of the network is the demarcation point between the access and core layers and helps to define and differentiate the core.

a. True

b. False

A. True

Answers to the Chapter 4 Q&A Section

1 Remedies for Buffer Overflow Condition include _____.

Increasing the size of the switch buffers
Increasing the size of the link to the servers
Creating multiple links
Setting higher priority for ports attached to the servers
Using a packet retry mechanism

2 A remote conversation takes place between a demand node and a resource node located in different _____.

Collision domains

3 Switched multiple segments enable local conversations between nodes in the same _____.

Collision domain

4 Define *local resource*

A resource node in the same collision domain as that of the demand node

5 Define *remote resource*

A resource node located in a different collision domain

6 Demand nodes include what type of nodes?

Workstations, personal computers, client applications, terminal servers

7 Resource nodes include what type of nodes?

Servers, WAN routers, minicomputers, or mainframe host

8 The large switched/minimal routing design scales well when VLANs are designed so that the majority of resources are available in the VLAN. Therefore, if this topology can be designed so that _____ percent of traffic is intra-VLAN and only _____ percent of traffic is inter-VLAN, the bandwidth needed for inter-VLAN routing is not a concern.

80, 20

9 In a hierarchical network design, distribution layer can be summarized as the layer that provides _____ connectivity.

Policy-based

10 In the campus environment, access-layer functions can include _____.

Shared bandwidth, switched bandwidth, MAC-layer filtering, and microsegmentation

Answers to the Chapter 5 "Do I Know This Already?" Quiz

1 The architecture of the Catalyst 5000 series switch supports which of the following media types?

a. Ethernet

b. Fast Ethernet

c. Token Ring

d. ATM

e. FDDI

f. PPP

A, B, C, D, and E

2 The Catalyst 5000 series switch architecture uses a store-and-forward model for input and output.

  a. True

  b. False

  A. True

3 The Management Bus carries configuration information from the _____ to each module and statistical information from each module to the NMP.

  a. SAINT

  b. EARL

  c. NMP

  d. CAL

  C. NMP

4 Using the Bus Arbiter, the bus supports a two-level priority request scheme.

  a. True

  b. False

  B. False (three-level)

5 The switching bus is _____ bits wide and operates at 25 MHz.

  a. 48

  b. 64

  c. 256

  d. 512

  A. 48

6 Each dedicated Ethernet and Fast Ethernet switch port has its own SAINT ASIC and _____ KB of dedicated frame buffer.

  a. 64

  b. 128

  c. 192

  d. 256

  C. 192

7 As a frame is received from the network and stored in the port's frame buffer, ASICs on each port encapsulate Ethernet frames with _____ bytes of information to indicate VLAN ID.

   a. 12

   b. 24

   c. 48

   d. 64

   A. 12

8 You can also configure static entries in the EARL table. The EARL stores up to _____ addresses.

   a. 16,000

   b. 32,000

   c. 64,000

   d. 128,000

   D. 128,000

9 The Catalyst 5000 series switch architecture enables media-rate performance not only for unicast traffic, but also for broadcast and multicast traffic.

   a. True

   b. False

   A. True

10 The SNMP agent executes in the _____.

   a. EARL

   b. CAL

   c. NMP

   d. SAINT

   C. NMP

Answers to the Chapter 5 Q&A Section

1 The Catalyst 5000 series architecture has three basic components: the _____ and _____, the _____ , and the _____.

Bus Arbiter and EARL, Port Interface, NMP

2 Supervisor II can forward up to _____ Mpps (with feature card 1 or 2), and the Supervisor III can forward up to _____ to _____ Mpps.

1; 2 to 3

3 It is theoretically possible to oversubscribe the backplane when the chassis is populated with 100 Mbps ports.

a. True

b. False

A. True

4 This intermodule communication occurs across the management bus, which is a serial bus operating at _____ kbps.

761

5 The EARL automatically learns source MAC addresses and associated _____ and saves them in a RAM address table with VLAN and port information.

VLANs

6 The EARL stores learned addresses for 300 seconds (5 minutes) by default, or _____ to _____ seconds if so configured by the user.

a. 20–100

b. 60–300

c. 60–600

d. 60–1200

D. 60–1200

7 When an Ethernet frame arrives at a port on the Fast Ethernet module, the port's _____ controller stores it in its receive buffer.

a. EARL

b. DMA

c. SAINT

d. CAL

B. DMA

8 When the entire frame is received and stored in the frame buffer, the SAINT ASIC posts a request to the _____ to transmit the frame across the high-speed switching bus.

Bus arbiter

9 On power-up or reset, the line module LCP executes boot code residing in _____.

Local ROM

10 A bus access arbitration scheme is implemented on the _____.

Supervisor engine

Answers to the Chapter 6 "Do I Know This Already?" Quiz

1 Which one of the following is an option currently available on the Supervisor engine?

a. Two 100BaseTX ports with SC connectors

b. Two SMF ports with RJ45 connectors

c. Two multimode fiber ports with RJ45 connectors

d. Two multimode fiber ports with SC connectors

A and D

2 The Catalyst 5000 series switch has environmental monitoring and reporting functions.

a. True

b. False

A. True

3 Online insertion and removal is supported on the Catalyst 5000 series switch for:

a. The fan trays only

b. The fan trays and redundant power supplies only

c. The fan trays and all switching modules only

d. The fan trays, redundant power supplies, and all switching modules

D. The fan trays, redundant power supplies, and all switching modules

4 On the Catalyst 5000 switch, the Supervisor engine:

a. Must be installed in slot 1

b. May be installed in either slot 1 or slot 2

c. May be installed in slots 1, 2, or 3

d. May be installed in any slot

A. Must be installed in slot 1

5 On the Catalyst 5500 switch, the Supervisor engine:

a. Must be installed in slot 1

b. May be installed in either slot 1 or slot 2

c. May be installed in slots 1, 2, or 3

d. May be installed in any slot

B. May be installed in either slot 1 or slot 2

6 The Catalyst 5000 series switch 10/100 Mbps Ethernet module:

a. Controls data access to the switching backplane

b. Uses RJ45 connectors to attach to Category 5 cable

c. Determines the destination of frames

d. Provides system processing and memory

B. Uses RJ45 connectors to attach to Category 5 cable

7 The Catalyst 5000 series switch Supervisor engine Status LED is red:

a. During system boot

b. If the module is disabled

c. If the redundant power supply is installed but not turned on

d. All of the above

D. All of the above

8 The Catalyst 5000 series switch Supervisor engine allows:

a. Two 100 Mbps Ethernet connections

b. Four 100 Mbps Ethernet connections

c. Two 10/100 Mbps Ethernet connections

d. Four 10/100 Mbps Ethernet connections

A. Two 100 Mbps Ethernet connections

 9 Maximum station-to-station cabling distances for the Catalyst 5000 series Ethernet switching modules are:

 a. 100 m for 100BaseTX half-duplex, and 200 m for 100BaseTX full-duplex

 b. 400 m for 10BaseFL half-duplex, and 200 m for 10BaseFL full-duplex

 c. 400 m for MMF 100BaseFX half-duplex, and 2 km for MMF 100BaseFX full-duplex

 d. 2000 m for SMF 100BaseFX half-duplex, and 2000 m for SMF 100BaseFX full-duplex

 C. 400 m for MMF 100BaseFX half-duplex, and 2 km for MMF 100BaseFX full-duplex

 10 The Catalyst 5002 supports:

 a. One Supervisor engine and one switching module

 b. Two Supervisor engines and one switching module

 c. One LS1010 module and one ATM LAN Emulation module

 d. One Supervisor engine and one LS1010 module

 A. One Supervisor engine and one switching module

Answers to the Chapter 6 Q&A Section

 1 The ASP module must be installed in slot _____.

 13

 2 The Catalyst 5500 backplane implements _____ 1.2-Gbps buses identical to the single bus used in the Catalyst 5000.

 3

 3 There are _____ MAC addresses available from an EPROM mounted on the backplane.

 1024

 4 The Catalyst 5000 supports the creation of up to _____ virtual LANs.

 1000

 5 The Catalyst 5002 switch is a Catalyst 5000 series switch with _____ slots.

 2

6 The Catalyst 2900 is a _____ port, fixed-configuration Fast Ethernet switch.

14

7 The Group Switching Fast Ethernet Module (100BaseTX 24 Port) requires NMP software Release _____ or later.

2.2(2)

8 The 12-port 100BaseFX Fast Ethernet Switching Module uses _____ connectors to attach to 62.5/125-micron multimode fiber.

SC

9 The multimode fiber-optic (MMF) (WS-X5006) Supervisor engines provide two half- and full-duplex Fast Ethernet, multimode fiber interfaces with SC connectors for connection distances up to _____ meters for half-duplex, and up to _____ kilometers for full duplex.

400 and 2

10 The Supervisor engine is the main system processor in the switch. It contains the Layer _____ switching engine, the network management processor for the system software, and the system memory components.

2

Answers to the Chapter 7 "Do I Know This Already?" Quiz

1 The SLIP connection *must* use the _____.

a. IP address 127.0.0.1

b. Console port

c. IP address of the administrator's PC as a default gateway

d. MAC address of the RSM

B. Console port

2 The system initiates a BOOTP or Reverse Address Resolution Protocol (RARP) request:

a. At the end of every system boot.

b. When the TFTP server IP address is set to 0.0.0.0.0.

c. When the sc0 interface IP address is set to 0.0.0.0.

d. All of the above.

C. When the sc0 interface IP address is set to 0.0.0.0.

3 Match each of the following commands with its description.

___**set**

___**show**

___**clear**

a. Used to overwrite or erase a parameter

b. Used to establish switch parameters

c. Used to verify a configuration

B, C, and A

4 Match each of the following command element descriptions with the syntax used to depict them.

Command element descriptions:
___Commands and keywords
___Prompt that indicates user level
___Prompt that indicates privileged level
___Arguments for which you supply values
___Indicator for optional parameter
___Separator for alternative but required keywords
___Sample console screen display
___Indicator for text you enter
___Indicator for nonprinting characters, such as passwords

Syntax:

a. Console>

b. Screen font

c. *Italic* font

d. Boldface font

e. Elements in square brackets ([ ])

f. Console >(enable)

g. Angle brackets (< >)

h. Boldface screen font

i. Vertical bars (|)

H, A, F, C, E, I, B, D, G

5 The **set interface** command:

   a. Can be used to configure static routes on the Catalyst 5000.

   b. Must be used to bring the sc0 interface up before you can use the serial console port after using the **clear config all** command.

   c. Can be used to enable SLIP.

   d. Can be used to assign network addresses and subnet masks for SLIP interfaces.

   D. Can be used to assign network addresses and subnet masks for SLIP interfaces.

6 Which command is used to copy a switch configuration to a file on a host?

   a. write terminal

   b. write network

   c. write config

   d. upload config

   B. **write network**

7 The default setting for port speed on a 10/100 Mbps Ethernet port is:

   a. 10 Mbps

   b. 100 Mbps

   c. Auto

   d. Desirable

   C. Auto

8 The default setting for port speed on Token Ring switching ports is:

   a. Half-duplex

   b. Full-duplex

   c. Auto

   d. Desirable

   C. Auto

9 The default setting for port mode on 10/100 Mbps Ethernet ports and Token Ring switching ports is:

   a. Half-duplex

   b. Full-duplex

   c. Auto

   d. Desirable

   C. Auto

10 The default setting for port mode on 10 Mbps Ethernet ports and 100 Mbps Fast Ethernet is:

a. Half-duplex

b. Full-duplex

c. Auto

d. Desirable

A. Half-duplex

Answers to the Chapter 7 Q&A Section

1 The default IP address of sc0 is _____.

0.0.0.0

2 The default sc0 interface is assigned to VLAN _____.

1

3 The default gateway on Catalyst switch is set to _____.

0.0.0.0 with a metric of 0

4 The Virtual Trunking Protocol (VTP) interval is ____ minutes.

5

5 All trunk-capable ports are set to _____ mode for trunking.

Auto

6 SNMP community defaults are set to these parameters:

Read-Only: _____

Read-Write: _____

Read-Write-All: _____

Public, Private, Secret

7 The command-line connection is set to _____ mode.

Normal

8 If you are connected to the command line through the console port and you enter the **slip attach** command, you will lose the console port connection.

 a. True

 b. False

 A. True

9 You can configure a BOOTP server with the MAC and IP addresses of the switch.

 a. True

 b. False

 A. True

10 The *read only* SNMP community string gives what access?

 This mode gives read access to all objects in the MIB except the community strings, but it does not allow write access.

Answers to the Chapter 8 "Do I Know This Already?" Quiz

1 ISL tagging:

 a. Is performed by the NMP software.

 b. Is performed by the client stations.

 c. Is performed by the network devices or server with ISL intelligence.

 d. Is effective between Catalyst 5000 switches only.

 C. Is performed by the network devices or server with ISL intelligence.

2 VLAN Trunk Protocol:

 a. Synchronizes the configuration of two connected Catalyst 5000s from nontrunk to trunk.

 b. Supports four RMON groups on all Ethernet and Fast Ethernet ports.

 c. Advertises on Catalyst 5000 trunk ports VLAN information to other Catalyst 5000s in the same management domain.

 d. Uses a data-link protocol with a multicast destination address of 01-00-0CC-CC-CC.

 C. Advertises on Catalyst 5000 trunk ports VLAN information to other Catalyst 5000s in the same management domain.

3 Hardware- and software-based broadcast/multicast packet suppression is available in the software release 2.2.

   a. True

   b. False

   A. True

4 CGMP is:

   a. A messaging format for routers to download MAC tables to enable Layer 2 switching in the router.

   b. A protocol that provides dynamic configuration, forwarding multicast traffic to only those ports that have IP multicast clients attached.

   c. A serial protocol for communications between routers and switches.

   d. An alternative protocol that can be used instead of SNMP to manage groups of routers or switches.

   B. A protocol that provides dynamic configuration, forwarding multicast traffic to only those ports that have IP multicast clients attached.

5 Multicast traffic in the Catalyst 5000 switch is:

   a. Handled by the EARL learning broadcast or multicast addresses.

   b. Flooded out each port within the VLAN if the destination address is unknown.

   c. Handled by the EARL if it is dynamically programmed by the SAGE ASIC.

   d. Routed by the IGMP protocol.

   A. Handled by the EARL learning broadcast or multicast addresses.

6 The **set vtp** command sets up the management domain.

   a. True

   b. False

   A. True

7 All switches in the same VTP domain will automatically share VLAN information using VTP if configured correctly.

   a. True

   b. False

   A. True

8 An ISL trunk port must be:

  a. On the Supervisor module.

  b. An FDDI or CDDI connection.

  c. A Fast Ethernet port.

  d. Capable of maintaining several instances of the Spanning-Tree Protocol.

  C. A Fast Ethernet port.

9 Fast EtherChannel:

  a. Uses two line modules that act as a single module.

  b. Is configured as separate instances of spanning tree per link.

  c. Treats two links as a single spanning tree.

  d. Uses Gigabit Ethernet.

  C. Treats two links as a single spanning tree.

10 To verify that the VLAN configuration is correct, enter the _____ command.

  a. show vtp

  b. show vlan trunk

  c. show vlan

  d. show domain

  C. **show vlan**

Answers to the Chapter 8 Q&A Section

1 VTP version 1 and VTP version 2 are interoperable on switches in the same VTP domain.

  a. True

  b. False

  B. False

2 In VTP version 1, the transparent mode inspects VTP messages for the domain name and version, and forwards a message only if _____.

  The version and domain name match.

3 VTP is transmitted on all trunk connections, including _____, _____, and _____.

  ISL, 802.10, and LAN Emulation (LANE)

4 Determine the MAC address-to-VLAN mapping by entering the _____ command.

show cam

5 VLANs can extend across an FDDI network by multiplexing switched packets over a CDDI/FDDI interface using the _____ protocol.

802.10

6 CDDI/FDDI modules also support one _____ VLAN, which handles all non-802.10 encapsulated FDDI traffic.

Native (nontrunk)

7 By default, broadcast/multicast suppression is _____.

Disabled

8 Using the _____ bit in the packet destination address, the broadcast/multicast suppression circuitry determines whether the packet is a unicast or broadcast/multicast packet.

Individual/Group

9 Because software broadcast/multicast suppression uses a packet-based method of measuring broadcast/multicast activity, the most significant implementation factor is setting a threshold value for the number of _____ allowed.

Broadcast packets per second

10 CGMP manages multicast traffic in Catalyst 5000 series switches by enabling directed switching of IP multicast traffic within a network at rates greater than 1 million packets per second.

   a. True

   b. False

   A. True

Answers to the Chapter 9 "Do I KnowThis Already?" Quiz

1 You can manage the Catalyst 5000 via which of the following?

   a. Via the command-line interface through a terminal attached to the console port

   b. By attaching a modem and using the Point-to-Point Protocol (PPP)

   c. By attaching a terminal to the console port and using the Cisco Discovery Protocol (CDP)

   d. Via the command-line interface through a terminal attached to the parallel port on the Supervisor engine front panel

   A. Via the command-line interface through a terminal attached to the console port

2 Which of the following is true of the Telnet capability on the Catalyst 5000?

  a. Telnet capability on the Catalyst 5000 is not supported.

  b. Telnet capability on the Catalyst 5000 is supported, but it does not allow any outgoing Telnet.

  c. Telnet capability on the Catalyst 5000 is supported and allows up to three outgoing Telnet connections.

  d. Telnet capability on the Catalyst 5000 is supported and allows up to eight outgoing Telnet connections.

  D. Telnet capability on the Catalyst 5000 is supported and allows up to eight outgoing Telnet connections.

3 Which of the following is true of the Embedded RMON feature on the Catalyst 5000?

  a. The Embedded RMON feature on the Catalyst 5000 requires the use of a dedicated RMON probe or network analyzer.

  b. The Embedded RMON feature on the Catalyst 5000 supports four RMON groups: Statistics, History, Alarms, and Events.

  c. The Embedded RMON feature on the Catalyst 5000 is contained in the EARL ASIC.

  d. The Embedded RMON feature on the Catalyst 5000 enables you to monitor traffic from across a VLAN to a single port, for analysis.

  B. The Embedded RMON feature on the Catalyst 5000 supports four RMON groups: Statistics, History, Alarms, and Events.

4 Which of the following items accurately completes the statement: "Switched Port Analyzer (SPAN) lets you monitor traffic _____"?

  a. For analysis by a network analyzer.

  b. For analysis by an RMON probe.

  c. From across a VLAN (multiple ports) to a single port, for analysis.

  d. All of the above

  D. All of the above

5 Which of the following items accurately completes the statement: "The Fast Ethernet SwitchProbe _____"?

  a. Collects statistics on four RMON groups: Statistics, History, Alarms, and Events.

  b. Works with VlanDirector to provide a view of switched internetwork traffic.

  c. Collects RMON2 statistics on all seven protocol layers.

  d. Can communicate with the network management station across the SPAN port while monitoring traffic on the same interface.

  C. Collects RMON2 statistics on all seven protocol layers.

6 Which of the following items accurately completes the statement: "The Cisco Discovery Protocol (CDP) _____"?

  a. Uses the network layer.

  b. Allows network management applications to discover Cisco devices.

  c. Is media-dependent.

  d. Is media- and protocol-independent.

  D. Is media- and protocol-independent.

7 Match the following network management application to its description:

CiscoWorks Switched Internetwork Solutions (CWSI)_____

CiscoView_____

VlanDirector_____

TrafficDirector_____

  a. Enables you to graphically display traffic levels

  b. Graphically represents Cisco products with IP address

  c. Includes three network management applications

  d. Enables you to use the GUI representation of switches to drag the appropriate ports into the desired VLAN

C, B, D, A

8 To establish an out-of-band connection on a Catalyst 5000 series switch, a 100 percent Hayes-compatible modem, a ____ cable, is used between the modem and the switch.

  a. Straight-through

  b. Cross-over

  c. Parallel cable

  d. A straight-through cable with a 9 pin D-type connector

A. Straight-through

9 Which of the following items accurately completes the statement: "The console port of the Catalyst 5000 is an _____"?

  a. EIA/TIA-232 DCE

  b. EIA/TIA-232 DTE

  c. EIA/TIA-256 DCE

  d. EIA/TIA-256 DTE

A. EIA/TIA-232 DCE

10 Which of the following items provides the correct syntax to enable support for RMON on a 5000 series switch?

a. set snmp rmon

b. set rmon enable

c. set snmp rmon enable

d. set snmp rmon enable sc0

C. **set snmp rmon enable**

Answers to the Chapter 9 Q&A Section

1 What is the default value for the read-only community string?

Public

2 What is the default value for the read-write community string?

Private

3 What is the default value for the read-write-all community string?

Secret

4 What is the syntax to enable SNMP on a Catalyst 5000 switch?

Set snmp community {read-only | read-write | read-write-all}

5 What is the syntax to enable RMON on a Catalyst 5000 switch?

Set snmp rmon enable

6 The Catalyst 5000 series switch console port is what type of interface?

EIA/TIA-232

7 What is the command to verify that RMON is enabled on the switch?

show snmp

8 What is the command to display CDP information about neighboring systems?

show cdp neighbor

9 The Catalyst 5000 series switch supports how many simultaneous Telnet sessions?

8

10 CDP operates at what layer of the OSI model?

The data link layer

Answers to the Chapter 10 "Do I Know This Already?" Quiz

1 A red PS2 LED indication on the Supervisor indicates:

   a. The power supply in slot 2 is not installed.

   b. The power supply in slot 1 is not installed.

   c. The power supply is in a load-sharing mode.

   d. The power supply in slot 2 has failed.

   D. The power supply in slot 2 has failed.

2 The most common UTP cable problems are:

   a. Broken wire at the punch-down block

   b. Broken wire in the patch cable connector

   c. Straight-through instead of crossover cable

   d. a, b, c

   e. a, b

   f. b, c

   g. c, a

   D. a, b, c

3 Which of the following is true about the Fan LED on the Supervisor module:

   a. It indicates whether the fan is operational.

   b. If the fan is operational, the fan LED is green.

   c. If the fan is not operational, the fan LED is red.

   d. All of the above.

   D. All of the above.

4 The **show log** command can be used to display errors.

   a. True

   b. False

   A. True

5 The console connection can be used to display testing status during boot process.

  a. True

  b. False

  A. True

6 The AC OK (or DC OK) is _____ if input is supplied and power is on.

  a. Red

  b. Green

  c. Yellow

  d. Orange

  B. Green

7 The fan OK LED is _____ when the power supply fan is operating properly.

  a. Red

  b. Green

  c. Yellow

  d. Orange

  B. Green

8 The Output Failed LED is _____ if the power supply is not within the normal regulated limits.

  a. Red

  b. Green

  c. Yellow

  d. Orange

  A. Red

9 The **sh trunk** command displays the encapsulation information, including trunking status (trunking/nontrunking).

  a. True

  b. False

  A. True

10 The **sh vlan** command displays the virtual LAN type, status, and assigned modules/ ports.

   a. True

   b. False

   A. True

Answers to the Chapter 10 Q&A Section

1 Explain the function of the **sh arp** command.

   It displays the contents of the ARP table and aging time.

2 Explain the function of the **sh atm** command.

   It displays the ATM interfaces, traffic, VC and VLAN information and status.

3 Explain the function of the **sh cam** command.

   It displays the CAM table.

4 Explain the function of the **sh config** command.

   It displays the current system configuration.

5 Explain the function of the **sh fddi** command.

   It displays the settings of the FDDI/CDDI module.

6 Explain the function of the **sh flash** command.

   It displays the flash code names, version numbers, and sizes.

7 Explain the function of the **sh int** command.

   It displays the Supervisor module network interface information.

8 Explain the function of the **sh ip route** command.

   It displays the IP route information.

9 Explain the function of the **sh log** command.

   It displays the system or module error log.

10 Explain the function of the **sh mac** command.

   It displays the MAC counters for all of the installed modules.

11 Explain the function of the **sh module** command.

   It displays module status and information (hardware/firmware/software).

12 Explain the function of the **sh netstat** command.

It displays statistics for the various TCP/IP stack protocols and state of active network connections.

13 Explain the function of the **sh port** command.

It displays the port status and counters for all installed modules.

14 Explain the function of the **sh spantree** command.

It displays the spanning-tree information for the VLANs, including port states.

Answers to the Chapter 11 "Do I Know This Already?" Quiz

1 What is APaRT, and what is its function?

It stands for Automated Packet Recognition and Translation. APaRT uses content-addressable memory (CAM) table entries on the Catalyst 5000 FDDI or CDDI module to associate a specific Layer 2 frame type with each MAC address.

2 What media/connectors are supported in the FDDI/CDDI cards?

Category 5 UTP with RJ-45 connector, multimode fiber with MIC connector, and single-mode fiber with ST connector.

3 What is the distance limitation on a CDDI module?

100 meters

4 What is the distance limitation on an FDDI SMF Module?

32 km

5 What is the protocol that is used to create FDDI VLANs?

802.10

6 What would the value of the SAID be (default) if you typed the command **set vlan 100** (while in enable mode)?

100,100

7 What is the command to translate an Ethernet VLAN to an FDDI VLAN?

set vlan ether_vlan_num translation fddi_vlan_num

8 If you disable APaRT, what happens to fddicheck?

It is disabled.

9 In what environment might you consider disabling APaRT?

In an IP-only environment

Answers to the Chapter 11 Q&A Section

1 The 4-byte SAID field allows for:

   a. 255 VLANs

   b. 1000 VLANs

   c. 2.32 billion VLANs

   d. 4.29 billion VLANs

   D. 4.29 billion VLANs

2 When creating FDDI VLANs, it is important to configure the SAID values.

   a. True

   b. False

   B. False: The SAID values are created by default.

3 When creating FDDI trunks, only one end of the trunk must be set to on.

   a. True

   b. False

   B. False: Both ends of the trunk must be set to on.

4 What is the distance limitation on an FDDI SMF Module?

   32 km

5 What would be the value of the SAID (default) if you typed the command **set vlan 100** (while in enable mode)?

   100,100

6 What is the command to translate an Ethernet VLAN to an FDDI VLAN?

   set vlan ether_vlan_num translation fddi_vlan_num

7 If you disable APaRT, what happens to fddicheck?

   It is disabled.

8 In what environment might you consider disabling APaRT?

   In an IP-only environment

9 The FDDI module's implementation of the IEEE 802.10 protocol:

a. Uses the ICV field of the IEEE 802.10 frame.

b. Uses the SAID field of the Protected Header in the IEEE 802.10 frame.

c. Uses the SAID field of the Clear Header in the IEEE 802.10 frame.

d. All of the above.

C. Uses the SAID field of the Clear Header in the IEEE 802.10 frame.

Answers to the Chapter 12 "Do I Know This Already?" Quiz

1 What is a LECS, and what is it used for?

LECS stands for LAN Emulation Configuration Server, and it is responsible for assigning each LEC to an emulated LAN (ELAN).

2 What devices can be LAN Emulation Clients (LECs)? Which devices can be LAN Emulation Servers (LESs)?

LECs: Router, switch, ATM switch, workstation
LESs: Router, switch, ATM switch

3 In the ATM address structure, what is an ESI?

End station identifier

4 What command is used from the Catalyst to access the LANE module?

session module_num

5 What is the maximum distance that can be achieved using an MMF ATM LANE Module?

2 km

6 What are the performance characteristics of the ATM LANE module with respect to throughput?

155 Mbps

7 What media types are available using LANE?

UTP, multimode fiber, single-mode fiber

8 What is the configuration command to enable an LES? What component of ATM LANE does this also enable?

lane server-bus ethernet *elan-name*

Cisco uses one command to enable both the LES and the BUS because they are a pair.

Answers to the Chapter 12 Q&A Section

1 The LANE protocol is implemented in what layer of the OSI model?

The data link layer

2 ILMI is used for what purpose?

To discover ATM addresses and servers

3 Transmission to unknown stations is performed by which component of LANE?

The BUS: Broadcast and Unknown Server

4 What is a LECS, and what is it used for?

It stands for LAN Emulation Configuration Server; it is responsible for assigning each LEC to an emulated LAN.

5 ATM LANE uses which ATM Adaptation Layer?

LANE uses AAL5 to perform its functions.

6 What devices can be a LANE Client (LEC)? What devices can be an LES?

LEC: Router, switch, ATM switch, workstation

LES: Router, switch, ATM switch

7 In the ATM address structure, what is an ESI?

It is an end station identifier.

8 What command is used from the Catalyst to access the LANE module?

session module_num

9 What is the maximum distance that can be achieved using an MMF ATM LANE Module?

2 km

10 What is SSRP, and what is it used for?

Simple Server Redundancy Protocol; it allows for backup LECS and LES/BUS.

11 What are the performance characteristics of the ATM LANE module with respect to throughput?

155 Mbps

12 The command-line interface (CLI) for the LANE Module is similar to what other interface?

Cisco router IOS software CLI

13 On a dual-PHY LANE module, can both interfaces be active at the same time?

Only one interface can be active at one time; only physical redundancy is provided, and manual intervention is required.

14 How many ATM LANE Modules can be installed in a Catalyst 5000 switch?

A maximum of three LANE modules can be installed.

15 What LANE component gets the first MAC address of the pool?

Every LEC gets the first MAC address of the pool.

16 How many LECS are needed for each individual administrative domain?

Only one LECS is used in a particular administrative domain.

17 How many MAC addresses are assigned to an individual ATM LANE Module?

A pool of 16 MAC addresses is assigned.

18 What function does SAR perform?

The segmentation and reassembly of cells

19 What media types are available using LANE?

UTP, multimode fiber, and single-mode fiber

Answers to the Chapter 13 "Do I Know This Already?" Quiz

1 How many MAC addresses are supported on the Catalyst 1900 switch?

1024

2 Name three features that are common to both the Catalyst 1900 and the Catalyst 2820 switch.

Any three of the following:

AUI port on back of switch
IEEE 802.1 STP support
Shared memory architecture
Connection to a redundant power system
Up to four VLANs allowing ports to be grouped into separate logical networks
Cisco Group Membership Protocol (CGMP)
Port Security
Flooding and broadcast control
Cisco Discovery Protocol
Embedded RMON support
SNMP support

3 What three types of modules are available for the Catalyst 2820 expansion slots?

ATM, Fast Ethernet, and FDDI

4 Where is the EIA/TIA-232 located on the Catalyst 1900 and what is it used for?

It is located on the back of the Catalyst 1900 and is used as the console connection.

5 Name three features that are implemented in the Embedded Control Unit (ECU).

The ECU subsystem is responsible for diagnostics and error handling, switch configuration, STP, in-band and out-of-band management, statistics reporting, and control of front panel display.

6 What mode of switching would you use if you were experiencing FCS or alignment errors?

Store-and-Forward

7 When implementing Port Security, what is the maximum number of addresses that can be associated with a secure port?

132

8 Assume that you've configured a Broadcast threshold of 500. What happens to broadcasts if you choose the block option and the threshold is exceeded?

The switch drops all broadcast packets received from a port when the rate of broadcasts exceeds the broadcast threshold.

9 What does the hold time mean when configuring CDP?

The hold time is the amount of time that CDP information is held.

10 How many VLANs can be configured on a Catalyst 2820 switch?

4

11 Can the ATM LANE module be configured from the menus directly?

No, it must be configured from the CLI.

12 What command verifies the LANE configuration?

show lane from the CLI

Answers to the Chapter 13 Q&A Section

1 How many expansion slots are available on the Catalyst 2820 switch?

There are two expansion slots on the Catalyst 2820.

2 What is the maximum amount of 100BaseTX ports that the Catalyst 1900 switch can provide?

Depending on which model of switch you order, two 100BaseTX are the maximum you can get.

3 When the System LED on a Catalyst 1900 switch is amber, what does this indicate?

The System LED is amber when the switch fails the POST.

4 What does a rapidly blinking activity LED on the Catalyst 2820 FDDI Module indicate?

A rapidly blinking activity light indicates high traffic.

5 What three modes can be indicated by the Port LEDs using the Mode button on the front of a Catalyst 1900?

The three modes are Port Status, Bandwidth Utilization, and Full-duplex status.

6 To initially configure the Catalyst 1900 switch, you must connect a terminal to which port?

The EIA/TIA-232 interface connector on the back of the switch

7 If the destination address of a packet resides on the same port as the source address, what happens to the packet?

It will be filtered and dropped.

8 What are the maximum instances of Spanning Tree Protocol that can run in a Catalyst 2820 switch?

There can only be one instance of STP for each VLAN configured—because the maximum number of VLANs you can have is 4, the maximum number of instances of STP is also 4.

9 You could create a collapsed backbone network with a Catalyst 1900 by doing what?

A collapsed backbone network can be created with a Catalyst 1900 by connecting it to a 100BaseT backbone switch or router.

10 By default, the broadcasts and multicasts in a Catalyst 2820 switch's VLAN are forwarded where?

To all ports in the VLAN

11 The source port filtering feature on a Catalyst 2820 or 1900 switch is used to do what?

This feature can be used to designate restricted static addresses for which you want packets forwarded only if the packets are received on specified ports.

12 What mode of switching would you use if you were experiencing FCS or alignment errors?

Store-and-forward   .

13 Under which menu option do you find the information about the switching mode of a Catalyst 2820 or 1900 switch?

From the Main Menu, select [S] for System Configuration menu. From this menu, you can check the switching mode of the switch.

14 What is the out-of-band management connector called?

The EIA/TIA-232 port or connector

15 What methods can be used for in-band management of the Catalyst 2820 and 1900?

Telnet and SNMP can be used for in-band management.

16 What must be done before you can use in-band management with the Catalyst 2820 or 1900 switch?

You must configure an IP address, a subnet mask, and a default route.

17 Which menu enables you to configure the read and write community strings?

The SNMP Management menu, which is a selection off the Network Management menu, which is a selection from the Main Menu

18 What is the main task that is performed using the Multicast Registration menu on a Catalyst 2820 or 1900 switch?

To register a multicast address

19 What does SPAN stand for, and what function does it provide?

SPAN stands for Switch Port Analyzer, and it allows mirroring of traffic from one or more ports to another port to be used with a protocol analyzer or other piece of diagnostic equipment.

20 How many MAC addresses are supported on the Catalyst 1900 switch?

A maximum of 1024 addresses are supported on the Catalyst 1900 switch.

21 Which LANE component can be configured on a Catalyst 2820 ATM LANE module?

Only a LAN Emulation Client (LEC) can be configured on a Catalyst 2820 ATM LANE module.

22 What command is used to display the status of the ATM LANE module in a Catalyst 2820 switch?

You can use the CLI command **show lane** or select option [L] from the ATM Port Configuration menu.

23 What is the ATM address commonly known as?

The ATM address is commonly known as the NSAP, or Network Service Access Point.

24 What is the theoretical effect of configuring full-duplex on a 100BaseT link to a server also running in full-duplex mode?

By running both ends of the link at full-duplex, you effectively double your link bandwidth to 200 Mbps.

25 What three types of modules are available for the Catalyst 2820 expansion slots?

ATM, Fast Ethernet, and FDDI

26 When implementing Port Security, what is the maximum number of addresses that can be associated with a secure port?

132 addresses

27 What does the hold time mean when configuring CDP?

The hold time is the amount of time that CDP information is held on the switch.

Answers to the Chapter 14 "Do I Know This Already?" Quiz

1 What size is the buffer space on a 10 Mbps port on the Catalyst 3000 switch?

192 KB

2 How many MAC addresses per port are supported on the Catalyst 3000 switch?

1700

3 Which switch in the Catalyst 3000 series has seven expansion slots?

Catalyst 3200

4 The Catalyst Matrix has how many SCSI ports?

The Matrix has eight SCSI ports.

5 What is the name of the switching bus in the Catalyst 3000 architecture, and how much switching bandwidth does it support?

The AXIS Bus, and it supports 480 Mbps.

6 What is the PFPA, and what purpose does it serve?

The Proprietary Fat Pipe ASIC is the interface between the AXIS Bus and High-Speed LAN ports.

7 What is the name of the switching mode that enables the switch to monitor errors and change from cut-through to store-and-forward and back?

It is called Auto mode.

8 Which takes precedence regarding port duplex mode: hardware control or software control?

Software control

9 What is the name of the menu that enables you to view VLAN configuration information?

The VLAN Configuration menu

10 How many filter types are available?

There are four filter types.

11 What is the meaning of the Broadcast Water Mark when configuring Broadcast Suppression?

The Broadcast Water Mark is a user-defined percentage level based on broadcast traffic compared to total traffic on that port. If broadcast traffic exceeds this level, packets are suppressed until they fall below that level.

Answers to the Chapter 14 Q&A Section

1 The port duplex mode is set from which configuration menu?

The Port Configuration menu

2 Does the Router Configuration menu provide for rebooting the router module without resetting the switch?

Yes; there is a menu selection for this on the Router Configuration Menu.

3 Which switch in the Catalyst 3000 series has seven expansion slots?

Catalyst 3200

4 What is the maximum number of ports that can be used for EtherChannel?

The maximum number is seven.

5 What is the name of the switching bus in the Catalyst 3000 architecture, and how much switching bandwidth does it support?

The AXIS Bus, and it supports 480 Mbps.

6 The Catalyst 3200 supports a range of how much capacity, where capacity equals the number of simultaneous conversations possible on each port times the speed of the port?

The capacity range of the Catalyst 3200 is 40 Mbps–700 Mbps.

7 What size is the packet buffer on a 100 Mbps port on a Catalyst 3000?

A 512 KB buffer

8 What is the name of the switching mode that enables the switch to monitor errors and change from cut-through to store-and-forward and back?

It is called Auto mode.

9 A single Catalyst 3000 supports how many switched ports without using expansion slots?

16 ports are standard.

10 What is the maximum bandwidth provided by the Catalyst StackPort module?

280 Mbps

11 What is the maximum length of the SCSI-2 cable used to interconnect Catalyst 3000 switches to the Matrix?

1 meter

12 What is the name of the menu that enables you to view VLAN configuration information?

The VLAN Configuration menu

13 How many filter types are available?

There are four filter types.

14 If a Catalyst 3000 had 8 MB of memory, how many MAC addresses would be supported?

10,000 MAC addresses would be supported.

Transparent and Source-Route Bridging

Background

Transparent bridges were first developed at Digital Equipment Corporation (Digital) in the early 1980s. Digital submitted its work to the Institute of Electrical and Electronic Engineers (IEEE), which incorporated the work into the IEEE 802.1 standard. Transparent bridges are very popular in Ethernet/IEEE 802.3 networks.

Technology Basics

Transparent bridges are so named because their presence and operation are transparent to network hosts. When transparent bridges are powered on, they learn the network's topology by analyzing the source address of incoming frames from all attached network nodes. If, for example, a bridge sees a frame arrive on Line 1 from Host A, the bridge concludes that Host A can be reached through the network connected to Line 1. Through this process, transparent bridges build a table, such as the one in Figure B-1.

Figure B-1   *Transparent Bridging Table*

Host Address	Network Number
15	1
17	1
12	2
13	2
18	1
9	1
14	3

The bridge uses its table as the basis for traffic forwarding. When a frame is received on one of the bridge's interfaces, the bridge looks up the frame's destination address in its internal table. If the table contains an association between the destination address and any of the bridge's ports (aside from the one on which the frame was received), the frame is forwarded out the indicated port. If no association is found, the frame is flooded to all ports except the port on which the frame was received. Broadcasts and multicasts are also flooded in this way.

Transparent bridges successfully isolate intrasegment traffic, thereby reducing the traffic seen on each individual segment. This usually improves network response times seen by the user. The extent to which traffic is reduced and to which response times are improved depends on the volume of intersegment traffic relative to the total traffic, as well as the volume of broadcast and multicast traffic.

Bridging Loops

Without a bridge-to-bridge protocol, the transparent bridge algorithm fails when there are multiple paths of bridges and local-area networks (LANs) between any two LANs in the internetwork. Figure B-2 illustrates such a bridging loop.

Figure B-2   *Inaccurate Forwarding and Learning in Transparent Bridging Environments*

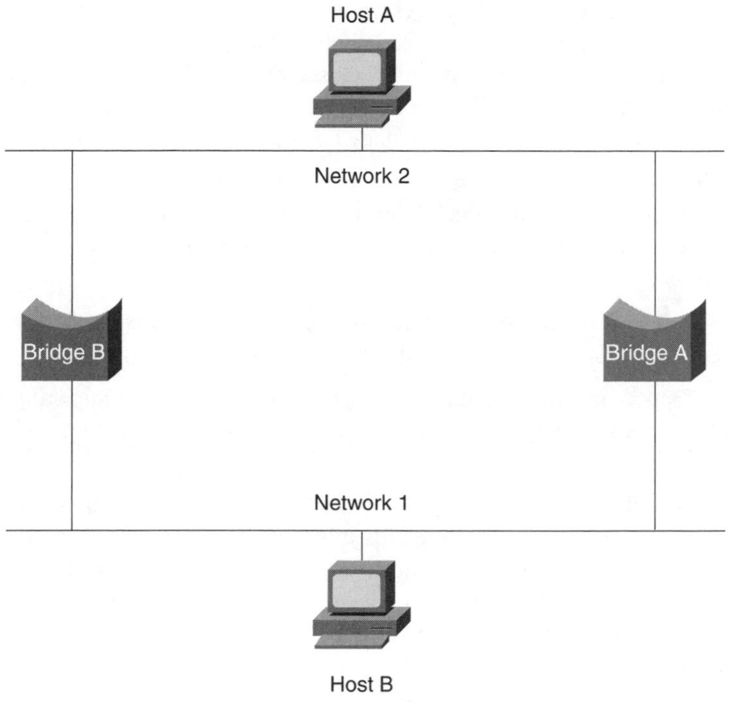

Host A

Network 2

Bridge B

Bridge A

Network 1

Host B

Suppose Host A sends a frame to Host B. Both bridges receive the frame and correctly conclude that Host A is on Network 2. Unfortunately, after Host B receives two copies of Host A's frame, both bridges will again receive the frame on their Network 1 interfaces because all hosts receive all messages on broadcast LANs. In some cases, the bridges will then change their internal tables to indicate that Host A is on Network 1. If so, when Host B replies to Host A's frame, both bridges will receive and subsequently drop the replies because their tables will indicate that the destination (Host A) is on the same network segment as the frame's source.

In addition to basic connectivity problems such as the one just described, the proliferation of broadcast messages in networks with loops represents a potentially serious network problem. Referring again to Figure B-2, assume that Host A's initial frame is a broadcast. Both bridges will forward the frames endlessly, using all available network bandwidth and blocking the transmission of other packets on both segments.

A topology with loops such as that shown in Figure B-2 can be useful as well as potentially harmful. A loop implies the existence of multiple paths through the internetwork. A network with multiple paths from source to destination can increase overall network fault tolerance through improved topological flexibility.

Spanning-Tree Algorithm

The spanning-tree algorithm (STA) was developed by Digital Equipment Corporation, a key Ethernet vendor, to preserve the benefits of loops while eliminating their problems. Digital's algorithm was subsequently revised by the IEEE 802 committee and was published in the IEEE 802.1d specification. The Digital algorithm and the IEEE 802.1d algorithm are not the same, nor are they compatible.

The STA designates a loop-free subset of the network's topology by placing those bridge ports that, if active, would create loops into a standby (blocking) condition. Blocked bridge ports can be activated in the event of primary link failure, providing a new path through the internetwork.

The STA uses a conclusion from graph theory as a basis for constructing a loop-free subset of the network's topology. Graph theory states the following:

> For any connected graph consisting of nodes and edges connecting pairs of nodes, there is a spanning tree of edges that maintains the connectivity of the graph but contains no loops.

Figure B-3 illustrates how the STA eliminates loops. The STA calls for each bridge to be assigned a unique identifier. Typically, this identifier is one of the bridge's *Media Access Control (MAC)* addresses plus a priority. Each port in every bridge is also assigned a unique (within that bridge) identifier (typically, its own MAC address). Finally, each bridge port is associated with a path cost. The path cost represents the cost of transmitting a frame onto a LAN through that port.

In Figure B-3, path costs are noted on the lines emanating from each bridge. Path costs are usually defaulted but can be assigned manually by network administrators.

Figure B-3 *Transparent Bridge Network Before Running STA*

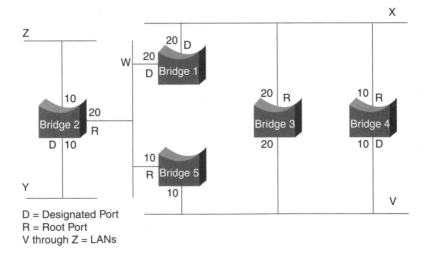

D = Designated Port
R = Root Port
V through Z = LANs

The first activity in spanning-tree computation involves the selection of the *root bridge*, which is the bridge with the lowest value bridge identifier. In Figure B-3, the root bridge is Bridge 1. Next, the *root port* on all other bridges is determined. A bridge's root port is the port through which the root bridge can be reached with the least aggregate path cost. This value (the least aggregate path cost to the root) is called the *root path cost*.

Finally, *designated bridges* and their *designated ports* are determined. A designated bridge is the bridge on each LAN that provides the minimum root path cost. A LAN's designated bridge is the only bridge allowed to forward frames to and from the LAN for which it is the designated bridge. A LAN's designated port is the port that connects it to the designated bridge.

In some cases, two or more bridges can have the same root path cost. For example, in Figure B-3, Bridges 4 and 5 can both reach Bridge 1 (the root bridge) with a path cost of 10. In this case, the bridge identifiers are used again, this time to determine the designated bridges. Bridge 4's LAN V port is selected over Bridge 5's LAN V port.

Using this process, all but one of the bridges directly connected to each LAN are eliminated, thereby removing all two-LAN loops. The STA also eliminates loops involving more than two LANs, while still preserving connectivity. Figure B-4 shows the results of applying the STA to the network shown in Figure B-3 and shows the tree topology more clearly. Comparing Figure B-3 to the pre-spanning-tree Figure B-4 shows that the STA has placed both Bridge 3 and Bridge 5's ports to LAN V in standby (blocking) mode.

Figure B-4   *Transparent Bridge Network After Running STA*

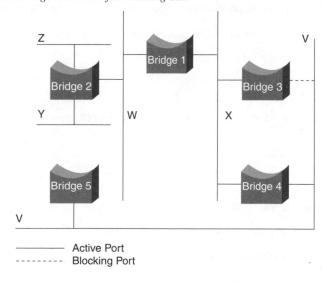

The spanning-tree calculation occurs when the bridge is powered up and whenever a topology change is detected. The calculation requires communication between the spanning-tree bridges, which is accomplished through configuration messages (sometimes called *bridge protocol data units*, or *BPDUs*). Configuration messages contain information identifying the bridge that is presumed to be the root (root identifier) and the distance from the sending bridge to the root bridge (root path cost). Configuration messages also contain the bridge and port identifier of the sending bridge and the age of information contained in the configuration message.

Bridges exchange configuration messages at regular intervals (typically 1 to 4 seconds). If a bridge fails (causing a topology change), neighboring bridges will soon detect the lack of configuration messages and will initiate a spanning-tree recalculation.

All transparent bridge topology decisions are made locally. Configuration messages are exchanged between neighboring bridges; no central authority on network topology or administration exists.

Frame Format

Transparent bridges exchange *configuration* messages and *topology change* messages. Configuration messages are sent between bridges to establish a network topology. Topology change messages are sent after a topology change has been detected to indicate that the STA should be rerun.

The IEEE 802.1d configuration message format is shown in Figure B-5.

Figure B-5 *Transparent Bridge Configuration Message Format*

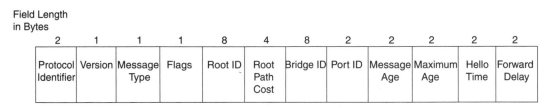

The fields of the transparent bridge configuration message are listed here:

- *Protocol identifier*—Contains the value zero.

- *Version*—Contains the value zero.

- *Message type*—Contains the value zero.

- *Flag*—A 1-byte field, of which only the first 2 bits are used. The topology change (TC) bit signals a topology change. The topology change acknowledgment (TCA) bit is set to acknowledge receipt of a configuration message with the TC bit set.

- *Root ID*—Identifies the root bridge by listing its 2-byte priority, followed by its 6-byte ID.

- *Root path cost*—Contains the cost of the path from the bridge sending the configuration message to the root bridge.

- *Bridge ID*—Identifies the priority and ID of the bridge sending the message.

- *Port ID*—Identifies the port from which the configuration message was sent. This field enables loops created by multiple attached bridges to be detected and dealt with.

- *Message age*—Specifies the amount of time since the root sent the configuration message on which the current configuration message is based.

- *Maximum age*—Indicates when the current configuration message should be deleted.

- *Hello time*—Provides the time period between root bridge configuration messages.

- *Forward delay*—Provides the length of time that bridges should wait before transitioning to a new state after a topology change. If a bridge transitions too soon, not all network links may be ready to change their state, and loops can result.

Topological change messages consist of only 4 bytes. They include a *protocol identifier* field, which contains the value zero; a *version* field, which contains the value zero; and a *message type* field, which contains the value 128.

Source-Route Bridging

The source-route bridging (SRB) algorithm was developed by IBM and was proposed to the IEEE 802.5 committee as the means to bridge between all local-area networks (LANs). The IEEE 802.5 committee subsequently adopted SRB into the IEEE 802.5 Token Ring LAN specification.

Since its initial proposal, IBM has offered a new bridging standard to the IEEE 802 committee: the *source-route transparent (SRT) bridging* solution. SRT bridging eliminates pure SRBs entirely, proposing that the two types of LAN bridges be transparent bridges and SRT bridges. Although SRT bridging has achieved support, SRBs are still widely deployed.

SRB Algorithm

SRBs are so named because they assume that the complete source-to-destination route is placed in all inter-LAN frames sent by the source. SRBs store and forward the frames as indicated by the route appearing in the appropriate frame field. Figure B-6 illustrates a sample SRB network.

Figure B-6   *Sample SRB Network*

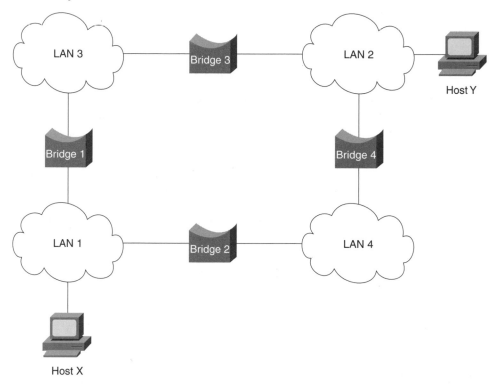

Referring to Figure B-6, assume that Host X wishes to send a frame to Host Y. Initially, Host X does not know whether Host Y resides on the same or a different LAN. To determine this, Host X sends out a test frame. If that frame returns to Host X without a positive indication that Host Y has seen it, Host X must assume that Host Y is on a remote segment.

To determine the exact remote location of Host Y, Host X sends an *explorer* frame. Each bridge receiving the explorer frame (Bridges 1 and 2, in this example) copies the frame onto all outbound ports. Route information is added to the explorer frames as they travel through the internetwork. When Host X's explorer frames reach Host Y, Host Y replies to each individually using the accumulated route information. Upon receipt of all response frames, Host X chooses a path based on some predetermined criteria.

In the example in Figure B-6, this process will yield two routes:

- LAN 1 to Bridge 1 to LAN 3 to Bridge 3 to LAN 2
- LAN 1 to Bridge 2 to LAN 4 to Bridge 4 to LAN 2

Host X must select one of these two routes. The IEEE 802.5 specification does not mandate the criteria that Host X should use in choosing a route, but it does make several suggestions, including the following:

- First frame received
- Response with the minimum number of hops
- Response with the largest allowed frame size
- Various combinations of the previous criteria

In most cases, the path contained in the first frame received will be used.

After a route is selected, it is inserted into frames destined for Host Y in the form of a *routing information field* (*RIF*). A RIF is included only in those frames destined for other LANs. The presence of routing information within the frame is indicated by the setting of the most significant bit within the source address field, called the *routing information indicator* (*RII*) bit.

Frame Format

The IEEE 802.5 RIF is structured as shown in Figure B-7.

Figure B-7 *IEEE 802.5 RIF*

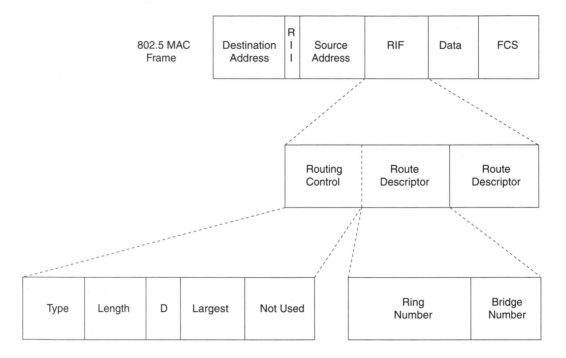

The fields of the RIF are listed here:

- The *routing control* field, which consists of the following subfields:

  — The *type* subfield in the RIF indicates whether the frame should be routed to a single node, a group of nodes that make up a spanning tree of the internetwork, or all nodes. The first type is called a *specifically routed* frame; the second type is called a *spanning-tree explorer*; and the third type is called an *all-paths explorer*. The spanning-tree explorer can be used as a transit mechanism for multicast frames. It can also be used as a replacement for the all-paths explorer in outbound route queries. In this case, the destination responds with an all-paths explorer.

  — The *length* subfield indicates the total length (in bytes) of the RIF.

— The *D* bit indicates the direction as to how the RIF should be read (forward or reverse) by the source route bridges.

— The *largest* field indicates the largest frame that can be handled along this route.

• The *route descriptor* field, of which there can be more than one. Each route descriptor field carries a ring number-bridge number pair that specifies a portion of a route. Routes, then, are simply alternating sequences of LAN and bridge numbers that start and end with LAN numbers.

Catalyst Switch Password Recovery Techniques

Catalyst 1200, 2900, 2926, and 5000 Password Recovery

To recover a lost password on Catalyst 1200, Catalyst 2900, Catalyst 2926, Catalyst 5000, and all concentrators, follow these steps:

1 You must be on the console.

2 Reboot the device.

3 When you see the password prompt, press Enter (null password for 30 seconds).

4 Type **Enable**.

5 When you see the password prompt, press Enter (null password for 30 seconds).

6 Change the password.

Catalyst 1600 Password Recovery

To recover a lost password on the Catalyst 1600, you need to push and hold the reset button on the switch until the LCD display displays "erasing mgmt passwd." If you let go at that point, the switch will reset and will come back without a password. This can also be achieved from TrueView.

Catalyst 1700, 1900, 2100, 2800, and 2820 Password Recovery

If you've lost the password on one of these Catalyst switches, contact Cisco's Technical Assistance Center (TAC), and open a case with a Cisco engineer. Provide the engineer with the switch serial number or MAC address (printed on the outside of some switches), and the engineer will supply a new password.

Catalyst 1800 Password Recovery

To recover a lost password on the Catalyst 1800, first look on the left side of the Catalyst 1800 switch. Two small black buttons should be mounted on a red holding device, located side by side inside the left cover. The black button located nearer to the front of the switch is the NMI switch.

To perform the password recovery, let the box boot up. When the box has finished booting up and asks for the password, press the NMI switch five times. This will reload the switch and reset the password to its default value of "public."

Catalyst 2600 Password Recovery

Press the System Request button to access the System Request Menu, and then Clear NVRAM.

CAUTION   This will clear the password but will also reset all configuration parameters to their default values, which means losing all options previously configured on the switch.

Catalyst 2900XL Password Recovery

If you lose the password for a Catalyst 2900XL switch, use the following procedure to recover the password:

1 Unplug the power cord from the back of the switch.

2 While holding down the Mode button, reconnect the power cord to the switch. You can release the Mode button a second or two after the LED above Port 1 x goes off.

3 Enter the **flash_init** command. The baud rate of the console port has now been reset to 9600; if your console stops working, reset its baud rate to 9600 as well.

4 Enter the **load_helper** command.

5 Enter the **dir flash** command.

6 Rename the configuration file; from "config.text" to "config.old," for example. Do this by entering the **rename flash:config.text flash:config.old** command.

7 Boot the system with the **boot** command.

8 Enter "**N**" when prompted to start the Setup program.

9 Enter "**N**" when asked if you want to continue with the configuration.

10 Enter "**en**" at the switch prompt.

11 Rename the configuration file with the **rename flash:config.old flash:config.text** command.

12 Copy the configuration file to memory using the **copy flash:config.text system:running-config**. Press Return in response to the two confirmation prompts.

13 The configuration file is now loaded, and you can configure a new password normally:

— Enter the **config terminal** command.

— Enter the **enable password** [*new_password*] command.

— Write the running configuration to the configuration file using the **write mem** command.

Catalyst 3000, 3100, and 3200 Password Recovery

If you lose the password for a Catalyst 3000, 3100, or 3200 switch, use the following procedure to recover the password:

1 Press the sys req button.

2 Move the arrow key to clear NVRAM.

3 Press Return.

4 The box will now reboot, with no password required.

Catalyst 3900 Password Recovery

If you lose the password for a Catalyst 3900 switch, use the following procedure to recover the password:

1 Press the sys req button to access the System Request menu.

2 Select **Clear the System Password**. This will clear only the system password. All other configuration parameters saved in NVRAM will be retained.

CAUTION   If the sys req button is pressed for more than 5 seconds, a download of the main image will be forced.

Configuring Spanning Tree
Understanding How Spanning-Tree Protocol Works

Configuring Spanning Tree is a white paper published by Cisco Systems.

STP is a link-management protocol that provides path redundancy while preventing undesirable loops in the network. For an Ethernet network to function properly, only one active path must exist between two stations. The Catalyst 5000 series switch uses STP (IEEE 802.1D bridge protocol) on all Ethernet, Fast Ethernet, Gigabit Ethernet, and Token Ring port-based VLANs. When you create fault-tolerant internetworks, you must have a loop-free path between all nodes in a network. In STP, an algorithm calculates the best loop-free path throughout a Catalyst 5000 series switched network. The Catalyst 5000 series switches send and receive spanning-tree packets at regular intervals. The switches do not forward the packets, but they use the packets to identify a loop-free path. The default configuration has STP enabled for all VLANs. Multiple active paths between stations cause loops in the network. If a loop exists in the network, you might receive duplicate messages. When loops occur, some switches see stations on both sides of the switch. This condition confuses the forwarding algorithm and enables duplicate frames to be forwarded.

To provide path redundancy, STP defines a tree that spans all switches in an extended network. STP forces certain redundant data paths into a standby (blocked) state. If one network segment in the STP becomes unreachable, or if STP costs change, the spanning-tree algorithm reconfigures the spanning-tree topology and reestablishes the link by activating the standby path.

STP operation is transparent to end stations, which do not detect whether they are connected to a single LAN segment or a switched LAN of multiple segments.

Election of the Root Switch

All switches in an extended LAN participating in STP gather information on other switches in the network through an exchange of data messages called *Bridge Protocol Data Units* (*BPDUs*). This exchange of messages results in the following actions:

- The election of a unique root switch for the stable spanning-tree network topology
- The election of a designated switch for every switched LAN segment

- The removal of loops in the switched network by placing redundant switch ports in a backup state

The STP root switch is the logical center of the spanning-tree topology in a switched network. All paths that are not needed to reach the root switch from anywhere in the switched network are placed in STP backup mode. Table D-1 describes the root switch variables that affect the entire spanning-tree performance.

Table D-1   *STP Root Switch Parameters*

Variable	Description
Hello Time	Determines how often the switch broadcasts its hello message to other switches.
Maximum Age Timer	Measures the age of the received protocol information recorded for a port and ensures that this information is discarded when its age limit exceeds the value of the maximum age parameter recorded by the switch. The timeout value is the maximum age parameter of the switches.
Forward Delay Timer	Monitors the time spent by a port in the learning and listening states. The timeout value is the forward delay parameter of the switches.

BPDUs contain information about the transmitting switch and its ports, including switch and port Media Access Control (MAC) addresses, switch priority, port priority, and port cost. The STP uses this information to elect the root switch and root port for the switched network, as well as the root port and designated port for each switched segment.

Figure D-1 shows how BPDUs enable an STP topology.

Figure D-1   *BPDUs Enabling a Stable STP Topology*

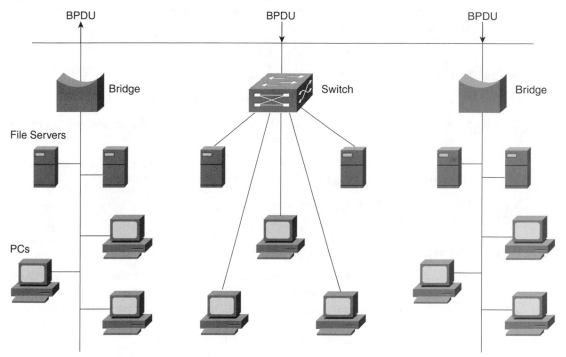

Bridge Protocol Data Units

The stable active topology of a switched network is determined by the following:

- The unique switch identifier (MAC address) associated with each switch

- The path cost to the root associated with each switch port

- The port identifier (MAC address) associated with each switch port

Each configuration BPDU contains the following minimal information:

- The unique identifier of the switch that the transmitting switch believes to be the root switch

- The cost of the path to the root from the transmitting port

- The identifier of the transmitting port

The switch sends configuration BPDUs to communicate and compute the spanning-tree topology. A MAC frame conveying a BPDU sends the switch group address to the destination address field. All switches connected to the LAN on which the frame is transmitted receive the BPDU. BPDUs are not directly forwarded by the switch, but the receiving switch uses the information in the frame to calculate a BPDU, and, if topology changes, to initiate a BPDU transmission.

A BPDU exchange results in the following:

- One switch is elected as the root switch.

- The shortest distance to the root switch is calculated for each switch.

- A designated switch is selected. This is the switch closest to the root switch through which frames will be forwarded to the root.

- A port for each switch is selected. This is the port that provides the best path from the switch to the root switch.

- Ports included in the STP are selected.

Creating a Stable STP Topology

If all switches are enabled with default settings, the switch with the lowest MAC address in the network becomes the root switch. In Figure D-2, Switch A is the root switch because it has the lowest MAC address. However, due to traffic patterns, the number of forwarding ports, or line types, Switch A might not be the ideal root switch. By increasing the priority (lowering the numerical priority number) of the ideal switch so that it becomes the root switch, you force an STP recalculation to form a new, stable topology.

Figure D-2   *Configuring a Stable Topology*

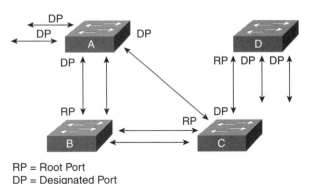

RP = Root Port
DP = Designated Port

When the stable STP topology is based on default parameters, the path between source and destination stations in a switched network might not be the most ideal. For instance, connecting higher-speed links to a port that has a higher number than the current root port can cause a root-port change. The goal is to make the fastest link the root port.

For example, assume that port 2 on Switch B is a fiber-optic link, and that port 1 on Switch B (an unshielded twisted-pair [UTP] link) is the root port. Network traffic might be more efficient over the high-speed fiber-optic link. By changing the Port Priority parameter for port 2 to a higher priority (a lower numerical value) than port 1, port 2 becomes the root port. The same change can occur by changing the Port Cost parameter for port 2 to a lower value than that of port 1.

STP Port States

Propagation delays can occur when protocol information passes through a switched LAN. As a result, topology changes can take place at different times and at different places in a switched network. When a switch port transitions directly from nonparticipation in the stable topology to the forwarding state, it can create temporary data loops. Ports must wait for new topology information to propagate through the switched LAN before starting to forward frames. They must allow the frame lifetime to expire for frames that have been forwarded using the old topology.

Each port on a switch using STP exists in one of the following five states:

- Blocking
- Listening
- Learning
- Forwarding
- Disabled

A port moves through these five states as follows:

- From initialization to blocking
- From blocking to listening (or to disabled)
- From listening to learning (or to disabled)
- From learning to forwarding (or to disabled)
- From forwarding to disabled

Figure D-3 illustrates how a port moves through the five states.

Figure D-3 *STP Port States*

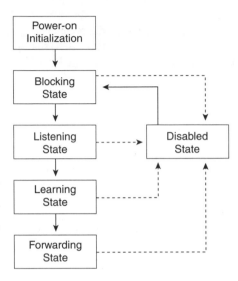

You can modify each port state by using management software. When you enable STP, every switch in the network goes through the blocking state and the transitory states of listening and learning at power-up. If properly configured, the ports then stabilize to the forwarding or blocking state.

When the spanning-tree algorithm places a port in the forwarding state, the following occurs:

- The port is put into the listening state while it waits for protocol information that suggests it should go to the blocking state.

- The port waits for the expiration of a protocol timer that moves the port to the learning state.

- In the learning state, the port continues to block frame forwarding as it learns station location information for the forwarding database.

- The expiration of a protocol timer moves the port to the forwarding state, where both learning and forwarding are enabled.

Blocking State

A port in the blocking state does not participate in frame forwarding, as shown in Figure D-4. After initialization, a BPDU is sent to each port in the switch. A switch initially assumes it is the root until it exchanges BPDUs with other switches. This exchange establishes which switch in the network is really the root. If only one switch resides in the network, no exchange occurs, the forward delay timer expires, and the ports move to the listening state. A switch always enters the blocking state following switch initialization.

Figure D-4   *Port 2 in Blocking State*

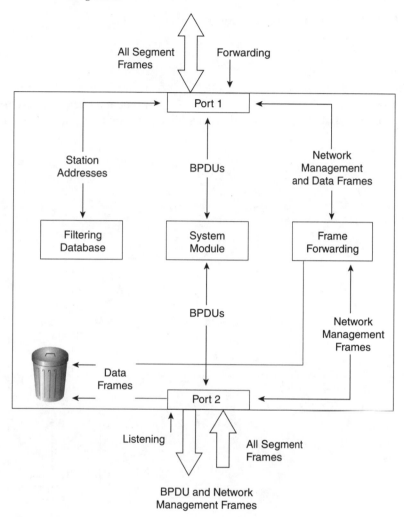

A port in the blocking state performs as follows:

- Discards frames received from the attached segment.

- Discards frames switched from another port for forwarding.

- Does not incorporate station location into its address database. (No learning occurs at this point, so there is no address database update.)

- Receives BPDUs and directs them to the system module.

- Does not transmit BPDUs received from the system module.
- Receives and responds to network management messages.

Listening State

The listening state is the first transitional state a port enters after the blocking state. The port enters this state when STP determines that the port should participate in frame forwarding. Learning is disabled in the listening state. Figure D-5 shows a port in the listening state.

Figure D-5   *Port 2 in Listening State*

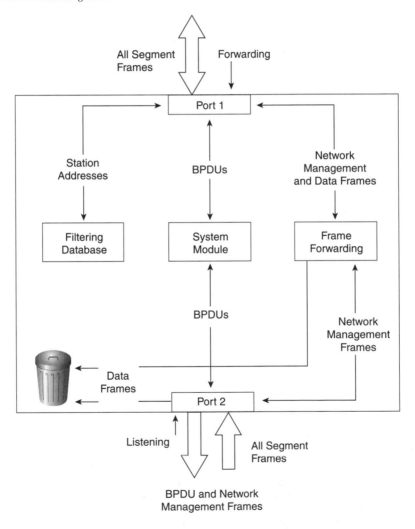

A port in the listening state performs as follows:

- Discards frames received from the attached segment.
- Discards frames switched from another port for forwarding.
- Does not incorporate station location into its address database. (No learning occurs at this point, so there is no address database update.)
- Receives BPDUs and directs them to the system module.
- Processes BPDUs received from the system module.
- Receives and responds to network management messages.

Learning State

A port in the learning state prepares to participate in frame forwarding. The port enters the learning state from the listening state.

A port in the learning state performs as follows:

- Discards frames received from the attached segment
- Discards frames switched from another port for forwarding
- Incorporates station location into its address database
- Receives BPDUs and directs them to the system module
- Receives, processes, and transmits BPDUs received from the system module
- Receives and responds to network management messages

Forwarding State

A port in the forwarding state forwards frames, as shown in Figure D-6. The port enters the forwarding state from the learning state.

Figure D-6 *Port 2 in Forwarding State*

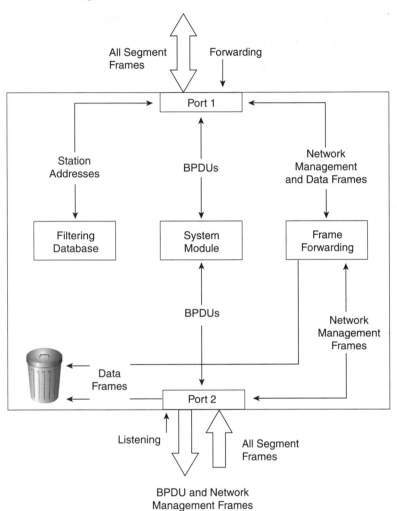

A port in the forwarding state performs as follows:

- Forwards frames received from the attached segment

- Forwards frames switched from another port for forwarding

- Incorporates station location information into its address database

- Receives BPDUs and directs them to the system module

- Processes BPDUs received from the system module

- Receives and responds to network management messages

CAUTION   Use the immediate-forwarding (portfast) mode only on ports connected to individual workstations to enable these ports to come up and go directly to the forwarding state, rather than having to go through the entire spanning-tree initialization process. To prevent illegal topologies, enable STP on ports connected to switches or other devices that forward messages.

Disabled State

A port in the disabled state does not participate in frame forwarding or STP, as shown in Figure D-7. A port in the disabled state is virtually nonoperational.

Figure D-7   *Port 2 in Disabled State*

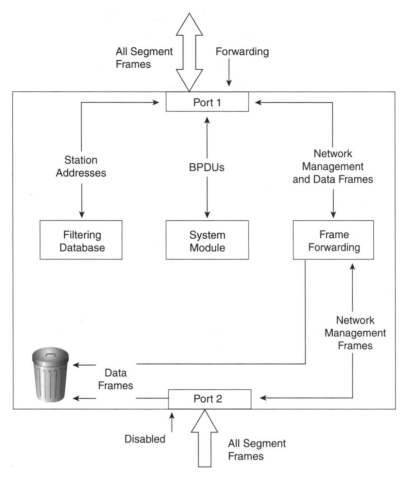

A disabled port performs as follows:

- Discards frames received from the attached segment.

- Discards frames switched from another port for forwarding.

- Does not incorporate station location into its address database. (No learning occurs, so there is no address database update.)

- Receives BPDUs, but does not direct them to the system module.

- Does not receive BPDUs for transmission from the system module.

- Receives and responds to network management messages.

Understanding How Spanning-Tree for Token Ring Works

Typically, each VLAN runs one instance of STP to prevent loops in the bridge topology. However, Token Ring runs STP both at the Token Ring Concentrator Relay Function (TrCRF) level and the Token Ring Bridge Relay Function (TrBRF) level. The TrCRF STP removes loops in the logical ring. The TrBRF STP is similar to the Ethernet STP, interacting with external bridges to remove loops from the bridge topology.

The Catalyst 5000 series Token Ring module supports these STPs:

- IEEE 802.1D STP

- IBM STP

- Cisco STP

The Catalyst 5000 series switch uses the IEEE 802.1D and IBM STPs on TrBRFs. The STP that runs on the TrCRF is either the Cisco or IEEE STP, depending on the bridging mode you configured for the TrCRF with the **set vlan** command.

CAUTION   Certain TrBRF STP and TrCRF bridge mode configurations are incompatible and can place the TrCRFs in a blocked state. For more information about these configurations, see the "Setting the Spanning-Tree Port State" section later in this appendix.

Default Spanning-Tree Configuration

Table D-2 shows the default STP configuration.

Table D-2   *STP Default Configuration*

Feature	Default Value
Enable state	STP enabled for all VLANs
Port priority	128
Port cost	62
Bridge priority	32,768

Configuring Spanning-Tree

The following sections describe how to configure STP on any Ethernet, Fast Ethernet, Gigabit Ethernet, and Token Ring port-based VLANs.

Enabling STP

To enable STP, perform this task in privileged mode:

Task	Command
Step 1 Enable spanning tree on the desired VLAN.	**set spantree enable** [*vlan*]
Step 2 Verify that spanning tree is enabled.	**show spantree** [*vlan*]

NOTE   STP is enabled by default on VLAN 1 and on all newly created VLANs.

Example D-1 shows how to enable spanning tree and verify that it is enabled:

Example D-1 *Enabling Spanning Tree*

```
Console> (enable) set spantree enable 100
Spantree 100 enabled.

Console> (enable) show spantree 100
VLAN 100
Spanning tree enabled
Spanning tree type        ieee
Designated Root           00-10-0d-40-34-63
Designated Root Priority  32768
Designated Root Cost      19
Designated Root Port      1/2
Root Max Age   20 sec    Hello Time 2  sec   Forward Delay 15 sec
Bridge ID MAC ADDR        00-10-0d-aa-cc-63
Bridge ID Priority        32768
Bridge Max Age 20 sec    Hello Time 2  sec   Forward Delay 15 sec
Port     Vlan Port-State     Cost   Priority Fast-Start  Group-method
-------- ---- ------------- ----- -------- ---------- -----------
 1/2     100  forwarding       19       32  disabled
Console> (enable)
```

Configuring the Port Priority

You can change the port priority of switch ports. The port with the lowest priority value forwards frames for all VLANs. The possible port priority range is 0 through 63; the default is 32. If all ports have the same priority value, the port with the lowest port number forwards frames.

To change the port priority for a port, perform this task in privileged mode:

Task	Command
Step 1 Change the port priority for a switch port.	**set spantree portpri** *mod_num/port_num priority* [*vlans*]
Step 2 Verify the port priority setting.	**show spantree** [*mod_num/port_num*]

Example D-2 shows how to change the port priority for a port and verify the configuration:

Example D-2 *Configuring Port Priority*

```
Console> (enable) set spantree portpri 1/2 20
Bridge port 1/2 port priority set to 20.

Console> (enable) show spantree 1/2
Port      Vlan Port-State      Cost  Priority  Fast-Start  Group-method
--------- ---- -------------   ----- --------  ----------  -----------
 1/2      1    blocking         19      20      disabled
 1/2      100  forwarding       19      20      disabled
 1/2      521  blocking         19      20      disabled
 1/2      522  blocking         19      20      disabled
 1/2      523  blocking         19      20      disabled
 1/2      524  blocking         19      20      disabled
 1/2      1003 not-connected    19      20      disabled
 1/2      1005 not-connected    19       4      disabled
Console> (enable)
```

Configuring the Port VLAN Priority

You can set the port priority for a port on a per-VLAN basis. The port with the lowest priority value for a specific VLAN forwards frames for that VLAN. The possible port-VLAN priority range is 0 through 63; the default is 32. If all ports have the same priority value for a particular VLAN, the port with the lowest port number forwards frames for that VLAN.

To change the port-VLAN priority for a port, perform this task in privileged mode:

Task	Command
Step 1 Change the port-VLAN priority for a VLAN on a switch port.	**set spantree portvlanpri** *mod_num/port_num priority* [*vlans*]
Step 2 Verify the port-VLAN priority setting.	**show spantree** [*mod_num/port_num*]

Example D-3 shows how to change the port-VLAN priority on a port and verify the configuration:

Example D-3 *Configuring Port-VLAN Priority*

```
Console> (enable) set spantree portvlanpri 1/2 1 100
Port 1/2 vlans 1-99,101-1004 using portpri 32.
Port 1/2 vlans 100 using portpri 1.
Port 1/2 vlans 1005 using portpri 4.

Console> (enable) show spantree 1/2
Port       Vlan  Port-State      Cost   Priority  Fast-Start  Group-method
---------  ----  --------------  -----  --------  ----------  ------------
  1/2      1     blocking          19        32   disabled

  1/2      100   forwarding        19         1   disabled
  1/2      521   blocking          19        32   disabled
  1/2      522   blocking          19        32   disabled
  1/2      523   blocking          19        32   disabled
  1/2      524   blocking          19        32   disabled
  1/2      1003  not-connected     19        32   disabled
  1/2      1005  not-connected     19         4   disabled
Console> (enable)
```

Configuring Port Cost

You can change the port cost of switch ports. Ports with lower port costs are more likely to be chosen to forward frames. Assign lower numbers to ports attached to faster media (such as full-duplex) and higher numbers to ports attached to slower media. The possible range is 1 to 65,535; the default differs for different media. Path cost is typically 1000 ÷ LAN speed in megabits per second.

To change the port cost for a port, perform this task in privileged mode:

Task	Command
Step 1 Change the port cost for a switch port.	**set spantree portcost** *mod_num/port_num cost*
Step 2 Verify the port cost setting.	**show spantree** [*mod_num/port_num*]

Example D-4 shows how to change the port cost on a port and verify the configuration:

Example D-4 *Changing the Port Cost*

```
Console> (enable) set spantree portcost 1/2 10
Spantree port 1/2 path cost set to 10.

Console> (enable) show spantree 1/2
Port       Vlan  Port-State     Cost   Priority  Fast-Start  Group-method
---------  ----  -------------  -----  --------  ----------  ------------
  1/2      1     forwarding      10       20     disabled
  1/2      100   forwarding      10       20     disabled
  1/2      521   forwarding      10       20     disabled
  1/2      522   forwarding      10       20     disabled
  1/2      523   forwarding      10       20     disabled
  1/2      524   forwarding      10       20     disabled
  1/2      1003  not-connected   10       20     disabled
  1/2      1005  not-connected   10        4     disabled
Console> (enable)
```

Configuring Port-VLAN Cost

You can change the port cost for a port on a per-VLAN basis. Ports with lower port-VLAN costs are more likely to be chosen to forward frames. You should assign lower numbers to ports attached to faster media (such as full-duplex) and higher numbers to ports attached to slower media. The possible range is 1 to 65,535; the default differs for different media.

To change the port-VLAN cost for a port, perform this task in privileged mode:

Task	Command
Step 1 Change the port-VLAN cost for a VLAN on a switch port.	**set spantree portvlancost** *mod_num/port_num* **cost** *cost* [*vlans*]
Step 2 Verify the port-VLAN cost setting.	**show spantree** [*mod_num/port_num*]

Example D-5 shows how to change the port-VLAN cost on a port and verify the configuration:

Example D-5 *Changing the Port-VLAN Cost on a Port*

```
Console> (enable) set spantree portvlancost 1/2 cost 10 100
Port 1/2 VLANs 1-99,101-1005 have path cost 19.
Port 1/2 VLANs 100 have path cost 10.

Console> (enable) show spantree 1/2
Port      Vlan  Port-State     Cost    Priority  Fast-Start  Group-method
--------- ----  -------------  -----   --------  ----------  ------------
 1/2        1   blocking          19         20  disabled

 1/2      100   forwarding        10         20  disabled
 1/2      521   blocking          19         20  disabled
 1/2      522   blocking          19         20  disabled
 1/2      523   blocking          19         20  disabled
 1/2      524   blocking          19         20  disabled
 1/2     1003   not-connected     19         20  disabled
 1/2     1005   not-connected     19          4  disabled
Console> (enable)
```

Configuring Spanning-Tree PortFast

With spanning-tree PortFast, a switch port connected to a single workstation or server can connect faster by causing spanning tree to enter the forwarding state immediately, bypassing the listening and learning states.

NOTE   Spanning-tree PortFast should be used only when connecting a single end station to a switch port. Otherwise, you might create a network loop.

To enable PortFast on a switch port, perform this task in privileged mode:

Task	Command
Step 1 Enable PortFast on a switch port connected to a single workstation or server.	**set spantree portfast** *mod_num/port_num* {**enable** | **disable**}
Step 2 Verify the PortFast setting.	**show spantree** [*mod_num/port_num*]

Example D-6 shows how to enable PortFast on a port and verify the configuration:

Example D-6 *Enabling PortFast*

```
Console> (enable) set spantree portfast 1/2 enable
Warning: Spantree port fast start should only be enabled on ports connected
to a single host.  Connecting hubs, concentrators, switches, bridges, etc. to
a fast start port can cause temporary spanning tree loops.  Use with caution.
Spantree port 1/2 fast start enabled.

Console> (enable) show spantree 1/2
Port       Vlan Port-State      Cost  Priority  Fast-Start  Group-method
---------- ---- --------------- ----- --------- ----------- ------------
 1/2       1    blocking          19        20  enabled
 1/2       100  forwarding        10        20  enabled
 1/2       521  blocking          19        20  enabled
 1/2       522  blocking          19        20  enabled
 1/2       523  blocking          19        20  enabled
 1/2       524  blocking          19        20  enabled
 1/2       1003 not-connected     19        20  enabled
 1/2       1005 not-connected     19         4  enabled
Console> (enable)
```

Configuring a Primary Root Switch

To configure a switch as the primary root switch, perform this task in privileged mode:

set spantree root *vlans* [**dia** *network_diameter*] [**hello** *hello_time*]

Example D-7 shows how to specify the primary root switch for VLANs 1 through 10:

Example D-7 *Specifying the Primary Root Switch for VLANs*

```
Console> (enable) set spantree root 1-10 dia 4
VLANs 1-10 bridge priority set to 8192
VLANs 1-10 bridge max aging time set to 14 seconds.
VLANs 1-10 bridge hello time set to 2 seconds.
VLANs 1-10 bridge forward delay set to 9 seconds.
Switch is now the root switch for active VLANs 1-6.
Console> (enable)
```

NOTE   Run the **set spantree root** command on backbone switches or distribution switches only, not on access switches.

The **set spantree root** command reduces the bridge priority (the value associated with the switch) from the default (32,768) to a significantly lower value, which enables the switch to become the root switch.

When you specify a switch as the primary root, the default bridge priority is modified so that it becomes the root for the specified VLANs. Set the bridge priority to 8192. If this setting does not result in the switch becoming a root, modify the bridge priority to be 100 less than the bridge priority of the current root switch. Because different VLANs could potentially have different root switches, the bridge VLAN-priority chosen makes this switch the root for all the VLANs specified. If reducing the bridge priority as low as 1 still does not make the switch the root switch, the system will display a message.

Configuring a Secondary Root Switch

To configure a switch as the secondary root switch, perform this task in privileged mode:

set spantree root [**secondary**] *vlans* [**dia** *network_diameter*] [**hello** *hello_time*]

Example D-8 shows how to specify the secondary root switch for VLANs 22 and 24:

Example D-8 *Specifying the Secondary Root Switch*

```
Console> (enable) set spantree root secondary 22,24 dia 5 hello 1
VLANs 22,24 bridge priority set to 16384.
VLANs 22,24 bridge max aging time set to 10 seconds.
VLANs 22,24 bridge hello time set to 1 second.
VLANs 22,24 bridge forward delay set to 7 seconds.
Console> (enable)
```

The **set spantree root secondary** command reduces the bridge priority to 16,384, making it the probable candidate to become the root switch if the primary root switch fails. You can run this command on more than one switch to create multiple backup switches in case the primary root switch fails.

Configuring STP for a TrBRF

You can configure the type of STP to be used by a TrBRF. Note that the following STP and bridge mode configurations are incompatible and can place logical ports in a blocked state:

- TrBRF is running the IBM STP, and the TrCRF is in SRT mode.
- TrBRF is running the IEEE STP, and the TrCRF is in SRB mode.

For more information, see the "Setting the Spanning-Tree Port State" section later in this appendix.

To specify a STP for a TrBRF, perform this task in privileged mode:

set vlan *vlan_num* [**stp** {**ieee** | **ibm**}]

Example D-9 shows how to specify the STP for a TrBRF:

Example D-9 *Specifying the STP for a TrBRF*

```
Console> (enable) set vlan 950 stp ieee
Vlan 950 configuration successful
Console> (enable)
```

Setting the Spanning-Tree Port State

When you enable STP, every switch in the network goes through the transitory listening and learning states at power-up. If properly configured, the logical ports then stabilize to the forwarding or blocking state. However, with TrBRFs and TrCRFs, the following exceptions require you to manually set the state of a logical port of a TrBRF:

- TrBRF is running the IBM STP, and the TrCRF is in SRT mode.

- TrBRF is running the IEEE STP, and the TrCRF is in SRB mode.

NOTE   If one of these configurations occurs, the logical ports are put in a blocked state and no STP is run.

You can use the **set spantree portstate** command to manually set the state of a logical port to blocked or forwarding mode.

To set the state of a logical port manually, perform this task in privileged mode:

> **set spantree portstate** *trcrf* {**auto** | **block** | **forward**} [*trbrf*]

NOTE   If you disable the STP state for a TrBRF using the **set spantree** command, the logical ports of the TrBRF are put in forwarding state, regardless of the state you configured using the **set spantree portstate** command.

Example D-10 shows how to set the STP state of a logical port:

Example D-10 *Setting the STP State*

```
Console> (enable) set spantree portstate 950 forward
Portstate successfully set for tokenring crf 950
Console> (enable)
```

Specifying the STP Functional Address for a TrBRF

To configure a TrBRF running IEEE STP to use the bridge functional address instead of the IEEE STP address, perform this task in privileged mode:

```
set spantree multicast-address vlan_num ibm
```

Configuring Additional STP Parameters

To configure additional STP parameters, perform one of these tasks in privileged mode:

Task	Command
Set the bridge forward delay for a VLAN.	**set spantree fwddelay** *delay* [*vlan*]
Set the bridge hello time for a VLAN.	**set spantree hello** *interval*
Set the bridge maximum aging time for a VLAN.	**set spantree maxage agingtime** [*vlan*]
Set the bridge priority for a VLAN.	**set spantree priority** *bridge_priority* [*vlan*]

Disabling STP

To disable STP, enter this command in privileged mode:

```
set spantree disable [vlan]
```

NOTE   In a Token Ring environment, if you disable STP for a TrBRF, then all TrCRFs with this TrBRF as a parent are set to the forwarding state.

Using Spanning-Tree UplinkFast Switchover

This section describes the operation and configuration of the UplinkFast feature (also known as spanning-tree UplinkFast Switchover).

Understanding How UplinkFast Works

UplinkFast provides fast convergence after a spanning-tree topology change and achieves load balancing between redundant links using uplink groups. An uplink group is a set of ports (per VLAN), only one of which is forwarding at any given time. Specifically, an uplink group consists of the root port (which is forwarding) and a set of blocked ports, except for self-looping ports. The uplink group provides an alternate path in case the currently forwarding link fails.

NOTE   UplinkFast is most useful in wiring-closet switches. This feature may not be useful for other types of applications.

Figure D-8 shows an example topology with no link failures. Switch A, the root switch, is connected directly to Switch B over link L1 and to Switch C over link L2. The port on Switch C that is connected directly to Switch B is in blocking state.

Figure D-8   *UplinkFast Example Before Direct Link Failure*

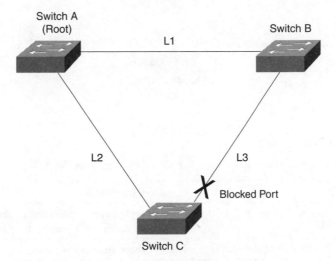

If Switch C detects a link failure on the currently active link L2 (a *direct* link failure), UplinkFast unblocks the blocked port on Switch C and transitions it to the forwarding state without going through the listening and learning states, as shown in Figure D-9. This switchover takes approximately 1 to 5 seconds.

Figure D-9 *UplinkFast Example After Direct Link Failure*

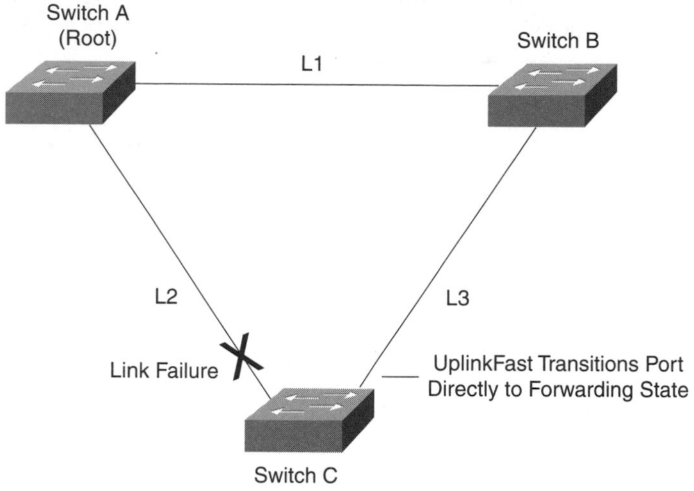

Configuring UplinkFast

To enable UplinkFast, perform this task in privileged mode:

Task	Command
Step 1 Enable UplinkFast on the switch.	**set spantree uplinkfast enable** [**rate** *station_update_rate*] [**all-protocols off**	**on**]
Step 2 Verify that UplinkFast is enabled.	**show spantree uplinkfast**

NOTE   When you enable the **set spantree uplinkfast** command, it affects all VLANs on a Catalyst 5000 series switch. You cannot configure UplinkFast on an individual VLAN.

The **set spantree uplinkfast enable** command increases the path cost of all ports on the switch, making it unlikely that the switch becomes the root switch. The *station_update_rate* value represents the number of multicast packets transmitted per 100 milliseconds (the default is 15 packets per millisecond).

Example D-11 shows how to enable UplinkFast with a station-update rate of 40 packets per 100 milliseconds. This example also shows how to verify that UplinkFast is enabled:

Example D-11 *Enabling UplinkFast*

```
Console> (enable) set spantree uplinkfast enable
VLANs 1-1005 bridge priority set to 49152.
The port cost and portvlancost of all ports set to above 3000.
Station update rate set to 15 packets/100ms.
uplinkfast all-protocols field set to off.
uplinkfast enabled for bridge.

Console> (enable) show spantree uplinkfast
Station update rate set to 15 packets/100ms.
uplinkfast all-protocols field set to off.
VLAN           port list
-----------------------------------------------
1              1/1(fwd),1/2
100            1/2(fwd)
521            1/1(fwd),1/2
522            1/1(fwd),1/2
523            1/1(fwd),1/2
524            1/1(fwd),1/2
Console> (enable)
```

Using Spanning-Tree BackboneFast Convergence

This section describes the function and configuration of the BackboneFast feature (also known as the spanning-tree BackboneFast Convergence feature).

Understanding How BackboneFast Works

BackboneFast is initiated when a root port or blocked port on a switch receives inferior BPDUs from its designated bridge. An inferior BPDU identifies one switch as both the root bridge and the designated bridge. When a switch receives an inferior BPDU, it indicates that a link to which the switch is not directly connected (an *indirect* link) has failed (that is, the designated bridge has lost its connection to the root bridge). Under normal spanning-tree rules, the switch ignores inferior BPDUs for the configured maximum aging time, as specified by the *agingtime* variable of the **set spantree maxage** command.

The switch tries to determine whether it has an alternate path to the root bridge. If the inferior BPDU arrives on a blocked port, the root port and other blocked ports on the switch become alternate paths to the root bridge. (Self-looped ports are not considered alternate paths to the root bridge.) If the inferior BPDU arrives on the root port, all blocked ports become alternate paths to the root bridge. If the inferior BPDU arrives on the root port and there are no blocked ports, the switch assumes that it has lost connectivity to the root bridge, causes the maximum aging time on the root to expire, and becomes the root switch according to normal spanning-tree rules.

If the switch has alternate paths to the root bridge, it uses these alternate paths to transmit a new kind of PDU called the *Root Link Query PDU*. The switch sends the Root Link Query PDU out all alternate paths to the root bridge. If the switch determines that it still has an alternate path to the root, it causes the maximum aging time on the ports on which it received the inferior BPDU to expire. If all the alternate paths to the root bridge indicate that the switch has lost connectivity to the root bridge, the switch causes the maximum aging times on the ports on which it received an inferior BPDU to expire. If one or more alternate paths can still connect to the root bridge, the switch makes all ports on which it received an inferior BPDU its designated ports and moves them out of the blocking state (if they were in blocking state), through the listening and learning states, and into the forwarding state.

Figure D-10 shows an example topology with no link failures. Switch A, the root switch, connects directly to Switch B over link L1 and to Switch C over link L2. The port on Switch C that connects directly to Switch B is in the blocking state.

Figure D-10 *BackboneFast Example Before Indirect Link Failure*

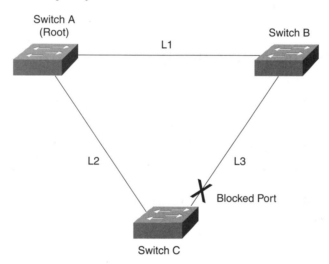

If link L1 fails, Switch C detects this failure as an indirect failure because it is not connected directly to link L1. Switch B no longer has a path to the root switch. BackboneFast enables the blocked port on Switch C to move immediately to the listening state without waiting for the maximum aging time for the port to expire. BackboneFast then transitions the port on Switch C to the forwarding state, providing a path from Switch B to Switch A. This switchover takes approximately 30 seconds. Figure D-11 shows how BackboneFast reconfigures the topology to account for the failure of link L1.

Figure D-11   *BackboneFast Example After Indirect Link Failure*

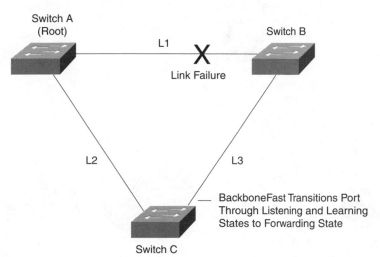

If a new switch is introduced into a shared-medium topology, BackboneFast is not activated. Figure D-12 shows a shared-medium topology in which a new switch is added. The new switch begins sending inferior BPDUs that say it is the root switch. However, the other switches ignore these inferior BPDUs, and the new switch learns that Switch B is the designated bridge to Switch A, the root switch.

Figure D-12 *Adding a Switch in a Shared-Medium Topology*

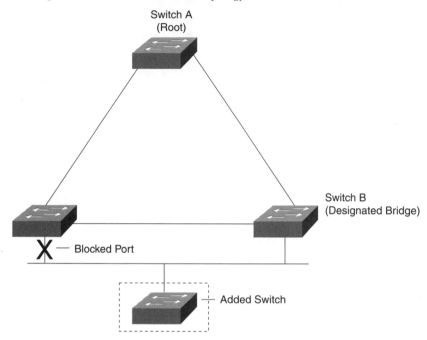

Configuring BackboneFast

This section describe how to configure BackboneFast Convergence.

Enabling BackboneFast

To enable BackboneFast, perform this task in privileged mode:

Task	Command
Step 1 Enable BackboneFast on the switch.	**set spantree backbonefast enable**
Step 2 Verify that BackboneFast is enabled.	**show spantree backbonefast**

NOTE For BackboneFast to work, you must enable it on all switches in the network. BackboneFast is not supported on Token Ring VLANs. This feature is supported for use with third-party switches.

Example D-12 shows how to enable BackboneFast on the switch and how to verify the configuration:

Example D-12 *Enabling BackboneFast*

```
Console> (enable) set spantree backbonefast enable
Backbonefast enabled for all VLANs

Console> (enable) show spantree backbonefast
Backbonefast is enabled.
Console> (enable)
```

Displaying BackboneFast Statistics

To display BackboneFast statistics, perform this task in privileged mode:

> **show spantree summary**

Example D-13 shows how to display BackboneFast statistics:

Example D-13 *Displaying Backbone Fast Statistics*

```
Console> (enable) show spantree summary
Summary of connected spanning tree ports by vlan
Uplinkfast disabled for bridge.
Backbonefast enabled for bridge.
Vlan  Blocking Listening Learning Forwarding STP Active
----- -------- --------- -------- ---------- ----------
    1        0         0        0          1          1
      Blocking Listening Learning Forwarding STP Active
----- -------- --------- -------- ---------- ----------
Total        0         0        0          1          1

BackboneFast statistics
-----------------------
Number of inferior BPDUs received (all VLANs)   : 0
Number of RLQ req PDUs received (all VLANs)     : 0
Number of RLQ res PDUs received (all VLANs)     : 0
Number of RLQ req PDUs transmitted (all VLANs)  : 0
Number of RLQ res PDUs transmitted (all VLANs)  : 0
Console> (enable)
```

Disabling BackboneFast

To disable BackboneFast, perform this task in privileged mode:

Task	Command
Step 1 Disable BackboneFast on the switch.	**set spantree backbonefast disable**
Step 2 Verify that BackboneFast is disabled.	**show spantree backbonefast**

Example D-14 shows how to disable BackboneFast on the switch and how to verify the configuration:

Example D-14 *Disabling BackboneFast*

```
Console> (enable) set spantree backbonefast disable
Backbonefast enabled for all VLANs

Console> (enable) show spantree backbonefast
Backbonefast is disabled.
Console> (enable)
```

ISL Functional Specification

Overview

ISL Functional Specification is a white paper published by Cisco Systems.

The Inter-Switch Link (ISL) is used to interconnect two VLAN-capable Ethernet switches using the Ethernet MAC and Ethernet media. The packets on the ISL link contain a standard Ethernet, FDDI, or Token Ring frame and the VLAN information associated with that frame. Some additional information is also present in the frame.

Functional Description

The ISL consists of three primary fields: the header, the original packet, and the FCS at the end. The header is further divided into fields as shown in Example E-1.

Example E-1 *ISL Header*

```
      0           1           2           3
      +---------+---------+---------+---------+
      |                  40                   |
      |                  DA                   |
      +---------+---------+---------+---------+
                    | 4 | 4 |         48
      DA(cont'd) |TYPE|USER|         SA
      +---------+---------+---------+---------+
      |                                       |
      |            SA (cont'd)                |
      +---------+---------+---------+---------+
      |         16        |    8    |    8    |
      |        LEN        |  0xAA   |  0xAA   |
      +---------+---------+---------+---------+
      |    8    |             24              |
      |  0x03   |            HSA              |
      +---------+---------+---------+---------+
      |       15        | 1 |       16        |
      |      VLAN       |BPDU|      INDX       |
      +---------+---------+---------+---------+
```

continues

Example E-1   *ISL Header (Continued)*

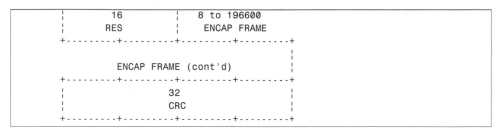

```
            16          8 to 196600
            RES           ENCAP FRAME
       +--------+--------+--------+--------+
                                           !
                                           !
            ENCAP FRAME (cont'd)           !
       +--------+--------+--------+--------+
       !             32                    !
       !             CRC                   !
       +--------+--------+--------+--------+
```

ISL Frame Format

The following is a diagram of the ISL frame and all its fields, including the number of bits in each field.

DA—Destination Address

The DA field of the ISL packet is a 40-bit destination address. This address is a multicast address and is currently set to be 0x01_00_0C_00_00. The first 40 bits of the DA field signal the receiver that the packet is in ISL format.

TYPE—Frame Type

The TYPE field indicates the type of frame that is encapsulated and could be used in the future to indicate alternative encapsulations. The following TYPE codes have been defined:

Code	Meaning
0000	Ethernet
0001	Token Ring
0010	FDDI
0011	ATM

USER—User-Defined Bits (TYPE Extension)

The USER bits are used to extend the meaning of the TYPE field. For example, Token Ring frames may have more than one type. The default USER field value is 0000. For Ethernet frames, two USER field values have been defined according to the following table. The USER field will be passed unchanged from the ISL packet to the internal packet headers in the switch.

For Ethernet frames, the USER field bits 0 and 1 indicate the priority of the packet as it passes through the switch. Whenever traffic can be handled in a manner that enables it to be forwarded more quickly, those packets with this bit set should take advantage of this quick path. It is not required that such paths be provided.

Code	Meaning
XX00	Normal priority
XX01	Priority 1
XX10	Priority 2
XX11	Highest priority

SA—Source Address

The SA field is the source address field of the ISL packet and is a 48-bit value. This should be set to the 802.3 MAC address of the switch port transmitting the frame. The receiving device may ignore the SA field of the frame.

LEN—Length

The LEN field is a 16-bit length of the packet in bytes, excluding the DA, T, U, SA, LEN, and CRC fields. The total length of the excluded fields is 18 bytes, so the LEN field is the total length minus 18 bytes. This field is stored as a 16-bit value.

AAA03

The AAAA03 field is an 18-bit constant value of 0xAAAA03.

HSA—High Bits of Source Address

The HSA field is the upper 3 bytes, the manufacturer's ID portion of the SA field. It must contain the value 0x00_00_0C.

VLAN—Virtual LAN ID

The VLAN field is the virtual LAN ID of the packet. This is a 15-bit value that is used to distinguish frames on different VLANs. This field is often referred to as the "color" of the packet.

BPDU—BPDU and CDP Indicator

The BPDU bit is set for all bridge protocol data units that are encapsulated by the ISL packet. The BPDUs are used by the spanning-tree algorithm to determine information about the topology of the network.

INDX—Index

The INDX field indicates the port index of the source of the packet as it exits the switch. This field is used for diagnostic purposes only and may be set to any value by other devices. It is a 16-bit value and is ignored in received packets.

RES—Reserved for Token Ring and FDDI

The RES field is used when Token Ring or FDDI packets are encapsulated with an ISL packet. In the case of Token Ring frames, the AC and FC fields are placed here. In the case of FDDI, the FC field is placed in the least significant byte of this field (for example, an FC of 0x12 would have a RES field of 0x0012). For Ethernet packets, the RES field should be set to all zeros.

ENCAP FRAME—Encapsulated Frame

The ENCAP FRAME is the encapsulated frame, including its own CRC value, completely unmodified. The internal frame must have a CRC value that is valid after the ISL encapsulation fields are removed. The length of this field can be from 1 to 24,575 bytes long to accommodate Ethernet, Token Ring, and FDDI frames. A receiving switch may strip off the ISL encapsulation fields and use this ENCAP FRAME as the frame is received, associating the appropriate VLAN and other values with the received frame, as indicated previously for switching purposes.

CRC—Frame Checksum

The CRC is a standard 32-bit CRC value calculated on the entire encapsulated frame, from the DA field to the ENCAP FRAME field. The receiving MAC will check this CRC and can discard packets that do not have a valid CRC on them. Note that this CRC is in addition to the one at the end of the ENCAP FRAME field.

ISL Frame Size

The ISL frame encapsulation is 30 bytes, and the minimum FDDI packet is 17 bytes; therefore, the minimum ISL encapsulated packet is 47 bytes. The maximum Token Ring packet is 18,000 bytes; therefore, the maximum ISL packet is 18,030 bytes. If only Ethernet packets are encapsulated, the range of ISL frame sizes is from 94 to 1548 bytes.

System Implications

The biggest implication for systems using ISL encapsulation is that the encapsulation is a total of 30 bytes and fragmentation is not required. Therefore, if the encapsulated packet is 1518 bytes long, the ISL packet will be 1548 bytes long. Additionally, if packets other than Ethernet packets are encapsulated, the maximum length can be greatly increased. This length change must be considered when evaluating whether a MAC can support ISL packets.

Another system implication is that ISL packets contain two CRC values: one on the internal encapsulated packet and another covering the entire ISL packet. If the original data does not contain a valid CRC, two will have to be calculated as the packet is transmitted.

INDEX

Numerics

A

G–H

I

M

N

P

T

W–Z

CCIE Professional Development

Cisco LAN Switching

Kennedy Clark, CCIE; Kevin Hamilton, CCIE

1-57870-094-9 • AVAILABLE NOW

This volume provides an in-depth analysis of Cisco LAN switching technologies, architectures, and deployments, including unique coverage of Catalyst network design essentials. Network designs and configuration examples are incorporated throughout to demonstrate the principles and enable easy translation of the material into practice in production networks.

Advanced IP Network Design

Alvaro Retana, CCIE; Don Slice, CCIE; and Russ White, CCIE

1-57870-097-3 • AVAILABLE NOW

Network engineers and managers can use these case studies, which highlight various network design goals, to explore issues including protocol choice, network stability, and growth. This book also includes theoretical discussion on advanced design topics.

Large-Scale IP Network Solutions

Khalid Raza, CCIE; and Mark Turner

1-57870-084-1 • AVAILABLE NOW

Network engineers can find solutions as their IP networks grow in size and complexity. Examine all the major IP protocols in-depth and learn about scalability, migration planning, network management, and security for large-scale networks.

Routing TCP/IP, Volume I

Jeff Doyle, CCIE

1-57870-041-8 • AVAILABLE NOW

This book takes the reader from a basic understanding of routers and routing protocols through a detailed examination of each of the IP interior routing protocols. Learn techniques for designing networks that maximize the efficiency of the protocol being used. Exercises and review questions provide core study for the CCIE Routing and Switching exam.

CISCO SYSTEMS

CISCO PRESS

www.ciscopress.com

Cisco Career Certifications

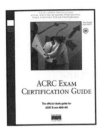

ACRC Exam Certification Guide
Clare Gough, CCIE

0-7357-0075-3 • AVAILABLE NOW   CCNP/CCDP

Scenario-based learning and exercises help you master ACRC exam topics, including standard and extended access lists, queuing, scalable routing protocols, route redistribution and summarization, dial-on-demand routing, dial backup, and the integration of bridging with a routed network.

Advanced Cisco Router Configuration
Cisco Systems, Inc., edited by Laura Chappell

1-57870-074-4 • AVAILABLE NOW

Based on the actual Cisco ACRC course, this book provides a thorough treatment of advanced network deployment issues. Learn to apply effective configuration techniques for solid network implementation and management as you prepare for CCNP and CCDP certifications. This book also includes chapter-ending tests for self-assessment.

Cisco Internetwork Troubleshooting
Edited by Laura Chappell

1-57870-092-2 • AVAILABLE NOW   CCNP

Based on the actual Cisco CIT course, this book covers troubleshooting methodology, routing and routed protocol troubleshooting, campus switch and VLAN troubleshooting, and Frame Relay and ISDN BRI problems. Master standard problem-solving using network troubleshooting tools and Cisco diagnostic tools as you prepare for CCNP certification.

Cisco Internetwork Design
Mathew Birkner, CCIE

1-57870-171-6 • November 1999 • AVAILABLE NOW   CCDP

Recommended and approved by Cisco Systems as official study material for CCDP candidates, this book is an in-depth and direct extension of the CID course taught by Cisco-approved training centers. This books contains case studies and exercises that foster an understanding of the application of the concepts, covering design issues for LANs, WANs, SNA, TCP/IP, and desktop protocols.

CISCO SYSTEMS
CISCO PRESS

www.ciscopress.com

Cisco Press Solutions

Enhanced IP Services for Cisco Networks
Donald C. Lee, CCIE

1-57870-106-6 • AVAILABLE NOW

This is a guide to improving your network's capabilities by understanding the new enabling and advanced Cisco IOS services that build more scalable, intelligent, and secure networks. Learn the technical details necessary to deploy Quality of Service, VPN technologies, IPsec, the IOS firewall and IOS Intrusion Detection. These services will allow you to extend the network to new frontiers securely, protect your network from attacks, and increase the sophistication of network services.

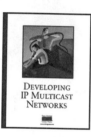

Developing IP Multicast Networks, Volume I
Beau Williamson, CCIE

1-57870-077-9 • AVAILABLE NOW

This book provides a solid foundation of IP multicast concepts and explains how to design and deploy the networks that will support appplications such as audio and video conferencing, distance-learning, and data replication. Includes an in-depth discussion of the PIM protocol used in Cisco routers and detailed coverage of the rules that control the creation and maintenance of Cisco mroute state entries.

OpenCable Architecture
Michael Adams

1-57870-135-X • AVAILABLE NOW

Whether you're a television, data communications, or telecommunications professional, or simply an interested business person, this book will help you understand the technical and business issues surrounding interactive television services. It will also provide you with an inside look at the combined efforts of the cable, data, and consumer electronics industries' efforts to develop those new services.

Designing Network Security
Merike Kaeo

1-57870-043-4 • AVAILABLE NOW

Designing Network Security is a practical guide designed to help you understand the fundamentals of securing your corporate infrastructure. This book takes a comprehensive look at underlying security technologies, the process of creating a security policy, and the practical requirements necessary to implement a corporate security policy.

www.ciscopress.com

Cisco Press Solutions

OSPF Network Design Solutions
Thomas M. Thomas II

1-57870-046-9 • **AVAILABLE NOW**

This comprehensive guide presents a detailed, applied look into the workings of the popular Open Shortest Path First protocol, demonstrating how to dramatically increase network performance and security, and how to most easily maintain large-scale networks. OSPF is thoroughly explained through exhaustive coverage of network design, deployment, management, and troubleshooting.

Top-Down Network Design
Priscilla Oppenheimer

1-57870-069-8 • **AVAILABLE NOW**

Building reliable, secure, and manageable networks is every network professional's goal. This practical guide teaches you a systematic method for network design that can be applied to campus LANs, remote-access networks, WAN links, and large-scale internetworks. Learn how to analyze business and technical requirements, examine traffic flow and Quality of Service requirements, and select protocols and technologies based on performance goals.

Internetworking SNA with Cisco Solutions
George Sackett and Nancy Sackett

1-57870-083-3 • **AVAILABLE NOW**

This comprehensive guide presents a practical approach to integrating SNA and TCP/IP networks. It provides readers with an understanding of internetworking terms, networking architectures, protocols, and implementations for internetworking SNA with Cisco routers.

For the latest on Cisco Press resources and Certification and Training guides, or for information on publishing opportunities, visit **www.ciscopress.com**.

Cisco Press

Staying Connected to Networkers

We want to hear from **you**! Help Cisco Press **stay connected** to the issues and challenges you face on a daily basis by registering your book and filling out our brief survey.

Complete and mail this form, or better yet, jump to **www.ciscopress.com** and do it online. Each complete entry will be eligible for our monthly drawing to **win a FREE book** from the Cisco Press Library.

Thank you for choosing Cisco Press to help you work the network.

Name _____

Address _____

City _____ State/Province _____

Country _____ Zip/Post code _____

E-mail address _____

May we contact you via e-mail for product updates and customer benefits?
❏ Yes   ❏ No

Where did you buy this product?
❏ Bookstore   ❏ Computer store   ❏ Electronics store
❏ Online retailer   ❏ Office supply store   ❏ Discount store
❏ Mail order   ❏ Class/Seminar
❏ Other _____

When did you buy this product? _____Month _____Year

What price did you pay for this product?
❏ Full retail price   ❏ Discounted price   ❏ Gift

How did you learn about this product?
❏ Friend   ❏ Store personnel   ❏ In-store ad
❏ Catalog   ❏ Postcard in the mail   ❏ Saw it on the shelf
❏ Magazine ad   ❏ Article or review   ❏ Used other products
❏ School   ❏ Professional Organization
❏ Other _____

What will this product be used for?
❏ Business use   ❏ Personal use   ❏ School/Education
❏ Other _____

How many years have you been employed in a computer-related industry?
❏ 2 years or less   ❏ 3-5 years   ❏ 5+ years

CISCO SYSTEMS

CISCO PRESS

www.ciscopress.com

www.ciscopress.com

Which best describes your job function?

❏ Corporate Management   ❏ Systems Engineering   ❏ IS Management

❏ Network Design   ❏ Network Support   ❏ Webmaster

❏ Marketing/Sales   ❏ Consultant   ❏ Student

❏ Professor/Teacher

❏ Other _____

What is your formal education background?

❏ High school   ❏ Vocational/Technical degree   ❏ Some college

❏ College degree   ❏ Masters degree   ❏ Professional or Doctoral degree

Have you purchased a Cisco Press product before?

❏ Yes   ❏ No

On what topics would you like to see more coverage?

_____

_____

Do you have any additional comments or suggestions?

_____

_____

CLSC Exam Certification Guide (0-7357-0875-4)

Cisco Press

201 West 103rd Street

Indianapolis, IN 46290

www.ciscopress.com

Place
Stamp
Here

Cisco Press

Customer Registration

P.O. Box 189014

Battle Creek, MI 49018-9947